About the Author

Born in Germany, Edgar Rothermich studied music a[t the] prestigious Tonmeister program at the Berlin Institut[e] University of Arts (UdK) in Berlin where he graduated [...] worked as a composer and music producer in Berlin, [...] where he continued his work on numerous projects i[n ...] Celestine Prophecy", "Outer Limits", "Babylon 5", "What the Bleep Do We Know", "Fuel", "Big Money Rustlas").

For over 20 years, Edgar has had a successful musical partnership with electronic music pioneer and founding Tangerine Dream member Christopher Franke.

In 2010 he started to release his solo records in the "Why Not ..." series with different styles and genres."Why Not Solo Piano", "Why Not Electronica", "Why Not Electronica Again", and "Why Not 90s Electronica". This previously unreleased album was produced in 1991/1992 by Christopher Franke. All albums are available on Amazon and iTunes, including the 2012 critically acclaimed release, the re-recording of the Blade Runner Soundtrack.

In addition to composing music, Edgar Rothermich is writing technical manuals with a unique style, focusing on rich graphics and diagrams to explain concepts and functionality of software applications under his popular GEM series (Graphically Enhanced Manuals). His best-selling titles are available as printed books on Amazon, as Multi-Touch eBooks on the iBooks Store, and as pdf downloads from his website.

Since 2017, Edgar Rothermich is Adjunct Professor at the Fullerton College Fine Arts Department.

www.DingDingMusic.com   GEM@DingDingMusic.com

About the Editor

Many thanks to Tressa Janik for editing and proofreading this manual.

Special Thanks

Special thanks to my beautiful wife, Li, for her love, support, and understanding during those long hours of working on the books. And not to forget my son, Winston. Waiting for him during soccer practice or Chinese class always gives me extra time to work on a few chapters.

The manual is based on Final Cut Pro X v10.3.3

Manual: Print Version 2017-0430

ISBN-13: 978-1544853505
ISBN-10: 1544853505

About the GEM (Graphically Enhanced Manuals)

UNDERSTAND, not just LEARN

What are Graphically Enhanced Manuals? They're a new type of manual with a visual approach that helps you UNDERSTAND a program, not just LEARN it. No need to read through 500 pages of dry text explanations. Rich graphics and diagrams help you to get that "aha" effect and make it easy to comprehend difficult concepts. The Graphically Enhanced Manuals help you master a program much faster with a much deeper understanding of concepts, features, and workflows in a very intuitive way that is easy to understand.

All titles are available in three different formats:

.... pdf downloads from my website www.DingDingMusic.com/Manuals

.... multi-touch iBooks on Apple's iBooks Store

.... printed books on Amazon.com

(some manuals are also available in Deutsch, Español, 简体中文)

For a list of all the available titles and bundles: www.DingDingMusic.com/Manuals

To be notified about new releases and updates, subscribe to subscribe@DingDingMusic.com

About the Formatting

I use a specific color code in my books:

Green colored text indicates keyboard shortcuts or mouse actions. I use the following abbreviations: **sh** (shift key), **ctr** (control key), **opt** (option key), **cmd** (command key). A plus (+) between the keys means that you have to press all those keys at the same time.
sh+opt+K means: Hold the shift and the option key while pressing the K key.

Brown colored text indicates Menu Commands with a greater sign (➤) indicating submenus.
Edit ➤ Source Media ➤ All means "Click on the Edit Menu, scroll down to Source Media, and select the submenu All.

Blue arrows indicate what happens if you click on an item or popup menu ●——➤

Table of Contents

1 - Introduction _____ 8

   The GEM Advantage -------------------------------------- 8
      Better Learning...9
      Better Value..9
      Self-published..10

   Final Cut Pro X - The App ------------------------------11
      A little bit of History......................................11

   Final Cut Pro X - My Books ----------------------------12
      FCPx Book..12
      FCPx-related Books.......................................12
      Audio Production Books..................................12
      What you will learn in this book........................13

2 - Getting Started _____ 14

   Get the App ---14
      Free Trial Version..14
      Purchase from the Mac App Store.....................15
      Additional Downloads...................................15
      Official User Guide.......................................16

   The User Interface ------------------------------------17
      Basic Workflow...17
      Types of Windows.......................................18
      Workspace..21

3 - FCPx Concepts _____ 30

   Basic Concepts---------------------------------------30
      Components...30
      Media Files and Clips....................................31
      Primary Storyline - no Tracks..........................35
      Magnetic Timeline......................................36
      Three Playback Formats...............................37
      Wide Gamut...38

   Advanced Concepts ----------------------------------39
      Databases and Metadata.............................39
      Rendering 44
      Clips and Timelines....................................48
      Where is the FCPx Project File?......................53
      Components & Terminology...........................56

4 -Basic Operations _____ 61

   Library---61
      Library Commands......................................61
      Library Properties.......................................64

   Events ---68
      Event Management.....................................69
      Inside the Event...72
      Browser UI...74

   Projects ---80
      First Project...81
      Project Management...................................85
      Timeline UI...87

   Viewer --92

Overview..92

SMPTE Reader..94

Transport Controls..96

Playhead and Skimmer..100

View Options..106

Inspector --**109**

Basics..109

Interface..111

5 - Importing Media _____**115**

Basics ---**115**

Overview..115

Supported Media Formats..116

Media Import Dialog ---**117**

Basics..117

Sidebar..119

Browser...120

Import Settings..124

Other Import Options --**131**

Finder - Drag and Drop..131

Browser - Drag and Drop...132

Motion...134

Record Voiceover..135

iMovie..136

XML..136

Camera Archive...137

Disk Images...138

6 - Organize Clips _____**139**

Introduction --**139**

Basic Workflow..139

Metadata Workflow...140

Metadata Types..143

Create Metadata --**144**

Info..144

Keywords...148

Ratings...155

Markers..158

Share Attributes..163

Filter Metadata --**165**

Basics..165

Filter Event Clips...166

Clip Filtering...169

Filter Window..172

Collections..175

Date and Time..181

Subclips --**182**

Virtual Subclips vs. Real Subclips......................................182

7 - Editing_____**184**

Placing Clips---**184**

#1 - What Clip to Place..184

#2 - How to Place the Clip 186

#3 - Where to Place the Clip...188

#4 - Consequences..190

Trimming Clips---**193**

Basics	193
Trimming Clips	197
Precision Editor	203
Other Edits	205

Editing Connected Clips ——————————————————— **206**
Basics	206
Editing	207

Adding Effects to a Clip —————————————————— **209**
Properties - Attributes - Parameters	210
Copy/Paste Attributes	213

8 - Audio   215

Concepts —————————————————————————— **215**
Before the Import	216
Audio Configuration	219
Summed Audio Clip vs. Audio Component Clips	221
Clip Structure	222

Edit - Trimming ———————————————————————— **224**
Standard Clip	224
Trimming Expanded Clips	226

Edit - Processing ——————————————————————— **229**
Basics	229
Inspector	230
The Virtual Mixer	232

Input Routing (Channel Configuration) ——————————— **236**
Basics	236
Setup	237

Audio Enhancements —————————————————————— **240**
Equalization	242
Audio Analysis	244

Audio Effects ———————————————————————— **248**
Effects Browser	249
Apply and Edit Effects	250
Manage Effects	254

Volume ——————————————————————————— **257**
Overview	257
Adjust Volume	258

Pan (Output Routing) —————————————————————— **263**
Concept	263
Signal Flow - Details	266

Surround ——————————————————————————— **270**
How to switch to Surround?	270
Surround Examples	273

9 - Roles & Lanes   274

Basics ——————————————————————————— **274**
Role Editor	276
Assign Roles	281

Lanes ——————————————————————————— **285**
Review	285
Understanding Lanes	289
All The Controls	295

Roles & Busses ———————————————————————— **298**
It's a Mixer	298

Compound Clips...302
Final Signal Flow Model...308

10 - Clips   311

Standard Clips ---311
Open Clip..312

Transitions - Titles - Generators ---------------------------313
Transitions..313
Titles...317
Generators..322

Compound Clips --323
Timeline vs. Browser...324
Editing Compound Clips..326
Standard Clip vs. Compound Clip...328

Synchronized Clips ---329
Layered Graphic Clips ---------------------------------------330
Audition Clips---331
Workflow...332

Multicam Clips--336
Concept...336
Create a MultiCam Clip..339
Edit a MultiCam Clip - Angle Editor.....................................342
Use a MultiCam Clip - Angle Viewer.....................................344
Use a MultiCam Clip - Timeline..348
Multi-channel Audio..350

Connected Storyline --352

11 - Animation (Automation)   354

Basics ---354
Math Background...354
Create Keyframes...356

Inspector --357
Dynamic Keyframe Area...357
Keyframe Buttons..358

Animation Editor --359
Interface..359
Managing Keyframes...361
Animation Editor Summary..367

Viewer - Onscreen Controls ---------------------------------368
Mechanism..369
Modules with Onscreen Controls...370

12 - Video Effects   372

Video Effects ---372
Conform..373
Fix...374
Built-in Video Effects...375
Additional Video Effects..381

Retime ---382
Basics..382
Retime Editor..383
Retime Effects...385

Color Correction ---390
Basics..390
Color Balance (Automatic Color Correction)........................391

Color Match 394
Color Correction 395
Video Scopes 402

13 - Export (Share) _____ 404

Basics -- 404
Share Concept 405

Configuration --- 406
Destinations and Bundles 406
Configuration Window 407
Shortcut Menu 412

Share a Project --- 413
What to Export 413
Share Dialog 414
Export Roles 415

Monitor --- 418
During the Export 418
After the Export 419

14 - Last But Not Least _____ 420

Relink Media -- 420
Missing Files 420
Relink Files Dialog 422

Key Commands --- 425
Command Editor 426

Touch Bar -- 429
Yes you Can 429
System Configuration 430
Final Cut Pro - Touch Bar Implementation 432

Preferences -- 436

Conclusion _____ 440

The GEM Advantage

If you've never read any of my other books and you aren't familiar with my Graphically Enhanced Manuals (GEM) series, let me explain my approach. As I mentioned at the beginning, my motto is:

"UNDERSTAND, not just LEARN"

Other manuals (original User Guide or third party books) often provide just a quick way to: "press here and then click there, then that will happen ... now click over there and something else will happen". This will go on for the next couple hundred pages and all you'll do is memorize lots of steps without understanding the reason for doing them in the first place. Even more problematic is that you are stuck when you try to perform a procedure and the promised outcome doesn't happen. You will have no understanding why it didn't happen and, most importantly, what to do in order to make it happen.

Don't get me wrong, I'll also explain all the necessary procedures, but beyond that, the understanding of the underlying concept so you'll know the reason why you have to click here or there. Teaching you "why" develops a much deeper understanding of the application that later enables you to react to "unexpected" situations based on your knowledge. In the end, you will master the application.

And how do I provide that understanding? The key element is the visual approach, presenting easy to understand diagrams that describe an underlying concept better than five pages of descriptions.

Here is a summary of the advantages of my Graphically Enhanced Manuals that set them apart from other books:

Better Learning

☑ Graphics, Graphics, Graphics

Every feature and concept is explained with rich graphics and illustrations that are not found in any other book or User Guide. These are not just a few screenshots with arrows in it. I take the time to create unique diagrams to illustrate the concepts and workflows.

☑ Knowledge and Understanding

The purpose of my manuals is to provide the reader with the knowledge and understanding of an app that is much more valuable than just listing and explaining a set of features.

☑ Comprehensive

For any given feature, I list every available command so you can decide which one to use in your workflow. Some of the information is not even found in the app's User Guide.

☑ For Beginners and Advanced Users

The graphical approach makes my manuals easy to understand for beginners, but still, the wealth of information and details provide plenty of material, even for the most advanced user.

Better Value

☑ Three formats

No other manual is available in all three formats: PDF (from my website), interactive multi-touch iBooks (on Apple's iBooks Store), and printed book (on Amazon).

☑ Interactive iBooks

No other manual is available in the enhanced iBook format. I include an extensive glossary, also with additional graphics. Every term throughout the content of the iBook is linked to the glossary term that lets you popup a window with the explanations without leaving the page you are currently reading. Every term lists all the entries in the book where it is used and links to other related terms.

☑ Up-to-date

No other manual stays up to date with the current version of the app. Due to the rapid update cycles of applications nowadays, most books by major publishers are already outdated by the time they are released. I constantly update my books to stay current with the latest version of an app.

☑ Free Updates (pdf, iBook only)

No other manual provides free updates, I do. Whenever I update a book, I email a free download link of the pdf file to current customers. iBooks customers will receive an automatic update notification and 24h after a new update, the printed book will be available on Amazon. They are print-on-demand books, which means, whenever you order a book on Amazon, you get the most recent version and not an outdated one sitting in a publisher's warehouse.

Self-published

As a self-published author, I can release my books without any restrictions imposed by a publisher. Rich, full-color graphics and interactive books are usually too expensive to produce for such a limited audience. However, I have read mountains of manuals throughout the 35 years of my professional career as a musician, composer, sound engineer, and teacher, and I am developing these Graphically Enhanced Manuals (GEM) based on that experience, the way I think a manual should be written. This is, as you can imagine, very time consuming and requires a lot of dedication.

However, not having a big publisher also means not having a big advertising budget and the connections to get my books in the available channels of libraries, book stores, and schools. Instead, as a self-published author, I rely on reviews, blogs, referrals, and word of mouth to continue this series.

If you like my "Graphically Enhanced Manuals", you can help me promote these books by referring them to others and maybe taking a minute and write a review on Amazon or the iBooks Store.

Thanks, I appreciate it:

amazon http://amzn.to/1sP8jvl   http://bit.ly/1oJ7ftQ

Disclaimer: As a non-native English speaker, I try my best to write my manuals with proper grammar and spelling. However, not having a major publisher also means that I don't have a big staff of editors and proofreaders at my disposal. So, if something slips through and it really bothers you, email me at <GrammarPolice@DingDingMusic.com> and I will fix it in the next update. Thanks!

Final Cut Pro X - The App

Who can describe better what Final Cut Pro is than Apple itself:

"Final Cut Pro X is a revolutionary application for creating, editing, and producing the highest-quality video. Final Cut Pro combines high-performance digital editing and native support for virtually any video format with easy-to-use and time-saving features that let you focus on storytelling."

A little bit of History

"Final Cut Pro X" (pronounced Final Cut Pro ten) was a major upgrade of Apple's successful video editing software "Final Cut Pro" (without the "X"). When the new version was released in the Summer of 2011, it created quite the sensation. Unfortunately, it wasn't for its groundbreaking new approach. Many professional editing features were missing in the original 10.0 version and some of the new concepts didn't resonate very well with the user base. However, Apple kept its promise and added most of the professional features since then and even changed some of the concepts due to user requests.

Final Cut Pro

This manual will help you learn, and more importantly, fully understand the concepts behind Final Cut Pro X (I use the short term "**FCPx**" throughout this manual). As I explained in the preface, my approach in writing manuals is to provide a visual understanding to create a more solid foundation for the actual learning process of the application. This is even more important with FCPx, especially if you come from the old version Final Cut Pro 7 ("FCP7") or any other video application.

It is often harder to learn a similar software than a brand new one, because it first requires some sort of "un-learning" of existing concepts and workflows that one has become accustomed to.

Releasing a FCPx manual that only tells you where to click in order to do the same process as in FCP7 or in a different video editing app wouldn't do it any justice. Although FCPx is just a video editing application that follows the main principles and workflows of other video editing software, it has some unique concepts and architecture that sets it apart from other apps. However, these concepts require some understanding before starting with any project in order to fully take advantage of those tools and incorporate them into your workflow.

I hope the many diagrams and graphics in this book (that you won't find in any other book or video) will help you better understand those concepts and amazing features. This visual approach will make it easy to quickly learn Final Cut Pro X.

BTW, it seems that Apple is slowly removing the number "X" from the name. The app in the Finder and also the Main Menu already uses just the name "Final Cut Pro" without the X.

FCPx Book

The original book that I released for FCPx had two volumes, "Final Cut Pro X - How it Works" and "Final Cut Pro X - The Details". For the revision of the book based on the release of FCPx v10.3, I decided to combine the entire content into a single book. I also removed the "X" in "Final Cut Pro X". As I just mentioned, it seems that Apple is slowly moving away from the "X"-business. "OS X" is now also just "macOS"

So that's why the new title is now:

"**Final Cut Pro 10.3 - How it Works**"

FCPx-related Books

Apple offers two applications that complement the video production process. I have written books for those as well:

- ● "**Motion 5 - How it Works**" explains this powerful motion graphics application with lots of background information that makes it understandable, even if you never used such an app.
- ● "**Compressor - How it Works**" explains this handy little application that provides the tools for a wide variety of file conversions and encoding procedures.

Audio Production Books

If you create your own soundtrack for your video production, then you might want to use Logic Pro X, GarageBand, or Pro Tools. I have written manuals for all these apps in my "Graphically Enhanced Manuals" series.

"Logic Pro X - The Details" has in-depth coverage of topics like "Working to Picture", "Synchronization", and how to use Final Cut XML to exchange audio tracks between FCPx and Logic Pro X.

For a list of all my books, go to my website www.DingDingMusic.com/Manuals/

What you will learn in this book

Although you can jump around between chapters and read the sections you are most interested in, depending on your prior experience with FCPx or video editing software in general. However, I strongly recommend you read and study the book in sequential order. There are so many places where I introduce features, elements, or workflows that are crucial in understanding various topics later on.

The visual component on this book makes it very easy to go through the pages and your experience and knowledge as a reader just determines the speed on how fast you learn or discover the individual features.

➡ *This is what you learn in the chapters:*

1 - Introduction: This is the chapter you are reading right now.

2 - Getting Started: The first step in getting to know FCPx, how it looks like, getting around the user interface and understanding the basic workflows.

3 - FCPx Concepts: Before diving head first into your first video project and showing you how to do video editing, I take my time to explain FCPx, what it is and what you should know about it. Take your time too to go through this chapter. Everything else later will make so much more sense.

4 - Basic Operations: The four corner stones of FCPx, Events, Projects, Library, and Inspector. This is the framework of your workflow, so I make sure in this chapter to properly explain these components.

5 - Importing Media: That's were it all starts, gather your material. There are many different ways how to get your files into FCPx and many different things to take into consideration when doing so.

6 - Organize Clips: This is the tedious not-so-productive part of organizing your material in FCPx before starting the video editing. However, this step contains the key elements of working efficiently and effortlessly later on by using your big helper - Metadata.

7 - Basic Editing: This is were the fun starts. Learning all the tools and procedures of video editing together with all the things that makes FCPx so special, or at least different.

8 - Audio: This chapter is dedicated to audio with lots of details not found in any other book. I will use my own models and signal flow diagrams to demonstrate what is really going on under the hood to better understand and control every aspect of your audio signal.

9 - Roles and Lanes: Roles and Lanes got a major boost in version 10.3. There is a lot to learn and to discover if you want take advantage of those amazing features.

10 - Clips: There are so many different types of Clips in FCPx and every type has its own little specialties, from minor differences to individual concepts and workflows. Learn them all to master them all.

11 - Animation (Automation): No matter whether you call this automation or animation, it is all about changing things automatically to really set your video project in motion.

12 - Video Effects: Once your basic editing is done, you want to make everything look nice. Lots of features and workflows how to "treat" the video visually.

13 - Export (Share): There are so many ways to share you newly edited Project with the world. Choose the destination that is right for you.

14 - Last But Not Least: This final chapter covers four very important topics. What to do with missing files, how to use Key Commands, the glorious Touch Bar, and a look at all the Preferences.

Get the App

Apple doesn't sell its software on physical discs anymore. All their apps are available only through downloads from the various online Apple Stores or from their website. This is also true for FCPx.

➡ *Requirements*

Before you download FCPx, make sure your computer meets the minimum system requirements.

As with any CPU intensive app, the better your machine, the better your overall experience. Here are the minimum requirements to run FCPx v10.3.

- OS X v10.11.4 or later
- 64bit processor
- 4GB of RAM (8GB recommended for 4K editing and 3D titles)
- OpenCL-capable graphics card or Intel HD Graphics 3000 or later
- 256MB of VRAM (1GB recommended for 4K editing and 3D titles)
- 4.15GB of disk space

As with any other Mac application, the localized versions are incorporated in the app and don't require any additional download. FCPx follows whatever language you are logged in with macOS and displays the app in that language. The supported language as of version 10.3 are:

▶ English, French, German, Japanese, Simplified Chinese, Spanish

Free Trial Version

Before you purchase FCPx, you can go to Apple's website and download a 30-day Free Trial version of the full featured FCPx app. http://www.apple.com/final-cut-pro/

http://www.apple.com/final-cut-pro/

Purchase from the Mac App Store

To purchase the app, you go through the same steps as with any other app purchases from the App Store:

- ☑ Go to the Mac App Store on your computer Menu ➤ App Store...
- ☑ Sign in with your Apple ID (this will be your virtual license key).
- ☑ Click the $299.99 price tag and follow the steps.
- ☑ The app will be downloaded to your computer.

One big advantage of the App Store system is that your purchase is registered with your Apple ID that you made the purchase with. That means, you can download the app to any computer that is signed in with the same Apple ID you made the purchase with. Any available update will also be available from the App Store application which makes it easy to stay current with the latest version of any app.

➡ *Pro Apps Bundle for Education*

For the education market, Apple also offers an amazing bundle of all its five professional production apps for **$199**. (which is a saving of $430).

The bundle includes Final Cut Pro X, Logic Pro X, Motion 5, Compressor 4, and MainStage 3.

http://www.apple.com/us-k12/shop/product/BMGE2/pro-apps-bundle-for-education

Additional Downloads

There is one big disadvantage to the online distribution model of software. Additional files in the 10s of gigabytes have to be downloaded over the internet.

➡ *Additional Content*

The size of the initial download for FCPx is already 4GB. Any additional files like effects or video codecs can be downloaded afterwards once you launched the app. The Final Cut Pro menu provides a command "Download Additional Content..." that opens the App Store application and displays any files that are available for download.

You can also download the Final Cut Pro Sound Effects separately as an installer file (637MB) from Apple's website at :

http://support.apple.com/kb/DL1394

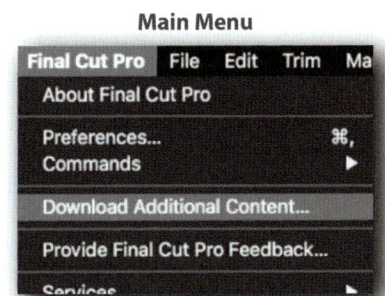

Main Menu

| Final Cut Pro | File | Edit | Trim | Ma |
| About Final Cut Pro |
| Preferences...   ⌘, |
| Commands   ▶ |
| Download Additional Content... |
| Provide Final Cut Pro Feedback... |
| Services   ▶ |

Official User Guide

There are multiple ways to access the official User Guide for FCPx from Apple:

➡ Help Viewer

"*Apple Help*" is a user help feature in macOS. It provides a special app, called "*Help Viewer*", that can display user guide information for a specific app in a floating window (the window was previously called "Help Center").

FCPx Help Menu

Most apps have a special "Help" command in the standard "Help" menu. The name of the command starts with the "name of the app", followed by the word "Help", for example, "*Final Cut Pro X Help*". The command launches the Help Viewer window, displaying the User Guide information for that app.

Help Viewer

The FCPx information displayed in the Help Viewer is pulled from the internet, so you have to be online to view the content.

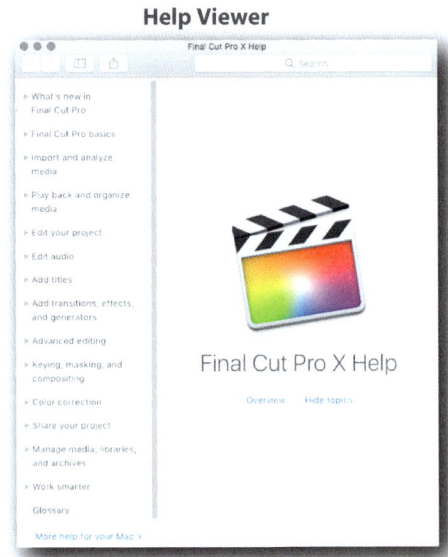

➡ Web Site

You can also access the Final Cut Pro X Help information on your web browser through the following URL:

http://help.apple.com/finalcutpro/mac/10.3/

Web Site

➡ PDF

The user guide is also available as a pdf download from Apple's website, but it might not be for the most recent version of FCPx:

http://manuals.info.apple.com/en_US/
final_cut_pro_x_user_guide.pdf

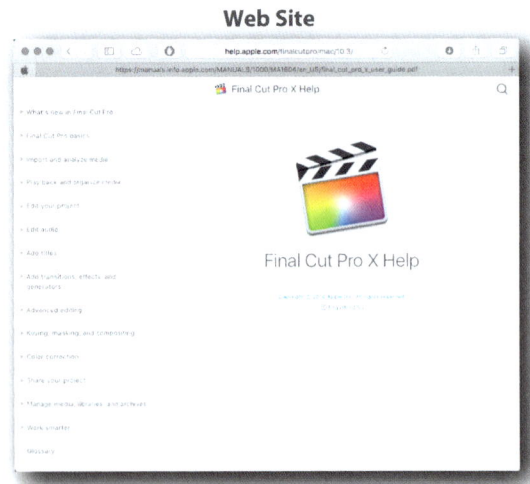

iBooks Store

➡ iBooks

Since April 2015, the FCPx User Guide is also available as an eBook from Apple's iBooks Store.

Search for Final Cut Pro X in Apple's iBooks Store or use the following URL in your web browser to link directly to the product:

https://itunes.apple.com/us/book/final-cut-pro-x-user-guide/id976299089?mt=11

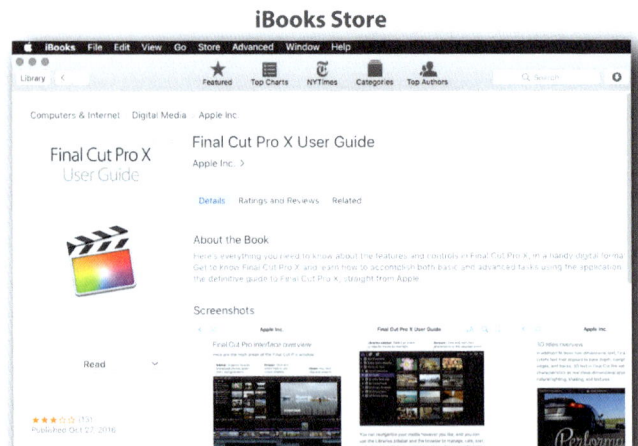

The User Interface

The problem with introducing the interface of an app early on in the book is that it shows components that will be explained later on in the book. So, hold on to those "question marks" and revisit this chapter during the course of this book to fill in the blanks.

Basic Workflow

Before learning the specific user interface elements of FCPx, let's have a quick look at the general concepts and workflow of a Video Editing software. It is the same in FCPx and basically any other Digital Video Editing software. We can break it down into five steps:

Import Media ❶

In order to create a new video, you have to import so-called Media Files (video, audio, images) into FCPx. They are the source material you will use to create your new video.

Prepare the Clips ❷

In this optional step, you can prepare the imported source material, referred to as Clips. This is done in the so-called Browser area in FCPx, where you can preview, mark, and even apply effects to the Clips.

Add Clips to a Timeline ❸

The actual movie is created in the so called Timeline area by adding Clips from the Browser to that Timeline. It represents the current video you are working on, your Video Project.

Edit Clips on the Timeline ❹

Once the Clips have been added to the Timeline, you can edit those Clips to fine-tune the sequence of the Clips, trimming them, and use effects and other creative tools.

Export the Timeline ❺

At any time during the editing process, you can export the Timeline as a new movie file, or to any other available file formats.

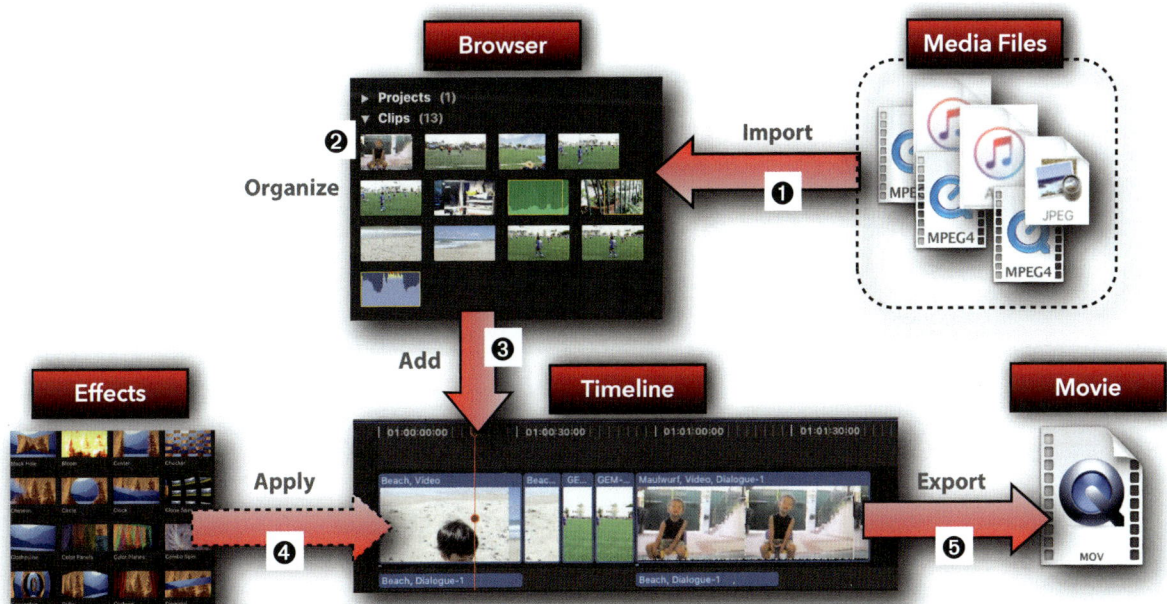

Types of Windows

When using FCPx, you have to familiarize yourself with the user interface, the different windows, to know which window contains specific elements or what windows open for specific tasks and the meaning and functionality of their parameters. But there is another aspect to the user interface that is often overlooked, different window types.

You have to be aware of the different types of windows, how they function differently when you interact with them.

FCPx uses three types of windows

- ☑ Multi-pane Window
- ☑ Standard Windows (Floating)
- ☑ Dialog Windows

➡ *Multi-pane Window - "Workspace"*

This is a popular user interface concept with a large window that is divided into sections, the so-called window panes. Instead of having multiple standalone windows that could easily clutter the computer screen, most of those often-used windows are displayed as window panes on that Multi-pane Window. Most window panes can be shown/hidden when needed and also individually resized to maximize the screen real estate.

🌑 Workspace

FCPx calls this multi-pane window the "Workspace" (blue frame), because that is where you spend most of your time working on your video project. It has four main window panes (I marked them in red) that you can show/hide, and they also can have additional "nested" window frames (marked in green) inside those window frames.

Workspace

➡ *Standard Windows (Floating)*

There are only a few additional standalone windows in FCPx that can be opened and closed in addition to the Workspace Window. They all have in common that they are so-called "Floating Window" that stay on top of the Workspace and not be covered by it. For example, the Preferences ❶, Keyword Editor, Record Voiceover, Filter, Find and Replace Title Text, Background Tasks, and all the Audio Effects windows ❷.

➡ *Dialog Windows*

There is one special kind of standalone window (used in most apps) that looks like a standard window but behaves differently, a so-called "modal window". If such a window is open, you cannot continue with FCPx until you close that window. It forces you to a "dialog", expects you to adjust some settings or at least close the window to continue with FCPx. There are different variations of a dialog:

▶ **Dialog Window**: These are mostly windows that let you configure or setup things, for example, Command Window ❸, Video Effects Presets, but also the standard Open Dialog, or the Media Import Dialog. Technically, all the small Alert Windows, that remind you of an error and mostly have an OK or Cancel Button, are also Dialog Windows.

▶ **Sheet ❹**: Sheets are small windows that slide out underneath a Window Title ❺. They also provide settings to configure a specific element in FCPx. Because this is a Dialog, you have to close the Sheet to continue with FCPx.

▶ **Popover ❻**: Popovers are Dialogs similar to Sheets, they are little windows that pop up right above a control or window element you clicked on, with a so-called "anchor" ❼, pointing at it. It indicates what the configuration is targeted at.

➡ Window-related topics

Here are two topics you have to know regarding windows:

◉ Key Window (key focus)

When working with multiple windows (separate windows or as part of window panes), it is always important to know which window is the "recipient" of any key stroke from your computer keyboard, either a Key Command or a text input. That window is called the "*Key Window*" or the one that has "*key focus*".

The Key Window usually has a highlighted Title Bar with its Title Bar Buttons colored ❶. However, not all windows follow that convention and if you use the "Graphite" Appearance selected in the General System Preferences, then it's hard to see at all.

Individual Window Panes can also have key focus. In the case of FCPx's Workspace Window, it displays a thin purple line (very subtle) at the top of the window pane. Here is a screenshot that shows the Browser ❷ selected or the Viewer ❸ selected.

◉ Full Screen

The standard Full Screen Mode only works in the Workspace Window in FCPx. However, there is an additional "Play Full Screen" Mode ⊡ in the Viewer that I cover later.

When Full Screen Mode is enabled, the window will take over the entire computer screen. The Main Menu also disappears, but moving the mouse to the top of your screen will temporarily slide out the Main Menu to access the Menu Commands.

You can toggle Full Screen Mode with the following commands:

- Title Bar Button: Instead of the Zoom Button ⊕ ❹, it turns into the "Enter Full Screen" button ◉ ❺ when you move your cursor over it. Once in Full Screen Mode, it changes to the "Exit Full Screen" button ◉ ❻ when moving over it.
- Menu Command *View ➤ Enter/Exit Full Screen*
- Key Command *ctr+cmd+F*
- Key Command *esc* also works as "Exit Full Screen Mode"

▶ Zoom Command

Please be aware of the special "Zoom Command", which is a standard feature in Mac apps. First of all, the term is all wrong because it "resizes" a window rather than "zooming" any object on it. The command toggles between the current window size and the maximum size the window can have on the screen. The command is available as Key Command *cmd+M*, from the Menu *Window ➤ Zoom*, by *double-clicking* on the Window Header, or *clicking* on the green Title Bar Button ⊕. On a window that uses the Full Screen Button (like the Workspace in FCPx), hold down the *option* key and the Full Screen Button ◉ switches to the Zoom Button ⊕.

Workspace

Now let's have a closer look at that Workspace window with its sheer endless possibilities of visible and hidden window panes. First, we will explore what window panes are available and then what commands to use to control the visibility of those windows.

➡ *Overview*

Here is the Workspace window showing the four main window panes and the various resize cursors that appear when you move the mouse over a specific border.

▶ **Outside Border**: Dragging the outside borders ❶ or the corners ❷ will resize the Workspace window, and with it, resizes all its visible window panes proportionally.

▶ **Divider Lines**: Dragging a divider line ❸ between window panes will resize the adjacent window panes proportionally without changing the size of the Workspace window itself.

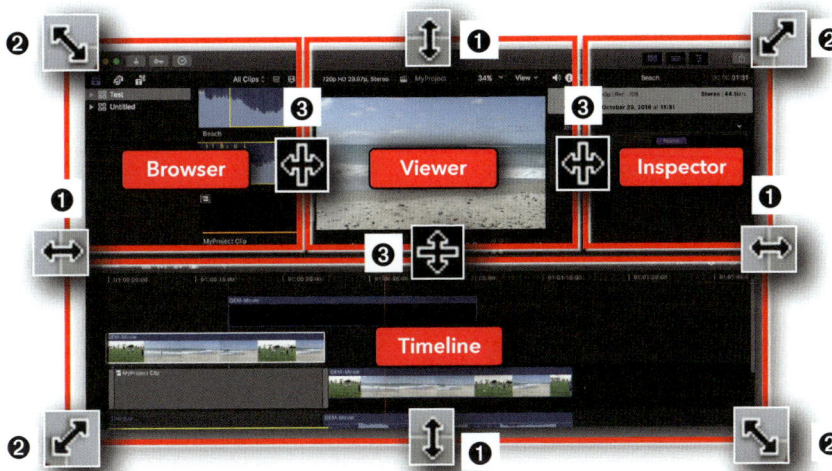

This is the Workspace window again with all the available nested window panes inside. Some window panes can be switched to different views, like switching to a different page.

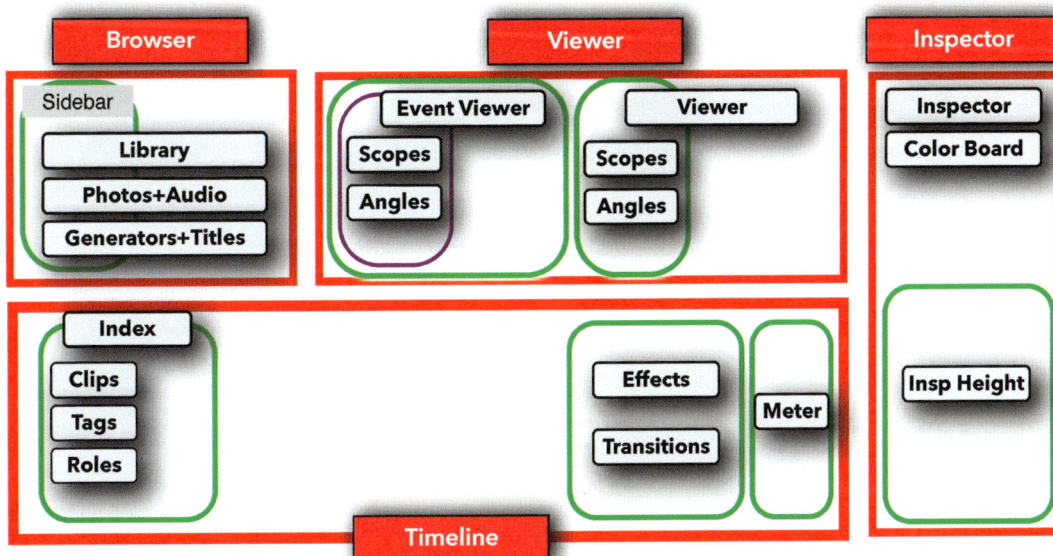

➡ *Four Main Window Panes*

Here is a quick look at the four main Window Panes and what nested window panes are available.

🟤 Browser

The Browser window is the place that lists all the material that is available for you to use in your video project.

▸ **Browser Views**: You can switch the Browser between three different views by *clicking* one of the three buttons in the upper-left corner, showing three types of content:

  - 🎬 **Libraries ❶**: This displays all the Active Libraries (a key component in FCPx that I discuss in the next chapter) and their content, the ones that are currently loaded.

  - 🎵 **Photos and Audio ❷**: This displays all the audio files and image files on your drives grouped by categories, mainly based on apps: Photos, iTunes, Logic Pro X, GarageBand.

  - 🅣 **Generators and Titles ❸**: This displays all the Generators and Titles that come pre-installed with FCPx.

▸ **Sidebar ❹**: The Browser has only one nested window pane that you can toggle on/off. When enabled, it shows the Sidebar where you select what is displayed in the Browser window for one of the three categories.

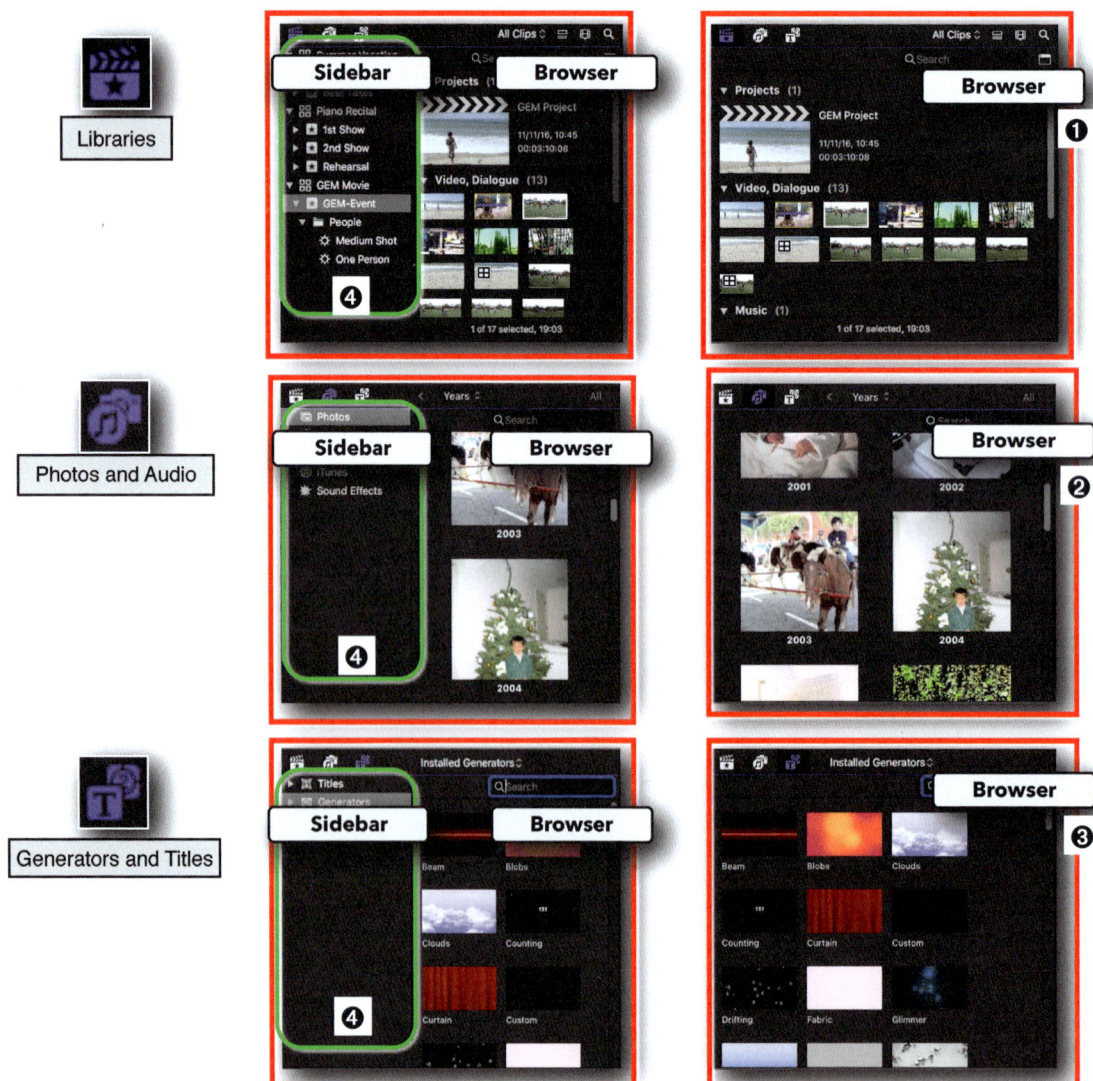

🌑 Timeline

The Timeline window shows the timeline of the Project that is currently selected in the Browser. It can also display the timeline of Compound Clips and even individual Clips as we will see later.

- ▶ **Timeline**: With no other nested window pane visible, the Timeline uses the entire space ❶.
- ▶ **Timeline Index**: The Timeline Index ❷ that slides out from the left shows additional information about the content on the Timeline. This window pane can switch between three different views ❸ to display Clips, Tags, or Roles.
- ▶ **Effects/Transitions**: The window pane to the right ❹ of the Timeline can be switched between two different views. It shows either the available Effects or the Transitions that can be applied to the Timeline Clips.
- ▶ **Audio Meters**: The window pane to the far right displays the Audio Meters ❺, the signal level of the currently played Clip (on the Timeline or the Browser).

("Toggle Inspector Height"): This is not an additional nested window pane, but a command that affects the Timeline pane by resizing its right border. The "*Toggle Inspector Height*" command extends the Inspector vertically ❻ to use the space of the Timeline window pane and "pushes" its border to the left ❼.

Toggle Inspector Height

🌐 Viewer

The Viewer is the "video screen" that plays the Clip(s). It has the most nested window panes, even a window pane in another window pane, so you have to pay attention to which window resizes which.

▶ **Viewer**: The Viewer pane ❶ plays either the Clips on the Timeline or the Clip that is selected in the Browser.

▶ **Scopes/Angles (Viewer)**: This nested pane has two views. It can either show the Scopes ❷ or the Angles ❸ of the Clip shown in the Viewer pane ❹ that is squeezed to the side.

▶ **Event Viewer**: The Event Viewer ❺ is also a nested window pane that resizes the Viewer pane ❻, but it has a different functionality than the Scopes and Angles. It provides a separate Viewer that only shows the Clip that is selected in the Browser ❼. If the Event Viewer ❺ is visible, then the regular Viewer pane ❻ only shows the Timeline Clips ❽.

▶ **Scope/Angles (Event Viewer)**: This is a nested window pane that is only available when the Event Viewer ❺ is visible. It shares its space only with the Event Viewer and doesn't affect the size of the standard Viewer pane ❻. It can display either Scopes ❾ or Angles ❿ for the Clip shown in the Event Viewer ❽.

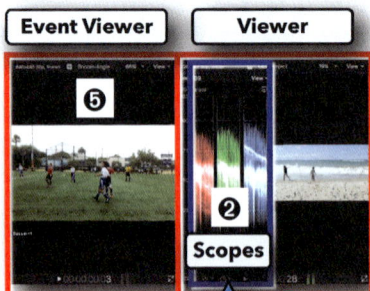

🙂 Inspector

The Inspector pane functions like a typical inspector, which is a window that displays its content based on the currently selected object (Library, Project, Clip) in another window (Browser, Timeline).

The Inspector has two specialties regarding the interface:

▶ **Inspector**: The Inspector window ❶ can be switched to different views, to show specific properties of the select object (Library, Project, Clip). These are the various Property views:

- 🔳 Library Property Inspector
- 🔳 Video Inspector
- 🔊 Audio Inspector
- ℹ️ Info Inspector
- ↕️ Share Inspector
- ◫ Transition Inspector
- ◉ Generator Inspector
- 🔤 Title Inspector
- ☰ Text Inspector

▶ **Color Board**: The Color Board ❷ is like a second page that can be displayed in the Inspector window. When selected, it shows the Color Board (controls for color correction), switching back shows the Inspector again.

▶ **Toggle Inspector Height**: As we have already seen in the Timeline pane, this command changes the borders between the Timeline and the Inspector. It extends the height ❸ of the Inspector pane taking over the space from the Timeline ❹.

- 🎛️ *Double-click* on the header of the Inspector to toggle the height
- 🎛️ Main Menu *View ➤ Toggle Inspector Height*
- 🎛️ Key Command *ctr+cmd+4*

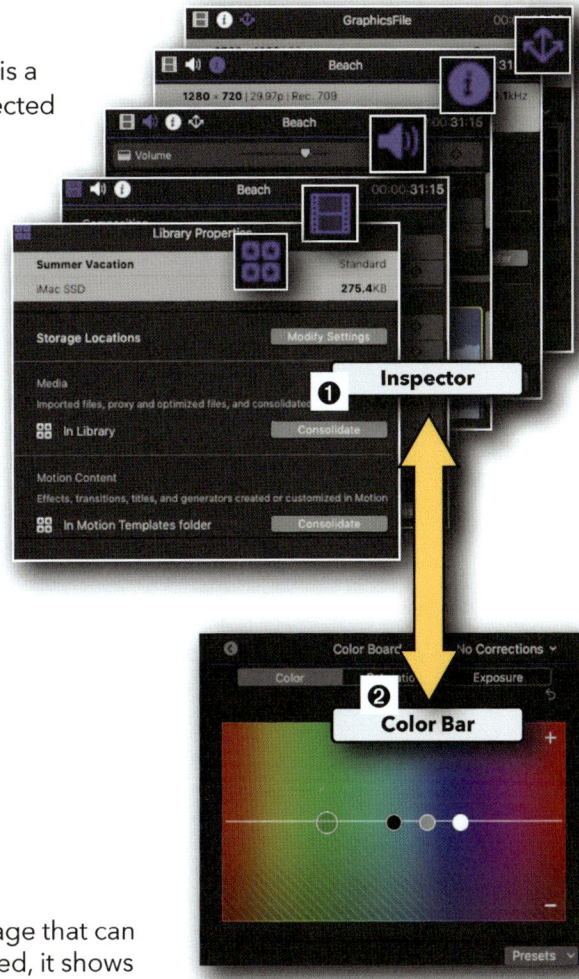

Toggle Inspector Height

➡ Commands

Now that we are familiar with the different window panes, let's look at the various commands how to show/hide those individual panes. Let me warn you, the location and functionality of the commands or the logic behind them can be confusing and, therefore, hard to remember. Let me try to break it down step-by-step.

🔮 Basic Considerations

There are a few things you have to be aware of about the implementation of the various commands:

▶ **Outcome**: There are basically two actions with a different outcome.
  - <u>Go To</u>: If the window pane was hidden, then this command will open it with key focus. If the window pane is already shown, then the command will give it key focus.
  - <u>Toggle</u>: A single command toggles two states. It will open a window pane (sometimes with a specific tab selected) if it was hidden and will hide it if it was open.

▶ **Type of Commands**: Most commands can be executed in different ways.
  - <u>Buttons</u>: Most buttons have different appearances to indicate if a window is shown, hidden, or has key focus. However, there seems to be too many inconsistencies to make sense out of many button appearances.
  - <u>Key Commands</u>: Many Key Commands are hard to remember, because they seem to be randomly assigned, maybe because some features were implemented later.
  - <u>Menu Commands</u>: Most commands are listed in the View Menu and Window Menu, however, there is no consistency why specific commands are in one or the other menu.

🔮 Key Commands

Here are all the default Key Commands that affect any of the window panes in the Workspace. A black button with the dotted lines indicates a toggle command, a white button indicates a GoTo command.

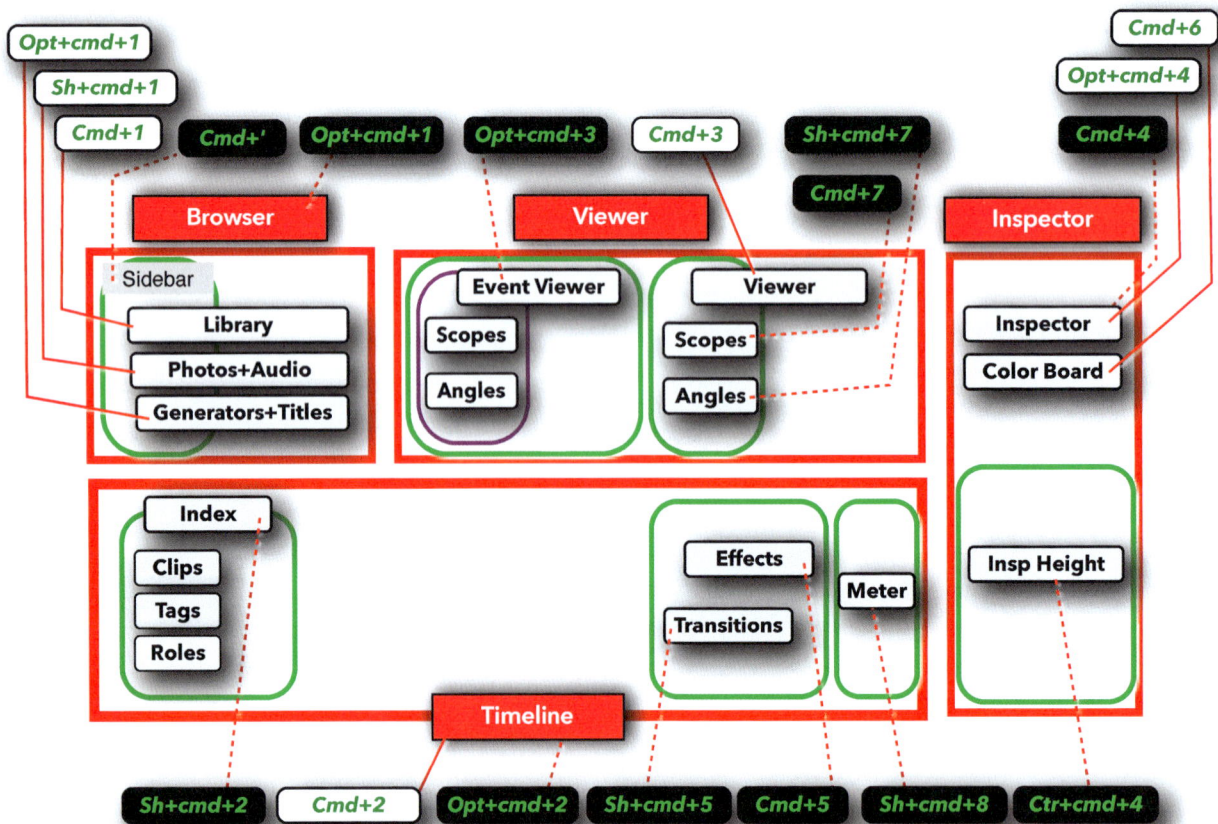

🌑 Menu Commands

The Menu Commands also try to be organized in a somewhat logical way, but there are too many exceptions that make it confusing:

▶ **Window ➤ Go To ❶**: The *Go To* submenu contains all the commands that open a window pane or switch to a specific view inside the window (and makes it the key window).

▶ **Window ➤ Show in Workspace ❷**: The *Show in Workspace* submenu contains all the commands that toggle a specific window pane (Show/Hide). It shows a checkmark in the menu if a window pane is already visible.

▶ **View ➤ Show in (Event) Viewer**: The two submenus contain the two commands to toggle the window pane for the Angles or the Video Scopes, separately for the Viewer ❸ and the Event Viewer ❹.

▶ **View ➤ Toggle Inspector Height ❺**: This toggle command is listed here "all by itself" in the View Menu. It is easier to just *double-click* the header of the Inspector, which has the same effect.

▶ **Timeline Index**: This Timeline Index submenu ❻ with the three commands should be in the "Show in Workspace" menu ❷, because it has a similar functionality like those commands. They toggle one of the three views in the Timeline Index (Clips, Tags, Roles). A checkmark indicates which of the three window panes is open.

▶ **Viewer Pane (View)**: The Viewer pane ❼ (and the Event Viewer pane) has a View Selector on top that also lists the two commands ❽ to toggle the Angles or the Video Scopes on/off. The status of the window pane is not indicated by a checkmark. Instead, the command changes to either "Show..." or "Hide...".

▶ **Viewer Pane (Magic Wand)**: The menu that opens when clicking on the Magic Wand ❾ icon ✦ (not available in the Event Viewer!) at the bottom also contains the command to toggle the Color Board ❿.

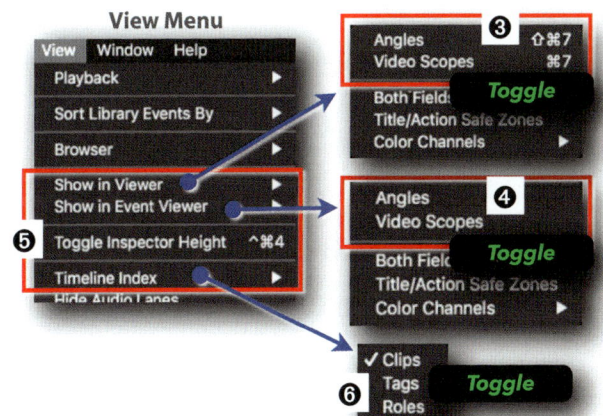

⚫ Buttons

Here are only the buttons that affect **WHAT** is displayed in the Workspace. They either show/hide a window pane or switch between the available views on a window pane. There are other buttons that determine **HOW** the content in a window pane is displayed. I cover that later in the individual chapters.

▶ **Main Window Panes ❶**: These three buttons on the Window Title Bar let you toggle the three main Window Panes. Please note that the Viewer Pane cannot be hidden and at least the Browser or the Timeline has to be open.

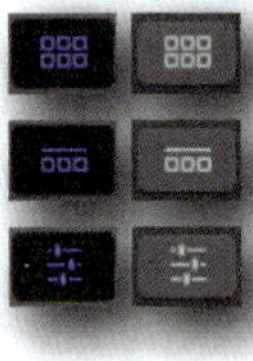

Browser
Timeline
Inspector

▶ **Inspector Views ❷**: These buttons on top of the Inspector let you switch between the different Inspector Views. The purple button indicates the active view. Only the relevant buttons for the current selection are displayed.

Video Inspector
Audio Inspector
Info Inspector
Share Inspector
Library Properties Inspector 
Others 

▶ **Browser Sidebar Views ❸**: These three buttons on top of the Browser let you switch between the different Browser Views. The purple button indicates the active view.

Libraries Sidebar
Photos and Audio Sidebar
Titles and Generators Sidebar

▶ **Timeline Index Pane ❹**: The Index button toggles the Timeline Index pane on (purple font) or off (white font).

▶ **Timeline Index Views ❺**: These three buttons on top of the Timeline Index pane lets you switch between the different Timeline Index Views. The purple font indicates the active view.

▶ **Effects/Transitions Pane ❻**: These two buttons toggle between the Effects and Transition pane. Purple indicates if a pane is visible.

Effects
Transitions

▶ **Audio Meter Pane ❼**: The tiny Level Meter at the bottom of the Viewer and Event Viewer also functions as a button to toggle the Audio Meter pane in the Timeline.

➡ Secondary Display

The Secondary Display View button ❶ in the upper right corner of the Workspace window is only displayed if you have a second computer monitor connected to your computer. Otherwise, there is no button ❷. The button allows you to "undock" one of the three window panes (Viewer, Browser, or Timeline) from the Workspace and move it to the secondary display. The window pane on the secondary display will use the entire screen real estate and cannot be resized.

Secondary Display

- 📌 *Click* on the Selector button ❸ ⌄ to choose which window pane you want to move to the secondary display. This will automatically enable the Secondary Display button.
- 📌 *Click* on the Secondary Display button to enable or disable it. The button turns purple if active.
- 📌 **Menu Command**: You can also select or deselect with the menu command *Window ➤ Show in Secondary Display ➤* to move one of the window panes to the secondary display. The menu is grayed out ❺ if no second display is connected.

Window Menu

➡ Workspaces Layout

The size and the location of the Workspace window and its window panes can be saved and later recalled. This lets you predefine specific layouts for specific tasks and quickly switch between them without constantly resizing and toggling window panes.

All the related commands are located in the *Window ➤ Workspaces ➤* submenu ❻

- ▶ **Custom Layouts ❼**: The section on top displays all the custom Workspace Layouts that you saved.
- ▶ **Factory Layouts ❽**: The four commands in the middle section are the Workspace Layouts that come preinstalled with FCPx.
- ▶ **Commands ❾**: The three commands at the bottom lets you manage the Workspace Layouts:
  - Save Workspace as...: Select this command to save the current layout of the Workspace (including Secondary Display placements). A dialog opens where you can enter a name for the Workspace Layout. The Workspace Layout is saved as a file with the file extension .fcpworkspace to the user directory *~/Library/Application Support/Final Cut Pro/Workspaces/*
  - Update "name of the current custom layout" Workspace: Select this command to save any changes to the layout since you opened it.
  - Open Workspace Folder in Finder: This opens the Finder location where FCPx stores the Workspace Layouts *~/Library/Application Support/Final Cut Pro/Workspaces/*. You can delete a file in this folder if you want to remove a Workspace Layout. You can also copy to or from other machines if you want to exchange Workspace Layouts.

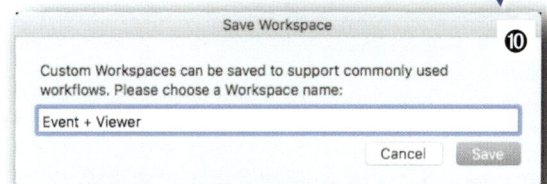

Basic Concepts

In this section, I provide information about the main concepts in FCPx to learn how FCPx works and to better understand the underlying procedures to improve your workflow and experience in FCPx.

Components

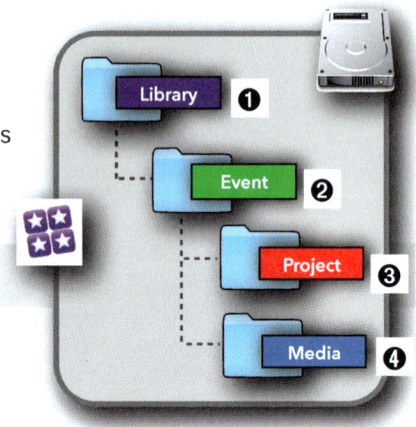

Here is a quick overview of the main components in FCPx:

➡ *Library* ❶

- ☑ **Organizational Tool**: Library is the tool that lets you organize all the elements of a specific video project. You can create separate Libraries for different video projects or split up big video projects into smaller Libraries to freely organize your "stuff" based on your personal workflow.

- ☑ **Hierarchy**: A Library is like a container that holds Events, which are sub-containers that hold Projects and Media, all the stuff related to a specific video project. A Library must contain at least one Event and can have as many Events as you want.

- ☑ **Single Library Files**: A Library is represented by a single Packaged-File ("LibraryName".fcpbundle) that contains all the necessary files "inside", but appears as a single file on the "outside" in the Finder.

- ☑ **Freely Move around**: You can freely move Library Files around in the Finder like any other files.

- ☑ **Libraries are like Documents**: You can open and close Libraries in FCPx like documents, have multiple Libraries open, and even move their content between open Libraries.

- ☑ **Flexible Data Management**: Libraries provide the mechanism to store specific data types (original media, rendered media, backups) in different locations to optimize data management needs.

➡ *Events* ❷

- ☑ **Storage Bin**: Events are folders that are contained inside Libraries and function like storage bins.

- ☑ **Unlimited Events**: There is no limit to the number of Events that can be contained in one library.

- ☑ **Content**: An Event can contain Media Files and Projects, but allows the user the flexibility how to spread the Media and Projects inside a Library across multiple Events.

➡ *Projects* ❸

- ☑ **Single Timeline**: A Project represents the sequence of Clips on a single Timeline, your video edit that you are working on with all the effects and creative tools. It becomes your final product that you export at the end.

- ☑ **"Sequence"**: You can create multiple Projects for different versions of your edit. They are similar to sequences in Final Cut Pro 7.

- ☑ **Inside Events**: A Project is created inside an Event, but can freely be moved between Events and even different Libraries.

➡ *Media* ❹

- ☑ **Inside Events**: Source Media Files that are used in your Library as part of your video project are stored as Clips inside a specific Event.

Media Files and Clips

Here is another fundamental concept that has to be understood when using FCPx or any other video editing software. The difference between the Media Files and and the Clips.

These are the terms you have to be familiar with in FCPx:

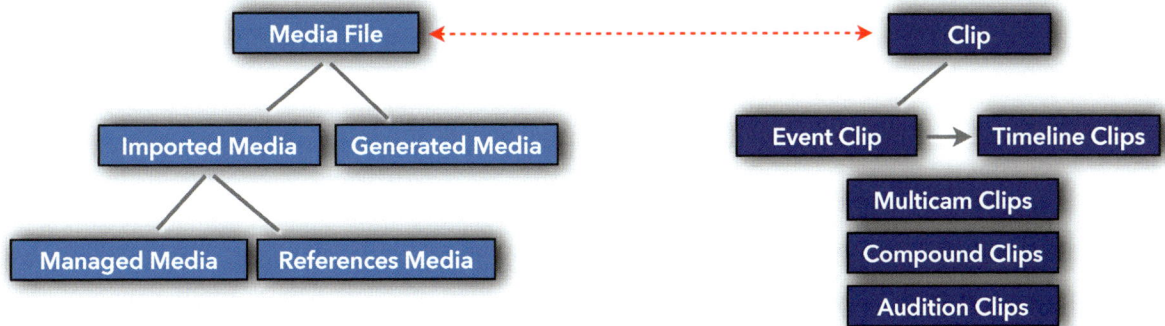

➡ *Files vs Clips*

FCPx relies on existing content. These are the so-called Source Files or Media Files that were created outside FCPx. For example, video files that were recorded on a camera, audio files from an audio recorder or a mixdown from a DAW, or images from a camera or a graphics app. FCPx can import all those Media Files to your Library (to a specific Event as we know by now).

Event Clip

For every Media File ❶ you import to your Library ❷, FCPx creates a Clip ❸ that is displayed in the Browser area ❹ (also referred to as an Event Clip). Each Clip is representing its parent source file. The Clips are linked to their source files. When you play back a Clip, FCPx plays back the original media file. When you change the Clip (i.e. shorten it), then FCPx only changes the way it plays back the source file, but never changes the original source file itself. This is a procedure called "*non-destructive editing*".

Timeline Clip

When you add a Clip from the Browser to the Timeline ❺, FCPx makes a copy of that Event Clip and it becomes a separate Clip, called a Timeline Clip ❻. Copying a Timeline Clip on the Timeline, will create yet another, separate Timeline Clip ❼. This makes it possible for you to edit those Clips individually and apply different effects while still linked to the same parent source file ❶.

Compound Clips, Multicam Clips

Compound Clips, Multicam Clips, and Audition Clips are special-purpose Clips that I cover later in the book.

➡ *Media Files*

As you have seen on the previous page, there are different kinds of Media Files (besides the file type).

🌑 Imported Media

The Imported Media represents all the source material that already exists outside of FCPx. To use that material in your video project, you have to import it to your Library, so FCPx can make those files available as Clips. There are two, let's call them mechanisms, for this import procedure that you have to choose from when importing files into FCPx:

> #### ▶ Managed Media
>
> When you choose "Copy to library" ❶, then the files on your hard drive ❷ that you want to import will be copied to the folder called "Original Media" ❸ inside the Event folder of the Library File you choose as the destination. The Clips that are created for those files ❹ are referenced to those new copied files ❸. This has the advantage that the media of a specific Library (also called "Assets") stays with the Library File ❺ when you move the Library File around in the Finder or to another drive.
>
> #### ▶ Referenced Media
>
> When you choose "Leave files in place" ❻, then FCPx does exactly that. The Library only stores the pathname ❼ (using a UNIX "trick" called Symbolic Links), where those files are located on your drive ❽ and the Clips ❾ that are created are referenced to those files. Please be aware that this has the danger that you will break that link when you move the Source Material ❽. However, in a multi-seat editing environment ❿, you can have often-used files (logos, sound effects, etc.) on a network storage without the need of having to create additional copies with every Library that needs those files. Later, you can convert Referenced Media into Managed Media at any time by copying files to the Library.

🌑 Generated Media

FCPx itself creates additional media files ⓫ for various purposes (Render Files, Analysis File, Proxy Files, etc.), which are stored inside the Library File. I will get into more details about that later.

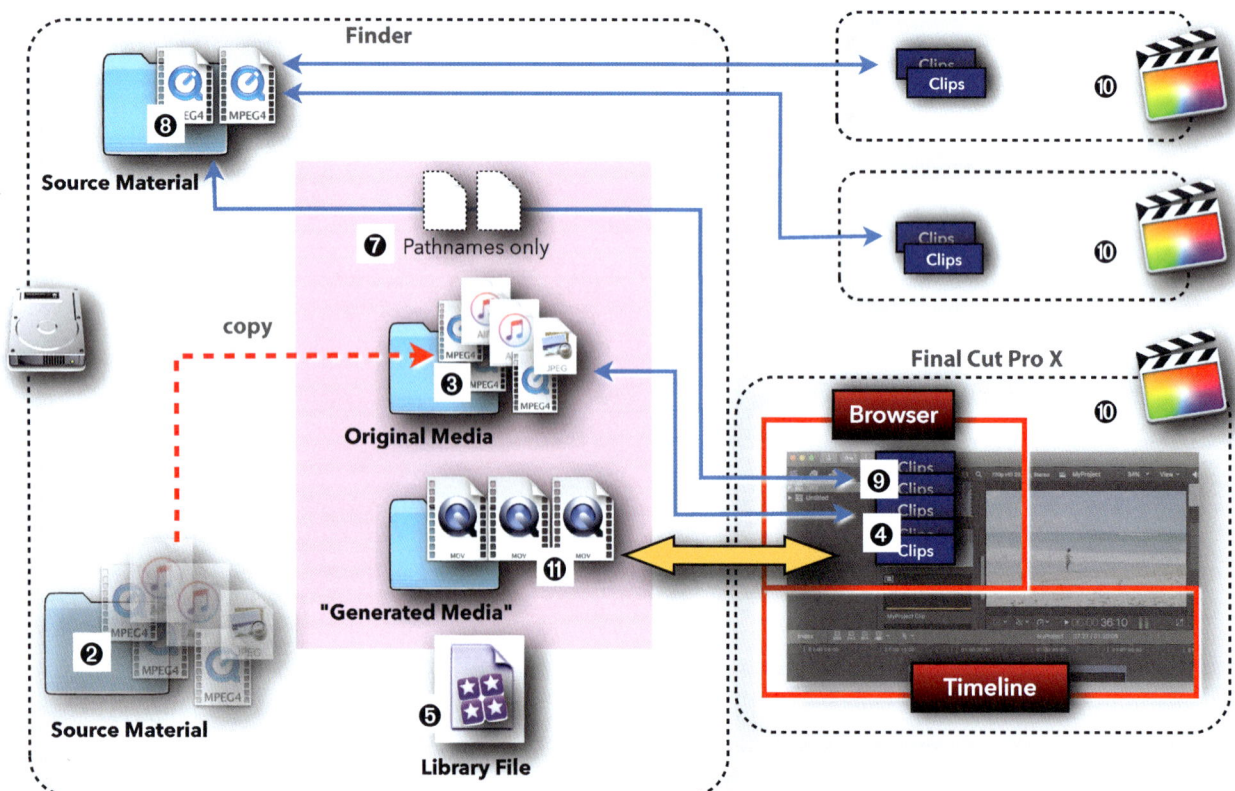

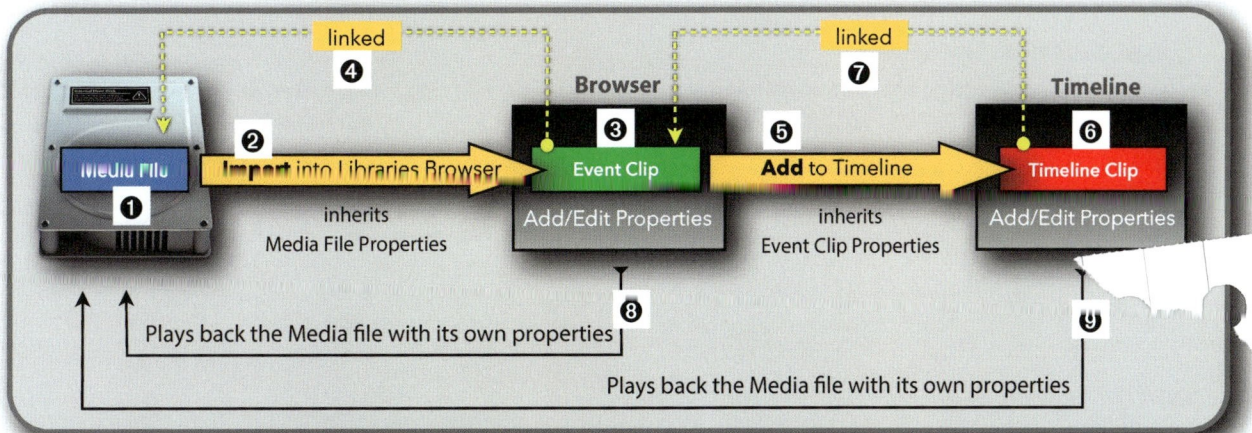

Basic Procedure

Here are the basic procedures when importing Media Files as Clips into FCPx and how they relate to the Media File.

Media File

The Media File ❶ contains its original properties the way it was recorded. It will never be changed as part of the non-destructive editing.

Event Clip

- ☑ When you import ❷ a Media File into FCPx, it creates an Event Clip ❸ that inherits all the properties of the Media Files (format, metadata, etc.) and stores them as its own properties.

- ☑ All those properties now belong to the Event Clip and you can view them in the Inspector where you can also add more or change the existing ones.

- ☑ The Event Clip ❸ is linked ❹ to its parent Media File ❶ and using the "Reveal in Finder" command in FCPx lets you see that media file in the Finder.

Timeline Clip

- ☑ When you add ❺ an Event Clip ❸ to the Timeline, FCPx creates another Clip, a Timeline Clip ❻ that inherits all the properties of that Event Clip (its format, metadata) and stores them as its own properties.

- ☑ All those properties now "belong" to the Timeline Clip and you can view them in the Inspector where you can also add more or change the existing ones.

- ☑ The Timeline Clip ❻ is linked ❼ to its parent Event Clip ❸ and using the "Reveal in Browser" command in FCPx lets you show that Event Clip in the Browser, which itself is linked ❹ to its parent Media File ❶.

Playback

- ▶ When you play back the Media File ❶ in the Finder (using QuickView), it plays back with its original properties as it was recorded.

- ▶ When you play back the Event Clip ❽ in FCPx, it plays back that same Media File, however, it applies its own properties, which means, it might change the playback parameters (i.e. 6dB louder, black and white, only play from 15s-32s, etc.).

- ▶ When you play back the Timeline Clip ❾ in FCPx, it plays back that same Media File, however, now it applies the properties stored with the Timeline Clip, which means, it changes the playback parameters based on those properties which might be different from the properties of the Event Clip (i.e. 10dB lower, half speed, only play the first 10s etc.).

➡ Multiple Timeline Clips

You can import a Media Clip only once into a specific Event ❶, but you can create multiple Timeline Clips from the same Event Clip ❷. There are two ways:

▸ **Add Again**: You can add an Event Clip ❷ multiple times ❸ ❹ to the Timeline if you need it at different spots on your video. All those Timeline Clips are linked to the same Event Clip but they contain their individual properties.

▸ **Copy Timeline Clip**: You can duplicate (copy) a Timeline Clip ❺ directly on the Timeline. The new Timeline Clip inherits the same properties (including the link to its Event Clip) and can now be edited individually.

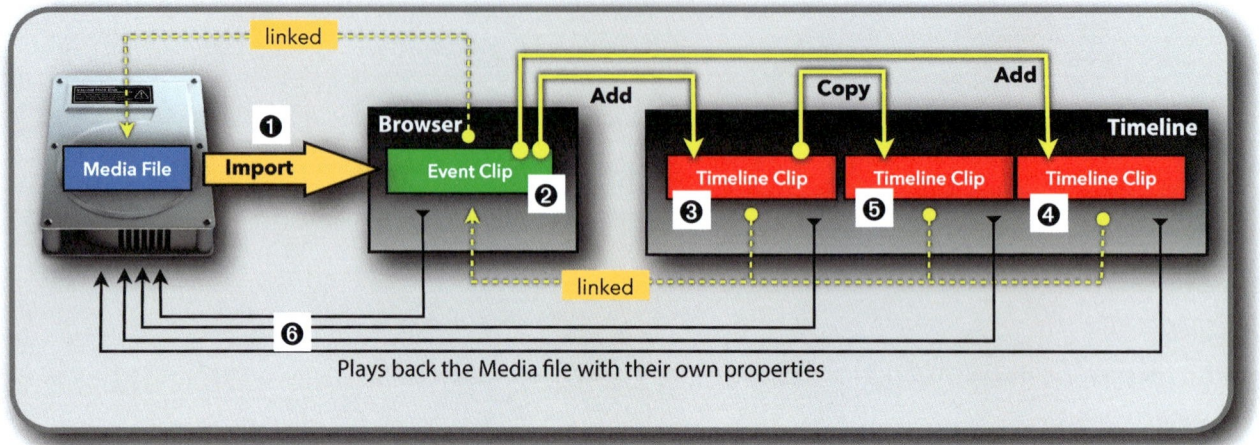

All the different Timeline Clips, linked to the same Media File, can play back that Media File differently ❻ based on their individual properties.

➡ Linked Clips/Files

To find the Media File that is linked to a specific Event Clip, select the Clip and use any of the following commands ❼:

- Key Command **sh+cmd+R**
- Main Menu Command *File ➤ Reveal in Finder*
- *Ctr+click* on the Clip and select from the *Shortcut Menu ➤ Reveal in Finder*

When you select a Timeline Clip, you can find all three of its references ❽:

▸ **Its linked Event Clip**:
- Main Menu *File ➤ Reveal in Browser*
- Key Command *sh+F*

▸ **Its Project**:
- Main Menu *File ➤ Reveal Project in Browser*
- Key Command *sh+opt+F*

▸ **Its linked Media File**:
- Main Menu *File ➤ Reveal in Finder*
- Key Command *sh+cmd+R*

Primary Storyline - no Tracks

➡ *Primary Storyline and Connected Clips*

Here is a special concept in FCPx that sets it apart form other video editing application: NO TRACKS.

Standard video editing applications work with the concept of Tracks ❶ on a Timeline. Using that approach, you could create a few video tracks and even more audio tracks to position your video and audio clips on that and arrange them in the correct sequence. However, FCPx doesn't use Tracks anymore, it uses a different approach with a single Track, the so-called **Primary Storyline** ❷.

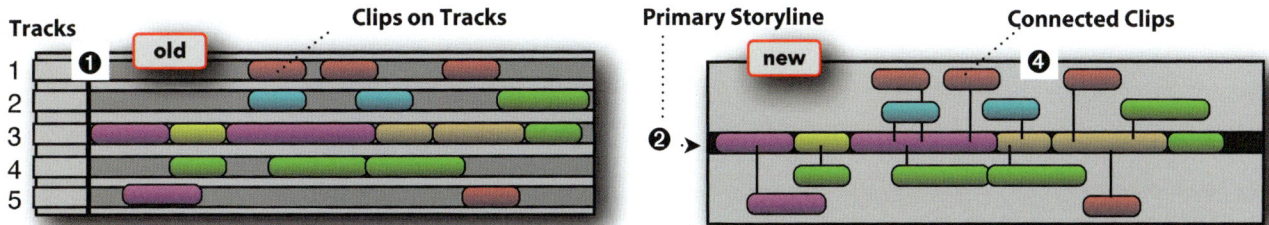

Here are some of the fundamental changes:

▶ **Primary Storyline** ❸: Instead of multiple Tracks on the Timeline, there is only one single "Track", the Primary Storyline, the black strip in the middle of the Timeline Area.

▶ **Connected Clips** ❹: Layered Clips are not placed on parallel tracks anymore, they are now "connected" to a Clip that is already placed on the Primary Storyline, becoming the so-called Connected Clips. When moving a Clip on the Primary Storyline, all its connected Clips move along with it, staying perfectly in sync (with commands to leave them in place if needed).

▶ **Audio and Video**: Connected Clips with video content are automatically placed above ❺ the Primary Storyline and Clips with audio-only

content are placed below ❻ the Primary Storyline. The top-most video has priority, but audio from all Clips will play at the same time.

▶ **No Colliding Clips**: Connected Clips are automatically stacked vertically to avoid any "collision" when moving them around, they move out of the way vertically.

▶ **Clips are Clips**: There is no distinction anymore between video tracks and audio tracks. Any Clip can be placed on the Primary Storyline or attached as Connected Clip. Even the editing procedures are virtually the same. The only difference of Clips is their content, what's inside (i.e. audio, video, graphics, and even more Clips).

Timeline with Clips on the Primary Storyline and Connected Clips attached to Clips on the Primary Storyline

Timeline with Clips and Connected Clips

Timeline with Clips on the Primary Storyline

Magnetic Timeline

The Magnetic Timeline was another buzzword that created quite a stir when it was introduced with the release of the original FCPx in 2011. It was a departure from the conventional way of editing Clips.

➡ The Old Way

Video editing applications (and most of the audio editing applications) are track-based. That means, you have several Tracks along the timeline and you can place your Clips on those Tracks anywhere along the time axis.

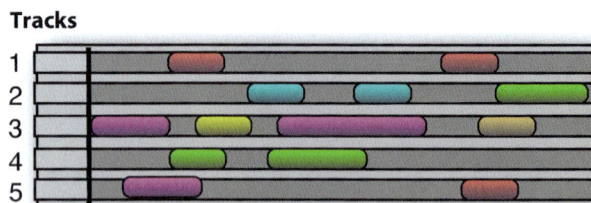

Tracks

➡ The FCPx Way

Not only reduces FCPx the concept of multiple Tracks to a single Track, the Primary Storyline, it imposes a strict rule for that ~~Track~~, I mean, Primary Storyline: NO GAPS.

When you place your first Clip on the Primary Storyline it automatically snaps to the beginning of the timeline. Now any additional Clip that you add to the Primary Storyline is placed at the end of the last Clip on the Primary Storyline, guaranteeing a continuous sequence of Clips without any gaps in between.

Primary Storyline

No Gaps !

😀 Attention

There are a few things you have to consider, or at least, be aware of about the concept of the Magnetic Timeline when editing your video. I will get into the details later in the Editing chapter, but here are just a few points up front:

▶ **Inserts**: You can insert Clips anywhere between existing Clips on the Primary Storyline, but all Clips after the insert are moved to the right accordingly.

▶ **Gap Clips**: FCPx provides two special Clips called a "Gap Clip" and a "Placeholder Clip" that function as "empty" Clips that you can place anywhere on the Primary Storyline to create space for later.

▶ **Connected Clips**: Be aware that Connected Clips move together with the Clip they are connected to on the Primary Storyline. This can be a good thing or a bad thing when Clips on the Primary Storyline are automatically moved due the Magnetic Timeline functionality.

▶ **Music Videos**: If you work on a video project that is based on a fixed timeline, like a music track, then the Magnetic Timeline concept could get in the way and you have to use specific technics to guarantee that everything stays in sync.

Three Playback Formats

➡ *Native and Resolution Independent*

One of the big advantages in FCPx is that it is resolution-independent and has native support for virtually all video formats. Here is what that means:

- ▸ **Native Support**: Native support means that you don't need to convert the source media files to a specific format that FCPx supports, just import them in FCPx and you are ready to go. You can edit all major professional camera formats from standard-definition to 6k RED RAW.
- ▸ **Resolution Independent**: When importing media files, you also don't have to worry about different resolutions of the source media files. FCPx handles everything when playing back your Clip with media up to 6K resolution and above.

➡ *Three Formats*

In addition to the Original Media ❶ file, FCPx can transcode ❷ any imported file to two additional formats. You can do that during the import or any time later:

Formats

- ▸ **Original Media**: Original Media ❸ are the files that are imported to FCPx. They are never changed based on the concept of non-destructive editing.
- ▸ **High Quality Media**: FCPx can convert the Original Media File to the Apple ProRes 422 ❹ format and store that file inside your Library File (or any location you define). This format is for optimized playback and editing operations.
- ▸ **Proxy Media**: FCPx can convert the Original Media File to the Apple ProRes 422 Proxy ❺ format and store that file inside your Library File (or any location you define). This format has a smaller file size with half the video resolution.

Switch between Formats

You can select from the Viewer's View Menu ❻ which format you want to use to switch at any time between the formats depending on your needs. Choose the high quality media for best picture results or switch to the Proxy format if you have a less powerful computer or less available storage space.

The Info Inspector ❼ has three indicators that let you know which files are available for a specific Clip.

Delete - re-transcode

You can delete the transcoded files at any time (for transfer or archiving) and re-transcode them whenever you need them again.

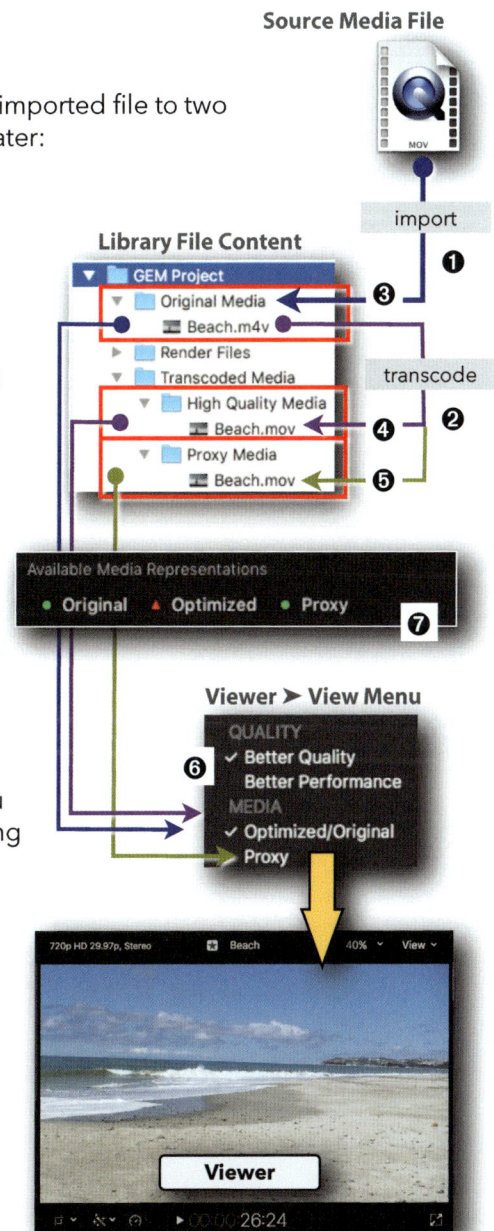

Wide Gamut

➡ About Color Space

The human eye can see many more colors than what computer screens or TV monitors can display. That's why there are different standards that define a specific range of colors (the so-called *Color Space*) that can be displayed on specific types of monitors.

When you produce video (i.e. in FCPx), you have to choose a Color Space depending on where your final product will be shown. For example, on a standard television, a high-definition television, or an Ultra-high screen.

The diagram on the right shows the range of colors the human eye ❶ can see. The smaller triangle ❷ marks the color space of HDTV (Rec. 709) and the bigger triangle ❸ marks the Wide Gamut color space (Rec. 2020).

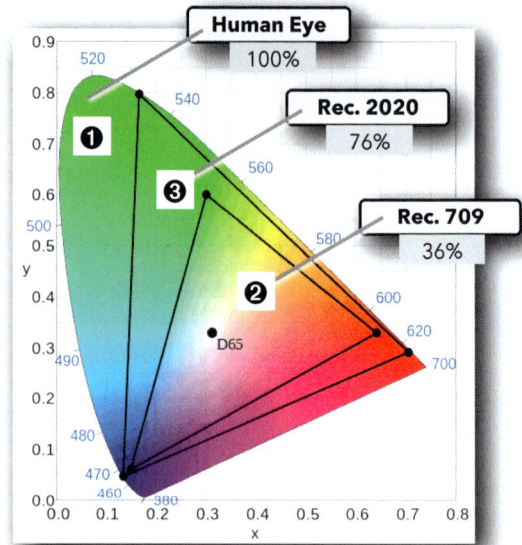

➡ FCPx Support

FCPx supports different color space formats ❹:

▶ **Rec. 601 (NTSC)** for standard definition based on the American TV standard NTSC.

▶ **REC. 601 (PAL)** for standard definition based on the European TV standard PAL.

▶ **REC. 709** for high definition up to 1080p. This is an RGB color space (same as sRGB), an ITU recommendation from 1990, created for HDTV.

▶ **REC. 2020** for video that was shot in Wide Gamut color space. This is an ITU recommendation from 2012 for 4K monitors and above.

Even log footage from ARRI, Blackmagic Design, Canon, Panasonic, and Sony cameras, including RED RAW footage can now be edited in real time in Wide Gamut space.

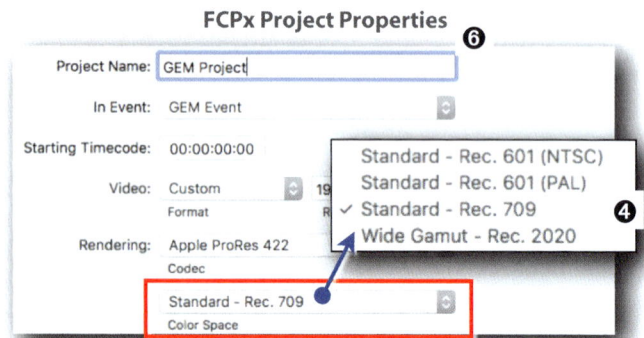

➡ FCPx - Rec. 2020 Advantages

▶ You can import, edit, and deliver in any standard, Rec.601, Rec. 709, and now also Rec. 2020.

▶ Color space can be configured in FCPx for the Library ❺ and Projects ❻.

▶ When set to Wide Gamut, you can properly view those FCPx Projects on supported Mac computers and external monitors.

▶ The FCPx Viewer provides a "Range Check" overlay that indicates "out of standard" areas in the video frame.

▶ The Video Scopes in FCPx display the currently selected color space in real time.

Databases and Metadata

The following information in this section is especially important, because I will explain the basic architecture of FCPx, what happens "behind the scene" when you perform the main tasks, like importing files, creating and editing Clips. That architecture is based on two main concepts, databases and metadata. Many of the features in FCPx like Keyword Collections, Smart Collections, Roles, or the powerful search functionality are based on the functionality of databases and metadata.

If you don't have any prior knowledge of how to use databases, then it might be a little bit challenging with all the non-video related "stuff", but the better you understand those concepts and techniques, the better you can use those features in FCPx when you edit your video project.

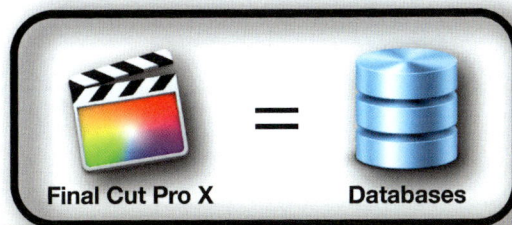

Final Cut Pro X = Databases

Final Cut Pro X is a Collection of Related Databases

Database

I will talk about databases a lot in this manual, because you have to understand that FCPx is based on databases. That means, the more you think in those terms when you are editing your video, the more efficient you will use FCPx.

Video Editing Tasks
=
Database Tasks

Metadata

Another term that we will use a lot in FCPx is Metadata. It provides the basis for the most powerful features in FCPx. Metadata means "data about data". A common type of metadata are ID3 tags in an mp3 file.

You add metadata (tags, descriptions, keyword, etc.) to your Clips, which are added as additional fields to the Clip's record in the databases, and any search for Clips or grouping is done automatically by applying a specific search query.

Metadata - The New Way to Organize and Find your Clips

To work with Metadata requires a rethinking of workflows and conventions that you might have used with other apps or the older Final Cut Pro 7. And again, the better you use Metadata in FCPx, the better and powerful its results will be.

➡ *Media Files vs. Clips*

🌐 Media File

The co-called "properties" of a media file ❶ are all the data contained in that file. There are two types of data, the Audio/Video data and the Metadata.

> ▶ **Audio/Video Data ❷**: The Audio/Video data determine how the media file looks and sounds when you play it back. For example, the video format, the audio format, aspect ration, duration, etc.

> ▶ **Metadata ❸**: Metadata is just additional, mostly text information. This can be anything from the the name of the file, to any description about the content, the author, the device that recorded it, etc.

When you open a Media File in QuickTime Player ❹ or iTunes, you can look up the properties for each individual file.

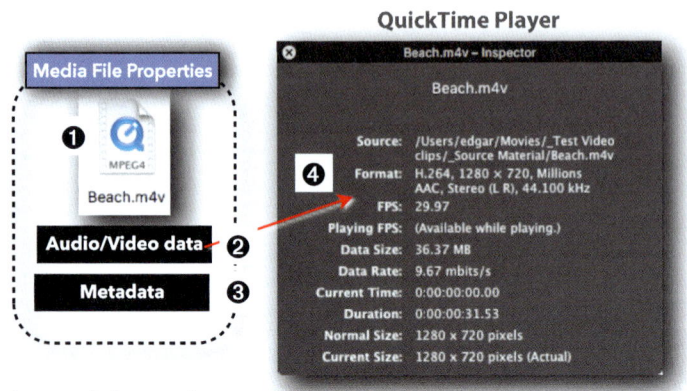

QuickTime Player

Beach.m4v – Inspector

Beach.m4v

Source:	/Users/edgar/Movies/_Test Video clips/_Source Material/Beach.m4v
Format:	H.264, 1280 × 720, Millions AAC, Stereo (L R), 44.100 kHz
FPS:	29.97
Playing FPS:	(Available while playing.)
Data Size:	36.37 MB
Data Rate:	9.67 mbits/s
Current Time:	0:00:00:00.00
Duration:	0:00:00:31.53
Normal Size:	1280 x 720 pixels
Current Size:	1280 x 720 pixels (Actual)

🌐 Clip

When importing Media Files into FCPx, it creates a Clip ❻ for each imported Media File ❺ and you can see those Clips in the FCPx Browser Pane.

What you don't see, but always have to be aware of when working in FCPx, is what happens with the underlying architecture of a database ❼ (actually multiple related databases). Here is the basic procedure:

> ▶ The Event ❼ in FCPx that you import your Media Files to is a database ❽.

> ▶ Whenever you import a Media File ❺, FCPx creates a new record ❾ in that database.

> ▶ Each record ❾ represents one Clip ❻, linked to its parent media file ❺.

> ▶ All the properties of a media file are copied to that specific record during the import procedure.

> ▶ The power and flexibility in FCPx is based on that database architecture. Think about it, when working with Clips in FCPx means, your video editing tasks are actually database tasks in the background.

Video Editing Tasks
=
Database Tasks

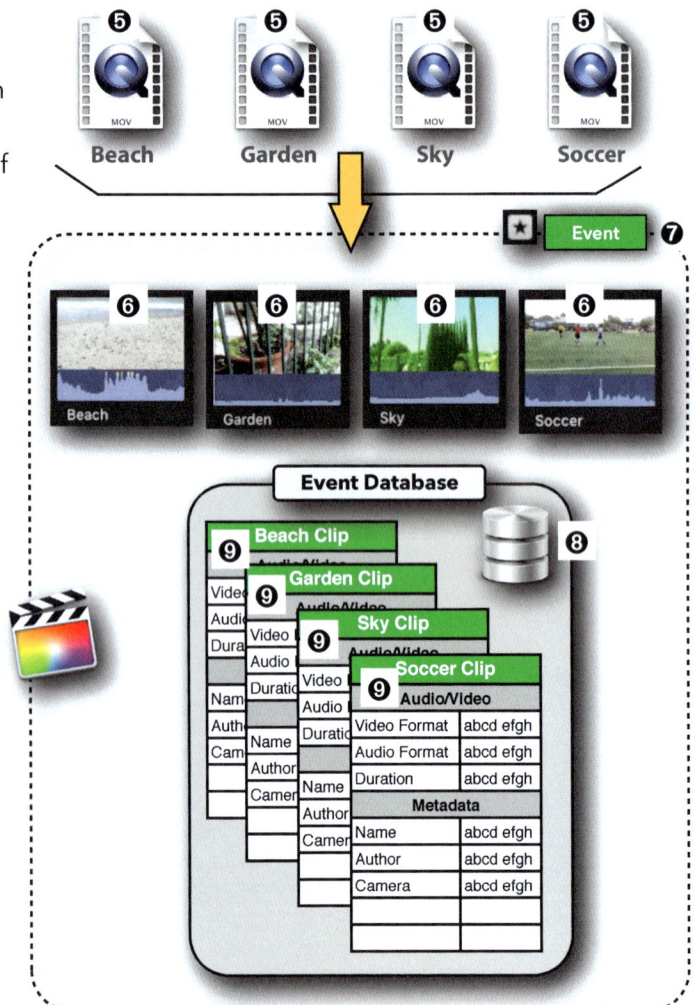

➡ *Event Database vs. Project Database*

Once you understand the basic concept that a Clip in FCPx relates to a record in a database, managed by FCPx in the background with all its properties that are stored in that record, we can go to the next revelation: In addition to Event Databases, there are also Project Databases.

Here is a screenshot of the Browser Pane and Timeline Pane, showing how their elements relate to the underlying databases:

🌐 Event ➤ Event Database

- ▸ Every Event ❶ that is listed in the Libraries Sidebar of the Browser in FCPx represents a database, that specific *Event Database* ❷.

- ▸ When you select that Event ❶ in the Sidebar, you will see all the Event Clips ❸ that are imported into that Event. Each Event Clip represents one record ❹ in that specific Event Database.

- ▸ When you select an Event Clip ❸ in the Browser, all its properties ❺ are displayed in the Inspector Pane ❻ of the FCPx Workspace window. The Inspector functions as the editor to view and edit the currently displayed record (Clip).

🌐 Project ➤ Project Database

- ▸ Every Project ❼ inside an Event that is listed in the FCPx Browser Pane also represents a database, that specific *Project Database* ❽.

- ▸ When you *double-click* on a Project ❼ in the Browser, it "opens" in the Timeline Pane ❾ with all the other Timeline Clips you have added and edited while working on your video.

- ▸ Each Clip ❾ on the Timeline represents a single record ❿ in that Project Database.

- ▸ When you select a Timeline Clip ❾, all its properties ⓫ are displayed in the Inspector Pane ❻ of the FCPx Workspace window. Now you can view and edit all the properties of that Timeline Clip.

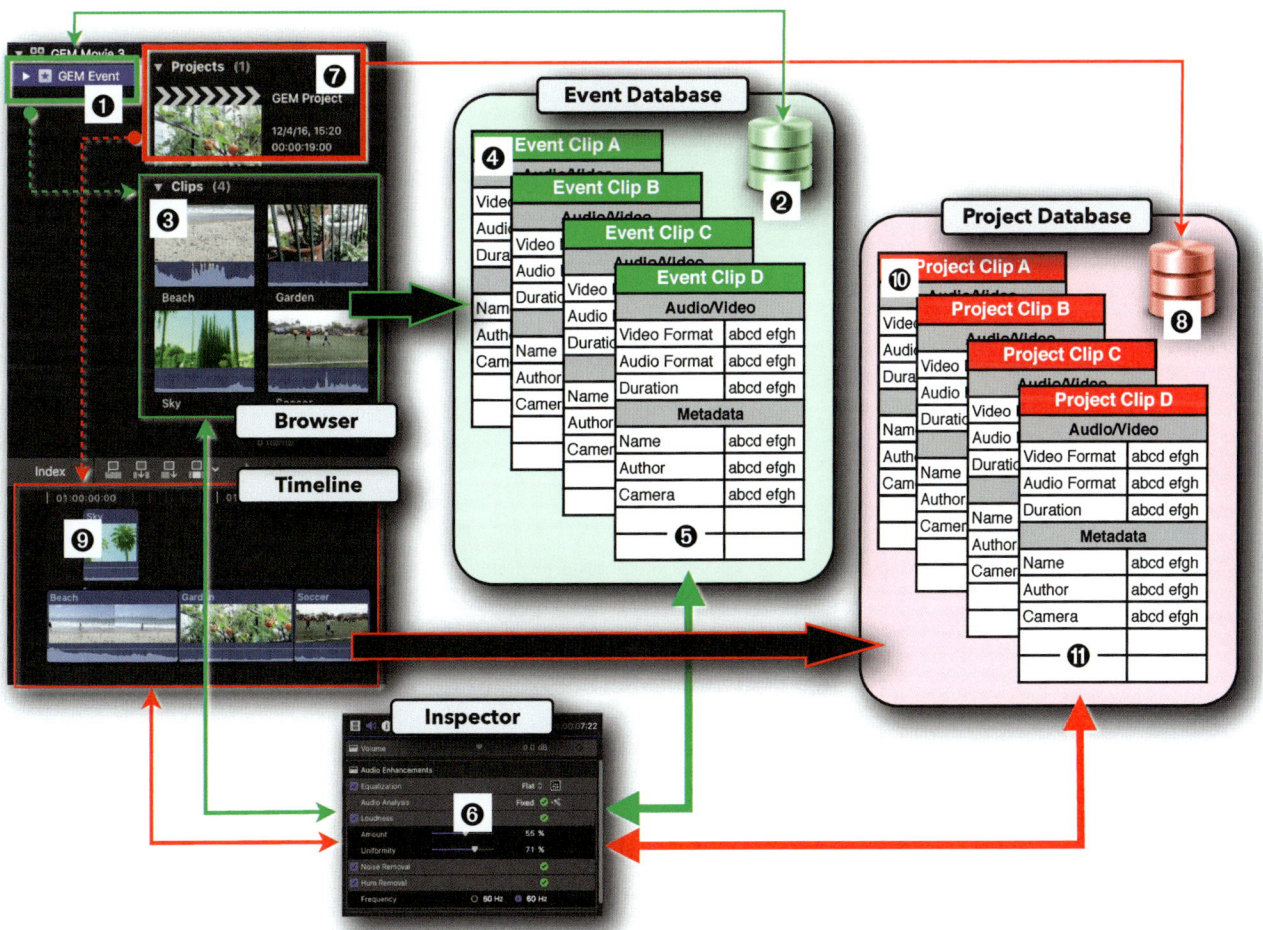

➡ *Library Database - Event Database - Project Database*

The Library itself, the container that holds all the elements of your video project, is also a database, which means that in FCPx you have three types of databases.

Here is the diagram again from earlier when I introduced the main components, showing those components and their hierarchy in FCPx.

- ▶ ❶ A Library contains one or multiple Events and each Event contains its Media Files and also one or multiple Projects.
- ▶ ❷ Now compare that concept to the FCPx user interface. I added the database symbols to indicate which component represents a database.
- ▶ ❸ The diagram on the right is a screenshot of the Finder that shows the "inside" of a Library File, containing all its elements. I color-coded the three database files accordingly. This is for demonstration purposes only and you should never mess around on that level anyway.

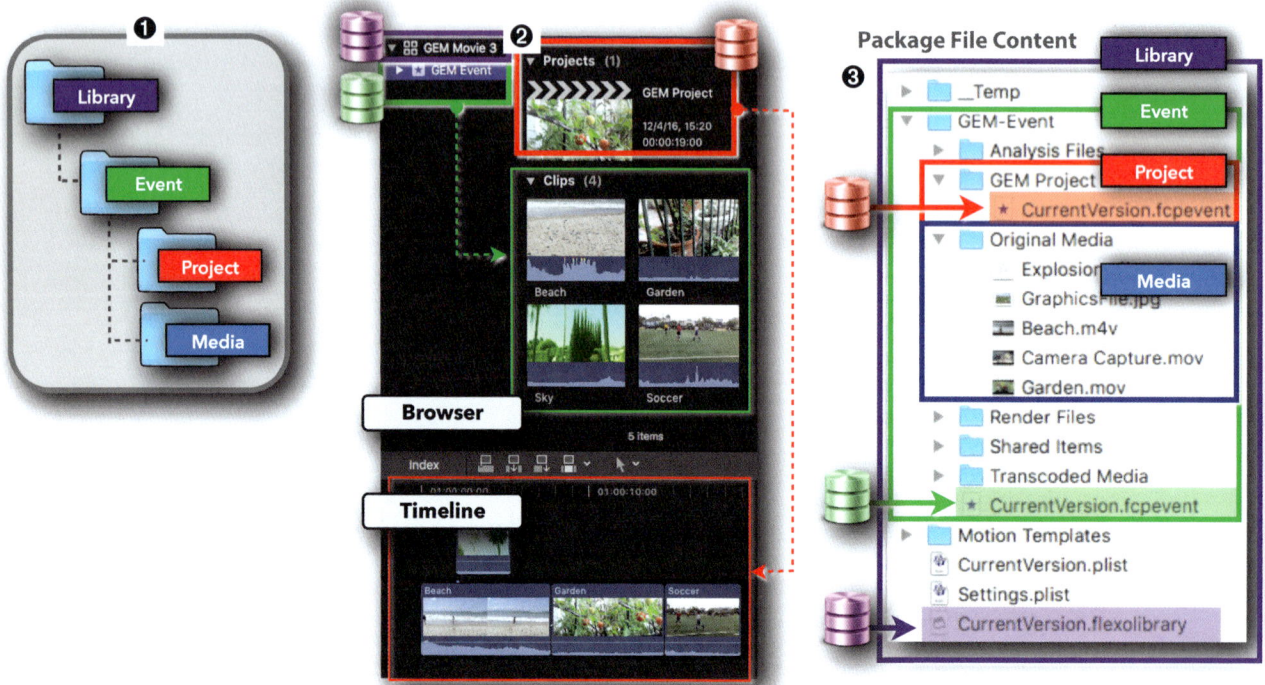

Here is a diagram with another example of a Library. It has two Events, the first Event ❹ (represented by the "**Event Database X**") contains one Project, "**Project Database Xa**" and the second Event ❺ (represented by the **Event Database Y**) has three Projects, represented by "**Project Database Ya**", "**Project Database Yb**", and "**Project Database Yc**".

From now on, you can think of a Library in a database-related way. Whenever you edit a Clip in that Library, remember that this Clip is represented by a record in one of the databases and if you edit that Clip, you edit the values of a field in that record.

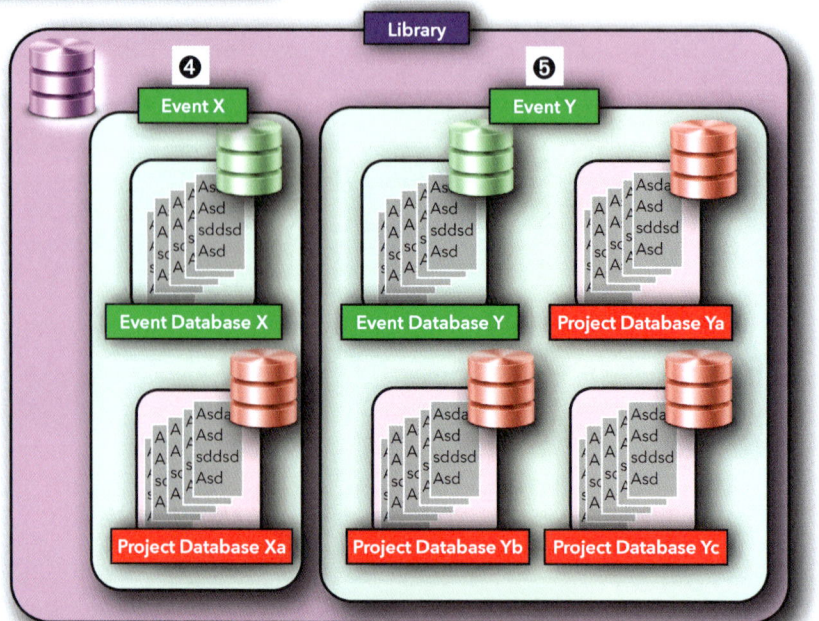

➡️ *Detailed Procedure*

Here is a diagram with more details and the "awareness" of databases.

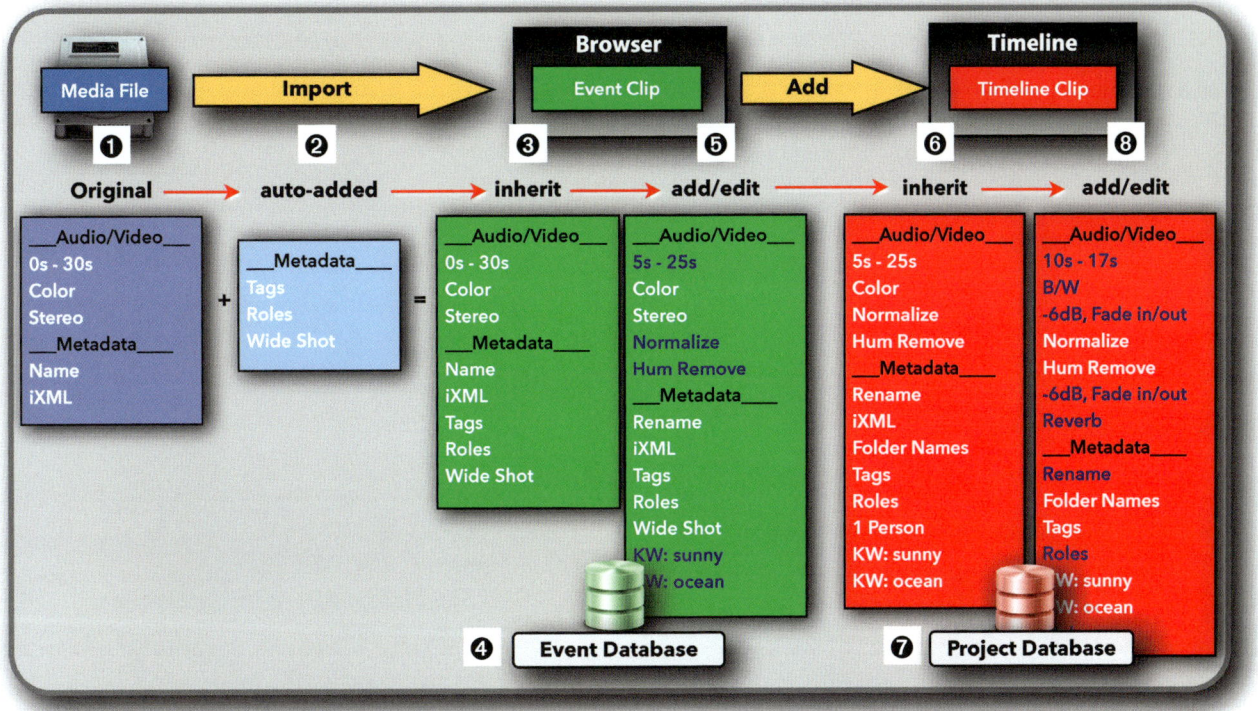

- The Media File ❶ contains its original data. The Audio/Video data determines the duration, the video standard, and audio format. In addition, the Metadata includes the file name and other data the recording device might have stored with the file (iXML, ID3 tags, etc.).

- During the import, FCPx can add additional Metadata ❷. It can analyze the file for specific parameters and add those as Metadata (Keywords) to the newly created Event Clip. For example, how many people are in the shot, is it a wide shot or close up, or assign Roles based on the content (Video, Dialog, Music, etc.).

- FCPx now creates the Event Clip ❸ and adds all that original data plus the auto-added data ❷ to that Event Clip.

  - **Database**: From a database point of view, this new Event Clip is a new record in the Event database ❹ and all the data are fields of that record with their corresponding field values.

- Like with any other database, you can change values ❺ for the various fields (i.e. change the phone number or the address of a contacts database) or add values to fields that were empty before. Whatever you change in the Event Clip (change the length, the volume, add

new Keywords) only affects the properties of that specific record in the Event database, that Event Clip, which is now independent from the original data of the Media File ❶. However, the record still has an entry that lists that parent Media File it is linked to.

- When you add the Event Clip to the Timeline ❻, FCPx creates a new Timeline Clip.

  - **Database**: The Project Timeline you are dragging the Clip to is a separate database, the Project Database ❼ (every Project in an Event is a separate database). FCPx basically takes the Event Clip (that record ❺ in the Event database ❹) and creates a new record entry ❻ in the Project database ❼ (represented by that Timeline Clip), copying over all the fields and values.

- Once you have a Timeline Clip placed on the Timeline, you can edit its properties ❽. All those changes are nothing other than changes in that specific record in the Project database ❼, which is now independent from the Event Clip (the record in the Event database ❹). However, the Timeline Clip record still has an entry that lists its parent Event Clip, which has entry for the pathname of its linked Media File, so the Timeline Clip can be played back properly.

Rendering

Rendering is a concept that is essential to all video editing software. A few things about the terminology:

▶ Rendering is just another word for "processing".

▶ Usually, you have a source data (i.e. a single video clip or an entire project) that you apply an effect to or export it to a specific format. You "render" it, which means you process the original data to get a new "rendered" data and store it as a rendered file(s).

➡ *Playback Procedures*

The process of rendering is something that FCPx requires under some circumstances to guarantee proper playback functionality of your Clips.

⚫ Standard Playback

Here is an example that does not require rendering:

▶ Let's assume you imported a Media File ❶ into the Libraries Browser.

▶ You place that Event Clip to the Project Timeline four times ❷, and as we know by now, they are all independent Clips with their own record in the Project Database.

▶ All four Clips are linked ❸ to the same Event Clip and use that one for playback, the same Original Media File ❶.

▶ All four Timeline Clips originally have the same properties (the same values in their database record) they inherited from their parent Event Clip. Therefore, when playing them back ❹, audio and video look and sound the same ❺.

▶ The exception in this example is the fourth Clip. On that one I increased the volume by 6dB ❻.

▶ **Real-time Playback Parameter**: Changing the audio playback level on a Clip is such a minor adjustment that FCPx can still play back the Original Media File and apply that changed Playback Parameter (level = +6dB) in real time ❼. Trimming a Clip is also one of those real-time playback parameters, because it just changes the position from where to where FCPx plays back that Media File.

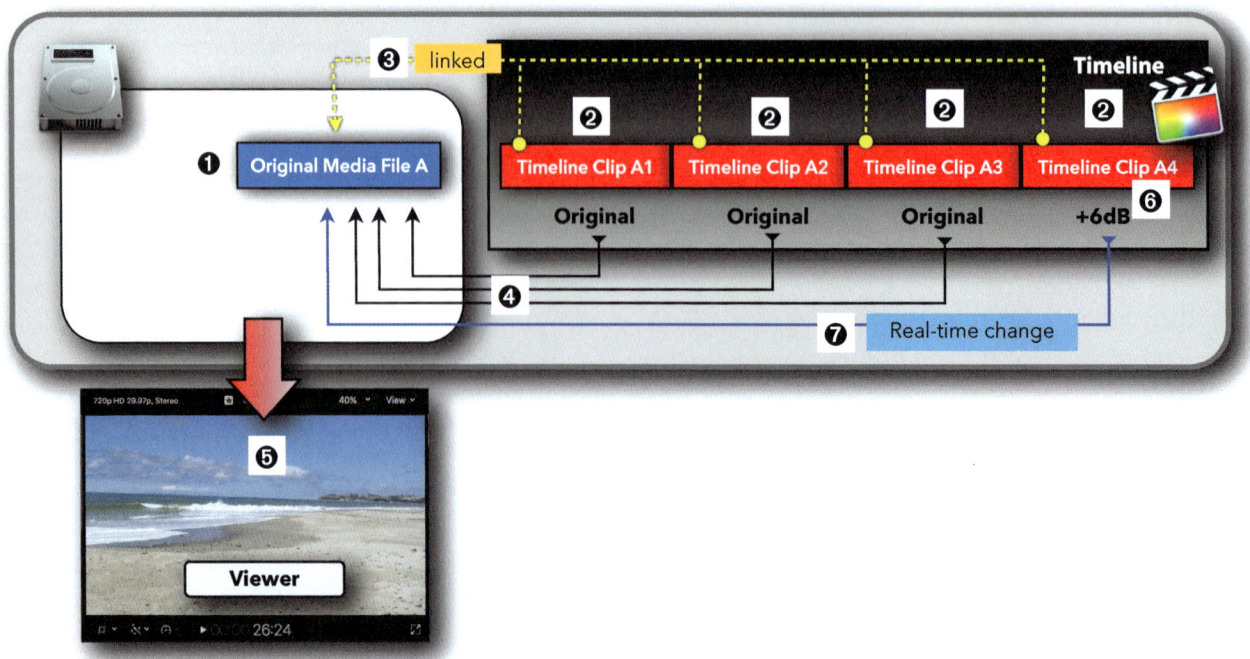

Rendered Playback

Now, when I apply edits to the Timeline Clips that FCPx cannot play back in real-time, it needs to render them. Here is the same example again:

▸ **Timeline Clip A1**: The first Clip ❶ is unchanged and it plays back from the Original Media File ❷.

▸ **Timeline Clip A2**: The second Clip ❸ has a +6dB volume adjustment, which can be applied in real-time ❹, still playing back from the Original Media File.

▸ **Timeline Clip A3**: On this Clip ❺, I add Reverb to it. Now, FCPx determines that this is too much processing to apply in real-time. If it is an "easy" process, it still can handle it, but the playback quality might suffer, depending on how much other processing is required in your Project. To avoid any issues, FCPx decides to "render" the effect, which means it processes that data and creates a new file with the applied effect, a new Render File ❻. Now, when you play back that Clip ❺, FCPx, uses that

specific Render File ❻ instead for playback. And when we think in database terms again, those changes (the existence of the Render File and its location) are stored in the Project Database record of that Timeline Clip.

▸ **Timeline Clip A4**: On this Clip ❼, I add a Color effect, and again, FCPx prefers to render the effect, processes that data and creates a new Render File ❽. Now, when you play back that Clip, FCPx uses that Render File instead of the Original Media File for playback.

▸ When you play back your Project, all the four Timeline Clips play back ❾ nicely, while FCPx uses the appropriate files, original or rendered for the individual Timeline Clips.

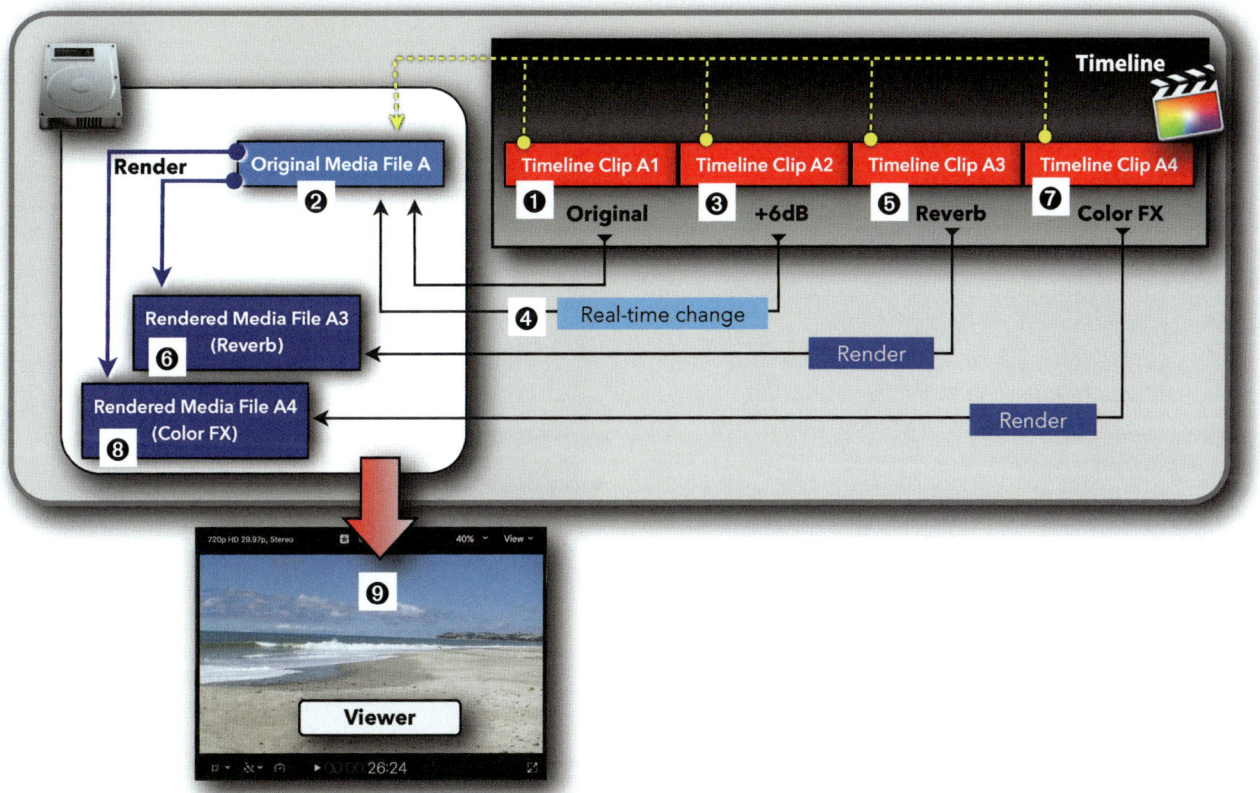

This is just the basic procedure about what happens in FCPx behind the scene regarding the rendering. There are a few controls in FCPx that are related to rendering and let you configure some part of them. Let's explore that next.

➡ *Render Configuration*

Info Inspector (Project)

🔮 Render File Quality

Because FCPx creates a new video file when rendering an effect, it gives you control over what format (quality) that video file will have. It is done on the Project level.

- ☑ Select the Project in the Browser Pane.
- ☑ Its properties will now be displayed in the Inspector (*cmd+4*).
- ☑ *Click* the Info Button 🔵 ❶ on the Inspector Header.
- ☑ When you *click* on the *Modify* button ❷, the Project Properties Sheet opens, which has a Rendering ❸ parameter with a popup menu to select from six different video formats ❹.

🔮 Dotted Render Line

Requires Rendering

Whenever FCPx decides that a Timeline Clip or a section of the Clip requires rendering, it displays a white dotted line ❺ on top of the Time Ruler to mark that section. Remember, you still might play back that Clip if the CPU of your computer can process the effects in real-time.

🔮 Manual vs. Automatic Rendering

FCPx Preferences ➤ Playback

You also have control over when FCPx renders the files:

The *FCPx Preferences ➤ Playback* (*cmd+,*) has two controls:

- ▶ **Background render ❻**: The checkbox toggles between manual rendering and automatic rendering. Please note that I use the term "automatic rendering" instead of "background rendering". Technically, the rendering doesn't happen in the background while you are working in FCPx in the foreground. You actually have to stop any editing before FCPx starts the processing of the render file. That means, you just tell FCPx to "automatically" start rendering when FCPx is in "idle mode".

- ▶ **Start after ❼**: Here you set the idle time (up to 999sec) that determines how long FCPx is waiting after your last interaction with FCPx before it starts the render process. This makes sure that no CPU power is used for rendering while working in FCPx. Of course, the render process can stop and pick up at any time. If you quit FCPx while still rendering, a little window ❽ pops up, reminding you that it cancels the tasks, but rendering will automatically pick up again when you launch FCPx the next time.

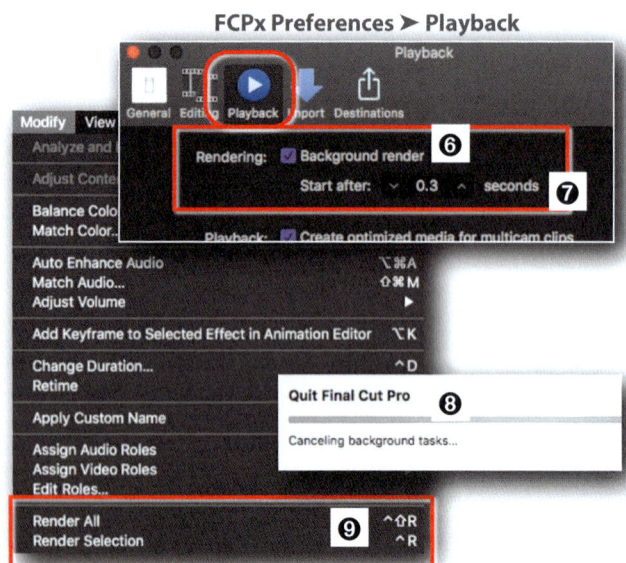

Here are two commands that let you start the render process manually ❾:

- ▶ **Manual Render All:** Menu Command *Modify ➤ Render All*, Key Command *sh+ctr+R*
- ▶ **Manual Render Selection only**: Menu Command *Modify ➤ Render Selection*, Key Command *sh++R*

Background Tasks Window

FCPx Workspace

Any ongoing rendering process is indicated in two places:

▶ **Background Tasks Button**: The Background Tasks Button ❶ is located in the upper-left corner of the FCPx Workspace window. This is the dynamic button, showing a dynamic pie chart ⬕ to indicate the progress of any ongoing background tasks, including rendering. It displays a checkmark if the process is done ✅. You can *click* on the button to open the Background Tasks Window.

Background Tasks Window

▶ **Background Tasks Window**: The Background Tasks Window ❷, that can also be opened from the Main Menu *Window ➤ Background Tasks* or the Key Command *opt+9*, shows the individual tasks ❸ and their progress. You can even pause ⏸ or stop ⊗ any process ❹.

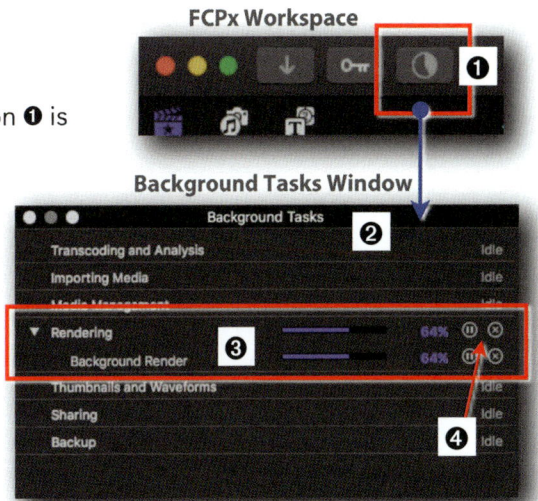

Share Render Files

Two things you have to be aware of when copying Clips that were rendered:

▶ **Same Library**: Render Files are shared between Events and Projects of the same Library.

▶ **Different Library**: Render Files are not copied when copying Clips between Libraries. They are re-rendered in the target Library.

Delete Rendered Files

Please keep in mind that render files can eat up a lot of storage space over time. With every new edit and new applied effect, a new render file is created and the old ones that became obsolete will not be deleted (so you can use the undo command).

Because Render Files belong to the so-called "Generated" files, they are not imported by the user, but created by FCPx. That means, FCPx can re-create them at any time if necessary. So you can go ahead and delete Render Files to free up disk space. There are two things to consider:

▶ **Generated Files**: FCPx has no "*Delete Render Files*" command, they are considered "generated files".

▶ **Library - Event - Project**: The delete command is under the File Menu, which is highly dynamic (contextual). You can delete the Render files from a specific Project, from all Projects in an Event, or from all Projects in a specific Library. You determine that by selecting that item in the Browser. The File Menu then changes the command accordingly:

❺ *Delete Generate Project Files...*

❻ *Delete Generate Event Files...*

❼ *Delete Generate Library Files...*

▶ From the Sheet that slides out underneath the Workspace, you can choose to delete the Render Files and have the option to select which type ❽:

• **Unused Only**: Only the Render Files that are not currently used by any Clips are deleted.

• **All**: All Render Files from the selected items are deleted.

Clips and Timelines

The concept I'm going to show in this section can be the cause of some confusion during editing if you are not familiar with it. It is what FCPx considers a Clip and a Project in regards to the Timeline.

➡ *Standard Clip*

FCPx uses a lot of different types of Clips for different purposes and we will get into that a little bit later. But first, let's look at the Standard Clip that is created when you import a Media File.

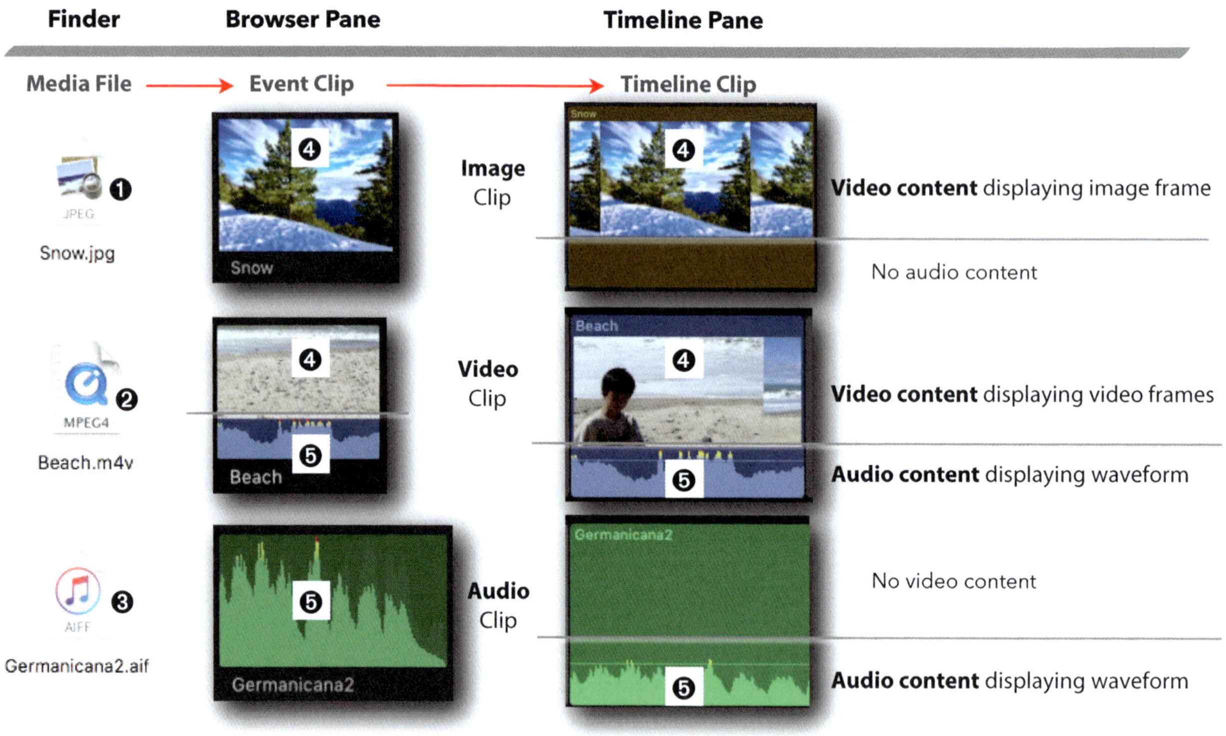

A few things to be aware of:

▶ **Media File**: What you are importing is a Media File, an image file ❶, video file ❷, or audio file ❷.
▶ **Media Content**: Depending on the Media File, it can have two types of content:
  • Video ❹: A video file, of course, has video content but an image file also has video content, just a single frame.
  • Audio ❺: A video file most likely also has audio content and an audio file, of course, has only audio content.
▶ **Single Clip**: FCPx creates a single Clip for every Media File you import into your Library. That Clip includes whatever content was included in the Media File. FCPx does not split the video and audio content of a file into two separate clips (you can do that later during editing if you need to).
▶ **Visual Content**: The content is always visible on the Clip, represented by a video image ❹ in the upper portion and the audio waveform ❺ in the lower portion of the thumbnail. The Clip Appearance Button 🎬 in the Browser and Timeline Header lets you adjust how and what you like to display on the thumbnail image.
▶ **Thumbnail Editing**: You can even perform edits directly on the thumbnails, for example, making Clip Ranges, assigning Keywords, and in the Timeline, you can even adjust the audio level, plus Fade-ins and Fade-outs directly on the waveform.

🌑 What is a Timeline?

Let's go over some procedures and terminology in this following example. Try to follow the train of thought to understand the underlying architecture in FCPx.

▶ **Video File**: "Beach.m4v" is a video file ❶. It is 31 seconds long.

▶ **View in QuickTime Player - visible timeline**: When you open ❷ the file in the QuickTime Player, you can see a timeline ❸ as part of the Navigation Controls. This is the timeline of that video "Beach", its *Source Timeline*.

▶ **Event Clip - no timeline?** When you import that video file ❶ into FCPx, it will show up in the Browser Pane as an Event Clip ❹, displayed as a thumbnail. It doesn't show any timeline.

▶ **Event Clip - invisible timeline**: The length of the thumbnail (or a longer filmstrip if it displays multiple thumbnails) in the Browser Pane represents an invisible timeline ❺ of that Clip, its Source Timeline. The left border of the thumbnail is the beginning of the timeline and the right border is the end of its timeline. You can click anywhere on the thumbnail between those borders (a Playhead appears) to play from that relative time position.

▶ **Project - free timeline**: When you create a new Project in FCPx, think of it as an "empty" video file. It has a timeline but no video content yet. If you would open that video file in the QuickTime Player you would see the Playhead moving along the Timeline but there would be no image, it's blank.

▶ **What is the Timeline Pane?** As I mentioned earlier, the Timeline Pane itself is not your Project, it is just a window pane in FCPx.

▶ **Open in Timeline**: You use an "Open" command to display specific content in that Timeline Pane. For example, *double-clicking* on a Project ❻ in the Browser Pane opens that Project in the Timeline Pane ❼. Now you are looking at that specific Project Timeline in the Timeline Pane. *Double-clicking* on another Project (in a different Event or different Library) will open that Project in the Timeline Pane, showing its specific Project Timeline.

▶ **Add to Timeline**: Once "something" (i.e. a Project) is opened in the Timeline Pane, you can add Clips ❽ to that Timeline ❾.

And here is the important revelation: A Project is only one component that you can open in the Timeline Pane. You can also "open Clips in the Timeline Pane", and that is the crucial part to wrap your head around to fully understand the concept and functionality of Clips, Projects, and Timelines in FCPx.

⬤ Timeline Pane (Basic Understanding)

Here are a few screenshots of the Timeline Pane to demonstrate its basic functionality.

When FCPx is open, but no Library is loaded ❶ (i.e. you closed all Libraries), then the Timeline Pane is completely blank ❷, only showing the Timeline Header with its controls.

Browser Pane   **Timeline Pane**

When you create a new Library with an Event but no Project ❸, then the Timeline Pane is still blank, but now displays a "New Project" button ❹ that you can click to create a new Project. This is the same view if that Event already has a Project created, but it wasn't opened before.

Once you created a new Project ❺ (visible in the Browser Pane and open it ❻) *double-click* on the Project or *ctr+click* on it and choose from the *Shortcut Menu ➤ Open Project*), the Timeline Pane will finally show a Timeline, an empty Timeline with the following elements in the three sections of the Timeline Area:

▶   **Header**: The name of the Project ❼ in the Header with its length (00:00)
▶   **Time Ruler**: The Time Ruler ❽ on top with the red Playhead at the beginning
▶   **Timeline Area**: The Primary Storyline ❾ (the black area) with the outline of an empty Clip at the beginning

Once you add Clips to the Timeline Area, two things will happen. The black movie slate icon in the Browser pane shows a thumbnail image ❿ and the Timeline Header now shows the duration ⓫ of the Project.

🌐 Timeline Pane (The Bigger Picture)

Once you understand the basic concept of the Timeline Pane, lets reveal its real functionality by following the next four points:

▶ A **Timeline** is a concept used in most video editing and also audio editing applications. It is a horizontal strip ❶ that displays elapsed time in a linear fashion from left to right. On top is a Time Ruler ❷ that functions as the time reference with dividers that reference the distance between those dividers to time units. The video ❸ and audio ❹ content are placed as Clips along that timeline and are, therefore, referenced to the time markers displayed in the Time Ruler.

▶ A **Project** ❺ in FCPx is a component that has a "built-in" Timeline with content aligned along that Timeline.

▶ A **Clip** ❻, as we have seen earlier in the QuickTime Player, is also a component that has a "built-in" Timeline with content aligned along that Timeline.

▶ The **Timeline Pane** ❼ in FCPx has no content, it is just a window pane that can display components with a "built-in" Timeline with video and audio content aligned to that timeline.

> **The Timeline Pane in FCPx can "open"**
> **any components that has a timeline**
> **with video and audio content aligned to that timeline**

Here is a summary of the two important concepts you have to understand in FCPx:

Concept 1

The important concept to understand about the Timeline Pane in FCPx is that it is not the same as your Project Timeline, it is only a window that can display a Project or a Clip.

Concept 2

And the important concept to understand about the Clips in FCPx is that you can also open them in the Timeline Pane like any other Project and even edit Clips in the Timeline Pane the same way you edit Projects.

Both, Projects and Clips, have a special "open" command that lets you display them in the Timeline Pane:

▶ **Open Project**: *Ctr-click* on a Project ❺ in the Browser Pane and choose from the *Shortcut Menu ➤ Open Project* ❽ (or just *double-click* on the Project).

▶ **Open Clip**: *Ctr-click* on an Event Clip ❻ in the Browser Pane or a Timeline Clip in the Timeline Pane and choose from the *Shortcut Menu ➤ Open Clip* ❾.

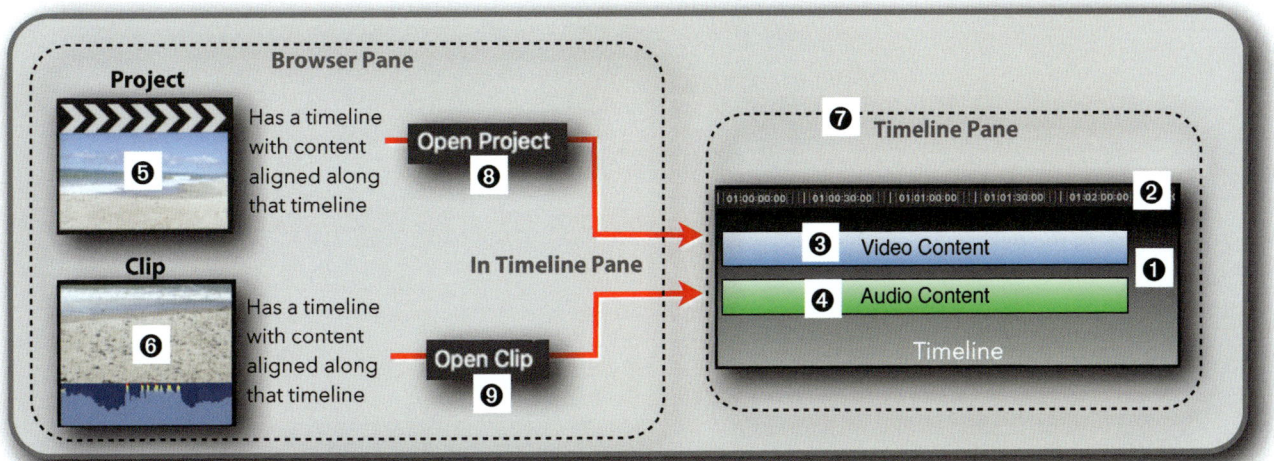

Open Clips in Timeline Pane

The concept of opening Clips in the Timeline Pane and even editing them is a very powerful feature in FCPx, especially with a specific type of Clip, so-called Compound Clips. I will discuss that later in the advanced editing chapter.

Here is a final screenshot on that topic to prepare your mindset and show you what to watch out for in the context of Clips, Projects, and the functionality of the Timeline Pane.

▶ **Open a Project ❶**: To open a Project in the Timeline Pane, you select it from the Browser Pane.

▶ **Open an Event Clip ❷**: To open an Event Clip in the Timeline Pane, you also select it from the Browser Pane. Pay attention to the following things:

- As a default, the Timeline displays the tracks of the parent Media Files the Clip is referenced to. For example, a Video Clip with the Clip Name and the added "- v1" for the video track ❸, and for the audio track ❹ the Clips Name and the added "- a1" for audio track.

- The Timeline Header shows "EventName | ClipName" ❺. In this example "My Event | Beach" to indicate that this is an Event Clip and the name of the Event it belongs to.

▶ **Open a Timeline Clip ❻**: Please make sure you understand the following procedure: By selecting the "*Open Clip*" command on a Timeline Clip that is currently the "content" of a Project displayed in the Timeline Pane ❼, you will change the view of the Timeline Pane and now display the content of that specific Timeline Clip.

- The Timeline again displays the tracks of the parent Media Files the Clip is referenced to.

- The Timeline Header shows "ProjectName | ClipName" ❽. In this example "My Project | Beach".

- The in and out markers ❾ show you the current trim boundaries with the media in the striped area that is not used in that edit.

Ctr+click on the left ◁ or right ▷ Timeline History Buttons next to the name in the Timeline Header to display a Shortcut Menu ❿ with all the components that you have displayed so far in the Timeline Pane. The names show the hierarchy (similar to the displayed name in the Header) and you can select an item to switch the view to that item.

Where is the FCPx Project File?

➡ #1 Databases

On the outside, FCPx looks like a video editing software, but its architecture regarding file management is based on a database. So technically, Final Cut Pro X is a database application with special tools to manage and manipulate its data (Clips, Projects, etc.). This is an important fact you always have to keep in mind when working in FCPx, as we will see when dealing with data and file management tasks.

Final Cut Pro X = **Database**

Final Cut Pro X is a Collection of Related Databases

➡ #2 Document-based vs. Library-based Applications

Here is something you have to be aware of when using any kind of apps, because it determines its functionality regarding file management.

🌑 Document Based Applications

A text application like *Word* or *Pages*, or a spreadsheet application like *Excel* or *Numbers* are so-called document-based applications.

- ☑ **Launch the App**: Launching the application will only open that application without any document.
- ☑ **Document**: The application lets you create documents (text, spreadsheets, etc.).
- ☑ **Open/Save**: You manually open document files to work on and save any edits back to that document file.
- ☑ **Multiple Documents Open**: You can have multiple documents open at a time, working on different spreadsheets, or text documents.

🌑 Library-based Applications

The iTunes or the Photos applications are so-called library-based applications.

- ☑ **Launch**: Launching the application will automatically show your music or your pictures.
- ☑ **Library**: Music and Photos are stored in a Library file, which is a database that the app opens when you launch it.
- ☐ ~~**Open/Save**~~: The app doesn't have an open or save command. The database is automatically loaded when you launch the app and any changes are saved immediately to the Library file.
- ☐ ~~**Multiple Documents Open**~~: You can technically create different Libraries (different databases) for iTunes or Photos, but you can only have one Library open at a time.

➡ **#3 Special Library-based Application**

Here is a diagram that shows the two types of applications.

Once a document-based application is launched ❶ you can open ❷ any document ❸ for that app, work on it, and save ❷ the edits back to the document file ❸.

When you launch a library-based application ❹, it automatically opens ❺ its Library file ❻ (the database). Any changes you make will automatically be saved ❺ back to the Library file ❻.

Document-based vs Library-based applications

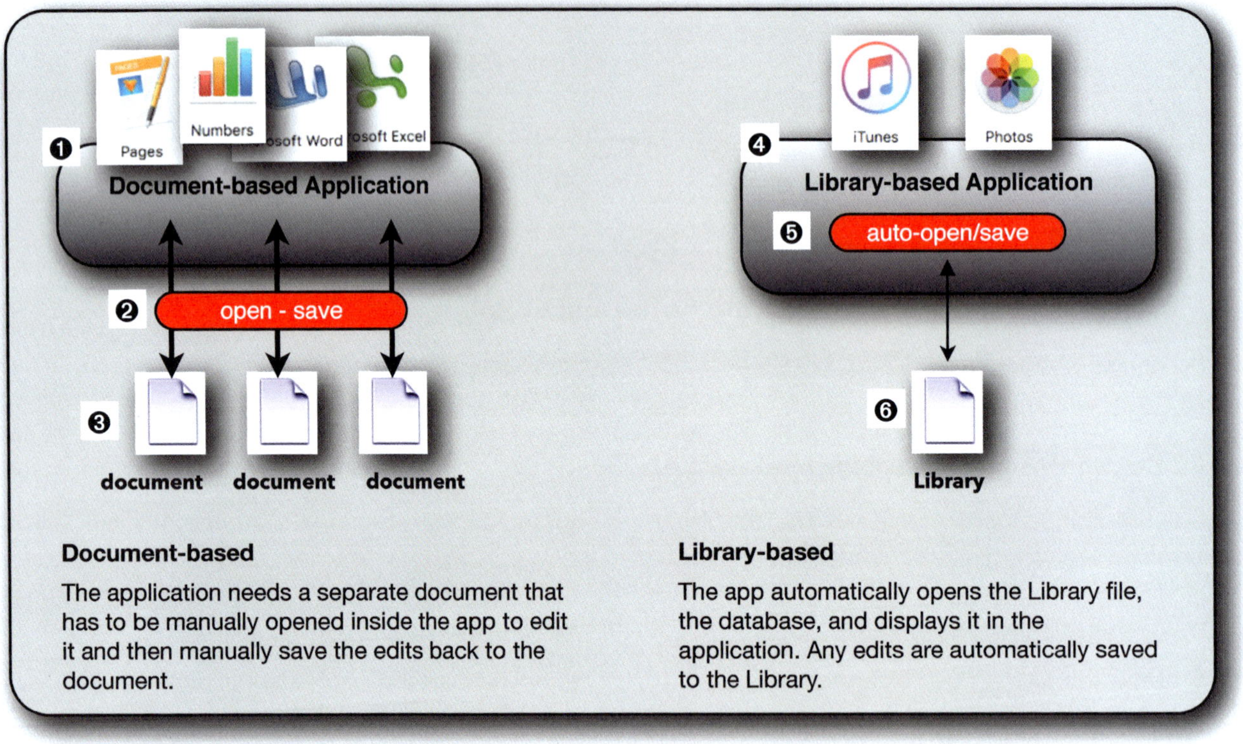

Document-based

The application needs a separate document that has to be manually opened inside the app to edit it and then manually save the edits back to the document.

Library-based

The app automatically opens the Library file, the database, and displays it in the application. Any edits are automatically saved to the Library.

Although technically, FCPx is a library-based application, it functions more like a hybrid, using the functionality of both concepts:

- ☑ FCPx is a library-based application ❼.
- ☑ FCPx saves its data to a Library file ❽.
- ☑ FCPx has a standard *File ➤ Open Library* command ❾ to manually open a specific Library file.
- ☑ FCPx lets you open multiple Libraries ❽ at a time.
- ☑ FCPx has no *File ➤ Save Library* command. All edits are saved automatically ❿ (immediately).

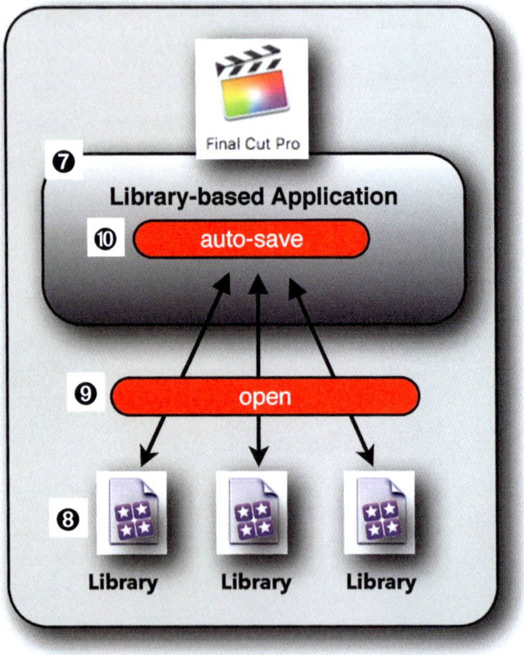

🔮 **Library File**

All the components that are related to a specific movie or video you are working on in FCPx are stored in a single Library File. So technically, the thing you are working on is not called a "*Project*", you are working "*on a Library*", or "*in a Library*". That sounds strange, but we will get more into specific terminology to find out what a Library actually is.

➡ #4 Package File

The Library File is a special type of file, a so-called "*Package File*". This is the concept of having a folder that can contain all types of files and other nested folders, but make it appear on the "outside" as a single file, a "self-contained file". Please note that incremental backup applications like TimeMachine or Carbon Copy Cloner recognizes those files as folders and, therefore, only backup the changed content inside and not the entire Package File every time.

> **A Package File is a Folder disguised as a File**

🌐 Applications

The concept of Package Files always has been used for applications in OSX. Every file that an application needs to run is "packaged" into a folder and converted so it looks like a single file on the "outside". This has some major advantages:

- ☑ An application can be conveniently treated (copy, move, delete) as a single file.
- ☑ All the required files are kept together inside the Package File.
- ☑ A Package File can still have a single unique extension like a regular file (but it is usually hidden in the Finder).
- ☑ Packaging a folder as a file reduces the "risk" that a user will open the folder, delete some files by accident, and leave the application corrupted.
- ☑ There is a "hidden" command that lets you "open" the Package File. ***Ctr+click*** on a file in the Finder to open its Shortcut Menu. If it has a "*Show Package Contents*" ❶ menu item, then it is a Package File and you can select that option to display its content in the Finder like a regular folder.

🌐 Documents

All the advantages of a Package File can also be used for any kind of non-application files, like documents or libraries. This is especially useful for documents that include "assets", additional content like audio, video, and graphics files, as they are used in FCPx. This content can be "embedded" in this folder-like Package File. On the Finder, it still looks like a single file.

When you ***ctr+click*** on a FCPx Library file ❷ and choose "Show Package Contents" ❸, the Finder will display all the enclosed content ❹ of that Library file. In addition to the convenience, one of the reason to have all those files "hidden" inside a Package is that you don't mess with them on the Finder level. The entire management of those files is handled through various commands on the FCPx interface ❺.

Warning: I will only show the content of the Library File in this manual to demonstrate the functionality and you should never alter those files (which could end up in a corrupted Library)! All the necessary tasks are handled through the FCPx user interface.

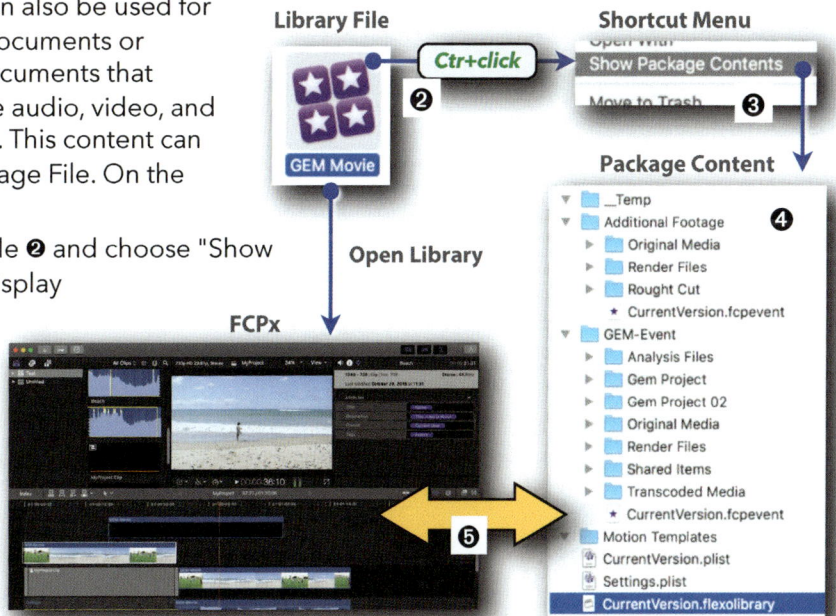

Components & Terminology

Here are the five main components in FCPx.

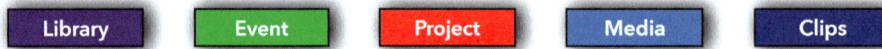

With the next few diagrams, I want to make sure you have a clear understanding on how those components relate to each other. Let's start again with the diagram that shows the typical workflow, where you import source media files into your FCPx and then add them to the Timeline to assemble your new video.

This is the typical workflow:

- When you first open FCPx, it automatically creates a so-called *Library* ❶ and an *Event* ❷. You can create more Libraries, all following the same file structure that I show now.

- Think of the Library as a container or a main folder ❸ that holds all the components related to that Library.

- An Event represents a nested folder ❹ inside that Library folder ❸. You can create multiple Events inside a Library to organize other components in a Library.

- When you import media ❺ (video, audio, images) into your current Library, you have to tell FCPx to which Event ❷ you want to assign those media files to. Those source files are stored in a subfolder ❻ (named "Original Media") inside that chosen Event folder ❹.

- For each source file, FCPx creates a Clip ❼ that is linked to its Parent Source File ❺. You only work with those Clips in FCPx, not the Media Files ❺ directly.

- When you want to create your new video in FCPx with those Clips ❼, you have to add them to a Timeline ❽. However, a new Library ❶ doesn't have a Timeline yet (only the empty Timeline area on the FCPx window). You have to manually create a new Project ❾ first, which will create an empty Timeline ❽, where you can now add the Clips ❼ to. So a Project is represented by a single Timeline, which is similar to a Sequence in older FCP7 versions.

- The same way you have to choose an Event to import Media Files to, you also have to choose an Event ❷ to create a Project in. You can create multiple Projects (each with their own Timeline) in an Event, which are subfolders ❿ stored inside the ❹ Event folder inside a Library folder ❸.

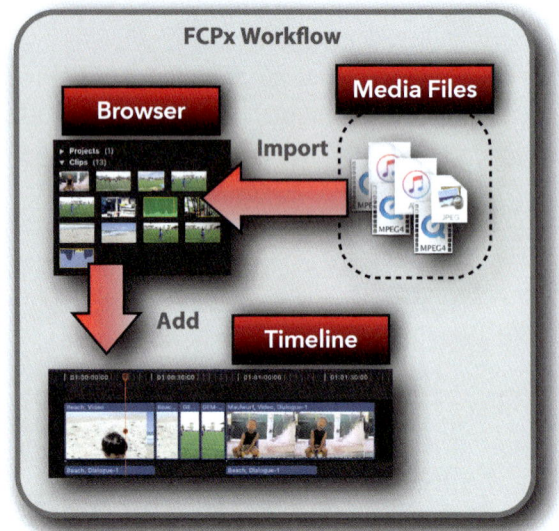

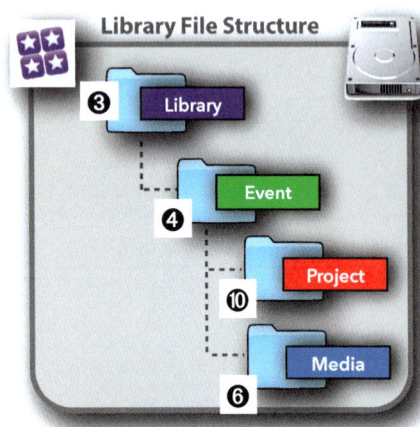

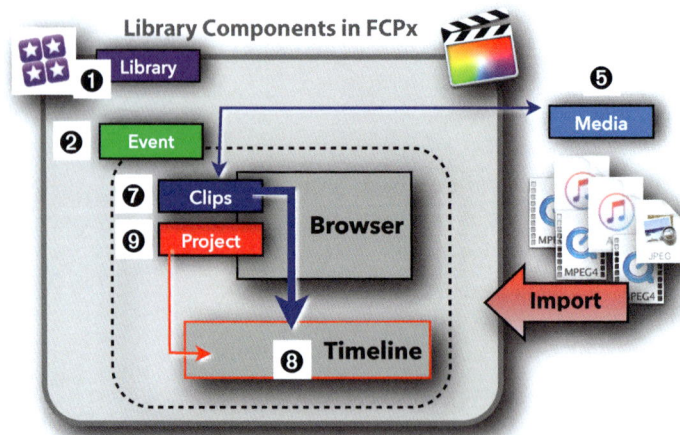

The reason why I spend that extra time on the details, is that you recognize those five components when working in FCPx and always be aware of the "big picture", how those components relate to each other. This is especially important when you later deal with more complex tasks and starting to do file management.

I will get into more specifics throughout the book when we learn all the different aspects about FCPx. Here are three examples where you encounter those components in your workflow.

Commands

These are some of the commands in FCPx that let you create the various components. They are also available from other menus or buttons:

▶ **New ❶**: The *File* ➤*New* contains the commands to create any of the three components: Library, Event, Project.

▶ **Open/Close ❷**: These two commands let you open additional FCPx Libraries or close the Library that is currently selected in FCPx.

▶ **Import ❸**: This command lets you import Media Files.

Interface Elements

The Browser pane in FCPx is one of the main interface elements that shows all the components currently available (loaded) in FCPx so you can access them and also manage them.

▶ **Library ❹**: All the Libraries that are open at the moment in FCPx are listed in the Browser Sidebar indicated by the Library icon ▦. The disclosure triangle lets you show/hide its Events.

▶ **Event ❺**: All the Events, indicated by the Event icon ★, that were created for a specific Library are listed in the Browser Sidebar, underneath their parent Library section.

▶ **Projects ❻**: All the Projects that were created for a specific Event are listed in the Browser window. The window displays all the Projects that "belong" to the Event(s) that is currently selected in the Sidebar.

▶ **Clips ❼**: All the Clips that were imported to a specific Event are also listed in the Browser window. The window displays all the Clips referenced to imported Media that "belong" to the Event(s) that is currently selected in the Sidebar.

Finder

Here is the diagram again that shows the file structure, the relationship between those components.

▶ **New Event**: Whenever you create a new Event ❽, it has to be assigned to a parent Library ❾.

▶ **New Project or Media**: Whenever you create a new Project ❿ or import Media ⓫, it has to be assigned to a parent Event ❽.

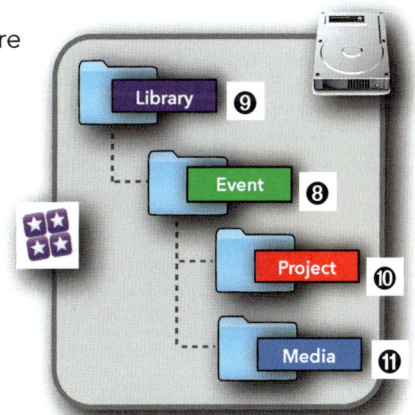

➡ *File Structure*

Once you understand the purpose of the different components and their relationship, you can ask yourself, what's the best way to use them. Here are three diagrams that show three examples of different Libraries to demonstrate different scenarios, something you have to consider before starting your FCPx video project.

Two things to be aware of:

😀 Work Stuff

If you think about it, when you work on a video project, you are mainly concerned with two components:

- ▸ `Media` **Clips**: All the Clips that you have available in FCPx are the material that you can use to create your new video. For example, the video footage, audio files, images, etc. Those Clips represent the Source Media you imported.

- ▸ `Project` **Timeline**: The Timeline is your work area where you create your new video. Remember, in FCPx, a Timeline represents one Project. One Project = One Timeline.

😀 Organize

Now think about the other two components, Library and Event. They are not really necessary for your work. They are more the organizational tools imposed by FCPx that give you options on how to organize the other two important work-related components, the Media and Project(s):

- ▸ `Library` **Library**: The Library represents your "document", the video project you are working on. This is the only component that is visible outside the FCPx app, as a file on the Finder that you can move around and treat like any other file. You decide how you want to organize your video project. You can work in one Library, or in bigger video projects, split it up into smaller Libraries. As we will see later, you can easily move components between Libraries.

- ▸ `Event` **Event**: The Events are the subfolders inside a Library, like bins, where you store your work-related stuff, the Media and Projects. How you organize them is up to you. You can put all the Media and the Project (the timeline) in one single Event ❶, even create multiple Projects ❷ (multiple Timelines) in that Event to create different versions of your video. Or maybe you can create multiple Events ❸ to organize your material differently. For example, one Event for the Media files and one Event for all the different Projects. Or, create one Event per movie reel, or a single Event for each day of shooting with all the footage of that day.

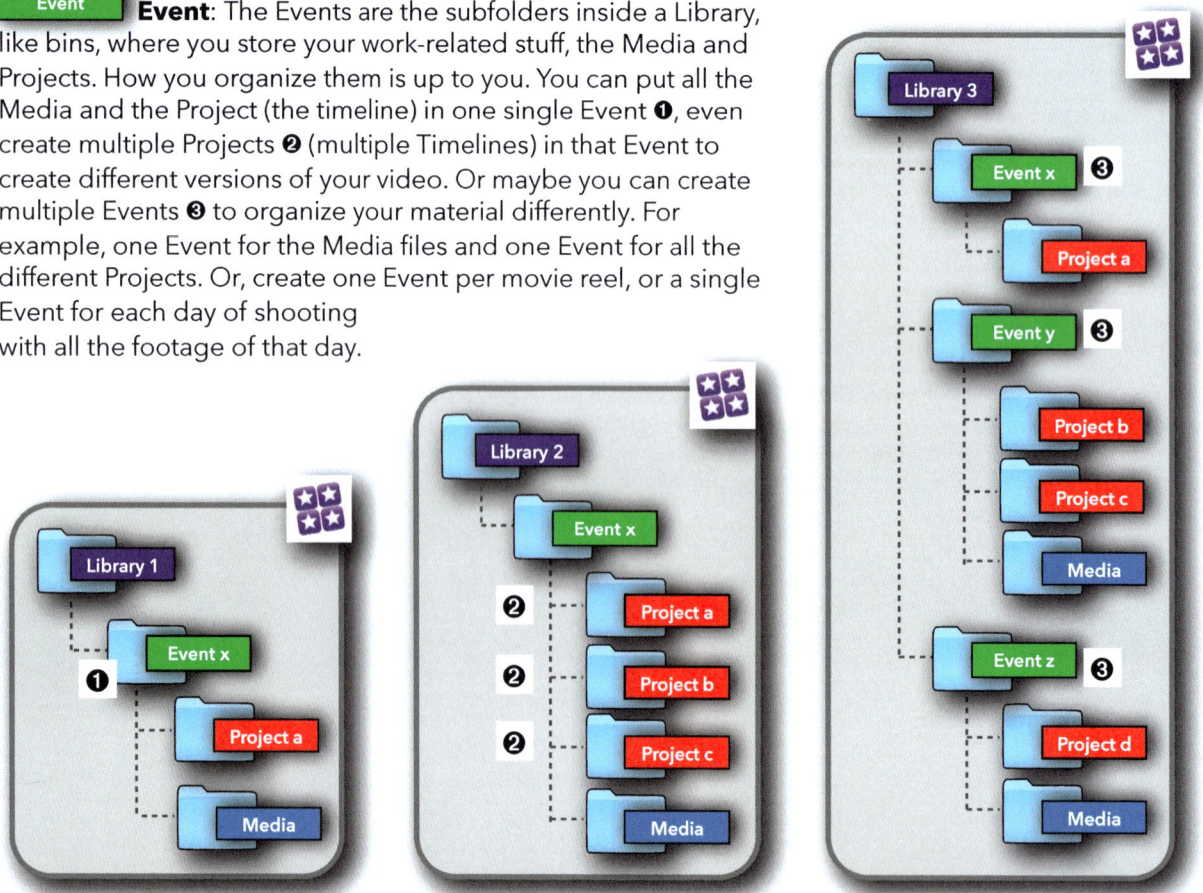

➡ The Finder Level

Let's have a look at those components on the Finder level. And again, "only looking, no touching"!

🌑 Finder Window

A FCPx Library file is easy to spot in a Finder

window by its unique file icon ❶
Although FCPx likes to store those Library Files in the user's Movie folder, you can place them wherever you want, on local drives, network drives, but not on iCloud.

🌑 Get Info Window

Ctr+click on a Library file and select Get Info to open the Get Info window.

> ▶ **Kind ❷**: In the General section, you can see what kind of file this is "*Final Cut Pro Library*".

> ▶ **Extension ❸**: The file extension is .fcpbundle, which is usually hidden in the Finder.

🌑 Package Content

Ctr+click on the Library file and select *Show Package Contents* to "open" the Library file.

> ▶ **Library Folder ❹**: The content that you see is the Library Folder. FCPx stores more files and folders for all different purposes as you work on a Library.

> ▶ **Event Folder ❺**: FCPx automatically names the Event Folder after the name you give it

in FCPx. The content of this folder is highly dynamic, depending on if you import Media, create Projects, or many other Event-related procedures.

> ▶ **Project Folder ❻**: A Project is located inside an Event Folder and FCPx automatically names the Project Folder after the name you give that Project in FCPx. There will be one Project Folder for each Project you create in that Event.

> ▶ **Media Folder ❼**: An Event Folder can have only one Media Folder with a fixed name "Original Media". It contains all the imported media files.

> ▶ **Database Files**: Remember, I stated at the beginning that FCPx is a database app. If you look at this Library folder, then you can see three database files: "*CurrentVersion.flexolibrary*" ❽ is the main database for this Library and located on the root level of the Library folder. Inside each Event Folder is a file called "*CurrentVersion.fcpevent*" ❾ that is the database for the Event and inside each Project folder is also a file called "*CurrentVersion.fcpevent*" ❿ that is the database for this Project.

➡ *Library or Project?*

After all this technical background, let's return to the original question, what we call that "thing" we are actually working on in FCPx, a Library or a Project? Here are a few terms and phrases:

- **Video Project**: FCPx is a video editing software. So I think a "Video Project" is a good term to call whatever we are working on in FCPx. Of course, there are a wide variety of different types of video projects, from home videos, wedding videos, trailers, commercials, documentaries, to full length feature films.

- **Video Project ➤ Library**: In a typical scenario, you want to have all the elements that belong to a specific Video Project stay together. That means, you want them to be saved together as one "entity" ❶ and when you need all the elements of that Video Project back in FCPx, you want to open ❷ that single "entity" to have everything back together with one click. FCPx calls this single "entity" a *Library* ❸, a term that is more common with computer and databases.

- **Library**: A single Library would represent a single Video Project. When you work on different Video Projects, you would create different Libraries ❹. But as I mentioned before, there is no strict rule. You could also divide a Video Project you are working on into smaller Libraries, which depends more on your personal preference and workflow.

- **Library ➤ Library File (Final Cut Pro Library)**: A Library, that single entity containing all the elements for a specific Video Project, is saved as a Library File ❺, also known as a "*Final Cut Pro Library*". This is the file you see in a Finder window, a Package File, containing all the individual elements ❶ of the Video Project.

- **Active Library**: When you open ❶ a Library File in FCPx, you make it an Active Library ❸ with access to all its components that are stored inside the Library File ❶ (Events, Projects, Media, etc.). You can freely open and close Libraries to quickly switch between Video Projects and also exchange components between Libraries.

- **Library ➤ Project**: "Project" is a very specific term in FCPx. It is a component ❻ of the Library that represents a single Timeline, a sequence of Clips ❼, a specific version of the video you are working on. You can have multiple Projects ❻ stored in a Library, but only one Project ❽ can be visible at a time in the Timeline Area ❾ that you watch in the Viewer ❿.

- **Export Project**: When you export ⓫ a Project (FCPx uses the term "Share"), you create a new video file of the Project ❽ that is currently displayed in the Timeline Area ❾.

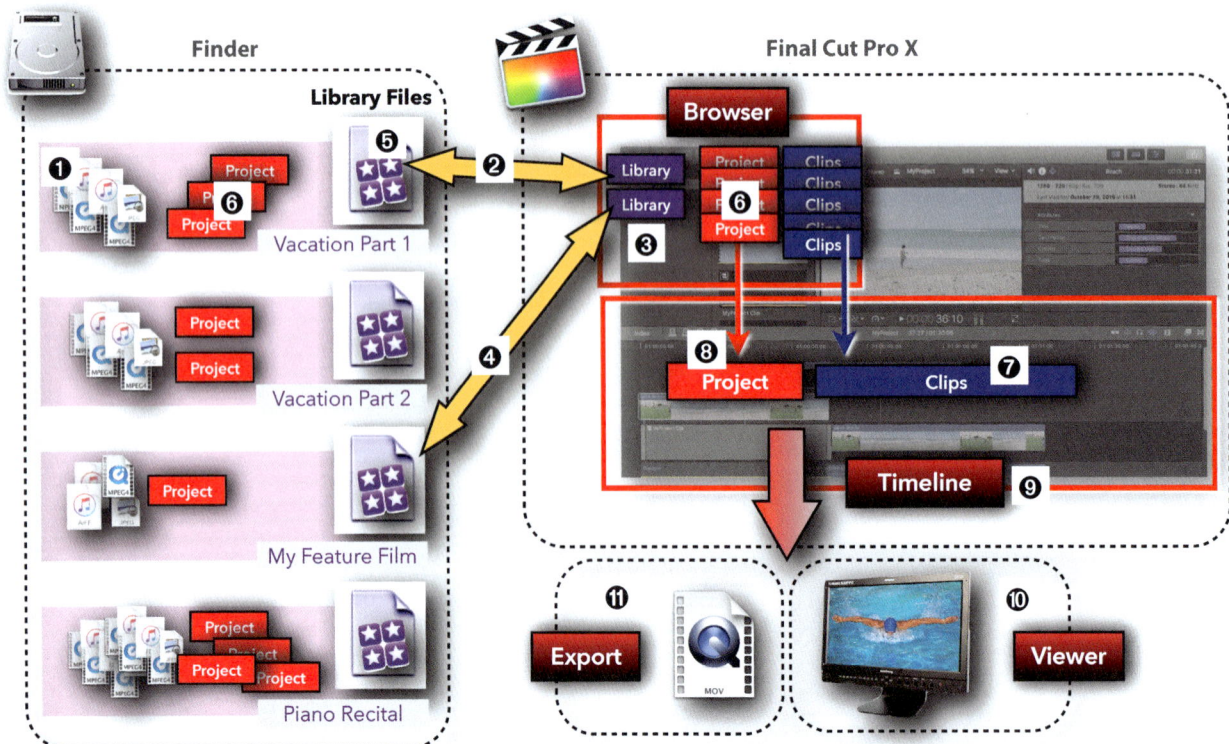

Library

Library Commands

Everything in FCPx starts with a Library as the top of the hierarchy when doing any work in FCPx. So let's look at the available commands related to those Libraries:

FCPx Main Menu

➡ **New Library**

A new Library is automatically created when you launch FCPx the first time. You can manually create new Libraries by using any of the following commands:

- Menu Command *File ➤ New ➤ Library* ❶
- Key Command (is not assigned by default)
- Menu Command *File ➤ Open Library ➤ Others ...* (*cmd+O*) and *click* the *New...* button ❷ in the Open Library Dialog

Open Library Dialog

Those commands open the standard Save Dialog ❸ with the following options:

- ▶ **Name**: Enter a name for the Library File. You can change that name at any time later in FCPx, which will update the file name in the Finder.
- ▶ **Tags**: Enter optional Finder Tag(s).
- ▶ **Location**: The default location for a new Library is the user's *Movies* folder ❹, but you can navigate to a different location to store the Library File on any of the connected volumes, except iCloud, which will prompt an alert ❺.

This document cannot be saved to iCloud Drive.

Select a local storage device, SAN, or supported SMB location.

Reveal in Finder

To find out where a Library File is stored on your drive, select it in the Browser Sidebar and then use any of the following commands, which opens its Finder window.

- Key Command *sh+cmd+R*
- Main Menu Command *File ➤ Reveal in Finder*
- *Ctr+click* on a Library in the Browser Sidebar and select from the *Shortcut Menu ➤ Reveal in Finder*

- You can also move the mouse over a Library in the Browser Sidebar and a Tooltip ❻ pops up with the name and the path where that Library File is located on your computer

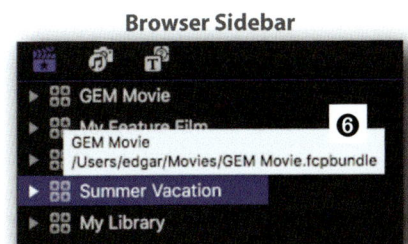

Browser Sidebar

GEM Movie
My Feature Film
GEM Movie
/Users/edgar/Movies/GEM Movie.fcpbundle
Summer Vacation
My Library

➡ Open

There are many different procedures on how to open Libraries in FCPx.

Dock

- ▸ **Launch from FCPx app**: When you launch the FCPx app, it opens the same Libraries that were open when you quit the app the last time. If no Library was open when you quit FCPx, then the *Open Library Dialog* ❽ opens (same as *cmd+O*).

- ▸ **Launch from Library File Finder**: *Double-clicking* on a Library File ❶ in the Finder will launch FCPx and only opens that Library. You can also *click* on a Library File in the *Final Cut Backups* folder inside the *Movies* folder to launch a specific Library Backup. More about that in the File Management chapter.

- ▸ **Launch from Dock**: When *ctr+clicking* on the FCPx icon in the Dock ❷, it opens a list with all the recently opened Libraries that you can select.

- ▸ **Empty Browser Sidebar**: If you close all the Libraries in FCPx, then an *Open Library* button ❸ appears in the Browser Sidebar that opens the Open Library Dialog when *clicked* on.

- ▸ **Open Library Command**: Use any of the commands in the Main Menu *File ➤ Open Library* submenu ❹.

Browser Sidebar

🔵 "Open Library" Command

The Menu Command *File ➤ Open Library ➤* ❹ opens a submenu with the following menu items:

- ▸ **"Recent Libraries"**: The top of the list displays all the Libraries that you had open recently.

- ▸ **Other...**: This command opens the "*Open Library Dialog*" ❽. See below.

- ▸ **From Backup...**: This command opens a Dialog ❺ with a popup menu ❻, listing all the available backup versions of the currently selected Library. The *Other...* button ❼ opens an Open Dialog with the Final Cut Backups folder selected.

- ▸ **Clear Recents**: This command removes all the Libraries from the top of this submenu.

FCPx Main Menu

🔵 Open Library Dialog

FCPx doesn't open the standard Open Dialog when using the Open command to navigate to a specific file. Instead, it opens the *Open Library Dialog* window ❽ with the following options:

- ▸ **List ❾**: The list shows all the Libraries that you had open recently, their name, modification date, and location. You can even sort by modification date. Select one or multiple Libraries (*cmd+click* or *sh+click*) and press the Choose button to open those Libraries. Selecting a single Library will display its location below.

Open Library Dialog

- ▸ **Locate... ❿**: This opens the standard Open Dialog where you navigate on the Finder level.

- ▸ **New... ⓫**: This opens the Save Dialog that lets you create a new Library.

➡ *Close*

You can close any Library that is currently open in FCPx. Select the Library in the Browser Sidebar and choose any of the two commands:

- 🔘 Main Menu Command *File ➤ Close Library "NameOfLibrary"* ❶
- 🔘 *Ctr+click* on a Library in the Browser Sidebar and select from the *Shortcut Menu ➤ Close Library "NameOfLibrary"* ❷

Shortcut Menu

Main Menu

➡ *Delete Library*

You cannot delete a Library from inside FCPx. There is no command for that, out of security reasons. Remember, deleting a Library would delete all its components inside (Projects, Events, Media, etc.).

The only way to delete a Library is to delete its Library File in the Finder ❸.

Finder

➡ *Delete Generated Library Files...*

There is a separate command in the File menu that lets you delete specific media files inside the Library File and also if they are referenced to a location outside the Library File. However, don't worry, because these are all files that can be recreated again at any time.

The page states that this will delete files "*inside and outside the library*". However, this does not refer to any referenced source media files (which will never be deleted), but to any files stored at an External Location defined in the Library Properties. See the next page.

Selecting the Main Menu Command *File ➤ Delete Generated Library Files...* ❹ opens a Sheet with the following options:

FCPx Main Menu

🔘 Delete Render Files ❺

This deletes all the files inside the folder "*Render Files ➤ High Quality Media*" ❻ of every Event folder inside that Library File. You can choose to delete *All* rendered files or the *Unused Only*. These are the ones that were created for a specific effect, but are not used anymore.

🔘 Delete Optimized Media ❼

This deletes all the files inside the folder "*Transcoded Media ➤ High Quality Media*" ❽ of every Event folder inside that Library File.

🔘 Delete Proxy Media ❾

This deletes all the files inside the folder "*Transcoded Media ➤ Proxy Media*" ❿ of every Event folder inside that Library File.

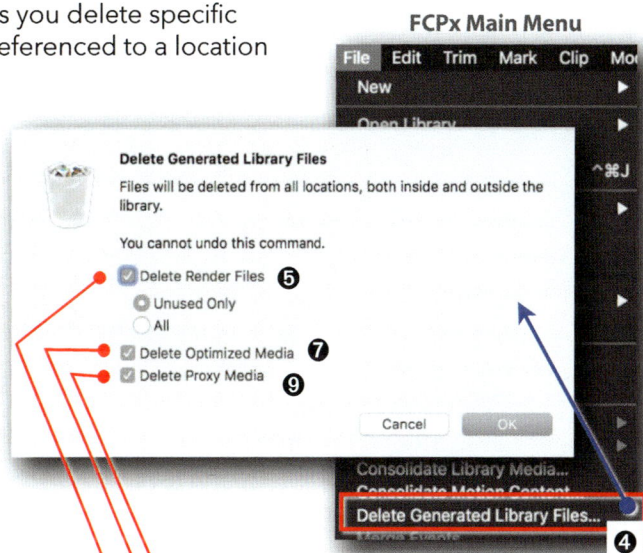

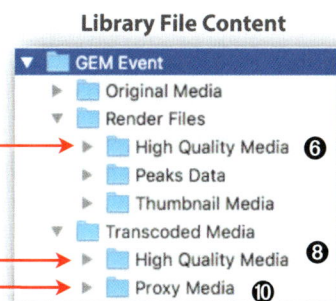

Library File Content

Library Properties

All the details about a specific Library and the file management inside that Library File (what components are stored where) are available in the Inspector on a page called *Library Properties*. You can access that view in two ways:

- Have any item of the Library selected in the Browser Sidebar and choose the Main Menu Command *File ➤ Library Properties (ctr+cmd+J)* ❶. This will open the Inspector pane in the Workspace (if it wasn't open yet) with the Library Properties view ⊞ ❷.
- While the Inspector pane is open (*cmd+4*) select the Library ❸ in the Browser Sidebar.

The Library Properties Inspector displays eight sections:

- **Header**
- **Media**
- **Motion Content**
- **Cache**
- **Backups**
- **Storage Used for Media and Motion Content**
- **Color Processing**

➡️ *Header* ❹

The Header lists four informations:

- ▶ **Name**: The name of the Library, identical with the name of the Library File on your drive.

- ▶ **Color Space**: This label on the right indicates what Color Processing ❺ you have selected for this Library (Standard, Wide Gamut, or any other color space) at the bottom of the Inspector.

- ▶ **Volume**: This is the name of the mounted volume. There is no indication if this is a local volume or a networked volume.

- ▶ **Size**: This indicates the size of the Library File. Please note that it displays the actual file size, which means that the source media files might not be included in that calculation if they are stored outside the Library File based on two scenarios:
  - You kept the source media files at their original location and created a reference to those files during the import.
  - You used an external storage location for the media file, which you set up in the next section under "Storage Location" ❻.

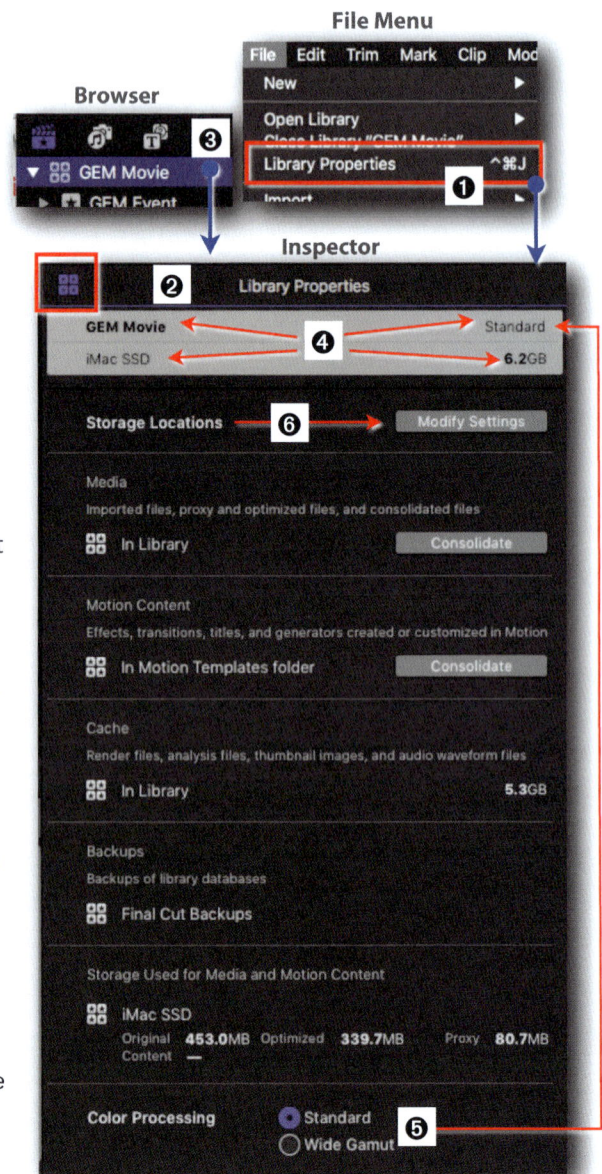

➡ *Storage Locations* ❶

This section only has one button that opens a sheet where you set the storage locations of four types of files. The next four sections in the Inspector ❷ show those four file types and the selected storage location.

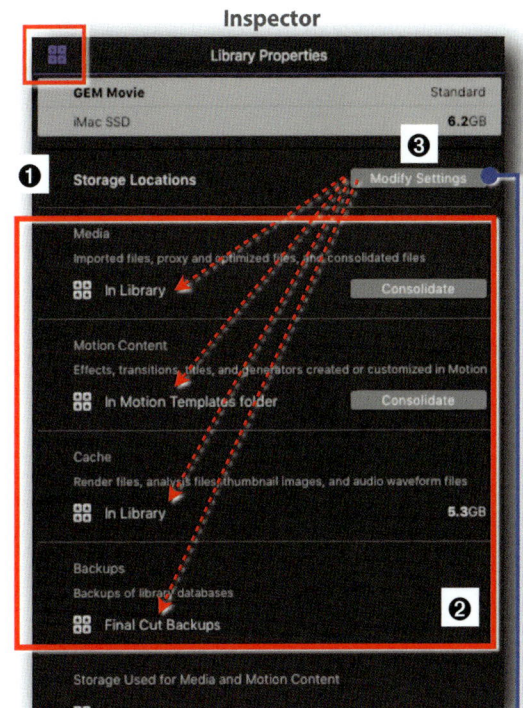

Click on the *Modify Settings* button ❸ to open the Sheet that slides out underneath the Workspace:

🌀 Media ❹

The default location to store the Media Files is "inside" the Library File. You can open the popup menu and select "Choose..." to navigate to any other location (i.e. bigger external hard drive or server).

SymLink: When you choose an External Location for the Media Files for your Library, FCPx will move the media files to that location. For each of those files, FCPx creates a SymLink, which looks like an Alias ❺ (that points to the file in the external storage location) and puts it inside the Original Media folder inside the Library File.

🌀 Motion Content ❻

The default location for Motion Content is "*In Motion Template folder*", which is a folder automatically created inside the user's Movies folder (*~/Movies/Motion Templates/*). You can choose to store those files inside the Library instead so they stay with the Library, which is useful if you exchange Library Files with other computers.

🌀 Cache ❼

The default location for the Cache Files (which are files generated by FCPx like render files, analysis files, thumbnail images, and audio waveform files) is inside the Library File. You can open this popup menu and select "Choose..." to navigate to any other location to store those files "outside" in a special Package File ❽ 📦 with the .fcpcache file extension.

🌀 Backups ❾

The default location for the Backup Files of the Library is the separate folder "Final Cut Backups" in the user's *Movies* folder (*~/Movies/Final Cut Backups/*). You can open the popup menu and select "Choose..." to select any other location or set it to "*Do not Save*", which will stop saving any backups for that Library.

Symlink File

Interview.mov

Cache File

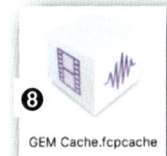

GEM Cache.fcpcache

Please note that you can mouse-over any of the menu selectors to display a Tooltip ❿ that displays the full pathname of that location.

➡ Media

The Media section in the Library Properties Inspector displays the current folder ❶ that is used by the Library to store the Media Files (Original, Optimized, and Proxy). In this example, I chose the location "My external FCPx SSD" (unfortunately, it doesn't say on which volume that folder is located).

If later, you want to "move" those files into the Library, you use the Consolidate command. **Click** on the *Consolidate* button ❷ to open a Sheet ❸ that lets you choose if you want to move the Optimized Media and the Proxy Media too.

Please note that changing the storage location of a Library after you have already imported some files only effects the newly imported files. That means, any files that were imported before as a referenced media file stay at their location. To also move them "inside" the Library, you have to use this "Consolidate" ❷ command.

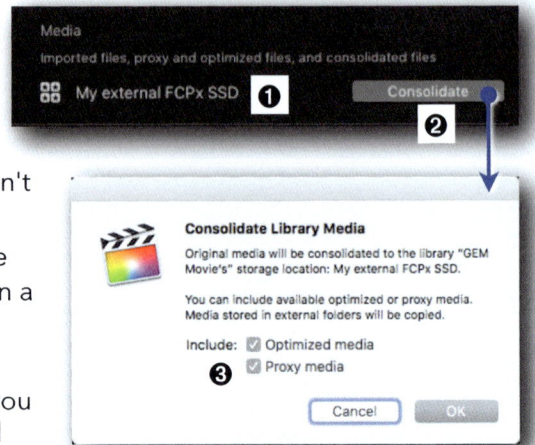

➡ Motion Content

The Motion Content section in the Library Properties Inspector displays the current folder ❹ that is used by the Library to store the Motion Content. It can be stored either in the Library (which makes it easy to move around) or in the default location *~/Movies/ Motion Templates/*. **Click** the *Consolidate* button ❺ to move the content to the currently set location in case they are not there yet.

An alert window tells you if Content will be moved ❻ or if there is nothing to move ❼.

➡ Cache

The Cache section in the Library Properties Inspector displays the current folder ❽ that is used by the Library to store its Cache Files (plus the file consumption). These are files that are generated by FCPx, for example, render files, analysis files, thumbnail images, and audio waveform files. They can be re-generated at any time.

The section has no *Consolidate* button, because whenever you change the location (with the *Modify Settings* button above), it always moves those files to the selected location.

When moved ❾ to a different location, FCPx creates a Package File ❿ with the name of the Library and the additional word "*Cache*", plus the file extension .fcpcache. It contains the Event Folder(s) ⓫ with the various subfolders containing the cache files (i.e. "Analysis Files" and "Render Files").

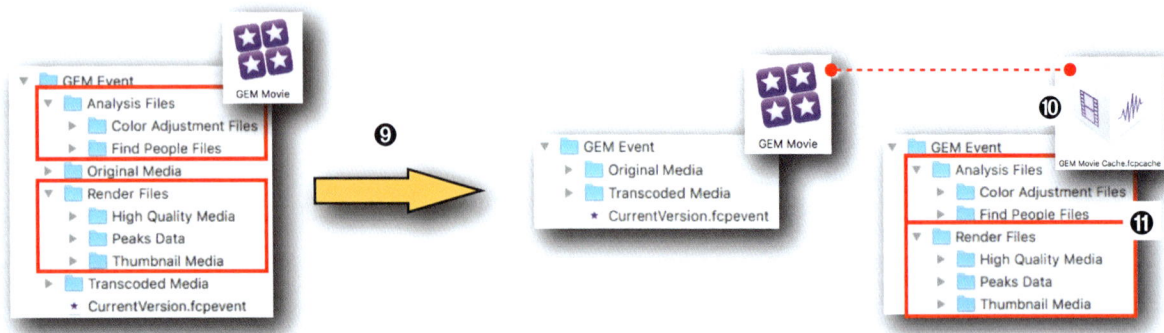

➡ Backups

The Backup section in the Library Properties Inspector displays the current folder ❶ that is used by the Library to store its Backup Files.

FCPx doesn't have a *Save Library* command, because every edit you perform will automatically be saved to your Library File. The Library Backup is an additional safety measure, that also allows you go back and open an earlier version, one of those Backup Libraries, in case you "went too far" during editing.

- ▸ FCPx makes backups of your Library at regular intervals.
- ▸ A backup is a standard Final Cut Library File, that you can open with the Open Backup procedure inside FCPx or by **double-clicking** on the file in the Finder.
- ▸ The files are stored by default in the user directory **~/Movies/Final Cut Backups/**, but you can change the location using the *Modify Settings* button in the Library Properties Inspector.
- ▸ The backup files only contain the Library Files without any media files.
- ▸ FCPx automatically deletes backup files after a few days.
- ▸ Incremental Backup software (TimeMachine, CarbonCopyCloner) treat the Library Package Files as a folder and, therefore, only backs up the changed files inside and not the entire Library File.

➡ Storage used for Media and Motion Contents

This section ❷ shows you how much storage is used by that Library, broken down by individual types of media.

➡ Color Processing

This section lets you switch the Color Space used for the Library.

- ▸ You can set the Color Space to Standard (Rec. 709) or Wide Gamut (Rec. 2020) ❸.
  - • **Rec. 709** is an RGB color space (known as sRGB), an ITU recommendation from 1990, created for HDTV.
  - • **Rec. 2020** is an ITU recommendation from 2012 for 4K monitors an above.
- ▸ An Alert Dialog ❹ pops up when you switch.
- ▸ The selected setting is displayed in the upper-right corner of the Library Properties Inspector ❺.
- ▸ The Color Space of a Project can only be set to Rec. 2020 when the Library is set to Wide Gamut.
- ▸ The *Range Check* ❻ options in the Viewer's View Menu indicates which Color Space has been selected.

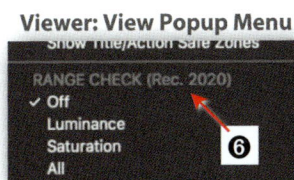

Now let's move on to the next level of the FCPx hierarchy, the Event, and explore the place in FCPx where it is located, the Browser Pane of the FCPx Workspace.

➡ *Default Browser*

Here is a screenshot of what the Browser looks like after we created our first Library with the name "GEM Movie".

To see these window elements, make sure that all the necessary interface elements are visible:

☑ **Browser Pane ❶**: The Browser Pane is one of the four main window panes in the FCPx Workspace. *Click* on the Browser Button [img] or use the Key Command *ctr+cmd+1* to make it visible.

☑ **Browser View ❷**: The Browser Pane can display three views, Libraries, Photos and Audio, and Titles and Generator. *Click* the Libraries Button [img] to switch to the Libraries View or use the Key Command *cmd+1*..

☑ **Sidebar ❸**: The Browser Pane has a nested window pane, the Sidebar that lets you select what is displayed in the Browser window. *Click* on the Libraries Browser Button [img] again to toggle the Sidebar or use the Key Command *cmd+'*.

FCPx Workspace

The Browser of our default Library displays the following three elements:

▶ **Sidebar**

The Sidebar contains three items:

- [img] ❹ This item represents our Library. It has a disclosure triangle to reveal all its components inside.

- [img] ❺ This is a folder item. A newly created Library automatically has a folder named "Smart Collections", which I discuss later.

- [img] ❻ This is the actual Event item. A newly created Library automatically creates an Event with the creation date used as the Event name.

▶ **Browser**

The Browser area doesn't contain anything yet.

[img] This is the only element displayed in the Browser area, the big *Import Media* button that opens the *Media Import Dialog* to add source media files to the Event.

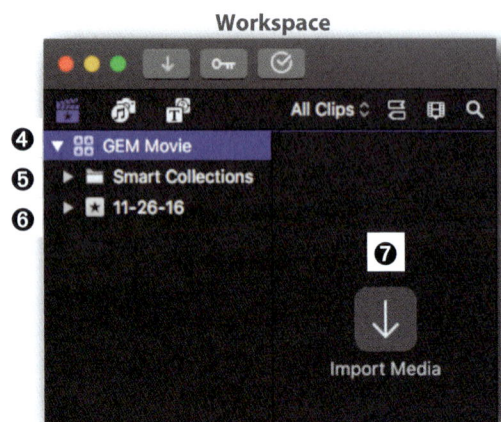

Workspace

Event Management

Now let me introduce the individual elements by going step-by-step and see what happens:

➡ *One Event*

Browser - Libraries Sidebar

In this screenshot, I deleted the folder *Smart Collections* that was automatically created, plus I renamed the Event to "GEM Event". A very basic structure ❶, one Library (GEM Movie) that includes one Event (GEM Event). An Event item in the Sidebar also has a disclosure triangle, but as you can see, it is open and no other items are inside yet.

Before exploring all the options that can be inside an Event, I first want to discuss the various commands and procedures related to the Event itself.

➡ *Create Event*

This is the most basic command that lets you add more Events to a Library. As we already learned, an Event is just a folder or a bin to organize the stuff that belongs to a Library (mainly Clips and Projects). You can create as many of those Events in a Library as you like.

Here are the available commands to add a new Event. Please note that if you have multiple Libraries open in the Sidebar, you have to select the target Library (or an item inside that Library) in which you want to create the new Event.

- Menu Command *File > New > Event...* ❷
- Key Command *opt+N*
- *Ctr-click* the Library (or any item inside the Library) in the Sidebar and select from the *Shortcut Menu ➤ New Event* ❷
- *Tap* the *New Event* button [★ New Event] ❹ on the Touch Bar

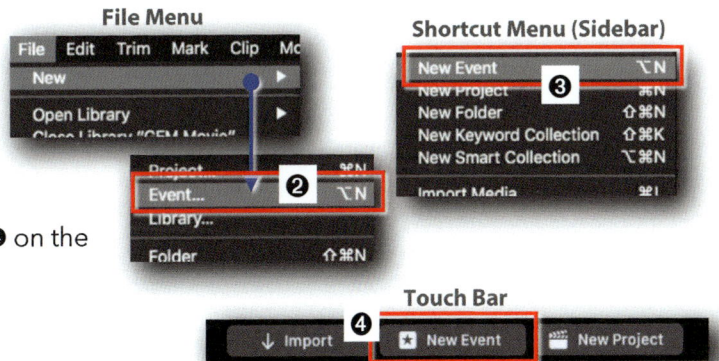

File Menu

Shortcut Menu (Sidebar)

Touch Bar

Any of those commands will slide out a Sheet underneath the Workspace to configure the new Event:

- ▶ **Event Name ❺**: Enter a name for the new Event. It can later be renamed in the Browser Sidebar at any time. Also, don't forget that you can also use emojis as characters to give it a more visual touch.

New Event Sheet

- ▶ **Library ❻**: The popup menu has the Library selected that was selected in the Browser Sidebar when you chose the New Event command. If you have other Libraries currently open in FCPx, then they will be listed in this popup menu and you can choose any of those as the Library the new Event is created in.

- ▶ **Create New Project ❼**: Enable this checkbox to create a new Project inside that new Event. I will discuss that option later.

➡ Multiple Events

In this screenshot, I created four Events ❶ in the "GEM Movie" Library. Look at the relationship between what is displayed on the Browser Sidebar ❷ and the content of the Library File in the Finder ❸.

Here is a recap about the file structure inside the package file of a Library File:

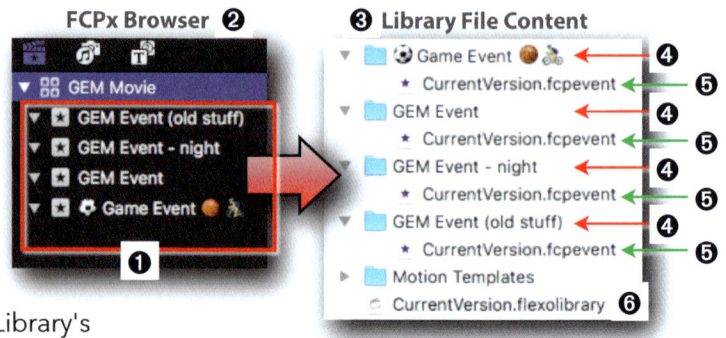

▸ For every Event that you create in the Workspace, FCPx will create a folder ❹ on your drive. It is located inside the Library's Package File on the top level.

▸ FCPx names the Event folder after the name you give the Event in the Browser Sidebar.

▸ As a default, an Event folder will contain the database file "*CurrentVersion.fcpevent*" ❺ where all the information related to that Event will be stored.

▸ Everything else related to an Event (media files, rendered files, transcoded media, etc.) will be stored later inside that Event folder.

▸ Pay attention to the file "CurrentVersion.flexolibrary" ❻, also on the top level of the Library Package File. This is the main database file for that Library.

➡ Rename Events

You can rename Events at any time.

▸ There is no specific Rename command, just select the Event in the Browser Sidebar, press **return**, type a new name, and hit **return** again.

▸ FCPx renames the Event folder inside the Library Package File accordingly and takes care of everything under the hood, so that all the references and connections stay in place.

▸ All the elements of a Library, the database entries and updates, are managed from the FCPx user interface. Never ever change the folder/file structure or rename anything inside the Library File on the Finder level or you end up with a corrupted Library!

➡ Sort Events

You can't freely move the order of the Events in the Sidebar. There is a separate command for the sort order that applies to the Events in all Libraries in the Sidebar.

📌 **Click** on any item in the Sidebar to open the **Shortcut Menu ➤ Sort Events By ➤** ❼. The submenu ❽ lets you choose to sort by Date or Name and set it to Ascending or Descending.

📌 Main Menu **View ➤ Sort Library Events By ➤** ❾.

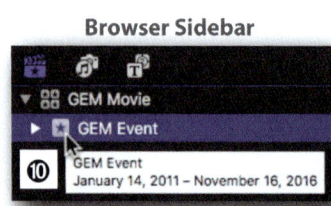

Event Date: The date for an Event is determined by the date you created the Event or the creation date of the Projects or referenced Media Files inside the Event. Mouse-over an Event in the Browser Sidebar and a Tooltip ❿ pops up with the name of the Events, plus its associated date. If the media files that its Clips are linked to have different creation dates, then you will see a data range for the oldest to the newest media files.

➡ Copy/Move Event(s) to Library ➤

You can easily copy or move Events and all their content between Libraries.

☑ Select one or multiple Events from a Library in the Browser Sidebar.

☑ Select the command *File ➤ Copy/Move Events to Library ➤* ❶. Please note that the name of the menu command changes from "Event" to "Event**s**" ❷ to indicate if multiple Events have been selected.

☑ The submenu ❸ lists all the currently open Libraries, plus a command "*New Library...*" to create a new Library if you want to copy or move the Events to a new Library.

☑ A Dialog ❹ pops up to inform you that the Original Media of those Events are copied/ moved and gives you the option with two checkboxes to include the Optimized Media and Proxy Media too (if available).

➡ Merge Events

You can select two or more Events in the Browser Sidebar and merge them together into one single Event. FCPx uses the Event on top as the target Event, which is automatically selected after the merge command, so you can rename it right away. The command will be executed without any additional dialog window. However, you can Undo (*cmd+Z*) that command.

📌 Menu Command *File ➤ Merge Events* ❺

📌 You can also *drag* one or multiple selected Events over another Event to merge them

➡ Delete Event(s)

Select the Event(s) and choose any of the following commands to delete an Event. A dialog ❻ opens that lets you confirm the action:

📌 Key Command *cmd+delete*

📌 Menu Command *File ➤ Move Event(s) to Trash* ❼

📌 *Ctr+click* on the selected Events and choose from the *Shortcut Menu ➤ Move Event(s) to Trash* ❽

You can use the Undo command (*cmd+Z*) if you hit the delete command by accident and move the Event back out from that Trash folder.

Although this command is called "Move to Trash", it will not move the Event to the Finder Trash (where you might recover it). Instead, it will be moved to a temporary "_Trash" folder inside the Library File, which will be deleted if you close FCPx.

Inside the Event

Each Event in the Browser Sidebar has a disclosure triangle to reveal what's inside. There are three types of items that can be listed under an Event: Folders, Keyword Collections, and Smart Collections.

➡️ *Overview*

🟤 **Browser Sidebar**

Folder ❶: A Folder is just an organizational tool like the folders in the Finder.

Create a folder item with those commands:

- *Ctr+click* the Event item and select from the *Shortcut Menu ➤ New Folder* ❷
- Main Menu *File ➤ New ➤ Folder* ❸
- Key Command *sh+cmd+N*

Keyword Collection ❹: Keyword Collections function as "virtual bins" based on the metadata like stored search commands. I will cover that later.

Create Keyword Collections with any of those commands:

- *Ctr+click* the Event item and select from the *Shortcut Menu ➤ New Keyword Collection* ❷
- Key Command *sh+cmd+K*
- Main Menu *File ➤ New ➤ Keyword Collection* ❸
- There are other procedures where FCPx automatically creates Keyword Collections

Smart Collection ❺: Smart Collections also function as "virtual bins" based on metadata that represent complex search queries. I will also cover that later.

Create Smart Collections with any of those commands:

- *Ctr+click* the Event item and select from the *Shortcut Menu ➤ New Smart Collection* ❷
- Key Command *opt+cmd+N*
- Main Menu *File ➤ New ➤ Smart Collection* ❸
- Open the Search window (*cmd+F*) and click the "New Smart Collection" button
- There are other procedures where FCPx automatically creates Keyword Collections

🟤 **Browser Area**

The Browser area always displays what is selected in the Sidebar, even if the Sidebar is hidden. So, whenever you look at the Browser, know what is selected in the Sidebar, which could be a single item or multiple items. The Library Browser shows two types of items, Projects and Clips.

Projects ❻: The same way an Event has to be created inside a specific Library, a Project has to be created inside an Event too. However, the Projects are not displayed in the Sidebar, they are displayed on top of the Browser area with the header "Projects" and the amount of Projects in parenthesis. A disclosure triangle can show/hide all the Projects for the current selection.

Clips ❼: Clips, the representation of media files, are imported to a specific Event and also displayed in the Browser area below the Projects when that Event is selected in the Sidebar. The section header "Clips" indicates the amount of Clips in the current selection.

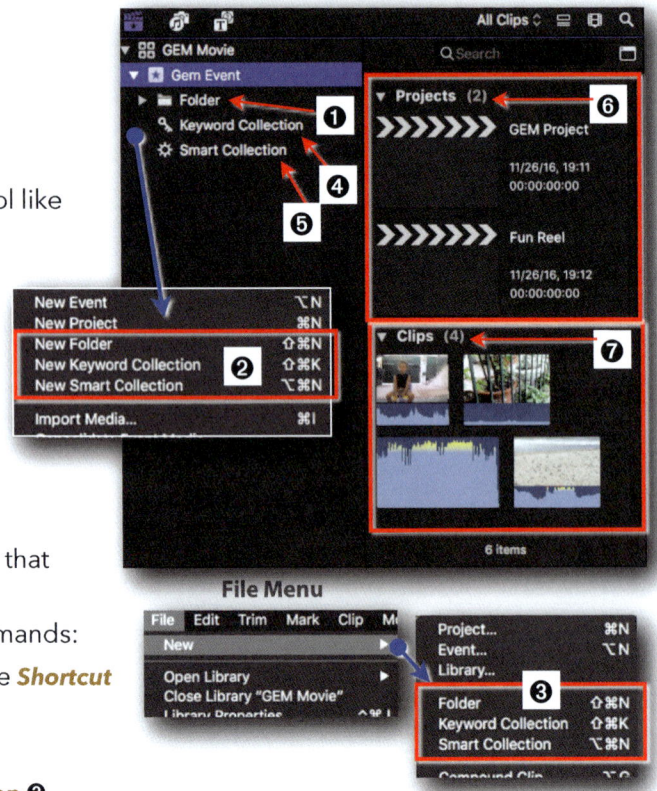

➡ Sidebar Rules

There are a lot of rules and techniques in the Sidebar that you should make yourself familiar with to structure and organize your Library.

Library

▸ The order of the Library items cannot be changed in the Sidebar. The last opened or created Library moves to the top.

▸ Mouse-over the Library item and a tooltip displays the name of the Library and the path where it is located on your drive.

Event

▸ Mouse-over the Event item and a tooltip displays the name of the Event and a date range, that represents the creation dates of the enclosed media.

▸ The order of the Event items can be set to Name or Date from the *Shortcut Menu ➤ Sort Events By ➤*. The date refers to the creation date of the enclosed media, which is shown in the tooltip.

▸ Any items inside an Event (Folders, Keyword Collections, Smart Collections) are sorted alphabetically.

▸ You can manually merge Events by *dragging* one Event (or a group of selected Events) over another Event. This works only inside the same Library.

Folder

▸ A Folder can not be created directly inside the Library's top level, only inside an Event (select the Event) or inside another Folder.

▸ There is one exception. Creating a Smart Collection on the Library level will create a Folder on the top level and puts the Smart Collections inside.

▸ The purpose of the Folders is mainly for organizing the Keyword Collections and Smart Collections. Therefore, you can *drag* those collections freely between Folders.

▸ You can only *drag* Smart Collections into the Folder that was automatically created on the top level of the Library.

▸ You can rename a Folder at any time. Select it, press *return*, type the name, and press *return* again. Of course, you can use your favorite emojis to indicate what a folder contains.

▸ Delete a folder(s) by selecting it and choose

📌 Main Menu *File ➤ Delete Folder(s)*

📌 Shortcut Menu *Delete Folder(s)*

📌 Key Command *cmd+delete* or ⓧ

Keyword Collection

▸ Keyword Collections can be created on any level except the top level of a Library.

▸ You can *drag* Keyword Collections freely between the Events or Folders of the current Library to move them around. *Dragging* them over items of a different Library will copy them.

▸ Delete a Keyword Collection(s) by selecting it and choose :

📌 Main Menu *File ➤ Delete Keyword Collection(s)*

📌 Shortcut Menu *Delete Keyword Collection(s)*

📌 Key Command *cmd+delete* or ⓧ

Smart Collection

▸ Smart Collections can be created on any level of a Library.

▸ You can *drag* Smart Collections freely between the Events or Folders of the current Library to move them around. *Dragging* them over items of a different Library will copy them.

▸ Delete a Smart Collection(s) by selecting it and choose:

📌 Main Menu *File ➤ Delete Smart Collection(s)*

📌 Shortcut Menu *Delete Smart Collection(s)*

📌 Key Command *cmd+delete* or ⓧ

Browser UI

The user interface of the Workspace in FCPx is extremely "dynamic" with all the different window panes and areas that are visible or not visible, depending on so many conditions. Here is an overview of the Browser Pane and how it is divided into individual areas.

➡ Overview

These are the main areas of the Browser

- ▶ **Browser Pane ❶**: The Browser Pane is that entire section, one of the four main window panes of the Workspace. There are actually three different Browsers, the Library Browser ▦, Photos and Audio Browser 🎵, and Titles and Generators Browser 🅣. We are looking at the Library Browser.
- ▶ **Sidebar ❷**: We just discussed the Sidebar, the nested window pane that can be toggled on/off. The screenshot below shows the Event "GEM Event" ❸ with an example of all the different items that can be organized inside that Event. The selection in the Sidebar determines what is displayed in the Browser area to the right.
- ▶ **Browser ❹**: The actual Browser area displays the content based on what is selected in the Sidebar ❷. It can be toggled between two different views:

  ▤ **List View ❺**

  ▥ **Filmstrip View ❻**
- ▶ **Header ❼**: The Header is always visible on top of the Browser. It contains the three View Buttons on the left to select the Browser View and on the right are various buttons, selectors, or controls that we discuss in a moment.
- ▶ **Status Bar ❽**: The Status Bar is always visible at the bottom of the Browser to provide information about the displayed items in the Browser. How many items are displayed, how many are selected, and what is the total length of all the selected Clips or Projects.

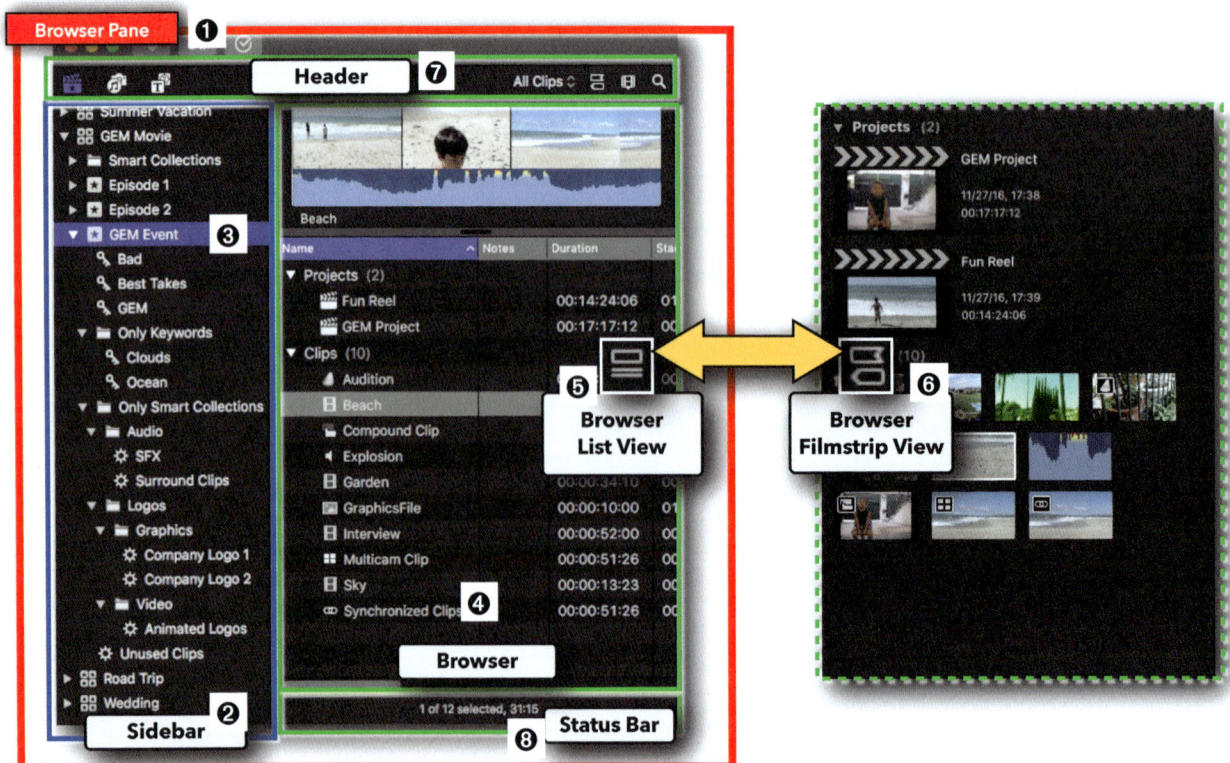

➡ Header Controls

The Library Browser has four controls in the upper-right corner of its Header. Two controls determine "what content is displayed" and the two determine "how the content is displayed".

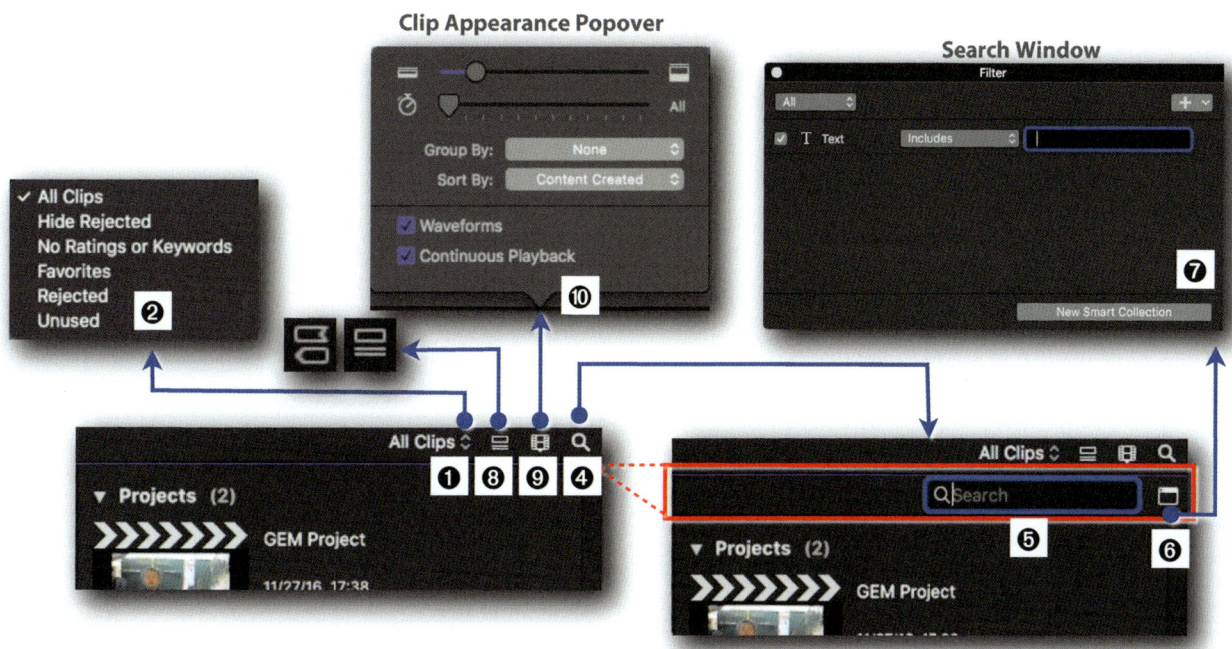

Clip Appearance Popover

Search Window

🌐 What Content is displayed?

The selection in the Sidebar determines what content is displayed in the Browser. In addition, the following two controls let you apply additional search filters that affect what is displayed, based on metadata. I will get into more details about that in the following chapter Organize your Clips. The most important fact about these two controls is that those filters are always active, so whenever you work in the Browser, keep an eye on them to make sure you know what content the Browser is showing to you.

▶ **Clip Filtering ❶**: This control is a selector that opens a popup menu ❷ with six options. The "All Clips" is not a label for that control, it is the name of the currently selected option. This way, you can always see the currently applied filter and if you squint your eyes, you will even see a tiny black line ❸ that underlines the displayed option.

▶ **Search Field ❹**: The Search button has a special functionality. It toggles an area that slides out underneath showing the Search Field ❺ and the *Filter HUD Button* ❻, that toggles the Search Window ❼.

🌐 How is the Content displayed?

The following two controls let you determine how the content in the Browser area is displayed.

▶ **Browser View ❽**: *Click* on this button to toggle the Browser view between List View and Filmstrip View. The icon shows what view you are switching to when you click on it. The toggle command is also available as Menu Command *View ➤ Browser ➤ Toggle Filmstrip/List View* and Key Command *opt+cmd+2*.

▶ **Clip Appearance ❾**: *Click* on this button to toggle a popover with six controls that determine the look and functionality of the displayed Clips.

➡ *Filmstrip View*

The Filmstrip View displays the current content in two sections, the Projects ❶ are listed on top and all the Clips ❷ are listed below.

🏀 Projects ❶

This is what you see in the Projects sections:

- ▶ The Projects are listed alphabetically.
- ▶ The number of displayed Projects are listed in parenthesis, next to the header.
- ▶ Each Project shows a thumbnail image of its timeline (black if the Project is empty ▦), the name of the Project, the date and time the Project was created, plus the length of the Project ❸.
- ▶ *Click* on a Project to display its properties in the Inspector and *double-click* on a Project to open it in the Timeline.

🏀 Clips ❷

There are many more controls to configure how to display the Clips in the Browser. They are available in the Clip Appearance Popover when you click on the Clip Appearance button.

- ▶ **Continuous Playback ❹**: This checkbox is the only setting that has nothing to do with the appearance. If enabled, the following will happen. If you play a Clip in the Browser and it reaches its end, FCPx will continue to play the next Clip, and then the next one.
- ▶ **Waveform ❺**: If enabled, a Video Clip displays the waveform ❻ in its thumbnail.
- ▶ **Track Height ❼**: The slider lets you set the Track Height. You will see the effect while *dragging* left and right.
- ▶ **Horizontal Clip Zoom ❽**: The slider sets the length of the filmstrip, which is a sequence of individual thumbnails. The number that is indicated next to the slider determines how many minutes are represented by one thumbnail segment. If the slider is set to "5s" and the Clip is 50s long, then the filmstrip is made of 10 thumbnail segments. Setting the slider all the way to the left shows "All", which means the entire Clips is represented by a single thumbnail.

Here are three screenshots ❾ of a Browser window that has three Clips with a length of 5s, 30s, and 50s. You can see the different appearances, the length of the filmstrips when the zoom slider is set to "All", "10s", and "5s". If a filmstrip has a ripped edge ❿ then it wraps around to the next line.

▶ **Group By ❶**: This popup menu provides various options ❷ on how to group the displayed Clips in the Browser area. The groups can be displayed in ascending or descending order ❸.

Here are a few examples with screenshots:

- **None ❹**: All the Clips are displayed under the header named "Clips" with the number of Clips in parentheses.
- **Content Created ❺**: All the Clips that were created on the same day are grouped together. The header lists the date with the amount of Clips in parentheses.
- **Duration ❻**: All the Clips are grouped by a specific range of their duration with Still Images (no duration) listed as a separate group.
- **File Type ❼**: All the Clips are grouped by their file type. If they don't have a specific file type (i.e. Compound Clip, Multicam Clip), then they are grouped under "No Data".
- **Reel ❽**: If the Clips have no information about a parameter that you've selected (i.e. Reel), then they are grouped together under "No Data".

    Attention: The label of each Group has a disclosure triangle that lets you show/hide the Clips in that Group by *clicking* on it. If you *opt+click* on any disclosure triangle, you toggle all the disclosure triangles at once ❾. For example, quickly close all groups and go through them one by one.

▶ **Sort By ❿**: In addition to the grouping of Clips, you can apply a sorting order inside each group by selecting an option from this popup menu and also set the ascending or descending order ⓫.

➡ List View

The List View is divided in two sections that can be re-seized by **dragging** the divider line ❶ in between. It displays all the Projects and Clips in a list form. The lower section displays all the Projects and Clips ❷ in a list and whatever item is selected in the list will be displayed as a filmstrip ❸ above.

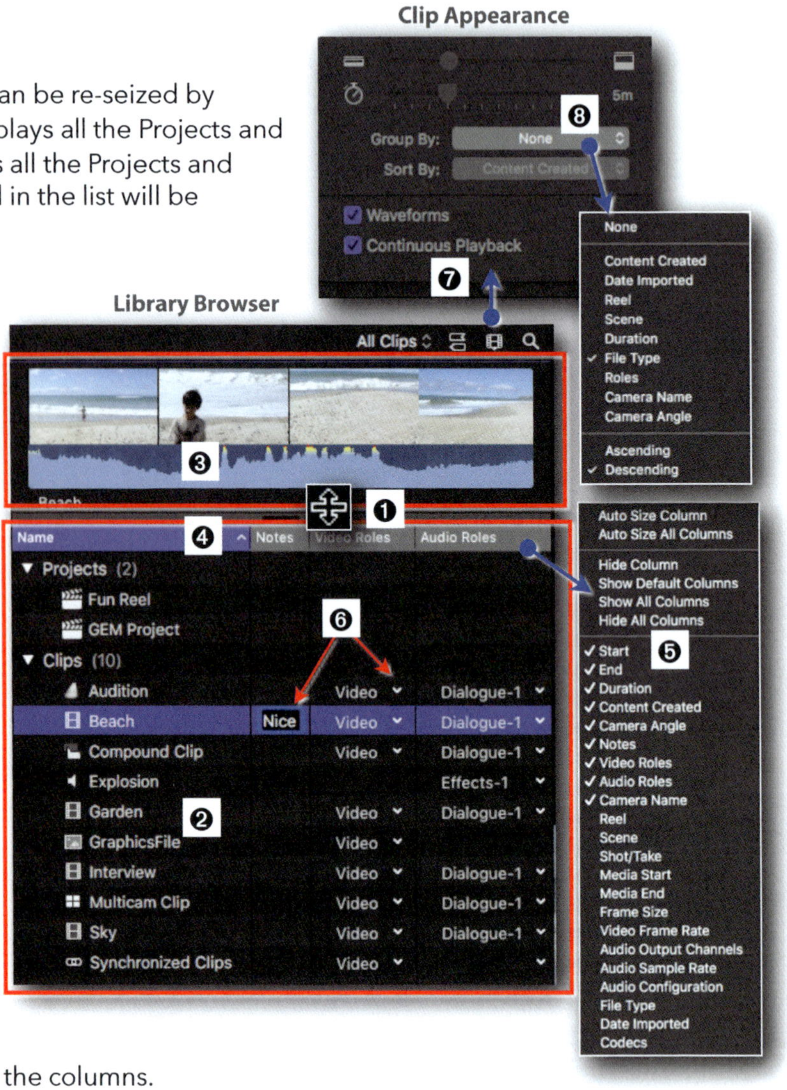

Clip Appearance

🔵 Filmstrip ❸

The length of the filmstrip automatically adjusts to the width of the browser window.

You have all the Clip editing tools available. **Click** on the filmstrip to play from that section, use the Skimming feature, make selections to create subclips or apply metadata and Markers. More about that in the Organize Clips chapter.

🔵 List ❷

You have most of the conventional list features:

Library Browser

▶ **Sort Order**: **Click** on a header ❹ (it turns purple) to sort the list by that field. Click the little arrow to toggle between ascending ⌄ and descending ⌃ order.

▶ **Column Order**: **Drag** the column header to rearrange the positions of the columns.

▶ **Column Width**: **Drag** the divider line between the column header to adjust the column width.

▶ **Column Selection**: **Ctr+click** on the column header to open a popup menu ❺, where you can select which columns to display, plus a few general resize and show/hide commands.

▶ **Time Display**: Please note that any time fields are displayed based on the time format set in the *Final Cut Pro ➤ Preferences ➤ General ➤ Time Display*.

▶ **Edit Fields**: In addition to renaming the Clips, you can edit the Notes fields ❻ (*click* on it and enter any text) and also reassign the Roles by selecting from the Roles popup menu in those fields.

🔵 Clip Appearance

The Clip Appearance popover ❼ only has three parameters available, Waveform, Continuous Playback, and Group By. The other ones are grayed out.

Library Browser

Grouped By ❽: This selector opens the same popup menu as in the Filmstrip View. It also works the same way, so the list is grouped into sections ❾ based on the selection from the popup menu and the sort order. The column header ❹ sorting now applies to each section individually.

➡ *Other Browser View Options*

There is one submenu in the Main Menu ***View ➤ Browser*** ❶ that also affects the user interface and behavior of the Browser with some of the options duplicating the controls in the Clip Appearance Popover ❷.

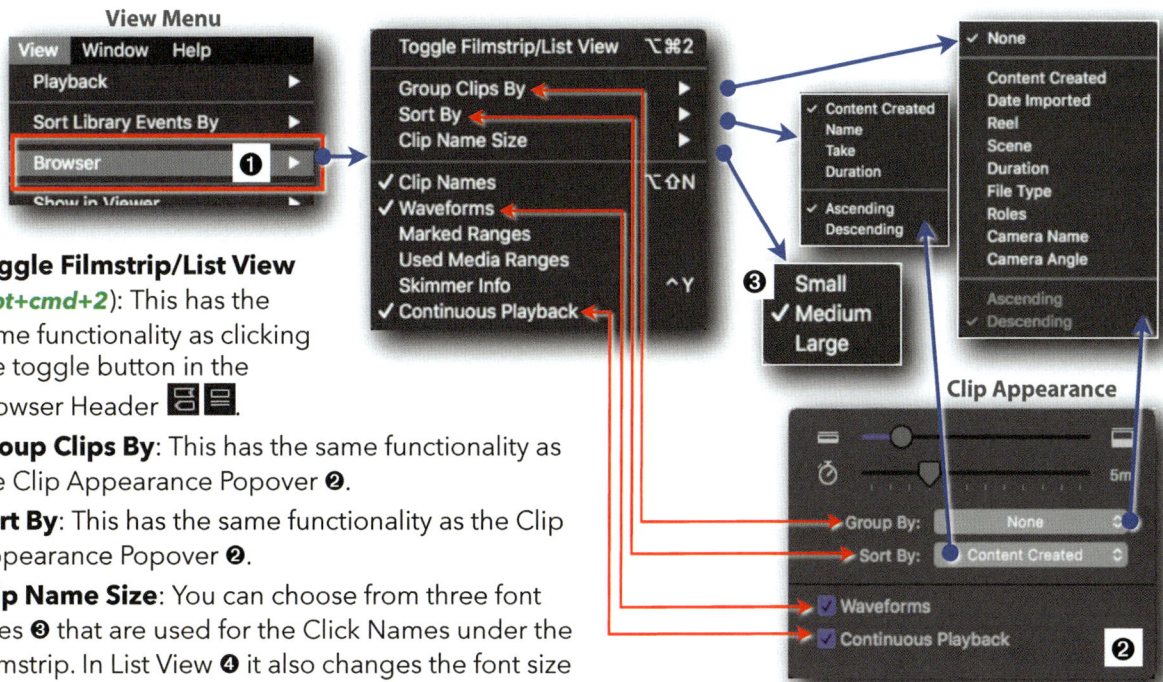

▸ **Toggle Filmstrip/List View** (***opt+cmd+2***): This has the same functionality as clicking the toggle button in the Browser Header ⯐⯑.

▸ **Group Clips By**: This has the same functionality as the Clip Appearance Popover ❷.

▸ **Sort By**: This has the same functionality as the Clip Appearance Popover ❷.

▸ **Clip Name Size**: You can choose from three font sizes ❸ that are used for the Click Names under the Filmstrip. In List View ❹ it also changes the font size for all the text in the list.

▸ **Clip Names** (***sh+opt+N***): If enabled, it displays the Clip Name below the Filmstrip. Clip Names will automatically be hidden in the Filmstrip View at smaller Clip Height.

▸ **Waveforms**: If enabled, a Video Clip displays the waveform ❺ in its thumbnail (same as popover ❷).

▸ **Marked Ranges**: If enabled a Clip will display the colored horizontal lines ❻ that mark various ranges: Orange = Used, Blue = Keyword, Purple = Analysis, Green = Favorite, Red = Rejected. Markers ❼ are always displayed and not affected by this setting.

▸ **Used Media Ranges**: If enabled, a Clip displays an orange line ❽ at the bottom of the thumbnail to mark the section that is used in a Project.

▸ **Skimmer Info** (***ctr+Y***): If enabled, a popover ❾ appears along the top of the Skimmer with the following information: Clip Name, timecode position, metadata. Of course, Skimming (***S***) has to be enabled too.

▸ **Continuous Playback**: If enabled and you play a Clip in the Browser, it will continue to play the next Clip when reaching the end of a Clip (same as Clip Appearance Popover ❷).

Projects

Before getting into the details about Projects, you have to have a clear understanding of what a Project is and also what it is not. For that, let's recap the FCPx architecture and see how the Projects fit into that:

▶ **Library**: A Library ❶ is just a tool that lets you organize all the elements of a specific video project. On your drive, the Library is stored as a Library File ❷, a Package File that contains all those elements inside.

▶ **Events**: Events ❸ can be created inside a Library ❶. They function as containers (like bins) to better organize the elements of a Library. On your drive, each Event is represented by an Event Folder ❹, stored inside the Library File ❷.

▶ **Media** (Clips): Media Files ❺ are imported into one of the Events ❸ inside a Library ❶. On your drive, they are stored in a separate folder ❻ inside that Event Folder and listed as Clips in the FCPx Browser ❺.

▶ **Projects**: Projects ❼ have to be created in your Library, also inside a specific Event ❸. The Projects are listed next to the Clips ❺ in the FCPx Browser. On your drive, each Project is represented by a separate Project Folder ❽ inside the Event Folder ❹ it is assigned to.

🔮 **Timeline**

Here is the important part to understand about the Timeline ❾. It is not a component of the Library like the Events, Clips, or Projects. It is just a section of the FCPx Workspace, displaying a timeline (plus other elements).

☑ **List Projects**: A Project ❼ "lives inside" a specific Event ❸. That means, you use the FCPx Browser to access the available Projects.

☑ **Open a Project**: You "open" a Project in the Timeline Pane ❾, displaying its Project Timeline ❿.

☑ **Work on a Project**: To work on a Project ❼ means to add Clips to its timeline ❿, arrange the sequence of the Clips, add effects, and do all your video editing magic.

☑ **Store the Project**: All the edits are automatically saved to its individual database file, stored inside the Project Folder ❽.

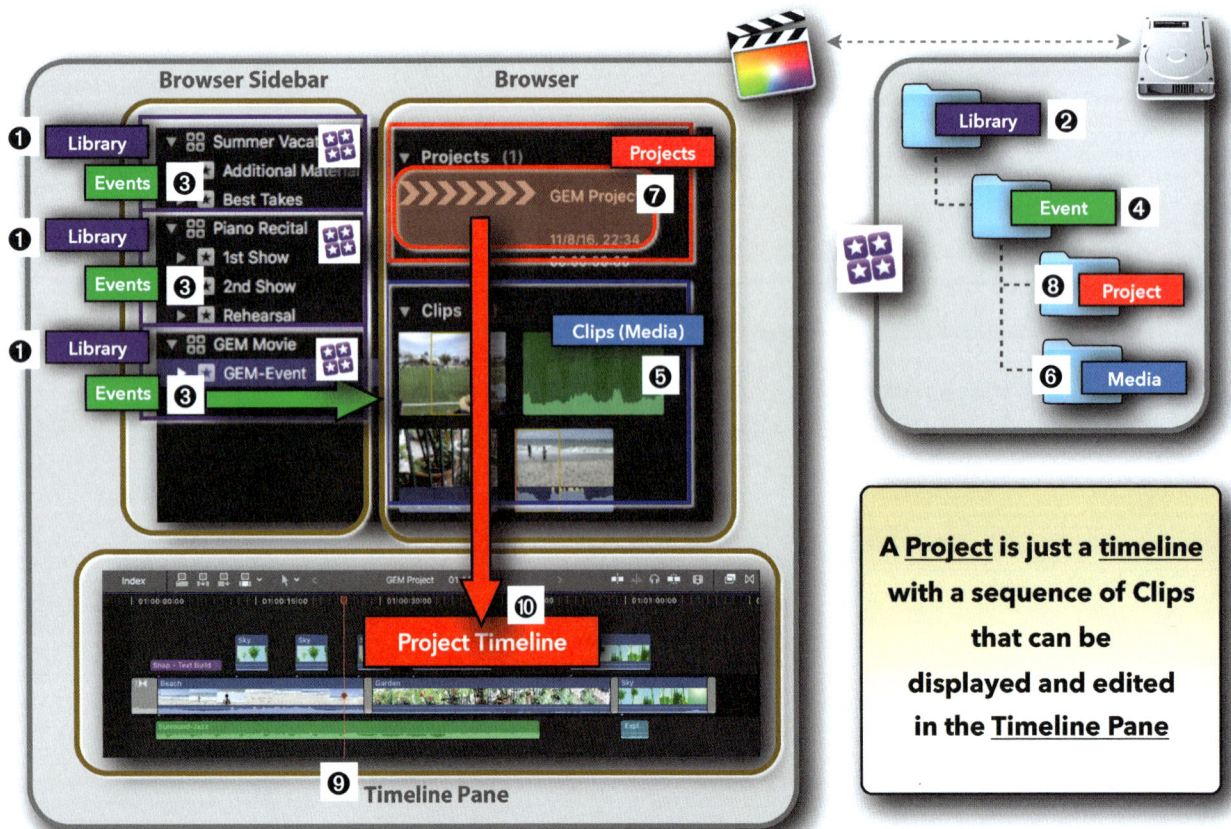

A **Project** is just a **timeline** with a sequence of Clips that can be displayed and edited in the **Timeline Pane**

First Project

In this section, we will explore the steps to create and setup our first Project.

➡ *Create a Project*

Here is a screenshot of a new Library ("GEM Library") with a single Event ("GEM Event") that has four Clips imported. The Browser displays those four Clips ❶, but there are no Projects, because you have to create them manually.

The Timeline Pane of the FCPx Workspace is empty if nothing has been selected yet to be displayed in that window. There is only one big "New Project" ❷ button.

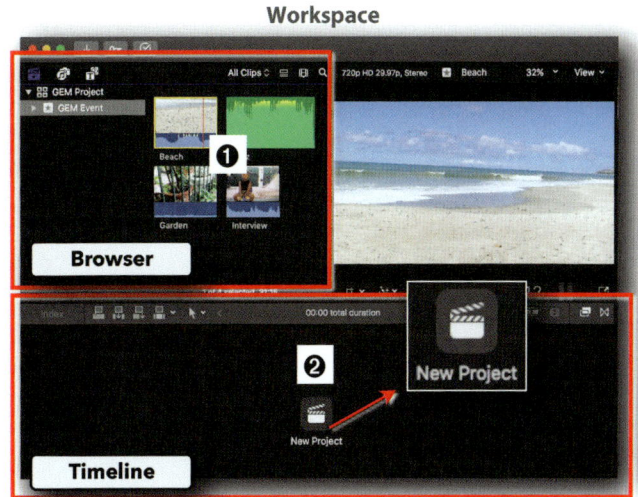

Workspace

Here are the available commands to add a new Project. Please note that if you have multiple Libraries open in the Sidebar, you have to select the target Library (or an item inside that Library) in which you want to create the new Project.

- Menu Command *File > New > Project...* ❸
- Key Command *cmd+N*
- *Ctr-click* the Library (or any item inside the Library) in in the Browser Sidebar and select from the
  Shortcut Menu ➤ New Project ❹
- *Tap* the *New Project* button [New Project] ❺ on the Touch Bar
- You also have the option to create a new Project at the time when you create a new Event by enabling the checkbox "Create New Project" ❻

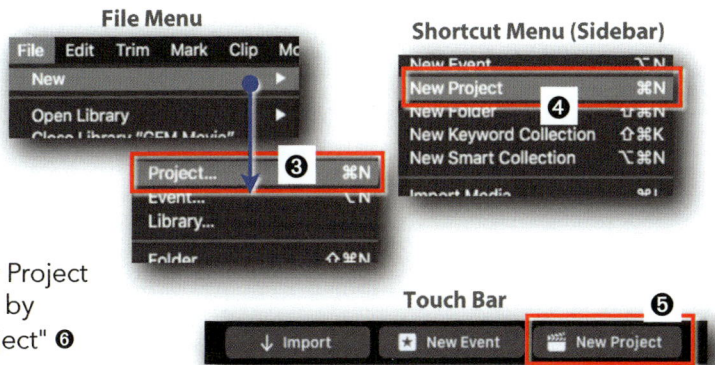

File Menu

Shortcut Menu (Sidebar)

Touch Bar

🎬 Create New Event and New Project

When enabling the checkbox "Create New Project" ❻, the following will happen:

- ☑ The sheet for setting up a new Event will expand, displaying the Project Properties ❼ to configure the new Project.
- ☑ You can *click* the "Use Custom Settings" ❽ to expand the sheet even more with additional settings.
- ☑ When *clicking* OK, the new Event will be created with a new Project, named "Untitled Project" in that Event.

➡ Project Properties

Any of the New Project commands will slide out a Sheet ❶ underneath the Workspace to let you configure the properties for the new Project that you are about to create.

The Properties for the new Project can be changed later in the Project Properties Sheet again by selecting the Project and using any of the commands:

- 🔘 Menu Command *Window* ➤ *Project Properties* ❷
- 🔘 Key Command *cmd+J*
- 🔘 *Click* on the purple Modify ❸ label in the Info Inspector ⓘ

🔵 Two Settings Views

The Project Properties Sheet has two views:

- ▶ **Automatic Settings** ❹: This sheet provides only the basic setting. The properties for Video, Audio, and Rendering are set automatically. *Click* the "Use Custom Settings" button in the lower-left corner to switch to the Custom Settings View.

- ▶ **Custom Settings** ❺: This sheet lists all the properties and lets you configure them individually. *Click* the "Use Automatic Settings" button to switch back to the Automatic. Settings View.

🔵 Automatic Settings

- ▶ **Project Name** ❻: This will set the name of the Project and also the name of the Projects Folder on your drive that will be created. You can rename the Project later in the FCPx Browser at any time.

- ▶ **In Event** ❼: Select the Event you want to save the Project to. The currently selected Event is automatically selected, but you can *click* on the selector to choose any other available Event. The popup menu displays all the Active Libraries and their Events.

- ▶ **Starting Timecode** ❽: Set the SMPTE start time for the Project Timeline.

- ▶ **Video** ❾: FCPx does not set the Video Properties for the Project yet. Later, when you drag your first Event Clip onto the Project Timeline, FCPx looks up the video properties of that first Clip and uses those settings as the Video Properties.

- ▶ **Audio and Rendering** ❿: FCPx sets the Render properties to ProRes 422s, which means that any video segments that are rendered during the editing of your Project will be saved in that format. The Audio properties are set to Stereo, 48kHz.

🎬 Custom Settings

Here is the list of all the parameters in the custom Project Properties Sheet:

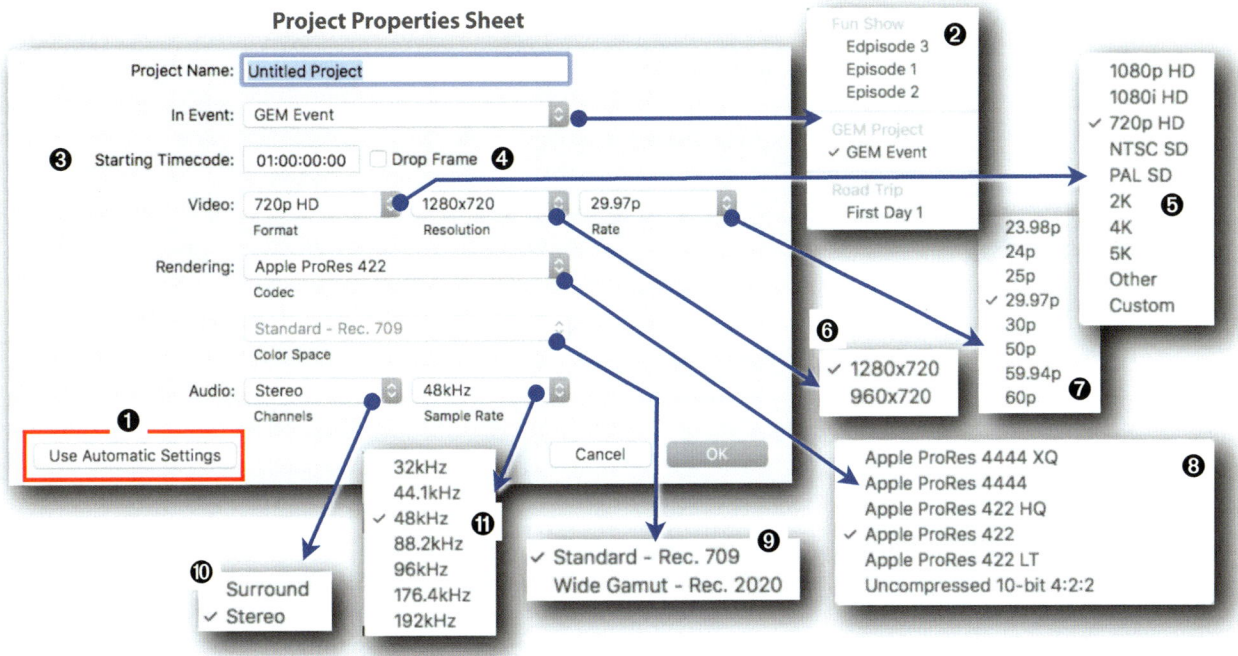

Project Properties Sheet

▶ **Project Name**: This will set the name of the Project and also the name of the Projects Folder on your drive that will be created. You can rename the Project later in the FCPx Browser at any time.

▶ **In Event ❷**: Select the Event you want to save the Project to. The currently selected Event is automatically selected, but you can *click* on the selector to choose any other Event. The popup menu displays all the Active Libraries and their Events.

▶ **Starting Timecode ❸**: Set the SMPTE start time for the Project Timeline.

▶ **Drop Frame ❹**: Enable this checkbox for video files that use the SMPTE drop frame format.

Video Properties:

▶ **Format ❺**: Select the video format that you plan to export your finished video to. This selection determines what options are available in the popup menus for Resolution, Rate, and Color Space.

▶ **Resolution ❻**: Choose the resolution of the video frame.

▶ **Rate ❼**: Choose the video frame rate (fps).

Render Properties:

▶ **Codec ❽**: Select from six different video codecs. Any video segment that is rendered during the editing of your Project will be saved in that format.

▶ **Color Space ❾**: The available options depend on the section in the Video Format popup menu. For example, Rec.601 (NTSC) or Rec.601 (PAL) for standard definition (PAL SD, or NTSC SD). For high definition formats the options will be the Rec.709 or Rec. 2020. However, you can only choose Rec. 2020 if the Color Processing of the Library is set to Wide Gamut (Rec.2020), instead of Standard (Rec. 709).

Audio Properties:

▶ **Channels ❿**: Set the channel configuration to Stereo or Surround.

▶ **Sample Rate ⓫**: Choose from 32kHz up to 192kHz, depending on what is supported by your audio interface.

➡ *What happened?*

Now let's have a look at what happened after we created our first Project.

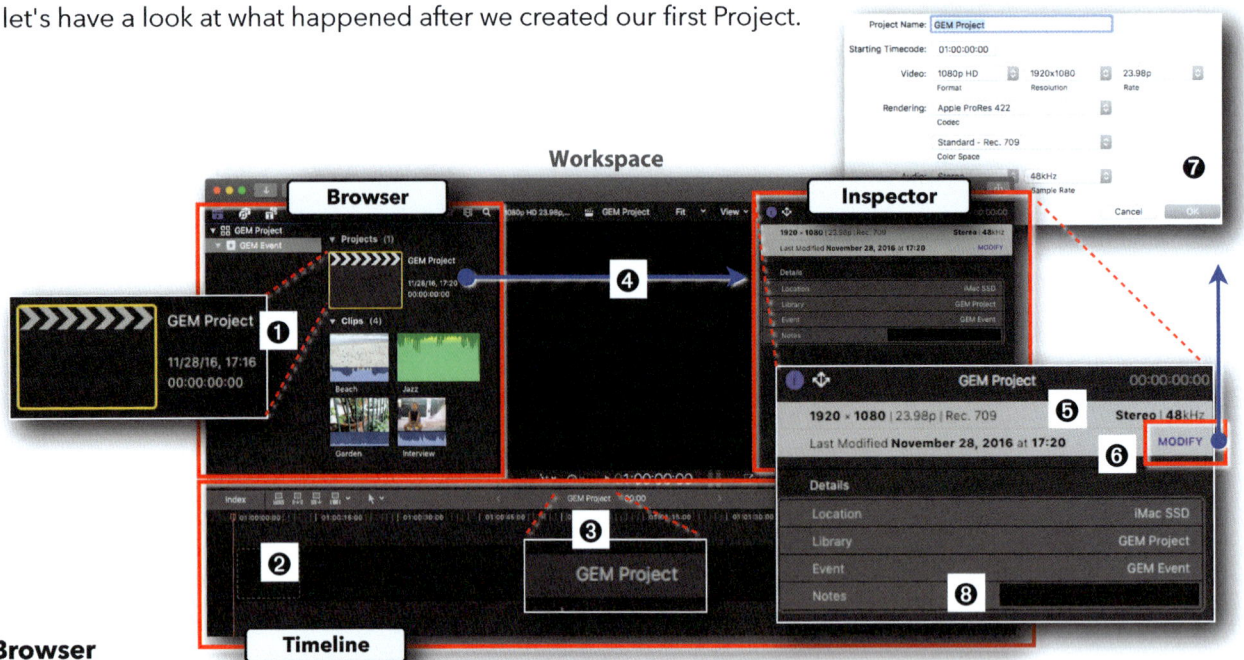

Workspace

🕱 Browser

The Browser now
lists the new Project ❶ with a black slate icon showing the Project Name, the creation date and time, plus the
duration, which is 0, because we haven't added any Clips to the
Project yet.

🕱 Timeline

The Timeline Pane displays the Project ❷, showing its name on the
Timeline Header ❸. The Project Timeline is empty, because we
haven't added any Clips to the Project yet.

🕱 Inspector

When we select the Project in the Browser ❹ and show the
Inspector Pane in the Workspace, it shows the following elements
in the Info Inspector ⓘ:

▸ The Project Header shows the name.

▸ The gray area below ❺ shows the Project Properties with
the modification date underneath.

▸ *Clicking* on the purple *MODIFY* ❻ button opens the Project
Properties Sheet ❼ again, with most of the properties we
had when creating the new Project. You can change those properties if needed.

▸ Details Section: The four lines below show the name of the Event and Library the Project belongs to,
plus the volume it is stored at. You can enter any comments into the Notes field ❽.

🕱 Finder

Here is a screenshot of the content of the Library File to show what happened on the Finder level.

▸ FCPx automatically creates a Project Folder ❾ for each Project that you create in a Library. In this
example, I created two more Projects named "Fun Reel" and "Long Version".

▸ The Project Folder is named after the Project and is stored inside the Event Folder it is assigned to.

▸ The Project Folder contains only one file, the database file that stores all the edits for the Project
made on its Project Timeline. Please note that the Project database file is also named
"CurrentVersion.fcpevent" ❿, and not "CurrentVersion.fcpproject" as you would have expected.

Project Management

➡ *Rename Project*

You can rename Projects at any time.

▶ Same as with the Events, there is no specific Rename command to rename a Project, just select the Project in the Browser, press **return**, type a new name, and hit **return** again.

▶ FCPx renames the Project Folder inside the Event Folder accordingly and takes care of everything under the hood, so that all the references and connections stay in place.

▶ And again, never ever change the folder/file structure or rename anything inside the Library File on the Finder level or you end up with a corrupted Library!

➡ *Copy/Move Project(s) to Library ➤*

You can easily copy or move Project(s) between Libraries.

☑ Select one or multiple Projects in the Browser.

☑ Select the command *File ➤ Copy/Move Project(s) to Library ➤* ❶. Please note that the name of the menu command changes from "Project" to "Project**s**" ❷ to indicate if multiple Projects have been selected.

☑ The submenu ❸ lists all the currently open Libraries, plus a command "*New Library...*", to create a new Library if you want to copy or move the Project(s) to a new Library.

☑ A Dialog ❹ pops up to inform you that the Original Media related to those Projects are copied/moved and gives you the option with two checkboxes to include the Optimized Media and Proxy Media too (if available).

🔘 Drag & Drop

You can also drag a Project or a group of selected Projects from the Browser direct over any Event in the Browser Sidebar. This could be to an Event from the same Library or a different Library.

▶ **Move**: *Drag* the Project(s) over

▶ **Copy**: *Opt+drag* the Project(s) over

A green plus icon ❺ appears at the mouse cursor as soon as you move over an Event, and a red tag with a number ❻ if you drag more than one Projects.

A warning dialog ❼ pops up if you drag Projects to a Library with a different Color Space.

File Menu

Drag multiple Project

Drag one Project

➡️ Duplicate Project

The Duplicate command creates a new Project in the same Event, a duplicate of the selected Project. This way, you can continue to work on two different versions of the Project. Keep in mind that any Compound Clips or Multicam Clips in that Project refer to the same instance.

Use any of the following commands:

- Key Command *cmd+D*
- Menu Command *Edit ➤ Duplicate Project* ❶
- *Ctr+click* on a Project and choose from the *Shortcut Menu ➤ Duplicate Project*

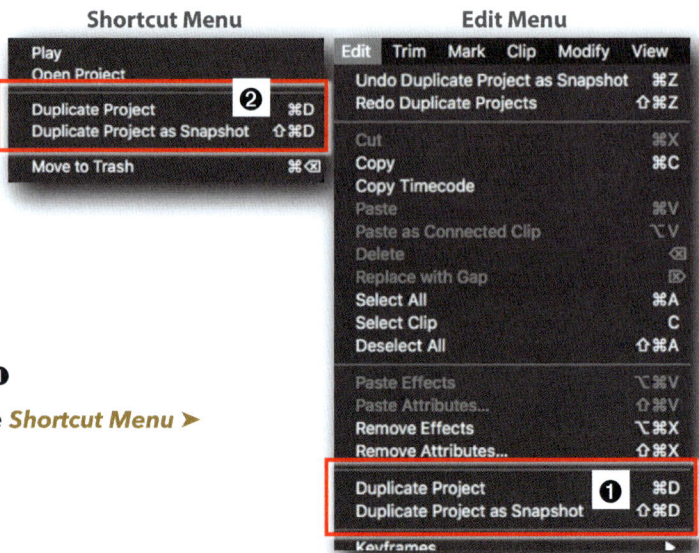

➡️ Duplicate Project as Snapshot

The *Duplicate Project as Snapshot* command also creates a new Project, a duplicate of the selected Project, but it has one important difference. Any Compound Clip or Multicam Clip will be copied as new (unlinked) instances in the new Project. This guarantees that editing the Compound or Multicam Clips in the original Project will not affect those Clips in the duplicated Project, it stays self-contained, like a "snapshot in time".

Use any of the following commands:

- Key Command *cmd+D*
- Menu Command *Edit ➤ Duplicate Project as Snapshot* ❶
- *Ctr+click* on a Project and choose from the *Shortcut Menu ➤ Duplicate Project as Snapshot* ❷

<u>Attention</u>: FCPx uses the same name for the duplicated Project, but adds the words "Snapshot" and the date and time. The full name is truncated in Filmstrip View ❸, but if you look at the Finder inside the Library File, you will see the entire Project Folder name ❹.

Shortcut Menu

Play
Open Project

Duplicate Project   ❷   ⌘D
Duplicate Project as Snapshot   ⇧⌘D

Move to Trash   ⌘⌫

Edit Menu

Edit Trim Mark Clip Modify View

Undo Duplicate Project as Snapshot   ⌘Z
Redo Duplicate Projects   ⇧⌘Z

Cut   ⌘X
Copy   ⌘C
Copy Timecode
Paste   ⌘V
Paste as Connected Clip   ⌥V
Delete   ⌫
Replace with Gap   ⌦
Select All   ⌘A
Select Clip   C
Deselect All   ⇧⌘A

Paste Effects   ⌥⌘V
Paste Attributes...   ⇧⌘V
Remove Effects   ⌥⌘X
Remove Attributes...   ⇧⌘X

Duplicate Project   ❶   ⌘D
Duplicate Project as Snapshot   ⇧⌘D

Keyframes   ▶

FCPx Browser

▼ Projects (2)

GEM Project
11/28/16, 21:06
00:15:45:00

GEM Project
Snapshot Nov 28, 20
11/28/16, 21:06   ❸
00:15:45:00

Finder

▼ 📁 GEM Event
    ★ CurrentVersion.fcpevent
  ▼ 📁 GEM Project
      ★ CurrentVersion.fcpevent
  ▼ 📁 GEM Project Snapshot Nov 28, 2016, 21/06/54
      ★ CurrentVersion.fcpevent   ❹

➡️ Delete Project(s)

Select the Project(s) and choose any of the following commands to delete it.

- Key Command *cmd+delete*
- Menu Command *File ➤ Move to Trash* ❺
- *Ctr+click* on a Project and choose from the *Shortcut Menu ➤ Move to Trash* ❻

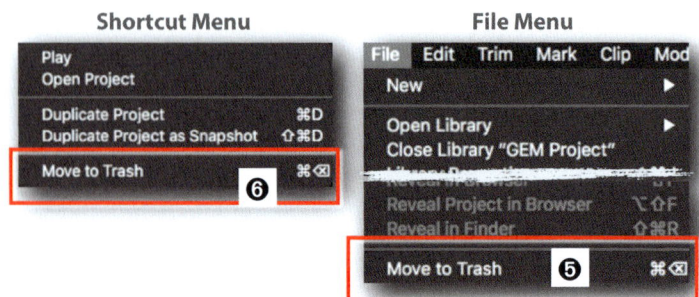

Shortcut Menu

Play
Open Project

Duplicate Project   ⌘D
Duplicate Project as Snapshot   ⇧⌘D

Move to Trash   ❻   ⌘⌫

File Menu

File Edit Trim Mark Clip Mod

New   ▶

Open Library   ▶
Close Library "GEM Project"
Reveal in Browser
Reveal Project in Browser   ⌥⇧F
Reveal in Finder   ⇧⌘R

Move to Trash   ❺   ⌘⌫

You can use the Undo command (*cmd+Z*) if you hit the delete command by accident and move the Project back out from that Trash folder. Although this command is called "Move to Trash", it will not move the Project to the Finder Trash (where you might recover it). Instead, it will be moved to a temporary "_Trash" folder inside the Library File, which will be deleted if you close FCPx.

Timeline UI

The **Browser** ❶ is only the container where you store the individual Projects ❷ (inside a specific Event). To work on the Project, you have to open the Project in the **Timeline** Pane ❸, where you do the actual video editing. You view your Timeline in the **Viewer** Pane ❹. The **Inspector** Pane ❺ helps you with specific editing task.

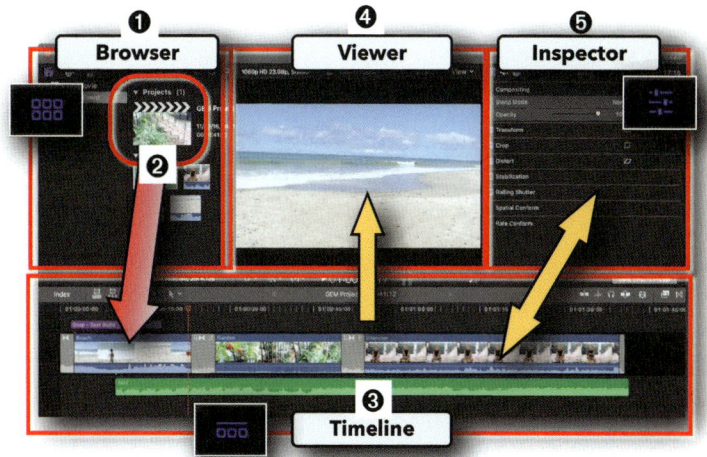

➡ **Open Project**

These are the commands to open a Project in the Timeline:

- *Double-click* on the Project ❷ in the Browser.
- *Ctr+click* on the Project in the Browser and choose from the *Shortcut Menu* ➤ *Open Project* ❻.
- *Ctr+click* on the Project and choose from the *Shortcut Menu* ➤ *Play*. This opens the Project in the Timeline and starts playing it right away.
- If a Project was already open before, then you can *ctr+clicking* the Timeline History Buttons ⟨ ⟩ on the Timeline Header and select it from the popup menu.

➡ **Main Areas**

The Timeline Pane has four main elements (not including the various window panes that can be opened inside the Timeline):

▸ **Header** ❼: This area was the *Toolbar* in previous FCPx versions. Now it functions as the header as part of the Timeline that provides buttons and controls for various purposes related to the Timeline.

▸ **Timeline Ruler** ❽: The ruler provides the time reference for your Project. You can choose from four different Time Displays in the *Final Cut Pro* ➤ *Preferences* ➤ *General*.

▸ **Primary Storyline** ❾: The black strip in the center of the Timeline Area is the Primary Storyline. This is where you place your Clips.

▸ **Playhead** ❿: The Playhead is the thin vertical line that spans across the Timeline with the Playhead Thumb ▮ on top in the ruler that you can *drag* left-right. It marks the position on the timeline that is currently displayed in the Viewer during pause or playback.

Timeline Pane

➡ *Timeline Header*

Here is just a quick overview with the elements on the header. I will discuss them in more details later.

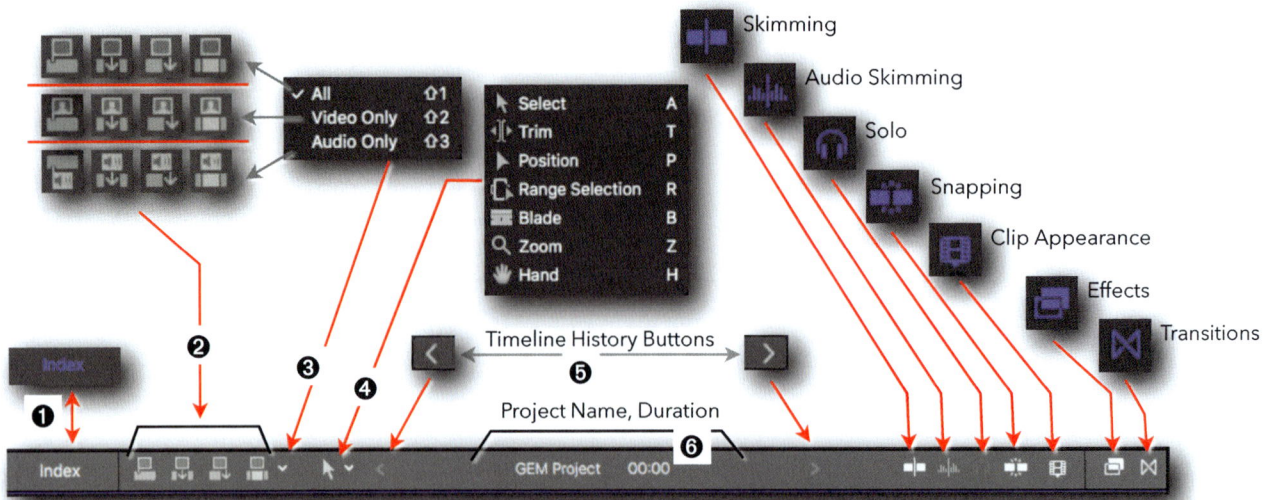

- **Index ❶** (*sh+cmd+2*): *Click* on the word "*INDEX*" to toggle the Timeline Index pane on the left of the Timeline.

- **Move Clips to Timeline Buttons ❷** (*Q*, *W*, *E*, *D*): *Click* on one of the four buttons to move the currently selected Clip(s) or Clip Range in the Browser to the Timeline. The different buttons determine where and how the Clip is placed on the timeline. Please note that the selector ⬇ to the right changes the appearance and function of those four buttons to indicate if you move the video, audio, or both components of a Clip.

- **Clip Type Selection ❸** (*sh+1*, *sh+2*, *sh+3*): *Click* to open a popup menu with three options that changes the functionality (and appearance) of those four buttons on the left.

- **Edit Tool Selector ❹**: *Click* the selector ⬇ to open a popup menu with seven options to change the mouse cursor to one of those Edit Tools. The currently selected tool is displayed next to the selector.

- **Timeline History Button ❺** (*View* ➤ *Timeline History Back/Forward cmd+} cmd+{*): FCPx remembers the Projects (or Clips) that you had previously open in the Timeline. Those arrows let you quickly step through those Project. *Ctr+click* on the arrow to open a popup menu, listing the names of those Projects or Clips.

- **Project Name and Duration ❻**: The center of the Timeline Header shows the name and duration of the Project (or Clip) displayed in the Timeline. The duration of a selected Clip in the timeline will be displayed in yellow font.

- **Skimming** (*View* ➤ *Skimming S*): *Click* to toggle a scrubbing feature, called the Skimmer. When enabled, moving the mouse across the timeline area "plays the content" corresponding to the position of your mouse and the speed of your mouse movement. The play position is indicated by a red Skimming line, which is independent from the Playhead.

- **Audio Skimming** (*View* ➤ *Audio Skimming sh+S*): This lets you turn on/off the audio signal during skimming if you need only a visual reference without the "noise".

- **Solo** (*Clip* ➤ *Solo opt+S*): When enabled, it solos the audio portion of the selected Clip and mutes the audio from other non-selected Clips when playing back.

- **Snapping** (*View* ➤ *Snapping N*): When you *drag* objects, the Playhead, or the Skimmer, then they will snap to the nearest object or Playhead.

- **Clip Appearance**: *Click* to open/close the Clip Appearance Popover.

- **Effects Browser** (*Window* ➤ *Show in Workspace* ➤ *Effects cmd+5*): *Click* to toggle the Effects Browser on the right of the Timeline.

- **Transitions Browser** (*Window* ➤ *Show in Workspace* ➤ *Transitions sh+cmd+5*): *Click* to toggle the Transitions Browser on the right of the Timeline.

➡ *Clip Appearance*

The Clip Appearance Popover in the Timeline Header determines the look of the Clips in the Timeline, the so-called Timeline Clips of your Project.

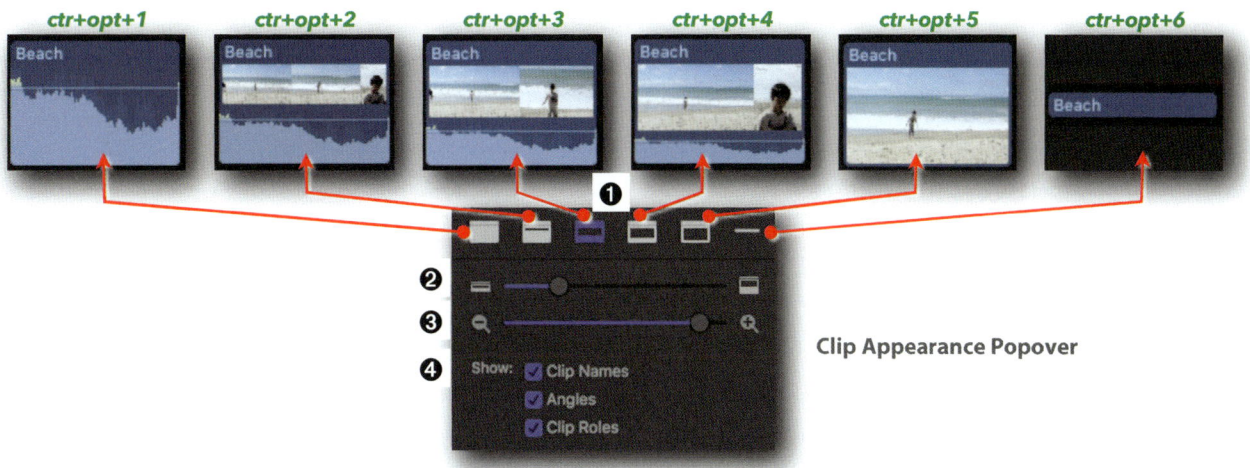

ctr+opt+1   *ctr+opt+2*   *ctr+opt+3*   *ctr+opt+4*   *ctr+opt+5*   *ctr+opt+6*

Clip Appearance Popover

- ▸ **Clip Appearance Buttons ❶**: *Click* on any of the six buttons to determine what content is displayed on the Clip. Use the Key Command *ctr+opt+ArrowUp* or *ctr+opt+ArrowDown* to step through the six types or use the dedicated Key Command:

  Audio only *ctr+opt+1*   Big video, small audio *ctr+opt+4*

  Big audio, small video *ctr+opt+2*   Video only *ctr+opt+5*

  Equal audio and video *ctr+opt+3*   Clip labels only *ctr+opt+6*

- ▸ **Clip Height Slider (vertical zoom) ❷**: *Drag* the slider left-right to zoom the timeline vertically. This changes the height of the Clips.

- ▸ **Clip Length Slider (horizontal zoom) ❸**: *Drag* the slider left-right to zoom the timeline horizontally. This changes the length of the filmstrips that represent the Clips.

- ▸ **Show Label ❹**: Choose what label to display on the Clip: "*Clip Names*", "*Clip Angles*", "*Clip Roles*".

➡ *Zoom your Project*

There are a few more additional commands for zooming the timeline horizontally:

- ▸ **Zoom In ❺**: This command zooms in by increments. *View ➤ Zoom In* or *cmd+EqualSign* or Spread Gesture on the track pad.

- ▸ **Zoom Out**: This command zooms out by increments. *View ➤ Zoom Out* or *cmd+MinusSign* or Pinch on the track pad.

- ▸ **Zoom to Fit**: This command zooms the timeline so the entire Project is visible (horizontally). *View ➤ Zoom to Fit* or *cmd+Minus*.

- ▸ **Zoom to Samples ❻**: Please note that this is a mode and not a command. If enabled (checkmark ✅), the Zoom In command has three more steps to zoom in even further, which is useful when doing precise audio editing.

- ▸ **Touch Bar**: *Tap* the Timeline View Button ▭ on the Touch Bar to bring up the overview where you can slide the left or right handles ❼ of the Zoom Range to zoom in/out of the Project.

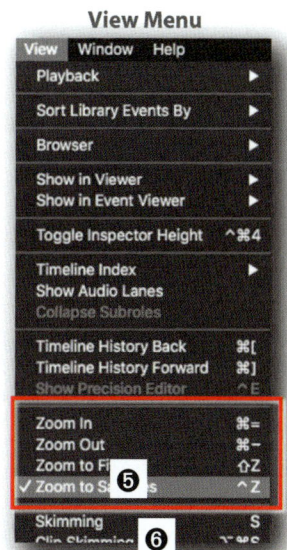

View Menu

Touch Bar

🌑 Zoom Center

A common issue when zooming in to a specific spot on the timeline is that the spot can move out of site and then you have to scroll the timeline left or right to find it and bring it back to the center. To avoid that, you can place the Playhead at that spot, because FCPx always keeps the Playhead visible and uses it as the center when zooming. This guarantees that the spot you need to zoom in stays visible.

However, if you have the Skimming enabled (*View* ➤*Skimming* or *S*), then the Skimmer position functions as the center instead of the Playhead.

🌑 Frame Indicator

Please note that when you zoom in far enough, you will see a shaded area on the Time Ruler ❶, or across the entire Timeline area ❷ (i.e. when the Blade Tool is selected). This indicates the range of a single video frame to show you the boundaries if you do video editing (i.e. trim, cut).

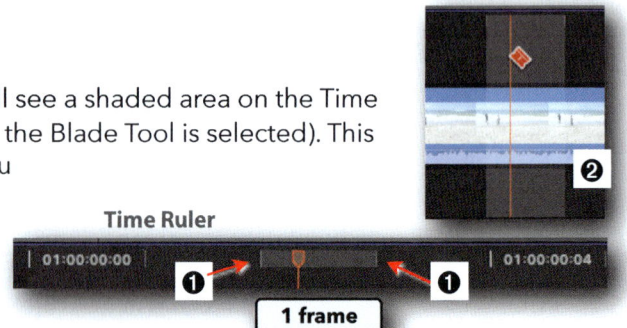

Time Ruler

➡️ *Window Panes*

In addition to the Timeline Area ❸ and the Timeline Header ❹, which are always visible in the Timeline Pane, you can toggle three additional window panes inside that Timeline Pane:

▶ **Timeline Index ❺**: The Timeline Index gives you an alternate view of your currently displayed Project while working in the Timeline.

- Toggle this window pane: *Window* ➤ *Show in Workspace* ➤ *Timeline Index* or *sh+cmd+2* or *click* the "*INDEX*" button ❻ on the Timeline Header.

▶ **Effects/Transitions Browser ❼**: The Browser pane can display either Effects or Transition, which you can apply to your Project by *dragging* them over Clips on the Timeline Area.

- Toggle the window pane: *Window* ➤ *Show in Workspace* ➤ *Effects* or *cmd+5* or *click* the Effects button 🔀 ❽ on the Timeline Header.

- Toggle the window pane: *Window* ➤ *Show in Workspace* ➤ *Transitions* or *sh+cmd+5* or *click* the Effects button 🔲 ❾ on the Timeline Header.

▶ **Audio Meters ❿**: The Audio Meters let you monitor the audio signal level of your Project. It automatically switches to stereo (two bars) or surround (6 bars) depending on the format of the Clip or Project.

- Toggle the window pane: *Window* ➤ *Show in Workspace* ➤ *Audio Meters* or *sh+cmd+8* or *double-click* or *click* on the tiny Audio Meters at the bottom of the Viewer Pane.

➡ Timeline Index

The Timeline Index provides an alternate view of the Project that is currently displayed in the Timeline Area. The window pane has three different views (Clips - Tags - Role) that can be accessed by clicking on their tabs in the header or selecting them from the Main Menu *Clip* ➤*Timeline Index* ➤ ❶.

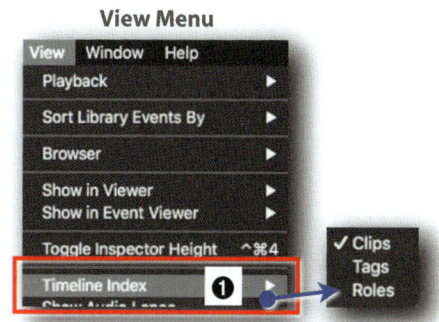

🌑 Clips ❷

This view shows all the Clips in your Project displayed as a chronological list.

- ▶ Each Clip is displayed as a separate row.
- ▶ You can display up to five columns in addition to the name field.
- ▶ *Right-click* on the column header to select from a popup menu ❺ which column to display.
- ▶ *Drag* the columns to reorder or *drag* the divider line to resize the columns.
- ▶ You can edit the fields for the Name, Notes, and Roles.
- ▶ The four buttons at the bottom ❻ let you filter the list to display only Video, Audio, Titles, or All Clips.
- ▶ A horizontal Playhead ❼ indicates the current Playhead Position.
- ▶ The Search field 🔍 at the top lets you display only the Clips that match that search criteria.

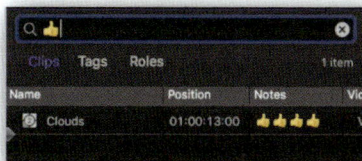

- ▶ Selecting a Clip in the list will select that Clip in the Timeline and moves the Playhead to the beginning of the Clip. You can also select multiple Clips for editing.

🌑 Tags ❸

The list shows all the tags that are assigned to any Clips in your Project, listed in chronological order.

- ▶ Selecting a Tag selects the Clip, Subclip (Clip Range), or Marker in the timeline with a white frame and moves the Playhead to the beginning of that frame.
- ▶ A horizontal Playhead indicates the current Playhead Position.
- ▶ Markers ❽ can be clicked (to change from to-do 🔲 to completed 🔲) and *double-clicked* to open the Marker Popover.
- ▶ The buttons 🔲 🔲 🔲 🔲 🔲 🔲 ❾ at the bottom lets you filter the list to show only the select Tag type.
- ▶ The Search Field 🔍 at the top lets you display only the Clips with a tag that match that search criteria.

🌑 Roles ❹

The Roles View does not represent a timeline list. It displays all the Roles that are used in the current Timeline Clips. It provides a lot of powerful features when working in your Timeline Project that I cover in the Roles chapter.

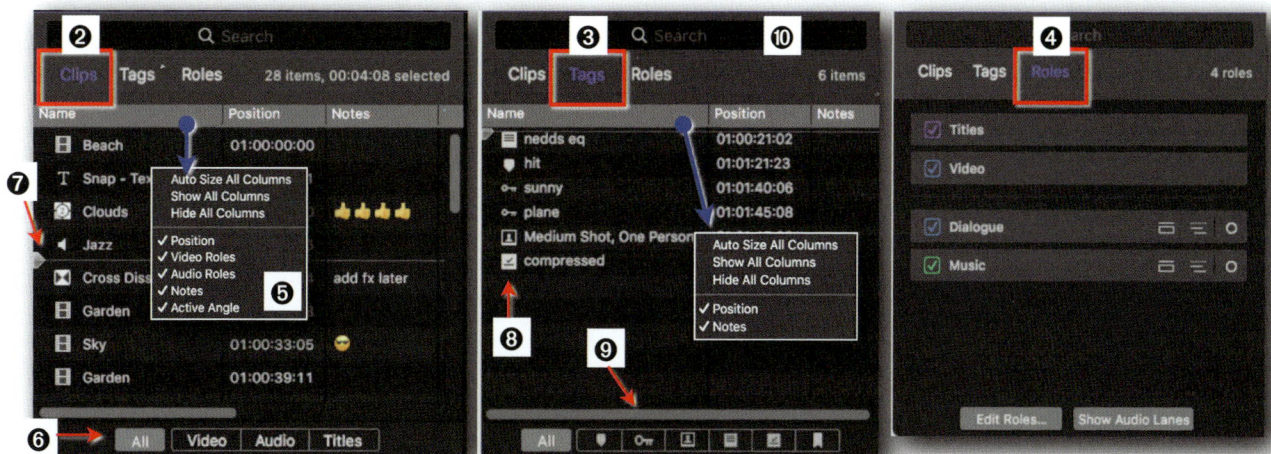

Overview

As we have already seen in the Interface chapter, the Viewer is a very "versatile" window with lots of combinations of what you can display.

➡ *Key Focus*

The most important aspect of the Viewer is that it has an additional Viewer, called the *Event Viewer*, that can be toggled on/off and shares the Viewer pane. When it is visible ❶, it only plays the Clip that is currently selected in the Browser ❷ and the Viewer ❸ itself displays the Clips from the Timeline ❹.

If only the Viewer ❺ is visible, then you have to pay attention to whether the Browser or the Timeline has key focus to determine what is displayed in the Viewer.

- ▶ **Browser - key focus**: If the Browser has key focus, it shows a thin purple line ❼ right below the three Browser buttons. In that status, the Viewer will display the Clips from the Browser.
- ▶ **Timeline - key focus**: If the Timeline has key focus, it shows a thin purple line ❽ right above the Timeline Ruler. Now, the Viewer will display the Clips from the Timeline ❾.

Viewer	Event Viewer
Always visible in the Workspace as one of the main window panes	Window pane can be added with the command Window ➤ Show in Workspace ➤ Event Viewer (ctr+cmd+3)
Displays the Event Clip that is currently selected in the Browser or the Clips playing in the Timeline, whichever has **key focus**. If the Event Viewer is visible, then it displays only the Timeline	Only displays the Event Clip that is currently selected in the Browser
Provides all the Viewer controls	Provides all the Viewer controls with the exception of Transform, Crop, Distort, Enhancement, and Retime button
Can be viewed individually in Play Full Screen Mode	Can be viewed individually in Play Full Screen Mode
Both Viewers can be placed together on a second display with the command Window ➤ Show Viewers on Secondary Display	
The Viewers can be displayed on an optional Broadcast Monitor with the command Window ➤ A/V Output	

➡ *Overview*

❶ Project/Clip: The top-center of the Viewer displays what is currently displayed:

> ▸ 🎬 The name of the Project with the Project icon, or
>
> ▸ ⭐ The name of the Clip with the Event icon

❷ Project/Clip Format: The upper-left corner displays the video and audio format of the currently played Project or Clip.

❸ Zoom Level: The percentage number displays the current Zoom Level. *Click* on the selector to open a popup menu where you can choose various Zoom Levels. "Fit" will auto-adjust the Zoom Level based on the size of the available window pane.

❹ View Options: *Click* on the selector to open a popup menu with a wide variety of important controls, for example, toggle nested window panes to show Video Scopes or Angles, and also choose the Playback Media (Original, Optimized, Proxy).

❺ Transform/Crop/Distort Button: This button changes to indicate which of the three video effects is currently selected from the popup menu. Transform 🔲, Crop 🔲 , or Distort 🔲 . The currently selected effect displays its onscreen controls in the Viewer to adjust the effect.

❻ Enhancement Button 🔧: *Click* on the button to open a popup menu with various commands for audio and video enhancement effects.

❼ Retiming Button 🕐: *Click* on the button to open a popup menu with various commands related to retiming (different playback speeds).

❽ Play/Pause Button ▶️⏸: This is the only visual Transport Control. It toggles between Playback Mode and Pause Mode.

❾ SMPTE Reader: The SMPTE Reader has two functions, it acts as a display for the Playhead Position, but can also be used for entering numeric values for Clip editing.

❿ Audio Meter: This is a tiny LED Meter to display the current audio signal. It automatically switches to stereo (2 bars) or surround (6 bars) depending on the audio format. You can also click on the meter to toggle the Audio Meter pane in the Timeline window.

⓫ Play Full Screen Button 🔲: Clicking on this button will switch the Viewer to full screen and starts playback.

Current Project/Clip Format   Currently displayed Project/Clip   Zoom Level   View Options

Retiming Button   SMPTE Reader   Play Full Screen Button

Enhancement Button   Play/Pause Button   Audio Meter

Transform/Crop/Distort Button

SMPTE Reader

Let's start with a closer look at the SMPTE Reader that has a lot of little details you have to pay attention to.

➡ Time Display Mode

The SMPTE Reader can display time in four different display modes. From the Preferences ❶ *Final Cut Pro* ➤ *Preferences* ➤ *General* ➤ *Time Display* (*cmd+,*) select one from the popup menu ❷. This setting also changes the time display on the Timeline Ruler in the Timeline Pane.

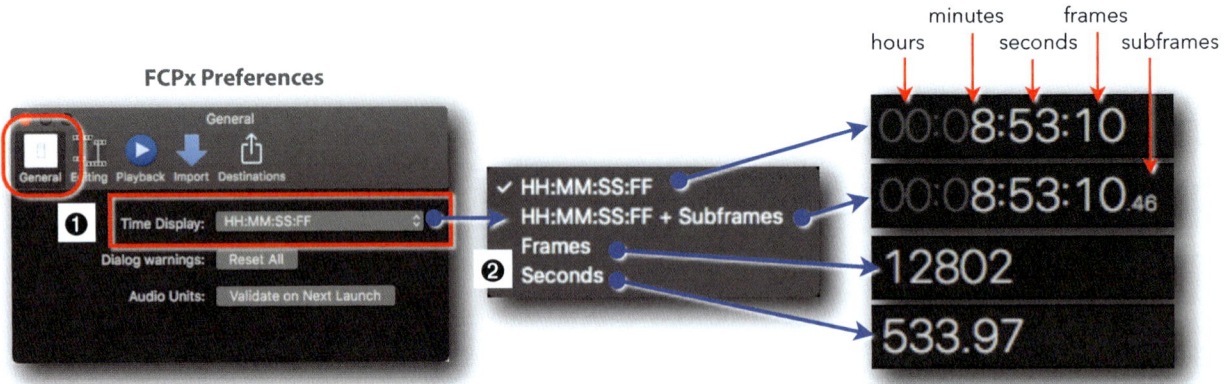

A few things to be aware of:
- ▶ The "unused" digits in a SMPTE display are grayed out for better readability.
- ▶ The number of frames in a second depends on the video frame rate (fps) of the Project or Clip.
- ▶ The number of subframes per video frame is 80.
- ▶ If the video frame of a Clip or Project is set to Drop Frame, then the colon between seconds and frames changes to a semicolon ❸.

➡ Position Display

As a display device, the SMPTE Reader can show the following information:
- ▶ As a default, it displays the current position of the Playhead ❶ or Skimmer.
- ▶ When *dragging* a Connected Clip in the Timeline, it displays the current start position ❺ of the Connected Clip while dragging.
- ▶ The display also acts as an input device, to enter time values for various editing procedures. During input mode, the display turns purple ❻, indicating that the SMPTE Reader has key focus.

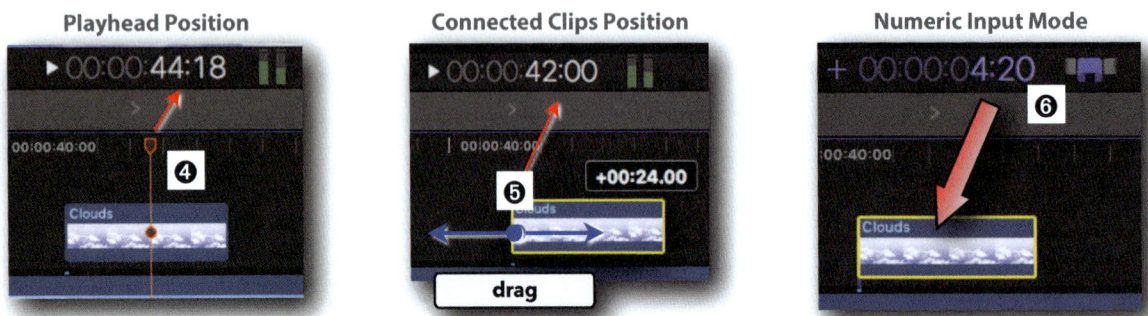

Playhead Position | Connected Clips Position | Numeric Input Mode

➡ Numeric Input Mode

You can use the SMPTE Reader as a numeric input device to enter exact time values for precise editing. There are some details you have to pay close attention to in order to avoid any confusion.

Move Playhead **to** 4s:20f ❶

`00:00:04:20` ⏻

🌑 Visual Feedback

The numeric input mode is indicated by three things:

▶ The display turns purple.

▶ The specific input mode is indicated by an icon on the right ❶.

▶ The display might have a plus or minus sign ❷ on the left if the edit adds or subtracts number values.

Move Playhead 4s:20f **to the right**

`+ 00:00:04:20` ⏻→

Move Playhead 4s:20f **to the left**

`— 00:00:04:20` ←⏻

❷

🌑 Input Conventions

Once you have entered a specific input mode, the following input conventions apply:

▶ Enter numbers, which will be added on the right moving left.

▶ Use the **period** key as a separator h.m.s.f.

▶ Press the **delete** key to delete the last entered digit.

▶ Press **esc** key to cancel the Numeric Input Mode.

▶ Press the Plus **+** key or Minus **-** Key to toggle between positive or negative values.

▶ Numbers bigger than the allowed values will be re-calculated. For example, entering "40" (in a 30fps setup) will result in 1:10 (1s:10f).

▶ You can copy the Timecode address with the command **Edit ➤ Copy Timecode** and paste timecode with the standard **cmd+V**.

Set Clip Length to 4s:20f

`00:00:04:20` ▮▮

Lengthen Clip by 4s:20f

`+ 00:00:04:20` ▮▮

Shorten Clip by 4s:20f

`— 00:00:04:20` ▮▮

🌑 Input Modes

You have to pay attention to two conditions::

▶ #1: How to enter the input mode ❸

▶ #2: What is selected ❹

🔘 **Reposition Playhead** ❺

- #1 **Click** on the SMPTE Reader
- #2 It doesn't matter what Clip is selected

🔘 **Resize Clip(s)** ❻

- #1 **Double+click** on the SMPTE Reader
- #2 One or multiple Clips have to be selected. This also applies to Event Clips in the Browser

🔘 **Trim Clips** ❼

- #1 Press **+** or **-** key
- #2 The outcome depends on what Edit Points are selected
  - Ripple Left Edit or Right Edit
  - Roll Edit
  - Slide Edit
  - Slip Edit

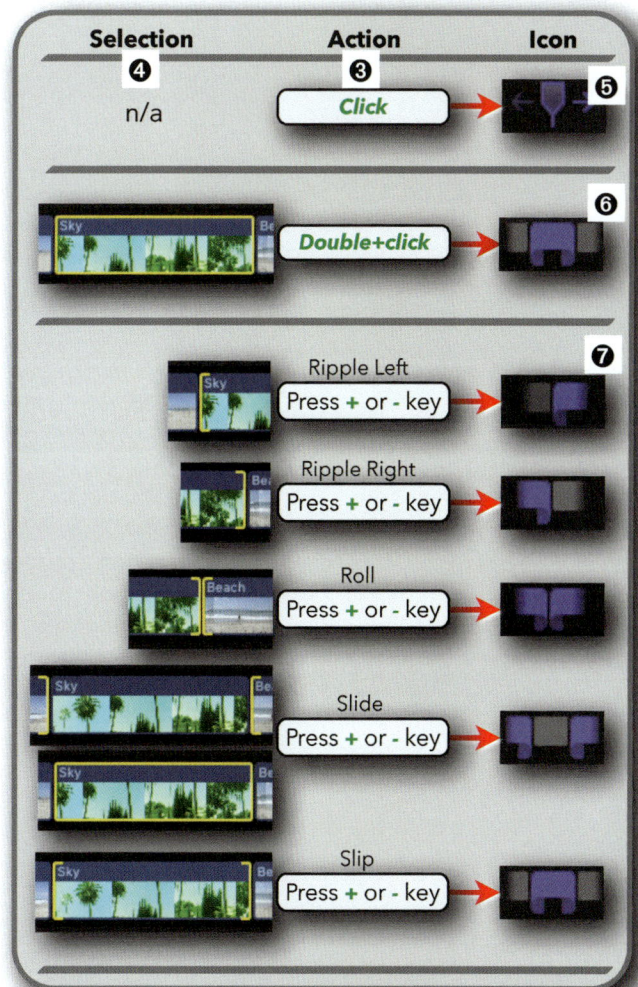

Selection ❹	Action ❸	Icon
n/a	Click	⟵⏻ ❺
Sky ... Be	Double+click	▮▮ ❻
Sky (Ripple Left)	Press + or - key	❼
Be (Ripple Right)	Press + or - key	
Beach (Roll)	Press + or - key	
Sky ... Be (Slide)	Press + or - key	
Sky ... Be (Slip)	Press + or - key	

Transport Controls

➡ *Playback Controls*

🟡 Play Buttons

There are only two buttons on the Viewer (and identical buttons on the Event Viewer) that affect the playback.

▶ **Play/Pause Button ❶**

The button toggles between two states:

- ▶ *Click* on the button to start playback of the Clip currently viewed in the Viewer

- ⏸ *Click* on the button to pause playback

▶ **Play Full Screen Button ❷**

- ⤢ *Clicking* on this button will switch the Viewer to full screen and starts playback from the Playhead Position. Same as *View ➤ Playback ➤ Play Full Screen* or *sh+cmd+F*. You can use any other playback commands while in Full Screen Mode (i.e. *J*, *K*, *L*).

Key Focus

When you click on a button or control in the Viewer or Event Viewer you affect that specific Viewer directly. For all other commands (Menu Commands, Key Commands), you have to keep the following thing in mind: If you have the Viewer and the Event Viewer visible in the Workspace, you have to tell FCPx which Viewer is the recipient of a command. And that is decided by the "key focus".

If the Browser has key focus, then the Event Viewer will receive the command. If the Timeline has key focus, then the Viewer will receive the command.

You can also click directly in one of the Viewers to give it key focus. You can see the thin purple line in the Event Viewer ❸ or the Viewer ❹, depending on which one you click to get key focus.

🟡 J K L

These three keys are used for various playback operations:

- 🔘 Press *L* to start Forward Playback.
- 🔘 Press *J* to start Reverse Playback. You can alternate between L and K to change the playback direction.
- 🔘 Press *K* to pause Playback.
- 🔘 Press *L* or *K* repeatedly again (and again) to increase the playback speed.
- 🔘 Hold *K* and then hold down *J* or *L* to play back at 1/2 speed.
- 🔘 Hold *K* and then press *J* or *L* to move the playhead by one frame forward or backwards.

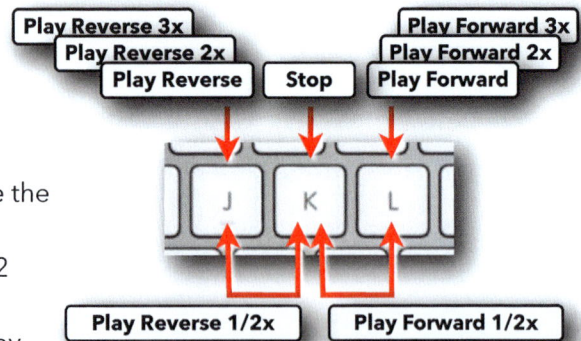

Play Commands

The various Menu Commands for playback are all located in the *View ➤ Playback ➤* submenu ❶:

▸ **Play** (*space*): This toggles between Play and Pause and has the same function as pressing the button in the Viewer ▶ ⏸, playing back at the Playhead or Skimmer position.

    • The Key Command *sh+spacebar* plays back in reverse.

▸ **Play Selection** (*/*): This starts playing from the currently selected Clip (marked with the yellow frame). Pressing while in playback mode, jumps to the beginning of the selection again while continuing to play.

▸ **Play Around** (*sh+?*): Starts playing from the Playhead or Skimmer position with a pre-roll amount set in *Final Cut Pro ➤ Preferences ➤ Playback ➤ Pre-Roll Duration* ❷ and continues to play beyond the Playhead or Skimmer position by the amount set in the *Final Cut Pro ➤ Preferences ➤ Playback ➤ Post-Roll Duration* ❸. The Touch Bar has a separate button ⟨⊹⟩ for that when in Timeline View ❹.

▸ **Play from Beginning** (*sh+ctrl+I*): Starts playing from the beginning of the Project in the Timeline or the selected Clip in the Browser. Pressing again while playing jumps back to the beginning while still in playback mode.

▸ **Play to End** (*sh+ctrl+O*): Starts playing from the current Playhead or Skimmer position to the end of the Selection.

▸ **Play Full Screen** (*sh+cmd+F*): This is the same function as pressing the Play Full Screen Button ⤢ in the lower right corner of the Viewer. Remember that you can use any other playback commands while in Full Screen Mode (i.e. *J*, *K*, *L*).

▸ **Loop Playback** (*cmd+L*): This is not a play command. It sets the playback mode. When enabled, it will play the entire Project or any selection in the Timeline or Browser in a continuous loop.

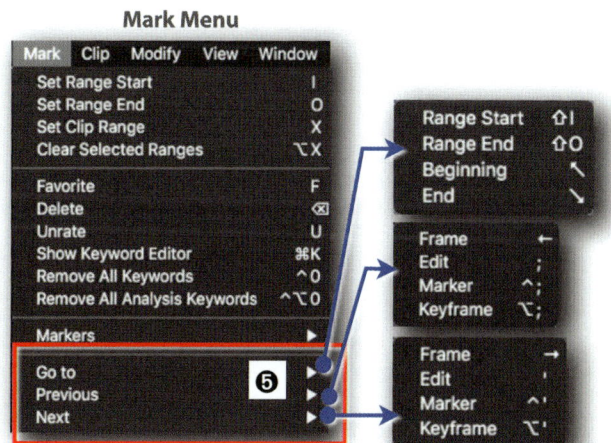

➡ Navigation Controls

Next are the various commands to position the Playhead or Skimmer.

Menu Commands and Key Commands

All the following commands are available from the Mark Menu ❺ and have corresponding (easy to remember) Key Commands.

▸ **Go to the Beginning of the Timeline**: Key Command *home* or Menu Command *Mark ➤ Go To ➤ Beginning*.

▸ **Go to the End of the Last Clip**: Key Command *end* or Menu Command *Mark ➤ Go To ➤ End*.

▸ **Go to Previous/Next Edit** (Clip Boundary): Key Command *ArrowUp* and *ArrowDown* or Key Command *;* and *'* .

▸ **Go to Previous/Next Frame**: Key Command *ArrowLeft* and *ArrowRight*.

▸ **Go to next 10 Frame**: Key Command *sh+ArrowLeft* and *sh+ArrowRight*.

▸ **Go to next Sub Frame**: Key Command *cmd+ArrowLeft* and *cmd+ArrowRight*.

▸ **Go to Previous/Next Marker**: Key Command *ctr+;* and *ctr+'* .

▸ **Go to Previous/Next Keyframe**: Key Command *opt+;* and *opt+'*.

🏅 Playhead Position - mouse

The most direct way to position the Playhead (or the Skimmer) is to move it there with the mouse using the following procedures. Some actions have different outcomes depending on the currently selected Cursor Tool: ▶Select Tool, ⫿⫿Trim Tool, ▶Position Tool, ⌟Range Tool, ▭Blade Tool, 🔍Zoom Tool, ✋Hand Tool.

Timeline

Timeline

- **Click** on the Time Ruler ❶ on top of the Timeline Area to move the Playhead to that click position. Can be used with any cursor tool.
- **Clicking** in the Timeline area ❷ (but not on a Clip) will also place the Playhead, except 🔍 ✋.
- **Opt+clicking** on a Clip ❸ will select the Clip and moves the Playhead to that click position, except ▭ 🔍 ✋.
- **Dragging** the Playhead Thumb ▼ ❹ along the Time Ruler slides the Playhead. This will "scrub" the video (the video plays back according to the speed and direction of the mouse movement), but not the audio portion.

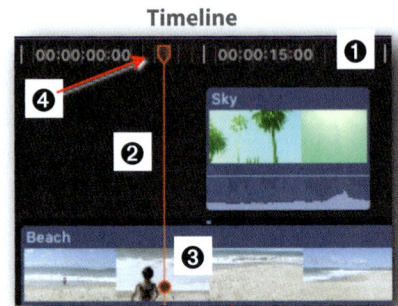

Browser

Browser

- **Click** on the Filmstrip ❺ of a Clip in the Browser window to move the Playhead to that click position.
- **Opt+click** on a Filmstrip to move the Playhead to that click position and remove any Range selections on that Clip.
- **Dragging** on the Filmstrip will create a selection (yellow frame) and positions the Playhead at the same time.

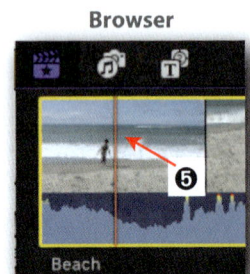

🏅 Playhead Position - numerically

You can position the Playhead numerically to an absolute position or move it to the left or right by a specific amount. First, you have to **click** on the SMPTE Reader to enter Numeric Input Mode ❻. The display turns purple (key focus) with a Playhead Thumb icon on the right.

SMPTE Reader

While in this mode, do any of the following actions:

- ▶ Type an absolute timecode address to move the Playhead to that position when you hit **enter**.
- ▶ Press the plus key to toggle the plus sign ❼ (and a right arrow next to the Playhead Thumb icon). The Playhead now moves by that amount to the right when you hit **enter**.
- ▶ Press the minus key to toggle the minus sign ❽ (and a left arrow next to the Playhead Thumb icon). The Playhead now moves by that amount to the left when you hit **enter**.

🏅 Timeline Index

The Timeline Index can also be used as a navigation tool. Open it by **clicking** the Index button in the upper-left corner of the Timeline (**sh+cmd+2**). Select the Clips tab to display a chronological list of all the Timeline Clips.

Timeline Index

- ▶ Selecting any Clip ❾ in the list will select that Clip in the Timeline ❿ and moves the Playhead to the beginning ⓫ of that Clip. Press the **ArrowUp** or **ArrowDown** key to step through the Clips in the list.

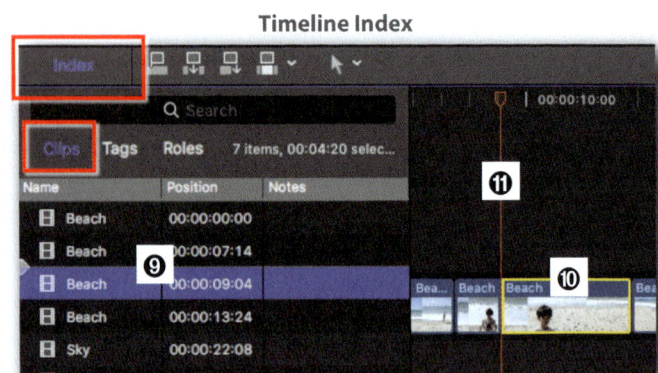

➡️ *Playhead Position Indicator*

FCPx adds a few visual indicators in the Viewer to mark specific positions of the Playhead or Skimmer.

- ▶ **Filmstrip Left ❶**: If the Playhead is positioned at the first frame of the Project Timeline (Key Command *home*) or the first frame of the Event Clip selected in the Browser.

- ▶ **Filmstrip Right ❷**: If the Playhead is positioned at the last frame of the Project Timeline (Key Command *end* and then press the *ArrowLeft* key) or the last frame of the Event Clip selected in the Browser.

- ▶ **Torn Edges Right ❸**: If the Playhead is positioned one frame after the last frame of the Project Timeline (Key command *end*).

- ▶ **Bracket Left ❹**: If the Playhead is positioned at the left Edit Point of a Timeline Clip.

- ▶ **Bracket Right ❺**: If the Playhead is positioned at the right Edit Point of a Timeline Clip.

- ▶ **Left Selection Boundary ❻**: If the Playhead on the Event Clip (in the Browser) is positioned at the start of a Clip Range (Keyword 🔑, Favorite ⭐, Rejected ❌).

- ▶ **Right Selection Boundary ❼**: If the Playhead is positioned at the end of a Clip Range.

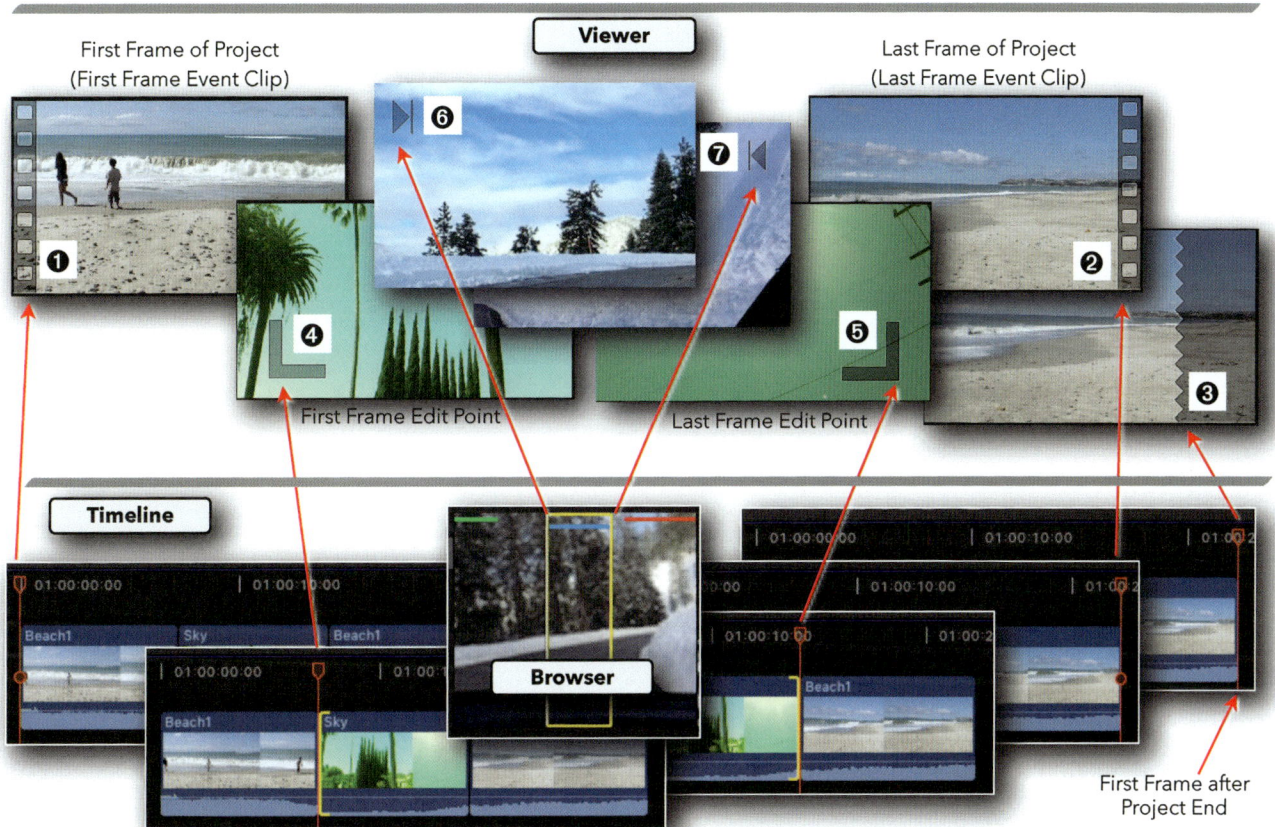

First Frame of Project (First Frame Event Clip)

Viewer

Last Frame of Project (Last Frame Event Clip)

First Frame Edit Point

Last Frame Edit Point

Timeline

Browser

First Frame after Project End

One special indication on the Viewer appears when you have a Project selected in the Timeline that is empty and place the Playhead at the beginning. In that case, the Viewer is black, displaying the filmstrip ❻ on the left and the torn edges ❼ on the right.

Timeline

Viewer

empty

Playhead and Skimmer

In this section, I want to introduce the Playhead and Skimming feature. These are very essential tools in every video editing application and you will use them all the time when working on your video project.

Most users might be already familiar with the concept, but the implementation in FCPx could be a bit confusing due to a lot of little details and some inconsistencies. So let's get to it step-by-step.

➡ *Basics*

Whatever you see on the Viewer is indicated by two components, a Time Display and a Playhead.

And here is the first advice. As we have already seen in earlier chapters, there are two "sources" that can feed the Viewer, the Browser Pane or the Timeline Pane. You have to pay attention to their differences regarding the Playhead and the Time Display.

🟡 Timeline Pane

The Timeline Pane has a visible Time Ruler ❶ on top that acts as the time axis of the timeline where you place the Timeline Clips ❷ in sequence. The Playhead ❸, that thin vertical line, moves along horizontally along the Time Ruler and that is the position that is displayed in the Viewer ❹. The SMPTE Reader ❺ in the Viewer is the time display that shows the current Playhead Position ❸.

🟡 Browser Pane

The Filmstrip of an Event Clip in the Browser Pane doesn't have a visual Time Ruler ❻. Instead, the length of the displayed thumbnail(s) represents the length (duration) of that Clip. However, it can still display a Playhead ❼, the thin vertical line, moving horizontally across the filmstrip while displaying its content in the Viewer ❽. The SMPTE Reader ❾, in this case, displays the Source Timecode of the Clip or the relative time from the beginning of the Clip.

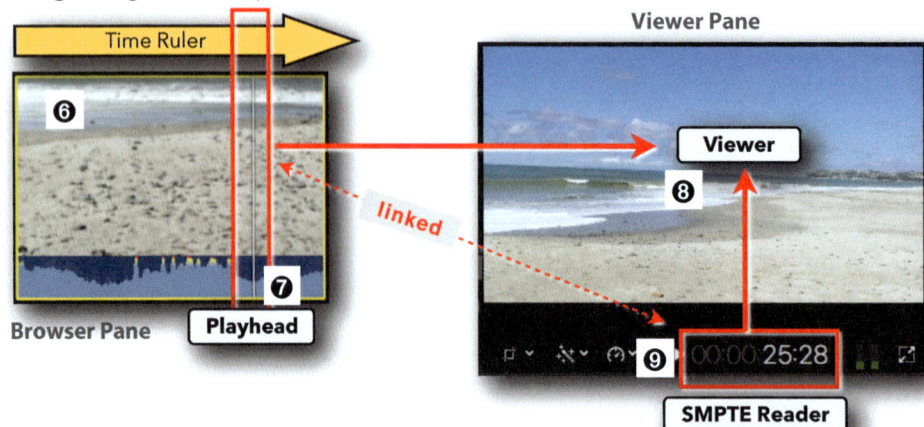

➡ Playhead - Basic Functionality

Here are the basic functions of a Playhead, and as I mentioned, they are slightly different in the Timeline Pane and the Browser Pane.

🌑 Timeline Pane

▶ **Display**: Whenever you play back your Project in the Timeline, the Playhead will follow, referencing what you see in the Viewer to the Time Ruler of your Project. Also, using any of the navigation commands in Pause Mode (Goto..., Next..., Previous...) will also move the Playhead accordingly.

▶ **Positioning**: You can click on the Timeline Pane to re-position the Playhead:

- *Click* anywhere in the Time Ruler ❶ during Pause Mode ⏸ When clicked during Play Mode ▶, the playback continues to play from the clicked position.

- *Drag* along the Time Ruler ❷ to "scrub" the video, which means the Viewer follows the position and speed of your mouse movement (without audio). *Dragging* during playback will scrub the video, including the audio signal.

- *Click* on the Timeline area outside a Clip ❸.

- *Opt+click* on the Timeline area on a Clip ❹. The Clip or the Clip Border will also be selected (yellow frame ❺). Please note that clicking on a Clip will only select the Clip without moving the Playhead, that's why you have to use the modifier key *option*.

🌑 Browser Pane

▶ **Display**: Whenever you play back an Event Clip in the Browser Pane, the Playhead will follow, referencing what you see in the Viewer to the position on the Event Clip. Also, using any of the navigation commands in Pause Mode (Go to..., Next..., Previous...) will also move the Playhead accordingly.

▶ **Positioning**: The Event Clip in the Browser Pane only has limited functionality:

- *Click* anywhere on the thumbnail ❻ during Pause Mode ⏸. When you click during Play Mode, then the playback will stop when you reposition the Playhead by clicking on the thumbnail.

- An optional popover can be displayed on top of the Playhead, showing the name, time positions and any available keywords at that position. The inconsistency here is that this popover is called the Skimmer Info that can be toggled with *View ➤ Browser ➤ Skimmer Info* or *ctr+Y* and is displayed even if the Skimming feature is disabled.

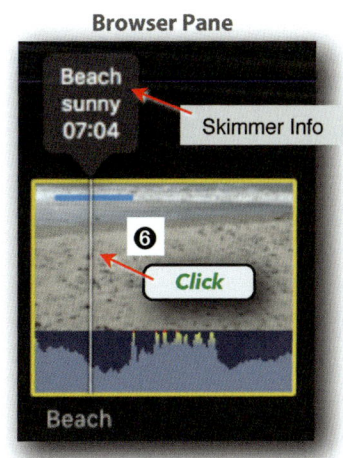

➡ *Skimmer - Basic Functionality*

When enabling Skimming, you add the following functionality, which is only available during Pause Mode ⏸. So remember, Skimming only works in Pause mode, not in Play Mode.

▶ **Skimmer**: Whenever you move the mouse cursor over the Timeline Area or any filmstrip in the Browser Pane, a second Playhead appears, a thin red line, called the Skimmer ❶. The waveform in the Audio Inspector has its own ("always-on") Skimming functionality.

▶ **Viewer / SMTPE Reader**: Whenever the Skimmer is visible, the Viewer ❷ and its SMPTE Reader ❸ ignore the Playhead ❹ position and switch to follow the Skimmer ❶ position.

▶ **Scrubbing**: The Skimmer follows the horizontal movement of the mouse cursor, which means the playback responds to the direction and speed of the mouse movement, a common editing procedure called "scrubbing".

▶ **Audio optional**: You can turn off the audio signal during scrubbing to concentrate on the visual part.

▶ **Editing Tool**: You can use the Skimmer also as an editing tool, for example, to set in and out points for a Clip Range.

▶ **Clip Skimming** (Timeline Pane only): This is a special Skimming mode I explain on the next page.

▶ **Play**: Use any of the play commands to start playback from the Skimmer Position (*spacebar*, *sh+spacebar*, *J*, *L*).

▶ **Editing**: Pressing the *I* key will select a Clip Range with the Skimmer Position as the in-point and pressing the *O* key will select a Clip Range with the Skimmer Position as the out-point.

▶ **Info Tag** (Browser Pane only): You can enable a little popover (the so-called Skimmer Info ❺) that shows up on top of the Skimmer to display the name of the Clip and the current time position of the Skimmer (plus any keywords if available).

▶ **Auto Key Focus**: This is an important little detail. Usually, a window or window pane only gets key focus when you click on it or select it with a command. The Skimmer, however, automatically switches the key focus between the Timeline Pane and the Browser Pane just by moving over the filmstrip of an Event Clip or moving over the Timeline Area. You can see that if you look closely at the thin purple line ❻ at the top of the Browser Pane of theTimeline Pane.

▶ **Zooming**: When you use a Zoom In and Zoom Out command *(cmd+=* and *cmd+-)*, FCPx does not just zoom in, it uses the Playhead as a center that stays visible regardless of how much you zoom in. However, if you have the Skimmer visible, then the Skimmer position functions as the center instead of the Playhead.

102   4 -Basic Operations

➡ Skimmer Controls

Here is how to access those Skimmer related controls:

🎯 Skimming

You toggle Skimming on/off with any of the following commands:

- Main Menu *View* ➤ *Skimming* ❶
- Key Command **S**
- *Click* the Skimming Button ❷ in the Timeline Header

🎯 Audio Skimming

You toggle the Audio Skimming on/off (only if Skimming is enabled) to disable the audio signal during skimming with any of the following commands:

- Main Menu *View* ➤ *Audio Skimming* ❸
- Key Command *sh+S*
- *Click* the Audio Skimming Button ❹ in the Timeline Header
- Turning off Skimming will also turn off the Audio Skimming Button if it was enabled, but leaves it checked in the View Menu (see Clip Skimmer below)

🎯 Skimmer Info

Please note that, when the Skimmer Info is enabled, it also displays the popover on the Playhead in the Event Clips, even if Skimming is turned off. Toggle the Skimmer Info with the following commands:

- Main Menu *View* ➤ *Browser* ➤ *Skimmer Info* ❺
- Key Command *ctr+Y*

🎯 Snapping

This is a useful feature when editing Clips on the Timeline, but it also affects both the Playhead and the Skimmer. When you move them close to an object (i.e. Clip Boundaries or Keyframes), the Playhead or Skimmer snaps to that object and also turns yellow to indicate that special status.

- Main Menu *View* ➤ *Snapping* ❻
- Key Command *N*
- *Click* the Snapping Button in the Timeline Header ❼

🎯 Clip Skimming

The implementation of the Clip Skimming is a little bit strange and you have to make sure to understand what is enabled and when. I'll explain that feature on the next page. Here are the Key commands to toggle it on/off.

- Main Menu *View* ➤ *Clip Skimming* ❽
- Key Command *sh+opt+S*

FCPx View Menu

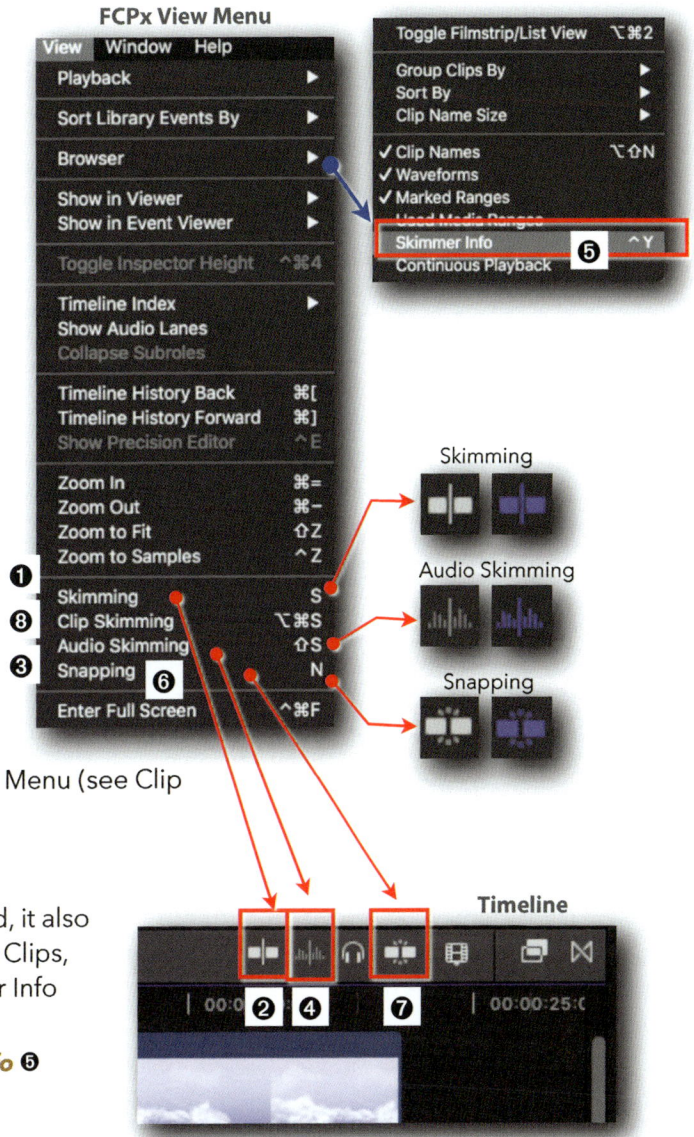

➡ Clip Skimming

Clip Skimming is an additional Skimming Mode that works only in the Timeline Pane and not for Event Clips in the Browser Pane. It can be activated independently of the regular Skimming function. Please pay attention to how it is implemented.

🔵 Functionality

Here is the concept of how Clip Skimming works if regular Skimming is already enabled:

▶ **Clip Skimming off**: This is the "standard" Skimming behavior. When moving the mouse cursor ❶ around in the Timeline, <u>ALL</u> the Clips are "played" ❷ indicated by the red Skimmer line going across all Clips. Only the horizontal position (time axis) is relevant.

▶ **Clip Skimming on**: Now, when moving the mouse cursor over a Clip ❸, only that Clip will be skimmed ("played") and all the other Clips that are "present" at that same time location are ignored. This is especially helpful when you want to check the footage of a Clip that is "covered" by a Connected Clip above ❹. Only the skimmed Clip will play as if the Connected Clip, a cut away or overlay, was not present. The red Skimmer line is now only visible on that Clip as an orange line ❺.
If you move the mouse over an area in the Timeline, not covering any Clip, then the standard red Skimmer ❻ line appears again, skimming all Clips.

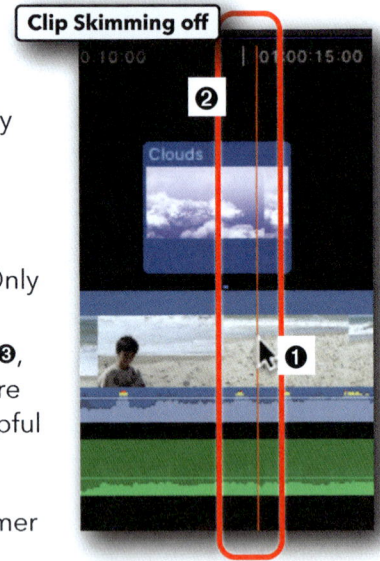

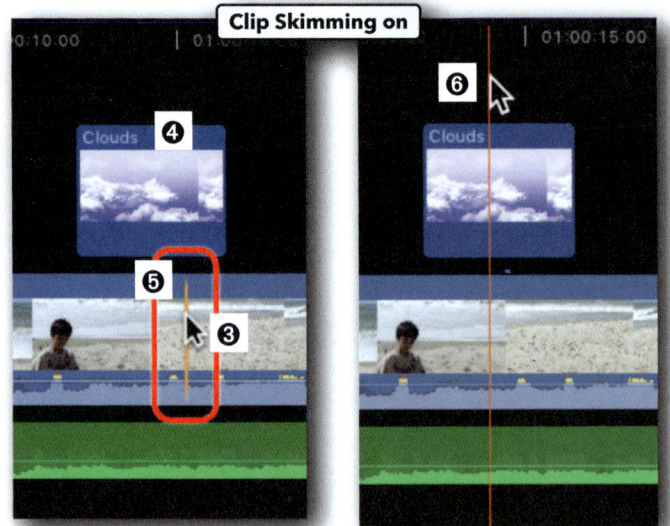

🔵 Implementation

The implementation of Clip Skimming is confusing, especially in regards to Audio Skimming. Here are the rules:

▶ Clip Skimming can be enabled independently from the standard Skimming.

▶ Clip Skimming can only be toggled with the Menu Command *View ➤ Clip Skimming* or Key Command *sh+opt+S*.

▶ There is no dedicated button for Clip Skimming and, therefore, no quick visual reference on the Timeline if it is enabled or not. However, you will notice it immediately when you move the mouse cursor over a Timeline Clip.

▶ The Skimming Button 🔲 (and its related commands) only toggle the standard Skimming and has no affect on the Clip Skimming functionality.

▶ The Audio Skimming feature is the most confusing, because the Audio Skimming Button ❼ 🔳 only toggles the audio signal for "standard" Skimming and does not (!) relate to the Audio Skimming on/off checkbox in the View Menu *View ➤ Audio Skimming* ❽. These are the three possible combinations:

- Checkmark ✅ and active button 🔳: Audio Skimming is enabled for Skimming and Clip Skimming

- Checkmark ✅ and inactive button 🔳: Audio Skimming is only enabled for Clip Skimming

- No checkmark ⬛ and inactive button 🔳: Audio Skimming is off for Skimming and Clip Skimming

➡ *Color Code*

Here is a final overview of the different appearances of the Playhead and Skimmer.

💀 Timeline

The Timeline has the most variations for the appearance of the Playhead and the Skimmer, so keep an eye on that.

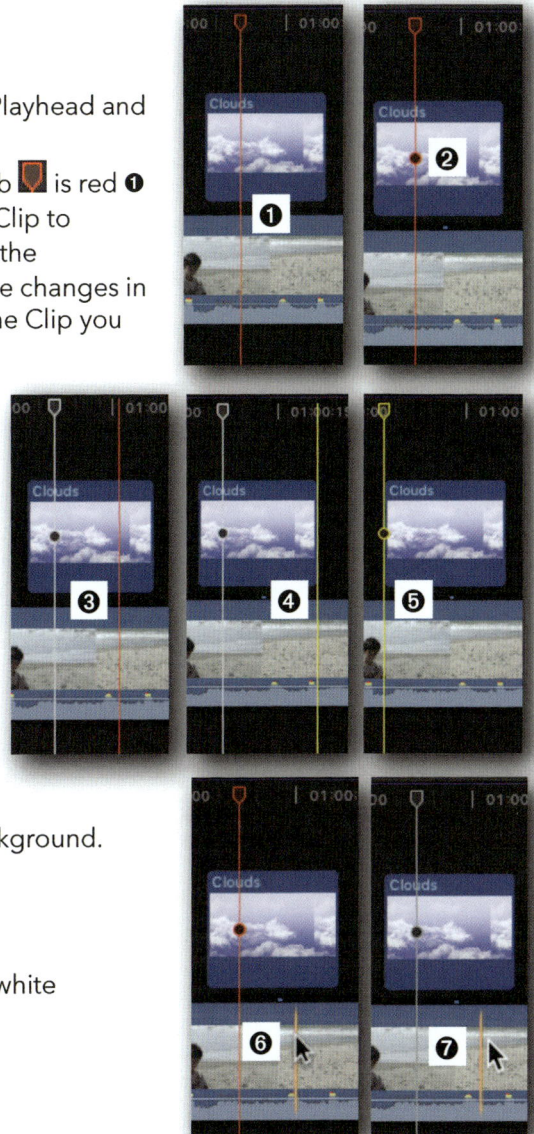

- ▸ **Skimming off** ▦: The Playhead with its Playhead Thumb 🔻 is red ❶ and, during Pause Mode ⏸, you will see a circle ❷ on a Clip to indicate if it is the Active Clip, the one that is selected in the Inspector. Or think the other way around, when you make changes in the Inspector, then this red circle indicates which Timeline Clip you are currently editing (if no Clip is selected).

- ▸ **Skimming On** ▦: The Playhead turns white ❸ if you enable the Skimming function. The Skimmer is red.

- ▸ **Snapping On** ▦: The Skimmer turns yellow ❹ if Snapping is enabled and it snaps to an object. The Playhead is also snapping to an object, but only turns yellow ❺ if Skimming is off.

- ▸ **Clip Skimming On**: The Clip Skimmer is always orange, but the color of the Playhead depends on if the "standard" Skimming feature is off ▦ (Playhead is red ❻) or turned on ▦ (Playhead is white ❼).

- ▸ **Inactive**: The Playhead always turns to a white thin line when you switch to a different app, but the FCPx Timeline window is still visible on your screen in the background.

💀 Timeline Index

The Timeline Index has only one kind of Playhead. It is always a white horizontal line with the Playhead Thumb on the left ❽.

💀 Browser Pane

The appearance of the Playhead and Skimmer has less variations and there is no Clip Skimming Mode.

- ▸ **Skimming Off** ▦: The Playhead is always a white line ❾.

- ▸ **Skimming On** ▦: The Skimmer is always a red line ❿ and the Playhead stays white.

- ▸ **Snapping On** ▦: Although the Snapping Mode is a feature of the Timeline, it also works for the Skimmer on the Filmstrips of Event Clips. It will snap to Clip Ranges (yellow borders), any of the Marked Ranges (the colored lines on top), the Used Range (the orange lines at the bottom), or Markers ⓫.

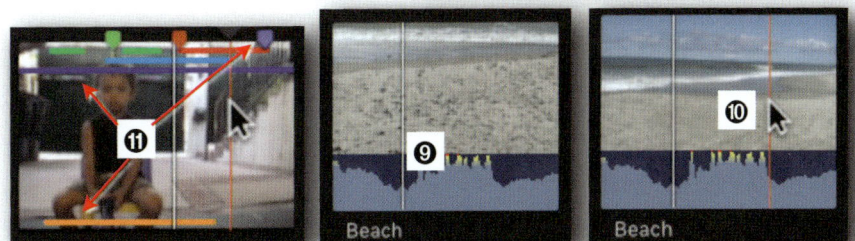

View Options

The View selector ❶ opens a popup menu ❷ with a wide variety of important commands and settings.

➡️ *Display*

The first section ❸ in the popup menu has three commands:

🏀 Show/Hide Video Scopes

This command toggles the Video Scopes Pane ❹ (*cmd+7*) inside the Viewer Pane. It replaces the Angles Pane if it was visible.

I will discuss the topic later in the book.

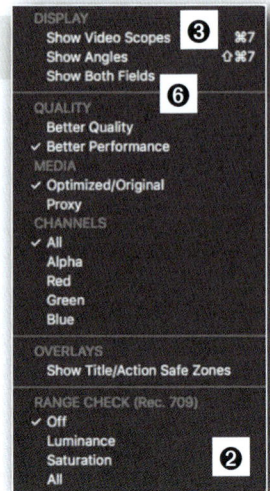

🏀 Show/Hide Angles

This command toggles the Angles Pane ❺ (*sh+cmd+7*) inside the Viewer Pane. It replaces the Video Scopes Pane if it was visible.

I will discuss the topic later in the book.

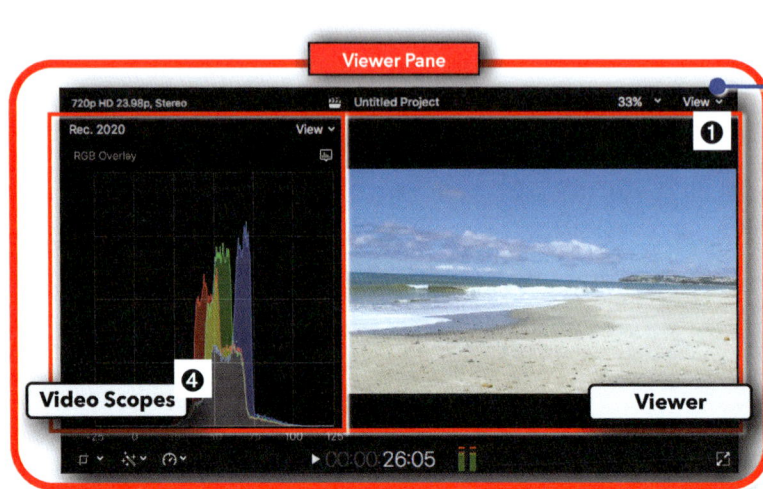

🏀 Show Both Fields ❻

This is an option you can check when working with interlaced video to show the even and odd fields of an interlaced video frame. It is off by default to prevent the additional required processing.

→ *Quality/Media*

This is a very important setting that you have to be aware of because it relates to one of the main concepts in FCPx. Here is a quick review:

- ▸ Whenever you import a source media file ❶, it is, by default, copied to the "Original Media" folder ❷ inside the Library File.
- ▸ As an option, FCPx can make two more copies of that media file to convert (transcode) ❸ it to a high resolution ProRes 422 file format (*Optimized*) and a lower resolution ProRes 422 Proxy format (*Proxy*). Those two files are stored in their separate "*Transcoded Media*" folder inside their subfolders "*High Quality Media*" ❹ and "*Proxy Media*" ❺.
- ▸ You create those extra two transcoded media files either during the import (with checkboxes ❺ in the Media Import Dialog) or later at any time (with the "Transcode Media" command), and also delete and re-generate them whenever you need it.
- ▸ When a Clip is selected in the Browser, the Info Inspector will display green/red indicators ❼ at the bottom to show which version (Original / Optimized / Proxy) is available or not.

⚫ Media ❽

Now these two menu items in the View popup menu of the Viewer determine which of the three file types FCPx should use during playback. Please note that this has no affect on your edits, because you are editing Clips and those Clips are just the representation of their corresponding Media Files. With this setting ❽, you tell FCPx which of the three versions to use when playing back the Clips.

- ▸ **Proxy**: FCPx will only use the Proxy files during playback. This way, you can edit your project only using Proxy Files when working on a computer with less power and storage capacity, i.e. for offline editing. You can open the Project later on a more powerful computer with the full-resolution Optimized Media. If a Clip doesn't have a corresponded Proxy file generated yet, then the Viewer will display a red "Missing Proxy" card ❾ and the Clips in the Browser and Timeline will also show that card ❿.
- ▸ **Optimized/Original**: This is the default setting. FCPx uses the Original Media for playback and if an Optimized (High Quality Media) file is available, it will automatically use those.

⚫ Quality ⓫

These two options are gray when Proxy is selected.

- ▸ **Better Quality**: FCPx displays full-resolution video in the Viewer, which might decrease playback performance, depending on your processor speed and source material.
- ▸ **Better Performance**: FCPx displays the video in the Viewer with reduced resolution to provide a better playback performance.

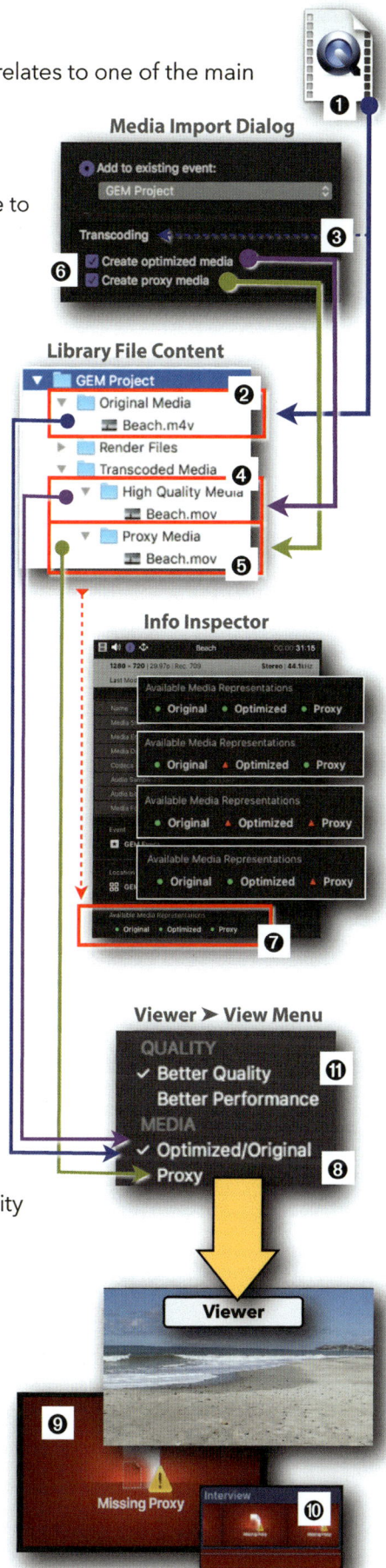

Media Import Dialog

Library File Content

Info Inspector

Viewer ➤ View Menu

➡ *Channels* ❶

Select if you want to display **All** channels of an RGB video signal in the Clip or display the individual channels **Alpha**, **Red**, **Green**, or **Blue**.

➡ *Overlays* ❷

Title-safe and Action-safe

This double-frame Overlay (not visible in the exported video) is a guide to keep specific elements in the picture away from the edges of the picture frame, because that area might not be visible when viewed on older (tube-based) TV sets.

- ▶ **Action Safe** ❸: The outer yellow frame is about 5% away from the picture frame. All the action (actors) should appear inside that frame.

- ▶ **Title Safe** ❹: The inner yellow frame is about 10% away from the picture frame. All titles, text, logos, and other important graphics should be placed inside this frame.

➡ *Range Check* ❺

The standard for the Color Space that you chose for a Project or Clip (Standard: Rec. 709 or Wide Gamut: Rec. 2020) only allows for a specific range of colors ("gamut") to be properly displayed. The title ❻ in the popup menu actually indicates the Color Standard of the currently selected Project (or Clip).

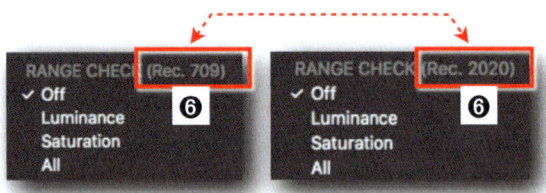

The Range Check feature is an overlay of patterns that indicates if areas of your picture are out of that color range. On the screenshot to the right, you see the overlaid pattern (animated zebra stripes ❼) indicating the trouble areas.

You can choose from four options:

- ▶ **Off**: No overlays.
- ▶ **Luminance**: This detects and indicates brightness (luma) values in the picture that are outside the limits of the Project's color space setting.
- ▶ **Saturation**: This detects color (chroma) values in the picture that are outside the limits of the Project's color space setting, including negative or extremely high R, G, or B values.
- ▶ **All**: This detects and indicates both, luma and chroma values, in the picture that are outside the limits of the Project's color space setting.

Basics

The Inspector Pane is one of the four main windows in the FCPx Workspace **❶**.

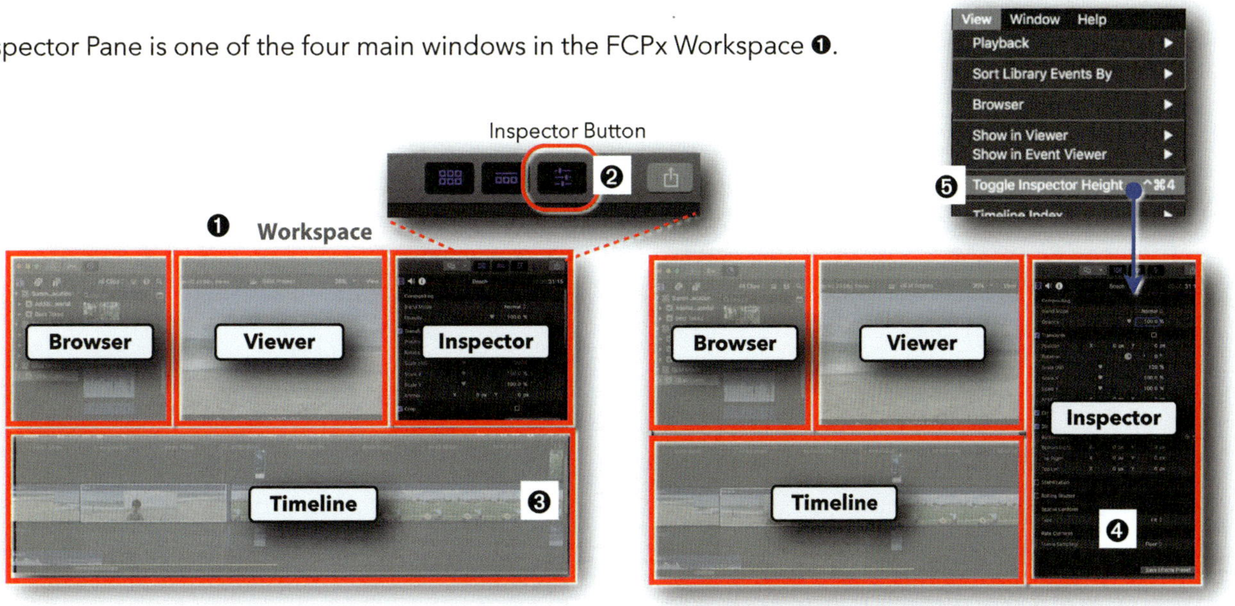

Inspector Button

❶ Workspace

Browser Viewer Inspector

Timeline **❸**

Browser Viewer

Inspector

Timeline

❹

➡️ *Open the Inspector Pane*

There are two types of commands to open the Inspector:

▶ **Toggle the window**: These commands will show/hide the window pane on the Workspace:

- Menu Command *Window ➤ Show In Workspace ➤ Inspector*
- Key Command *cmd+4*
- *Click* on the Inspector Button in the upper-right corner of the Workspace **❷**

▶ **Open the window**: These commands will open the window in the Workspace or, if it was open already, give it key focus:

- Menu Command *Window ➤ Go To ➤ Inspector*
- Key Command *opt+cmd+4*

💀 **Specialties**

▶ **Toggle Height**: Per default, the Timeline Pane uses the lower section of the Workspace from the left to the right **❸** window border. However, you can toggle the height of the Inspector to extend all the way to the bottom of the Workspace window **❹**, reducing the size of the Timeline Pane. Use any of the following commands to toggle the height:

- *Double-click* the Inspector Header
- Menu Command *View ➤ Toggle Inspector Height* **❺**
- Key Command *ctr+cmd+4*

▶ **No Secondary Display**: The Inspector is the only one of the four window panes that cannot be moved to the Secondary Display.

▶ **Color Board**: The Inspector Pane is also used to display the Color Board (*cmd+6*). You can switch it back to the Inspector with the *opt+cmd+4* command.

➡ *Concept*

The Inspector is not just another window, it is a special concept used in many applications. You select an object inside the app (i.e. a word processor, a graphics app, etc.) and the Inspector window displays the properties (the various parameters) of that object and lets you change those parameters, for example, color, font, size, etc.

⚫ Display

What is displayed:

▶ **Selected Object**: The Inspector ❶ in FCPx automatically displays the details of an object that is selected in either the Browser Pane ❷ or the Timeline Pane ❸.

▶ **Dynamic Display**: Selecting a different object ❹ will automatically switch the Inspector to show the properties of the currently selected object.

▶ **Object Types**: You can select a variety of objects ❺, for example, Clips, Projects, Libraries, etc. Whatever is selected, the Inspector shows the detailed information about those objects in its window.

▶ **Nothing to Select**: If no object is selected or an object is selected that the Inspector "doesn't know" (i.e. Events), then the Inspector will be blank and shows the text "*Nothing to Inspect*" ❻.

▶ **Properties**: The details of an object that are displayed in the Inspector are called its "Properties" ❼, all the characteristics and parameters that define that object. For example, a Clip has a specific resolution, frame rate, audio channels, metadata, etc.

▶ **Window Views**: Instead of having one long list of parameters, the Inspector groups all those properties into separate window views ❽, for example, Video, Audio, Info, etc.

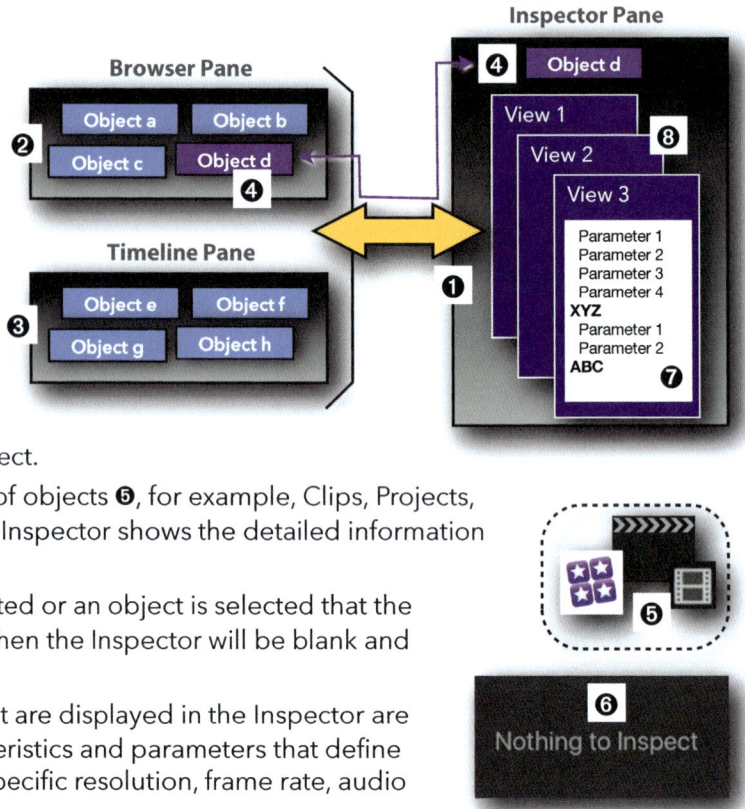

⚫ Edit

Some of the properties that are displayed in the Inspector are read only, but many can be edited.

▶ **Edit Single Objects**: The Inspector is the place where you do a lot of editing. Once an object is selected and displayed in the Inspector, you can go ahead and change the various parameters ❼.

▶ **Edit Multiple Objects**: You can even do "batch editing" by selecting, for example, multiple Clips, edit a parameter and that change is applied to all the currently selected Clips. There are special indications for those kind of edits that I will explain later.

⚫ What is selected

Because the displayed content of the Inspector is dynamic, you always have to keep an eye on what is currently selected to know what the Inspector is actually displaying. Otherwise, you can make big edits without realizing that you have changed to a total different Clip from what you have intended to.

Look out for the following things:

- The Inspector Header
- Purple selection (in list view) ❾
- Yellow frame around a Clip ❿
- A little circle on the Playhead in the Timeline ⓫

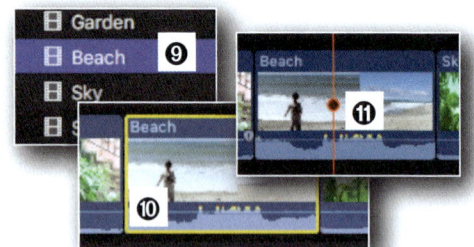

Interface

The information presented in the Inspector window can be overwhelming at times with so many parameters and controls and sometimes even hidden controls where you have to know how to get to them. So let's go over some key interface elements to learn your way around the Inspector.

➡ Header

The header has the following elements:

▸ **View Buttons**: On the left are the various buttons ❶ that let you switch to those specific views that are available for that object. The purple one is the currently selected view.

▸ **Title ❷**: The Name in the middle is the name of the object, i.e. Clip Name, Project Name.

▸ **Time Display ❸**: Some objects have a time display on the right to indicate their duration.

▸ **Toggle Height**: Don't forget that you can also *double+click* on that header to toggle the height of the Inspector.

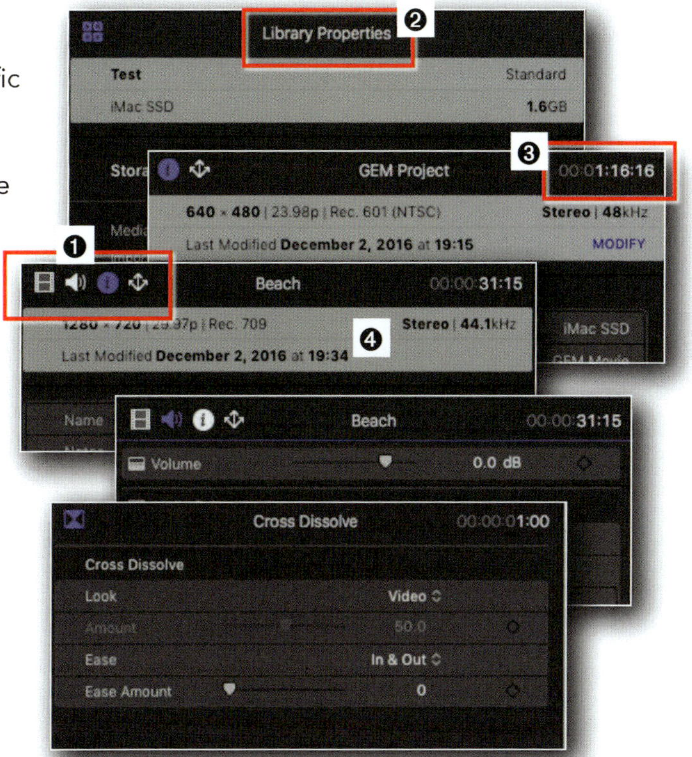

➡ View Buttons

Here is a list of the various views that you will encounter on the Inspector:

- Library
- Video
- Audio
- Info
- Share
- Generator
- Title
- Text
- Transition

➡ Main Properties

Some views display a gray area ❹ below the header with information about their main properties:

▸ Video Format
▸ Audio Format
▸ Modification Date

➡ *Sections*

All the controls on a specific page are organized in sections. Sometimes, you have to be adventurous to "unfold" all the available controls that might not be visible right away. Here are a few examples:

🔮 Show/Hide Button (mouse-over)

When you mouse-over on the right side of some components ❶, a *Show* button ❷ appears. ***Click*** on it to expand that component, revealing more controls ❸. Now, when you mouse-over that same spot, a *Hide* button ❹ appears that collapses ❶ the component when you ***click*** on it.

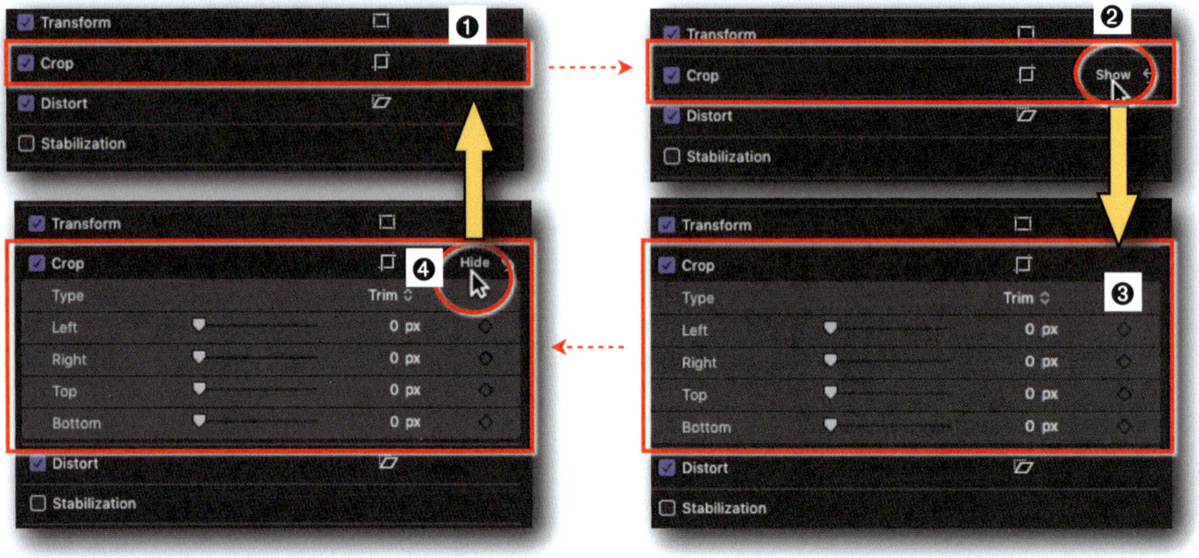

🔮 Nested Controls

The Audio Enhancements Module ❺ is an example of nested controls. ***Click*** on the right side (red dot ❻) to reveal the Equalization and Audio Analysis controls. ***Click*** on the Audio Analysis (blue dot ❼) to reveal three more controls, and each of those can be ***clicked*** (green dot ❽) to reveal their controls.

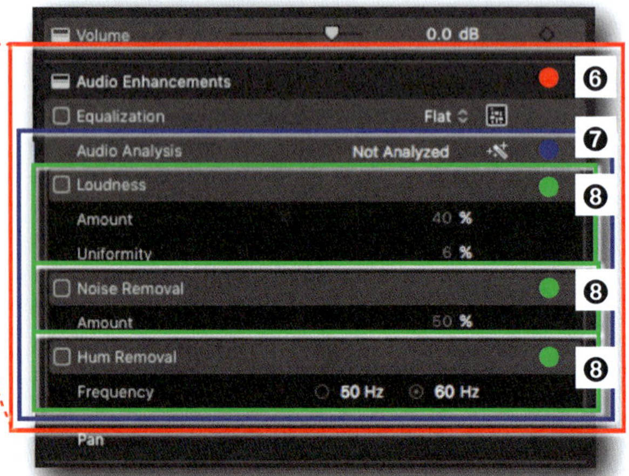

🔮 Adjustable Divider Line

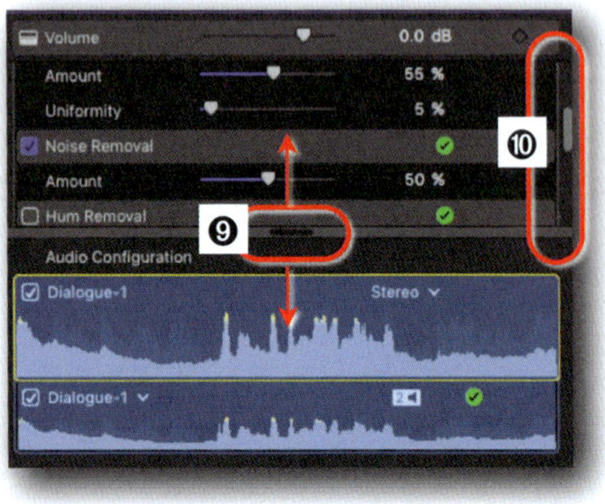

The Audio Inspector has a divider ❾ that you can ***drag*** up/down to adjust the height of the upper and lower section proportionally. If the upper or lower sections gets to small to show all its controls, then a scroll bar ❿ appears on its right to scroll through the parameters.

➡ Controls

The Inspector has a wide variety of controls that lets you edit all kinds of parameters. The same concept applies here, be adventurous. Not only are lots of elements hidden and you have to mouse-over to make them visible, very often a little icon or a text is actually a button that you can click on.

🔘 Dialog Buttons

The big gray buttons ❶ usually open a Dialog to setup or change various configurations.

🔘 Text Entry

The Info Inspector shows most of the metadata, which is displayed as a two-column list. Any value field that has a black box ❷ is most likely editable. *Click* on it and it becomes active with a blue frame around it, indicating its current key focus status.

🔘 Number Entry

Many numbers ❸ can be adjusted the usual way:
- *Click* on the number to have it selected, type a value and hit *enter*.
- *Click-hold* on a number and *drag* it up/down. *Opt+drag* for a finer resolution.

🔘 Sliders

If a number value has a corresponding slider ❹ next to it, then you can *drag* the slider knob left/right.

🔘 Buttons (visible/hidden)

Most icons ❺ are active buttons that sometimes change their appearance to indicate their status 🔲 🔳. Some controls like the "Add/Remove Keyframe" ◈ or Rest Button ↩ only appear when you mouse-over them.

🔘 Plugin Button

Click on the Plugin Button ❻ 🔲 to open the Plugin Window ❼ for that effect.

🔘 Popup Menus

Any down-arrow ⌄ or double-arrow ⌃⌄ indicates an available popup menu ❽.

🔘 Motion Controls

Titles and Generators are mostly based on Motion effects and often provide a wide variety of controls ❾ that lets you adjust the effect.

🔘 Audio Parameters

The Audio Inspector displays the waveform at the bottom with their own controls, including the always-on Skimming feature ❿ when you move the mouse over the waveform.

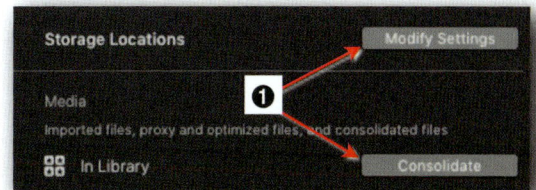

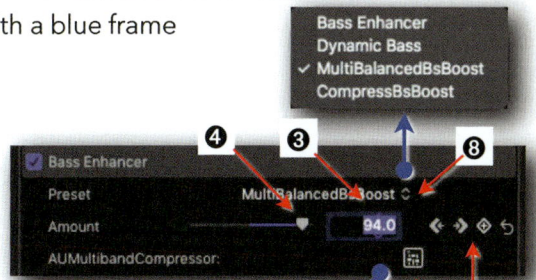

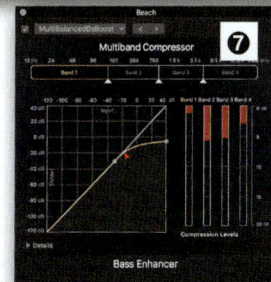

Plugin Window

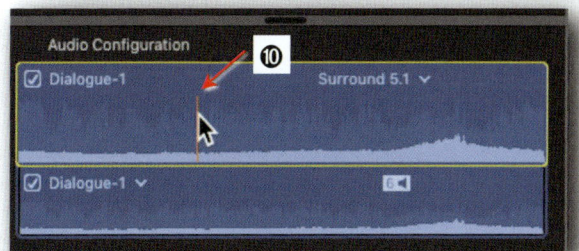

➡ *Batch Editing*

There is one special procedure in the Inspector and that is Batch Editing. That means, instead of selecting one item (i.e. a Clip) and edit it in the Inspector, you select multiple items (multiple Clips) and edit all of them at once. However, there are a few things to pay attention to.

🌑 Inspector Header

If you have more than one item selected, then you will see that right away in the Inspector Header. Instead of displaying the name of the selected item, it will display "Inspecting n items" ❶ ("n" indicating the number of selected items).

🌑 Same Values

If the current values of all the selected Clips are the same, then you wouldn't notice any difference. The values are displayed.

🌑 Display Different Values

If the selected Clips have different values for a specific parameter, then it depends on what type of display it is to indicate that condition.

- ▶ **Text Field**: The field shows the label "Multiple Values" ❷.
- ▶ **Checkbox**: A checkbox shows a hyphen ❸.
- ▶ **Popup Menu 1**: Some popup menus show the item "Mixed" ❹.
- ▶ **Popup Menu 2**: Other popup menus just have a hyphen ❺ next to the arrow button.
- ▶ **Number Value**: Instead of a number, you will see a hyphen ❻ and if the value has a Slider, then it will be grayed out ❼.
- ▶ **Audio Waveform**: The waveform area will show an empty grid ❽ instead of the audio waveform.

🌑 Edit Different Value

Indicating that the selected Clips have different values for a specific parameter is only half the story. The important question is, how do you edit those parameters and what will happen if you do so?

- ▶ **On/Off Status**: Setting a checkbox to either on or off will set all selected Clips to that status.
- ▶ **Selection**: Selecting a specific item from the popup menu will set that selection on all selected Clips.
- ▶ **Number Values**: You have two options when editing number values:
  - Apply Absolute Value: When you click on the number field and enter a numeric value, then that will be applied to all selected Clips.
  - Apply Relative Offset: When you slide the number up/down ❾, then that amount (i.e. +10) will be applied as an offset to the parameter value of all selected Clips, keeping their relative values intact.
- ▶ **Channel Selection**: If the Audio Channel Configurations of the selected Clips don't match, then you cannot make any appropriate selection and the popup menu shows you a label ❿ telling you exactly that.

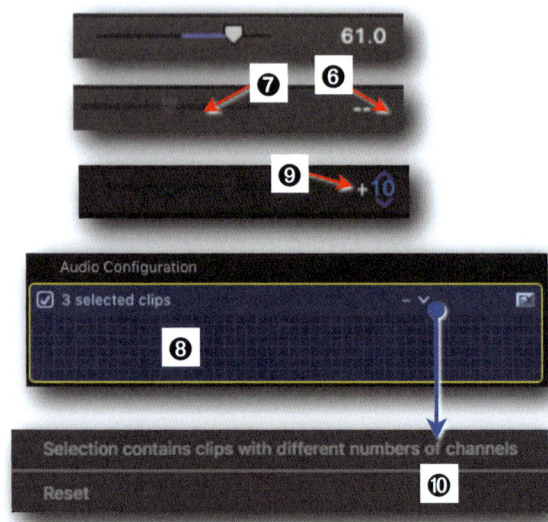

Basics

Overview

There are a wide variety of procedures on how and what to import, the procedure that is also referred to as "Ingesting". Let's start with an Overview:

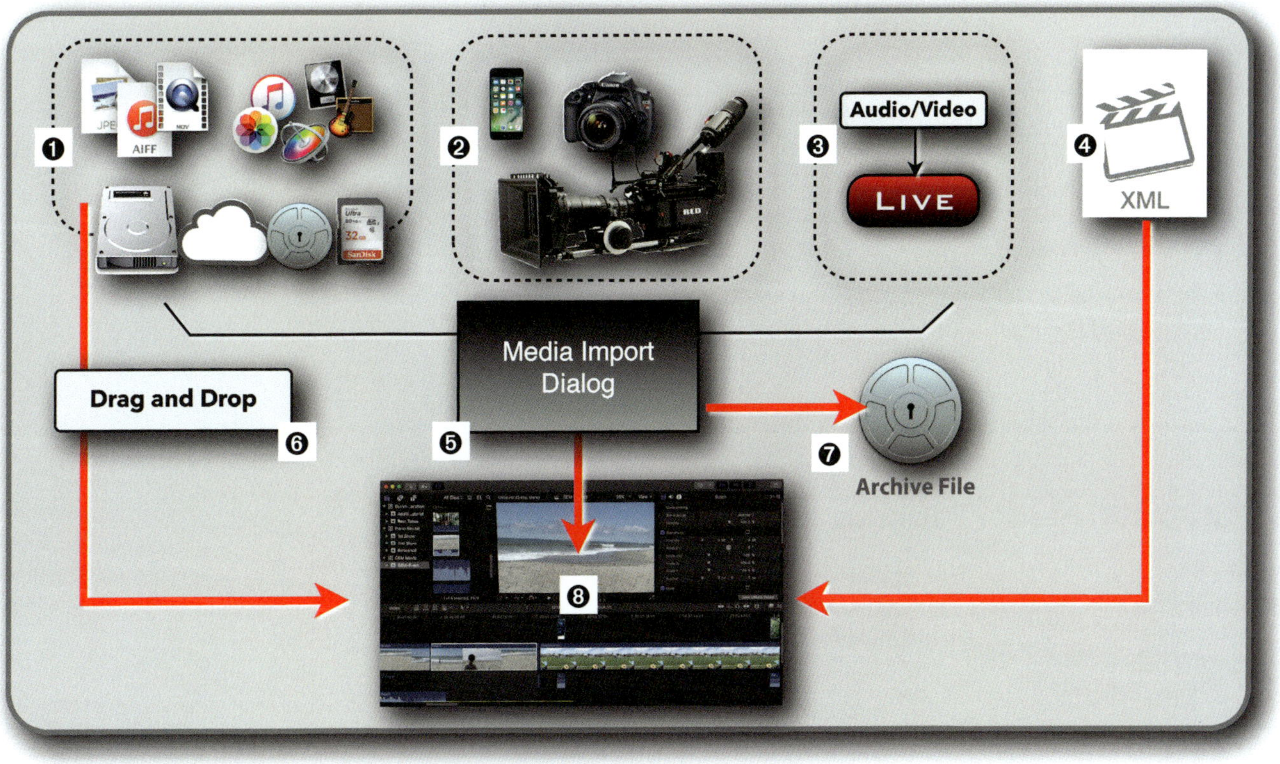

▶ **Source**: Here are the different types of sources from where you can import material to your FCPx Library:
  - Devices ❶: Any storage device that contains media files and can be mounted on your computer can be used as a source to import those files into FCPx.
  - Cameras ❷: Media from file-based or tape-based cameras can be imported into FCPx.
  - Live Recording ❸: You can use a connected camera to record audio/video directly into FCPx.
  - XML ❹: XML is a standard that lets you exchange Libraries, Events, Projects, and Clips between applications that support the XML standard. So technically, this can also be considered an import option.

▶ **Import Procedure**: There are two basic import procedures:
  - Media Import Dialog ❺: The Media Import Dialog is a window in FCPx with a wide variety of controls and settings that are used for most import procedures.
  - Drag and Drop ❻: You can also use simple drag and drop procedures to import media files from your Finder ❶ or from the Media Browser inside FCPx.

▶ **Archive ❼**: This is a special procedure that allows you to import media from cameras ❷ and store them to an Archive File on your drive, instead of importing them into an Active Library ❽.

➡ *Import What?*

Whenever you import media into FCPx, keep in mind what you are importing:

▶ **Video Stream**: This procedure captures a video stream from a tape-based camera that you are playing back or use the live video stream from a camera. FCPx creates a new media file and a corresponding Clip in FCPx.

▶ **Single Media File**: This procedure lets you import a single media file. FCPx copies that file to your Library File and creates a corresponding Clip in FCPx.

▶ **Multiple Media Files**: This procedure lets you import multiple media files at once. FCPx copies those files to your Library File and creates corresponding Clips in FCPx.

▶ **Portion of a Media File**: This is a very powerful procedure that lets you select a portion of the media file and copies only that section to a new media file in your Library File with its corresponding Clip. Here are some useful Key Commands when operating with Ranges:

Single Range

- *Drag* on the filmstrip to create a range, indicated by a yellow frame
- *Drag* the borders of a single range to trim the range
- *Opt+drag* to create a new range
- Position the Skimmer and press the key *I* or *O* to extend the start and end to that position

Multiple Range

- *Cmd+drag* to create an additional range on the same filmstrip
- *Cmd+drag* the borders to trim the range (if there are multiple selections)
- *Cmd+click* on the inside frame to toggle between active/inactive. Inactive selections are dimmed and will not be imported

Supported Media Formats

Here is a list of supported file formats.

💀 **Video formats**

QuickTime formats, H.264

Apple ProRes (all versions), Apple Animation codec, Apple Intermediate codec

AVC-Intra, AVC-LongG, AVCHD (including AVCCAM, AVCHD Lite, and NXCAM)

DV (including DVCAM, DVCPRO, and DVCPRO50), DVCPRO HD, HDV

Iframe, Motion JPEG (OpenDML only), MPEG IMX (D-10)

Uncompressed 10-bit 4:2:2, Uncompressed 8-bit 4:2:2

XAVC (including XAVC-S), XDCAM HD/EX/HD422

REDCODE RAW (R3D)

💀 **Audio formats**

AAC, AIFF, BWF, CAF, MP3, MP4, WAV

No Protected audio files

💀 **Still-image formats**

JPEG, PNG, GIF, TIFF, RAW, BMP, TGA, PSD (static and layered)

💀 **Container formats**

MOV (QuickTime), AVI, MP4, 3GP, MXF, MTS/M2TS

For a list of the currently supported formats, go to Apple's website:

▶ **Supported Cameras**: https://support.apple.com/en-us/HT204203
▶ **Supported Media Formats**: https://support.apple.com/kb/PH12754?locale=en_US

Media Import Dialog

Let's start with the Media Import Dialog, the main import procedure.

Basics

➡ Open Commands

The Media Import Dialog ❶ can be opened with any of the following commands, and remember, this is a dialog window, which means that all other FCPx actions are blocked (even turned black) until you close the dialog again:

Attention: If Keyword Collection(s) 🔍 are selected in the Libraries Sidebar ❽ of the Browser when opening the Media Import Dialog, then all the media that you will import next will have those Keyword(s) ▣ assigned to those imported Clips.

- 📌 Empty Event ❷: Whenever you select an Event in the Browser Sidebar that doesn't have any Clips imported yet, FCPx will display a big Import Media button in the Browser. *Click* on it to open the Media Import Dialog.

- 📌 Media Import Button ❸: The Media Import Button ⬇ is always displayed in the upper-left corner of the Workspace window, next to the three Title Bar Buttons.

- 📌 Key Command ❹: *cmd+I* (also closes the dialog).

- 📌 Menu Command ❺: *File ➤ Import ➤ Media*.

- 📌 Shortcut Menu ❻: *Ctr+click* on an item in the Browser Sidebar to open its Shortcut Menu and select *Import Media*.

- 📌 Touch Bar ❼: The Touch Bar will display the Import Button if you select any item in the Sidebar of the Library Browser.

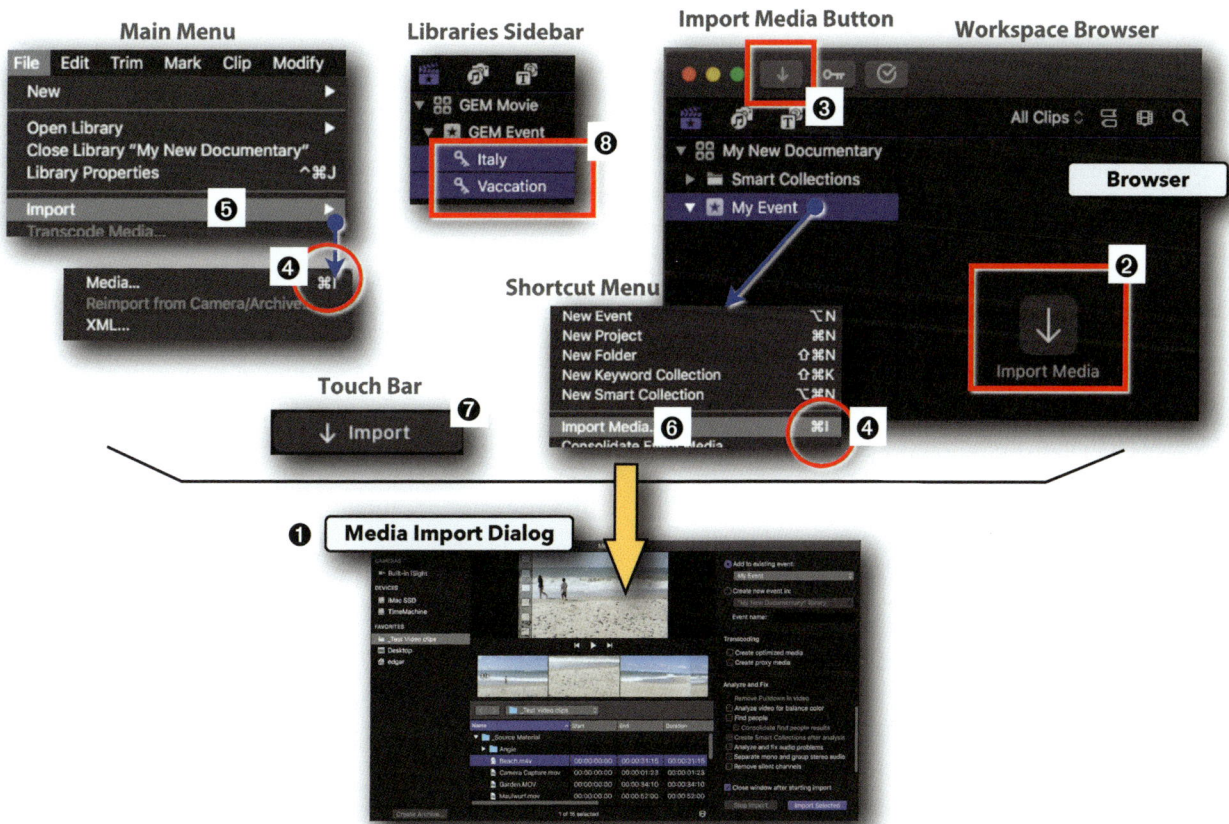

➡ Interface

The Media Import Dialog is divided into three window panes, Sidebar, Browser, and Import Settings.

🔵 Sidebar

All the available sources on your computer, from where you can import Media Files, are listed in the Sidebar ❶. They are grouped together by two categories, Cameras and Devices, plus the category Favorites, where you can place folders that you often need to access (similar to the Finder Sidebar functionality).

🔵 Browser

The window pane in the middle is the Browser ❷ that shows the content of whatever source is selected in the Sidebar ❶. You can navigate deeper in the folder structure to find the media files you want to import.

Media Import Dialog

Sidebar   Browser   Import Settings

▶ **Filmstrip/Viewer**: Depending on the selected source, the Browser will also display a Filmstrip ❸ and a Viewer ❹ that lets you preview the files before you import them, even select a range to import only a portion of a source file.

🔵 Import Settings

The window pane on the right contains all the settings ❺ to configure how the files are imported. The Import Buttons ❻ at the bottom of the Settings pane ("Import", "Import All", or "Import Selected") start the import procedure and the "*Stop Import*" button stops the capture from a tape-based or live camera.

The Media Import Dialog doesn't have a Cancel button to close it if you don't want to import anything. Just *click* on the red Title Bar Button or use the Key Command *cmd+W* or *cmd+I*.

Background Tasks Button

Background Tasks Window

Background Tasks

Even if the Media Import Dialog closes, the actual import might still be going on in the background, depending on the amount of files and process required.

This ongoing process will be indicated by the Background Tasks Button in the upper-left corner of the Workspace window. It turns into a circular progress indicator ❼ 🕐. You can *click* on the button to open the Background Tasks Window ❽ that shows the details of the import procedure. The Background Tasks Button turns to its regular appearance ❾ ☑ (checkmark) to indicate that all the processes are completed.

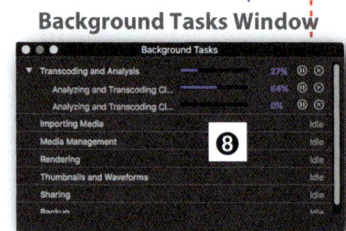

Sidebar

The Sidebar of the Media Import Dialog looks and functions similarly to the Finder's Sidebar or the Sidebar in iTunes. Those items represent folders or volumes that contain files. Selecting an item will display that content in the Browser pane to the right.

➡ Categories

All the sources in the Sidebar are grouped into three categories:

🔘 Cameras ❶

Any camera, tape-based or file-based ❷, that is connected to your computer is automatically listed in this section, including the built-in iSight camera on your computer, and even your connected iPhone, which is technically a file-based camera. *Ctr+click* on an item to open its Shortcut Menu that lets you rename the device.

🔘 Devices ❸

This section lists all the mounted storage devices ❹:

> ▶ Mounted local drives
>
> ▶ Mounted network drives
>
> ▶ Mounted (inserted) memory cards

🔘 Favorites ❺

This is a user-definable section that can list aliases of any folder of a Device that is listed in the Devices category. This is useful for folders with media content that you often need to access, like logos, SFX, background music, etc. The Desktop and home folder ❻ of your user directory is already added by default.

▶ **Add a folder to the Favorites**: There are two ways to add a folder to the Favorites category:

   📌 Navigate to the folder in the Browser pane on the right and drag it onto the *FAVORITES* label. The cursor will change to a green plus icon 🟢 ❼ to indicate that action when you release the mouse.

   📌 *Ctr+click* on the folder in the Browser pane and select from the *Shortcut Menu ➤ Favorite* ❽.

▶ **Remove folder from Favorites**: To remove an item from the Favorites category *ctr+click* on it and select from the *Shortcut Menu ➤ Remove from Sidebar* ❾.

▶ **Reveal in Finder**: If you want to know where a folder in the Favorites category is located on your drive, *ctr+click* on it and select from the *Shortcut Menu ➤ Reveal in Finder* ❿.

▶ **Attention**: A few things to be aware of.

   • If a Favorites icon is representing a folder on a drive that is currently unmounted, then you will not get any indication for that. Using the *Reveal in Finder* command will also not pop up an alert window.

   • Moving the original folder or renaming the original folder a Favorites icon is pointing to, will break the link and you have to remove it and add it again.

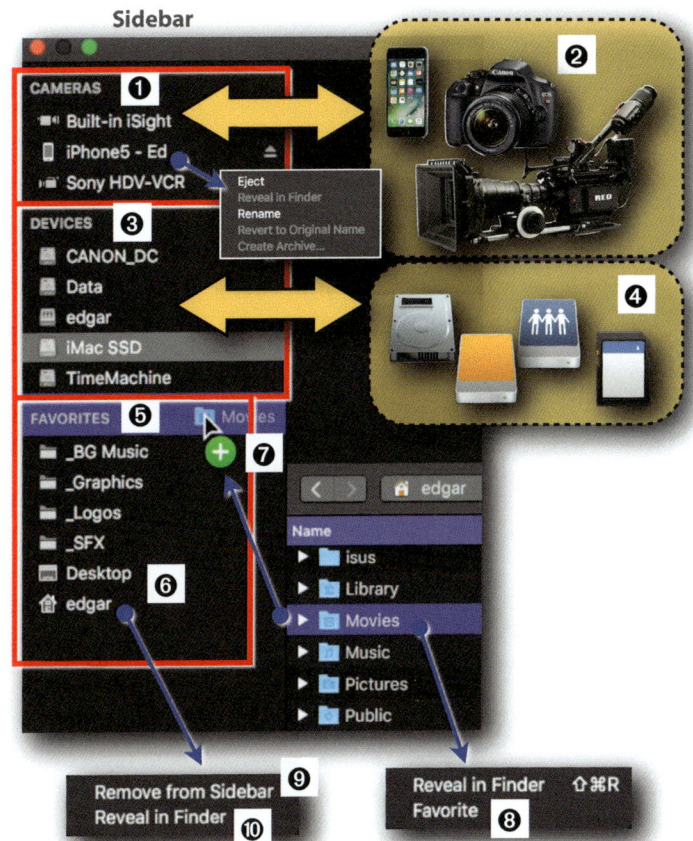

Browser

While the appearance of the sidebar on the left doesn't change much, the Browser in the middle is highly dynamic, displaying up to three sections.

🌑 List View ❶

The List View is the default for most selected sources.

▶ **View**: The bottom section lists all the available files ❹ and selecting a file will display it as a filmstrip ❺ in the middle section (you can skim over the strip) and also in the Viewer ❻ above.

▶ **Import**: The Import Button ❼ will be labeled "*Import Selected*" when you select specific Clips (***cmd+click***), or "*Import All*" when you select all Clips (or none).

- Range Selection: On filmstrips of file-based cameras or Camera Archives, you can even ***drag*** ❽ one or multiple (***cmd+drag***) ranges marked as yellow frames and also adjust the borders (***opt+cmd+drag***) to select only those sections and import them as individual Clips. The popover ❾ indicates the timecode of the dragged position.

🌑 Filmstrip View ❷

When a file-based camera is selected in the Sidebar, then the Browser has the option to toggle between List View 🖳 and Filmstrip View 🖾.

▶ **View**: Now all Clips are displayed as filmstrips (displayed as a sequence of thumbnails) and whichever you select is displayed in the Viewer above.

▶ **Import**: The Import Button ❼ is labeled "*Import Selected*" or "*Import All*".

🌑 Viewer Only ❸

When a tape-based camera or a camera in live-mode is selected, then the Browser will only display the Viewer with the optional transport controls.

▶ **View**: The Viewer shows either the live feed of the camera or the signal when playing back the tape.

▶ **Import**: Now the Import Button is only labeled "Import" ❿ that will start the capture process and the button next to it is labeled "Stop Import". It will be active during the recording to stop the capturing and create the new quicktime file.

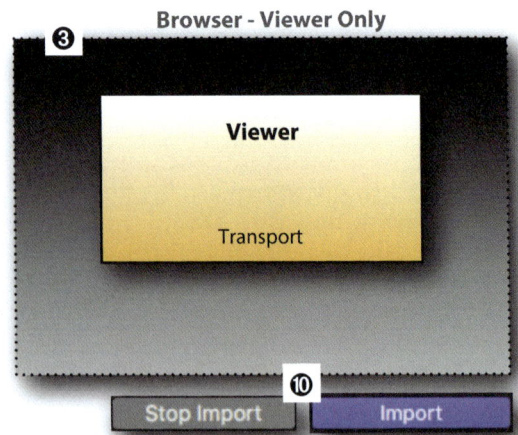

Browser - List View

Browser - Filmstrip View

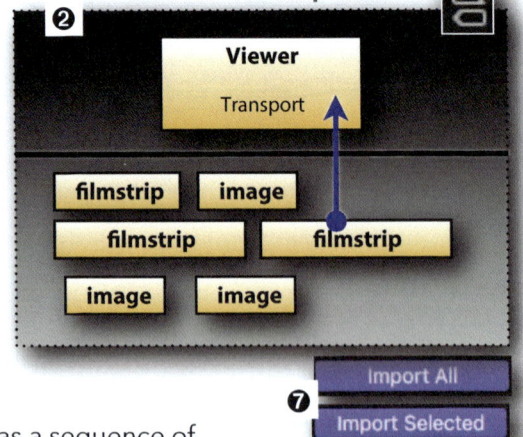

Browser - Viewer Only

5 - Importing Media

➡ *Devices*

Here is how you select items from the Devices category:

▶ Selecting an item ❶ from the Devices category in the Sidebar displays the content of that directory in the Browser to the right ❷. Anything that you can "mount" on your computer will show up in the list and you can import from there.

- ☑ Internal drive or mounted external drive
- ☑ Network Volumes
- ☑ iCloud (or any cloud-base storage) if you can mount it on the Finder
- ☑ Memory Card inserted into a card slot or connected card reader

▶ You can navigate to a specific folder:

- *Double-click* a folder in the list or *click* on the disclosure triangle to reveal its content.
- The popup menu ❸ above lets you go to a different level in the folder hierarchy.
- The left ◁ and right ▷ arrow buttons ❹ jump to the previous and next viewed folder in the browsing history.

▶ Selecting a media file will display it above as a single Filmstrip ❺, plus a Viewer ❻.

▶ If the selected file is a video file, then the Viewer will display the Playback controls ❼.

▶ The single filmstrip in the middle can be "skimmed" when *dragging* the mouse over it. A Skimmer Info tag ❽ displays the name and the position of the Clip. The Viewer ❻ above follows the skimming position.

▶ The Appearance Button 🎞 ❾ in the lower-right corner opens the Clip Appearance popover, which lets you show/hide the waveform in the filmstrip.

▶ The Browser lists the items with Metadata columns that function in a standard way. *Click* a column header to sort the items, move or resize the columns and *ctr+click* on the header to open a popup menu ❿ to show/hide specific metadata columns.

▶ Select a single or multiple files. The standard selection commands apply. *Sh+click* to select contiguous items or *cmd+click* to select (deselect) multiple non-contiguous items. *Cmd+A* selects all items.

▶ Please note that from Devices you cannot import a range selection of a file (Subclip). You can only import entire files (Clips).

▶ Once you made the selection (and configured the Import Settings), you can click the Import Button ⓫ to start the import procedure.

➡ Cameras (file-based)

FCPx supports the Picture-Transfer-Protocol (PTP), which lets you display all the files on a connected camera directly in the Media Import Dialog where you can select and import them.

▶ **View Mode**: The files can be displayed in two different Views. *Click* on the View Mode button ❶ in the lower-right corner to toggle between List View ❹ 🔲 and Filmstrip View ❻ 🔳.

▶ **Display Selection**: On top of the Browser is a popup menu ❷ that lets you choose if you want to display only Videos, Photos, or All Clips.

▶ **Status Bar**: The bottom of the Browser ❸ shows how many items are displayed and how many are selected. The time value next to it indicates the length of the selected Clip(s). If multiple Clips are selected, then it displays the combined length. If you *drag* a range ❾ on a Clip, then that time value will display the length of that range.

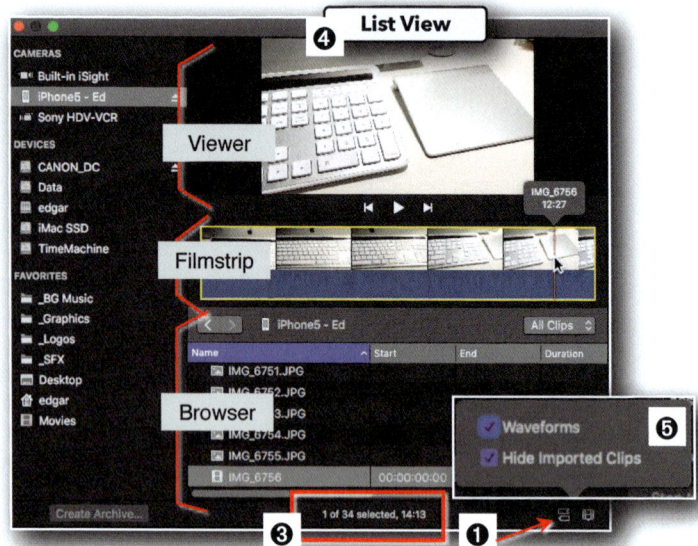

🔘 List View ❹ 🔲

▶ The List View has three sections, the Browser, the Filmstrip, and the Viewer. This is the same view we just saw in the view for Devices and it functions the same way.

▶ The Appearance Button 🔳 opens a popover ❺ with two checkboxes to choose if you want to display any Waveforms on the Clip and if you want to hide Clips that were already imported.

🔘 Filmstrip View ❻ 🔳

▶ The Filmstrip View only has two sections. The lower part displays all the available media files (photos and videos) as filmstrip thumbnails and the upper part displays the Viewer with the transport controls.

▶ The skimming ❼ works on all filmstrips the same as with the single filmstrip in List View.

▶ The Appearance Button 🔳 opens the Clip Appearance popover ❽ that also has the two checkboxes plus a slider to set the Clip Height and a slider to adjust the visible length of the filmstrips. You set what length a single thumbnail segment represents, from "All" (one thumbnail segment represents the entire Clip) to 1/2 second (i.e. an 8 second clip will have 16 thumbnail segments).

▶ You can *drag* a range on the filmstrip to import only a portion of the Clip. The selection is indicated by a yellow frame ❾. *Opt+cmd+drag* the borders ❿ ⟷ to adjust the range, *opt+drag* to create a new selection, or use the Key Command *I* and *O* to set the in-point or out-point to the Skimmer position. The Skimmer Info popover (*ctr+Y*) displays the Skimmer Position and the Help Tag displays the length of the current selection. A white line ⓫ indicates if a section of that media file has already been imported.

➡ Cameras (tape-based)

The Browser Pane is quite different when selecting a tape-based camera (with a Firewire connection or Thunderbolt-to-Firewire adapter).

▸ The Media Import Dialog displays only the Viewer ❶.

▸ The Transport Controls ❷ at the bottom let you remote control the camera (also use the Key Command **J**, **K**, and **L**). The playback status ❸ and the timecode ❹ will be displayed at the top.

▸ Once you configure the Import Setting on the right pane, you can *click* the *Import* button ❺. This will start the playback of the camera and imports the signal from the camera.

▸ During the Import, the status display shows the label "Importing" and the elapsed time ❻.

▸ FCPx detects any timecode interruptions on the tape and creates separate Clips for those sections.

▸ *Click* the *Stop Import* button ❼ (or press *esc*) to stop the import (or the tape reaches the end, or you drive gets full). This will save the new Media File to the selected Event and creates an Event Clip from that file and places it in that Event in the Workspace Browser.

➡ Camera (live)

"Importing" a live video signal from a connected iSight camera or any other camera that outputs a live video signal means that you are "recording" video directly into FCPx, into the selected Event of your Library.

▸ The Media Import Dialog displays only the Viewer ❽ with the live signal from the selected video camera. The playback controls are grayed out.

▸ Once you configured the Import Setting on the right pane, you can *click* the Import Button ❾ to start recording. A label appears in the upper left corner, "Importing" with the elapsed time ❿.

▸ Press the *Stop Import* button ⓫ to stop the recording.

Import Settings

The right window pane on the Media Import Dialog contains all the settings that determine what happens during the import procedure.

Import Settings

🌑 Mandatory Settings ❶

The first two sections have to be selected for any import and that's why they are radio buttons, with one option pre-selected.

🌑 Optional Settings ❷

Most of the settings have checkboxes, which means, they are optional. Many of those procedures can also be performed after a Clip has been imported.

> ▸ **Show/Hide**: The Settings pane shows scroll bars when the Media Import Dialog isn't high enough. You can decrease the required vertical space by hiding individual sections. When you move the mouse over any of the sections, a "*Hide*" label ❸ will appear. *Click* on it to hide those settings, which leaves only the header visible. Moving the mouse over that header again will display a "*Show*" label ❹ that lets you show those settings again. FCPx remembers not only the checkbox configuration, but also which section is hidden.

🌑 Commands

The bottom of the window pane lists the *Import* Button ❺ and the *Stop Import* Button ❻. You can also *double-click* on a file to start the import.

The Stop Button is only needed when getting media off a tape-based camera or live-video camera.

Pay attention to the label on the button, which indicates the type of import:

Import	Imports live video or tape-based video
Import All	Imports all displayed media files in the Browser
Import Selected	Imports all selected media files in the Browser
Stop Import	

The checkbox "*Close window after starting import*" ❼ does exactly that. This way you don't have to wait for the import to finish in order to continue to work in FCPx. The import progress is indicated by the appearance of the Background Tasks Button ❽ 🕐 ⊘ on the Workspace window and also displayed in more detail in the Background Tasks Window (by *double-clicking* on the Background Task Button).

Workspace Window

Background Tasks Button ❽

➡️ *Event Selection*

In FCPx, any media file has to be imported to a specific Event of a Library. This determines the folder where the imported file is stored in (the Event folder inside that Library File).

This first section in the Settings pane let's you do exactly that, select an Event. You have two options:

🔘 Add to Existing Event

Click on the selector to open a popup menu ❶ that lists all the Active Libraries (the ones that are currently open in FCPx) and all the Events in those Libraries. Choose one Event as the destination for the file import.

🔘 Create a new Event

This option lets you add a new Event in any of the Active Libraries. That Event will be created during the import procedure and the imported media files will be assigned to it.

- *Click* on the selector to open a popup menu ❷ with a list of all the available Libraries ❷ where you want to create the new Event in.
- Type a name in the text field ❸ for the new Event. You can always change the name of the Event later.

➡️ *Files*

This option determines if you import the Clip as a Managed Clip or a Referenced Clip. As I explained already in the Getting Started chapter, all the Clips in your Library are linked to a source file on your drive. That source file can be located inside the Library File (a so-called Managed Clip) or it can be located anywhere on your drive (a so-called Referenced Clip).

🔘 Copy to library - Managed Media ❹

During the import, all source files are copied into the "Original Media" folder ❺ inside the selected Event folder inside the Library File. The new Clip that is created during the import is linked to that new source file.

Please note that in the Library Properties *File ➤ Library Properties ➤ Storage Locations* you can choose to store the Media Files of a Library to a different location outside the Library File ❻. In that case, the option *Copy to library* ❹ changes to *Copy to "name of external storage location"* ❼.

🔘 Leave files in place - Referenced Media ❽

During the import procedure, FCPx leaves the source files at their original location and only creates a special file, called a Symbolic Link (Symlink) ❾, and stores it in the Original Media folder of the Event folder. This file functions similar to an Alias. It points to the original source file, wherever that one is located on your drive. This is a dangerous situation, because if you move the original source file, the link will be broken and you can't play the Clip. However, at any time, you can convert a Referenced Clip to a Managed Clip, placing a real copy in the Library File with the command *File > Consolidate Event Files*.

Please note that this option is not available for import from tape-based cameras.

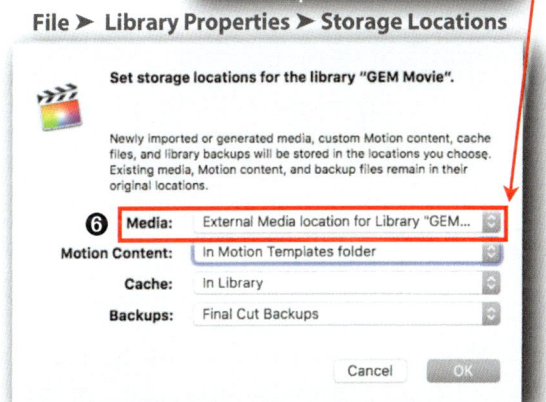

File ➤ Library Properties ➤ Storage Locations

Set storage locations for the library "GEM Movie".

Newly imported or generated media, custom Motion content, cache files, and library backups will be stored in the locations you choose. Existing media, Motion content, and backup files remain in their original locations.

❻ Media: External Media location for Library "GEM...
Motion Content: In Motion Templates folder
Cache: In Library
Backups: Final Cut Backups

Cancel   OK

Library File

▼ 📁 GEM Event
  ▼ 📁 Original Media
    ❾ → 🎞️ Sky.mov
    ❺ → 🎞️ Garden.mov

➡ *Keywords*

These two settings relate to a powerful feature in FCPx called "Keyword Collections" and the topic of metadata that I will discuss later in more detail.

🌑 From Finder Tags ❶

The Finder has a feature that lets you assign so-called Tags to any file. These are metadata that can be used to better organize or search files. You can use the "Edit Tags" button ❷ in the Finder Toolbar or the Contextual Menu to select or create new Tags ❸. Those Tags can also be displayed in the Finder's List View ❹.

FCPx can detect if your source media files have any of those Finder Tags assigned to them, and if so, imports those tags and assigns them to the Clips as metadata ❺ 🔑. In addition, FCPx creates Keyword Collections ❻ 🔑, listed in the Workspace Browser's Libraries Sidebar under the Event. This enables you to quickly search for Clips that contain those Keywords.

🌑 From Folders ❼

If you select, instead of single file, complete folders that contain the source media files, then FCPx uses the name of those folders (if they are meaningful names) and assigns them as Keyword metadata ❽ 🔑 to the Clips during the import procedure. FCPx also creates new Keyword Collections ❾ 🔑 for those names added to the Libraries Sidebar in the Workspace Browser.

If imported source media files are contained in nested folders (folders inside folders), then FCPx assigns a Keyword for each folder name in that folder hierarchy.

Clips in the Browser have a blue line across the filmstrip ⓫ to indicate that they contain Keyword metadata.

➡ Audio Roles

Whenever you import media files (video, audio, graphics), FCPx analyzes its content (including any existing metadata) and assigns so-called "Roles" to the video component and audio components (a topic I cover later). It uses one of the five default Roles for the assignments: Video, Titles, Dialogue, Music, or Effect.

This Audio Role setting in the Media Import Dialog provides some additional controls on how FCPx specifically assigns the Audio Roles during the import of source media files:

🌑 Assign Role

- ▸ The default setting is "Automatically"❶, where FCPx assigns the Role based on how it analyzes the audio content.

- ▸ You can choose from the popup menu any of the three default Roles ❷ (Dialogue, Effects, or Music) to ignore the analysis and assign that Role to the audio components of the imported media files.

- ▸ If you have created custom Roles in the Role Editor Dialog (*Modify ➤ Edit Roles...*), then those Roles will be listed in the popup menu at the bottom for you to choose from ❸.

🌑 Assign iXML track name if available

Some recording devices support the iXML standard (established in 2004) that allows the user to assign metadata tags to the individual audio channels it records. If you enabled this checkbox ❹, FCPx uses these tags and assigns them as Subroles to the audio component during import. For example, if an audio channel was labeled "Lav Mic 1", then the imported audio components will have that Subrole assigned to it automatically.

Whatever Roles are assigned to the audio components, they will also color those components based on the settings in the Role Editor Dialog (*Modify ➤ Edit Roles...*).

➡ Transcoding

FCPx is "resolution independent", which means you can mix and match different audio and video formats in your Project and it transcodes them on the fly. However, to optimize the performance, FCPx can convert its Clips to two additional formats and you can choose later which one to use for playback.

The two extra transcoded copies of the original file can be created during the import process by selecting these two checkboxes. Keep in mind that you can also do the transcoding process later.

The availability of those three formats is displayed in the Info Inspector with a green dot ❺ (or red if not available).

🌑 Create optimized media ❻

This creates a copy of the file in Apple Pro Res 422 format that will be stored inside the *Library File ➤ "Event Folder" ➤ Transcoded Media ➤ High Quality Media ➤ ❼*.

🌑 Create proxy media ❽

This creates a copy of the file in the lower resolution Apple Pro Res 422 Proxy format that will be stored inside the *Library File ➤ "Event Folder" ➤ Transcoded Media ➤ Proxy Media ➤ ❾*.

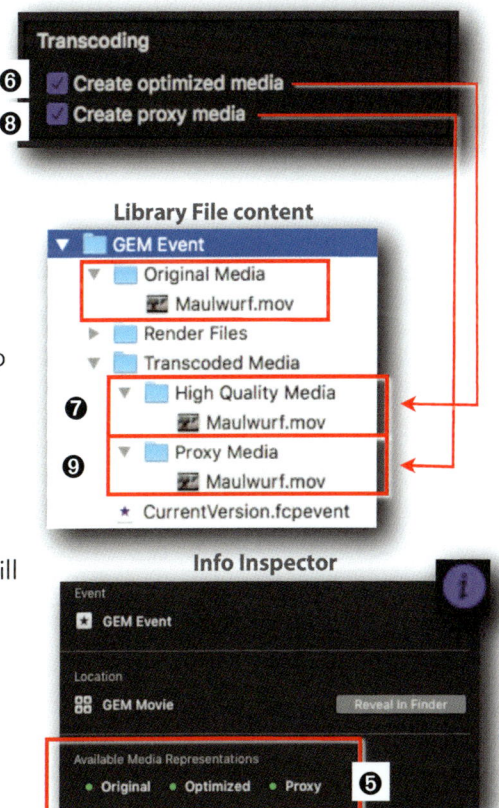

➡ *Analyze and Fix*

Many of the settings in this section require some understanding of topics that I discuss in more detail later in the book, so I will only explain the basic functionality of those checkboxes.

The first four checkboxes affect the video/image and the other three the audio portion of the imported source media files.

Video Analysis

🌐 **Remove Pulldown in video**

This options is only available for tape-based cameras. It removes pulldown patterns when checked.

🌐 **Analyze video for balance color**

If enabled, FCPx analyzes the video clip to detect color balance and also contrast. Please note that FCPx adds an effect to the Clip based on the analysis that later can be modified or disabled.

▸ The analysis data is stored inside the Library File's Event folder **Analysis Files ➤ Color Adjustment Files ➤ "ClipName".cbal ❶**. That file will be deleted if you delete the Clip from the Event.

▸ You can toggle this Automatic Color Correction on/off with the following commands:

- 📌 **Click** on the Magic Wand Button ❷ 🪄 in the Viewer and select/deselect the Balance Color ❸ option.

- 📌 Use the Key Command **opt+cmd+B**.

- 📌 When the Clip is opened in the Timeline ❹, you will see in the Video Inspector ❺ a checkbox labeled "Balance Color" ❻ under the Effects section (move the mouse over the Effects section and **click** on "*Show*" in case it is hidden). That section also shows a label that indicates if the Clip was "Analyzed" ❼ or "Not Analyzed" ❽.

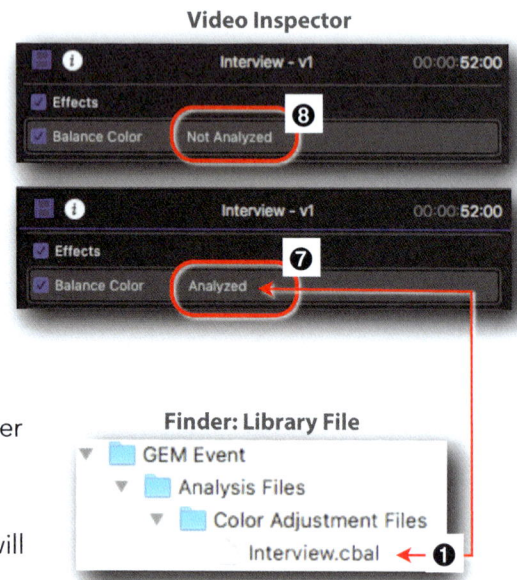

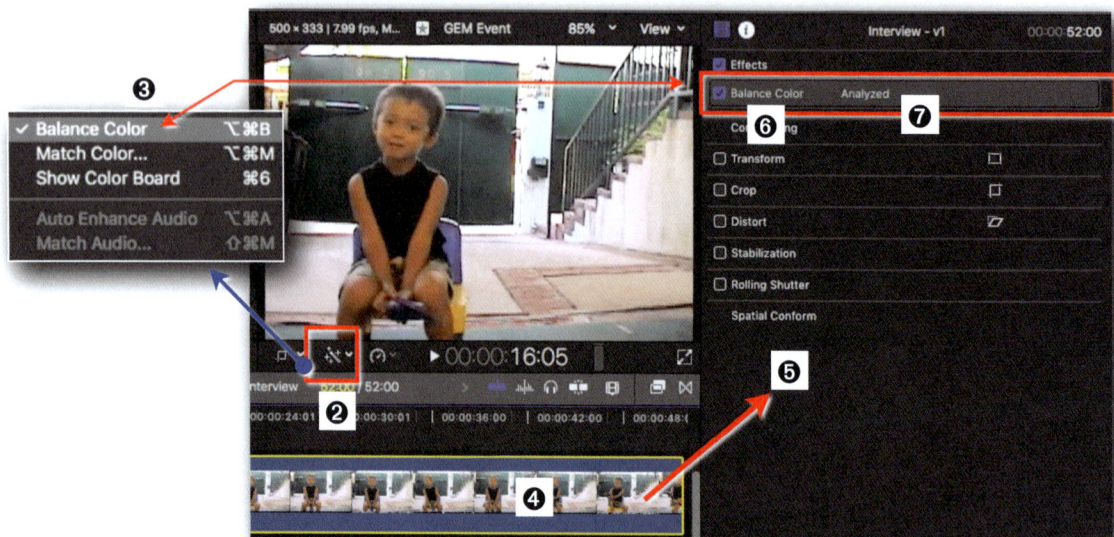

Video Inspector

Finder: Library File

Find People

If enabled, FCPx analyzes the source media files to check how many people are in the shot (One Person, Two Persons, or Group) and what type of shot it is (Close Up Shot, Medium Shot, or Wide Shot).

▶ The analysis data is stored inside the Library File's Event folder *Analysis Files ➤ Find People Files ➤ "ClipName".fppl* ❶. That file will be deleted if you delete the Clip from the Event.

▶ The Analysis Keywords are added to the Clip and can be viewed in the Browser by opening the disclosure triangle ❷ 🖽.

▶ Clips with Analysis Keywords have a purple line on top ❸.

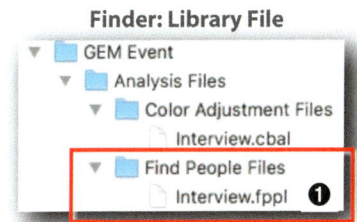

Finder: Library File

Consolidate find people results

If enabled, FCPx uses only one Person Type analysis keyword (One Person, Two Persons, or Group) and one Shot Type (Close Up Shot, Medium Shot, or Wide Shot) for every 2-minute segment of the video. If multiple people types and shot type occur during a 2-minute segment, then FCPx chooses the one with the most people and the widest shot.

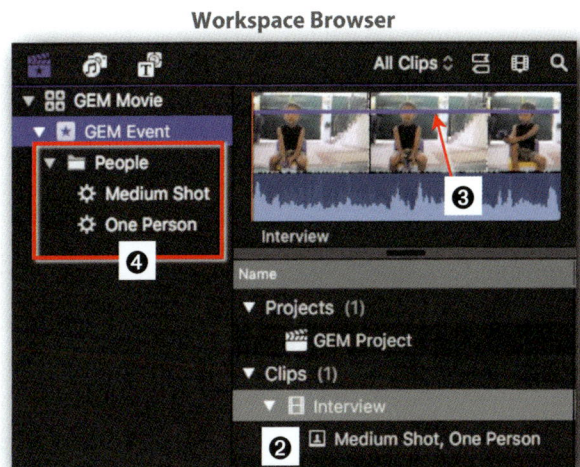

Workspace Browser

Create Smart Collections after analysis

If enabled, FCPx creates a Smart Collection ⚙ ❹ for each Analysis Keyword and places them in alphabetical order in the Libraries Sidebar under the Event, inside a People folder.

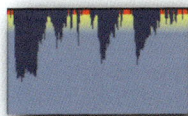

Audio Analysis

Analyze and fix audio problems

Same as with video analysis, FCPx adds effects to the Clip based on the analysis that later can be modified or disabled. To see the actual Audio Enhancements effects, you have to dig a little bit into the Inspector:

Audio Inspector

With the Clip selected, show the Audio Inspector 🔊. Move the mouse over the Audio Enhancements section ❺ and click on "*Show*". This reveals two sections inside ❻, the "*Equalization*" and the "*Audio Analysis*". It indicates if the Clip was "Analyzed" or "Not Analyzed" ❼. Move the mouse over the Audio Analysis section and click on "*Show*" ❽. Now this reveals its three components ❾, Loudness, Noise Removal, Hum Removal. Move the

mouse over each of those sections and click on "Show" ❿ to reveal their individual controls ⓫.

FCPx analyzes the audio signal for hum, noise, and loudness (these are the three components available under the **Audio Enhancements ➤ Audio Analysis**) and automatically fixes any detected problems. The label "Not Analyzed"❶ then changes to "Fixed" ❷ with a green checkmark, or other indicator ❸ (yellow or red).

Making the three modules ❹ visible in the Audio Inspector shows you how FCPx sets those parameters. You can manually adjust those controls or re-analyze at any time.

There is much more to the Audio Analysis which I cover in the Audio chapter.

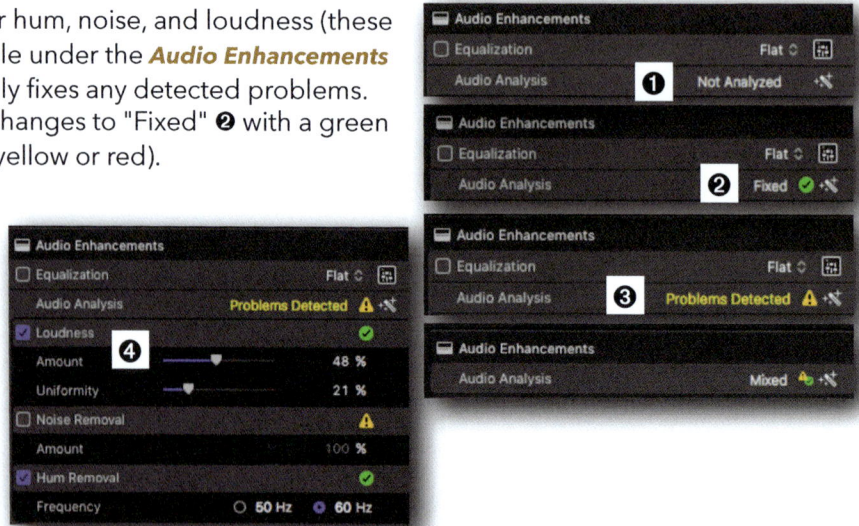

Separate mono and group stereo audio

If an audio file or the audio track of a video file has multiple channels, then FCPx analyzes if those channels are related or not. Based on that analysis, it creates the appropriate channel configuration, combining channels into mono, dual mono, stereo, surround, or any combination of that.

Here is an example of an audio track with 7 channels ❺ that FCPx groups into 5 audio components of 3 mono channels and 2 stereo channels ❻.

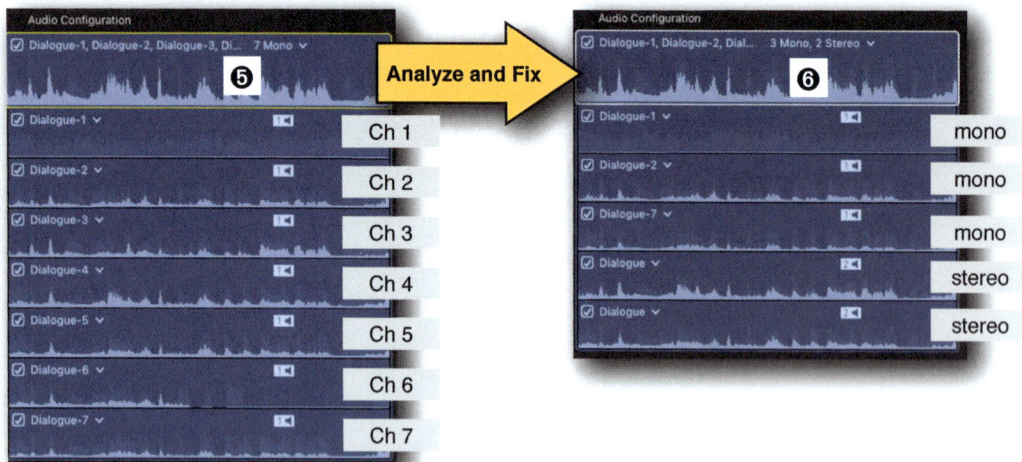

Remove silent channels

If an audio file or the audio track of a video file has a channel with no signal (silent channel ❼), then FCPx will not import ❽ that audio channel during the import.

Here is an example of an audio track with two channels where the second channel has no signal.

Other Import Options

Finder - Drag and Drop

Instead of using the Media Import Dialog to import source media files into your Library, you can also drag files directly from the Finder into FCPx. You have to be aware of two things:

- ☑️ **Destination**: Onto which part, the window element in FCPx, do you drop the file?
- ☑️ **Setting**: What import settings do you apply for this kind of import?

Workspace

➡️ *Destination*

You can drag a file (and even a folder) onto four different areas in the FCPx Workspace:

🔘 **Browser**

Drag a file or folder from the Finder ❶ onto the Browser pane ❷.

🔘 **Libraries Sidebar - Event**

Drag a file or a folder from the Finder onto a specific Event ❸ in the Libraries Sidebar.

🔘 **Libraries Sidebar - Keyword Collection**

Drag a file or a folder from the Finder onto a Keyword Collection ❹ 📷 in the Libraries Sidebar.
The file(s) will be added to the Event the Keyword Collection belongs to and have that specific Keyword 🔑 added to the Clip(s).

🔘 **Timeline**

Drag a single or multiple files (no folders) from the Finder onto the Timeline pane ❺. The same positioning procedures apply as if you would drag a Clip from the Browser to the Timeline (Connect, Insert, Append, Replace). The Clip will be added to the Event ❻ the Project belongs to.

➡️ *Import Settings*

The Import Preferences (*Final Cut Pro X ➤ Preferences...*) ❼ provide the same list of Import Settings as the Media Import Dialog (with the exception of the Event selection). These are the settings that are automatically applied to the source media file when imported using the drag and drop procedure.

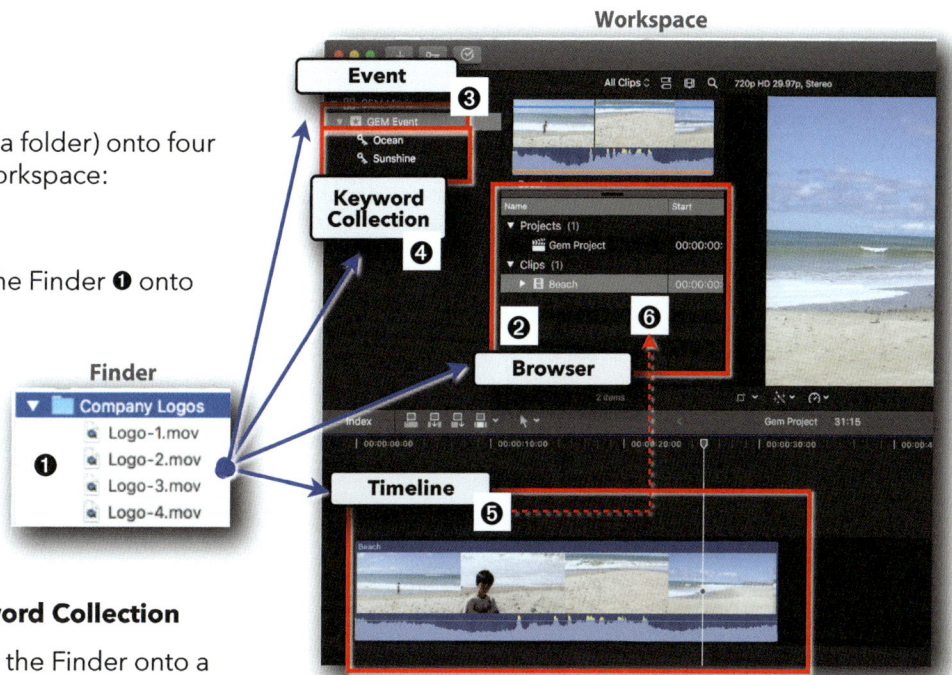

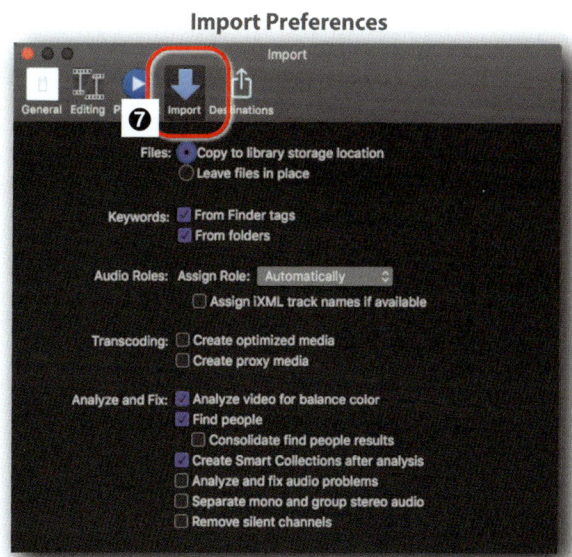

Import Preferences

Browser - Drag and Drop

This is another way to import source media files into your Library via drag and drop, but this time, you can access the material from inside the FCPx Workspace.

➡ *Photos and Audio Browser*

Click on the *Photos and Audio Sidebar* button ❶ 🎵 in the Workspace Browser. You will see a list of apps ❷ in the Sidebar from where you can import media files from.

🔮 Source

The Sidebar lists all the applications that have related media files available. *Click* on an item to view those media files in the Browser ❸ on the right. Please note the top of the Browser ❹ where you have one or two filters and a search field ❺ 🔍 to narrow down the displayed items in the Browser.

- ▶ **Photos** (and iPhoto if installed): Select Photos and Videos from your Photos Library.
- ▶ **iTunes**: Select songs from your iTunes Library. Protected audio files are not displayed in the Browser because you cannot import and use them in your video project (due to copyright restrictions).
- ▶ **GarageBand**, **Logic Pro X** (if installed): This lists all the mixes that were bounced from Logic or GarageBand using the "Share to Media Browser" command. Those audio files are stored in a special "Preview" folder inside a Logic or GarageBand Project File.
- ▶ **Sound Effects**: These are sound effects and other audio files that come preinstalled with FCPx. It also lists existing sound libraries that were installed on your drive by Logic, iLife, iMovie, or FCP7.

🔮 Destination

You can drag a file or a group of selected files from the Browser window to two destinations. You can also *opt+drag* ↔ a range ❻ to import a portion of the media files.

- ▶ **Timeline**: *Drag* the file(s) onto the Timeline pane ❼. The same positioning procedures applies as if you would drag a Clip from the Browser to the Timeline (Connect, Insert, Append, Replace). The Clip will be added to the Event the Project belongs to.

- ▶ **Sidebar**: You cannot *drag* a file to an Event in the Libraries Sidebar, because the Photos and Audio Sidebar is currently displayed. However, FCPx has a little trick. *Drag* the file(s) to the left over the Sidebar area anyways and the Browser temporarily switches to the Libraries Sidebar (neat, isn't it?). Now, while still pressing down the mouse button, you can drag the file(s) over an Event ❽ or over a Keyword Collection ❾ if you want to add that Keyword to the Clip(s).

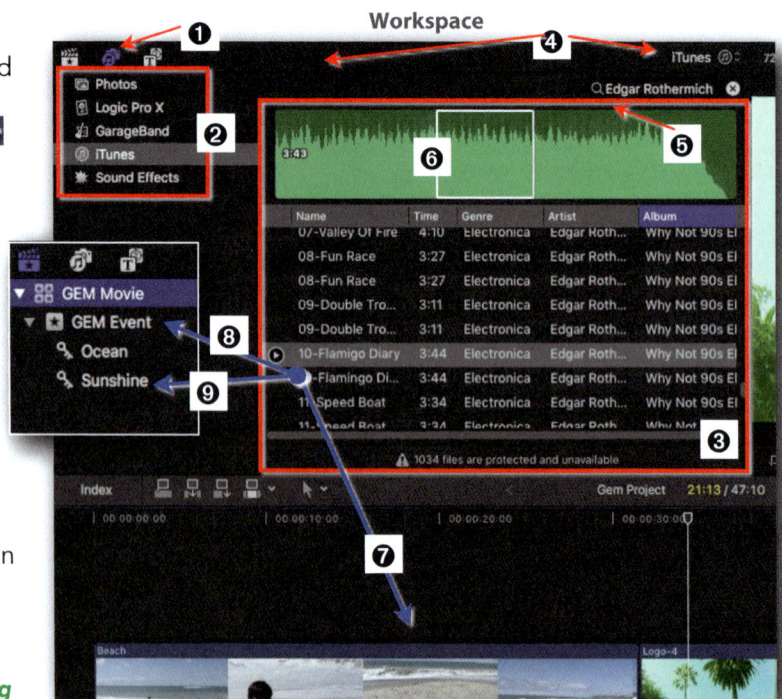

🔮 Import Settings

Most of the Import Settings configured in the Import Preferences (*Final Cut Pro X ➤ Preferences...*) also applies to this type of import.

🔊 Sound Effects

The Sound Effects ❿ item has a great feature for your own sound library.

▶ **Available Sounds**: The audio files that you see in the Browser ❶ are the audio files that are stored in the system directory */Library/Audio/Apple Loops/Apple/Final Cut Pro Sound Effects/*

- If those files weren't downloaded during the FCPx installation, go to the Main Menu *Final Cut Pro ➤ Download Additional Content...*
- You can also download the dmg file (637MB) from Apple's website at http://support.apple.com/kb/DL1394

▶ **Sound Effects Menu**: *Click* on the selector ❷ in the upper-right corner of the Browser to open the Sound Effects Menu.

- The menu lists the main folder "Effects" ❸ with the "Final Cut Pro Sound Effects" ❹ folder as a subfolder with additional subfolders representing its individual sound categories ❺. This is the same folder structor of the actual folder in the Finder.
- In addition to the "Final Cut Pro Sound Effects" folder, there might be other folders that FCPx recognizes. For example, you will see the "Theme Music" folder if you have iMovies installed on your computer.

▶ **Browser**: The displayed items in the Browser depend on the following selection:

- You can select specific folders ❸ ❹ ❺ in the menu to display only that content in the Browser.
- The Browser has three Columns ❻ (Name - Time - Genre) with the standard controls like other lists. *Drag* the Column Header left/right to reorder them or *click* on the Column Header to determine the sorting order (ascending 🔽, descending 🔼).
- You can use the search field ❼ to filter out the displayed files in the Browser, even search for Genre names (which are the category folders).
- Move the mouse over a row and the Play/Pause Button ❽ ▶ ⏸ appears to preview the audio file.

▶ **Roles**: FCPx automatically assigns the Effects Role to the audio files when you import them into your Project.

Add Custom Files/Folders to the Effects Menu

If you have your own sound effects library or folders with music cues that you often use in your video projects, then you can also add them to the Sound Effects Menu, so you can conveniently search, preview, and import those files within FCPx without switching to the Finder:

- ☑ Create an Alias (this way you don't have to copy the files) of the top folder of you library. The folder can be on an internal drive, external drive, or network drive.
- ☑ *Drag* the Alias (I named it "--- GEM Sound Effects ---") into the original Final Cut Pro Sound Effects folder */Library/Audio/Apple Loops/Apple/Final Cut Pro Sound Effects/*
- ☑ Relaunch FCPx and you will see that folder ❾ in the Effects Menu, including its internal folder structure.
- ☑ You can make changes in your original folder and they will show up in the Effects Menu via the Alias.

➡️ *Titles and Generators Browser*

Adding Titles or Generators to your Project is technically also an import procedure, although there are no source media files imported to your Event. Therefore, they don't show up in the Libraries Browser as separate items, but they are still considered Clips that you can drag directly to the Timeline (of a Project or a Clip).

Click on the *Titles and Generators Sidebar* button ❶ 🔲 in the Browser and you will see the two items in the Sidebar ❷.

🔵 Source

The Sidebar lists the Titles and the Generator items. ***Click*** on an item to view their available content in the Browser ❸ on the right. The disclosure triangle reveals the various categories.

Please note the top of the Browser ❹ where you have a filter menu and a search field ❺ 🔍 to narrow down the displayed items in the Browser.

- ▶ **Titles**
- ▶ **Generators**

🔵 Destination

The Timeline ❻ is the only destination you can ***drag*** those Clip to. The same positioning procedure apply as if you would drag a Clip from the Browser to the Timeline (Connect, Insert, Append, Replace). The Clip will be added to the Event the Project belongs to.

The Import Preferences (***Final Cut Pro X ➤ Preferences...***) have no effect on this "import".

Workspace

Motion

You can also "import" Titles and Generators from the Motion app to FCPx, although this procedure is called "publishing".

- ▶ **Edit Titles and Generators**: You can open any of the available Titles and Generators in the FCPx Browser directly in Motion (***ctr+click*** and select "Open copy in Motion") and edit them. Now you have the choice to save them (overwrite) or use the *Save as* to create a new one. They will be "published" and show up in FCPx in the Titles and Generators Browser.

- ▶ **Create new Titles and Generators**: You can start creating your own Titles and Generators in Motion from scratch and when you save them, they will also be published to FCPx. You can even create your own categories ❼.

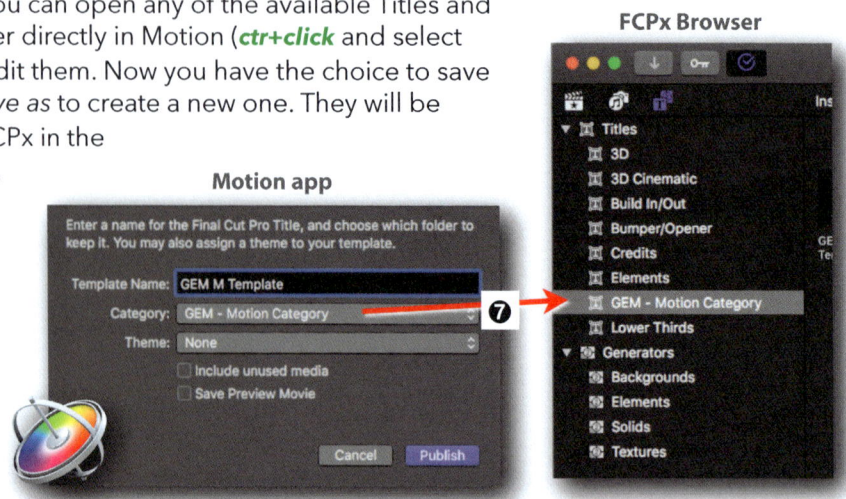

Motion app

FCPx Browser

Record Voiceover

Another way to "import" audio into your Project is to record live directly into FCPx. This comes in handy when you want to record some quick voiceover audio into your project during editing.

Open the Record Voiceover Window ❶ from the Main Menu *Window ➤ Record Audio* (Key Command *opt+cmd+8*).

➡ Setup

These are the available controls and settings:

▶ **Record Button**: *Click* on the button, hit the **space** key, or **sh+opt+A** to toggle recording on/off.

▶ **Meters**: The audio meters (mono or stereo) let you monitor the input level to avoid clipping (red meter segment).

▶ **Input Gain**: The slider lets you adjust the sensitivity (-12dB ... +12dB) of the input device.

▶ **Name**: Enter a name for the Clip that will be created.

Advanced Settings:

Click on the disclosure triangle to reveal more parameters:

▶ **Input**: The popup menu ❷ displays all the available Input Sources connected to your computer. The menu provides a submenu ❸ to select a specific channel from that input device. This setting is remembered the next time you open the Record Voiceover Window.

▶ **Monitor**: Select "off" to mute the output device to avoid possible audio feedback or choose "on" if you are using headphones.

▶ **Gain**: Set the monitor output level between -∞dB ... +12dB. This is disabled if the Monitor is set to off.

▶ **Countdown to record**: If enabled, FCPx starts 4 seconds before the Playhead start position and displays a countdown on the Viewer ❹ when you start recording in order to cue the start of the recording.

▶ **Mute Project while recording**: If enabled, all audio from your current Project is muted during the recording.

▶ **Create Audition from takes**: If enabled, FCPx creates an Audition Clip ❺ 🟡 if you record multiple times (from the same start position). This is a single Clip that contains every take (recording pass), so you can select later, at any time, which take to use.

▶ **Event**: Select any of the available Events from the popup menu you want to assign that new Clip to.

▶ **Role**: Assign a Role to that Clip.

Record Voiceover Window

Viewer with Voiceover Countdown indicator

Audition Clip

➡ *Recording Procedure*

The following will happen when you hit record *sh+opt+A*:

- ☑ The Record Button changes from this ⬤ to that ⬤ (which are just two random icons with no relation to anything in the audio world regarding "recording". Obviously the universal color for recording, RED, was not available).

- ☑ If the Countdown is enabled, then the playback starts 4 seconds before the Playhead start position and records at the start position. If the Countdown is not enabled, then recording starts immediately at the Playhead start position.

- ☑ The audio from the selected Input Device will be recorded as a wav file into the current Event's Original Media folder. The name of the file will start with "ClipName-1" and counts up with each following recording.

- ☑ The Bit Depth and Sample Rate is determined by the Input Device.

- ☑ The new Clip will always be placed on the Timeline as a Connected Clip starting at the Playhead position. If there was no Clip on the Primary Storyline, a Placeholder Clip will be created that the Voiceover clip connects to.

- ☑ The Clip will also be placed in the Libraries Browser.

- ☑ The Playhead returns to the start point when you stop, and any additional recording will be added, if selected, to an Audition (a Clip that contains all the takes you record at that position).

- ☑ You only can record to an existing Project, but not to the the Browser.

iMovie

There is no command in FCPx to import or open an iMovie Project directly in FCPx.

To open an iMovie Project, you have to initiate it from the iMovie app itself by using the command *File ➤ Send Movie to Final Cut Pro* ❶. This will convert the iMovie to a standard FCPx Library that you can then open in FCPx.

XML

XML is a file format that lets you exchange FCPx Libraries, Events, Projects, and Clips between FCPx and third-party applications and devices. For example, send a Project to Logic Pro X for mixing and import it back again with the mixed audio.

To import an XML file (with the file extension *.fcpxml*) use the Menu Command *File ➤ Import ➤ XML...* ❷. That opens a standard Import Dialog ❸ to navigate to the file, or just *double-click* on a fcpxml file ❹. XML files of a Project can be imported into an existing Event.

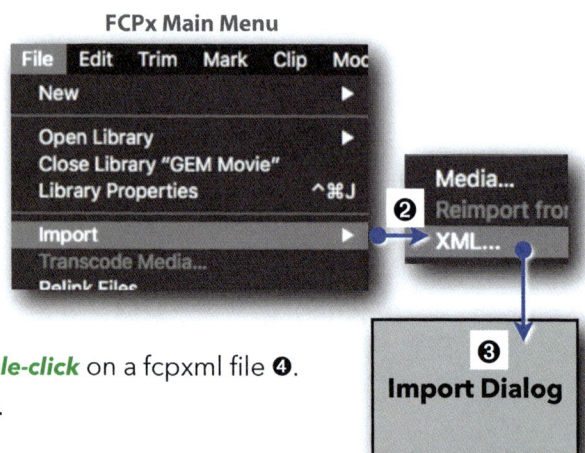

Camera Archive

So far, all the material we imported were imported to a specific Event of an Active Library, currently open in FCPx. However, the Camera Archive lets you import/capture footage of a camera, create new source media files, but instead of importing it into your Library, it stores them as a Package File to any location on your drive. This way, FCPx acts as a pure capture utility to get the footage/files off the camera for later use. No clips will be created and nothing will be added to the Libraries Browser in FCPx.

➡ *Create Camera Archive*

This is the procedure:

☑ Open the Media Import Dialog ⬇ (***cmd+I***).

☑ Select the tape-based camera ❶ in the Sidebar.

☑ The "*Create Archive...*" button in the lower-left corner should now be active Create Archive... .

☑ ***Click*** on "*Create Archive...*" button ❷, which slides out a sheet ❸ that lets you set three things:

  • Enter a name for the Archive File.

  • Navigate where you want to store that file.

  • A checkbox lets you automatically add that Archive File to the Favorites category in the Sidebar of the Media Import Dialog.

☑ Once you ***click*** Create ❹, the tape will rewind to the beginning, starts playing ❺ and captures the video to the newly created Archive File.

☑ The video is saved as one .mov file. If the video tape wasn't recorded in one pass and has multiple (Rec-Stop) sections, then FCPx detects those timecode interruptions on the tape and creates individual movie files for each section.

☑ The new Archive File ❻ (with the file extension .fcparch) is actually a Package File that you can open with the Finder's "*Show Package Contents*" command to reveal the movie file(s) inside ❼.

☑ You can let the tape run to the end or click the *Stop Import* button ❽ Stop Import to do exactly that. A dialog window ❾ lets you choose to keep what you have captured so far or delete the file.

☑ Please note that the Import Settings don't apply to this type of import.

Media Import Dialog

Create As: Indoor Shoot
Where: 🎬 Movies

☑ Add Camera Archive to Favorites

Cancel   Create ❹

Archiving (Rewind)... ❺
Archiving (0:07 m)...

Stop Import ❽

Import Stopped ❾
Archiving has been stopped before reaching the end of tape. Would you like to keep the archive "GEM Archive 1" with the clips captured this far?

Move to Trash   Keep Archive

Show Package Contents

📄 FCArchMetadata.plist
🎞 2006-01-21 19_16_33.mov ❼
🎞 2006-12-05 05_03_25.mov

Indoor Shoot.fcarch ❻

➡️ *Import from Camera Archive*

Importing source media files from a Camera Archive is similar to importing any other files from a Device. In the Sidebar ❶, select the drive you stored the Archive files in and navigate in the Browser ❷ to that location. The Media Import Dialog sees those Camera Archives as folders ❸ and you can click on the disclosure triangle ❹ to reveal their content to select the files you want to import.

Remember that you can **drag** one or multiple selections on the filmstrip to import only sections of the source media.

Media Import a Dialog

Disk Images

You don't need the Camera Archive feature for archiving file-based camera content. You can also copy the files to a folder on your drive and create a Disk Image instead.

- ☑️ Launch the Disk Utility app */Applications/Utilities/Disk Utility*.
- ☑️ Use the command *File ➤ New Image ➤ Image from Folder...*
- ☑️ Select the folder with all the media files you want to create the Disk Image for. It can also be password protected for "sensitive" footage.
- ☑️ You can move, copy, archive the disk image file (.dmg) that contains all the images of the original folder like any other file on the Finder.

Disk Utility app

To import files from a Disk Image ❼, just **double-click** the file to mount it ❽ and it will show up as a Volume under the DEVICES category ❾ in the Media Import Sidebar. Select the files ❿ that you want to import.

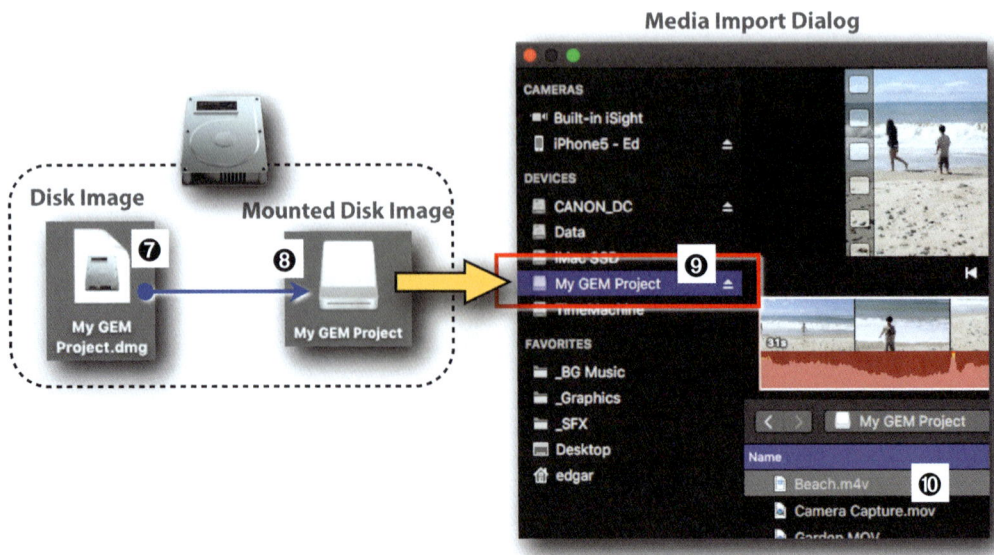

Media Import Dialog

After you imported your media files and have all the Clips in your Browser Pane, there is one additional step before you start with the video editing process and that is the procedure where you (or your assistant) organizes the Clips, the Event Clips to be specific. Although this step is not as exciting as the editing process itself, it is necessary to save you a lot of time later during editing.

Warning

This procedure of organizing Clips in FCPx is all about metadata and the mindset of using metadata as your virtual assistant. If you are not familiar with those concepts and workflows or still might be used to the old fashion way of organizing your Clips manually with bins, then this chapter is especially import for you.

Introduction

Basic Workflow

Think about the situation you might be facing at the beginning of a video editing project:
- You come back from your vacation with lots of videos from all the amazing places
- You just finished a weeding shoot
- You received the dailies from the location of a movie production
- You got a 3TB drive with all the footage of a documentary the producer shot over the last five years

➡ *Two Tasks*

The main challenge in all those productions, no matter how big or small, is to organize the footage before you start editing. There are two common steps that are used:

Grouping

This is the most basic organizational tool, also used for everything else in life. You group things together based on categories. In a video production, you create folders or bins with specific labels (i.e. outdoor, good, action, sunset, car ride, actor A, actor B, etc.) and put all the related files or clips in the related bins.

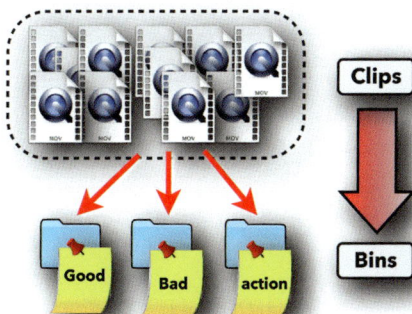

Creating Subclips

If you have longer clips that include multiple scenes or scenes that fit multiple labels, then you might want to cut up those clips into smaller chunks, so-called *Subclips*, so they better fit your labeling system.

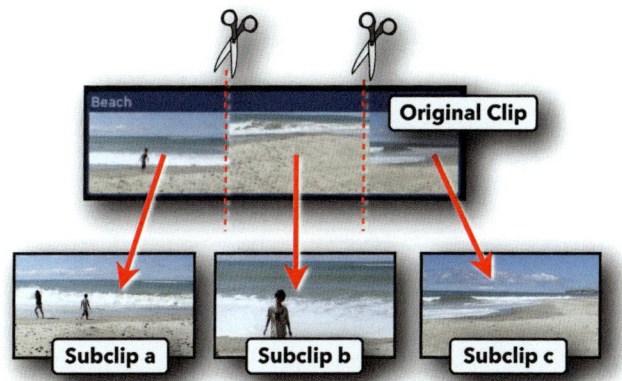

Metadata Workflow

FCPx provides those same two organizational workflows of **Grouping Clips** and **Creating Subclips**, but it uses metadata for those tasks. There are a lot of new and different techniques and workflows involved with that concept, which requires the proper understanding and adaption of that specific "mindset" to utilize the "Power of Metadata".

I will start with a basic overview before getting into all the necessary details that, unfortunately, do not have much to do with the creative part of video editing, but more so with the technical data management skills. . However, that has become one of the important requirements for a modern day video editor.

➡ *What is Metadata?*

Here is a simple analogy to demonstrate what Metadata is and the two types of Metadata we will use in FCPx to organize our Clips:

🌑 Data (Content) ❶

The data itself is the actual content of an item. In this example, let's look at a book and a Clip:

▶ **Book**: The content of a book, its data, are the pages ❷ with the written words on it.

▶ **Clip**: The content of a Clip, its data, are the bits ❸ stored in the linked source media file.

🌑 Metadata (Entire Content) ❹

In addition to the content, the <u>data</u>, you need the <u>metadata</u>, the "data about the data". This is information that applies to the entire content as a whole.

▶ **Book**: The metadata ❺ for a book is usually the title of the book, the author, the publisher, etc., everything about that book.

▶ **Clip**: The metadata ❻ for a file is usually the name of the Clip, the filetype, creation data, etc. This is the information about that Clip as a whole.

🌑 Metadata (Sections of the Content) ❼

While the metadata usually provides information about the entire content, you can create a different type of metadata, that provides information only for a section of the content.

▶ **Book**: The information could be a description of the individual chapters or descriptions of a range of pages ❽.

▶ **Clip**: For a Clip, you could have information about specific sections ❾ ❿ ⓫ in that Clip.

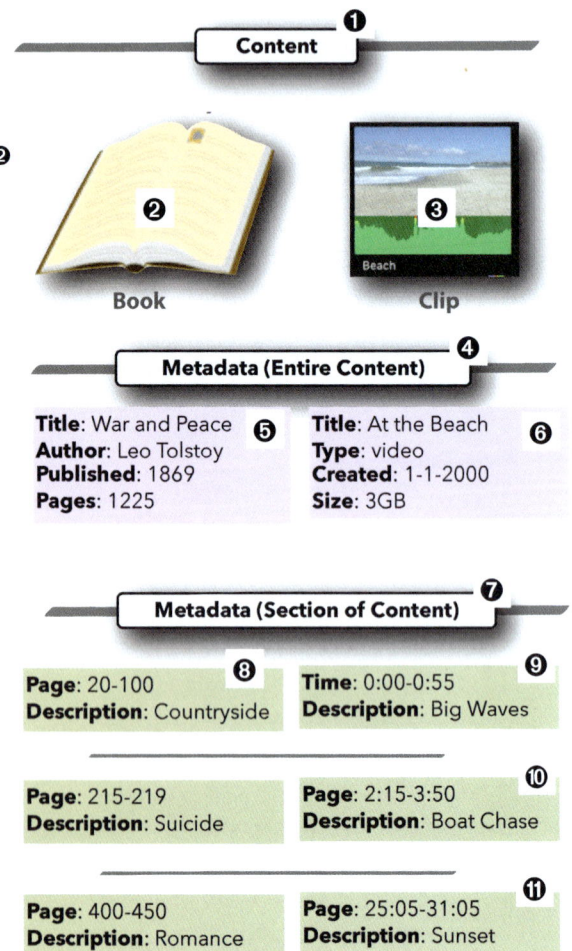

Content ❶

Book ❷   **Clip** ❸

Metadata (Entire Content) ❹

Title: War and Peace ❺
Author: Leo Tolstoy
Published: 1869
Pages: 1225

Title: At the Beach ❻
Type: video
Created: 1-1-2000
Size: 3GB

Metadata (Section of Content) ❼

Page: 20-100 ❽
Description: Countryside

Time: 0:00-0:55 ❾
Description: Big Waves

Page: 215-219
Description: Suicide

Page: 2:15-3:50 ❿
Description: Boat Chase

Page: 400-450
Description: Romance

Page: 25:05-31:05 ⓫
Description: Sunset

The important thing to understand is that Metadata is a **set of value pairs** ❺. There are two fields, the PropertyName (or Field Name) and the value for that property, the PropertyValue, for example, "Title: At the Beach". The entire list of those pairs make up the MetadataSet that applies to the entire content ❸.

On the other hand, the Metadata for a each section of the content represents its own set of value pairs, multiple MetadataSets ❾ ❿ ⓫ each one applying only to that section of the content, that specific range.

➡️ *Recognizing Metatdata*

Before learning how to create those Metadata, I want to first show you how to find and properly read (recognize) the various Metadata in FCPx. We have to pay attention to two things:

- ▸ **PropertyName vs. PropertyValues**
- ▸ **MetadataSet for the EntireClip vs. MetadataSet for a ClipRange**

🔵 Info Inspector

Selecting an Event Clip ❶ in the Browser Pane will display a wide range of data for that Clip in the Inspector Pane ❷ (where you can also edit most of that data). **Click** the Info Button 🔵 in the Inspector Header to switch the view to the Info Inspector.

These are the two things you will see:

- ▸ **PropertyName - PropertyValue**: The displayed list shows the name of the Properties (PropertyNames) in the left column ❸ and the value for each of those Properties (PropertyValue) in the right column ❹.

- ▸ **MetadataSet for EntireClip**: Please note that the Info Inspector only shows the MetadataSet for the entire content ❺, but cannot display any MetadataSets for any sections of the Clip.

🔵 Browser Pane in List View 🖼️

The List View in the Browser Pane also shows the Metadata, but differently.

- ▸ **PropertyName - PropertyValue**: The List View uses a spreadsheet type of list. The header (first row) shows the PropertyNames, each column a different Property ❻, and the rows underneath under each column show their PropertyValues ❼, each row for a different Clip (or Subclip).

- ▸ **MetadataSet for EntireClip and ClipRange**: The Info Inspector ❷ can only show one Clip at a time and, therefore, shows the MetadataSet of only one Clip at a time. The Libraries Browser, on the other hand, can show multiple Clips (depending on what is selected in the Sidebar), each row representing a separate Clip, displaying the Metatdata Set for that Clip. If the Row has a disclosure triangle ❾ on the left, then it means that there are also MetadataSets for sections of the Clip (ClipRange) ❿. When the disclosure triangle is opened 🔽, you will see that the name field is indented on the left ⓫ and most of their fields are empty, because the MetadataSet of a ClipRange only has a few Properties.

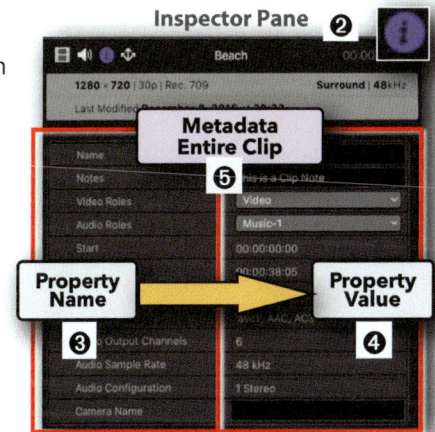

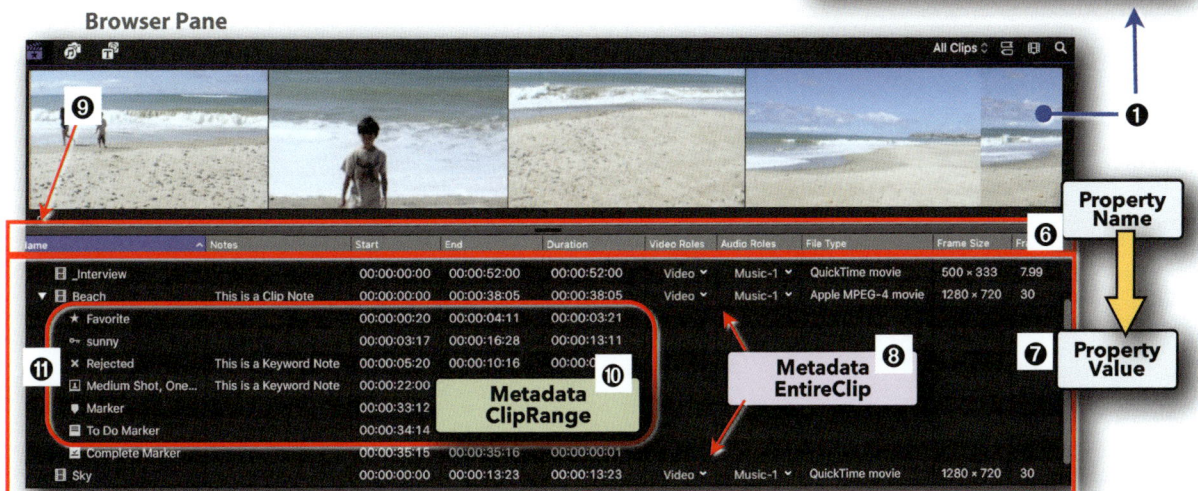

Inspector Pane

Browser Pane

Step 1: Organize
Step 2: Search

Yes, it all might sound a little technical so far, but when you look at those interface elements in FCPx through the eyes (and mindset) of a database structure, then life in FCPx becomes much easier, and especially more powerful. Remember, the reason behind all that is not because we are neat freaks. To organize your Clips with the underlying architecture of databases and metadata is only step 1, the preparation to create the foundation for step 2, searching and finding the right Clips (and finding them fast), are techniques we will learn later in this chapter.

Info Inspector

Here is a side-by-side view of the Info Inspector and the database structure behind it.

Info Inspector

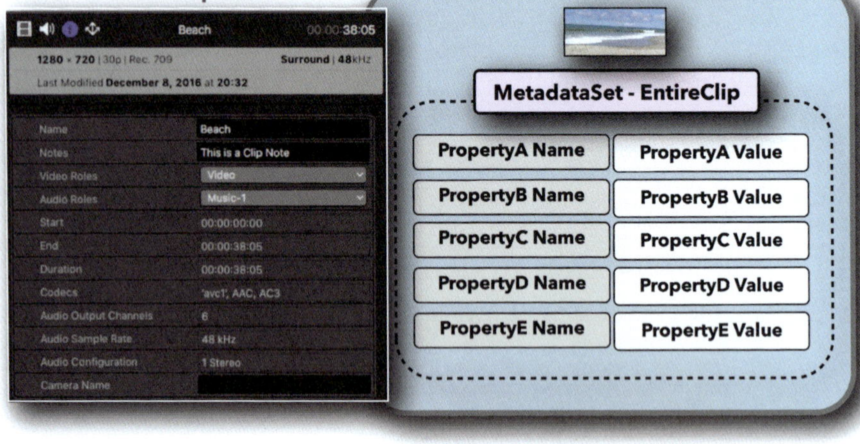

Browser Pane

Here is a side-by-side view of the Browser Pane in List View and the database structure behind it.

Browser Pane (List View)

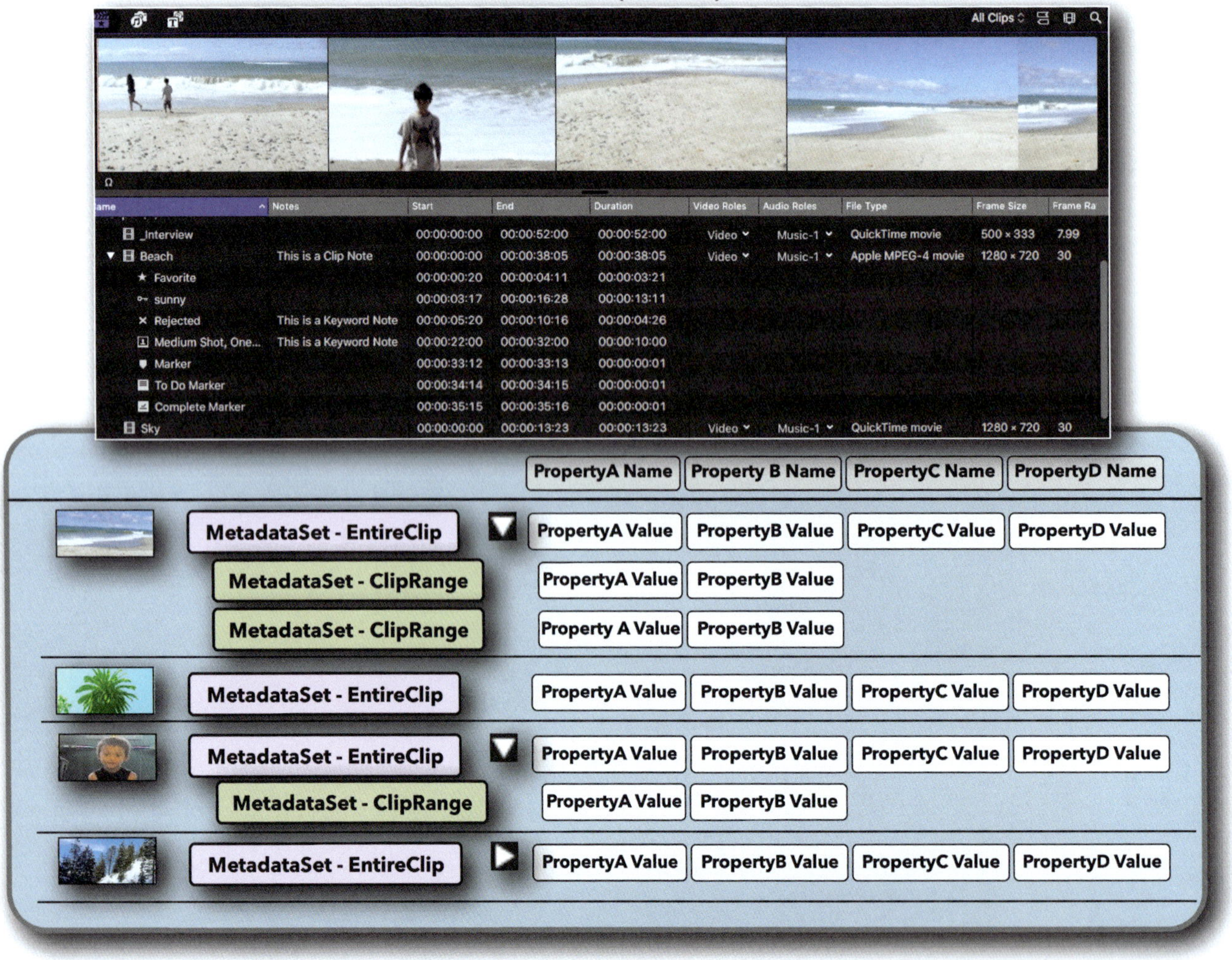

Metadata Types

There are two more aspects I want to point out about metadata before getting into the details on how to create them. Who creates the Metadata and what types of Metadata are available?

➡ Who Creates Metadata for a Clip?

Think of four sources that can enter metadata to a Clip:

- ▶ **Imported Metadata ❶**: As we discussed already in the previous chapter about Importing, you can take metadata that already exist in the media file (Name, Camera, iXML, etc.) and store them with the Clips to its MetadataSet-EntireClip or MetadataSet-ClipRange as Keywords ⚷
- ▶ **Analyzed Metadata ❷**: Also, during the import procedure or any time after you imported a Clip, you can let FCPx analyze the media file and add its "findings" (i.e. how many people are in the shot and what type of shot) as so-called *Analysis Keywords* ▣. Please note that these are stored as a "MetadataSet-ClipRange".
- ▶ **Manually added Metadata ❸**: You have extreme freedom to add your own metatdata to any Clip, either as MetadataSet-EntireClips or the different types of MetadataSet-ClipRange ⚷ ★ ✕ ☑ ▤ ⬛
- ▶ **Externally added Metadata ❹**: There are also third-party solutions that let you import log files from cameras or script editors on the set to match that data with the imported Clips.

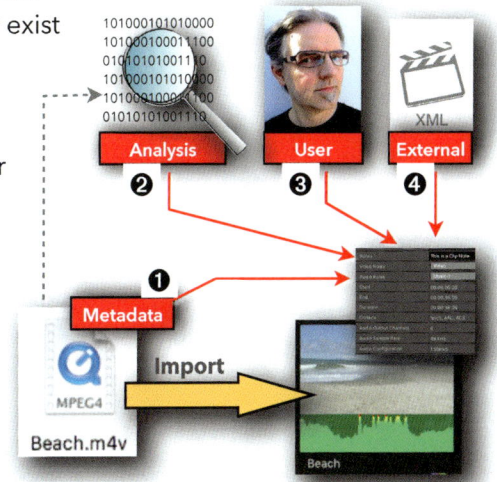

➡ What types of Metadata are available

When dealing with metadata, always be aware if it applies to the entire Clip (*MetadataSet-EntireClip*) or only to a section of the Clip (*MetadataSet-ClipRange*).

🌑 MetadataSet-EntireClip

This type of metadata applies to the entire Clip:

- ▶ **Info ❺**: You can type any text into the field of a PropertyValue (that is editable) and even create your own Properties.

🌑 MetadataSet-ClipRange

These types of metadata apply to a ClipRange and, therefore, requires you to make a selection on the thumbnail of the Event Clip first to specify the range. They function as virtual Subclips.

- ▶ **Keywords ❻** ⚷: You can apply a single (or multiple) word or phrase to that range and also add searchable notes to that Keyword.
- ▶ **Ratings ❼** ★ ✕: There are two types of Ratings that you apply to a section of a Clip (ClipRange), *Favorite* and *Rejected*. Although their default names are "Favorite" and "Rejected", you can rename each one to any (searchable) word you like.
- ▶ **Markers ❽** ☑ ▤ ⬛: There are different types of Markers (which are a single-address ClipRange) that you can also rename freely.

Create Metadata

Info

We already talked about the Info Inspector a few times, the place where you view and edit "Info"- Metadata, any type of "Information" about the Clip, the entire Clip. Let's have a closer look at that Inspector.

➡ *Terminology*

The crucial part is to know all the terminology you will encounter in the Info Inspector:

Database ❶: I can't repeat it enough, FCPx is based on a collection of relational databases. Every component is actually a database, the Library, its Events, its Projects.

Database Record: Think of each Event Clip (that belongs to a specific Event) as a single record stored in that Event database.

Field (Property) ❷: Each record in a database has fields. For example, in a contacts database, the fields are "Name", "Address", "Phone No", "Email", etc. In FCPx, where each Event Clip is a record entry in its Event Database, the fields are "Names", "Video Roles", "Start", "End", "Duration", etc. FCPx also calls these fields Properties.

PropertyName - PropertyValue ❸: We already discussed that each Property is a value pair, the two columns displayed in the Info Inspector. You have the name of the Property (PropertyName) on the left and its corresponding value (PropertyValue) on the right, which can be blank.

Custom Metadata Field ❹: In addition to the 300 fields (Properties) that are available by default, you can create your custom Properties, called "Custom Metadata Field".

Custom Metadata Field Dialog ❺: This is a little window the lets you create a new field by giving it a PropertyName (and a Description), for example, "GEM-Show Episode".

Metadata: The Event Database contains a lot of data, and the data that contains the general information about a record in that database is referred to as the Metadata.

MetadataSet ❻: Because the term Metadata could refer to an individual Property or to all the Properties of a single record (EntireClip), I use the term "MetadataSet" to refer to the list of all the Properties of a Clip.

Metadata View ❼: Because not all Properties are relevant for each Clip and the list in the Info Inspector would be way to long to scroll through, the Info Inspector uses Metadata Views, which are collections of Properties that are displayed in the Info Inspector. You select from a list of Metadata Views to only show the Properties that you want to see.

Metadata View Dialog ❽: This is a window that lets you configure your own Custom Metadata Views (in addition to the 11 Metadata Views), to show exactly the Properties in the Info Inspector you want to see.

Custom Name ❾: This is a feature that lets FCPx automatically enter the value for the "Name" field based on a macro script that you define.

Naming Presets Dialog ❿: This is the window that lets you configure that macro for the Custom Name.

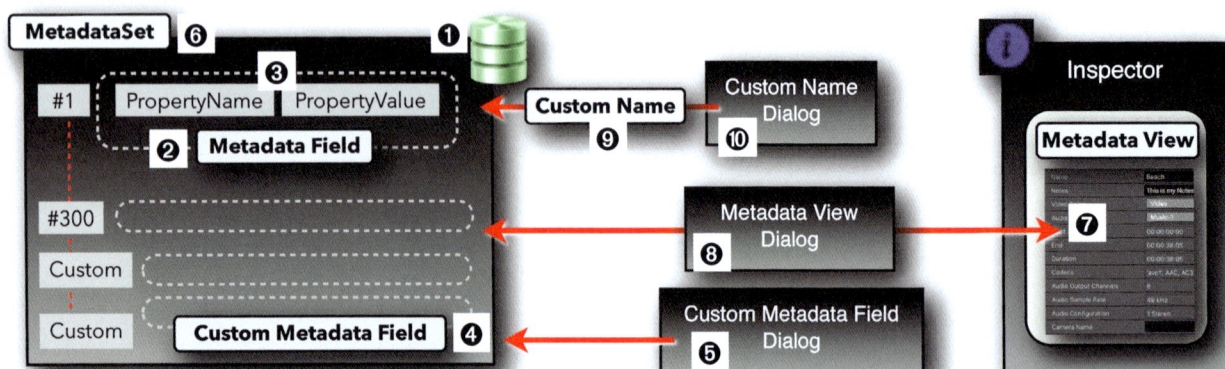

➡ Windows and Dialogs

Here are the screenshots of the popup menus and dialogs to show you how to access the various elements.

▶ **Metadata View Selector** ☑ ❶: The selector in the lower left corner of the Info Inspector shows the currently selected Metadata View ❹.

▶ The popup menu has the following menu items:

- **Add Custom Metadata Field... ❷**: The item on top opens the Custom Metadata Field Dialog where you enter the Name of the new Property and a short "Description" for that Property. This is not the PropertyValue, it is an additional field that is only displayed in the Metadata View Dialog ❻.

- **Metadata Views ❸**: The middle section of the popup menu lists all the Metadata Views that you can select. These are the 11 default views, plus any custom views you've created. The currently selected one (with the checkmark) is currently used in the Info Inspector ❹.

- **Rearrange Rows**: You can *drag* the individual rows (Properties) up/down to rearrange the list.

- **Save/Edit Metadata View ❺**: The two commands at the bottom of the popup menu let you either create a new Metadata View under a different name (Save As...) or open the Metadata View Dialog (Edit...).

▶ **Metadata View Dialog ❻**: This dialog provides all the commands to create a new Metadata View or edit the currently selected one (see next page for details).

▶ **Custom Name Selector ❼** ☑ Pay attention to the inconsistency with the two selectors. The left one ❶ opens a popup menu and its label changes to show the currently selected Metadata View in the Inspector. The button on the right ❼ also opens a popup menu, but its label is always the same "Apply Custom Name", because its menu items are commands that change the value of the "Name" Property, the name of the Clip(s). Please note that you can have multiple Clips selected in the Browser and that command then applies to all of them. This is a really powerful "scripted" Batch Renaming feature. In the Naming Preset Dialog ❽, you can create your own macro script for a Custom Name, which will then be listed in this popup menu.

▶ **Naming Preset Dialog ❽**: The *Edit* and *New* command ❾ in the popup menu both open the same *Naming Preset Dialog*. The window lets you create your own Custom Names by drag and drop "tokens" that act as variables for metadata. When dealing with a big dataset of clips, this can save hours of prep work with easy to use scripting.

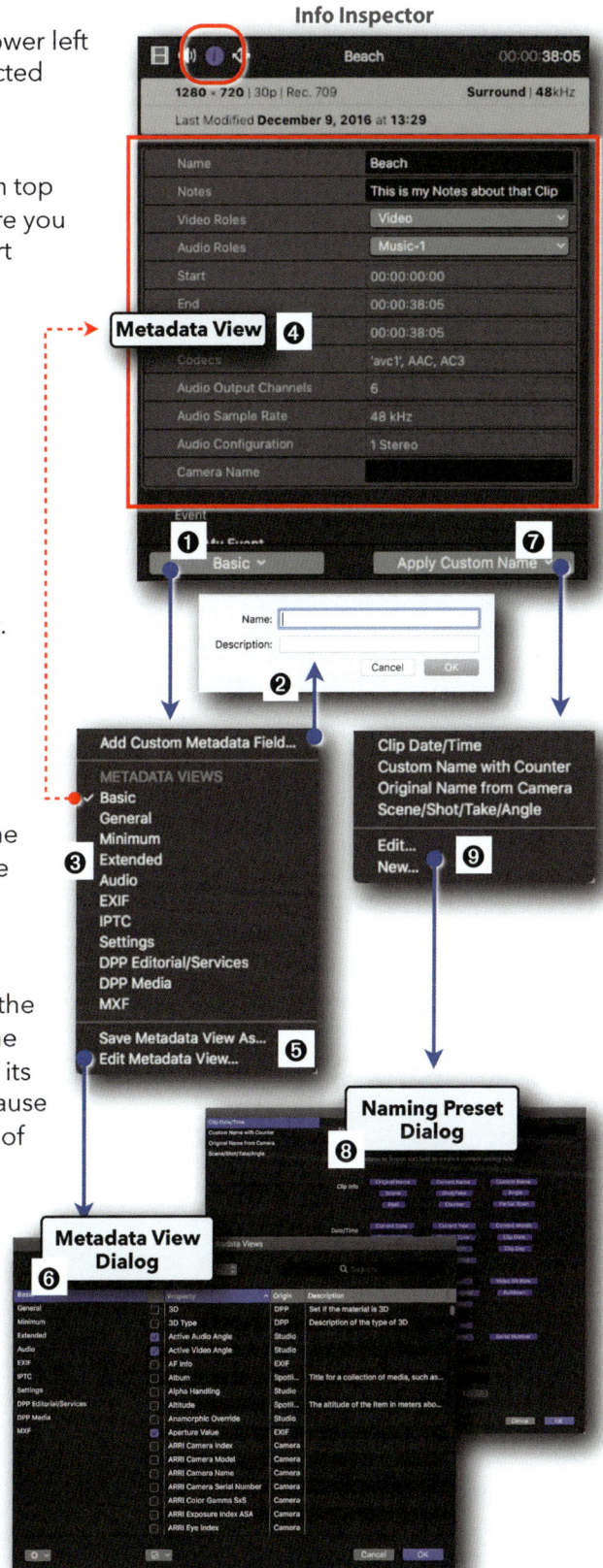

➡ *Metadata View Dialog*

I don't want to cover all 300 Metadata Fields, but let's have a little peek and encourage you to play with it. This is also a good place to learn more about your Clips by looking at what information they already come with (imported metadata). After all, those are the parameters that you can search for later.

▶ **Sidebar ❶**: The sidebar lists all the available Metadata Views, original and custom ones.

▶ **Browser ❷**: The Browser on the right displays the Properties with four columns. Please note that there are no PropertyValues here. This is just for configuration and entering data. *Click* on any column ❷ to sort the list. The little triangle in the header toggles the ascending ⏷ or descending ⏶ sort order.

- Checkbox: The checkboxes indicate if that specific Property is displayed ☑ or not displayed ☐ in the Metadata View that is currently selected in the Sidebar ❶. *Click* on it to change its status. The button below has two commands to "Check all" or "Uncheck All" ❹.

- Property: This is the name of the Metadata Field (Property). *Ctr+click* on a custom Property ❺ and a popup menu lists two commands to Edit (opens a Dialog sheet ❻) or Delete that Field.

- Origin: This field indicates the category of the Property.

- Description: Some Properties provide a short description in that field about what the property is for or where it came from.

▶ **Property Type Selection ❼**: You can filter out a specific category of Properties to be displayed in the Browser by selecting one from the popup menu. This lets you check on a specific category without scrolling through the long list.

▶ **Search Field ❽**: You can enter a word or phrase in the Search Box to search the currently displayed list in the Browser. This applies to the Property and Description field.

▶ **Action Button ❾**: The Action Button in the lower-left corner reveals four commands to manage the Views (New, Save As, Restore, Delete) and one command to add a new Metadata field "Add Custom Metadata Field".

▶ **Add Custom Metadata Field ❿**: This opens the same little dialog window we saw on the previous page to create custom Properties, and also, when editing custom Properties on this window ❻. You can use this one to completely customize the MetadataSet to your own production needs. For example, create a field for actors, for locations, maybe even licensing info to mark public domain cues (image, audio, or stock footage), anything. Later, with a click of a button you can select only the clips that meet those criteria.

Metadata View Dialog

6 - Organize Clips

➡ *Data Entry*

Here are a few things you have to keep in mind when entering using the Metatdata type "Info":

😊 Value Pair

As we know by now, a MetadataSet for a single Clip has about 300 Properties, each one represented by two values, the name of the Property (PropertyName ❶) and the actual data for that Property (PropertyValue ❷), which, of course can be blank ❸ if it doesn't contain any data.

😊 Read Only

Most metadata that has been retrieved from the media file during import are read only ❹, which means you cannot change their PropertyValues.

😊 Entry Methods

Properties that can be edited ❺ by the user have a black entry box (*click* on it and enter text), a popup menu, or a checkbox.

😊 Browser Pane - List View

As we have already discussed, the List View in the Browser Pane also displays the metadata, here in a spreadsheet style where the header shows the PropertyNames ❻ and the rows below represent the individual Clips with their PropertyValues ❼ in the corresponding columns.

The List View provides a fixed set of 22 Properties ❽ and you can *ctr+click* on a header to choose from the popup menu which of those Properties you want to display in that list. Think of it as a different kind of configurable Metadata View.

Browser Pane - List View

😊 Batch Editing

I already mentioned in a previous chapter the capability of batch editing in the Inspector. You just select multiple Clips in the Browser Pane and whatever you enter in a PropertyValue field will apply to all the selected Clips. Be careful, if the selected Clips have existing PropertyValues and they are different, then you will see a shaded text "*Multiple Values*" in the black box ❾.

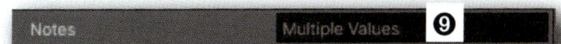

😊 Emojis

Don't forget that you can also use emojis in any text entry field in FCPx. You can even search ❿ for specific emojis in your Metadata.

Keywords

➡ Comparison

Let's start with a comparison of the two types of metadata, the "Info" MetadataSet and the "Keyword" MetadataSet:

🌑 Info MetadataSet

- The Info MetadataSet has about 300 Properties.
- The Metadata applies to the whole Clip (EntireClip).
- The Properties can be viewed in the Info Inspector and some Properties are also displayed in the Browser Pane's List View.

🌑 Keyword MetadataSet

- The Keyword MetadataSet ❾ has only six Properties.
- The Metadata applies only to a section of the Clip (ClipRange).
- You can create as many Keyword MetadataSets for a Clip as you like.
- The Metadata is displayed numerically in the Browser Pane in List View ❷ (not in the Info Inspector!), and visually, directly on the Clip's thumbnail as a blue line ❸.

➡ Terminology

Be careful with the term "keyword", because it means three things. So whenever you use word keyword (or I use it in this manual), you have to make sure to know what it is referring to. For example, if you say "I added the keywords *Big Trees* and *snow* to a section of a Clip", then the term keyword can mean three different things:

▶ **MetadataSet**: Adding a Keyword means, creating a Keyword MetadataSet ❶ that is displayed as a single row ❷ in the Browser's List View with its six Properties and also as a blue line ❸ on top of the thumbnail of the Event Clip.

▶ **Name Field**: The "Keywords" can be one or many words that are added to a single field ❹ (the Name Property) of that one MetadataSet, displayed under the Name column ❺ in that row ❷ of the List View.

▶ **Words**: A Keyword could mean only one of the words in that Name Field ❻, for example, "snow" ❼.

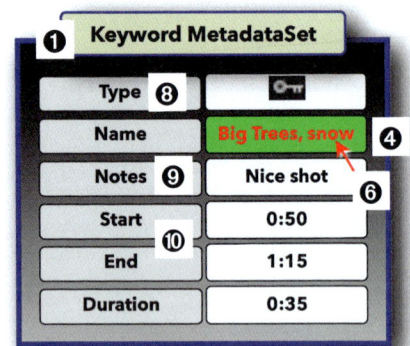

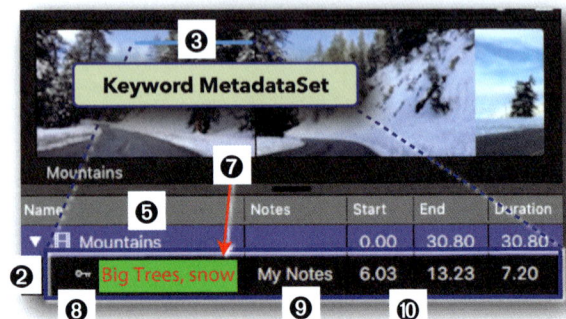

Browser Pane's List View

➡ MetadataSet

The Keyword MetadataSet has six Properties.

- ☑ **Type ❽**: Analysis 🔳 or Standard 🔑.
- ☑ **Name ❺**: The actual keyword can be a word ("snow") or phrase ("Bit Trees"), or multiple words/phrases separated by commas ("Big Trees, snow").
- ☑ **Notes ❾**: The Keyword MetadataSet has its own Note Property where you can enter any text.
- ☑ **Start ❿**: This is the Start Time of the ClipRange that you defined for the Keyword.
- ☑ **Stop**: This is the End Time of the ClipRange that you defined for the Keyword.
- ☑ **Duration**: This is just the calculation "End Time minus Start Time".

➡️ *Two Types of Keywords*

There are two types of Keyword MetadataSets. The functionality is virtually the same once they are created, their only difference is who created them and when.

🖼️ **Analysis Keywords**: Created by FCPx with the Analysis procedure.

🔑 **Standard Keywords**: Created by FCPx during the import or created manually by the user.

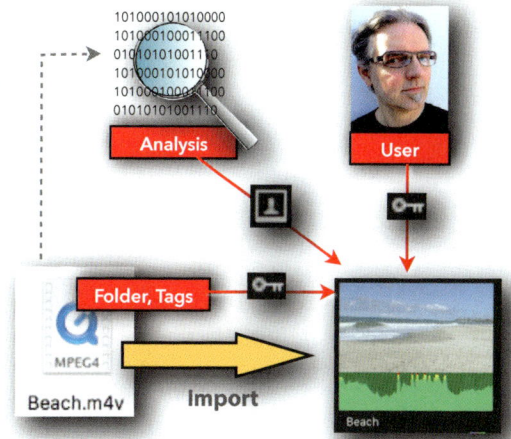

➡️ *Analysis Keywords* 🖼️

Analysis Keywords, also referred to as "People" and marked with the people icon 🖼️ in the Browser Pane's List View, are automatically created by FCPx, if you tell it to do so.

▶ **Create**: The Media Import Dialog (*cmd+I*) and the *Preferences ➤ Import* have two checkboxes ❶ "Find people" and "Consolidate find people results" that initiate an analysis process during the file import. You can also perform the analysis any time after the import by *ctr+clicking* on the Clip(s) and select from the *Shortcut Menu ➤ Analyze and Fix...* ❷, which opens a Sheet with the same two checkboxes ❸.

▶ **Procedure**: FCPx analyzes the video content to see how many people are in the shot and what kind of angle it is. For any detected section (ClipRange), FCPx creates a separate Keyword MetadataSet ❹ that is added as a separate row in the Browser Pane's List View below the Clip 🖼️. The row displays the six Properties of the Keyword MetadataSet. The icon 🖼️ in the Name field functions as the KeywordType Property.

▶ **Keyword**: Depending on the analysis results, FCPx enters the following words as the value for the KeywordName ❺: One Person, Two Persons, Group, Close Up Shot, Medium Shot, or Wide Shot.

▶ **Visual Indicator**: The thumbnail of the Event Clip indicates the ClipRange for that Keyword MetadataSet with a purple line on top ❻, and its Start-End numbers displayed in the MetadataSet row ❼.

▶ **Edit**: You cannot edit the range ❼ (Start - End) of the Keyword or the keyword names ❺.

▶ **Notes**: One of the Properties of a Keyword MetadataSet is the Notes field ❽, where you can enter any kind of text that you can later search for.

▶ **Delete**: You can delete the Analysis Keyword MetadataSet by *ctr+clicking* on its row in the Browser's List View and select from the *Shortcut Menu ➤ Remove Analysis Keywords* ❾ or from the Main Menu *Mark ➤ Remove All Analysis Keywords* (*ctr+opt+0*)

Media Import Dialog

Event Clip

Name	Notes	Start	End	Duration
▼ 🎬 Beach		0.00	38.17	38.17
🖼️ Medium Shot, One Person	My Notes	22.00	32.00	10.00

➡ *Standard Keywords* 🔑

There are two ways as to how Standard Keywords are created, as "Imported Keywords" or "User-created Keywords".

🌑 Imported Keywords

Although Keywords are usually created manually by the user, there is one exception where FCPx automatically creates a Keyword MetadataSet.

> ▶ **Import**: The Media Import Dialog (*cmd+I*) and the *Preferences ➤ Import* have two checkboxes ❶ "From Finder tags" and "From folders". When enabled, FCPx creates a single Keyword MetadataSet ❷ (if data is detected), and in the KeywordName field, it adds all the Finder Tags and the enclosed Folder Names (that are found from that media file) as words or phrases, separated by commas.

> ▶ **One Keyword MetadataSet**: FCPx creates only a single MetadataSet, represented by a single row 🔑 below the Clip ❷ in the Browser's List View and all the words are added as keywords to the Name field ❸ of that MetadataSet, in this example, the folder name "*GEM Production*" and the Finder Tags "*Best*" and "*Red*".

> ▶ **Import Only**: Please note that this MetadataSet can only be created during the import, but not after the Clip has been created.

> ▶ **Duration**: Remember that a *Keyword MetadataSet* belongs to the type of metadata that applies only to a specific Clip Range instead of the entire Clip (like the *Info MetadataSet*). However, if you look at the Start and End Property ❹ of that Keyword MetadataSet in the List View, you will see that the ClipRange happens to be from the beginning to the end of the Clip, so technically it also applies to the entire Clip.

> ▶ **Blue Keyword Line**: Because the Keyword applies to the entire Clip, the blue line ❺, indicating a Standard Keyword, spans across the entire thumbnail of the Event Clip. More about that line later.

> ▶ **No indication**: There is no indication that tells you that this MetadataSet was automatically created by FCPx during the import. It has the same keyword icon ❷ 🔑 as the user-created Keywords ❻ in the Browser's List View.

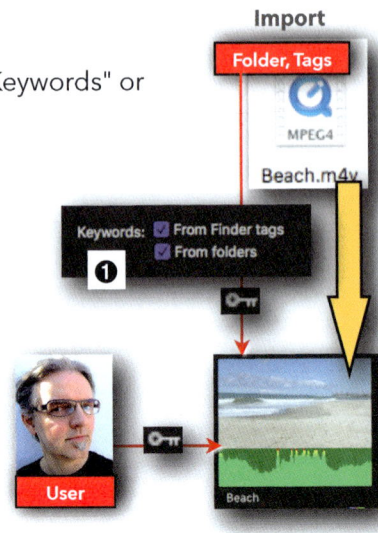

🌑 User-created Keywords

To manually create a Keyword MetadataSet, you have to follow these four steps:

> ☑ **Define the Selection**: On the thumbnail of the Event Clip, *drag* a selection.

> ☑ **Open the Keyword Editor**: Use any of the commands:
>> 🌀 *Click* on the Keyword Editor Button 🔑 in the upper left corner of the Workspace Window
>> 🌀 Key Command *cmd+K*
>> 🌀 Menu Command *Mark ➤ Show/Hide Keyword Editor*

> ☑ **Enter the Keywords**: Type the words(s) in the text field. Again, this can be a single word or phrase, or multiple words or phrases, separated by commas; In this example, *Big Wave* and an emoji 🏖 ❼. They are all added to the Name field and all apply to that ClipRange of that Keyword MetadataSet.

> ☑ **Enter**: Press *enter* and the Keyword MetadataSet is created and visible in the Browser's List View as a new row ❻ below the Clip ▼.

➡ *Keyword Editor*

Let's have a closer look at the Keyword Editor. It is such an important component in FCPx that it even has its own button ❶ in the upper-left corner of the Workspace window.

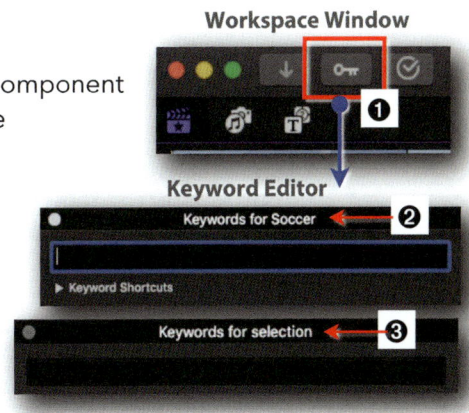
Keyword Editor

- ▸ The Keyword Editor is a floating window
- ▸ You toggle the visibility of the window with the following commands:

  - 💡 ***Click*** on the Keyword Editor Button 🔑
  - 💡 Key Command ***cmd+K***
  - 💡 Menu Command *Mark ➤ Show/Hide Keyword Editor*
  - 💡 ***Ctr+click*** on the Keyword row and select from the *Shortcut Menu ➤ Show/Hide Keyword Editor*
  - 💡 ***Double-click*** on a Keyword icon 🔑 in the Browser's List View

- ▸ Pay attention to the window title, because it displays the name of the currently selected Clip ❷, the one you are editing. If multiple Clips are selected, then the title displays "Keyword for selection" ❸.

🔘 Enter Keywords

The Text Entry box is where you type in your keywords for the currently selected Keyword MetadataSet(s), the row that is selected in the Browser's List View. This is what gets entered in the Name field of that Keyword MetadataSet.

Here is the procedure:

- ▸ **Key Focus**: Make sure the text entry box has key focus, indicated by the blue frame and blinking insert cursor ❹.
- ▸ **Single Entry**: Type in the word ("sunny") or phrases ("Big Sailing Boat") and hit ***enter*** (or the ***comma***). This will create the new Keyword MetadataSet displayed as a new row ❺ under ▼ the Clip in the Browser's List View with the word displayed in the Name field ❻.
- ▸ **Multiple Entries**: If you want to assign multiple words or phrase to that Keyword MetadataSet, then type it in the text box of the Keyword Editor next to the existing word and press ***enter*** or ***comma*** again ("Sunny, waves, ⛱, Big Sailing Boat") ❼. Every time you hit enter, the word will be added to the name field of that MetadataSet, the row in the List Browser ❽.
- ▸ **Tokens**: You notice that the entry field changes each word or phrase into a purple label once you press ***enter***. These are so-called Tokens. The Tokens automatically re-arrange when you enter multiple words or phrases to be listed alphabetically.
- ▸ **Remove Tokens**: To delete a word, you ***click*** on that token to select it (or hit ***enter*** to select all tokens) and press the ***delete*** key. You can also click next to the last Token and press ***delete***.

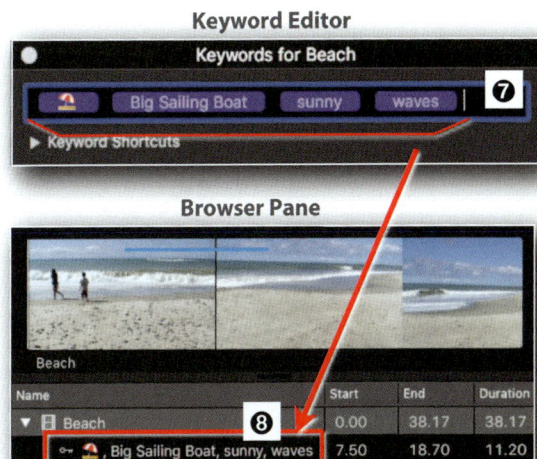
Keyword Editor / Browser Pane

🌑 Keyword Shortcuts

The Keyword Editor has an additional functionality. **Click** on the disclosure triangle ❶ 🔽 below the text entry field to extend the window and reveal the Keyword Shortcuts.

▶ **Nine Slots**: The Keyword Editor provides nine slots, representing the nine Keyword Shortcuts that let you pre-configure specific keywords you often use when organizing your Clips.

▶ **Button and Text Field**: Each slot has a text field ❷ to enter words or phrases and a button ❸ that is assigned to a Key Command (*ctr+1 ... ctr+9*), which is printed on the button.

▶ **Create Keyword Shortcuts**: You can enter words or phrases ❹ the same way as in the main text field above. The entered words are listed as purple Tokens. They are stored with FCPx and, therefore, available with any Library you have open.

▶ **Use Keyword Shortcuts**: You can assign the words or phrases of a Keyword Shortcut to a new Clip Range (or selected row, the Keyword MetadataSet) by **clicking** on their corresponding button when the Keyword Editor is open. In addition, if you remember the assignments, you can just use their Key Commands (*ctr+1 ... ctr+9*) without having the window open.

▶ **Remove Keyword Shortcuts**: To delete individual words, **click** the token and press the **delete** key.

▶ **Remove all Keywords**: The slot in the lower-right corner is a command ❺ (*ctr+0* button), a special Keyword Shortcut. It also affects the currently selected row(s), but instead of adding preconfigured words to that MetadataSet, it will remove all the existing words ❻ and, therefore, delete the entire row ❼, that individual Keyword MetadataSet (you can use the Undo command *cmd+Z*). This command is also available from the two Menu Commands:

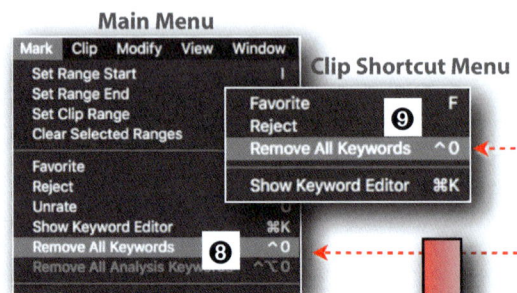

🎚 Main Menu *Mark ➤ Remove All Keywords* ❽

🎚 *Ctr+click* on the row of a Keyword MetadataSet and select from the *Shortcut Menu ➤ Remove All Keywords* ❾

🌑 Keyword Collection 🔑

For every Keyword (single word or phrase) you create on a Clip, FCPx automatically creates an individual Keyword Collection with that name ❿. These are pre-configured search queries that can be used as virtual bins. More on that later in this chapter.

➡ Create a Clip Range

The first step to create a new Keyword MetadataSet is to mark the Clip Range, a selection on the thumbnail of the Event Clip. There are quite a few commands you can use to do that:

▸ **Set Single Selection**:

- 📌 *Drag* along the thumbnail and the selection will be displayed as a yellow frame **❶**. The cursor changes to the Resize Tool 🔀 during the dragging and a little black help tag displays the length of the selection.

- 📌 You can also set the Range in real time. *Click* on the thumbnail and start the playback from that position (press the *spacebar*). Pressing the *I* key at any time will set the start of the Range at the Playhead position and pressing the *O* key will set the end position of the Range.

▸ **Adjust Single Selection**:

- 📌 Move the cursor over a left or right border of the yellow frame (the cursor changes to the Resize Tool 🔀) and *drag* it left or right.

- 📌 You can also press the *I* and *O* keys to adjust the borders to the current Playhead (or Skimmer) position (also in real time).

- 📌 *Opt+I* will set the left border to the beginning and *opt+O* will set the right border to the end of the Clip.

- 📌 You can also just redraw the selection again as long as you *drag* outside an existing yellow frame. To start the redraw inside a yellow frame, use *opt+drag*.

- 📌 Press the *X* key to select the entire Clip as the Clip Range. Now the entire Clip has a yellow frame around it.

- 📌 Press *opt+X* to remove any existing yellow frame.

▸ **Multiple Selections**:

- 📌 *Cmd+drag* lets you create additional selections (new yellow frames) without deleting any existing selections. Assigning a Keyword with the Keyword Editor (i.e. "running") will create a Keyword MetadataSet for each Range with the same keyword name **❸**. The three blue lines on the thumbnails indicate the ClipRanges **❹**.

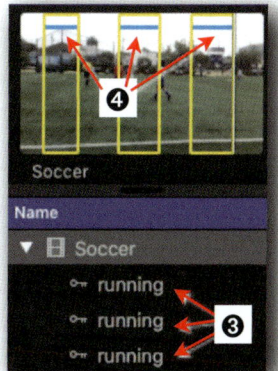

🎾 Overlapping Keywords

Please pay close attention to overlapping ClipRanges for Keywords:

▸ The first screenshot has two Keyword MetadataSets as you can see on the two rows. The first one **❺** ("running") is from 2s - 15s and the second one **❻** I created when a foul happened, with a duration of 6s - 10s.

- As you can see, Keyword ClipRanges can overlap showing the two rows with their start and stop time, but the blue line **❼** on the thumbnail shows only one combined line.

▸ Now look at the second screenshot to see what happens if you delete the Keyword "foul":

- The MetadataSet with the keyword "foul" is deleted, but the original MetadataSet ("running") is split into two MetadataSets (two rows) with the same keyword, one from 2s - 6s **❽** and the second one from 10s - 15s **❾**, leaving a gap at the position of the deleted keyword "foul", as you can see on the blue line.

Editing Keywords

You cannot edit the beginning and end position of a Keyword MetadataSet once it is created. However, you can edit individual keywords, the purple Tokens. Here is an example:

- ☑ You created a keyword "*runing*" ❶ instead of "*running*"
- ☑ ***Double-click*** on the purple token ❷
- ☑ The token changes to the standard text ❸ that you can edit
- ☑ Hit ***return*** and the word turns into a token again ❹ and is updated in the List View

Remove Keywords

When using commands for removing Keywords, you have to pay attention to what exactly is removed. For example, when you ***ctr+click*** on the Keyword row in the Browser's List View, you can select from the ***Shortcut Menu ➤ Remove all Keywords***. But remember, I discussed earlier that the term "keyword" could mean three things. Which one do you think the menu command is referring to. The **MetadataSet** represented by the row, the **Name Field** in that MetadataSet, or the **Words** in the Name Field? The correct answer is "<u>all of the above</u>". The command is deleting the complete MetadataSet, but only that single one, that row, and not any other Keywords the Clip might have.

- ▸ If you use the Main Menu Command ***Mark ➤ Remove All Keywords***, then you can select one or multiple rows in a Clip to delete them or select the Clip itself (the main row above) to delete all rows that represent Keyword MetadataSets.

- ▸ ***Double-click*** on a row and it opens the Keyword Editor with all the keywords of that MetadataSet displayed in the text entry field of the Key Editor. Now you can delete individual Keywords, the purple Tokens. Deleting the last Token, will delete the entire MetadataSet, the row.

- ▸ Please note that the Keyword Collection in the Libraries Sidebar (that we discuss later in this chapter) will not be deleted when you delete the actual Keyword metadata from a Clip.

➡ *View Options*

There are a few options you should enable when creating Keyword ClipRanges.

- ▸ **Skimming** ▦: It is a good idea to enable the Skimming feature (Key Command **S**), so when you move over the thumbnail (without clicking) you see the video in the Viewer at the current cursor position. Please note that Skimming is always enabled when you ***click-drag*** along the thumbnail.

- ▸ **Skimmer Info**: The Skimmer Info is a popover (***ctr+Y***) that appears above or below the Skimmer to display information about the current Skimmer Position. As a default, it displays the name ❺ of the Clip and current time position ❻ of the Skimmer. In addition, it displays a separate line with all the Keywords ❼ (of all MetadataSets) and another line with all the Analysis Keywords ❽ at the current Skimmer Position ❻. The info tag updates automatically when you move horizontally across the thumbnail. Toggle the Skimmer Info with the Key Command ***ctr+Y*** or from the Main Menu ***View ➤ Browser ➤ Skimmer Info*** ❾.

- ▸ **Marked Ranges**: In order to see all the colored lines for Keywords, Analysis Keywords, and other metadata indicators on the thumbnail, have the option ***View ➤ Browser ➤ Marked Ranges*** ❿ enabled (default).

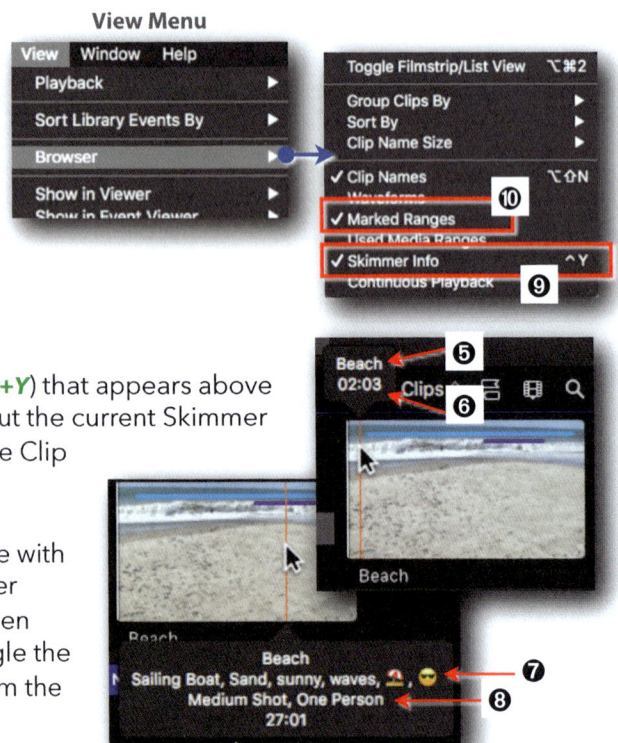

6 - Organize Clips

Ratings

Ratings are another type of metadata in FCPx. It also has a few specialties you have to be aware of, so I like to use the underlaying model I used for Keywords to show what Ratings are and how they work.

➡ *Basic Concept*

🔘 Two Ratings only

The concept of Ratings in FCPx is similar to other rating mechanisms like in iTunes or the Photos app. You select the item and grade it by giving it one star, two stars, or as many grades the ratings system allows.

Instead of allowing multiple stars/grades, FCPx only provides two grades, and instead of an amount of stars, it uses two symbols, representing the two grades like a "thumbs up" and "thumbs down" rating.

FCPx calls them Favorite ⭐ and Rejected ❌.

> Rating Types:
> ⭐ **Favorite** - ❌ **Rejected**

🔘 Rate Sections (ClipRange)

On Amazon you can also rate books, which applies to the entire book. You can't give a 5-star rating to the first two chapters but for the last 100 pages give it a 2-star rating. However, that is exactly what you can do with the Ratings feature in FCPx. Instead of rating an entire Clip, you define a section of a Clip first (the ClipRange) and apply the rating to that section. If you like that section you rate it as a Favorite ⭐ and if you don't like it, you rate it as Rejected ❌. This way, you can skim through the Event Clips and quickly mark the good sections that you might use in the edit and mark the bad sections that you might not use in the edit, because of shaky camera, or bad dialog, etc.

Similar to the sections that have keywords assigned to them and are marked with a blue line, each Ratings sections is also marked with a line on the thumbnail, this time, a green line ❶ for the Favorite ratings and a red line ❷ for the Rejected ratings. Each line represents an individual MetadataSet that is displayed as a separate row ❸ in the Browser Pane's List View below the row that represents the entire Clip ❹.

➡ Create Ratings MetadataSets

Let's look at the Ratings MetadataSet ❶ to understand the structure and functionality of the Ratings feature.

🔵 Type

The TypeField ❷ can only have one of two entries, which determines if the MetadataSet is a <u>Favorite</u> ⭐ or a <u>Rejected</u> ❌ FCPx has two separate commands, one creates a MetadataSet with the TypeField set to Favorite and another command creates a MetadataSet with the TypeField set to Rejected.

▶ **Favorite**:
> 📌 Key Command *F*
> 📌 Main Menu *Mark ➤ Favorite* ❸

▶ **Rejected**:
> 📌 Key Command *delete*
> 📌 Main Menu *Mark ➤ Reject* ❹

Attention: Three things to be aware of:

- You can change a Favorite rating to a Rejected rating and vice versa by selecting a row of that Ratings MetadataSet and use the command for Favorite ❸ or Reject ❹ or by *ctr+clicking* on the row and selecting from the *Shortcut Menu ➤ Reject* ❺ or *Shortcut Menu ➤ Favorite* ❻. The menu is context sensitive and only shows the opposite rating.

- You can even *ctr+click* on the row of a Keyword MetadataSet and choose either *Favorite* or *Reject* ❼ and FCPx will create a new Ratings MetadataSet (a new row) with the same ClipRange.

- Please note that you can search later for all the Clips that have a Favorite or Rejected rating. More about that later in this chapter.

Main Menu / Shortcut Menu

🔵 Name

FCPx automatically enters a name for the MetadataSet, which is either "Favorite" or "Rejected" ❽ depending on which type you created.

▶ **Rename**: You can rename "Favorite" or "Rejected" to any other name, which is a good idea, because you can search for that text later. Select the row, press *enter* (so the name will be highlighted ❾), type the new name and press *enter* again.

Attention: Two things to be aware of:

- If you use any command to create or change the rating, then FCPx will overwrite your custom name to "Favorite" or "Rejected" again.

- You can also search for the text in the Name field.

🔵 Notes

You can also add some comments in the Notes field ❿ that you can search for.

🔵 Start - Stop - Duration

These three fields show the Start, End, and Duration ⓫ of the ClipRange for that rating. They are read only and cannot be edited.

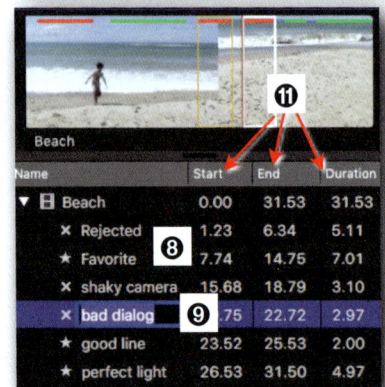

⚫ Remove Ratings

You don't use the delete key to remove Ratings, instead, it has its own command (using two different terms!):

- 📌 Select one or multiple rows of a Ratings MetadataSet and choose the Menu Command *Mark ➤ Unrate* ❶
- 📌 Select one or multiple rows of a Ratings MetadataSet and choose the Key Command *U*
- 📌 *Ctr+click* on a Favorite or Reject row and choose from the *Shortcut Menu ➤ Unmark* ❷

Main Menu

Mark	Clip	Modify	View	Window
Set Range Start				I
Set Range End				O
Set Clip Range				X
Clear Selected Ranges				⌥X
Favorite				F
Reject				⌫
Unrate ❶				U
Show Keyword Editor				⌘K

⚫ No Overlap

Unlike Keywords, Ratings can't overlap, which makes sense. Either a section is good (Favorite) or bad (Rejected), or undecided if you don't assign any Ratings at all.

Shortcut Menu

Reject		Favorite		F
Unmark ❷	U	Unmark ❷		U
Remove All Keywords	^0	Remove All Keywords		^0
Show Keyword Editor	⌘K	Show Keyword Editor		⌘K

Here is an example with two ClipRanges marked as Favorite, which is indicated by the two green lines ❸. Now I drag a new selection that overlaps the first line ❹ and the second line ❺.

- ▶ **Option 1** ⭐: If I assign a Favorite (*F*) to that new selection, then the two original ClipRanges are merged together into one single Favorite Rating. Look what happened to the MetadataSet, the row. The two ratings that I have named ❼, "Big Waves" and "Seagulls", are merged into a single MetadataSet, one row, with the generic name "Favorite" ❽.

- ▶ **Option 2** ❎: If I assign a Rejected Rating (*delete*) to the new section, then a new Rejected MetadataSet for that ClipRange is created (a new row ❾), indicated by the new red line ❿ and the two existing Ratings remain, but trimmed accordingly.

⚫ Event Clips Only

When you move an Event Clip or the Project Timeline, then that new Timeline Clip will not inherit the Ratings metadata. They only have a functionality in the Browser Pane for organizing and selecting Clips.

Markers

Four Types of Markers

- Standard Marker
- Notes Marker (To Do)
- Notes Marker (Completed)
- Chapter Marker

Markers are another type of metadata that also creates a set of metadata, let's call it "*Marker MetadataSet*". It's main difference compared to Keyword and Ratings MetadataSets, it marks only one time position on the Clip instead of a section, a ClipRange.

You can use those Markers for all kinds of purposes. For example, mark a specific spot on the Clip (and add notes and instructions to it) that you can easily search for later. Mark spots for synchronizations (door slams) or use them to create chapters that are carried over to your exported file (QuickTIme, Podcast, DVD, etc.).

➡ Overview

Here are some basic characteristics about Markers:

- ▶ **Type Field ❶**: FCPx provides four types of Markers
  - • Standard Marker
  - • To Do Marker
  - • Completed Marker
  - • Chapter Marker (Timeline Clips only)
- ▶ **Name Field ❷**: Whenever you create new Markers, regardless what type, FCPx automatically names them sequentially Marker 1, Marker 2, etc. ❸. You can rename them (select the row, press enter, type, press enter) and later, search for that name or phrase.
- ▶ **Indicator**: The four Marker types have individually colored indicators on top of the thumbnail of the Clip ❹ 🔖🔖🔖🔖. The rows ❸ (representing the Marker MetadataSet) in the Browser Panes's List View (and the Timeline Index on the Timeline Pane) display icons 🔖📄✅🔖 in front of the name, which are different from the colored icons on the Clip.
- ▶ **Notes**: You can enter comments in the Notes field ❺ that you can search for later.
- ▶ **Start - End - Duration Field**: Although Markers define only a single position on the Clip, its MetadataSet still has the three fields, Start - End - Duration, because technically, that one position is actually a ClipRange with a duration of 1 frame ❻.
- ▶ **Convert Markers**: You can change the value of the Type Field of a Marker MetadataSet, which means, changing, for example, a Standard Marker to a To-Do Marker, or a To-Do Marker to a Completed Marker while keeping the other values.
- ▶ **Multiple Markers**: You can create as many Markers as you want as long as they are placed on a different position along the Clip.
- ▶ **Event Clip ➤ Timeline Clip**: Markers, like Keywords, will be copied over with a Clip when you *drag* an Event Clip to the Project Timeline and it becomes a Timeline Clip.
- ▶ **Timeline Clips**: Unlike Keywords, new Markers can also be created on Timeline Clips.
- ▶ **Chapter Markers**: The fourth Marker type, Chapter Marker 🔖, can only be created on a Timeline Clip and not on an Event Clip in the Browser Pane.

Marker MetadataSet

Type	🔖📄✅🔖	❶
Name	Marker 1	❷
Notes	First Wave	❺
Start	1:00:20:15	
End	1:00:20:16	
Duration	0:00:00:01	❻

Beach

Name		Start	End	Duration
▼ 🗄 Beach		0.00	31.53	31.53
	🔖 Marker 1	5.51	5.54	0.03
	📄 Marker 2	12.45	12.48	0.03
	✅ Marker 3	20.32	20.35	0.03

❸

➡️ *Create/Manage Markers*

A variety of commands lets you manage Markers through Key Commands, Main Menus and Shortcut Menus:

▶ **Create**: A Marker will always be created at the current Playhead/Skimmer position in Stop or Play mode, on the Event Clip in the Libraries Browser or on a Timeline Clip in the Timeline. This creates a purple Standard Marker ❶ 🔖 on the thumbnail and a new row ❷ (the MetadataSet) in the List View.

- 🔘 Key Command *M*
- 🔘 Menu Command ❸ *Mark ➤ Markers ➤ Add Marker*

▶ **Create with Marker Window**: This command creates the Marker and automatically opens the Marker Window ❹, so you can enter a name right away ❺, choose a different type ❻ of Marker and also delete the Marker.

- 🔘 Key Command *opt+M*
- 🔘 Menu Command *Mark ➤ Markers ➤ Add Marker and Modify*

▶ **Modify**: The Modify command opens the Marker Window ❹.

- 🔘 *Click* on the Marker, either on the Clip ❶ or in the List ❷ (this will move the Playhead to that position), and use the Key Command *sh+M*, or Menu Command *Mark ➤ Markers ➤ Modify Marker*
- 🔘 *Double-click* the Marker on the Clip ❶
- 🔘 *Ctr+click* on a Marker (on the Clip or the List) and choose from the *Shortcut Menu ➤ Modify Marker* ❼

▶ **Name**: You can rename a Marker directly in the List View ❽. Select the row, press *enter*, type the name, and hit enter *again*. Or you can enter it in the Marker Window ❺.

▶ **Delete**: You can delete a single Marker (or all the Markers in a selection) by selecting them and then use any of the following commands:

- 🔘 Key Command *ctr+M* (*sh+ctr+M*)
- 🔘 Menu Command ❸ *Mark ➤ Markers ➤ Delete Marker* (*Delete Markers in Selection*)
- 🔘 *Ctr+click* the Marker ❼ (on the thumbnail or the List) and select from the *Shortcut Menu ➤ Delete Marker*
- 🔘 Open the Marker Window for a Clip and *click* on the Delete ❾ button

▶ **Nudge**: You can nudge a selected (or multiple selected) Markers left or right by 1 frame (or 1 subframe for audio only Clips).

- 🔘 Key Command *ctr+,* or *ctr+.*
- 🔘 Main Menu ❸ *Mark ➤ Nudge Marker Left/Right*

▶ **Copy/Cut-Paste**: If you have named a Marker and don't want to repeatedly do that for a series of Markers, you can just copy-paste Markers.

- 🔘 *Ctr+click* on a Marker in the List View or directly on the thumbnail of the Clip and select from the *Shortcut Menu ➤ Cut/Copy Marker* ❼. Now use the Playhead or Skimmer to position it on the thumbnail and use the standard Key Command *cmd+V* to paste a New Marker there. You can quickly paste the same Marker at different positions by simply move the Playhead or Skimmer and press *cmd+V* again

▶ **Move**: You cannot move a Marker to a new position (besides the Nudge command), but the Cut-Paste procedure will do the trick.

➡ *Marker Window*

Now let's have a closer look at that Marker Window. It is a popover window with its typical "anchor" ❶ (the arrow) pointing at the Marker it is referring to.

- ▶ **Marker Type ❷**: The three tabs on top of the window let you choose the Marker Type.

  - Standard Marker ▢: This selection creates a Standard Marker with a purple indicator on the thumbnail of the Clip and this icon ▢ in the List.

  - To Do Marker ▢: This selection creates a To Do Marker with a red indicator ▢ on the thumbnail of the Clip and this icon ▢ in the List.

  - Chapter Marker ▢: Chapter Markers are only available for Timeline Clips and, therefore, the Chapter Marker Button is grayed out.

- ▶ **To Do - Complete**: The checkbox "Completed" is only visible if a To Do Marker ❸ is selected.

  ☐ Completed ❹ :The Marker is a "To Do" Marker with the red Marker ▢ on the thumbnail and this icon in the List View ▢.

  ☑ Completed ❺ :The Marker is a "Completed" Marker with the green Marker ▢ on the thumbnail and this icon in the List View ▢.

- ▶ **Name ❻**: FCPx automatically enters a default name for all Markers (Marker 1, Marker 2, etc.). When you open the Marker Window for a Marker with a default name, then the name will be selected, so you can type your custom name right away. When opening the Marker Window for a Marker that already has a custom name, then the name will not be selected. The text field will have key focus with the insertion point blinking at the end of the name. Please note that you can search for Marker names.

- ▶ **Position ❼**: The SMPTE time location of the marker is just a read-only display. You have to use the Nudge command or cut/paste if you want to move an existing Marker.

- ▶ **Delete ❽**: *Click* this button to delete this Marker.

➡ Marker Conversion

Besides the different types of Marker Icons, there is one place that could cause confusion and that is the Shortcut Menu that opens when you **ctr+click** on a Marker, either on the Clip's thumbnail or its row in the List View.

Pay attention to the two menu items in the middle, "To Do" and "Completed". Their appearance is context sensitive. It changes depending on what Marker you clicked. You also have to know what happens when you click on any of the two menu items.

- ▸ You ctr+clicked on a Standard Marker 🔖 and this is what you see ❶:
    - ◉ *Clicking* on "To Do" will change it to a To Do Marker 🔲.

- ▸ You ctr+clicked on a To Do Marker 🔲, indicated by the checkmark and this is what you see ❷. Now you have two options:
    - ◉ *Clicking* on "To Do" will uncheck it and change it back to a Standard Marker 🔖.
    - ◉ *Clicking* on "Complete" will enable (check) that option, which means it turns into a Completed Marker ☑.

- ▸ You ctr+clicked on a Completed Marker ☑, indicated by both checkmarks and this is what you see ❸. Now you have these two options:
    - ◉ *Clicking* on "To Do" will uncheck both (!) and change it back to a Standard Marker 🔖.
    - ◉ *Clicking* on "Complete" will only uncheck that option, which means it turns it back to a To Do Marker 🔲.

Makes sense? It might be easier just to open the Marker Window and use the controls there.

➡ Markers on Timeline Clips

Although, in this Organize Clips chapter, we only focus on the Browser Pane and its Event Clips, I will briefly go over topics about the Markers in the Timeline Pane.

◉ Timeline Clips

A few things about the Markers and the Timeline Clips:

- ▸ When you add ❹ an Event Clip to the Project Timeline, it becomes an independent Timeline Clip which inherits all the Markers ❺ (the Marker MetadataSets).

- ▸ You can edit those inherited Markers (which are now metadata of the Timeline Clip), convert them, rename them, or delete them.

- ▸ The Marker Window functions the same way for Markers on a Timeline Clip.

- ▸ In addition, now you can also create Chapter Markers ❻ 🔖 on Timeline Clips, which are not available for Event Clips.

Timeline Index

The Timeline Index has a few specialties about the Markers:

▶ Select the *Tags* tab ❶ to view all the Markers and Keywords metadata of all Clips in the currently displayed Timeline.

▶ The Filter Buttons ❷ at the bottom let you display only one type of Marker ▼ ▣ ▣ ▮ (or Keywords ⊙ 🖾).

▶ The icons for the To Do Marker ▣ and Completed Marker ▣ in the Timeline Index function as active buttons ❹. *Click* on them to toggle the Marker between ▣ and ▣. It will change the Marker on the Timeline Clip accordingly between "To Do" ▼ and "Completed" ▼.

▶ Markers (and Keywords) can have comments entered in their Notes field. Those notes are inherited by the Timeline Clip from the Event Clip and you can edit them in the Timeline Index or add new comments ❺. You can even search for those entries with the Search field ❻ in the Timeline Index .

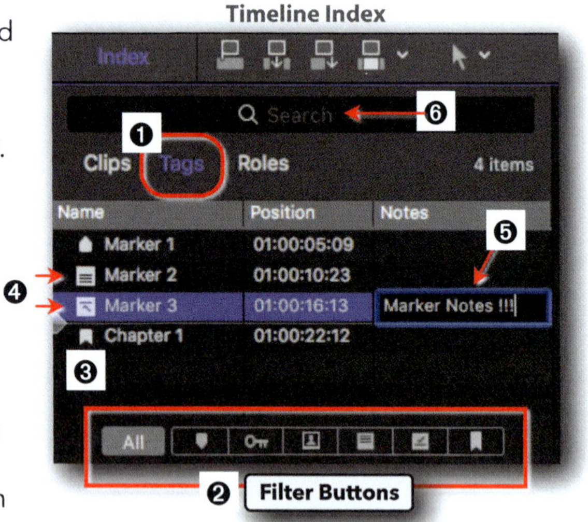

Timeline Index

Chapter Markers

Here are the details about the special Chapter Markers:

▶ Chapter Markers can only be created on Timeline Clips.

▶ Chapter Markers are mainly used when exporting your Timeline Project, because you can embed them with the exported video. A checkbox ❼ in the Settings of the Share Dialog determines if the Chapter Markers are included in the exported video.

▶ Embedded Chapter Markers are supported by a wide variety of applications (Quicktime, iTunes, DVD Player) and devices (iDevices, DVD players). They are embedded as metadata in mp4, m4v, and mov export formats. Use them as chapters in a quicktime movie, chapters for podcasts, and even chapters used in Compressor for encoding purposes. Chapter Markers can also be used for subtitles when exporting a project to DVD or Blu-ray.

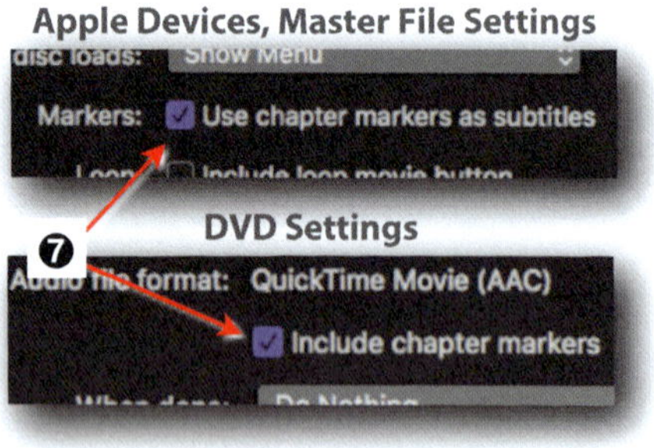

▶ When selecting a Chapter Marker ❽ on the Timeline Clip, an attached Poster Frame pin (Chapter Marker Thumbnail ❾) will be displayed. You can drag that orange pin left or right to position it on a frame. This frame becomes the Poster Frame that is displayed later on the QuickTime video or DVD as the Marker reference in the QuickTime movie.

▶ The default position of the Chapter Marker Thumbnail is 11 frames next to the Marker but you can *drag* the pin left and right to choose any frame. The Viewer will display the frame of the pin position when dragging. You can *drag* the pin anywhere from the beginning to the end of the Primary Storyline. If the Marker is on a Connected Storyline, then you can move the pin between the beginning and end of that storyline.

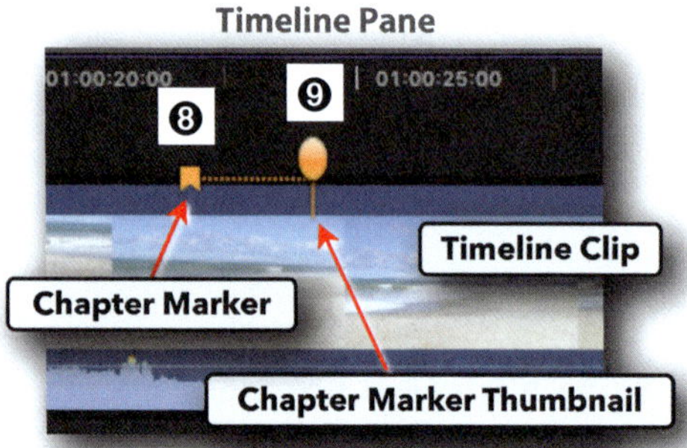

Apple Devices, Master File Settings

Timeline Pane

Share Attributes

Share Attributes are another collection of metadata (a MetadataSet ❶), but they function a little bit different than the MetadataSets for Keywords, Ratings, and Markers.

➡ *Concept*

🌐 Database Structure

The best way to understand what Share Attributes are and how they work is to think of them in terms of metadata stored in a database, the way we explored Keywords, Ratings, and Markers.

- ▶ **20 Properties (Attributes) ❷**: "Share Attributes" is a MetadataSet with 20 Properties (or database fields), here they are called Attributes.

- ▶ **Event Clips and Projects**: Unlike with the other MetadataSets (Keywords, Ratings, Markers) that you have to create manually for a Clip, the Share MetadataSet is by default part of each Event Clip and Project.

- ▶ **View MetadataSet**: To view (and edit) the MetadataSet, select the Event Clip or Project in the Browser Pane and *click* on the Share tab ❸ 🔽 in the Inspector. This will switch its view to the Share Inspector.

- ▶ **Value Pairs**: Similar to the Info Inspector, the Properties (Attributes) of the MetadataSet are displayed as a list with two columns. The left column shows the AttributeName ❹ (the label) and the right column shows the corresponding AttributeValue ❺.

🌐 Functionality

Here is how you use the Share Attributes:

- ▶ **Export Embedded Metadata (Attributes)**: Think about the Tracks in your iTunes Library, which have embedded metadata. For example, Artist Name, Genre, Composer, Comment, etc. This is what FCPx calls the Attributes (Properties in the Share MetadataSet). FCPx can embed those Attributes in the new video file that is created when you export (FCPx calls this "Share") an Event Clip or a Project. For Example, when you export your Project and share that media file to a social media site, then those embedded Attributes will be keywords that users can search for.

- ▶ **Global Configuration - Show/Hide Attributes**: You can configure which Attributes you want to embed. If you don't need all 20, then select the ones you want. This is a global setting and applies to all exports in FCPx.

- ▶ **Individual Configuration - Enter AttributeValues**: The second element you can pre-configure is the actual value of each Attribute. FCPx utilizes Tokens, the same concept used in the Keyword Editor. They function as variables (placeholders), that look up the actual value during the export when the Attribute is being created. Most Attributes already have a default Token ❻. For example, the logged-in user is entered as the Creator and Producer, and the name of the Project or Event Clip is entered as the Title, etc. A special dialog, the "*Edit Share Fields Dialog*", lets you change the pre-configuration.

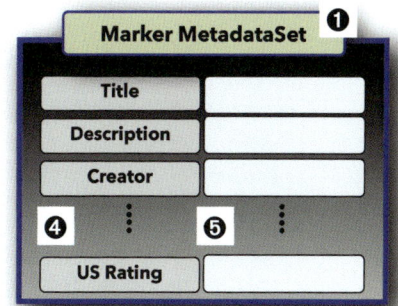

➡ Manage Share Attributes

Here are the three windows that you use to manage Share Attributes

🏆 Share Inspector

The Share Inspector lets you perform three tasks:

▶ **Show/Hide Attributes**: *Click* on the arrow button ❶ 🔽 in the upper-right corner to open a popup menu with various commands that determine what Attributes are displayed in the Share Inspector:

- ❷ Select "*Show All Fields*" to display all 20 Attribute Fields or select "*Show Default Fields*" to display only the first four (grayed out) Fields.

- ❸ *Click* on any Attribute to toggle its state between shown (☑) and hidden.

- ❹ Select the command "*Save as Default*" to save the current set of Attributes. You can later recall that default set with the command "*Update to Default*".

▶ **Enter AttributesValues ❺**: Some Fields already have a value (a Token). You can enter a new word or word phrase into the fields. You can also enter the name of one of the Tokens. If FCPx recognizes the phrase, it creates that Token.

▶ **Pre-configure AttributeValues ❻**: The command "Edit Share Fields" at the bottom of the popup menu opens that dialog.

🏆 Edit Share Fields Dialog

This dialog displays all the 20 Attribute Fields in the left Sidebar ❼ and when you select one, the Browser on the right ❽ lets you pre-configure that Attribute value. These are the default values that are displayed in the Share Inspector ❺ and also in the Share Dialog ❿.

▶ **Format**: This is the text field for the Attribute that is selected in the Sidebar.

▶ **Example**: This "translates" the token and displays the actual Text that will be embedded for that Attribute.

▶ **Token**: There are 18 Tokens divided into three groups (Info, Date/Time, US Rating). Just *drag* them to the Format text field. These 18 Tokens are pre-defined and cannot be changed.

▶ **Custom Name**: This is the only token that can be defined by the user. Just enter the word or word phrase what the "Custom Name" Token should represent.

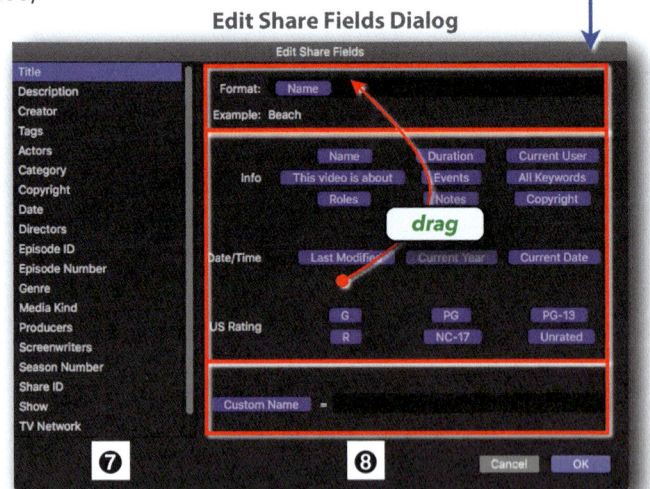

🏆 Share Dialog: Info Tab

When selecting a Destination to share ❾ an Event Clip or a Project, the Share Dialog will open. When selecting the Info tab ❿, all the Attributes are listed with their assigned values based on the Tokens. You still can edit the values before starting the export process.

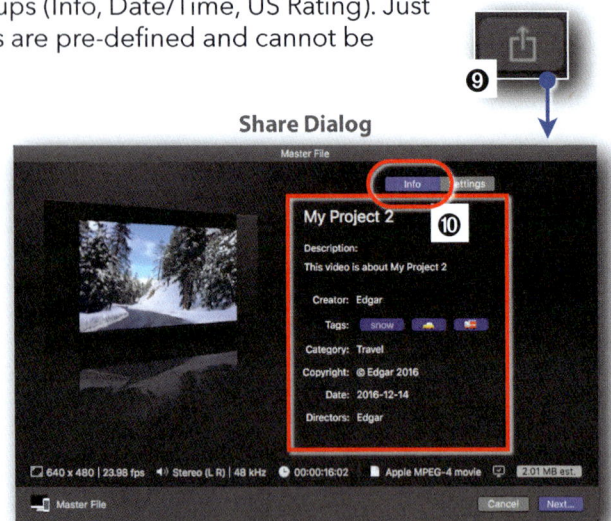

Share Inspector

Edit Share Fields Dialog

Share Dialog

Basics

So far in this chapter, we learned all the procedures on how to add various metadata to our Event Clips. However, this is only half the story of our organizational procedure. Marking Clips or sections of a Clip and labeling them helps us only if we look at the individual labels to find the ones we are looking for. This is the old "analog" way of doing things. But now, with all the labels in the digital form as metadata, we can utilize powerful search procedures in FCPx to find the right Clips.

➡ *Search*

Here is a diagram that shows the "digital mindset" you need when working in FCPx. On one side, you fill the database ❶ with metadata, and later, you use filter/search techniques ❷ to "unleash the amazing power" of the system, using our "digital mindset".

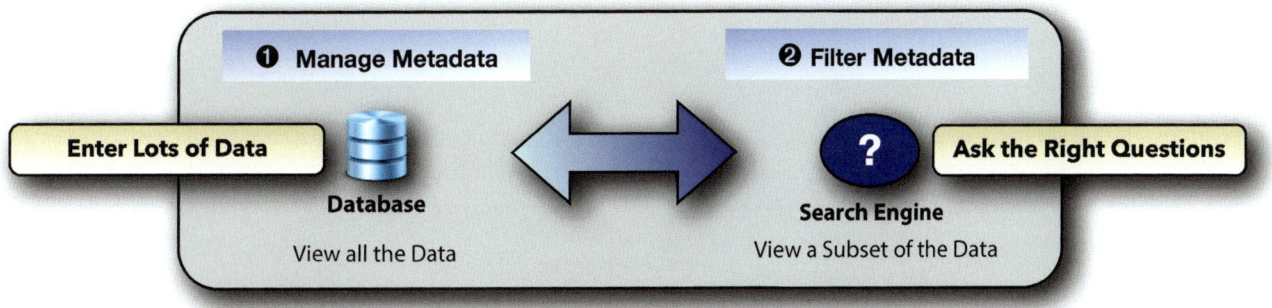

🔵 Manage Metadata

As we know from Google experience, a search engine is only as good as the available datasets. In other words, the more available data and descriptions, the better the search results will be. In FCPx, that is your first task: <u>Enter lots of Metadata</u>.

🔵 Filter Metadata

But even with all the available data on the Internet, people can't find what they are looking for. The reason for this is that they often don't know how to properly search for it.

The same applies to FCPx, the art of searching, and that is what we will discuss in this section "<u>Ask the right questions</u>".

It sounds simple, but this is where many FCPx users might have a problem initially.

If you organize your own files, then the only thing you have to do is to remember where you put those files. If you are dealing with databases to organize your things (by entering locations, descriptions, and all that metadata), then you have to train yourself to think in terms of database queries. You must learn how to "ask those questions" in the form of logical queries. This is the crucial element in FCPx. Yes, FCPx doesn't have traditional bins and the ability to organize your things the old fashion way, but in order to use FCPx, you have to embrace (learn and master) the new thinking in order to fully use the underlying power of database file management in FCPx.

Filter Event Clips

Let's look at the difference between two simple words "Find" and "Filter" and why it is relevant to differentiate between them when it comes to Metadata.

▶ **Find**: This is a very generic term. Mainly, it is used when looking for an object or objects.

▶ **Filter**: This is a more specific term in the context of search.

➡ *Find vs. Filter*

When you enter the Find command in FCPx (*cmd+F*), a window pops up that is called "Filter". You might think "Find" and "Filter" have the same first letter, they are kind of the same thing so not a big deal. However, it is a big deal that *cmd+F* brings up a "Filter window" and not a "Find window".

- With Find, you are looking for one or multiple objects in some defined space, for example, your living room, your garden, or your pdf file.
- With Filter, the space you are searching is a database, i.e. the Event Database with all your 200 imported Clips. When you work in FCPx and you search for Clips that have a 2-person close-up in it, you are filtering the database. You say to FCPx: "*Please Mrs. Event database, instead of displaying all 200 Event Clips in the Libraries Browser, display only the Clips that have a 2-person close-up in it.*" As a result, you are still looking at the Libraries Browser (database), but now only 15 Event Clips might be displayed. These 15 Clips are filtered out of the 200 available Clips.

🔮 The Difference

▶ In **Find**, when you can't get a result, you <u>extend the space</u> you are searching while keeping the search criteria (car keys not found in the kitchen, let's look in the bathroom).

▶ With **Filter**, you stay in the <u>same space</u> (the database), but you change the search criteria.

Database (Event)

❶ All Clips
❷ Clips that match **Metadata A**
❸ Clips that match **Metadata A+B**
❹ Clips that match **Metadata A+B+C**

This model shows how the filter process works regarding the database.

❶ You are looking at the entire database that has a record for each of your Clips (no filter applied). The Libraries Browser displays all the Clips.

❷ You filter out Clips that match a specific **Metadata A** (Camera "X"): The Libraries Browser now displays a subset, only Clips from Camera X.

❸ From that subset, you filter out the Clips that match **Metadata B** (date "July"): The Libraries Browser now displays only Clips that were shot on Camera "X" on the date "July".

❹ From that subset, you filter out the Clips that match **Metadata C** (Keyword "good"): The Libraries Browser now displays only Clips that were shot on Camera "X" on the date "July" with a keyword "good".

The previous example had three applied filters. Every time you apply another filter, the group that matches that criteria gets smaller or there are no matches at all. The order of the filter doesn't matter (A+B+C, or C+A+B). Just think for a moment how that applies to the daily workflow in FCPx and you will realize the potential power versus the limitation of a conventional file organization system where you create your own folders (bins) structure manually.

Here is an example: You are shooting with three cameras (X, Y, Z) on three days (a, b, c).

▶ **Manual Organization**: Once you imported the files, you might organize the Clips by camera and date and create two extra bins to place the good and bad takes in.

▶ **Metadata Organization**: You apply Metadata to each Clip. FCPx applies the Metadata for Camera and Data automatically because it comes from the Camera. You only have to apply the Ratings Metadata to tag the Clips as the good or bad takes.

Camera X		
Date a	Date b	Date c
good	good	good
bad	bad	bad

Camera Y		
Date a	Date b	Date c
good	good	good
bad	bad	bad

Camera Z		
Date a	Date b	Date c
good	good	good
bad	bad	bad

Doing the FCPx Metadata prep work might save you time in comparison with older FCP organizational schemes. No need to create bin structures and move files around. But the real advantage kicks in when you are looking/searching for Clips:

Here is what you have to do with a fixed bin structure:

☑ Screening all good takes from Date a requires you to look in three bins.

☑ Screening all takes from Date a requires you to look in six bins.

☑ Screening all good takes requires you to look in nine bins.

A Metadata based solution is quite different:

☑ You always look at one "bin", the Libraries Browser (database).

☑ Any possible scenario that you might be looking for is just a combination of filters applied to the Libraries Browser.

☑ Recurring searches can be saved for quick retrieval. Those little macros are called "Collections" ❶ (like virtual bins).

As you can see, the key to success when dealing with Metadata is:

• Have as much Metadata as possible -
Manage Metadata ❷

• Ask the right questions -
Filter Metadata ❸

Libraries Browser

Name	Rating	Date	Notes	❷
Clips	****	5-10	funny	
Clips	*	5-10	good	
Clips	****	5-11	funny	
Clips	****	5-11	Forget .	
Clips	*	6-03..	Better..	
Clips	****	6-03	Much b	

❸

?? Apply Metadata Filter

❶

Collection

Think about it, without Google having those huge data sets, you couldn't find anything. On the other hand, all that data wouldn't be useful if you didn't know how to construct a proper search query (from a simple to a complex search string).

➡ *Filter Event Clips*

The main area where you use the Metadata filter technique is in the Browser Pane. This is where you organize the Clips by applying useful Metadata and then hopefully find the right Clip(s) through metadata filtering to be used in the Timeline Project.

Now that we know that we always look at the same database(s), just through "filtered glasses", the next important fact to keep in mind is that the different Filters are **always active** (independent for each Event)!

> **Always be aware of filters, always keep an eye on them!**

These are the different filter areas:

▶ **❶ Event** ⬛: First, which Event (database) is selected in the Libraries Sidebar? Please note that you can select multiple Events, which means that you can search in multiple databases at the same time.

▶ **❷ Collections** 🔑 ⚙: The Keyword Collections and Smart Collection are listed in the Libraries Sidebar below the Events or inside nested Folders. You can select multiple Collections. More about Collections in a moment.

▶ **❸ Clip Filtering**: This popup menu in the header of the Browser Pane provides six different filter settings.

```
✓ All Clips
  Hide Rejected
  No Ratings or Keywords
  Favorites
  Rejected
  Unused
```

▶ **❹ Search/Filter** 🔍: This is the most powerful filter tool. It is linked to the Filter window that might be closed, but its content is always active. The search field (toggle it with the magnifying glass button) displays Metadata icons to indicate any filters that are currently active.

You can also search for a text string. For example, if you rename a Favorite Marker "funny quote", then you could enter the word "funny quote" in the search field and that Clip (and any other clip containing the phrase "funny quote") would be filtered out and displayed in the Libraries Browser.

▶ **❺ Clip** 🎬: The displayed Clips in the Libraries Browser are the result of all the applied filters above (1 - 4).

▶ **❻ ClipRange (Metadata)** 🔑: If a Clip has ClipRanges defined by any of the MetadataSets (indicated by a disclosure triangle ▼), then you can select any of those rows to display that section of the Clip (that ClipRange).

Here is a screenshot of the Browser Pane that shows the sections of the six filter elements you have to keep an eye on. Whatever element 1-4 you selected or made filter settings, only those Clips and related ClipRanges are displayed in the Libraries Browser based on the search/filter configuration.

Again, please keep in mind that filtering in FCPx is not one long search string that you have to rewrite every time you want to change one search criteria. Instead, each filter element (1-4) is independent and you can change one without changing the others just to modify the search result.

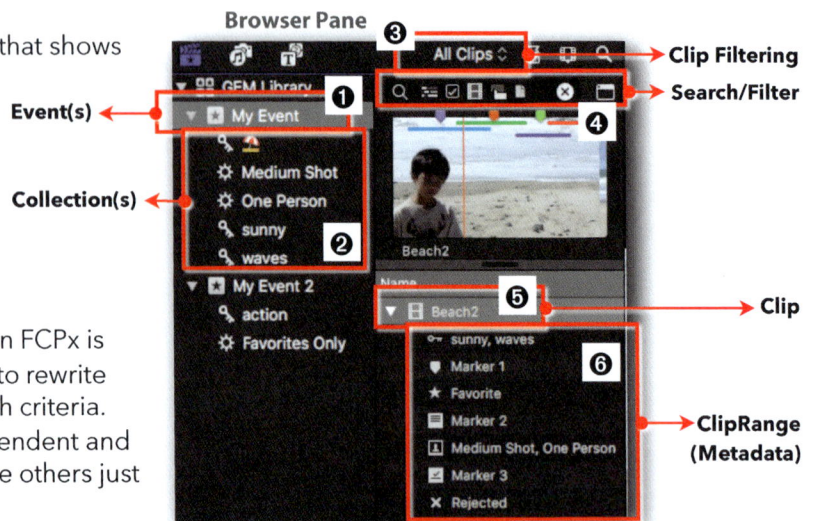

Clip Filtering

The Clip Filtering feature is not just a simple selection from the popup menu to tell FCPx which Clips to show and which ones to hide. This is the first example that demonstrates the power of metadata combined with search queries that enables you to organize and review your Clips in a way that is not possible with the old-fashion bins.

➡ Overview

Here is the basic concept:

▸ The area with the double arrow ❶ ⬍ in the Browser Pane header displays what is currently selected in the popup menu ❷. Always keep an eye on that one.

▸ The default selection is "All Clips", and if another option is displayed in the header, it means that you might see only a (filtered) subset of your Clips in the Browser.

▸ *Click* on the double arrow ⬍ to open the popup menu and select any of the six options.

The selected option will change not only **what** is displayed in the Browser (match or no match), but also **how** it is displayed. This is something you fully have to understand in order to use it.

➡ Clip Filtering Options

I will introduce the six options in a different order than they are listed in the popup menu to demonstrate the functionality of the Clip Filtering step-by-step.

⬤ All Clips

"All Clips" is the default setting. However, you still won't see all Clips if you've enabled any other filter options (i.e. in the Filter Window). So "All Clips" only refers to this filter element, meaning, "*Clip Filtering is off*".

⬤ Unused

"Unused" mans "*not used in any Project of this Library*". Please note that this means not only "the entire Clip was not used", but also if there are any sections of a Clip that weren't used, if you used only a ClipRange. Look at the following example:

▸ **All Clips**: The Browser with no filter ("All Clips" ❸) shows the Clip "Beach" ❹ with a length of 38s. The ClipRange marked as "Used" is from 8s - 17s ❺, indicated by a white frame ❻.

▸ **Unused** ❼: Now the Browser shows two (!) Beach Clips, but if you look at the Start-End times, you see that the first Clip is from 0s - 8s and the second Clip is from 17s - 38s. FCPx automatically created two virtual Subclips, one for the section before ❾ the used ClipRange and one for the section after ❿. These virtual Subclips are based on the search criteria "Filter the unused", or in other words, "*Show only the footage (ClipRanges) that have not been used in the Project*". There is no other indication besides the filter setting ❼ that these two Clips you are seeing are Subclips ❾ and not the original full-length Clip ❹.

Example

For the other four Clip Filtering options I will use the same Beach Clip (Clip Filtering set to "All Clips" ❶), but now I marked it with five Ratings Metadata. Two ClipRanges with Favorite ⭐ and three ClipRange with Rejected ❌. You will see on the first screenshot the Main Clip "Beach" ❷ and the five metadata-based ClipRanges underneath as five additional rows ❸. The Clip thumbnail shows the two green and three red lines ❹. On the second screenshot I just selected all the five rows for the ClipRanges, so you can see the white frames ❺, indicating the sections on the Clip. Please pay attention to those sections in order to understand what happens next when we apply the various Clip Filtering options.

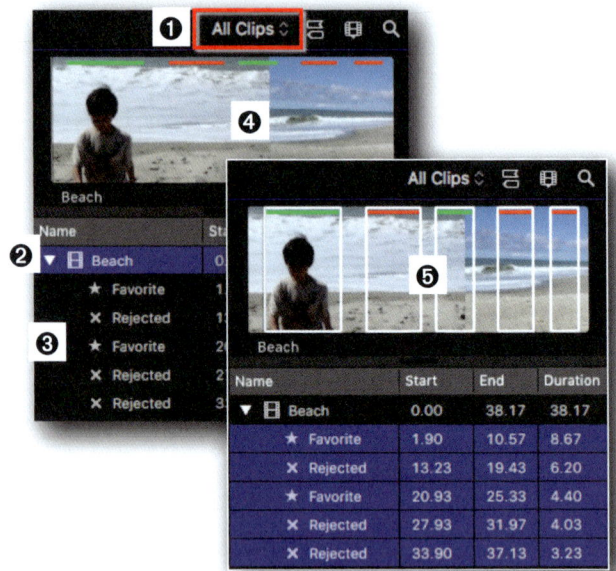

🌑 Favorites

When I select "Favorites" ❻ from the Clip Filtering popup menu, FCPx again changes the display in the Browser and shows virtual Subclips based on the filter selection.

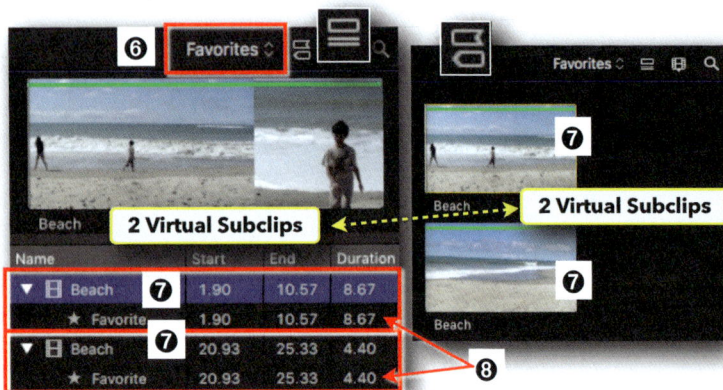

Because we had two ClipRanges marked as Favorite, FCPx shows these two ClipRanges as Clips ❼ 🎞, but they are, again, virtual Subclips. Just refer to the Start-End values, they match exactly the Start-End values of the two Favorite ❸ rows ⭐ when filtering was set to *All Clips*.

These two virtual Subclips also display the additional row ❽ for the Favorite metadata inside ⭐, matching the same length. The green line also spans the entire Subclip.

🌑 Rejected

When I select "Rejected" ❾ from the Clip Filtering, then the filtering process happens accordingly.

Because we had three ClipRanges marked as Rejected, FCPx shows these three ClipRanges as Clips ❿ 🎞, which are again virtual Subclips. Refer to the Start-End values, they match exactly the Start-End values of the three Rejected rows ❸ ⭐ when filtering was set to All Clips.

These three virtual Subclips also display the additional row for the Rejected metadata inside ❌, matching the same length. The red line also spans the entire Subclip.

🕱 Hide Rejected

The outcome when selecting "Hide Rejected" ❶ is a little bit more tricky. FCPx shows four Clips 🎞 with the same name "Beach", and yes you guessed it, these are four virtual Subclips ❷ that FCPx created based on the metadata in the original "Beach" Clip ❸. Look at that Clip again with the three red Rejected ClipRanges ❹ ❺ ❻ and follow how FCPx creates those individual Subclips:

- Subclip #1: From the beginning of the Clip Beach up to the beginning of the first Rejected ClipRange ❹: 0-13.
- Subclip #2: From the end of the 1st Rejected ClipRange ❹ to the beginning of the 2nd Rejected ClipRange ❺:19-27.
- Subclip #3: From the end of the 2nd Rejected ClipRange ❺ to the beginning of the 3rd Rejected ClipRange ❻: 31-33.
- Subclip #4: From the end of the 3rd Rejected ClipRange ❻ to the end of the Clip: 37-38.

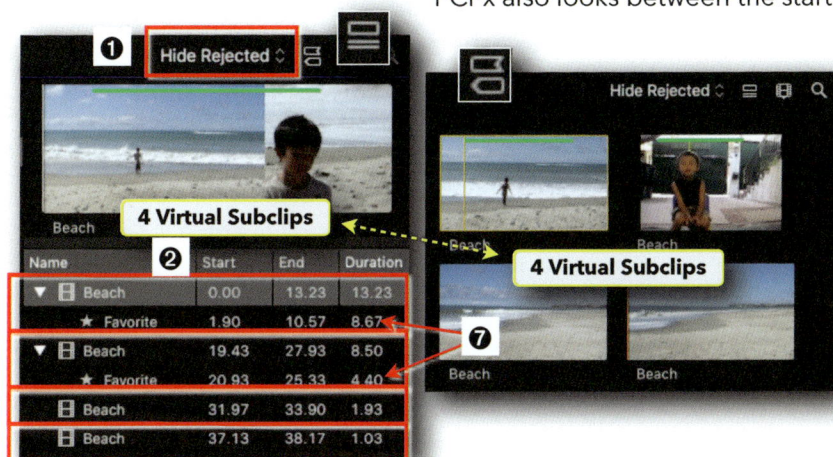

FCPx also looks between the start and end of each Subclip and if during those sections are any metadata on the original Clip ❸, then that metadata is also listed as ClipRanges with their related row ❼. In this example, I don't have any Keywords or Markers to keep it easier to follow, but that metadata would also be displayed on the virtual Subclips as additional rows.

🕱 No Ratings or Keywords

The "No Ratings or Keywords" ❽ filter works similar as the hide Rejected. Now FCPx starts looking from the beginning to the end of the original Clip and creates a virtual Subclip for any section that doesn't have a green (Favorite ⭐), red (Rejected ❌), or blue (Keywords 🔑) line. In our example, there are a total of six Clips ❾ 🎞 all with the same name "Beach", the six virtual Subclips. This time, none of them have additional rows of metadata, but if I had Markers (which are not included in the filter), then those would be displayed as additional rows (🔖 🟦 🟦) and tags on the Clip (🟪 🟧 🟩). This option is useful if you want to review any section on any Clip that hasn't been marked yet.

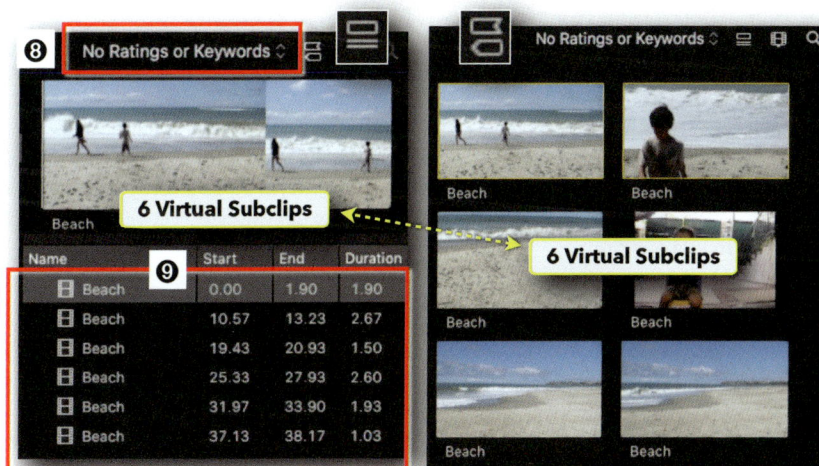

Please note that I demonstrated the Clip Filtering with just one Clip. Image you have hundreds of Clips in the Browser, how fast and efficient can you organize, review, and mark your material. Also, don't forget the Continuous Playback feature (Main Menu *View* ➤ *Browser* ➤ *Continuous Playback*) that plays from one Subclip to the next Subclip.

Filter Window

The Filter Window lets you create a so-called weighted search, which is a complex search by combining multiple search criteria. Let's find out what that means.

The Filter Window is a floating window that FCPx calls the "Filter HUD" (Heads Up Display). You can open it with any of the following commands:

- Main Menu *Edit ➤ Find...*
- Key Command *cmd+F*
- You need two buttons. First, *click* on the Search Button ❶ 🔍, which acts as a show/hide button that opens the Search Field ❺ underneath. The Search Field has a toggle button on the right ❷ 🖾 to show/hide the Filter HUD ❸ when you *click* on it.

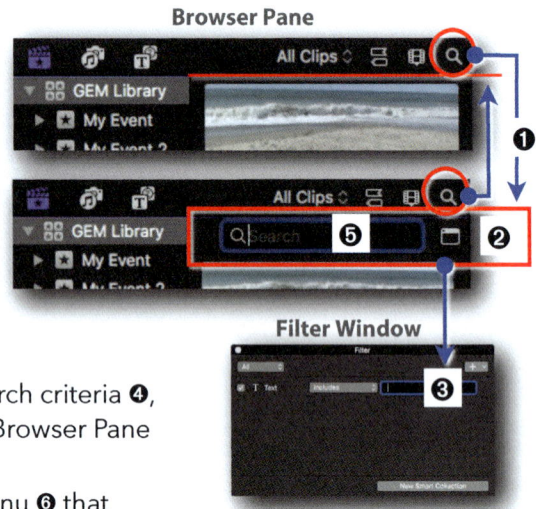

Browser Pane

Filter Window

➡ Basic Operations

- ▶ The default view of the Filter Window only lists one search criteria ❹, Text. This is the same field as the Search Field ❺ in the Browser Pane header.

- ▶ You can add more search criteria from the + popup menu ❻ that provides a total of eleven Metadata types. You can also add multiple search criteria of the same type if needed for your search query.

- ▶ The All-Any popup menu ❼ determines if the search should consider "All" criteria or "Any" of them.

- ▶ The checkbox ❽ on the left of each criteria lets you disable that criteria without removing it.

- ▶ The minus button ❾ at the right of each search criteria line lets you delete that line (except the Text item).

- ▶ Each search criteria has additional popup menus, checkboxes, and fields ❿ to define the condition in more detail.

- ▶ The currently displayed search criteria in the Filter Window "belongs" to the Event that is currently selected. Switching to a different Event and opening the Filter Window, will display the search criteria that was selected under that Event, or it shows the default view if nothing was configured.

- ▶ The "*New Smart Collection*" ⓫ button creates a new Smart Collection (named "Untitled") that stores the current search query. This functions as a search preset, a virtual bin that I explain in the next section. Please pay attention to what is currently selected in the Libraries Sidebar of the Browser Pane:
  - If an Event is selected, then the new Smart Collection is placed below that Event.
  - If a Library is selected, then the new Smart Collection is placed inside a Folder named "Smart Collections" underneath that Library.

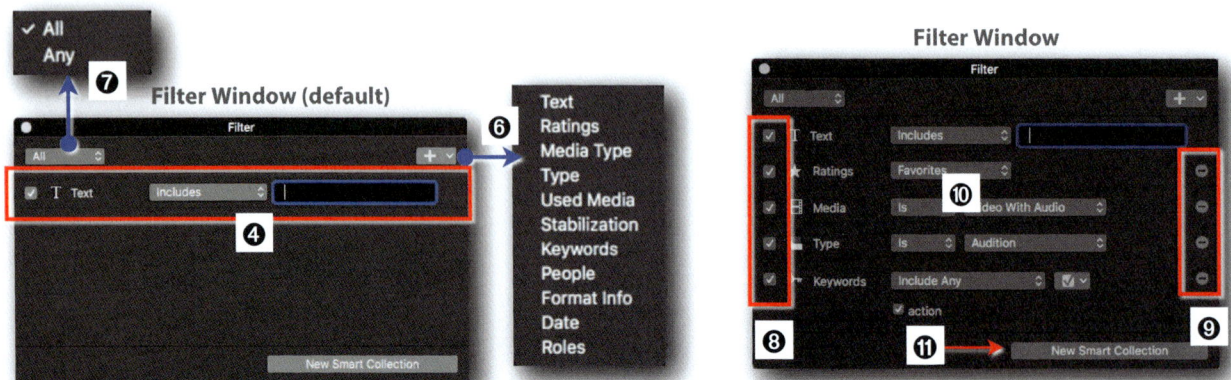

Filter Window (default)

Filter Window

Search Field vs. Filter Window

Pay attention to the relationship between the Search Field in the Libraries Browser and the Filter Window.

▸ If you enter only text in the Search Field ❶ and open the Filter Window, then that text is already entered in the search criteria *Text* ❷. Changing the text in one area updates it in the other area.

▸ Adding more criteria ❸ in the Filter Window will indicate each one with its corresponding icon ❹ in the Search Field and any text criteria is now only indicated by the Text icon.

▸ *Clicking* on the X Button ❺ in the Search Field will remove all search criteria in the Filter Window!

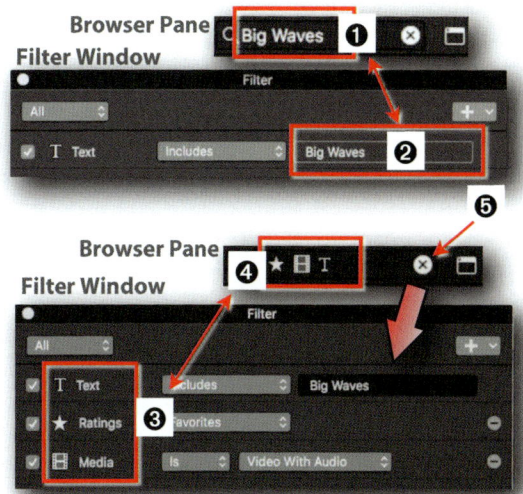

➡ *Individual Search Criteria*

Text

The Text criteria contains a text field to enter a word or phrase to search for. This searches for the name of Clips, but also any text in their metadata. The popup menu determines the condition. This is the default criteria that is always visible when opening the Filter Window (it doesn't have a minus button to remove it).

Ratings

The Ratings criteria only contains the popup menu to choose *Favorite* or *Rejected*.

Media

The Media criteria lets you filter out Clips based on their content. Is it a Clip with video and audio, video only, audio only, or is it an image (Stills)?

Type

The Type criteria lets you filter out based on what type of Clip it is or if it is a Project. This way you can search for just the Projects in your Library or everything except ("Is Not") Projects. Remember, you can add a criteria multiple times, so you can search for multiple types. For example, create one criteria to search for Compound Clips and one to search for Multicam Clips.

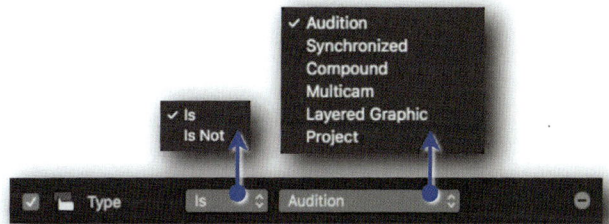

Used Media

The Used Media criteria lets you search for Clips or ClipRanges that are either used or not used in any Project.

Stabilization

The Stabilization criteria searches for the Analysis Keywords "Excessive Shake" that FCPx automatically assigns when it analyzes a Clip.

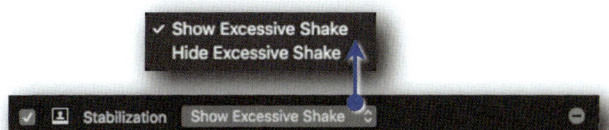

Keywords ⚿

The Keywords criteria automatically displays a checkbox for each existing Keyword Collection listed in the Libraries Sidebar under the current Event. That means this criteria is Event-based, displaying different checkboxes (Keywords) for different Events.

The popup menu ☑️∨ quickly lets you check or uncheck all the checkboxes, which comes in handy if you have an extensive list of Keyword Collections.

People 🖼

The People criteria searches for any of the six Analysis Keywords that FCPx automatically assigns when analyzing a Clip to determine how many people are in the shot and what angle the shot is.

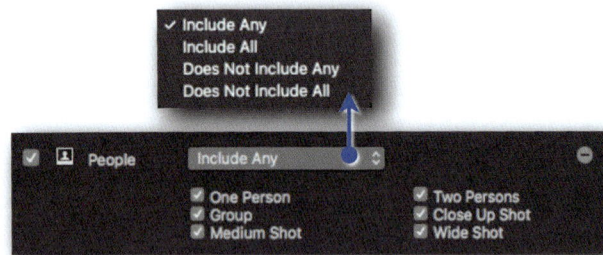

Format 🖺

The Format criteria, lets you choose from nine formats, for example, "Audio Sample Rate", and then you type the value for what you are looking for (i.e. 48kHz). And again, add multiple criteria to search for Clips that match, for example, a specific frame size, frame rate, and sample rate.

Date 🕐

The Date criteria lets you narrow down a search based on a wide variety of date-related settings.

Roles ☰

The Roles criteria functions similar to the Keywords criteria. It dynamically adds checkboxes. Here, it adds a checkbox for each Role and Subrole, but now it is Library-based, which means, the Roles you defined in the Role Editor (*Modify ➤ Edit Roles...*) are specific to the currently selected Library.

Collections

Collections are a powerful feature in FCPx in the context of metadata. Whatever search you create to filter Event Clips based on metadata can be saved as a preset called a Collection. You don't have to re-create that search again. Just click on that Collection and you have all your Event Clips instantly filtered, so the Browser only shows you the relevant Clips that you searched for.

Think of Collections as **virtual bins**.

Create specific Searches to filter Metadata → Save as presets

➡ Overview

▸ There are two types of Collections:

⚙ **Smart Collections**

🔑 **Keyword Collections**

🌑 Basic Rules

Collections have specific rules about their location.

▸ Collections are listed in the Libraries Sidebar ❶ of the Browser Pane

▸ Collections are listed "inside" Events ❷ 🌟 when you open the disclosure triangle ▼

▸ Collections can be placed inside folders ❸ or nested folders

▸ On the Library level, there is one folder on top named "Smart Collections" that can contain Smart Collections ❹

▸ Collections can be moved (*drag*) and copied (*opt+drag*) in the Sidebar between Events, Libraries, and Folder locations

🌑 Delete Collections

You have multiple ways to delete Smart Collections and Keyword Collections. Pay attention to the "dynamic" naming of the menu command. It detects if you select one or many collections ❺. If you selected both types, then the command says Delete Items ❻. To delete multiple selected Collections, they have to belong to the same Library.

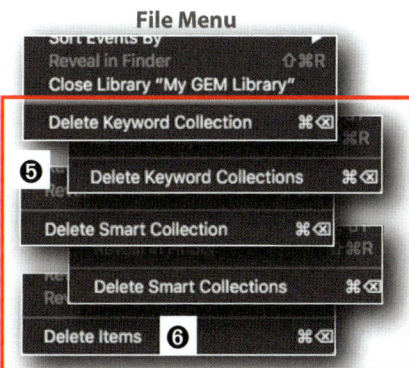

File Menu

- 🌑 Key Command *cmd+delete*
- 🌑 Menu Command *File ➤ Delete Keyword Collection(s) / Smart Collection(s) / Items*
- 🌑 *Ctr+click* on the selected Collections and choose from the Shortcut *Menu ➤ Delete Keyword Collection(s) / Smart Collection(s) / Items*

Libraries Sidebar

➡ *Smart Collection* ⚙

A Smart Collection is nothing more than a stored search configuration from the Filter Window.

🔮 Create a Smart Collection

There are four ways a Smart Collection can be created:

▸ **Default**: When you create a new Library, FCPx automatically creates a folder ❶ in the Libraries Sidebar below that Library with five preconfigured Smart Collections.

▸ **Analysis**: As we discussed in the Import chapter, during the import of a Clip or any time after a Clip has been imported, you can perform an Analysis procedure (Menu Command *Modify ➤ Analyze and Fix...*) ❷. FCPx creates MetadataSets, so-called Analysis Keywords ❸ 🖼 for the section of the Clip where it detects people or camera angles. There is an additional checkbox in the setup window that lets FCPx automatically create a Smart Collection ⚙ for each one and places it in individual subfolders "*People*" and "*Stabilization*" ❹.

▸ **Filter Window**: Open the Filter Window by *clicking* the Filter HUD Button ❺ 🖼 and setup the search criteria (as we have just discussed). When you *click* the "*New Smart Collection*" button ❻, a new Smart Collection named "Untitled" will be created and placed at the currently selected location in the Libraries Sidebar (Library, Event, Folder).

▸ **Empty Smart Collection**: You can create a new empty Smart Collection named "Untitled", which also will be placed at the currently selected Sidebar position.

📌 Menu Command *Edit ➤ New ➤ New Smart Collection*

📌 *Ctr+click* anywhere in the Sidebar and choose from the *Shortcut Menu ➤ New Smart Collection*

📌 Key Command *opt+cmd+N*

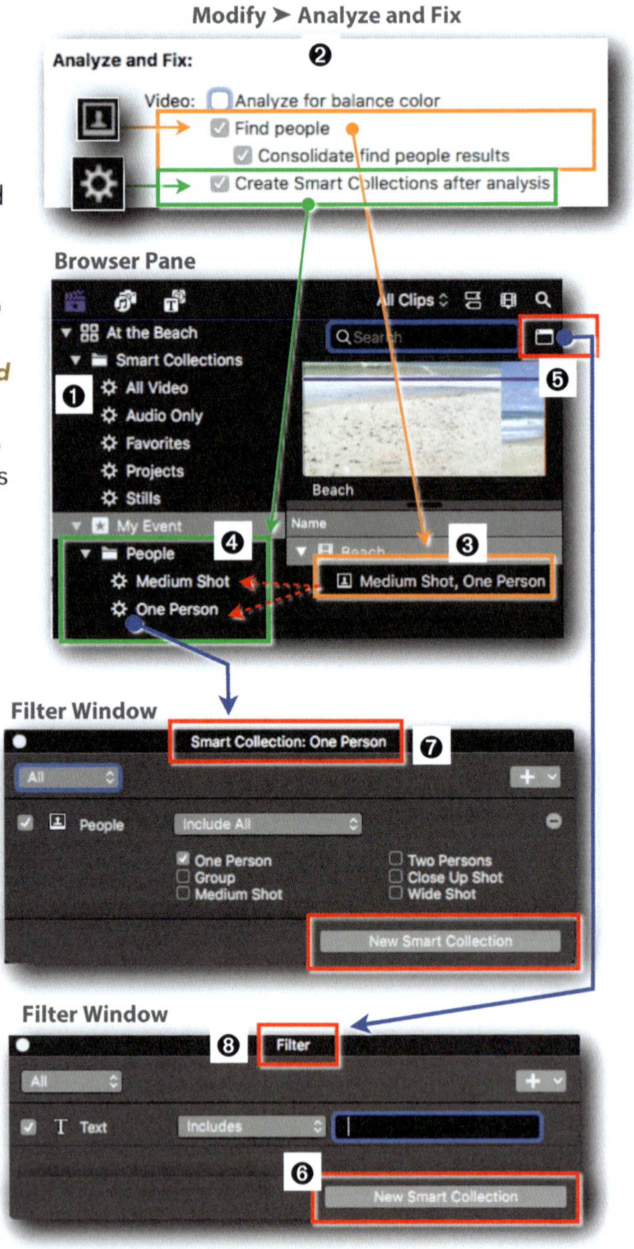

Modify ➤ Analyze and Fix

🔮 Edit a Smart Collection

To edit a Smart Collection, a newly created one ("Untitled") or an existing one, means to change the search criteria that it represents. There is only one command to do that. *Double-click* on the Smart Collection ⚙ in the Sidebar, which will open the Filter Window, displaying the search criteria of that Smart Collection.

▸ **Title Bar**: The title bar of the Filter Window displays the name of the Smart Collection you just "opened" ❼. When you open the Filter Window from the Filter HUD Button ❺, its title bar is "Filter" ❽.

▸ **No Save**: There is no save command. Whatever you change in the Filter Window updates the Smart Collection instantly. When done, close the Filter Window right away, to avoid any "accidents".

▸ **Rename**: You can rename the Smart Collection directly in the Libraries Sidebar. Select it, press *return* (it becomes highlighted), enter a name, press *return* again.

➡ *Keyword Collection*

A Keyword Collection is technically also a Smart Collection. It just has a single search criteria: "Filter all the Event Clips that match the single Keyword xyz". The name of a Keyword Collection conveniently tells you what Keyword it is filtering when you select it.

⬤ Create Keyword Collections

There are two ways to create a Keyword Collection:

▶ **Metadata**: Creating a new Keyword Metadata (*cmd+K*) for an Event Clip in the Browser will automatically create a Keyword Collection in the Event named after that Keyword. Remember, a Keyword MetadataSet (the single row 🔑 in the Libraries Browser) can have multiple Keywords (word or phrase) separated by a comma. Each one of those words or phrases generates a separate Keyword Collection 🔑 in the Sidebar.

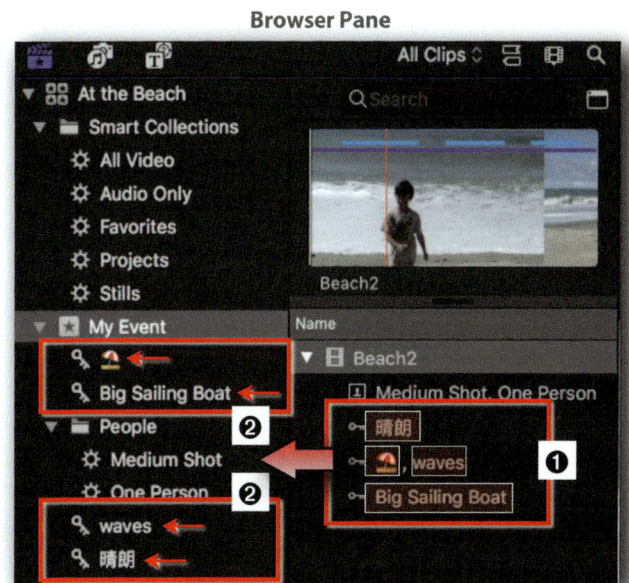
Browser Pane

Look at the screenshot on the right. I created three ClipRanges, representing three Keyword MetadataSets (three rows🔑 ❶). The second Keyword row contains two phrases (an emoji "⛱" and the word "waves"), so there are a total of four Keyword Collections in the Sidebar: "⛱", "Big Sailing Boat", "waves", "晴朗" ❷.

▶ **Empty Keyword Collection**: You can create a new empty Keyword Collection, which will be placed at the current location (except directly under the Library). Because that "empty" Keyword Collection is named "Untitled", it is a Smart Collection with the search criteria "Keyword = Untitled", so you have to rename it to a keyword that actually exists in any of the Clips.

    🎚 Menu Command *Edit ➤ New ➤ New Keyword Collection*

    🎚 *Ctr+click* anywhere in the Sidebar (except on a Library) and choose from the *Shortcut Menu ➤ New Keyword Collection*

    🎚 Key Command *opt+cmd+N*

⬤ Editing

While the Smart Collections are just presets with a specific search query, the Keyword Collections 🔑 are connected to their corresponding Keyword metadata 🔑.

▶ **Rename Keyword Collection 🔑**: Renaming a Keyword Collection ❷, for example, "waves" to "big waves", will change all the Clips that have Keyword Metadata ❶ with the word "waves" to the word "big waves". This can be used as a powerful "search and replace" feature.

▶ **Rename Keyword 🔑**: Renaming an existing Keyword in a Clip, for example, from "waves" to "big waves", will not update the Keyword Collection named "waves". Instead it creates a new Keyword Collection named "big waves" and leaves the (now orphaned) Keyword Collection "waves".

▶ **Delete Keyword Collection 🔑**: Be careful with this delete command! Deleting a Keyword Collection in the Sidebar will delete their corresponding word in the Keyword Metadata of every Event Clip!

▶ **Delete Keywords 🔑**: Deleting a Keyword Metadata will not delete the Keyword Collection with that name. The Keyword Collection becomes an orphaned search query with no search results (searching for a keyword that no Clips are assigned to), so that one you can delete manually from the Sidebar.

Workflow Tips

In addition to using the Keyword Editor or Keyword Shortcut to assigned Keyword metadata to a Clip or ClipRange, you can also use any of the Keyword Collections in the Sidebar.

▶ **Keyword Assignment during Import**: You can assign Keyword metadata to Clips directly during the import, depending on what import procedure you are using. In those cases, the ClipRange spans over the entire Clip.

- You already have one or multiple Keyword Collections in your Event ❶. Select one or multiple Keyword Collections ❷ before using the Import command ❸ (*cmd+I* or clicking on the Import Button ↓). FCPx will create a single Keyword MetadataSet for each imported Clip with all the Keywords added to that Metadata (one row). In this example, I imported the Clip "Beach" ❹ and "Mountain" ❺.

- When you *drag* a Media File directly from the Finder onto the Browser Pane, *drag* the file(s) onto a specific Keyword Collection and FCPx creates a MetadataSet for each file with a single MetadataSet with that Keyword.

- This also works when dragging content from the Photos and Audio Sidebar ❻ to an Event. Remember, FCPx has a neat little trick, when *dragging* a file from the *Photos and Audio Browser* to the left over the Sidebar ❼ (you see a little ghost Clip attached to the mouse pointer). The Browser Pane changes to the Libraries Browser, now showing the Libraries Sidebar. While still pressing down the mouse (during the dragging), move over a Keyword Collection and release the mouse. The Clip will be imported into your Event with that Keyword assigned as a Keyword MetadataSet.

Photos and Audio Browser

▶ **Drag and Drop Clips**: Let's say, you create a couple of new Keyword Collections in the Event (*File ➤ New ➤ Keyword Collection*) and name them "Outtakes", "B-Roll", "funny", etc., whatever categories you might use in your video production. You can also create Folders (*File ➤ New ➤ Folder*) in the Libraries Sidebar to organize your Keyword Collections. All these Keyword Collections function as your virtual bins. Now you just *drag* Clips ❽ over specific Keyword Collections ❾ and the name of the Keyword Collection will be assigned to those Clips as a Keyword metadata. It is like dragging the Clips into a bin. Later, whenever you select a Keyword Collection in the Libraries Sidebar, the Browser will only display the Clips and ClipRanges that have that Keyword assigned to them. It is like opening and displaying the content of those virtual bins.

➡ *Virtual Bins*

Here are five examples to demonstrate the concept of virtual bins

◉ No Filter

In this example, there are no filters applied. I selected the Event ❶ in the Sidebar and you see all the six Clips in that Event with sections of those Clips marked as ClipRanges and assigned Keywords ▣ and Analysis Keywords ▣ ❷. They are visible as rows in List View and as blue and purple lines in Filmstrip View ❸.

◉ Keyword Collection "action"

In this example, I have the Keyword Collection "action" ❹ selected in the Sidebar. The Browser now only shows two Clips ❺. However, these are not the entire Clips, but only ClipRanges that match the selected Keyword ▣ "action". The Filmstrip View ❻ also shows the two ClipRanges, and this time, you can see the blue line across the entire thumbnail, which is a sign that these are ClipRanges and not entire Clips.

◉ Smart Collection "One Person"

In this example, I have the Smart Collection "One Person" ❼ selected in the Sidebar. The Browser now only shows two Clips ❽. Again, these are not the entire Clips, but only ClipRanges that match the search query of this Smart Collection, which is: "People = One Person". The Filmstrip View ❾ also shows the two ClipRanges, and this time, you can see the purple line across the entire thumbnail.

⦿ Multiple Collections Selected

In this example, I selected three Collections ❶ in the Sidebar. The Browser now shows all the ClipRanges that match any of those selected Collections ❷. The reason you see some Clips twice ("Beach" ❸ and "Garden" ❹), is because those Clips have two ClipRanges that match any of those Collections. The Filmstrip View ❺ also shows all those ClipRanges and you can see by the blue or purple line on the thumbnail, which one is marked as a Standard Keyword and which one an Analysis Keyword.

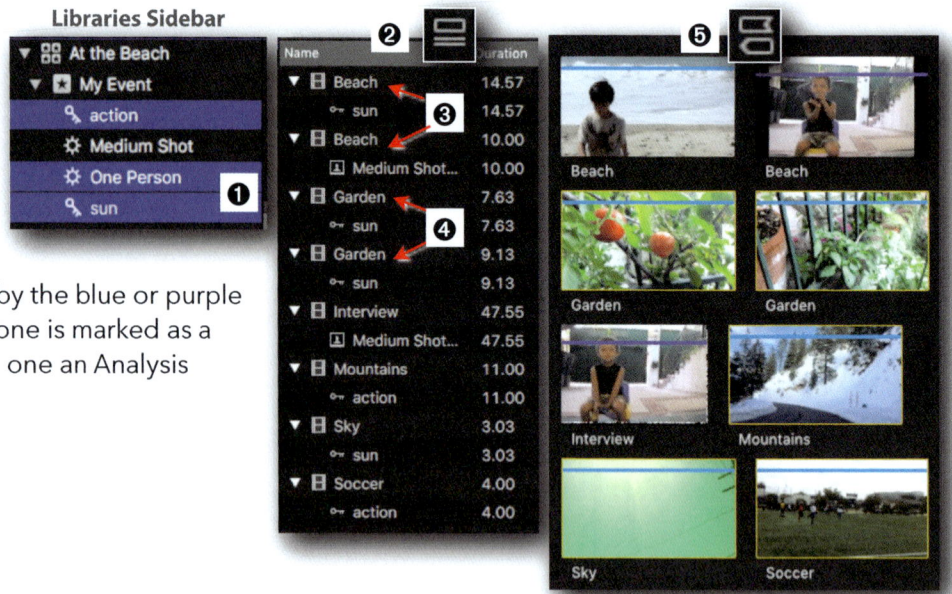

⦿ Keyword Collection vs. Smart Collection

Here is an additional example to demonstrate the difference (or similarity) of Keyword Collections and Smart Collections.

▶ **Keyword Collection**: The name of the Keyword Collection is the keyword name that is filtered out. In this example, it is "action" ❻. Selecting the Keyword Collection "action" will display all the ClipRanges in the Browser that are marked with the keyword "action" ❼.

▶ **Smart Collection**: The name of the Smart Collection is just a description. In this case, I named it "Search KW: "action" ❽. When you *double-click* on that Smart Collection, the Filter Window ❾ opens, showing the search criteria. Here, I configured it that it has the same functionality as the Keyword Collection "action" ❻. It has only a single criteria, "Keywords" ❿, which shows all the keywords that are used in this Event. I checked "action", which means selecting this Smart Collection will filter out (only show) the ClipRanges with the keyword metadata "action" ❼ assigned to them.

Date and Time

Virtually any Media File carries the basic Metadata of Date and Time when it was created. That data is imported with the Media File and saved with the Event Clip as part of its Metadata. This lets you search, find, and organize your Clips by date and time. It is part of the important Metadata Management.

There are two aspects to consider:

▶ The date and time information is coming from the internal clock of the device (computer, camera, phone) that created the file. If that clock was incorrect, because it is not running accurately or wasn't set correctly by the user, then you might run into problems, i.e. searching for the Clips that were shot on 2017-0115 doesn't help if the camera printed 1990-0101 on the file because the clock was never set in the first place.

▶ When shooting a 3 camera setup where you want to synchronize the Clips later in Multicam by date, you'll run into trouble in FCPx if the camera clocks weren't set correctly.

For those situations, FCPx provides a feature to adjust the Date and Time for Clips in case they've been imported with the wrong date and time data.

Main Menu

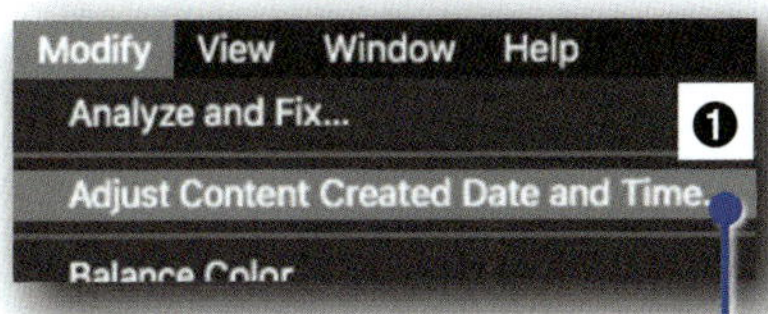

☑ Select one or many Event Clips (not available for Timeline Clips).

☑ Select the Menu Command *Modify ➤ Adjust Content Created Date and Time ...* ❶ or use a Key Command (unassigned by default) which slides out a sheet ❷ with the parameters to configure.

☑ Set the new date and time ❸ and click OK.

☑ Optional, select the checkbox ❹ if you also want to save the new date and time to the Source Media File. Not all Media Files will allow you to change their creation date. In some cases, FCPx will prompt an Alert Window ❺, explaining the problem.

☑ You can see the new date and time for the Event Clip in the FCPx Inspector if the Property "Content Created" ❻ is displayed in your Metadata View.

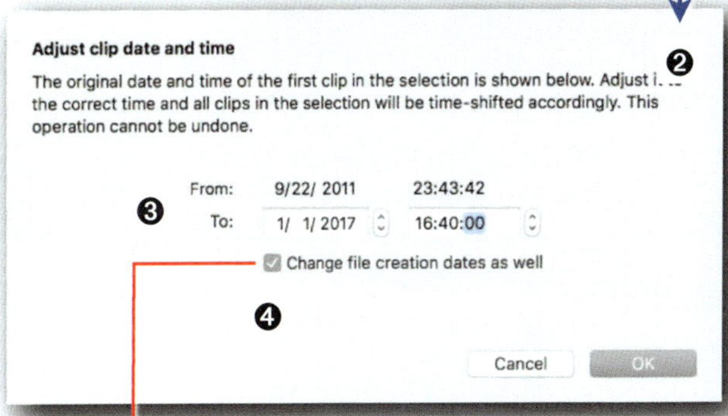

Info Inspector

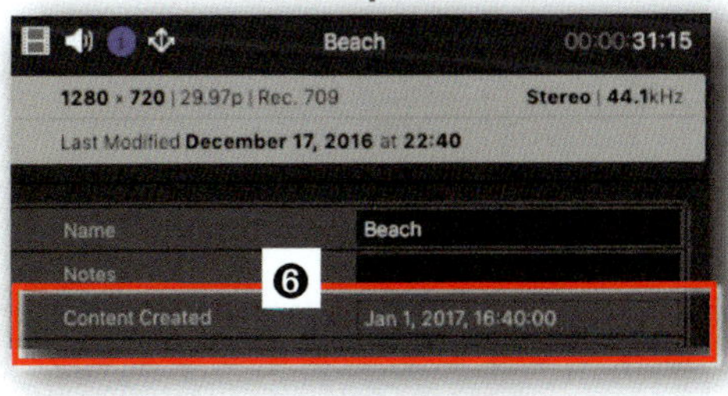

Attention: You can apply those changes to all different Clip types in the Libraries Browser, but there are differences:

▶ **Regular Clip** (video, audio, graphic): The selected Clip will be modified.

▶ **Compound Clip**: This will change the Compound Clip (the "container"), but not any of the enclosed Clips.

▶ **Audition**: Be careful. An Audition is just a window to a Clip (or possible others in that Audition). Selecting an Audition Clip will apply the date change only to the "Pick", the visible Clip in the Audition, not the other Clips in that Audition (see the section about Audition in a later chapter).

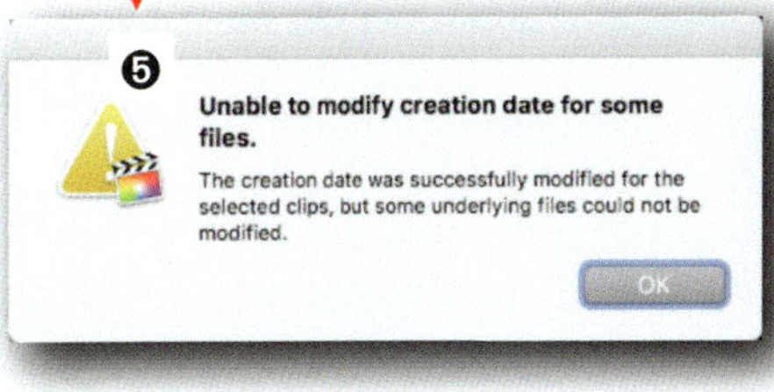

Let's talk about Subclips for a moment. It is a very common element when editing video, but the term "Subclip" itself is not even mentioned once in the official FCPx user guide. How come?

"Subclip" itself is just a term. It means a section of a Clip. Let's say you have an Event Clip that is 3 minutes long. It has some sections that are useful and some sections that you might not use for editing. So you just cut it up into sections, smaller Clips. Voilà, you got yourself some Subclips.

A Subclip is a section of an Event Clip

Event Clip

Subclip 1

Subclip 2

Subclip 3

Subclip 4

Virtual Subclips vs. Real Subclips

There is one main reason why you should cut the original Clips into smaller, separate Subclips. You can group them together by categories, store them in separate so-called bins. However, we spent this entire chapter to learn all the advantages of metadata and search queries to eliminate the somewhat restricted workflow of subclips and bins. However, if you still need to cut up a Clip into separate Subclips, you still can do that in FCPx.

😀 Virtual Subclips (Metadata-based)

The concept of Virtual Subclips is what we discussed in this chapter. It involves three steps:

- ☑ **ClipRange**: You create a selection on the Event Clip by dragging a ClipRange that represents your Subclip.
- ☑ **Metadata**: You assign metadata to that ClipRange (Ratings, Keywords), which functions as a label for that specific Virtual Subclip.
- ☑ **Filtering**: You use various search commands (Metadata, Clip Filtering, Collections) to filter out specific metadata and, therefore, only display the ClipRanges that match the current search criteria, which represents your Virtual Subclips.

😀 Real Subclips (independent)

You can still create separate Subclips in FCPx by using a special form of Clips, the so-called Compound Clips. It requires only two steps:

- ☑ **ClipRange**: The first step is the same where you create a selection on the Event Clip by dragging a ClipRange that represents your Subclip.
- ☑ **New Compound Clip**: You use a commands to create a new Compound Clip that acts as your dedicated Subclip, always visible in the Browser without the need of any search query.

➡ Create Compound Clip based Subclips

I will discuss the Compound Clip later in the book, here is just a quick step-by-step instruction on how to create Subclips with it.

Browser Pane

🔵 Define

On the filmstrip thumbnail in the Browser you drag a ClipRange ❶ for the section that should be your Subclip and choose any of the commands to create a Compound Clip:

- 🔵 Key Command **opt+G**
- 🔵 Menu Command **File ➤ New ➤ New Compound Clip...**
- 🔵 **Ctr+click** on the selection and choose from the **Shortcut Menu ➤ New Compound Clip...** ❷

🔵 Configure

The command opens a Sheet ❸ that lets you configure the properties of the Compound Clip. Just enter a new name ❹ and click OK.

🔵 Display

The new Compound Clip will be displayed right away in the Browser. In this example, I created three Compound Clips (Subclips) ❺ and as you can see they have their own icon 🔲 that is also displayed in the upper-left corner of the thumbnail ❻. If you look at the Start-End values ❼, you will see the time reference of the original Clip, because the Compound Clip inherited the original Source Timecode from its parent Clip "Beach".

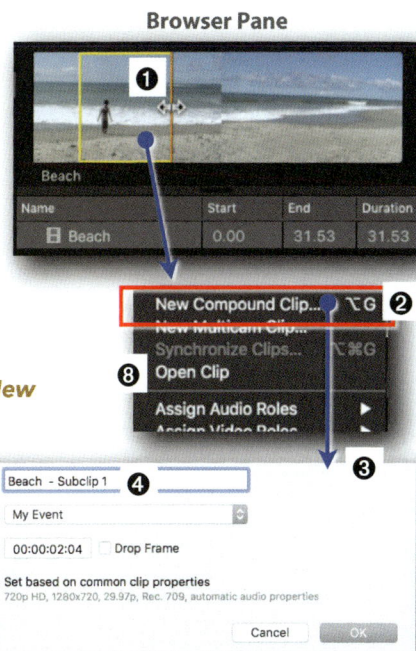

Browser Pane - List View

Browser Pane - Filmstrip View

🔵 Advanced

If you **ctr+click** on the Event Clip and choose from the **Shortcut Menu ➤ Open Clip** ❽, it will open that Clip in the Timeline Pane. Now, if you **ctr+click** on a Compound Clip and choose the **Shortcut Menu ➤ Open Clip**, you will see the "true identity" of that Compound Clip, a trimmed section ❾ of its Parent Clip ❿.

Compound Clip displayed as Timeline Clip in the Timeline Pane

Placing Clips

Now that we've organized all our source material as Event Clips in the Browser, we can finally go to the next level and create our new video by placing the Clips onto the Timeline.

In order to do that, we have to ask ourselves four fundamental questions:

?	**What**	#1 - **What** Clip(s) from the Browser do we want to place onto the Timeline?
🔧	**How**	#2 - **How** do we move the Clip(s), with what command or action?
→	**Where**	#3 - **Where** on the Timeline do we want the Clip to be placed?
⚡	**Consequences**	#4 - What are the **Consequences** to the existing Clips on the Timeline?

#1 - **What** Clip to Place

Before we can place Event Clips to the Timeline, we have to find them. This is where all the searching and filtering comes into place that we learned in the previous chapter. Once you find the Clip(s) in the Browser that you want for your edit, you have to make the first choice:

Browser Pane

💡 Use Entire Clip

You can select the entire Event Clip in the Browser, the Filmstrip ❶, or the list entry ❷ and move it to the Timeline.

💡 Use Clip Range (Subclip)

You don't have to move the entire Clip and trim it on the Timeline. That's what all the preparation time was for. All the sections that you marked on the Clips using the metadata (Keyword and Ratings) now function as Subclips. You move only those sections of a Clip (like pre-trimmed) onto the Timeline. You can use the ClipRanges, the yellow frames in the Filmstrips ❸ or the separate rows ❹ of a Clip that are (hopefully) nicely labeled, so you know exactly which Subclip to grab.

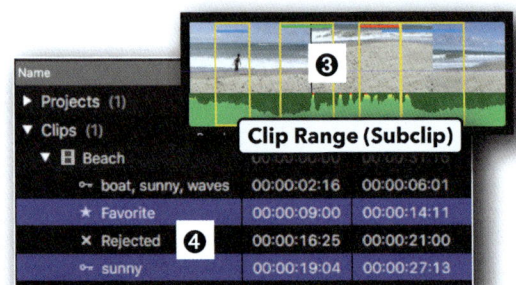

➡ *Content Filter*

The Question about "What Clip" to place goes one step deeper with the question, "What content of that Clip". Here is what that means:

Once you have found the Event Clips and they are displayed in the Browser, you have to keep an important little detail in mind before you actually move any Clip to the Timeline. Remember, placing an Event Clip ❶ from the Browser to the Timeline creates a new Clip, a so-called Timeline Clip ❷, which is a copy of the Event Clip. However, that copy procedure has one important element, a Content Filter ❸ that determines which content of the Event Clip will be copied.

You can set the filter to any of these three option:

▸ **Use All** (default): The entire content, its Video and Audio portion ❹ is copied.

▸ **Use Video Only**: Only the Video content ❺ of the Clip is copied.

▸ **Use Audio Only**: Only the Audio content ❻ of the Clip is copied.

Whatever method you are using (which we will look at in a moment) to place a Clip on the Timeline, that command is always executed with the currently set Content Filter. Please note that this filter doesn't apply when dragging Clips from the Photos and Audio Browser or the Finder!

You can change the filter in three different ways.

- Select a Menu Command *Edit ➤ Source Media ➤* ❼
- Use a Key Command: All *sh+1*, Video Only *sh+2*, Audio Only *sh+3*
- *Click* on the selector ❽ ⌄ in the Timeline Pane Header to select the filter setting from that popup menu

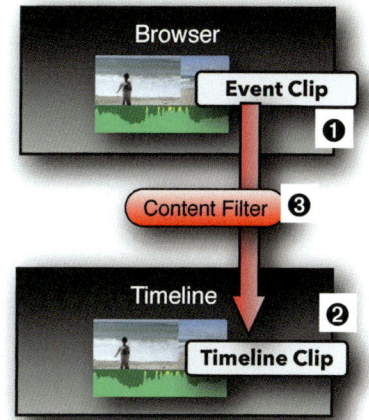

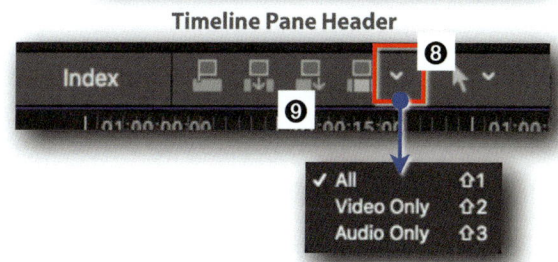

The four buttons ❾ next to the selector that determine the placement method change their appearance, depending on the current filter setting ❿.

#2 - <u>How</u> to Place the Clip

There are two methods to move Event Clip(s) or Subclip(s) from the Browser onto the Timeline:

▶ **Commands ❶**: You can choose from a variety of commands to move the Event Clip that is selected in the Browser directly onto the Timeline.

▶ **Drag-and-Drop ❷**: You can use your mouse to drag a Clip from the Libraries Browser directly onto the Project Timeline. Remember that you can also drag files directly from the Media Browser (Audio and Photos, Titles and Generator) or from the Finder.

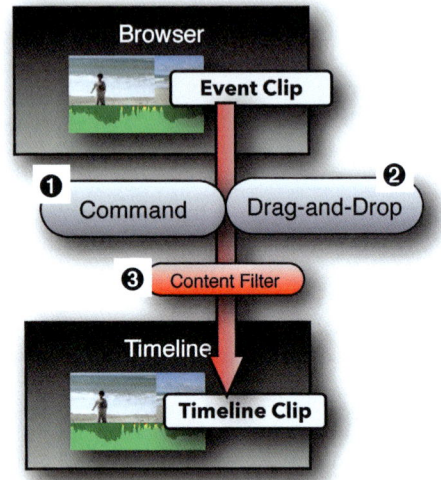

➡ *Use a Command*

There is not just one command but multiple commands (different methods) for placing a Clip onto the Timeline. How many, depends on how you count. Here is just an overview of those commands and we will get into the details as to what they exactly do in a moment.

- ◉ There are four main methods: **Connect** - **Insert** - **Append** - **Overwrite**
- ◉ Two of those methods have a "variation": **Backtimed Connect** - **Backtimed Overwrite**

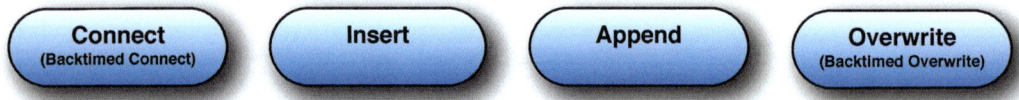

There are three ways to initiate those commands. Remember content filter ❸ always applies.

▶ **Menu Command ❹**: Select a Menu Command (in the Edit Menu)
▶ **Button ❺**: Click on one of the four buttons in the Timeline Header
▶ **Key Command ❻**: Use any of the available Key Commands

Commands:	**Connect**	**Insert**	**Append**	**Overwrite**
❹ Edit Menu:	*Connect to Primary Storyline*	*Insert*	*Append to Storyline*	*Overwrite*
❺ Button:				
❻ Key Command:	Q	W	E	D
Key Command:	*sh+Q*			*sh+D*
	Backtimed Connect			Backtimed Overwrite

➡ Use Drag-and-Drop

Instead of selecting the Event Clip(s) in the Browser and initiating one of the commands, you can use the mouse and just *drag* the Event Clip(s) down onto the Timeline. This is a more direct way.

A few things to pay attention to:

Browser

● **Drag Entire Clip(s)**

- You can *drag* an entire Clip by dragging its entry ❶ in the Browser's List View to the Timeline.
- You can select multiple Clips first, then *dragging* one Clip will move all the selected Clips with them.
- You can't drag the Filmstrip ❷ of the Event Clip, because this dragging action will create a Clip Range instead.

● **Drag Clip Range(s)**

- You can *drag* the entry in the Browser's List View that represents a Clip Range ❸. For example, a selection marked as a Keyword or Favorite.
- You can select multiple entries ❹ in the List View to drag multiple Clip Ranges to the Timeline.
- Once you select one or multiple entries in the List View, then those Clip Ranges will be displayed as white frames ❺ on the filmstrip. You can *drag* those frames to the Timeline.

● **Drag ad-hoc Clip Range(s)**

- You can also define ad-hoc Range(s) ❻ on the Filmstrip and *drag* those sections of the Clip (yellow frames) down to the Project Timeline.
- When dragging multiple Clip Ranges from the Filmstrip, then the mouse cursor will indicate the number of Clip Ranges with a red label ❼.
- When you move those Clips or Clip Ranges over the Timeline, you will see them as individual Clips ❽ added to the Timeline.

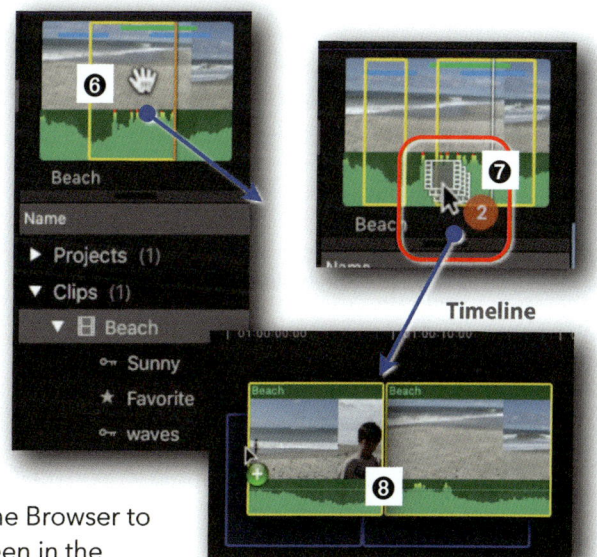

Timeline

Other Drag-and-Drop Procedures (not from the Libraries Browser)

The proper way in FCPx is to first import the Media Files into Events and then drag those Event Clips from the Browser to the Timeline. But there are two exceptions as we have seen in the Import chapter:

▶ **Media Browser**: *Drag* Media Files to the Timeline from the Media Browser (Photos and Audio 🎵, or Titles and Generators 🎬).

▶ **Finder**: *Drag* Media Files to the Timeline from the Finder.

Remember, moving Files to a Project in the Timeline Pane will add those Clips automatically to the same Event that this Project belongs to. The other Import settings in the Preferences window also apply to those files (Organize, Transcode, Analyze).

#3 - <u>Where</u> to Place the Clip

Now we have all those different options on "how" to move Event Clips from the Browser to the Timeline, the next question is, "where" exactly on the Timeline will the Clip be positioned.

➡ *Using Drag-and-Drop*

If you choose drag-and-drop to move the Clip(s) from the Libraries Browser to the Project Timeline, then your mouse position determines where the target position will be on the Timeline. Playhead/Skimmer or any existing Range selection will be ignored.

➡ *Using Commands*

If you are using any of the commands to move Event Clips to the Timeline, then you have to be aware of two possible target positions on the Project Timeline that determine were the new Clip(s) is placed: **Playhead/Skimmer** or a **Range**.

Those two possible target positions apply when using three of the four methods to add an Event Clip to the Timeline ❶:

Add Clip Methods

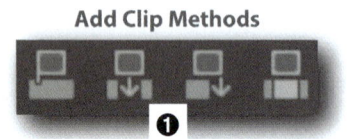

❶

▶   **Connect** (Key Command *Q* like in "qonnect")

▶   **Insert** (Key Command *W* like in "wedge")

▶   **Overwrite** (Key Command *D* like in "destructive")

The "Append" method always places the Clip(s) at the end of the last Clip on the Primary Storyline.

💡 Playhead / Skimmer

The Event Clip from the Browser will be placed at the current position of the Playhead ❷.

If a Skimmer is visible, then its position has priority over the Playhead.

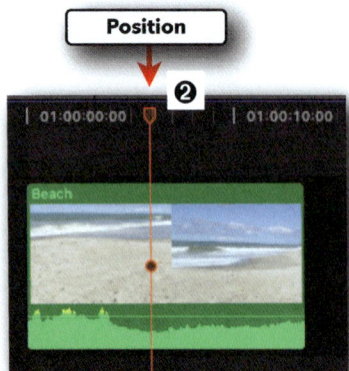

💡 Selected Range

If a Range ❸ is selected in the Timeline (which can even span across more than one Timeline Clip), then the target position for the placement of the new Clip is the left border ❹ of the Range (or the right border ❺ for backtimed operations).

However, a selected Range also determines how much (the length) of the Event Clip will be added to the Timeline. It uses only as much of the Event Clip to "fill" the current Range ❻. This is also referred to as a "3-point Edit".

Define a Range with the Key Command *I* and *O* at the Playhead position or use the Range Tool (*R*) 📷

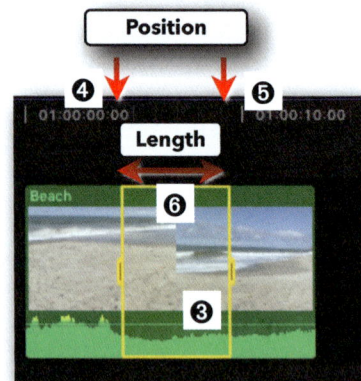

Here is an example to illustrate the placement.

🟡 Regular Methods

▶ **Playhead**: The Event Clip B ❶ will be placed at the Playhead/Skimmer Position ❷ using the entire length of the Clip ❸. What happens to the existing Timeline Clip A will be determined by the method you chose 🔲Connect, 🔽 Insert, 🔲Overwrite.

▶ **Range**: This a Selected Range, the Event Clip will be placed at the left border ❹ of the Range, but this time, only as much of the Event Clip is used to fill the Range ❺.

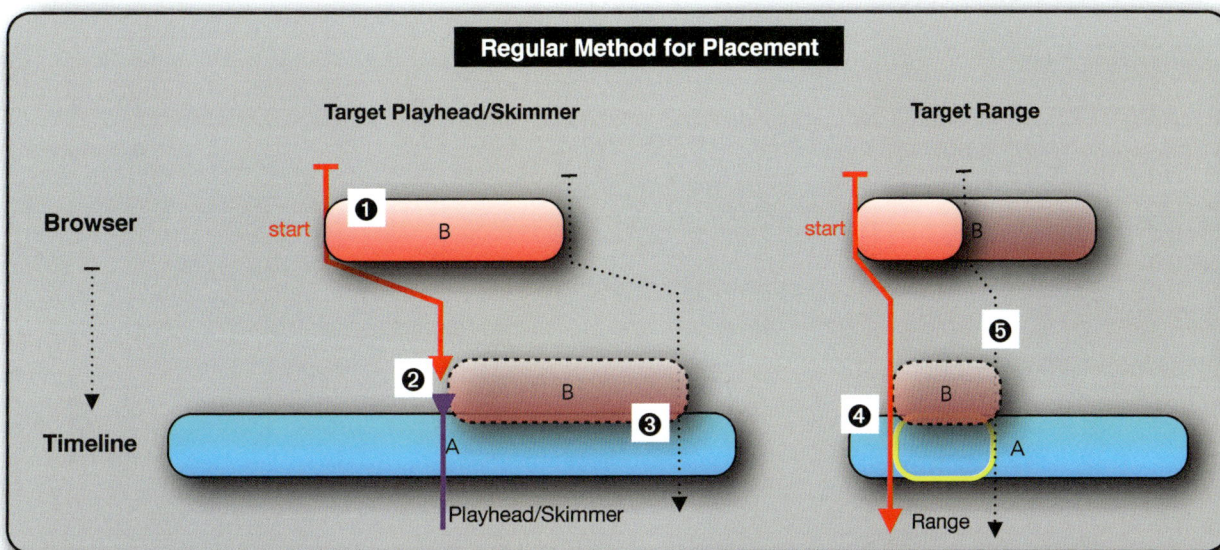

Regular Method for Placement

🟡 Backtimed Methods

▶ **Playhead**: This time the end of Event Clip B ❻ is positioned at the Playhead/Skimmer, using this as an alignment point. The start position of this new Timeline Clip on the Timeline depends on the actual length of the Event Clip.

▶ **Range**: The end of the Event Clip ❽ will be positioned at the end of the selected Range ❾ and only as much of the Event Clip is "used" prior to that end position to fill the Range ❿.

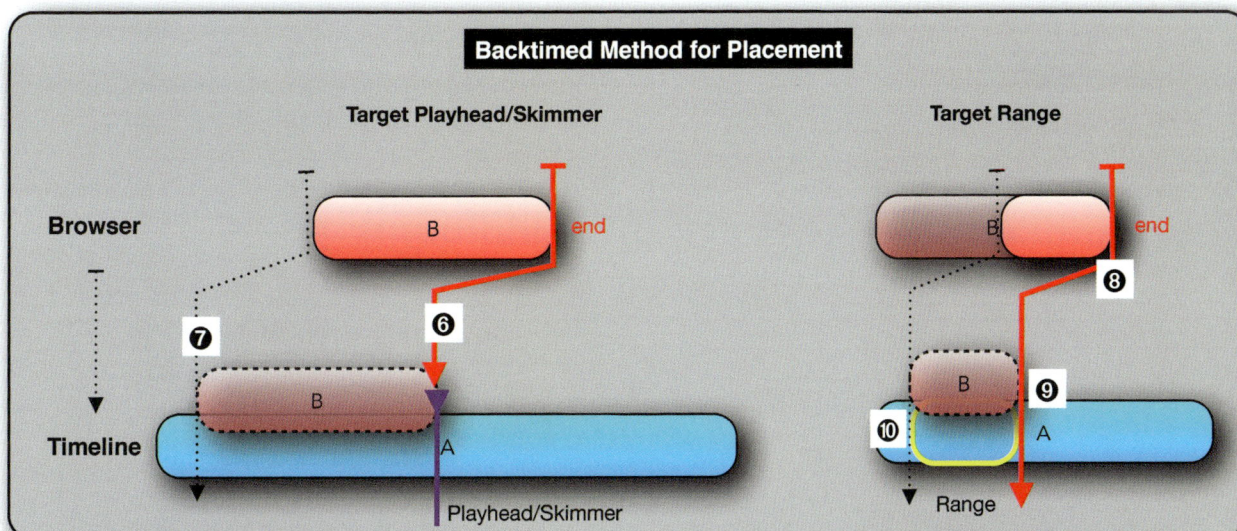

Backtimed Method for Placement

#4 - Consequences

Now in this last step of the four considerations when placing Clips on the Timeline, we will look at what happens on the Timeline when using the various commands, the "consequences" of that action. Needless to say, this is the most important step to make sure that the outcome is exactly what we wanted. Otherwise, you could really mess up your video edit.

Two types of "Consequences"

There are two types of consequences when you place an Event Clip onto the Timeline (the Primary Storyline) and neither one of them is "better" than the other. They both have pros and cons and it just depends on what you need for that particular edit.

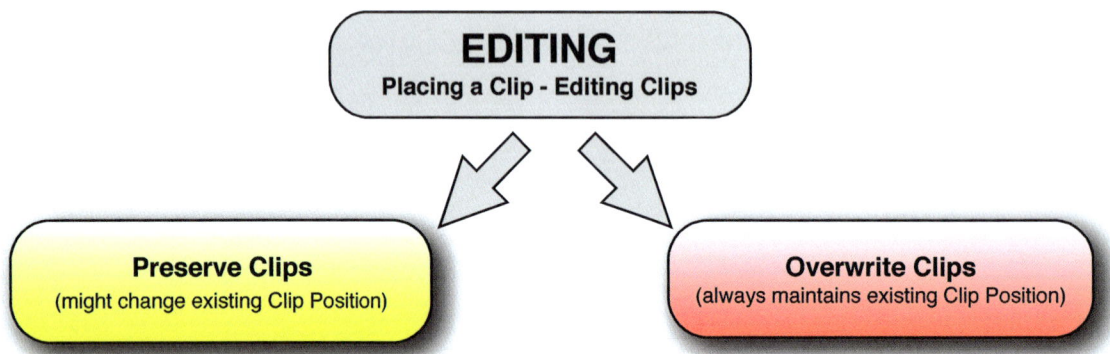

```
                          EDITING
                  Placing a Clip - Editing Clips


      Preserve Clips                            Overwrite Clips
  (might change existing Clip Position)    (always maintains existing Clip Position)
```

This is the **default** behavior in FCPx when placing Clips or editing Clips on the Timeline. Clips will not be overwritten. They will automatically be moved out of the way when inserting new Clips. Or when moving a Clip out of a sequence or deleting it, the gap will close up, moving the rest of the Clips to the left, always guaranteeing that the Clips on the Timeline stay connected. It is the so-called "Magnetic Timeline".

This is the **exception** in FCPx when placing Clips or editing Clips on the Timeline. This time, placing a Clip on the Timeline will OVERWRITE whatever Clip is there and when moving a Clip, the rest of the Timeline Clips will not try to close the empty space, instead, FCPx will leave a "Gap Clip" behind if necessary. Nothing gets shifted on the Timeline, which might be exactly what you want, you have all the existing Clips on your Timeline locked to their timecode position, for example, with a music video.

Commands

This is the command that preserves Clips, but might change Clip position:

Insert in Primary Storyline - *W*

Tools

This is the cursor tool that preserves Clips, but might change Clip position:

Select Tool - *A*

Commands

This is the command that might overwrite Clips, but preserves any Clip position:

Overwrite Storyline - *D*

Tools

This is the cursor tool that might overwrite Clips, but preserves any Clip position:

Position Tool - *P*

We've seen many different ways to move Clips from the Libraries Browser and place them on the Project Timeline. Now, let's explore the different "Consequences" on the Timeline. You have to be aware of what happens to the existing Clips on the Timeline and how they "react" to the "intruder".

And again, those consequences are different if you are using commands or drag-and-drop.

➡ *Using Commands*

Connect	Insert	Append	Overwrite

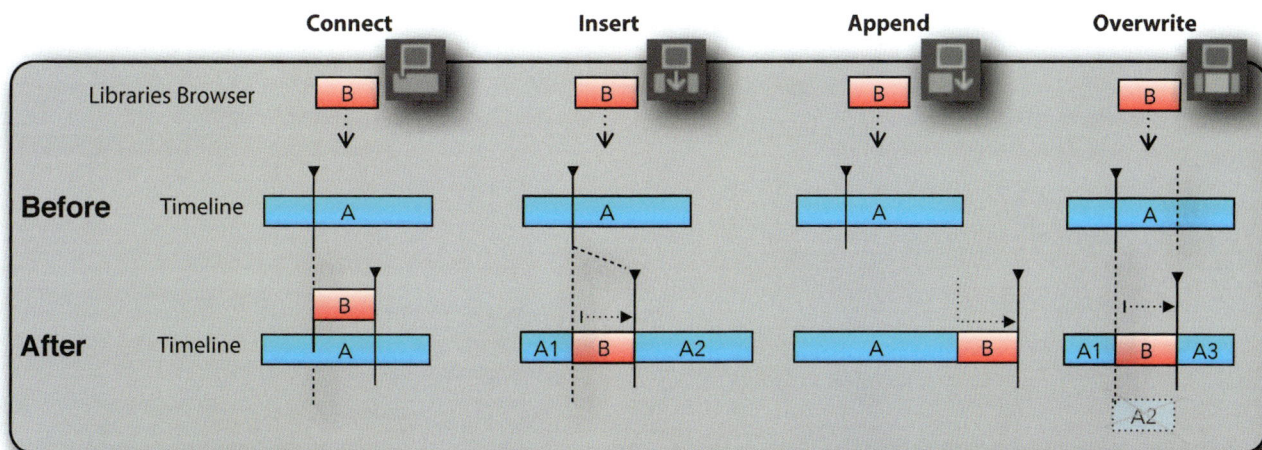

The new Clip (B) gets connected to the Primary Storyline at the Playhead position. The Playhead moves to the end of the new Clip (this is actually a Preference settings "*Position Playhead after Edit Operation*" ❶)

The Timeline Clip (A) gets cut at the Playhead position and the new Clip (B) gets inserted, moving the rest of the Clip A to the right. Everything else after that gets moved to the right with it.

The new Clip (B) gets added to the end of the LAST Clip in the Primary Storyline. The original Playhead position is ignored.

The new Clip (B) overwrites the Timeline Clip at the Playhead position. If Clip B is longer than Clip A, then it continues to overwrite into the next Clip on the Timeline too.

Backtimed Connect **Backtimed Overwrite**

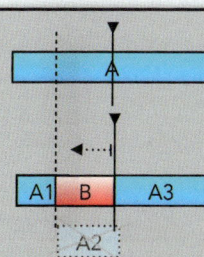

If the Playhead is located later than the end of the last Clip on the Timeline, then FCPx inserts a "Gap Clip" first before adding the new Clip (except for the Append command).

🕹 **Using Still Images**

When putting a still image onto the Timeline, which technically has no duration, then FCPx will create a Timeline Clip with the length that is set in the Preferences window ❷.

Preferences ➤ Editing

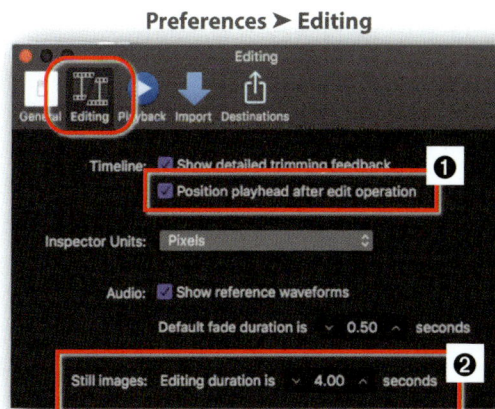

➡ *Using Drag-and-Drop*

The current Tool that is used to drag an Event Clip onto the Primary Storyline determines which "consequence" it has. ***Click*** on the Tool Selector Button ❶ in the Timeline Pane Header to choose from the Tools popup menu ❷.

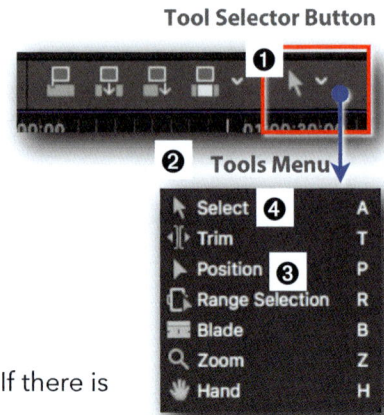

❷ **Tools Menu**

▲ Select ❹		A
◀|▶ Trim		T
▶ Position ❸		P
⌐ Range Selection		R
▦ Blade		B
🔍 Zoom		Z
✋ Hand		H

> ▶ Position   P
>
> **Overwrite Clips**
> (always maintains existing Clip Position)

🔵 **Position Tool ❸ ▷ is selected**

Wherever you drop the Clip on the Timeline, that is exactly where it will be. If there is anything in the way, it will be overwritten.

▶ If you drop the Clip after the last Clip on the Timeline, then FCPx will create a "Gap Clip" to fill the space.

▶ If you drop the Clip on top of an existing Clip, then that Clip will be overwritten for the duration of the new Clip (Overwrite functionality).

▶ If you drop the Clip above or below the Primary Storyline, then the new Clip will become a Connected Clip (Connect functionality).

> ▲ Select   A
>
> **Preserve Clips**
> (might change existing Clip Position)

🔵 **Select Tool ❹ ▲ is selected (or another Tool besides the Position Tool)**

Now Clips are moving out of the way to make room or closing up to fix any possible gap (Magnetic Timeline).

▶ If you drop the new Clip after the last existing Clip on the Timeline, then the new Clip will be appended to the end of the last Clip. It is not possible to create a gap, on purpose or by accident (Append functionality).

▶ If you place the Clip between two adjacent Clips on the Timeline, then the right Clip (and all the rest of the Clips in the Project Timeline) will move to the right to make space for the new Clip. Everything snaps into place to make sure that there are no gaps (Insert functionality).

▶ It is not possible to split an existing Clip with drag-and-drop. For that you have to use the Insert command with the Playhead.

▶ If you place the Clip on top of a Timeline Clip, then that Clip will be dimmed and a popup menu opens ❺ with the following options:

> Replace   ❺
> Replace from Start
> Replace from End
> Replace with Retime to Fit
> Replace and Add to Audition

• **Replace**: Replaces the Timeline Clip with the new Clip. The rest of the Clips will be shifted to adjust the new length, longer or shorter.

• **Replace from Start**

If the new Clip is longer than the Timeline Clip: Replaces the Timeline Clip with footage from the new Clip starting at the first frame for the length of the Timeline Clip to make sure that the length of the sequence doesn't change.

If the new Clip is shorter than the Timeline Clip: An Alert Window will pop up to remind you that the new Clip isn't long enough and, therefore, the sequence will be shortened after the replacement.

• **Replace from End**

If the new Clip is longer than the existing Clip: Replaces the existing Clip with footage from the new Clip, starting at the last frame for as long as the length of the existing Clip to make sure that the length of the sequence doesn't change.

If the new Clip is shorter than the existing Clip: An Alert Window will pop up to remind you that the new Clip isn't long enough and, therefore, the sequence will be shortened after the replacement.

• **Replace with Retime to Fit**: Time expands or compresses the new Clip to fit the space.

• **Replace and Add to Audition**: Keeps the Timeline Clip as an Audition Clip (see Clips chapter).

Once most of the Event Clips are placed from the Browser to the Timeline, the next step begins - trimming the Timeline Clips. Of course, new Clips can be added to the Timeline from the Browser (or directly from the Finder) at any time during editing.

Basics

Let's first look at some features and workflows related to the trimming procedure

➡ *Magnetic Timeline*

The default Clip behavior on the Timeline is that adjacent Clips on the Primary Storyline always stay attached to each other without leaving a gap (this is called the "Magnetic Timeline"). Any change you make on the Primary Storyline that affects the length of the existing Clip (lengthen, shortening, inserting, removing) will automatically be compensated by FCPx by nicely moving other stuff around.

However, sometimes you specifically need to leave a gap between Clips. For this purpose there are two kinds of special Clips, the *Gap Clips* and *Placeholder Clips*.

Gap Clip ❶

Gap Clip

This is just a gray Clip on the Timeline. FCPx creates those Gap Clips automatically (under some circumstances) or you can create a 3s Gap Clip manually at the current Playhead position with the following commands:

- Menu Command *Edit* ➤ *Insert Generator* ➤ *Gap*
- Key Command *opt+W*.

The Viewer displays a black background or any other of the choices from the *Preferences* ➤ *Playback* ➤ *Player Background* menu ❷.

Preference ➤ Playback

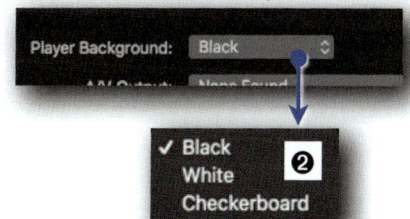

Player Background: Black

✓ Black   ❷
  White
  Checkerboard

Placeholder Clip ❸

Placeholder Clip

A Placeholder Clip is similar to a Gap Clip but more sophisticated. You can assign it some properties (in the Generator Inspector 🔲 ❹) to indicate what it is holding the place for (wide shot, close up, day, night etc.). Create a 3s Placeholder Clip at the current Playhead position with the following commands:

- Menu Command *Edit* ➤ *Insert Generator* ➤ *Placeholder*
- Key Command *opt+cmd+W*

Inspector Pane

Placeholder	00:00:03:00
Published Parameters	❹
Framing	Long Shot (LS)
People	2
Gender	Men and Women
Background	Pastoral
Sky	Sunny Day
Interior	☐
View Notes	☐

Gap Clips and Placeholder Clips can be named, have Metadata, and they show up in the Timeline Index list like any other Clips.

➡ Edit Tools

The various types of mouse cursors you use for editing in the Timeline are called the *Tools* or *Edit Tools*, the icons the cursor changes to indicate its functionality when clicking or dragging.

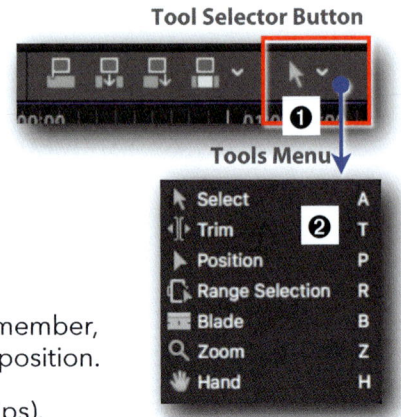

Tool Selector Button

Tools Menu

Select (*A*): All-purpose tool, including for ripple trimming.

Trim (*T*): For most of the trimming needs.

Position (*P*): Move or trim Clips without affecting the Timeline. Remember, this is the Tool that potentially overwrites Clips, but maintains any Clip position.

Range Selection (*R*): Select a Clip Range (even across multiple Clips).

Blade (*B*): Like a scissors tool to split Clips.

Zoom (*Z*): Zoom in (*drag*) and out (*opt+drag*) of the Timeline. Also use *click* and *opt+click*.

Hand (*H*): *Drag* the Timeline (functions like the scroll bar).

Switch to a specific Tool

- **Click** the Tool Selector ☑ ❶ on the Timeline Pane Header to open the popup menu ❷ and select the Tool
- Use their corresponding Key Commands.
- Use the Touch Bar buttons
  If the Timeline has key focus, then the Touch Bar switches to a view ❸ that also lets you select Edit Tools

- ☑ The first button on the left of the Touch Bar, next to the esc button, shows the currently selected Edit Tool ❹.
- ☑ **Tap** on the Edit Tool Button to switch to a different Touch Bar view ❺ that shows the seven Edit Tools. The currently selected Tool is highlighted.
- ☑ **Tap** on any of the buttons ❻ to select that Edit Tool (which also closes that View), or tap the Close Button ⊗ to return to the previous view.

Touch Bar (Timeline View)

Edit Tools

Temporary Edit Tool

You can also use the Tools as "temporary Tools". Instead of switching the Tools back and forth, you can hold the corresponding Key Command temporarily while doing the task (cutting, trimming, selecting) and when you're done, let the key go and it will return to the Tool it had before.

➡ Snapping

If Snapping is enabled, then objects, borders, or the Playhead/Skimmer snap to important positions (start, end of Clips/Selections, Playhead, Markers, Keyframes, etc.) when moving/dragging across the Timeline.

Timeline Pane Header

Snapping Button

Toggle Snapping on/off with any of the three commands:

- **Click** the Snapping Button ❼ in the upper-right corner of the Timeline Pane Header
- Menu Command *View ➤ Snapping*
- Key Command *N* (can be temporarily toggled by holding down the *N* key)

➡️ *Trimming Techniques with Edit Points*

There are a few trimming techniques that most of the video editing applications use. These are the ones based on what part of a Clip will be trimmed and what the effect is on the adjacent Clips.

The yellow brackets represent the Edit Point. That's the to-be-edited part of the Clip(s).

Ripple Left	Ripple Right	Roll	Slide	Slip

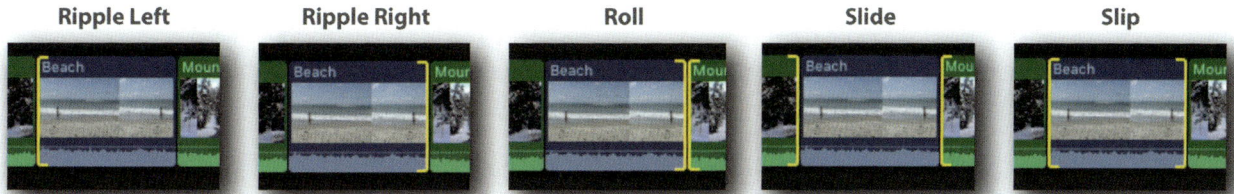

🔵 Ripple

You shorten or lengthen one end of the Clip (left or right) while the adjacent Clip stays "attached", meaning that they get moved to the left or the right on the Timeline to compensate the time difference (except with the Position Tool). Other Clips on the Timeline will shift accordingly.

🔵 Roll

You move two adjacent borders of two Clips together. So one Clip gets shortened while the other one gets lengthened or vice versa. Surrounding Clips will not be affected. Other Timeline Clips stay untouched.

🔵 Slide

This time, the Clip in itself stays untouched (same in, out, length) but you move it, as it is, to the left or the right on the Timeline. Therefore, the edges of the Clips to the left and to the right are shortened or lengthened. The rest of the Timeline stays untouched.

🔵 Slip

You are not moving the Clip. The length of the Clip stays the same and the surrounding Clips and the rest of the Timeline stays untouched. You are only moving the "portion of the media" underneath the Clip, if there is footage (also called "Media Handle") available on both ends.

➡️ *End of Range:*

The yellow Edit Point turns to a red border to indicate that there is no more footage (Media Handle) at that side of the Clip.

Potential danger with Connected Clips

You have to pay attention to Connected Clips when trimming Clips in the Primary Storyline.

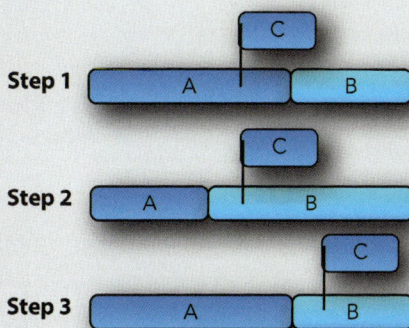

Step 1 — You have Clip A followed by Clip B. Clip A has a connected Clip C that stays in sync wherever you move Clip A.

Step 2 — When you shorten Clip A, Clip B will follow (Ripple or Roll). However, the Connected Clip C has the "rug pulled out from under it," because this time, it stays in sync with the Timeline and finds a new "mate", Clip B, which it happily attaches to.

Step 3 — Now, if you extend Clip A, Clip B will be pushed to the right. But this time, the Connected Clip C decides to stick with Clip B and moves with it!

If you did those three steps just to try an edit and you didn't pay attention, then you would have moved Clip C out of its original position. If Clip C was a SFX or a cued music track, then … you messed up.

➡ *Trim Info*

A black popover ❶ on top of the Edit Point displays the Timeline position of the Edit Point and the timing offset of your movement. Its "Anchor" ❷ (that little triangle) points at the Edit Point it is referring to.

Whatever Time Display setting is selected in the Preferences (*Preferences ➤ General ➤ Time Display* ❸), also applies to this little help tag.

Preferences ➤ General

➡ *Split Screen Editing (Two-up Display)*

Enable "Show detailed trimming feedback" in the *Preferences ➤ Editing* window to display a so-called Two-up Display in the Viewer when performing a trim with the mouse. Now the left display ❺ shows the last frame of the left Clip and the right display ❻ shows the first frame of the right Clip at the Edit Point.

You can temporarily turn the Two-up Display on by holding down the *option* key while trimming. Using the *option* key when the feature is disabled, toggles the Viewer from displaying the "last frame left Clip" to the "first frame right Clip".

Preferences ➤ Editing

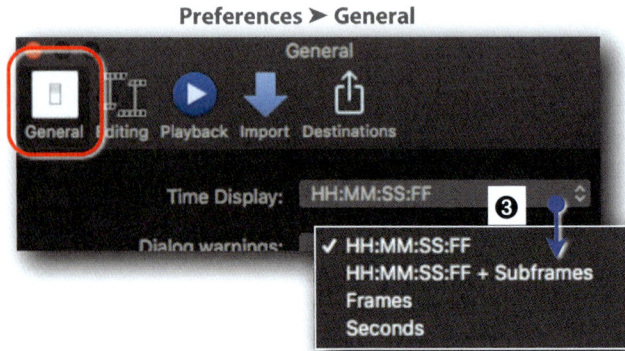

Viewer

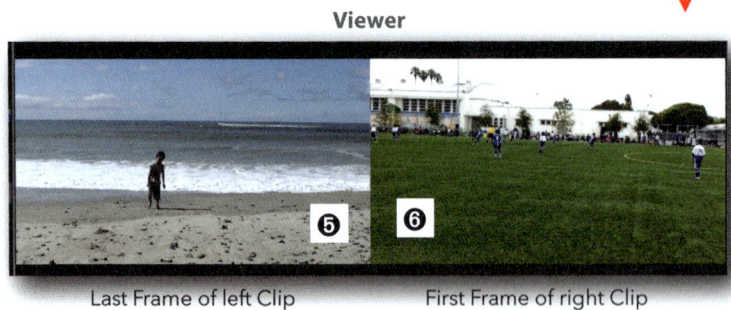

Last Frame of left Clip   First Frame of right Clip

➡ *Clip Selections vs. Range Selection*

Please note the difference between a Clip Selection (the whole Clip) and a Range Selection (any portion of it).

Click on a Timeline Clip with the Select Tool to select that Clip. The Clip will have a yellow frame around it ❼.

Press *C* when you mouse over the Timeline Clip to select that Clip.

Clip Selection

Range Selection

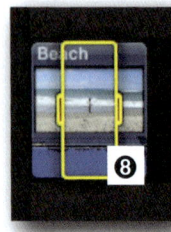

Click or drag with the Range Tool to make a Range Selection, even across multiple Clips. The Range Selection has a yellow border with handles on its side ❽.

Press *X* when mousing-over the Clip to select the entire Clip as a Range. The cursor changes to a Range Tool. Press *opt+X* to clear the selected Range. (Also works in the Libraries Browser).

What are the different trimming techniques? There are so many ways to do the same edits that it can be a bit overwhelming. Here are just a few:

- ▶ **Mouse**: Just drag around the edges of the Clip that you want to trim with the mouse and the correct cursor tool.
- ▶ **SMPTE**: Enter a precise time value of how much you want to trim.
- ▶ **Nudging**: Use Key Commands with predefined time values.
- ▶ **Playhead/Range/Duration**: Use the Playhead or a selected Range for the trim position, or enter a Clip duration.
- ▶ **Split**: Cut up an existing Clip at a specific edit point.

So in all, how many methods are available, and which one is the best to use? More importantly, do they have different effects or limitations?

Let's divide all these trimming techniques into two groups that determine how you perform the various edits. Editing with **Commands** and editing with the **Mouse**.

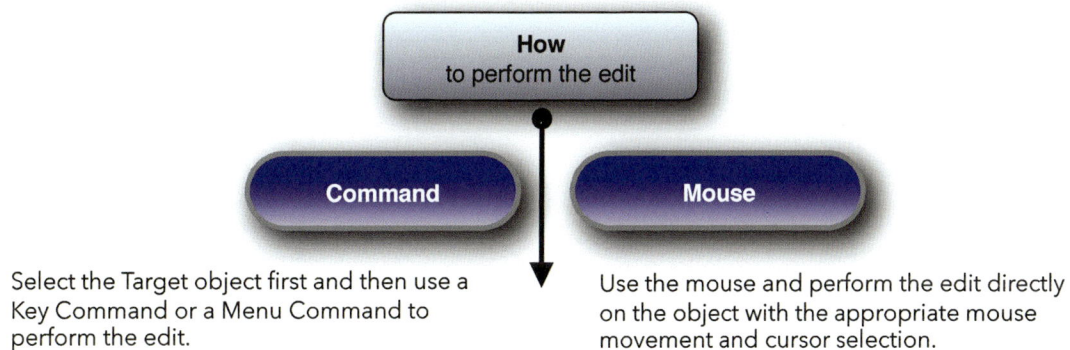

```
           ┌──────────────────┐
           │       How        │
           │ to perform the edit │
           └──────────────────┘
                    │
      ┌─────────────┴─────────────┐
  ( Command )                ( Mouse )
```

Select the Target object first and then use a Key Command or a Menu Command to perform the edit.

Use the mouse and perform the edit directly on the object with the appropriate mouse movement and cursor selection.

➡ Using Commands

When using a command (Key Command, Menu Command, or Touch Bar buttons), you have to be aware of what the Target object will be for your command. That depends mainly on what is selected. It sounds trivial but being aware of what is affected by the command you are using is very crucial, because the same command can have different outcomes depending on what is selected. Especially with very complex editing sessions, you want to avoid editing (changing) something by accident, that you might not even realize at that moment.

Let's look at four different scenarios that might be selected and see what commands are available:

- ▶ #1 **Nothing** is selected
- ▶ #2 **Clip** is selected
- ▶ #3 **Range** is selected
- ▶ #4 **Edit Point** is selected

⚙ #1 - Nothing is selected

In this scenario, no Timeline Clip is selected. However, even if there is no specific Timeline Clip selected, a command will still apply its edit to a specific Clip. In this case, it is the top-most Clip at the current Playhead/Skimmer position.

▶ **Target Indication**

FCPx has a little hint, a red dot on the Playhead that indicates which Clip is the target for any trim edit (and also any edit in the Inspector).

As you can see in the first screenshot, the red dot is on the "Beach" Clip ❶, but in the second screenshot, the target is the Connected Clip "Mountains" ❷, because it is the top-most Clip at this Timeline location.

▶ **Touch Bar**

Please note that when the Timeline Pane is selected, the Touch Bar will have three buttons ❸ on the right for the Trim Commands. With these commands, you can also trim to the Skimmer position.

Touch Bar (Timeline View)

❸ Trim Buttons

▶ **Commands**

Here are the various trim commands. They are all located in the Trim Menu ❹:

- **Trim Start**: The target Clip in the Timeline gets its left edge trimmed to the Playhead position. Any gap will be closed.
  - 📌 Key Command **opt+[**
  - 📌 Menu Command *Edit ➤ Trim Start*
  - 📌 *Tap* the Trim Start Button ▪[on the Touch Bar
- **Trim End**: The target Clip in the Timeline gets its right edge trimmed to the Playhead position. Any gap will be closed.
  - 📌 Key Command **opt+]**
  - 📌 Menu Command *Edit ➤ Trim End*
  - 📌 *Tap* the Trim End Button]▪ on the Touch Bar
- **Trim to Playhead**: The target Clip in the Timeline has its right or left edge trimmed to the Playhead position, depending on which side of the Playhead is closer.
  - 📌 Key Command **opt+**
  - 📌 Menu Command *Edit ➤ Trim To Playhead*
  - 📌 *Tap* the Trim To Playhead Button ⊡ on the Touch Bar
- **Blade**: Be careful, this is an exception. This command is applied to the Clip at the Primary Storyline and not the Clip with the red dot ⊙. The Clip gets cut at the Playhead or Skimmer position, creating two Clips. No change in the Timeline.
  - 📌 Key Command **cmd+B**
  - 📌 Menu Command *Edit ➤ Blade*

  To split all Clips at the Playhead/Skimmer position:
  - 📌 Key Command **sh+cmd+B**
  - 📌 Menu Command *Edit ➤ Blade ALL*

Main Menu

Trim	Mark	Clip	Modif
Blade			⌘B
Blade All			⇧⌘B
Join Clips			
❹			
Trim Start			⌥[
Trim End			⌥]
Trim To Playhead			⌥\\
Extend Edit			⇧X

👆 #2 - A Clip is Selected

In this scenario, a Clip(s) is selected and, therefore, only that Clip(s) will be affected by the command.

- ▶ **Trim**: All the Trim commands from the previous section, where no Clip was selected, also apply when a Clip is selected as long as the Playhead is positioned over it.

- ▶ **Duration**: Changing the duration of a Clip is the same as trimming the end of a Clip. There are four ways to initiate that command:
  - 📌 *Double-click* on the SMPTE Reader to enter the duration as an absolute time value. Any of the other three commands follow the same procedure. The display changes to the Numeric Input Mode (purple) with the following sign 🔲 ❶. Type in a number value and press *return*
  - 📌 Key Command *ctr+D*
  - 📌 Main Menu *Modify ➤ Change Duration...*
  - 📌 *Ctr+click* on the Clip and choose the *Shortcut Menu ➤ Change Duration...*

SMPTE Reader

00:00:04:25 ❶

- ▶ **Move by Nudge Value**: This procedure moves the selected Clip(s) left or right by the nudge value amount (connected Clips will move in sync). Be careful, every Clip in the way will be overwritten and potential Gap Clips are left behind. Connected Clips in the way will be "taken over"!

  - Nudge 1 frame left or right with **,** and **.** (the keys with the < and > character). Also available from the Main Menu *Trim ➤ Nudge Left/Right* ❷.
  - Nudge 10 frames left or right with the Key Command *sh+,* (shift and the comma key) *and sh+.* (shift and the period key).
  - Nudge 1 subframe (1/80 frame) left or right with *opt+,* (option and the comma key) and *opt+.* (option and the period key).

Trim Menu

Trim	Mark	Clip	Modif
Blade			⌘B
Blade All			⇧⌘B
Join Clips			
Trim Start			⌥[
Trim End			⌥]
Trim To Playhead			⌥\
Extend Edit			⇧X
Align Audio to Video			
Nudge Left	❷		,
Nudge Right			.

- ▶ **Move by Numeric Value**: When a Clip is selected and you press the **+** or **-** key, the SMPTE Reader changes to Numeric Input Mode. The little sign 🔲 now looks like a "Slide" symbol ❸, because you are performing a Slide Edit.

+ 00:00:02:10 ❸

- ▶ **Delete**: The selected Clip(s) and its Connected Clips will be deleted and any gap will be closed up by the surrounded Clips if it was on the Primary Storyline ("Ripple Delete"). Be careful, deleting a Clip on the Primary Storyline will also delete all its Connected Clips.
  - 📌 Main Menu *Edit ➤ Delete* (*delete* ⌫) ❹
  - 📌 Main Menu *Edit ➤ Cut* (*cmd+X*)

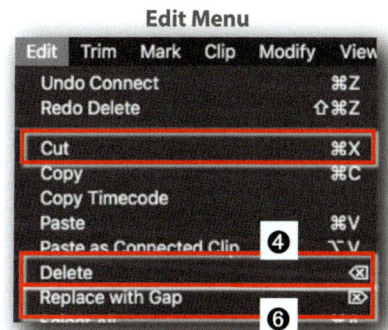

Edit Menu

Edit	Trim	Mark	Clip	Modify	View
Undo Connect					⌘Z
Redo Delete					⇧⌘Z
Cut					⌘X
Copy					⌘C
Copy Timecode					
Paste					⌘V
Paste as Connected Clip	❹				⌥⌘V
Delete					⌫
Replace with Gap	❻				⌦

- ▶ **Delete without Connecting Clips**: There is one procedure that lets you delete a Clip on the Primary Storyline without deleting any Connected Clips that are connected to that Clip.
  - 📌 Holding down the "Tilde" key (the ~ above the tab key) or the Disconnect Button on the Touch Bar 🔲 and the "temporarily disconnect" symbol 🔲 ❺ is added to (most of) the Edit Tools. Now, when pressing the *delete* key, only that selected Clip on the Primary Storyline will be deleted, the Connected Clip remains at its position and re-connects to the Clip that will move to that space.

- ▶ **Replace with Gap**: This command also deletes the selected Clip(s), but it replaces it with a Gap Clip to ensure that no other Clips are moved to close the gap.
  - 📌 Main Menu *Edit ➤ Replace with Gap* ❻
  - 📌 Key Command *ForwardDelete* ⌦

😒 #3 - A Range is Selected

In this scenario, the Range Selection ❶ is used as a guide to trim the start time of the Clip to the left border of the Range Selection ❷ and at the same time trim the end time of the Clip to the right border of the Range Selection ❸.

- ▶ **Trim To Selection**: Drag a Range with the Range Tool 🔲, which can span across multiple Clips, and use any of the following commands:
  - 📌 Menu Command *Edit ➤ Trim to Selection*
  - 📌 Key Command *opt+*

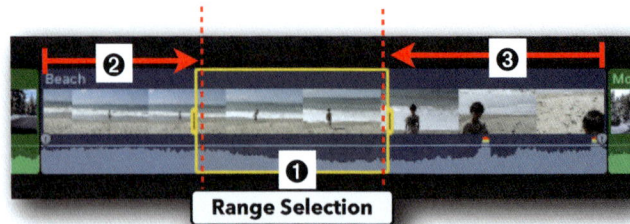

😒 #4 - Edit Points are Selected

In this scenario, you select the specific Edit Point with the Trim Tool 🔳 first and then type in the SMPTE Reader the amount of time that you want to shift that Edit Point. This method is for more precise trimming.

- ☑️ ***Click*** on the area of the Clip with the Trim Tool 🔳 to get the yellow bracket(s), the Edit Point, indicating what trimming technique will be performed on what Clip.
- ☑️ Press the plus or minus key ❺, depending on what direction you want to move the Edit Point. This sets the SMPTE Reader into Numeric Input Mode (purple display).
- ☑️ Enter the amount you want to trim on the keyboard ❻. The numbers, including a graphical indication of the trimming mode ❼, will be displayed in the SMPTE Reader.
  - Press **+** or **-** at any time to change the moving direction (as long as you are in Numeric Input Mode). Start from right (frames) to left. "23" means "23 frames", "213" means "2sec 13frames". Use the decimal point as a value divider "1." means "1sec 00frames". The number entry has some sort of intelligence. If you work in a 30f format and you type in "35", the display will automatically display "1s 5frames".
- ☑️ Press ***enter*** to execute that edit or press ***esc*** to abort the process.

Extend Edit is an additional command that moves the selected Edit Point (the yellow bracket) to the current Playhead/Skimmer position.

- 📌 Menu Command *Trim ➤ Extend Edit*
- 📌 Key Command *sh+X*

➡️ **Using the Mouse**

Trimming with commands allows very accurate editing, but it requires a two step process of selecting the target first and then applying the command. Trimming with the mouse, on the other hand, is a more direct and intuitive method, because you are performing your edit right there at your finger tips.

The mouse cursor in FCPx changes its function (and appearance) depending on where you move the mouse over (so-called Click Zones). It requires much less switching of the Cursor Tools. You can even temporarily switch to a different Edit Tool by holding down the same key that you would normally use to permanently switch to that Tool, perform the action, and then release the key.

The important thing, however, is that you always have to be aware of what the current selected Edit Tool is.

⊚ Edit Points

⟨⏐⟩ Trim Tool

The mouse cursor automatically changes to a different icon when moved over specific areas of the Clip to indicate the current trimming mode. The Clip Skimming is automatically enabled with the Trim Tool, indicated by the orange Skimmer. Once you **click** or **drag** on that position, the yellow bracket(s), the Edit Point appears and lets you perform that trim edit. **Cmd+drag** lets you trim with a finer resolution.

- ▶ **Ripple Left**: *Click* close to the left border of a Clip with the Trim Tool ⟨⏐⟩
- ▶ **Ripple Right**: *Click* close to the right border of a Clip with the Trim Tool ⟨⏐⟩
- ▶ **Roll**: *Click* between two adjacent Clips with the Trim Tool ⟨⏐⟩
- ▶ **Slip**: *Click* on the Clip with the Trim Tool ⟨⏐⟩
- ▶ **Slide**: *Opt+click* on the Clip with the Trim Tool ⟨⏐⟩

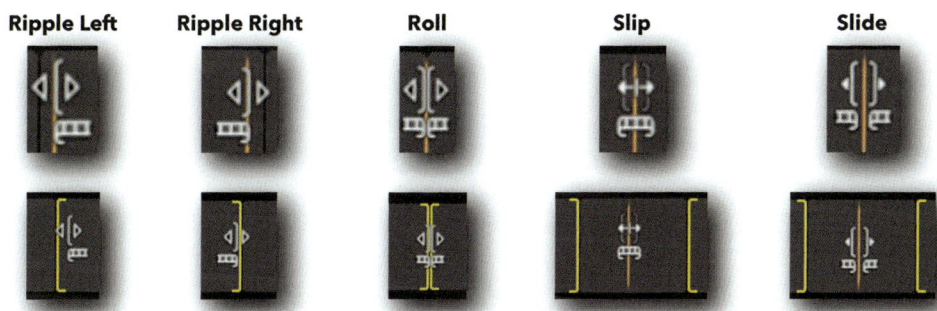

Ripple Left	Ripple Right	Roll	Slip	Slide

Ripple Left and Ripple Right can also be performed with the Select Tool ⬉. The Edit Tool automatically changes to that Tool when moving close to the left or right border of a Clip.

▶ Position Tool

The Position Tool provides a special type of trimming:

- ▶ The only trim edits you can perform with the Position Tool is Ripple Left and Ripple Right.
- ▶ When you shorten a Clip (on the left or right border), then the adjacent Clip stays fixed. This is the exception to the Magnetic Timeline if you want to make sure that existing Clips stay locked to the timeline. The shortened area will be filled with a Gap Clip.
- ▶ You cannot extend the left or right border into the adjacent Clip unless you extend into a Gap Clip.

Ripple Left   Ripple Right

💀 Split Clips

📷 Blade Tool

This trimming command allows you to split a selected Clip into two. Like the Trim Tool, the Blade Tool has its built-in Clip Skimming (always on) so you can see in the Viewer and the SMPTE Reader where you split the Clip.

There are three appearance of the Blade Tool:

▶ **Red Blade**: This indicates an inactive Clip when you move anywhere in the Timeline area outside a Clip. A click will only move the Playhead to that position.

▶ **Black Blade**: This indicates an active Blade, when you move the cursor over a Clip (Primary Storyline or Connected Clip). Click on it to split that Clip.

▶ **Double Blade** (red or black): The cursor switches to this tool when you hold down the *shift* key. Now all Clips along the Playhead or Skimmer will be split.

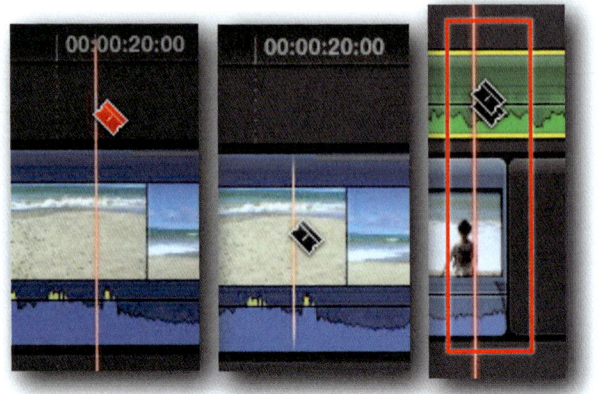

💀 Moving Clips

Besides trimming Clips in their position, you can also move Clip(s) around.

▶ Select Tool

▶ **Move any Clip(s)**: *Drag* the selection only between existing Clips. Any necessary gap will be closed or Clips will be moved out of the way.

▶ **Copy any Clip(s)**: *Opt+drag* the selected Clip(s). Same dragging behavior.

▶ *Position Tool*

▶ **Move any Clip(s)**: *Drag* the selection freely to any position on the Timeline. Any existing Clips will not change their position but might be (partially) overwritten. Gap Clips will be inserted if necessary.

▶ **Copy any Clip(s)**: *Opt+drag* the selected Clip(s). Again, all the existing Clips will not change their position but might be (partially) overwritten. Gap Clips will be inserted if necessary.

Precision Editor

The Precision Editor is not a separate Editor window, it is just an expanded view of the Timeline to provide a more visualized trimming in the Primary Storyline.

Active Edit Point Handle   Edit Point Handles

🔘 Open Precision Editor

- *Double-click* on an Edit Point ❶ between two Clips in the Primary Storyline (with Pointer or Trim Tool).
- Select an Edit Point (not the whole Clip) and use the command from the Main Menu *View ➤ Show Precision Editor* or Key Command *ctr+E*.

The Precision Editor splits the Primary Storyline into two lanes. All the Clips up to the Edit Point are placed on the upper lane ❷ and the remaining Clips on the lower lane ❸. The trimmed ("not used") portion of the outgoing Clip and incoming Clip (the "Media Handles") will also be visible, but slightly dimmed ❹. Between the two lanes is a center line ❺ that has an Edit Point Handle at each Edit Point of two adjacent Clips. The Handle for the current Edit Point is bigger and has a vertical Edit Line, marking the edit position ❻.

Now you can perform Ripple Edits and Roll Edits while you see the whole portion ("Handle") of the outgoing and incoming Clip. The Viewer will display a split view to show the last (outgoing) and first (incoming) frame of the edit.

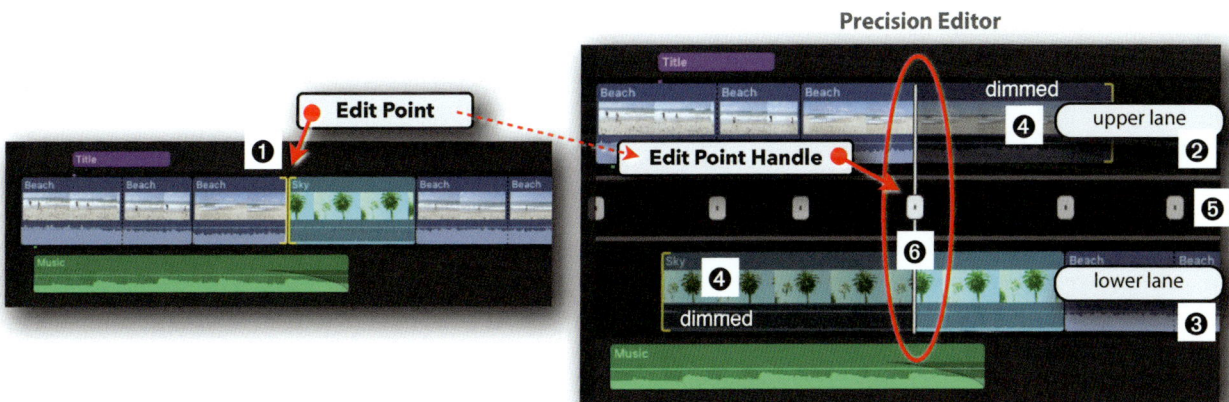

Precision Editor

🔘 Select Different Edit Point

- *Click* on any of the other Edit Point Handles in the center lane to have the Precision Editor split the lane there
- Key Command *ArrowUp* and *ArrowDown*

🔘 Close the Precision Editor

- *Double-click* on the Edit Point Handle
- Main Menu *View ➤ Hide Precision Editor*
- Key Command *ctr+E* or *esc*

The Precision Editor provides a few unique editing techniques. I'll demonstrate how it works in the diagrams below:

- ▶ The upper Clip is the outgoing Clip with the dimmed portion to the right
- ▶ The lower Clip is the incoming Clip with the dimmed portion to the left
- ▶ The Brackets are the Edit Points (they are yellow in FCPx when selected)

- ▶ In the middle is the active Edit Point Handle and the vertical Edit Line that marks the split
- ▶ All the elements in gray are unaffected by the dragging action, they aren't moving
- ▶ All the elements in red are moving with the blue arrow indicating where you are click-dragging

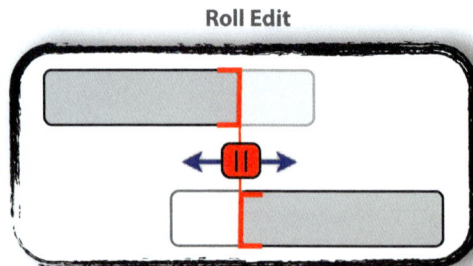

Roll Edit

Dragging the Edit Marker Handle in the center moves both Edit Points with it in the opposite direction. The Clips don't change their position only their Edit Points.

Ripple Edit outgoing

You're moving the Edit Point of the outgoing Clip (top). The Clip itself won't move. The lower Clip, however, is attached to the (moving) Edit Point and, therefore, moves that whole Clip with it (and the rest of the sequence to the right).

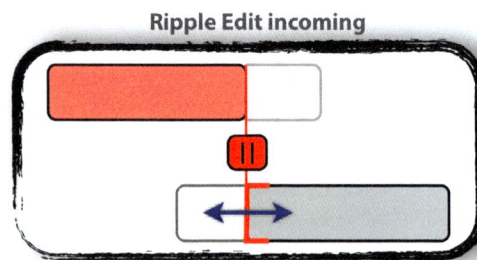

Ripple Edit incoming

You're moving the Edit Point of the incoming Clip (bottom). The Clip itself won't move. However, the upper Clip is attached to the (moving) Edit Point, moving the whole Clip with it (and all the Clips on the left).

Ripple Edit outgoing

You select the outgoing Edit Point, but this time you don't drag that Edit Point against the Clip. Instead, you drag the Clip against the Edit Point (moving all the Clips to the left with it).

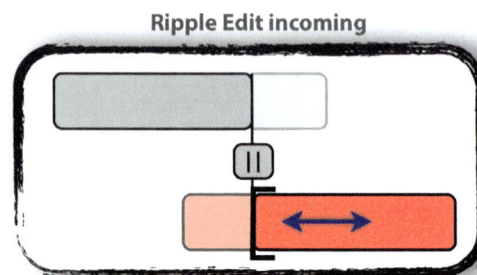

Ripple Edit incoming

You select the incoming Edit Point but this time you don't drag that Edit Point against the Clip. Instead, you drag the Clip against the Edit Point (moving the rest of the sequence with it).

- 💡 **Transitions**: The Precision Editor provides additional editing features when editing Transitions.
- 💡 **Skim Edits**: You can also skim in the used and unused (dimmed) area of the Clip to find the in or out point. Hit the spacebar to play that portion. Once you locate the frame, *click* the mouse and the Edit Point jumps to that position.
- 💡 **Numeric Edits**: You can also use all the numeric entries of timecode values in the SMPTE Reader to precisely move the selected Edit Point(s).

➡ Copy Paste

When editing your video in the Timeline, you can also use standard copy-paste procedures:

- ▸ **Cut**: You can select one or multiple Timeline Clips and use the standard Cut command (*Edit ➤ Cut* or *cmd+X* ❶) to copy those Clips to the clipboard and remove them from the Timeline. The Primary Storyline fills the gaps (Magnetic Timeline).

- ▸ **Copy**: You can select one or multiple Timeline Clips (or Event Clips) and use the standard Copy command (*Edit ➤ Copy* or *cmd+C* ❶) to copy those Clips to the clipboard.

- ▸ **Paste**: Use the standard Paste command (*Edit ➤ Paste* or *cmd+V* ❷) to place the Clips that are currently on the clipboard to the Primary Storyline at the current Playhead/Skimmer position. This functions as an Insert command, which will move any other Clips on the Primary Storyline to the right.

- ▸ **Paste as Connected Clip**: Use this Paste as Connected Clip command (*Edit ➤ Paste as Connected Clip* or *opt+V* ❷) to place the Clips that are currently on the clipboard as Connected Clips at the current Playhead/Skimmer position attached to the Clip on the Primary Storyline at that position.

Edit Menu

➡ Disable/Enable Clip

You can disable selected Clips, which means the video signal will be black and the audio signal is muted. The Clip turns darker in the Timeline ❸.

The following commands toggle the status:

- Key Command *V*
- Main Menu *Clip ➤ Disable/Enable Clip*
- *Ctr+click* on the Timeline Clip and select from the *Shortcut Menu ➤ Disable/Enable*

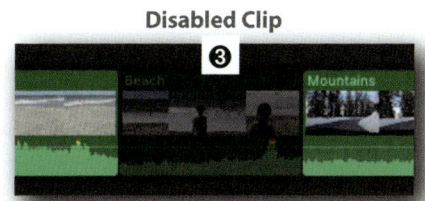

Disabled Clip

➡ Rename Clip

Here is one very simple but effective edit command, renaming the Clip.

You can rename a Timeline Clip in the following areas:

- **Timeline**: *Ctr+click* on the Timeline Clip and select from the *Shortcut Menu ➤ Rename Clip* ❹
- **Timeline Index**: *Double-click* the name in the list and type the new name in the entry field ❺
- **Inspector**: Select the Clip and display the Info tab 🔵 in the Inspector window. Type the name in the first field ❻.

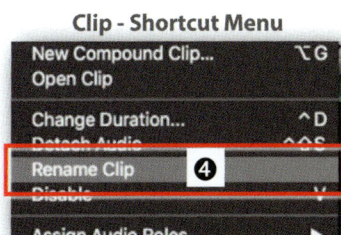

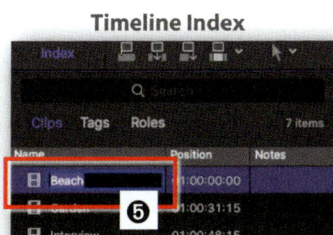

Clip - Shortcut Menu **Timeline Index** **Inspector - Info**

Basics

The concept of Connected Clips has great advantages when editing your video project, however, they come with special "rules and regulations" you have to pay attention to during editing.

➡ Place a Connected Clip

There are two ways to move a Clip from the Browser Pane to the Timeline as a Connected Clip.

▸ **Command**: Select the Clip in the Browser, position the Playhead on the Timeline where you want to position it, and use any of the Connect commands. Clips with video content are automatically placed above the Primary Storyline (used for "cutaways", "B-roll"), Clips with audio-only content are automatically placed below the Primary Storyline. These are the available commands.

- *Click* on the Connect Button 🖵 in the Timeline Pane Header
- Main Menu *Edit* ➤ *Connect to Primary Storyline*
- Key Command *Q*

▸ **Drag-and-Drop**: Instead of using a command, just *drag* the Clip from the Browser onto the Timeline at the position you want.

➡ Connection Point (Line)

The connection between a Connected Clip and its Parent Clip on the Primary Storyline is indicated by a Connection Point ❶ above or below the Parent Clip. If the Connected Clip is selected, then the entire Connection Line ❷ is displayed.

A few things about this "connection":

▸ **Move Parent Clip**: Moving a Parent Clip on the Primary Storyline will together move all the Connected Clips that are attached to that Parent Clip. They stay in sync.

▸ **Move Connected Clip**: Moving a Connected Clip will not move its Parent Clip. The Connected Clip can be moved independently and its Connection Point will attach to the new position on the Parent Clip or any Clip on the Primary Storyline that you move it over to.

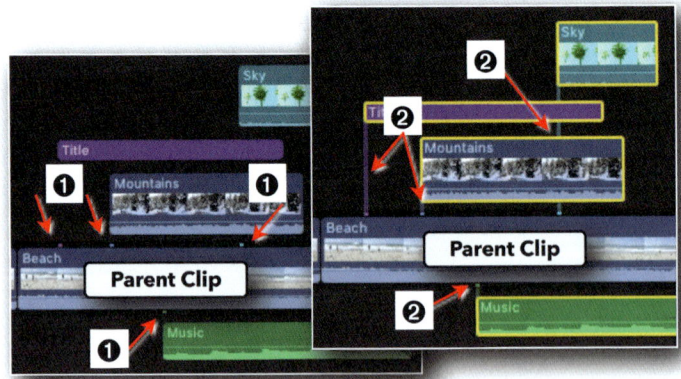

🔘 Connection Line - Default Position

As a default, the Connection Point is positioned at the first frame ❸ of the Connected Clip.

🔘 Connection Line - Custom Position

If you have, for example, an audio clip as a Connected Clip to the Parent Clip on the Primary Storyline that needs to start before that Clip, but still needs to be connected to that specific Parent Clip, then you need to place the Connection Point later on the Parent Clip ❹ before moving the Connected Clip to the left. *Opt+cmd+click* anywhere on the Connected Clip to place the Connection Point to that position in reference to the Parent Clip (without changing the sync between the Connected Clip and its Parent Clip).

Editing

Here are the various editing tasks that involve Connected Clips.

➡ *Edit Connected Clips*

Editing Connected Clips is simple:

🌑 No Magnetic Timeline

Connected Clips are "independent Clips" that don't follow the Magnetic Timeline. You can freely edit them (move, trim, etc.) without affecting any other Clip. Only the Connection Point might be repositioned to adjust to the edit.

➡ *Edit Parent Clip*

Editing the Parent Clip on the Primary Storyline a Connected Clip is attached to is more critical and requires special attention.

- ▶ **Delete**: Deleting a Clip on the Primary Storyline will delete all its Connected Clips.
- ▶ **Move**: Moving a Clip on the Primary Storyline will move all its Connected Clips with it.
- ▶ **Trim**: Trimming the Start Point of a Parent Clip to the right will adjust the Connection Point so it stays with the Parent Clip (without changing their relative position). However, moving the End Point to the left over a Connection Point, will keep the Connected Clip at its absolute position and re-attaches it to that new Clip "underneath".
- ▶ **Split**: Splitting a Parent Clip has no affect on the Connected Clip. It will be attached to the portion of the Clip where the Connecting Point is attached to.

🌑 Disconnect Mode 🔌

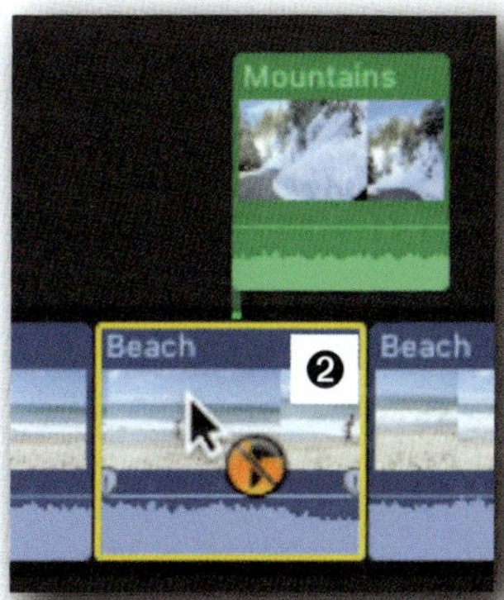

FCPx provides a tool to temporarily disconnect the "bond" between Connected Clips and their Parent Clips and lets you edit the Parent Clip on the Primary Storyline without affecting the Connected Clip. During that time, the Connected Clips are temporarily connected to the Timeline instead and keep that time position regardless of the edit on the Parent Clip.

You can switch to this Disconnect Mode in two ways:

- 📌 Hold down the Grave Accent (`) key, the one above the tab key, also referred to as the "Tilde" key (~).
- 📌 Press the Disconnect Button ❶ on the Touch Bar.

Touch Bar

A special icon ❷ 🔌 appears at the Edit Tool (cursor) to indicate that you are editing in Disconnect Mode.

- ▶ **Delete/Move/Trim**: When deleting, moving, trimming, and even choosing a different Clip from an Audition Clip on the Primary Storyline will not affect the Connected Clips. They will re-connect to whatever Clips move into the position on the Primary Storyline. If there are no Clips on the Primary Storyline to connect to, then FCPx creates a Gap Clip in that place and the Connected Clip will attach to that Gap Clip.

➡ *Edit both Clips*

Moving a Parent Clip will move all its Connected Clips, but copying a Parent Clip (*opt+drag*) will not copy its Connected Clip. For that, you have to select the Parent Clip and its Connected Clip(s).

➡ *Move up-down*

When you move an Event Clip to the Timeline, you can put the Clip on the Primary Storyline or attach it as a Connected Clip to a Parent Clip on the Primary Storyline. Once positioned, you still can exchange the position of a Clip between being a Connected Clip or a Clip on the Primary Storyline.

🌑 Primary Storyline -> Connected

These are the commands to change (move vertically) a Clip from the Primary Storyline to a Connected Clip:

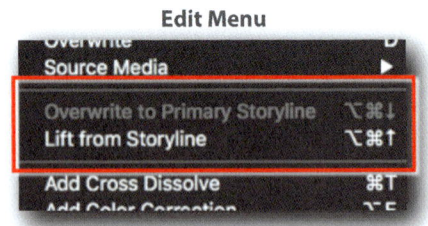

- *Drag* the Clip up or down from the Primary Storyline
- Key command *opt+cmd+ArrowUp*
- Main Menu *Edit ➤ Lift from Storyline*
- *Ctr+click* on the Clip and choose from the *Shortcut Menu ➤ Lift from Storyline*

Please pay attention to the different outcomes what happens to that "vacant" spot on the Primary Storyline:

- **Select Tool** ⬆: When using the *drag* procedure with the Select Tool, then the space on the Primary Storyline is filled with the Clips on the right, moving to the left to fill the gap (Magnetic Storyline). The new Connected Clip (and any existing Clips at that position) will attach to the new Clip that moved to that position on the Primary Storyline.

- **Position Tool** ⬆: When using the *drag* procedure with the Position Tool, then the vacant spot on the Primary Storyline is filled with a new Gap Clip. No Clips on the Primary Storyline will be moved. The new Connected Clip (and any existing Clips at that position) will attach to the new Gap Clip that moved to that position on the Primary Storyline. This is also the effect when using the Key Command *opt+cmd+ArrowUp* and the Menu Commands *Lift from Storyline*.

🌑 Connected -> Storyline

This command, moving the Clip in the opposite direction, is called "Overwrite to Primary Storyline", which moves the Connected Clip to the Primary Storyline.

These are the commands:

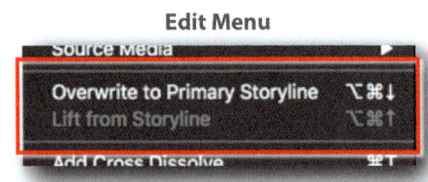

- *Drag* the Connected Clip onto the Primary Storyline
- Key command *opt+cmd+ArrowDown*
- Main Menu *Edit ➤ Overwrite to Primary Storyline*
- *Ctr+click* on the Clip and choose from the *Shortcut Menu ➤ Overwrite to Primary Storyline*

The outcome also has some specialties you have to pay attention to:

- Using the drag-and-drop action with the mouse follows the basic move procedures. If you use the Position Tool ⬆, then Clips will be overwritten, and using the Select Tool ⬆ will only let you insert the Clip between two Clips on the Primary Storyline.

- Using any of the commands, will overwrite (replace) the existing Clip(s) on the Primary Storyline, but only the video content. The original Video expands its audio content and continues that portion during the duration for the newly inserted Clip.

Adding Effects to a Clip

In addition to creating the sequence of Clips and trimming them on the Timeline, a big portion of your video editing will be the "treatment" of the individual Clips with all the available effects, for audio and video.

I touched the topic of Clip Properties before, but especially in the context of editing in the Timeline, it is very important to understand what is affecting what and at what level when it comes to applying effects to your Clips. Here is the underlying concept again with a different diagram.

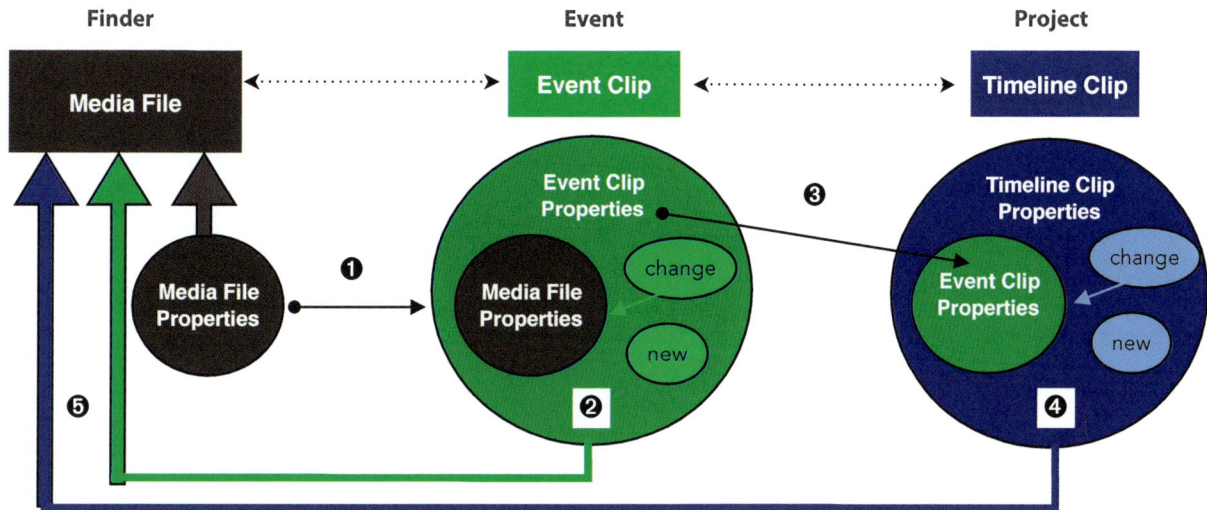

❶ You import a Media File into an Event. An Event Clip is created in the Browser that is linked to that Media File. The Event Clip inherits the original Properties of the Media File. It is like a one time "lookup".

❷ The Event Clip Properties can now be edited in the Inspector. You can change the inherited Properties and add new ones.

❸ Now, when you drag an Event Clip onto the Project Timeline, a Timeline Clip is created on the Timeline that is linked to the Event Clip. This Timeline Clip inherits the Properties of the Event Clip. Part of the Properties is the location of the Source Media File that the Event Clip is linked to. Again, this is a one time lookup.
It is very important to understand that this copy procedure of the Properties is a one time "lookup" at the moment when the Timeline Clip is created. Any changes made in the Event Clip later on are not reflected in that Timeline Clip.

❹ The Timeline Clip Properties can now be edited in the Inspector. Those changes are unique to that Timeline Clip. Any Clip that is placed on the Timeline carries its individual Properties that can be edited. Every time you drag an Event Clip from the

Browser to the Timeline or copy a Timeline Clip on the Timeline, you create a new Timeline Clip. Each of those "new" Timeline Clips has its own Properties that can be edited independently in the Inspector or the Timeline.

❺ If you play back the original Media File in the Finder (with QuickView), its own playback Properties apply. When you play back the Event Clip, then any playback instruction stored in the Event Clip Properties will apply when playing back the Media File. (i.e. play at -6dB). When you play back the Timeline Clip, any playback instruction stored in the Timeline Clip Properties will apply when playing back the Media File. (i.e. play with reverb and change the color tone of the video). Of course, all those instructions are non-destructive playback instructions. The Media File stays untouched. Please note that this model doesn't take the concept of rendering into account.

Editing the Properties for the Event Clip or the Timeline Clip is straight forward. You have the Inspector open *cmd+4* and select the Clip. The Inspector displays the information from whatever Clip is selected and you go ahead and make any necessary changes in the Inspector.

Properties - Attributes - Parameters

We haven't talked about databases for a while. Let's quickly recap a few facts, because they are important for understanding the concept of adding effects to your Clips.

▶ Each Event Clip ❶ and Timeline Clip ❷ represents a record in one of the databases (saved in your Library File) that stores all the properties for each individual Clip.

▶ The Inspector Pane ❸ displays all those Properties when you select a Clip.

▶ All the Properties are grouped into separate views in the Inspector. For example, the Info Inspector 🛈 lists most of the metadata, the Audio Inspector 🔊 lists all the audio related attributes and the Video Inspector ▦ lists all the video related attributes.

▶ The Inspector not only displays all the properties, it also lets you edit most of the Parameters.

▶ BTW, all those terms like Properties, Attributes, and Parameters, refer to the same thing, the individual data sets, pieces of information that make up the characteristics of those Clips.

➡ Adding Effects

Here is the basic concept on how to add an Effect to a Timeline Clip.

▶ All the available Audio and Video Effects are located in the Effects Browser ❹ ▦ (*cmd+5*).

▶ You *drag* an Effect from the Effects Browser directly onto a Timeline Clip ❺ to add it to that Clip (or *double-click* the Effect to apply it to every selected Timeline Clip).

▶ The new Effect becomes an independent Attribute with all its parameters displayed in the Inspector ❻ (when that Timeline Clip is selected).

▶ To edit the Effect, you adjust its parameters in the Inspector.

▶ Some parameters are also available as onscreen controls ❼ in the Viewer, that lets you adjust some effects visually on the actual video frame.

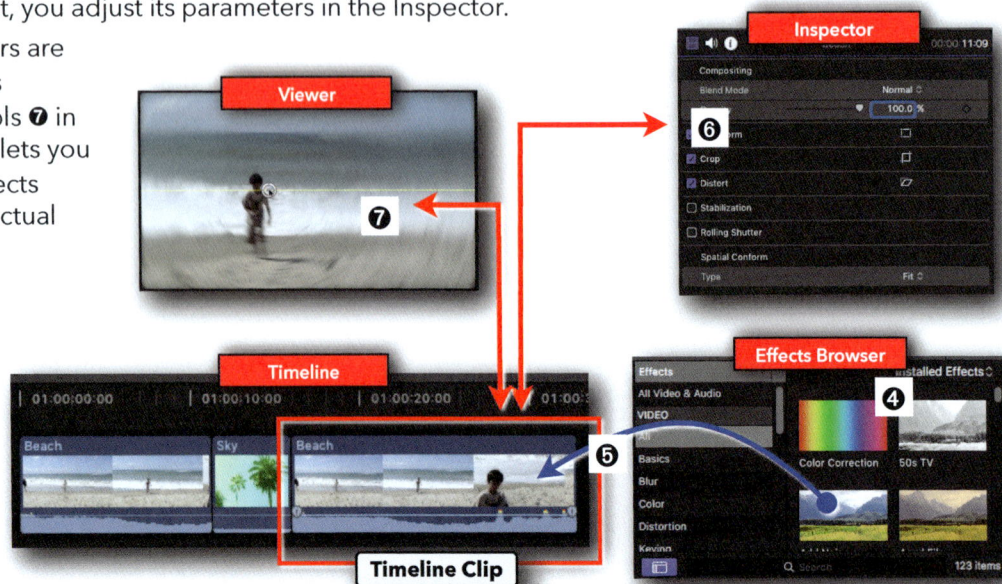

➡ *Event Clip vs. Timeline Clip*

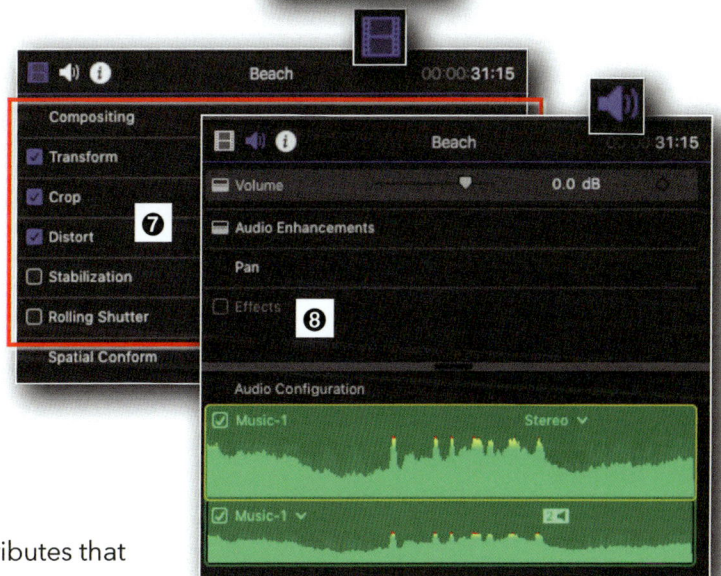

Here is a little detail I want to point out about the difference between the Event Clips and Timeline Clips regarding their Audio and Video Attributes.

🌐 Event Clips ❶

Usually, adding effects to your Clips is something that you do in the Timeline when working on your video edit. That means, any effects are added to the Timeline Clips. The Event Clips, on the other hand, represent the raw material that you gather in the Browser Pane so you can use it later for your edit by moving the Event Clips onto the Project Timeline. You cannot directly add effects to Event Clips in the Browser (you would have to open them in the Timeline or create Compound Clips, which I cover later). Instead of adding effects to Event Clips, you mainly "prepare" them for editing, which includes marking sections in the Clip and adding metadata. Therefore, there are only a few Attributes available in the Inspector.

- ▶ **Video Inspector** ▣: The Video Inspector only provides one Attribute, the Spatial Conform ❷. There are no other video attributes and you cannot add any Video Effects to it.

- ▶ **Audio Inspector** 🔊: The Audio Inspector has three Attributes ❸ (Volume, Audio Enhancements, Pan) plus the Audio Configurations with the waveforms at the bottom ❹. These parameters are mainly used for fixing any issues with the audio signal. You can optimize it during the preparation process, so you don't have to deal with issues (i.e. remove hum, adjust low volume, etc.) later when you are in the more creative/productive stage during editing. The Effects module ❺ is grayed out, because you are also not allowed to add any Audio Effects to the Event Clip.

🌐 Timeline Clips ❻

Here is a screenshot of the Audio and Video Attributes that are available as a default on a Timeline Clip:

- ▶ **Video Inspector** ▣: In addition to the Spatial Conform Attribute, you have six more default Attributes ❼ available in the Video Inspector. Any additional Video Effect that you add to the Timeline Clip will be later displayed at the top as its own module providing all the parameters for editing.

- ▶ **Audio Inspector** 🔊: The Audio Inspector shows the same Audio Attributes as the Event Clip ❽. Any adjustments that you did in the Event Clip (i.e. decrease volume -10dB) will be inherited when you move it to the Timeline and it becomes a Timeline Clip. Any Audio Effects that you add to the Timeline Clip will be added later to the bottom Effects section ❽ as its own module providing all its parameters.

➡ *Additional Effects*

Please refer to the Basic Operations chapter where I show the special interface elements of the Inspector. I will cover the specific Audio and Video Effects later in separate chapters. With the following screenshots, I want to show you how the additional Effects that you add to a Timeline Clip will be displayed in the Inspector.

▸ If you have added any Video Effects to the Timeline Clip, a new Effects section ❶ will be displayed on top of the Video Inspector.

▸ If you have added any Audio Effects to the Timeline Clip, then the Effects section will be enabled ❷. Remember, the Audio Inspector always shows that Effects section.

▸ The Effects section has a purple checkbox ❸ that lets you enable/disable all video or audio Effects for that Timeline Clip.

▸ *Double-click* on the header, next to the Effects label, or mouse-over the right side of the header and *click* on the "*Show*" button to toggle the visibility ❹ of all the effects that you added to that Timeline Clip.

▸ Each Effect, is represented by a separate Module. Here, I have two Video Effects ❺ and two Audio Effects ❻ with similar interface functionalities.

  • Toggle the purple checkbox ❼ to enable/ disable just that Effect.

  • *Click* the "*Show*" button to reveal the individual parameters for that effect.

▸ You can drag the header of an Effects Module up/down to rearrange the order of the effects, which could make a difference, depending on the used effects.

▸ Select an Effects module (shows yellow frame) and press *delete* to remove that module.

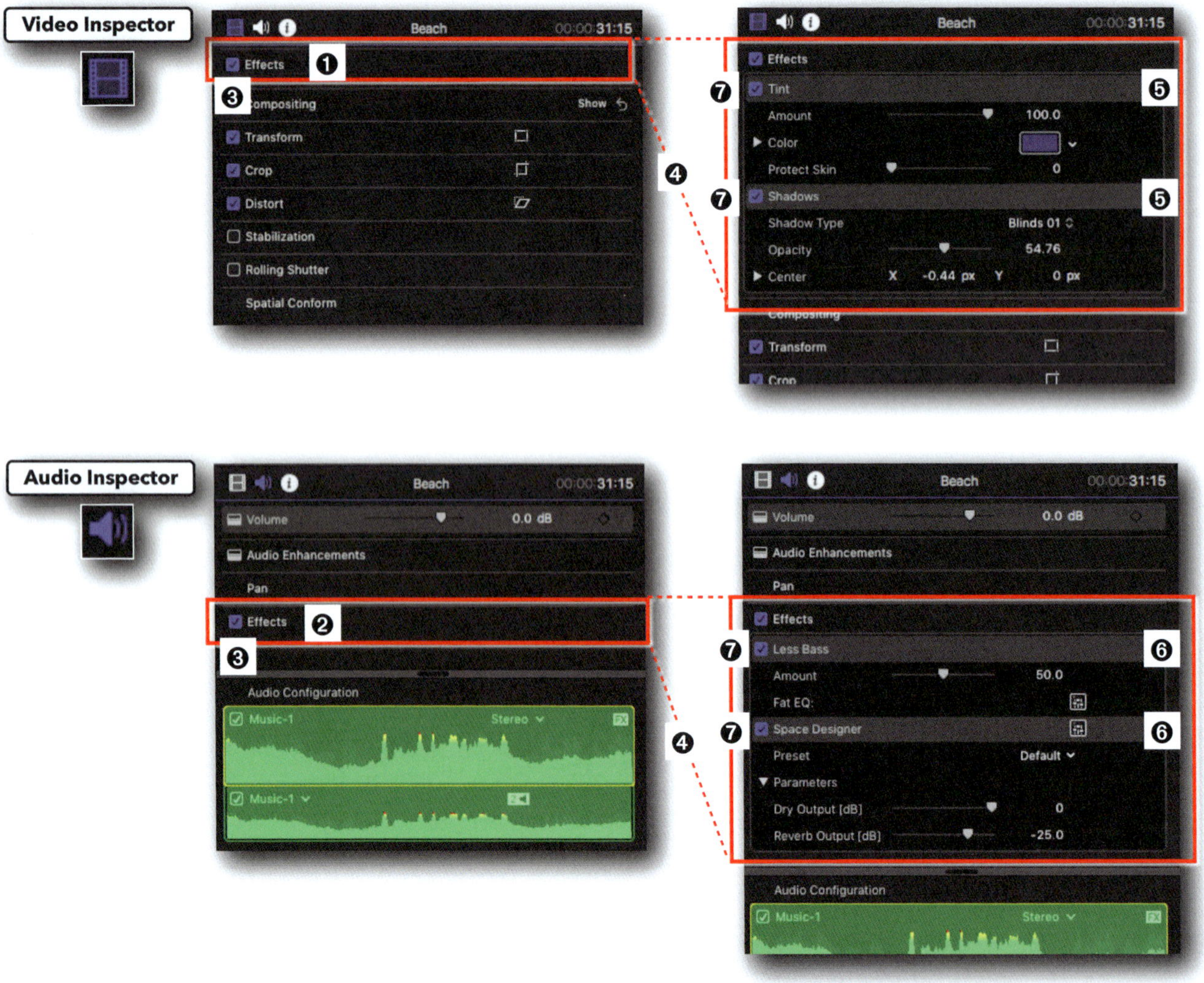

Copy/Paste Attributes

➡ *Terminology*

Before introducing a great workflow in FCPx regarding the Effects, we have to go over some terminology to avoid any possible confusion.

🌑 Attributes

The video signal and audio signal of a Clip has specific characteristics, the so-called Properties. For example, the audio signal is defined by its level, pan position, frequency response, etc. and the video signal is defined by its format, color, size, etc. When you play back a Clip unaltered, it plays back with its default properties.

FCPx provides various so-called Attributes that can change those Properties. For example, the Attribute "Volume" changes the signal level, the Attribute "Crop" cuts out a portion of the video frame. To do any of those alterations, which is referred to as "applying an Effect", you change the various Parameters of an Attribute.

So, think of an Attributes ❶ as a set of Parameters (one or multiple) that alters a specific aspect of the appearance or the sound of a Clip.

🌑 Parameters

Parameters ❷ are the individual controls like numeric values, sliders, checkboxes, menus, that belong to a specific Attribute.

🌑 Default Attributes ❸

The Default Attributes are all the Attributes that are always listed in the Inspector when you select a Clip.

🌑 Added Attributes (Effects) ❹

When you add a Video or Audio Effect to a Timeline Clip, it will show up as a new Attribute in the Inspector when you select that Clip.

🌑 Effects

The generic term" Effect" is used in FCPx in different ways:

- All the added Attributes of a Clip are listed in the Inspector under the Module labeled Effects ❺, either on top (for the Video Inspector) or the bottom (for the Audio Inspector).
- The Effects Browser in FCPx lists all the available Video and Audio Effects that you can add to a Timeline Clip.
- FCPx also uses the word "Effects" ❻ in two commands "Paste Effects" and "Remove Effects", which refers to the sum of all the Attributes.

➡ Copy - Paste - Remove

This is the standard procedure for altering your Timeline Clip:

- ☑️ Use any of the available Default Attributes in the Inspector and change their Parameters.
- ☑️ *Drag* additional Effects from the Effects Browser onto the Timeline Clip. Every new Effect will show up as an Added Attribute in the Inspector where you can adjust their Parameters.

And this is what you can do in addition, regarding the Effect.

▶ **Copy**: When you select a Timeline Clip ❶ and use the standard copy command (*Edit ➤ Copy* or *cmd+C*), the entire Clip, including its Video and Audio Attributes are copied to the clipboard ❷. This can be used to paste a copy of that Clip as a new Timeline Clip at another position on the Timeline. However, FCPx has two commands to use only the Attributes and "paste" them onto any existing Timeline Clips ❸.

▶ **Paste Effects** ❹: This command uses all Video and Audio Attributes of the Clip that has been copied to the clipboard ❷ and adds them to the currently selected Timeline Clip(s) ❸. Default Attributes will be overwritten.

▶ **Paste Attributes...** ❺: This command opens a Dialog ❻ with a list of all the Video and Audio Attributes of the Clip on the clipboard ❷. You can pick which Attributes you want to add to the currently selected Clip(s) ❸ and which Default Attribute you want to overwrite.

▶ **Remove Effects** ❼: This command does two things. It removes all the Video and Audio Effects that have been added to the currently selected Timeline Clip ❸ (Added Attributes). In addition, all the Default Attributes that can't be removed are reset to their default setting.

▶ **Remove Attributes...** ❽: This command opens a Dialog ❾ with a list of all the Video and Audio Attributes of the currently selected Timeline Clip ❸. You can pick which Attribute you want to remove. Again, selected Added Attributes, (the added Video and Audio Effects) are removed and selected Default Attributes are reset to their default values.

▶ **Save Effects Preset**: The bottom of the Inspector has a button "Save Effects Preset" ❿ that saves all the current Attributes as a *Final Cut Pro Effects Preset* file that will be available in the Effects Browser, so you can apply it to any Timeline Clip later in any Project or Library.

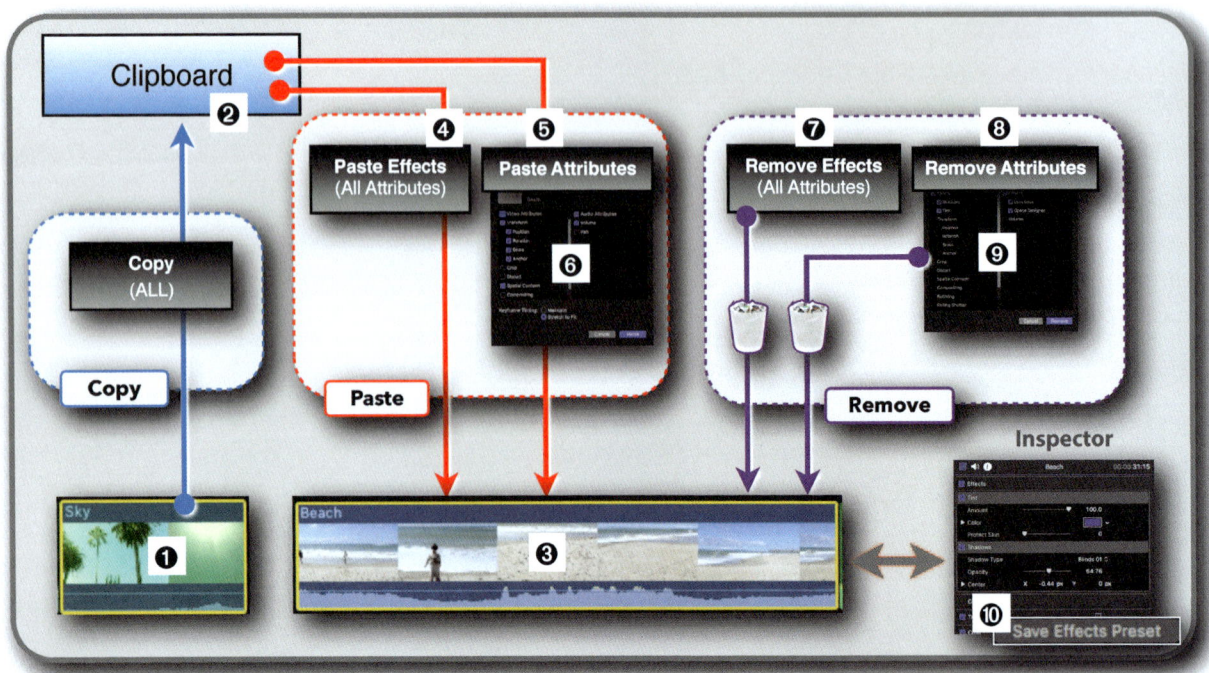

In this chapter, I want to talk about the other component in video production that often gets a little bit neglected, and that is, AUDIO.

Be careful, the way FCPx handles audio is quite different from other video editing software, including its own predecessor FCP7. If you don't take the time to explore and learn these new features and workflows you will be confused or even get stuck when dealing with the audio portion of your project.

I will start this chapter by taking the time to first talk about some fundamentals about audio and the underlying concepts in FCPx regarding audio. This will hopefully make it much easier later on to understand the functionality of the various controls, buttons, and menus in FCPx and easier to learn how to use them properly.

Concepts

In this section, I will lay the groundwork and go over the basic concepts and the terminology that is used when dealing with audio. The main problem with terminology is that different people often have a different understanding of what specific terms mean.

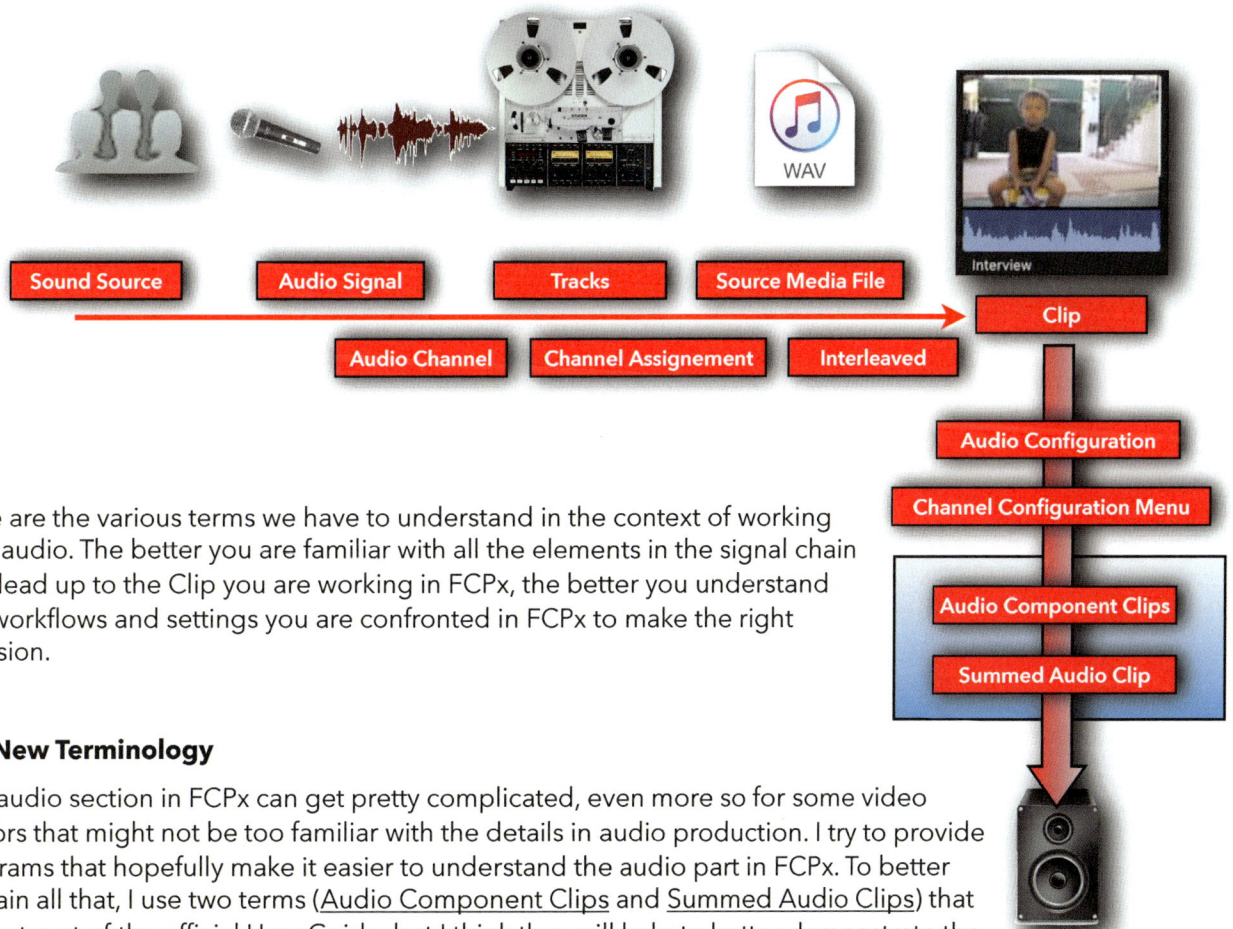

Here are the various terms we have to understand in the context of working with audio. The better you are familiar with all the elements in the signal chain that lead up to the Clip you are working in FCPx, the better you understand the workflows and settings you are confronted in FCPx to make the right decision.

🌑 New Terminology

The audio section in FCPx can get pretty complicated, even more so for some video editors that might not be too familiar with the details in audio production. I try to provide diagrams that hopefully make it easier to understand the audio part in FCPx. To better explain all that, I use two terms (Audio Component Clips and Summed Audio Clips) that are not part of the official User Guide, but I think they will help to better demonstrate the special and sometimes unique concepts and audio workflows in FCPx.

Before the Import

➡ *Where do Source Media Files Come From?*

We talked a lot about Source Media Files already in this book. These are the files that contain the video and/or audio that you import into your video as Clips. But where do these Source Media Files come from? Let's have a look at the audio portion of those files, because that has a lot to do with the understanding of how to use audio in FCPX.

🌐 Sound Source ❶

It all starts with a sound source that produces the actual audio signal. This can be an acoustic sound source or an electronic sound source:

▶ **Acoustic Sound Source**: An example would be non-musical sources like the dialog from an actor or natural sounds like thunder, door slams, or animal sounds. Musical sounds would be something from any kind of musical instruments or singers.

▶ **Electronic Sound Source**: Examples would be electronic instruments or the audio output of any type of audio device like CD-player or your computer.

🌐 Audio Signal ❷

The Audio Signal is simply the signal that is produced by the sound source. Please note that a single person or a single instrument produces an audio signal the same way as a big orchestra. So the audio signal itself is the single acoustic occurrence at a time, the signal that you capture, regardless of how many individuals or things "cause" that sound.

🌐 Tracks ❸

If you want to capture a sound source, you have to record its audio signal with any type of recording device. That could be a field recorder, a multi-track recorder, a dedicated Digital Audio Workstation (like Logic Pro or Pro Tools), and most of the video cameras can also record audio signals.

All those devices have so-called Tracks where they record the audio signal of a sound source onto. If the recording device provides multiple tracks, then you can record multiple signals from different sources (i.e. different microphones) at the same time, or later (a process called overdubbing).

🌐 Source Media File ❹

The recording device has to create the Source Media Files so FCPx can import them. It either automatically creates them or you manually have to save the recorded Tracks as those files.

🌐 Audio Channels ❺

Whoever creates the Source Media Files ❹ has to determine <u>how</u> to save the Audio Signals ❷ that were recorded on the Tracks ❸ of the recording device to the Source Media File. This is the part that many users are not aware of, but it is crucial in understanding many audio features in FCPx. So let's look into that next.

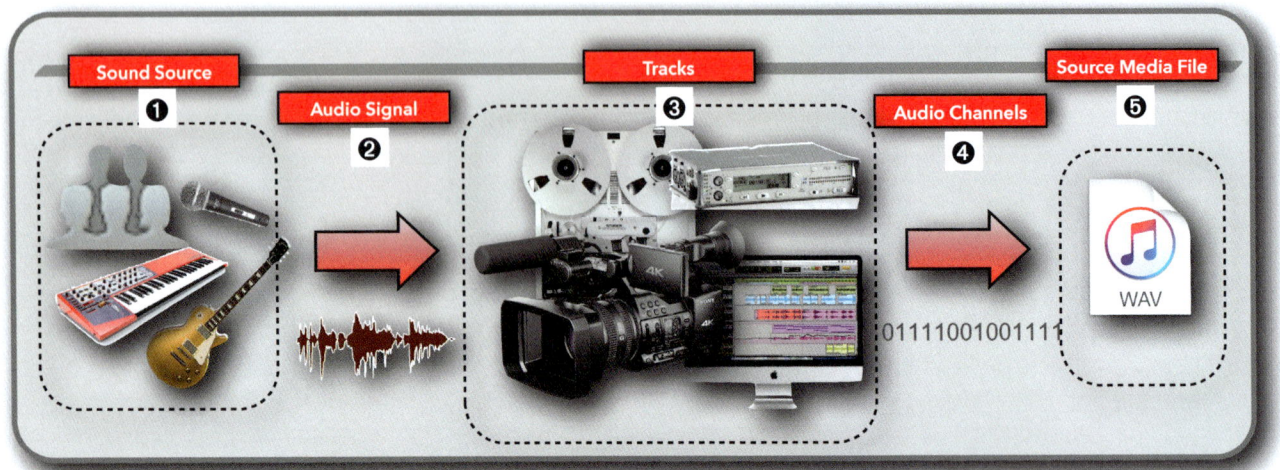

➡ *Channels and Channel Formats*

Video files and audio files are the two types of Source Media Files we are interested in right now, because they contain audio signals. The big question is, how is the audio signal stored on those files.

🔊 Audio Channel ❶

"Audio Channel" is the most important term in the context of Source Media Files. It is the direct translation of the previous terms we just discussed.

For example, 1 Audio Signal (from one or many "sound sources") is recorded on 1 Track of a recording device that saves it to a file, the Source Media File, as 1 Audio Channel. So, always think about an Audio Channel as the carrier of a single audio signal. And again, that single audio signal can be the recording of a cricket, an explosion, or the signal of symphony orchestra recorded with a single microphone.

🔊 Interleaved

The term "interleaved" is another one of those words that many users are confused about. First of all, it has nothing to do with "stereo", the word "interleave" just means "to combine". In this context, it describes what happens when you have more than one Audio Track on your recorder and want to save them to a single audio file.

- ▶ **Split**: You can create separate files (also referred to as "Split" files), one file ❷ for each audio channel and, therefore, each audio file containing one audio signal ❸.
- ▶ **Interleaved ❹**: You can save all channels (2, 4, 6, 7, etc.) into a single audio file ❺ by combining the data (not mixing the audio!) of all audio signals ❻, a process called "interleave".

🔊 Channel Assignment

Every Source Media File that carries more than one Audio Channel is an interleaved file and those files can contain an additional piece of important information: "What is the relationship between all those contained Audio Channels"?

- ▶ **Unassigned ❼**: If the file doesn't include any assignment information, then it means that the included audio channels are just independent mono signals. For example, a field recorder might record multiple sources (boom mic, Lav mic1, Lav mic2, etc.), but they are all independent mono signals.
- ▶ **Assigned ❽**: If, for example, an audio file contains the two channels of a stereo signal, then it can assign those channels. That means, it includes the information that channel 1 is the "Left" signal and channel 2 is the "Right" signal ❾. For a multichannel audio file it can include the channel assignments for that specific surround format (5.1 L, R, Ls, Rs, C, LFE ❿).

So the term "Stereo Interleave" means that a single file contains two audio channels that are assigned as a stereo signal. Also, don't confuse the term "Stereo Interleave" with the term "Joint Stereo", which is a process to data-compress audio files (i.e. mp3), where components of a signal that appear in the left and right channel are encoded as a mono signal.

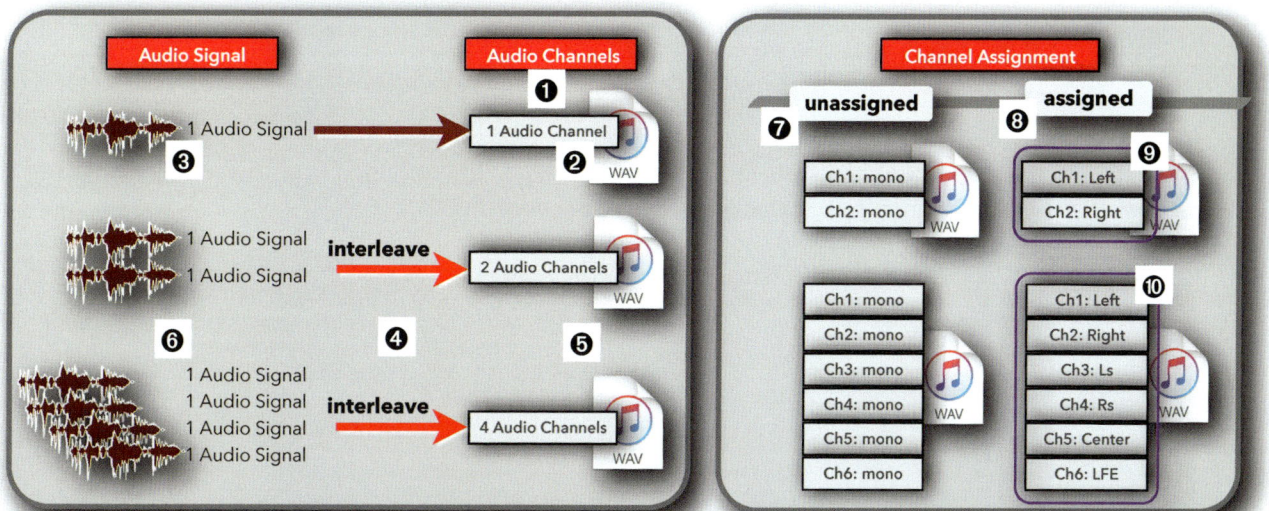

Here is an example of seven files to show what all that looks like in "real life":

- ▶ **Get Info Window**: The screenshots on the left show the Get Info window of the individual Source Media File in the Finder (*cmd+I*). In the "*More Info*" section it will show how many audio channels ❶ are embedded in that single file.

- ▶ **Format Inspector**: When you launch the file with the QuickTime Player and open its Inspector (*cmd+I*), you will see the screenshots with the black background ❷. It shows the assignment of the audio channels. If the channels are unassigned, it says "Mono" or "n channels" (marked in red), if the channels are assigned, then it displays the name of the individual assignments (marked in purple).

- ▶ **Audio Setting**: The screenshots below the one with the black background shows the *Properties* window (*cmd+J*) when you launch the file in the old QuickTime Player 7. It displays the names of the individual Channel Assignments ❸. If the channels are unassigned, then it says "Mono" (marked in red ❻), if the channels are assigned, then the column shows their names (marked in purple ❽).

- **1 Channel**: A file with a single channel ❶ is always mono and, therefore, there is no available channel assignment ❸.

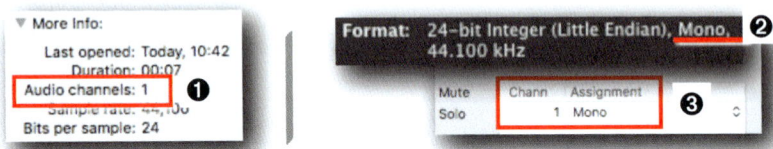

- **2 Channels**: The file on the right (that has a channel assignment) indicates that this is a stereo file ❹ and the label "Left" and "Right" ❺ is shown in the Assignment column.

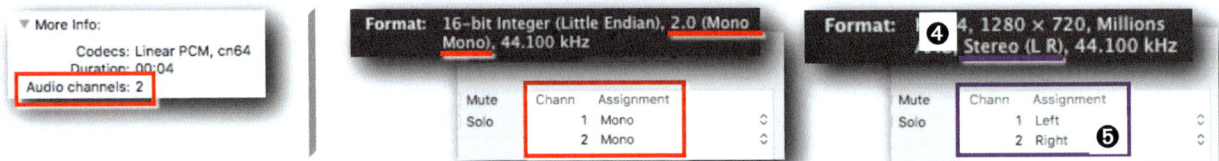

- **6 Channels**: The unassigned version of this 6 channels file (on the left ❻) just lists the 6 mono channels. The assigned version (on the right) indicates that this is a 5.1 surround format with the abbreviated channel indicator ❼ and the full labels ❽ in the Properties window.

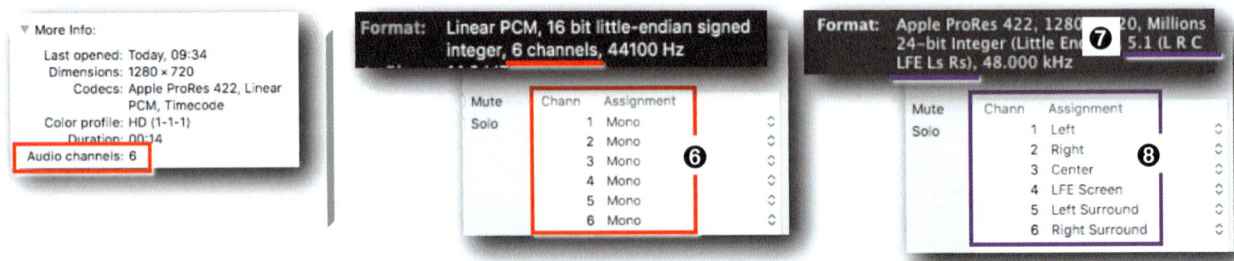

- **7 Channels**: This file contains 7 channels ❾. The file on the left is unassigned (7 mono channels) and the file on the right has those 7 channels assigned as a 6.1 surround format ❿.

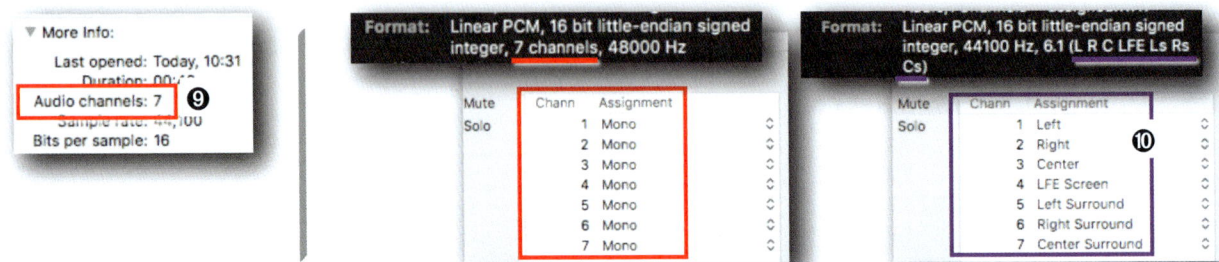

Audio Configuration

Now, with that understanding of Source Media Files and their assigned or unassigned Audio Channels, let's see how all that translates to FCPx.

- ☑ In the example below, I import two Source Media Files into FCPx, "Beach" ❶ and "Sky" ❷.
- ☑ As you can see from the screenshots, *Beach* has 2 Audio Channels (assigned as Stereo ❸) and *Sky* has 6 Audio Channels (assigned as 5.1 ❹)
- ☑ The first thing I do after the import is select each Event Clip and look at their Audio Properties by selecting the Audio Inspector ❺ 🔊 in FCPx.

🌐 Audio Configuration

The bottom of the Audio Inspector has a section labeled "Audio Configuration" ❻. This is the area you really should know inside out when it comes to controlling every aspect of audio in your video project. Not only does it show some waveforms, it is packed with tons of little controls, badges, and functionality. You can **drag** the divider line ❼ at the top of the section up/down to adjust its height proportionally to the other modules above in the Audio Inspector.

🌐 Channel Configuration Menu

The first element you should check in the Audio Configuration section for a new Event Clip is the label ❽ in the upper right corner of the first waveform. It has a downward arrow 🔽 to indicate that **clicking** on it opens a popup menu, the *Channel Configuration Menu*.

As you can see on the screenshots, both Clips have different menu items ❾ ❿, which has to do with the Audio Channels and the Channel Assignment that FCPx detected in those files during the import.

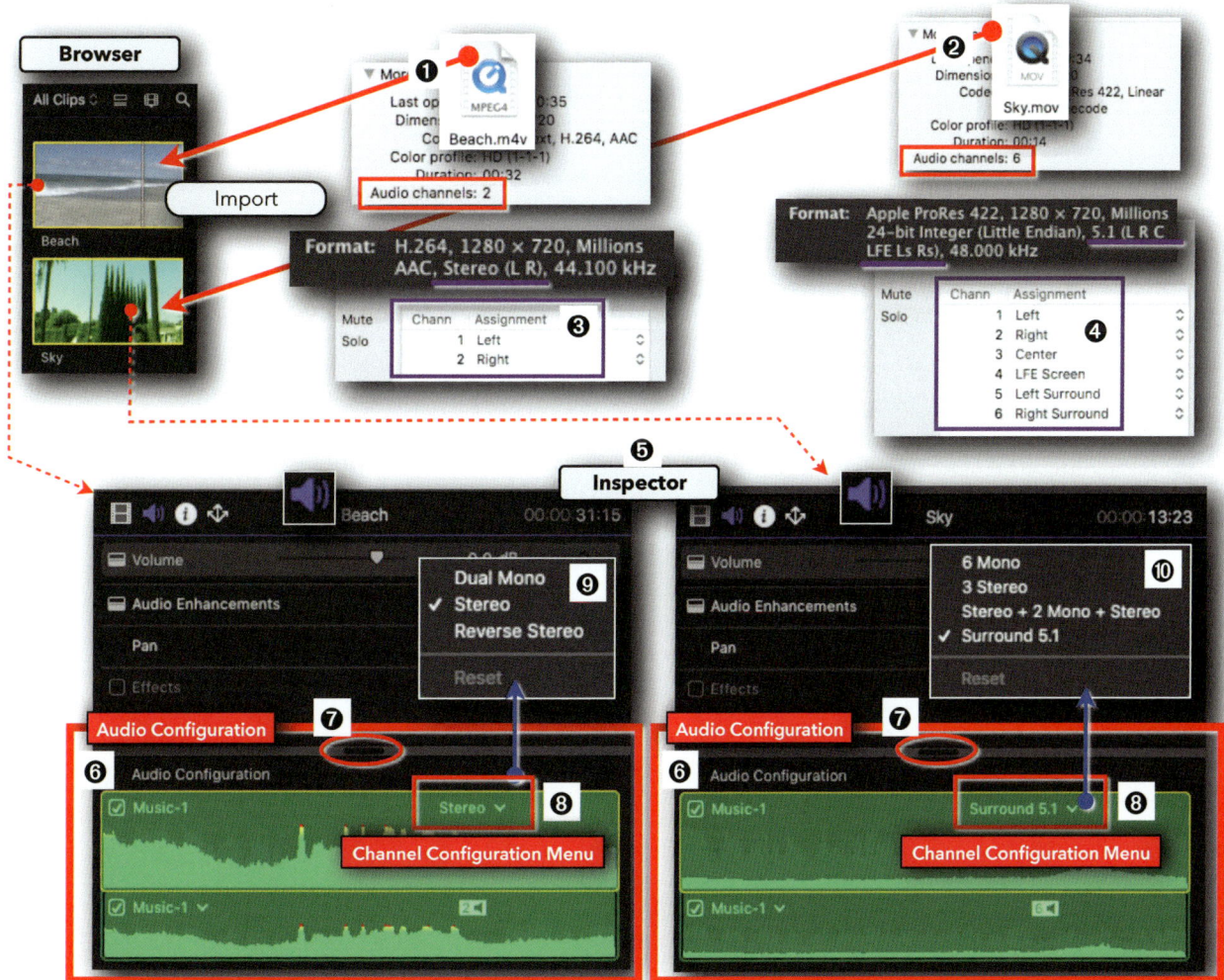

➡ *Channel Configuration*

Channel Configuration means, how to group (configure) the existing Audio Channels of a Clip, actually the audio channels of its referenced Source Media File. Of course, the more Audio Channels a Clip has, the more variations there are to group them. FCPx can create three types of groups:

▶ **Mono**: That Group contains only <u>one</u> Audio Channel

▶ **Stereo**: That Group contains <u>two</u> Audio Channels

▶ **Surround**: That Group contains <u>all</u> Audio Channels of a Clip

Here are the four Channel Configurations FCPx created from the *Sky* Clip, which has 6 Audio Channels ❶:

• **6 Mono ❷**: This configuration has six groups. Each group contains 1 Audio Channel

• **3 Stereo ❸**: This configuration has three groups. Each group has 2 Audio Channels

• **Stereo + 2 Mono + Stereo ❹**: This configuration has four groups. One group with 2 Audio Channels, two groups with 1 Audio Channel, and another group with 2 Audio Channels.

• **Surround 5.1 ❺**: This configuration only has a single group. It contains all 6 Audio Channels.

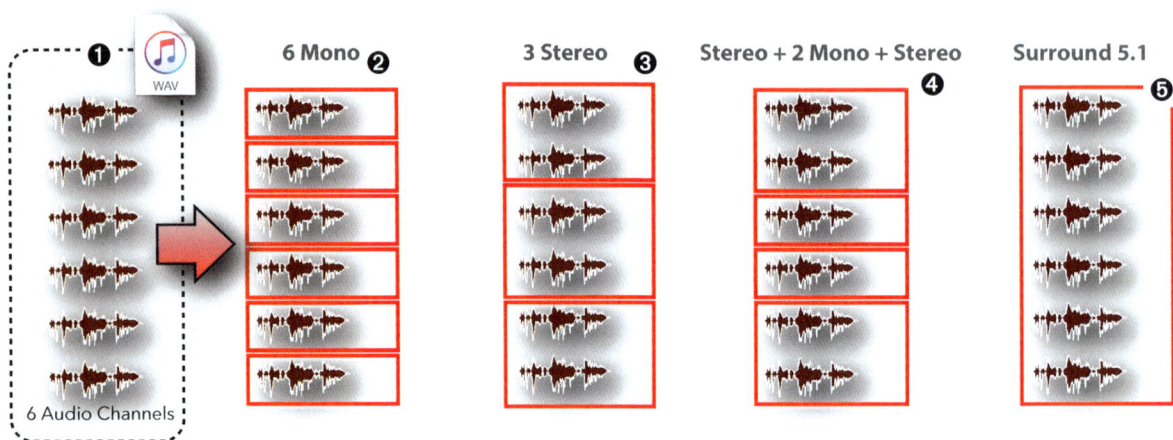

And here are the two important elements to pay attention to:

🟤 **Audio Component Clips ❻**

Each group of 1, 2, or all Audio Channels is displayed in the Inspector's Audio Configuration section as a single waveform, the so-called "*Audio Component Clips*" that represent those groups of combined Audio Channels.

🟤 **Summed Audio Clip ❼**

The first (slightly taller) waveform that is displayed on top of the Audio Configuration section is special. I call this in my manual the "*Summed Audio Clip*" because the single waveform it displays is the sum of all (active) Audio Component Clips.

Summed Audio Clip vs. Audio Component Clips

FCPx provides some extremely flexible and powerful audio features that I will cover in this chapter. However, they are all based on the proper understanding of those waveforms you see in the Audio Inspector. So, let's have another look at those important elements in the Audio Configuration section with two examples:

▶ **Audio Configuration**: The Audio Configuration section ❶ in the Audio Inspector is the area that lets you configure the Channel Assignments of the currently selected Clip (Event Clip or Timeline Clip).

▶ **Summed Audio Clip**: The first waveform that is displayed a little bit taller than the waveforms below represents the Summed Audio Clip ❷. This is the same waveform that is displayed on the Event Clip ❸ or Timeline Clip, representing all the enabled audio channels summed together. The waveform will change accordingly ❹.

▶ **Audio Component Clip**: All the Clips with the waveforms that are displayed below the first waveform are the so-called Audio Component Clips ❺, that represent groups of Audio Channels ❻. The little speaker symbol ❼ indicates how many Audio Channels are included in each Audio Component 1◀ 2◀ 6◀.

▶ **Channel Configuration Menu**: The Channel Configuration Menu ❽ shows the current Channel Configuration and lets you change it to a different Channel Configuration by selecting a different one from its menu ❾.

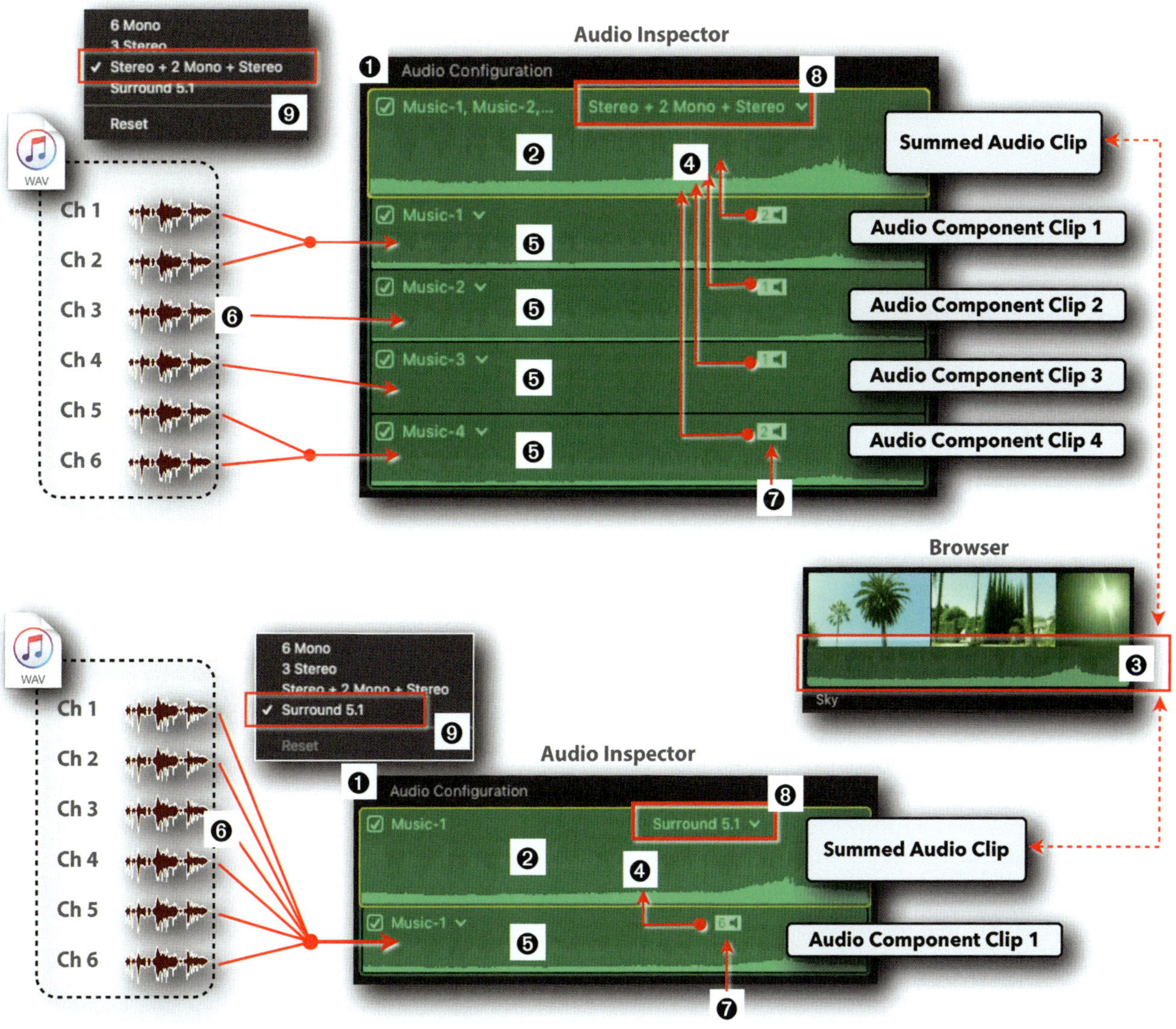

Clip Structure

Now that we've learned about the Audio Components and what they are (grouped Audio Channels in a Clip), I want to revisit the general topic about Clips to "update" our understanding about Clips in regards to audio.

➡ Single, Combined Clip (Standard Clip)

The diagram below shows a Video Clip, an Image Clip, and an Audio Clip, what they look like in the Browser and on the Timeline. These are the *Standard Clips* (we learn about *Compound Clips* and others later).

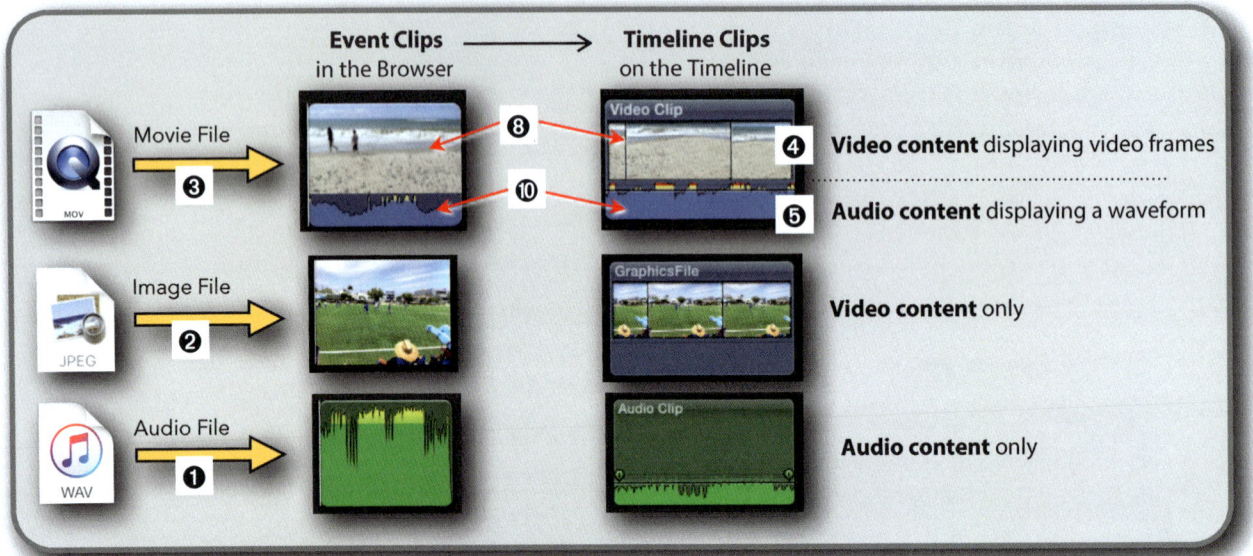

While a Clip, imported from an audio file ❶, only contains audio material and a Clip imported from an image file ❷ only contains video material (one video frame), a Clip imported from a movie file ❸, on the other hand, can include both elements, the video material ❹ and the audio material ❺. FCPx introduced this new concept that a movie file (with video and audio content) translates into a single Clip when it is imported in FCPx. It has the big advantage that you edit one Clip and don't have to deal with a separate Video Clip and Audio Clip, always trying to maintain the sync between them. However, such a Clip that contains video and audio material has more than these two elements.

Here is a simple model of such a Clip ❸ that shows its basic structure. I will use this model in this chapter to better explain the various features.

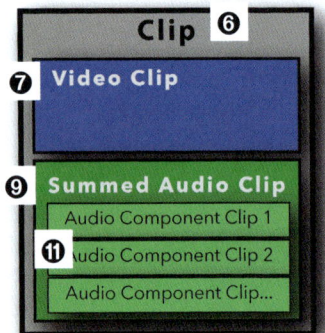

- ▶ **Clip ❻**: The Clip itself functions as the main Container that includes the audio and video material.

- ▶ **Video Clip ❼**: Inside the Clip is a separate container only for the video material. Think about a nested Video Clip. This is the section that you see at the top of a Clip as thumbnails, the video frames ❽.

- ▶ **Summed Audio Clip ❾**: The audio material of the Clip is also stored inside as another separate container, think about a nested Audio Clip. This is the section that you see at the bottom of a Clip as the audio waveform ❿.

- ▶ **Audio Component Clips ⓫**: This is the part that makes the audio portion special (which is where you have to pay attention to). The Summed Audio Clip ❾ (the container inside the Clip container ❻) stores additional nested containers inside, which are the Audio Component Clips that we just learned about. We also learned that these Audio Components inside a Clip change whenever you select a different Audio Configuration for that Clip.

➡ *Clip Editing*

Here is a brief overview of the power of this Clip structure when it comes to editing a Clip. I will go into more details throughout this chapter.

🟡 Trimming

When you want to trim a Clip, you can trim each "container" separately.

- ▶   ❶ Trim the Clip as a whole with all its content trimmed accordingly
- ▶   ❷ Trim the Video Clip and Summed Audio Clip separately
- ▶   ❸ Trim each Audio Component Clip separately

🟡 Processing

This part is extremely flexible regarding the audio material in your video project, because you can process (apply effects) to the Summed Audio Clip and in addition (!), each individual Audio Component Clip can be processed separately. This will function as your powerful (and slightly complex) virtual mixer.

- ▶   ❹ Edit the Video Properties of the Video Clip.
- ▶   ❺ Edit the Audio Properties of the Summed Audio Clip.
- ▶   ❻ Edit the Audio Properties of each Audio Component Clip separately !!!

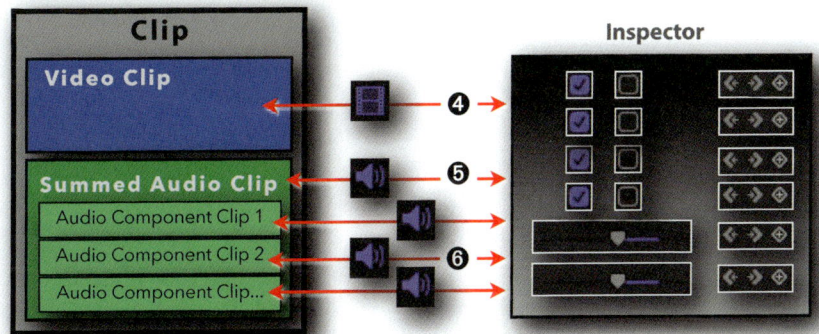

🟡 Roles

Roles are another powerful feature in
FCPx, especially in combination with the Audio Components as we will see in the Roles chapter.

Here are a few things up-front to be aware of:

- ▶   ❼ Video Roles are assigned to the Video Clip.
- ▶   ❽ When assigning Audio Roles to the Summed Audio Clip, they will actually be assigned to the individual Audio Component Clips of that Clip. This will overwrite any previous Role assignments of the individual Audio Component Clips.
- ▶   ❾ You can also change the Role Assignment of individual Audio Component Clips.
- ▶   Be careful, changing the Channel Configuration will also reset the current Role assignments on the Audio Components Clips.

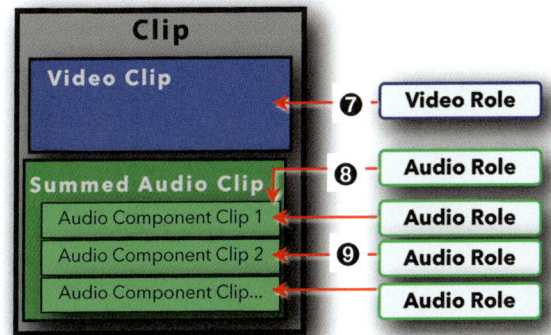

Standard Clip

Clip ❺

Video Clip

Summed Audio Clip
- Audio Component Clip 1
- Audio Component Clip 2
- Audio Component Clip...

➡️ *Display Options*

Here is a look at the Standard Clip ❶ and the three variations, how you can view such a Clip on the Timeline. You can toggle to any of the three display variations with a specific command (*Detach Audio* ❷, *Expand Audio* ❸, *Expand Audio Components* ❹). This also works for an audio-only Clip, where the Video Clip section will be blank.

First, I show the four display options of a Clip based on the model of a Clip ❺ that I just introduced. Below that are the screenshots of the individual Clips (Default ❻, Detach Audio ❼, Expand Audio ❽, Expand Audio Components ❾).

Default ❶ (combined)	Detach Audio ❷	Expand Audio ❸	Expand Audio Components ❹

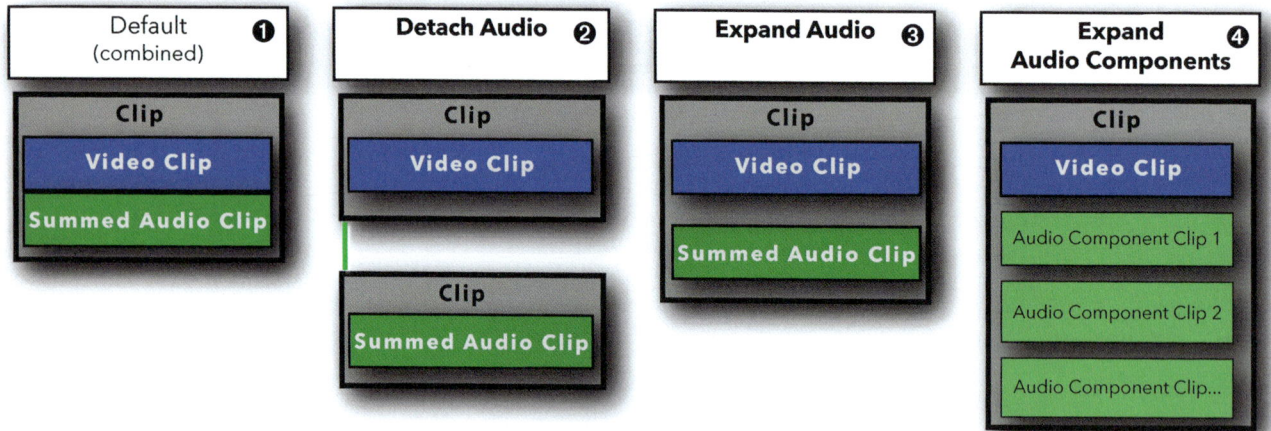

❷ Detach Audio   ^⇧S   ❸ Expand Audio   ^S   ❹ Expand Audio Components   ^⌥S

One single Clip. This is the default view.	The Summed Audio Clip is **detached** as a separate Connected Clip.	The Clip appears as a single object that can be moved and treated as one, but the Video Clip and the Summed Audio Clip can be trimmed separately.	The Clip also appears as a single object that can be moved as one, but instead of the Summed Audio Clip, all its separate Audio Component Clips are displayed, which can be trimmed separately.

   ❻      ❼      ❽      ❾

Detach Audio

Use any of the following commands:

- Main Menu *Clip* ➤ *Detach Audio*
- *Ctr+click* on the Clip and use the Shortcut Menu *Detach Audio*
- Key Command *sh+ctr+S*

This is the more radical approach, which breaks up the Clip into a separate Video Clip ❶ and Audio Clip ❷. Both Clips will have the same name. This command cannot be reversed later, only with the Undo command.

If the Clip is located on the Primary Storyline, then the new Video Clip stays on the Primary Storyline and the Summed Audio Clip will become a Connected Clip below ❸. If the Clip is already a Connected Clip, then both new Clips end up being Connected Clips, connected to their original Clip on the Primary Storyline.

Expand/Collapse Audio

Use any of the following commands:

- Main Menu *Clip* ➤ *Expand/Collapse Audio*
- Shortcut Menu *Expand/Collapse Audio*
- Key Command *ctr+S*
- *Double-click* on the waveform

This command also breaks apart the Video and Audio portion of the Clip, but only visually. This is just a pure display feature that can be toggled with the same command. Please note that the expanded Audio Clip is still one unit indicated by the vertically expanded Primary Storyline ❹ to display the video and audio portion.

Expand/Collapse Audio Components

Use any of the following commands:

- Main Menu *Clip* ➤ *Expand/Collapse Audio Components*
- Shortcut Menu *Expand/Collapse Audio Components*
- Key Command *ctr+opt+S*
- *Opt+double-click* on the waveform

This display option is a variation of the "Expand Audio" command. Now, the audio content is broken up into the individual "Audio Component Clips" ❺. The example on the right displays a 5.1 surround mix with a Channel Configuration of three Audio Components, each one including 2 Audio Channels. Please note that Audio Component Clips have a special badge ❻ in the Clip Header, a filmstrip 🎞 (if it is part of a video+audio Clip) or a speaker 🔈 (if it is part of an audio-only Clip), to indicate that each Clip is an Audio Component Clip and not a Summed Audio Clip ❼.

The Clip Menu ❽ and the Shortcut Menu ❾ contain all the commands for those options.

The Clip Menu has a fourth command called "*Break Apart Clip Items*" ❿.

🌑 Break Apart Clip Items

This is a special command that is used for Compound Clips, Audition Clips, or Connected Storylines, which I cover in the Clips chapter. However, the command can also be used on Standard Clips ❶. Think of a different name for the command, like "**Detach Audio Components**", and you will understand its functionality.

Like the *Detach Audio* ❷ command that creates a separate Connected Clip out of the Summed Audio Clip, the *Break Apart Clip Items* ❸ command creates separate Connected Clips for each Audio Component of that Clip.

This command is not available from the Shortcut Menu, only from the Main Menu and as a Key Command:

- 📌 Main Menu *Clip* ➤ *Break Apart Clip Items*
- 📌 Key Command *sh+ctr+G*

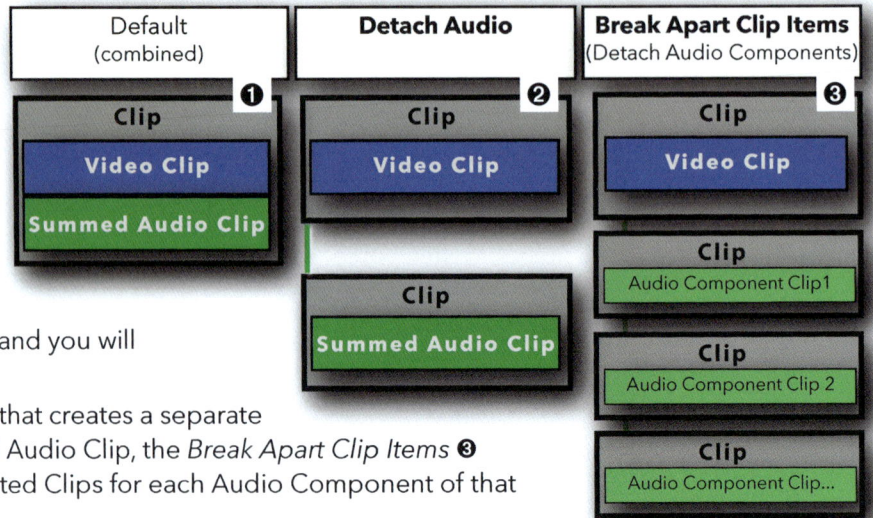

Default (combined)	Detach Audio	Break Apart Clip Items (Detach Audio Components)
Clip ❶	**Clip** ❷	**Clip** ❸
Video Clip	Video Clip	Video Clip
Summed Audio Clip		
	Clip	**Clip**
	Summed Audio Clip	Audio Component Clip1
		Clip
		Audio Component Clip 2
		Clip
		Audio Component Clip...

Trimming Expanded Clips

When editing a Standard Clip, all the trimming commands are applied to the video and audio content as one. But sometimes it is necessary to treat them individually. To detach the Audio to create a separate Connected Clip for the audio component would work, because it creates two independent Clips, however, that defeats the advantage of having a combined Clip in the first place.

By using the "Expand" command, the Clip keeps the video and audio elements together (as one Standard Clip) while still allowing you to trim the these elements separately.

➡ *Trimming*

🌑 Expand Audio

Here is a simple example of how to trim the expanded Audio Clip (Summed Audio Clip) of a Clip, separately from the Video Clip.

- ▶ The first Clip (*Sky*) is expanded ❹. Please note that the Primary Storyline (black area) is getting stretched vertically to accommodate the expanded Clip.

- ▶ In this screenshot, I trimmed only the Audio Clip of the *Sky* Clip and extending it to the right ❺ to play it longer than its sibling Video Clip.

- ▶ In this screenshot, I also expanded the second Clip (*Beach*) and trimmed its Audio Clip to start earlier ❻, creating an audio overlap between the two Clips. Please note that the Primary Storyline stretches vertically even further. Any overlapping Clips will automatically be displayed, stacked on top of each other, in a very clean visual way.

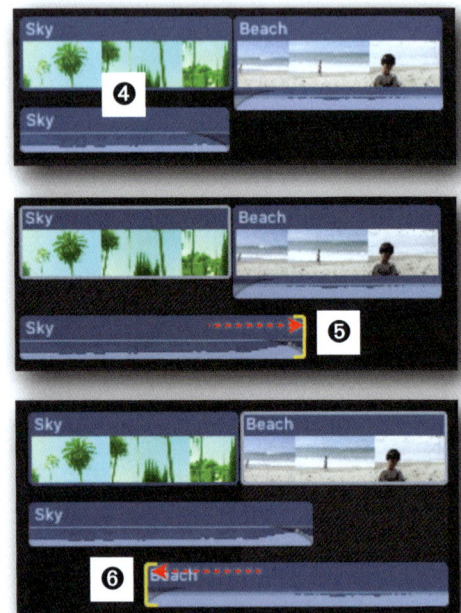

🦴 Expanded Audio Components

With the *Expand Audio Components* command, you can also trim the video and audio portion independently. However, you can take it one step further and trim the individual Audio Components of that Clip. You can trim each individual Audio Component Clip against the Video Clip and against each other.

Timeline

▶ On the left screenshot, the Clip is expanded, displaying its three Audio Component Clips ❶ (indicated by their special badge 🎞️). Here, they are grouped as three stereo channels. Visually, they indicate that they are still part of one combined Video Clip by the vertically stretched Primary Storyline.

▶ On the right screenshot, I trimmed the three Audio Component Clips separately ❷. Please note that there is no indication what these Audio Components Clips represent (mono, stereo, etc.). They all have the same Clip name. You have to select them and look up the information in the Audio Inspector or apply Roles (enable *Show Role Names* in the Clip Appearance Window 🎞️).

There are a few little details in the Audio Inspector you have to be aware of regarding Audio Components that have been trimmed separately. Below is an example of the same *Sky* Clip where I trimmed the three Audio Component Clips separately. The left screenshot shows the Timeline and the right screenshot shows the Audio Inspector.

▶ First, the Inspector labels the Audio Components with the name of the Subroles ❸. The first Clip, the Summed Audio Clip, lists the names of all Subroles ❹ used by its Audio Components.

▶ The displayed Clips in the Inspector are divided into an upper lane ❺ and a lower lane ❻, which is not apparent unless you trim an Audio Component. The upper lanes display all the controls (checkbox, pop menu) and badges (channel indication, FX, etc.). The lower lane displays the actual waveform (I increased the waveform here to make it visible) and indicates the trimmed area as a dark section. Moving over with your mouse on the lower lane will display the orange Clip Skimmer ❼. Audio Skimming has to be enabled in the Main Menu (*View ➤ Audio Skimming*) to hear it.

▶ If you look closely at the left and right screenshot, you will notice the following discrepancy. The Clips in the Inspector are always auto-zoomed ❽ to fit the length of the Inspector width. However, this width doesn't reflect the parent Clip ❾. It is the width from the left-most position to the right-most position ❿ of any of the Audio Component Clips and not the length of the Video Clip ❾ (which could be different). The horizontal area not shown in the Inspector is shaded dark on the Timeline ⓫.

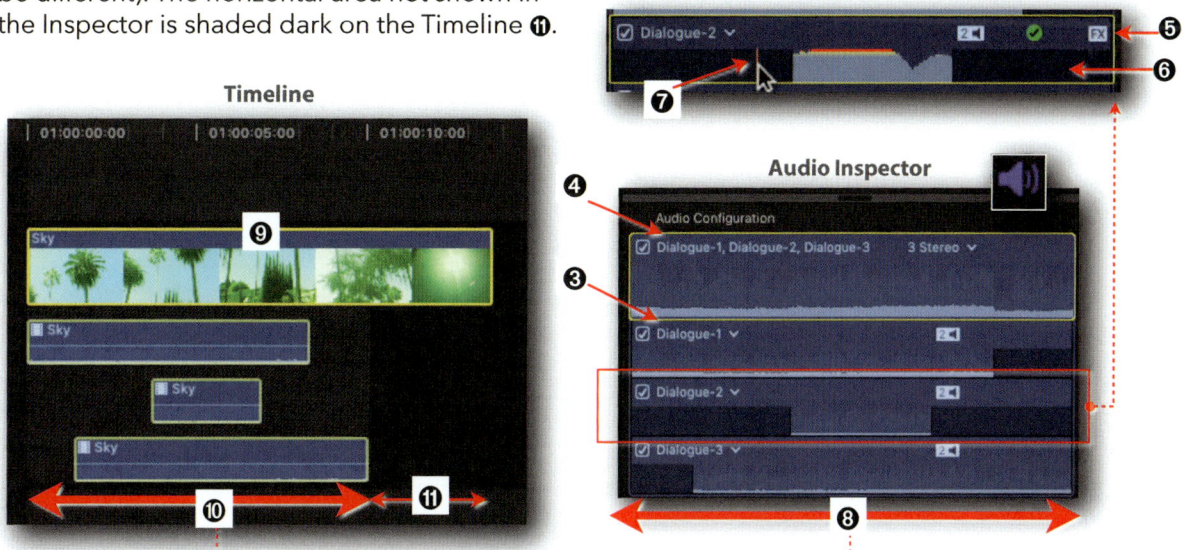

Timeline

Audio Inspector

➡ Advanced Trimming

You can take the trimming techniques even further in the *Expand Audio Components* view.

▸ The Clip in this screenshot contains two Audio Component Clips ❶.

▸ As we have seen in the previous example, you can trim the beginning and end of each Audio Component Clip individually. In this example, the first Component Clip starts later and stops earlier ❷.

▸ Switching the cursor to the Range Tool 🔲 (Key Command *R*) lets you *drag* a Range Selection ❸ on the Audio Component.

▸ Using the Disable Command (Shortcut Menu, Clip Menu, or Key Command *V*) disables only that selected Range. The Audio Component now shows that muted section as a dimmed area ❹.

▸ To enable a section again. Create a range over that area and use the Disable command again.

▸ You can mark multiple selections with the Range Tool on any Component and disable those sections ❺ very quickly to mute parts of specific Audio Component Clips.

▸ Unfortunately, disabled ranges are not indicated on the Audio Component Clips in the Inspector.

▸ You can also use the Range Tool to mark a section and quickly change the level just for that section of the Audio Components Clip by *dragging* the volume automation line up or down ❻. This creates keyframes (part of the Audio Automation I cover in the Automation chapter).

These trimming techniques for Clips with multichannel audio content are very quick and efficient. Everything is contained in a single Clip. You just *Expand* the Audio Components, do the edit, and *Collapse* the Audio Component again.

➡ Playback

There are a few playback features that you can use directly in the Inspector:

▸ **Clip Skimming**: Clip Skimming is always active when you move the mouse over the waveform of a Summed Audio Clip or Audio Component Clip in the Audio Inspector. However, you will only hear the sound if Audio Skimming is activated in the Main Menu *View ▸ Audio Skimming*, regardless of the Audio Skimming Button 🎚.

▸ **Key Focus**: Please note that using Clip Skimming on the Audio Components in the Inspector automatically switches key focus to the Inspector pane without actually clicking on that window.

▸ **Playback Controls**: If you have the mouse positioned over the waveform in the Audio Inspector, you can use the standard playback controls to play only that Summed Audio Clip or any of the Audio Component Clips (Solo Play). Key command *spacebar*, *J*, *K*, *L*.

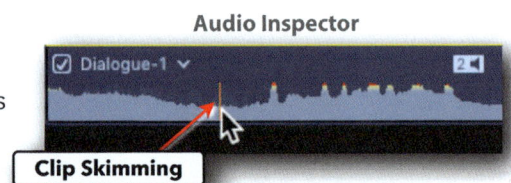

Basics

Apple made a bold move and eliminated the FCP7 concept of tracks ❶, replacing it with the Primary Storyline ❺. Besides messing up some common workflows that editors are used to, this change creates a big headache on the audio side too. In the audio world (Pro Tools, Logic Pro), everything is still based on tracks and it is the common "hand shake" between the video and audio world along with established file exchange formats.

Audio Clips were placed on audio tracks in the video app that were connected to mixer channel strips to do basic audio mixing in the video project.

The various audio clips could be placed on predetermined tracks (Dialog, SFX, Foley, Music, etc.) to get everything better organized. Those tracks could be handed over to the ProTools guy for mixing.

💀 The Inspector is the new Mixer

To better understand the audio concept in FCPx, think of it as a transition from an analog to a digital mindset. The analog way was track-based where you had tracks ❶ (on a video machine or an audio

multitrack machine) that carried the signal. The signal from the audio output was routed through a mixer ❷ where you balanced the signal and inserted FX for further signal processing. The mixed output signal was then sent out to the destination ❸ like speakers, ❹ another recording device, or exported to a file. This concept is simulated in virtually all DAWs (Digital Audio Workstations). FCPx now takes it to a different level when it comes to editing and mixing audio.

The individual audio signal(s), embedded in the Source Media File as Audio Channels, are represented as Clips ❺ in FCPx. These Clips are Objects that you select to display their parameters in the Inspector Window ❻. Every conventional audio processing task (level, fx, routing, etc.) is done by editing the Clip's parameters (its Properties) in the Inspector. Those parameters also determine where the audio signal of each Clip is routed to ❼.

In addition to the Properties that determine the more conventional parameters like volume and effects, each Clip contains special metadata ❽ that provides powerful functionality and flexibility that is not possible with a standard mixer.

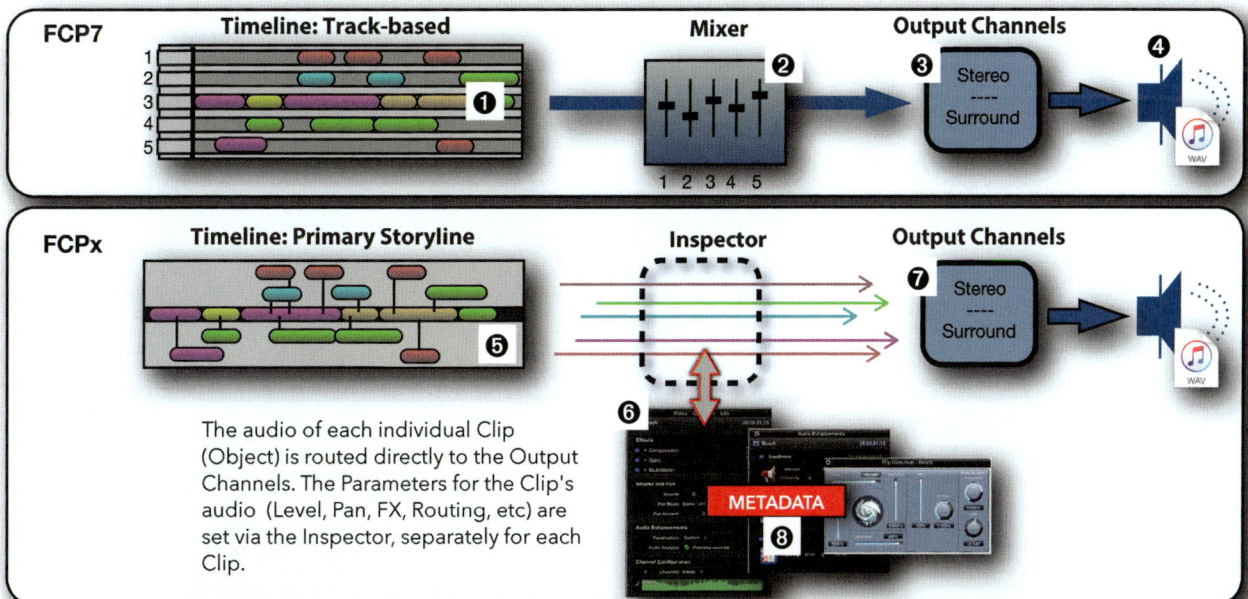

The audio of each individual Clip (Object) is routed directly to the Output Channels. The Parameters for the Clip's audio (Level, Pan, FX, Routing, etc) are set via the Inspector, separately for each Clip.

Inspector

Now let's have a look at our new mixer, the Inspector, and see how that thing could possibly replace an audio mixer.

The basic procedure of mixing an audio track is now the same as editing an object in a computer application like Photoshop, a word processor, or a layout application.

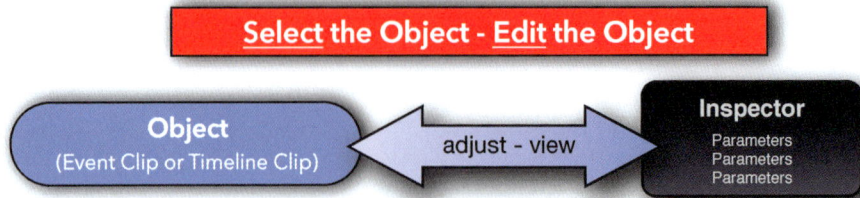

Select the Object - Edit the Object

Object (Event Clip or Timeline Clip) ◄— adjust - view —► **Inspector** Parameters Parameters Parameters

These are the necessary steps:

☑ **Select the Object** (or multiple objects)

This means, selecting a Clip first. This could be either an Event Clip or a Timeline Clip. We already learned that we can even select individual Audio Components inside a Clip.

☑ **Open the Inspector**

We also discussed earlier that the Inspector is a special window common in many applications. It lets you view and adjust the parameters of a selected Object.

☑ **View Parameter Values**

Having the Inspector window open while selecting different Objects, lets you view the values of their parameters.

☑ **Adjust Parameter Values**

Adjusting the values of the available parameters in the Inspector will apply those changes to the currently selected Object(s). Always make sure to know what Object (what Clip or Component Clip) is the selected one (key focus).

If any Object is selected that has audio content (Video Clip with audio content or Audio Clip), then the Inspector shows the Audio tab 🔊 in the header that switches to the Audio Inspector, listing all the available Audio Attributes. Their parameters are grouped in Modules. A Timeline Clip has an additional Module not available on an Event Clip. This is the Effects Module that functions like an Effects Rack where you can add additional audio effect modules to further process the currently selected Audio Clip or Audio Component.

Event Clip
- ▶ ❶ Volume
- ▶ ❷ Audio Enhancements
- ▶ ❸ Pan
- ▶ ❹ (Effects disabled)
- ▶ ❺ Audio Configuration

Timeline Clip
- ▶ ❻ Volume
- ▶ ❼ Audio Enhancements
- ▶ ❽ Pan
- ▶ ❾ **Effects**
- ▶ ❿ Audio Configuration

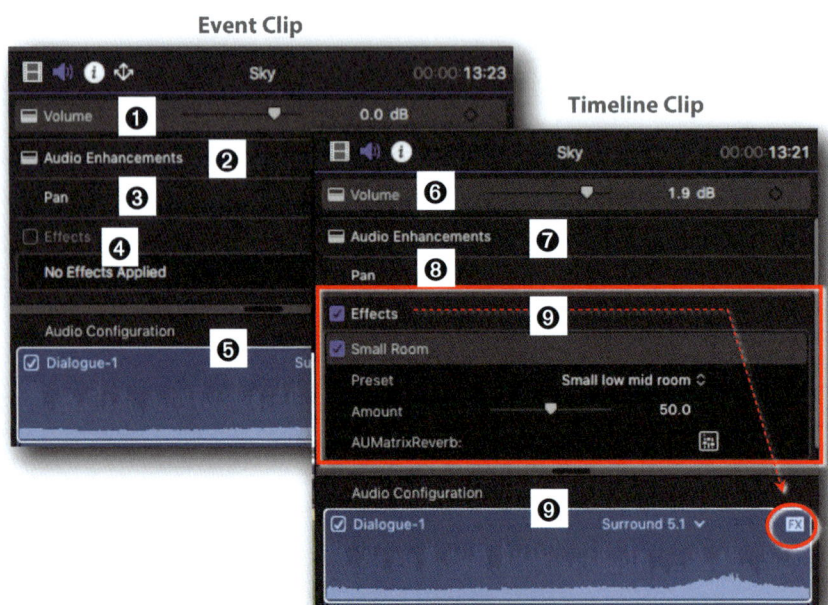

➡ Show/Hide Parameters

The Audio (and Video) Inspector is divided into individual sections, the Modules, that represent specific Audio Attributes. The Modules display the various Parameters that can be shown/hidden by **double-clicking** on the Module header or by mousing over the header, which reveals a "*Show*" ❶ or "*Hide*" ❷ button that can be clicked on.

➡ "Target" Clip

Whenever you use the Inspector to view and/or adjust Parameters, be aware of two things:

- ☑ What object is selected?
- ☑ Is the selected object an Event Clip or a Timeline Clip?

This sounds trivial but keep in mind:

- ▸ You don't want to change values in the Inspector and find out later that you edited the wrong Clip. Always keep an eye on what Clip(s) is selected.
- ▸ You can select multiple Clips and change their Parameters simultaneously.
- ▸ There are three types of indications that let you know what Clip the Inspector is currently displaying and, therefore, which Clip is receiving the changes you make in the Inspector:
  - • Selecting a Clip will add a yellow frame ❸ around it. It makes it the Target Clip.
  - • If you want to edit the Clip's parameters, you have to select the Inspector. This changes the key focus from the Timeline (or Browser) to the Inspector. The yellow frame that indicated the selected Clip(s) changes to a white frame ❹, still the Target Clip.
  - • If no Clip is selected, then the Playhead will display a red dot ❺ to indicate which Clip is the Target Clip.
- ▸ Another thing to remember. Event Clips and Timeline Clips have their own properties. Moving an Event Clip to the Timeline creates an independent Timeline Clip that inherits the Event Clip properties. All subsequent changes in the Timeline Clip do not affect its Parent Event Clip. Same thing when copying (duplicating) Timeline Clips on the Timeline itself. This creates a new independent Timeline Clip. So be aware of where you make audio adjustments and why. For example, if Event Clips need some basic treatment (channel assignment, level was to low or too hot), those can be made to the Event Clips so when it is time to drag them onto the timeline, those parameters will be "carried over."

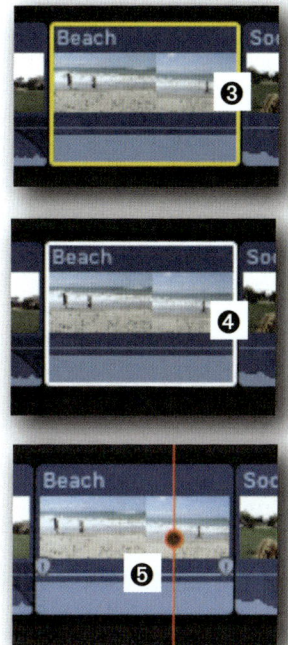

➡ Additional Controls

The Inspector is the place where you view and edit all the parameters. However, the Timeline Clip itself also has two areas where you can view and edit parameters. Those parameters correspond to the parameters displayed in the Inspector and are updated on either side.

- ▸ **Volume Display**: This lane displays the level for the Clip Volume ❻ including any Keyframes plus Fade Handles ❼. Please note that the two Fade Handles are unique to the Timeline Clip and are NOT available in the Inspector!
- ▸ **Audio Animation Lane**: Animation Lanes (*Show/Hide Audio Animation*) display any parameters as a function over time plus any available Keyframes ❽. See the Animation chapter for details.

The Virtual Mixer

This section is very important, because I will introduce a model that I use to explain how the new "Inspector-based Audio Mixer" functions in FCPx. Instead of just listing where individual parameters (volume, pan, fx, etc.) are located in the Inspector, I will use this model to show how these controls relate to a more conventional concept of using a signal flow.

In the previous section of this chapter, I already introduced a model to show that the audio content of a Clip can be viewed as two types of Clips.

- The **Audio Components Clips ❶** represent individual groups of Audio Channels, containing one or multiple Audio Channels of that Clip.

- The **Summed Audio Clip ❷** represents all Audio Component Clips summed together as a single Audio Clip.

➡ *Audio Inspector*

The diagram below shows two important aspects of the Audio Inspector:

▶ **What do you see?** A Clip can either show the Summed Audio Clip in Collapsed View ❸ or Expanded Audio View ❹, or it can display the Audio Component Clips in Expand Audio Components View ❺ (always watch out for the special badge on the Clip). However, the Audio Inspector always displays both types of Clips. The Summed Audio Clip on top ❻ with all Audio Components below ❼.

▶ **What do you edit?** The Inspector usually displays the parameters of the currently selected object, which is a Clip or a Project. However, the Audio Inspector is special. The object can be either the selected Summed Audio Clip ❻, or one of the selected Audio Component Clips ❼. Each one has its own sets of parameters ❽ that is displayed when you select that specific Clip, either in the Timeline or Browser, or by clicking on one of the waveform in the Audio Inspector (indicated by a yellow frame around it).

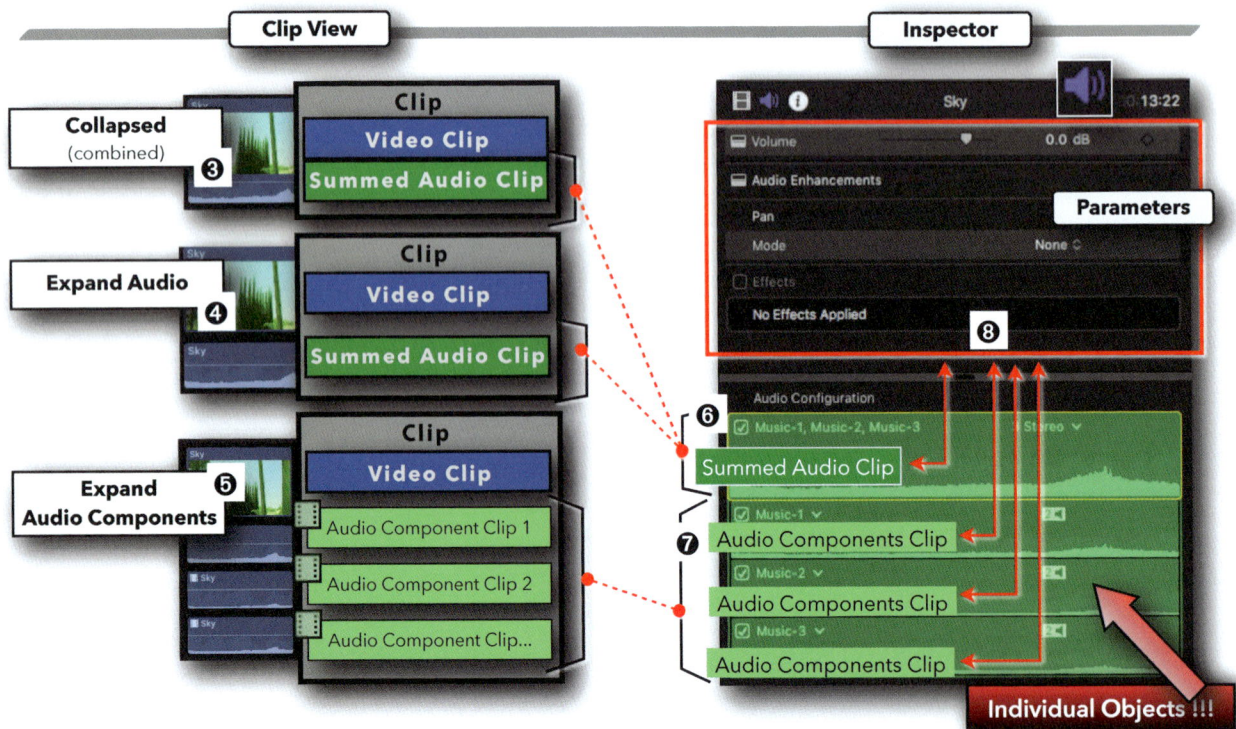

➡ Signal Flow

In this diagram I try to "translate" the object-based concept of Clips into the traditional form of a signal flow diagram the way it is used in mixing consoles. Whenever you look at the Inspector and edit some parameters, think about this underlying signal flow to help you "visualize" what happens to the signal.

> **Each Clip represents a little Audio Mixer**

You can think of a Clip ❶ as a little audio mixer with the Audio Component Clips as individual Channel Strips ❷ that are routed to a Master Channel Strip ❸, the Summed Audio Clip. Let's look at the elements with the following example:

▶ **Source Media File ❹**: This is the Source Media File the Clip is referenced to.

▶ **Audio Channels ❺**: One of the properties of the Source Media File, as we discussed earlier, is the amount of embedded Audio Channels. In this example, the file has 6 Audio Channels, which are routed to the input of the Channel Strips ❷.

▶ **Channel Configuration**: The Audio Inspector provides the important Channel Configuration Selector ❻ in the upper-right corner of the Summed Audio Clip. It determines how the Audio Channels ❺ are grouped (routed) into Audio Components.

▶ **Audio Component Clips**: Each Audio Component Clip ❼ represents an individual Channel Strip ❷. When you select an Audio Component Clip, then all parameters displayed in the Inspector ❽ represent individual controls only for that Channel Strip (volume, effects, pan, etc.).

▶ **Summed Audio Clip**: The output of each Channel Strip ❸ (Audio Components ❼) is routed to the Master Channel Strip ❸, which represents the Summed Audio Clip ❾. The same applies here. When you select the Summed Audio Clip, the Inspector now displays the parameters ❽ just for that Channel Strip (volume, effects, pan, etc.).

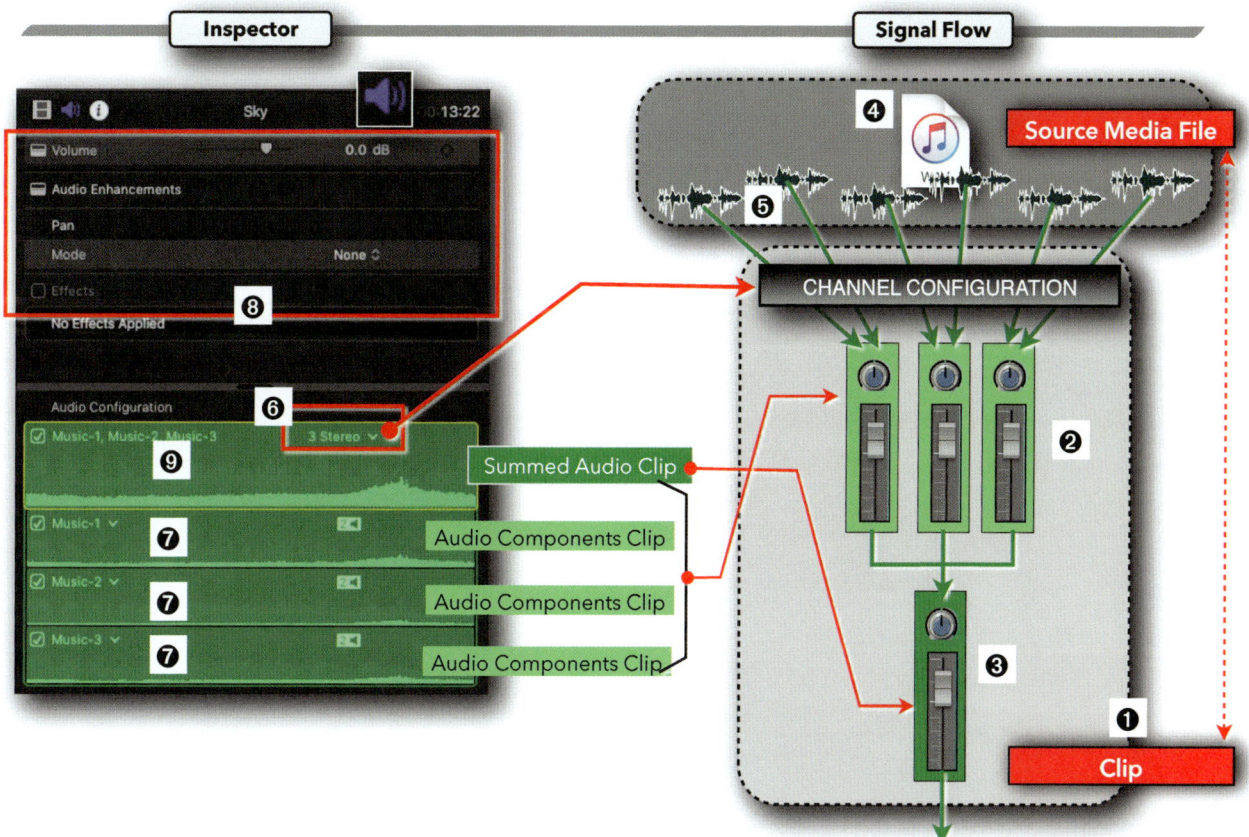

➡ **What is selected**

As I already mentioned, the most important thing when looking at the Audio Inspector is to "see" what parameters it is displaying, which means what is currently selected.

There are multiple "signs" that indicate the currently selected object.

▶ **Summed Audio Clip**:

- The header for the Volume and Audio Enhancements Module shows a symbol ❶ 🔲 that resembles that upper Clip.

- The Inspector places a yellow frame ❷ around the Summed Audio Clip. It doesn't display the name of the Clip, only the names of the Audio Roles (more about that later). The Inspector header ❸ displays the name of the Clip.

- The Collapsed View ❹ of the Clip (Event Clip or Timeline Clip) has the yellow frame to indicate that it is selected (it turns to a white frame when it doesn't have focus).

- If no Clip is selected, then positioning the Playhead over a Clip will show a red circle ❺ to indicate that this is the selected Clip.

- If Expand Audio View ❻ is enabled, then selecting the Summed Audio Clip will also select the corresponding Video Clip.

▶ **Audio Components Clip**:

- The header for the Volume and Audio Enhancements Module shows a symbol ❼ 🔲 that resembles the lower Clip, the individual Audio Component Clips. However, it doesn't indicate which Audio Component Clip is selected.

- The Inspector places a yellow frame ❽ around the Audio Component Clip. Again, only the Inspector header displays the Clip name ❾.

- With Expand Audio Components View ❿ enabled, the yellow frame (or white frame) indicates which Audio Component Clip is selected.

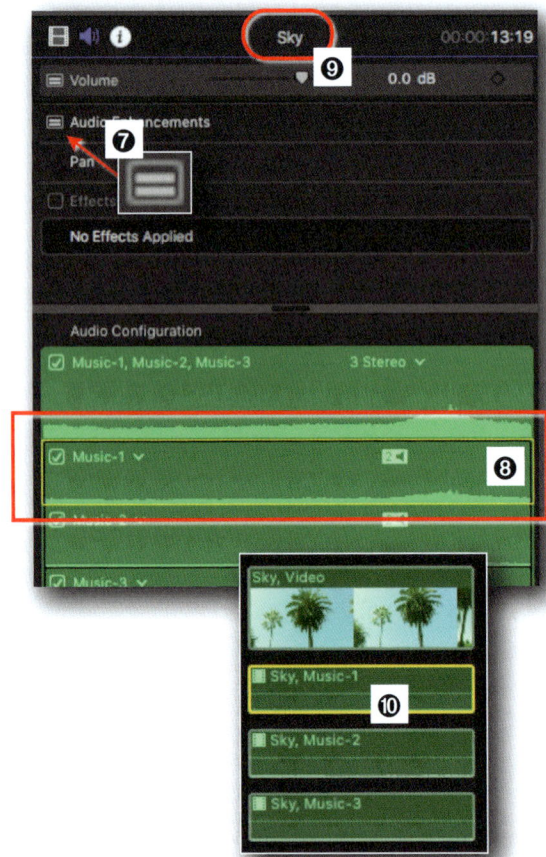

➡ Modules

A few considerations about the Audio Inspector:

- ▸ The Audio Inspector has four Modules that contain all the controls similar to the controls on a Channel Strip.
- ▸ The screenshot on the left ❶ shows the view when you open the Audio Inspector on a new Clip with all the Modules disabled and collapsed (parameters hidden).
- ▸ The screenshot on the right ❷ shows the Audio Inspector with the Modules expanded and loaded up.
- ▸ The audio signal passes through all the Modules and the order of the modules is very important. Unfortunately the displayed order on the Inspector (from top to bottom) is not the order of the actual signal flow. The diagram on the left ❸ shows the correct order: Audio Enhancements ➤ Effects ➤ Volume ➤ Pan (Output Routing).

🔵 Detailed Mini Mixer

Here is the same model of the Mini Mixer ❹ again that represents the audio signal flow "inside" a single Clip. This time, I added the individual Modules on the Channel Strips. As you can see, you have quite the control over the audio signal of a single Clip. That detailed control is available for each individual Clip (that has audio content) in your video project, so you get an idea how powerful this is. I will cover each Module separately, but here is a quick introduction:

- ▸ **Audio Enhancements ❺**: This Module provides basic signal processing that is mainly used for quick fixes, mostly during the prep work in the Libraries Browser.
- ▸ **Effects ❻**: This module functions as your FX Rack where you can add additional Effects Modules from the Effects Browser in FCPx.
- ▸ **Volume ❼**: This is the easiest Module that contains only a single control, a slider that controls the signal level.
- ▸ **Pan ❽**: This is arguably the most complex module that requires some "dedication" to decipher what is going on there.

The first step in any signal flow diagram, or when looking at Channel Strips on a mixer, is the input assignment or input routing. In FCPx this is the step called "Channel Configuration" that we already discussed a few times.

Basics

🔵 Concept

▸ Every Source Media File ❶ with audio content has as a specific amount of embedded Audio Channels ❷.

▸ FCPx "looks" at those Audio Channels and creates the so-called Channel Configurations ❸, which are listed in the Channel Configuration Menu.

▸ The Channel Configurations represent different ways on how to group the existing Audio Channels of a file into individual Audio Components ❹. You cannot group them manually, only choose from the existing options in the Channel Configuration Menu.

▸ Based on our mini-mixer model (Audio Components = Channel Strips), the Channel Configuration on a Clip ❺ determines two things:

☑ How many Channel Strips (Audio Components) are created ❻?

☑ How many audio inputs will each Channel Strip (Audio Component) have ❼? 1◀ 2◀ 6◀

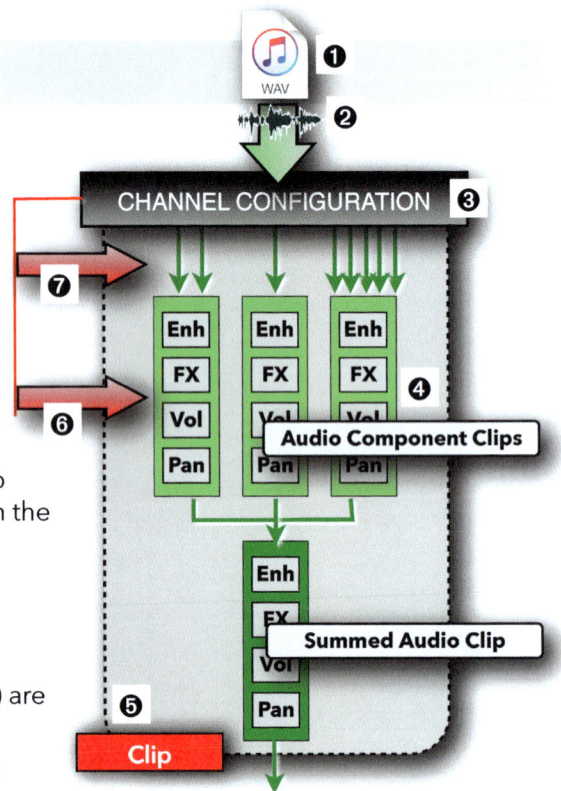

> **Channel Configuration:**
>
> How many Channel Strips (Audio Components) are created?
>
> How many audio inputs per Channel Strip?

🔵 Things to be aware of

▸ FCPx provides two options (during the import or later) that let it perform additional analysis to create better Channel Configurations.

▸ The selected Channel Configuration is part of each Clip instance. That means, once you copy a Clip, you can set the Channel Configuration independently for each Clip.

▸ *Important*: Choosing a different Channel Configuration from the popup menu of a Clip will reset any audio processing you have set on the current Audio Components, i.e. any applied Effects, Pan, Roles, etc. Even the audio analysis (see Audio Enhancements) will be reset.. Basically choosing a different Channel Configuration creates a new mixer with new default Channel Strips.

Setup

➡ Channel Analysis

FCPx creates the various Channel Configuration options and puts them into the Channel Configuration Menu ❶ for you to choose from ❸. Those configurations FCPx comes up with are based on two checkboxes ❷ in the Import Media Dialog under the "Analyze and Fix" section:

- ▸ **None selected** ❸ ⬛ ⬛: FCPx only uses the amount of Audio Channels found in the Source Media File to determine the various Channel Configurations.

- ▸ **Separate mono and group stereo audio** ❹ ☑: FCPx looks at any channel assignment in the Source Media File to determine what Channel Configurations to create. This special option ❺ will be displayed as separate entry in the popup menu, which will be selected as the default Channel Configuration.

- ▸ **Remove silent channels** ❻ ☑: Any Audio Channel that doesn't carry an audio signal (silent) will not be taken into consideration when FCPx decides on the Channel Configurations.

- ▸ **Both selected** ❼ ☑ ☑: FCPx looks at the file's channel assignment or format information, but ignores any silent Audio Channel when determining the Channel Configurations.

Media Import Dialog

Please note:

- ▸ The two checkboxes are available in the Media Import Dialog ❷ (*cmd+I*) and the *Preferences ➤ Import* for applying the settings to files that you drag into FCPx.

- ▸ You can apply the analysis after the import by *ctr+clicking* on the Clip and select from the *Shortcut Menu ➤ Analyze and Fix...* or from the Main Menu *Modify ➤ Analyze and Fix...* and choose from the sheet ❽.

- ▸ Only Event Clips can be re-analyzed, but not Timeline Clips.

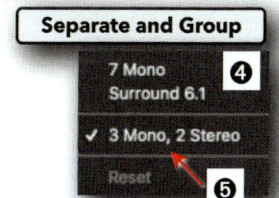

➡ Channel Configuration Menu

On the right are four screenshots of the Channel Configuration Menu for an audio file that has 7 Audio Channels, with one of them having no signal. You can see the different configurations FCPx comes up with, depending on the checkbox settings.

- ▸ **Available Configuration**: The menu lists in the upper section ❹ the configurations depending on the Source Media File.

- ▸ **Default Configuration**: FCPx picks one of the configurations as the default ☑.

- ▸ **Analyzed Configuration**: If you use the Analyze feature "Separate Mono and group Stereo" (the first checkbox), then the popup menu lists that Configuration separated by divider lines ❺.

- ▸ **Reset**: Once you choose from the menu a different configuration than the default configuration, then clicking the *Reset* ❾ command in the menu selects the Default Channel Configuration again.

Audio Inspector   **Channel Configuration popup menu**

Separate and Group ❹ / 3 Mono, 2 Stereo ❺ / Remove Silent ❻ / Separate and Group + Remove Silent ❼ / Reset ❾

8 - Audio   237

➡ *Examples (Mini-mixer Model)*

In the previous example, you can see on the various Channel Configuration Menus that there are a total of eight different Channel Configurations that FCPx can come up with for that one audio file. Here are eight diagrams that show the audio signal flow (based on the mini-mixer model) for those eight configurations to see what's changing "inside" a Clip when you change Channel Configurations.

▶ For the Surround ❶ configurations, you have only one Channel Strip (Audio Component) with all the Audio Channels feeding into that one Channel Strip.

▶ For the Mono ❷ configurations, each Audio Channel is feeding into its own Channel Strip (Audio Component). That means, you will have as many individual Audio Components as Audio Channels.

▶ The other four configurations are a mixture ❸ of Mono Channel Strips (1 Audio Channel Input) and Stereo Channel Strips (2 Audio Channel Inputs).

▶ Please note that the order of the Channel Strips (which means, the order of the Audio Component Clips from top to bottom in the Audio Inspector) is important. It follows how the Audio Channels are numbered ❹ in the Audio File.

▶ The speaker icon on each Audio Component Clip in the Audio Inspector indicates the number of audio inputs [1◀] [2◀] [6◀].

▶ Keep in mind that in each Clip, its Channel Strips (represented by the Audio Components) route their audio signal to a Master Channel Strip ❺ (represented by the Summed Audio Clip) of that Clip. The output of that Master Channel Strip is summed together with the output of all the other Clips in your Project.

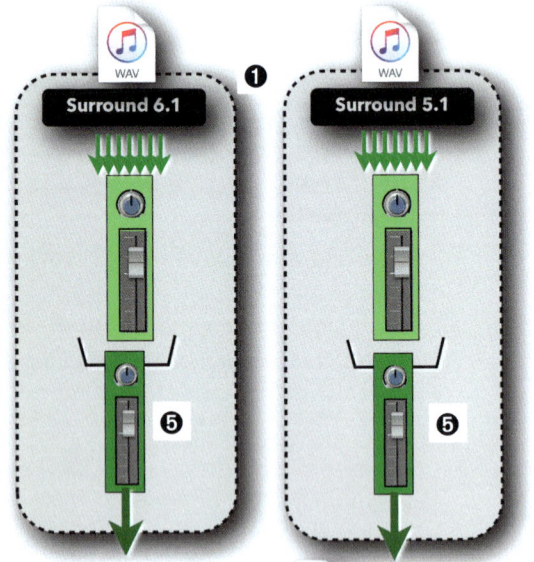

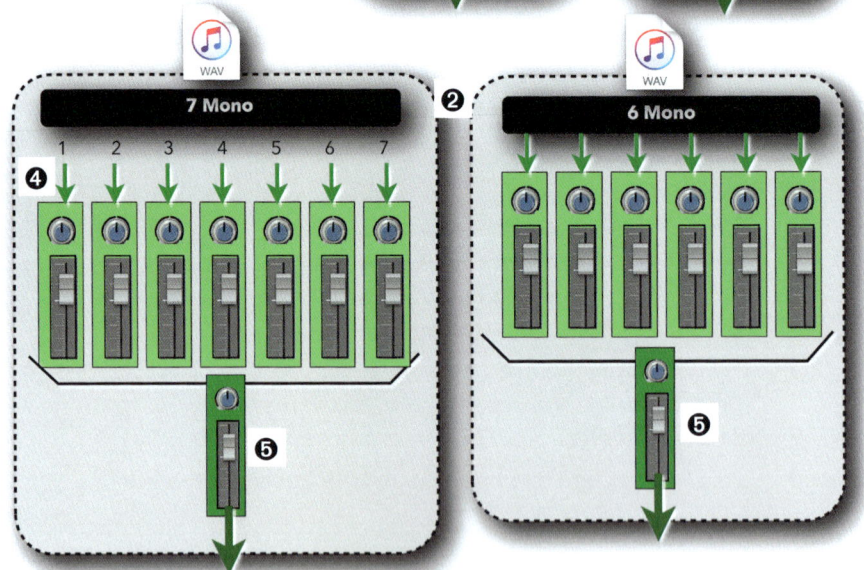

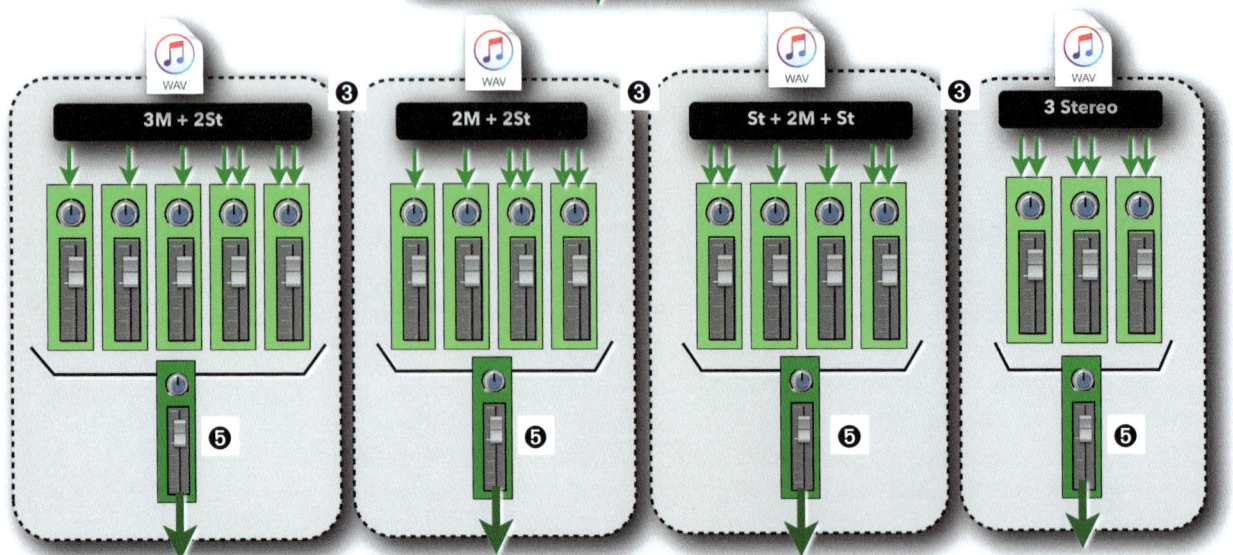

➡ *Other Channel Configurations*

Pay close attention to the Channel Configuration Menu, because there are other menu items that can pop up.

⚙ Reverse Stereo

In addition to *Stereo* or *Dual Mono* options, a Source Media File with two Audio Channels also has the option called "Reverse Stereo" **❶**. A better label would be "L-R Swap", because FCPx just flips the left and right channels.

⚙ Stereo Panner

The selected Channel Configuration also has an affect on the Pan Control:

- ▸ **Mono Channel Strip**: If you have an Audio Component Clip with a single Audio Channel input ⬚❷, then the Pan Control (when set to Stereo Left-Right) functions as a true L-R Panner **❸**.

- ▸ **Stereo Channel Strip**: If you have an Audio Component Clip with two Audio Channels as its input ⬚**❹**, then the Pan Control (when set to Stereo Left-Right) functions as a Stereo Balancer **❺**, which is completely different from a true Stereo Panner.

⚙ Mono Input

In addition to the input routing, the Channel Configuration can also affect the output routing of the audio signal for that specific Clip. If the Source Media File contains only a single Audio Channel **❻**, then there is technically only one Channel Configuration possible. One Audio Channel feeding that one signal into a single Channel Strip **❼** (Audio Component Clip) that feeds into the Master Channel Strip **❽** (Summed Audio Clip).

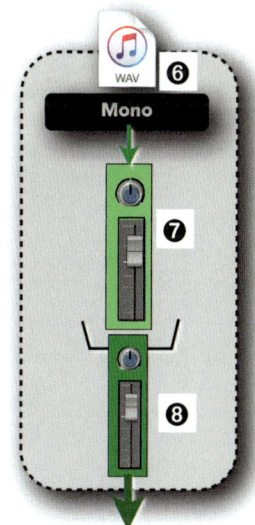

Therefore, you would expect to have only one option in the Channel Configuration popup menu ... wrong. You have seven options. In addition to the obvious "Mono" option, the popup menu lists all the channels of a 5.1 surround format **❾**. This lets you route that one audio signal directly to a specific output channel of a surround output.

More about that later.

Audio Enhancements

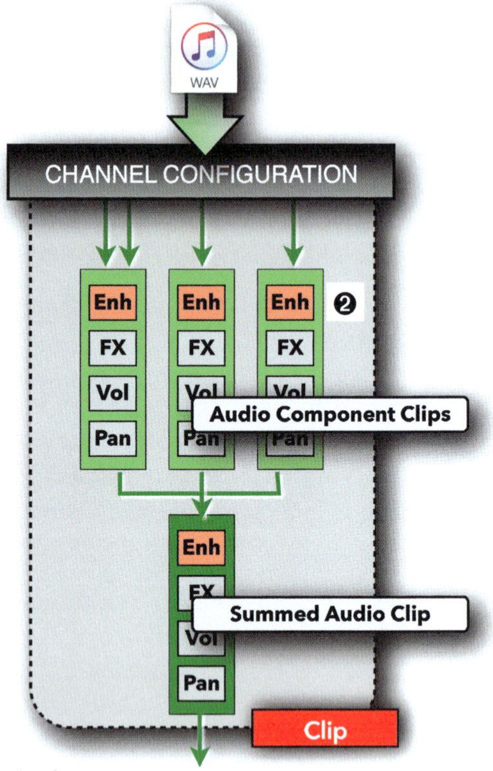

➡ Placement

Despite the fact that the Audio Enhancements Module is listed as the second module ❶ in the Audio Inspector after the Volume Module, it is actually the first module ❷ on the Channel Strip, the first signal processing stage the incoming audio signal(s) is passing through.

CHANNEL CONFIGURATION

Audio Component Clips

Summed Audio Clip

Clip

➡ Submodules

The Audio Enhancements Module contains five separate modules:

☑ **Equalization** ❸: You can use a graphical equalizer to tweak the frequency response.

☑ **Audio Analysis** ❹: This is a special module that lets FCPx automatically set the next three modules.

☑ **Loudness** ❺: You can adjust the overall loudness of the signal, which is basically a Compressor functionality.

☑ **Noise Removal** ❻: You can remove some background noise, which is basically an Expander/Gate functionality.

☑ **Hum Removal** ❼: You can remove 50Hz or 60Hz hum noise caused by ground loops, which is basically a so-called Notch Filter (removing only a very narrow frequency band).

➡ Interface

The interface implementation on how to access those Submodules is a little bit strange:

▸ When you open the Audio Inspector, you only see the header, labeled "Audio Enhancements" ❶.

▸ *Double-click* on the header or *click* on the "Show" button ❽ that appears when you mouse over it. This reveals the first two Modules ❾, *Equalization* and *Audio Analysis*.

▸ *Click* on the "Show" ❿ button that appears when you mouse over the "Analysis" header to reveal the remaining three modules, *Loudness* ❺, *Noise Removal* ❻, and *Hum Removal* ❼.

▸ You can mouse over each header of the three modules to reveal the Show/Hide Button. *Click* on it to reveal their parameters.

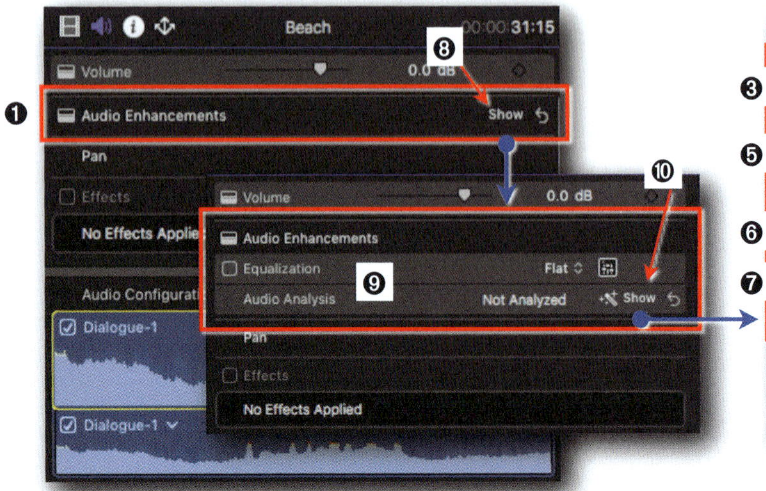

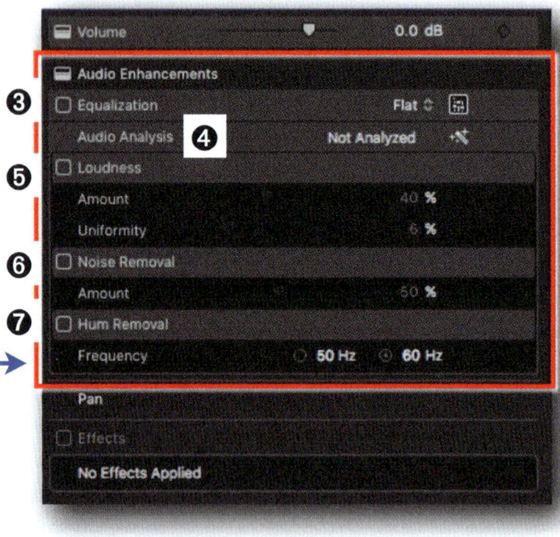

➡ *Audio Component Clip vs. Summed Audio Clip*

Here is an important fact about the implementation of the Audio Enhancements Module that could cause some confusion. However, because we discussed the topic of the Audio Component Clips vs. the Summed Audio Clips quite a bit and now understand their functionality regarding the signal flow "inside" a Clip, the following explanation should be easy to follow.

> **The Audio Enhancements Module is only available on the individual Audio Component Clips and not on the Summed Audio Clip**

💀 Single Audio Component Clip

If you have chosen a Channel Configuration that only has a single Audio Component (i.e. Stereo ❶, or 5.1), then the Audio Inspector shows all the submodules ❷ when you select the Summed Audio Clip ❸ (indicated by the 🗔 icon). However, these are only "remote controls" ❹ of that single Audio Component Clip ⓫. Select it ⓫ (indicated by the 🗔) and changing a parameter in one of the submodules ❷ will reflect the changes in the other (see it to believe it).

💀 Multiple Audio Component Clips

When you have a Channel Configuration selected that has more than one Audio Component ❼, then the Audio Enhancements module shows only the Audio Analysis Module ❽ when you select the Summed Audio Clip ❾ 🗔

However, this is again just a remote trigger ❿ to start the Audio Analysis on all its Audio Component Clips.

More about that in a moment.

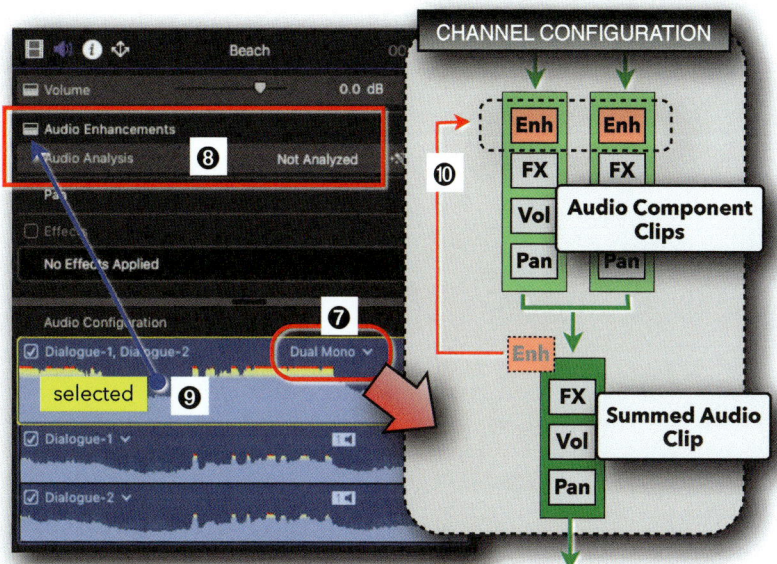

Equalization

The Equalization Module only has one row with three controls:

▶ **On/Off ❶** ☑ ▢: This checkbox lets you bypass the Equalization Module.

▶ **Preset Menu ❷** ⬍: This button shows the currently selected EQ Preset. *Click* on it to open the Preset Menu and select a Preset.

▶ **Plugin Window Button ❸** ▦: *Click* on this button to toggle a separate floating window ❹ with the user interface to adjust the EQ parameters.

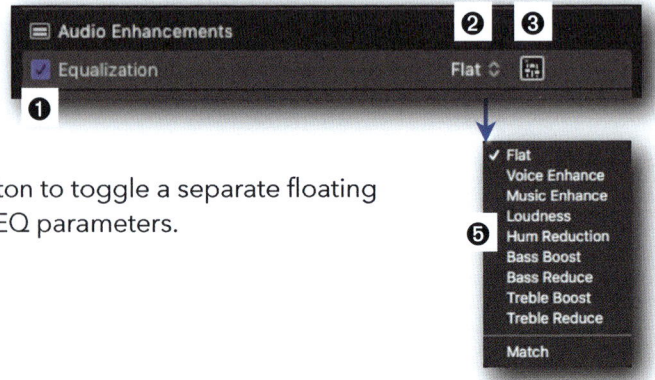

➡ Preset Menu

The popup menu ❺ lists several items:

▶ **Flat**: This means the EQ parameters are set to the default (all sliders at 0dB, same as bypassed).

▶ "**EQ Presets**": In addition, there are 8 Presets for specific situations that you can try. If you have the EQ window open, you can see the adjustments.

▶ **(edited)**: The word "(edited)" is added to the Preset name if you made any adjustments to that Preset.

▶ **Match**: This is a special feature if you want to match the sound characteristics (EQ) of a specific audio Clip (Timeline Clip only) to another reference Clip that you like.

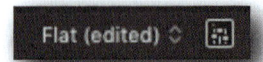

➡ Graphic Equalizer Window

The controls are pretty straight forward:

▶ The EQ window can be switched between a 10 band EQ (default) and a 31 band EQ ❻. The Presets only apply to the 10 Band EQ.

▶ *Drag* the individual slider up/down to set the level of a band ❼ or enter the level numerically in the entry box in the lower right corner ❽ for the selected frequency band.

▶ *Ctr+drag* from left to right lets you draw the slider positions.

▶ *Sh+opt+drag* lets you drag a selection of sliders (a blue frame appears) and then move them up/down as a group.

▶ The "Flatten EQ" button ❾ resets all the sliders to 0dB.

▶ You can leave multiple EQ windows open to make adjustments to two or more Clips while playing. The window header displays the name of the Clip it belongs to and the bottom displays the Role of that particular Audio Component Clip.

▶ The Header ❿ lists the On/Off checkbox (same as the one on the Inspector Module), the Preset Menu and the arrow buttons to step through the Presets.

▶ The EQ will affect the overall level, which you can see instantly on the Clip's waveform.

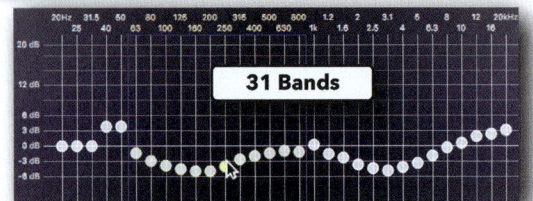

➡ *Match Audio*

Sometimes you want the sound of one Clip to sound like the sound of another clip. For example, you have a poor sounding music cue that you want to sound like a great sounding music cue. Or you have two video clips that where shot on different days and they sound differently because the microphone was not correctly placed or it was a different microphone altogether. In those cases you have two options. You have a lot of experience and know what frequency bands to tweak or you do a trial and error.

FCPx provides a third option: Match Audio.

These are the easy steps (the procedure is based on computer analysis, so your milage may vary):

☑ Select the Timeline Clip (no Event Clip) that you want to adjust.

☑ Select Match Audio with any of the following commands:

- 🎚 Select *Match* from the EQ Preset popup menu
- 🎚 Select *Match Audio...* ❶ from the Enhancements Menu button below the Viewer Pane
- 🎚 Select from the Main Menu *Modify ➤ Match Audio...*
- 🎚 Use the Key Command *sh+cmd+M*

Viewer Pane

☑ The Viewer changes to a split screen and displays a message "*Choose a Clip that has the audio you want to match*". The *Cancel* button aborts the procedure.

☑ Mouse over a Clip that has the audio you want to us as a reference

- The mouse cursor ❷ now has a little EQ icon 🎛 and a Skimming bar (to listen to the audio).

☑ *Click* on the Clip

- The text under the Viewer now displays the purple "*Apply Match*" button.

☑ *Click* the *Apply Match* button ❸.

- The matched EQ has been applied to the Audio Clip.

☑ The Equalization Module header has changed to display a little microphone icon ❹ 🎤. *Click* it if you want to repeat the procedure with a different reference Clip (if you weren't satisfied with the result).

☑ The Equalization Module displays the Plugin Button ❺, however, it will now open the "Match EQ" plugin ❻ instead of the Graphics Equalizer plugin. You can tweak those parameters further if you like.

> The instructions for Match EQ Plugin are found in the user guide "Logic Pro X Instruments"
>
> https://itunes.apple.com/us/book/logic-pro-x-instruments/id960809171?mt=11

Match EQ Plugin

Audio Analysis

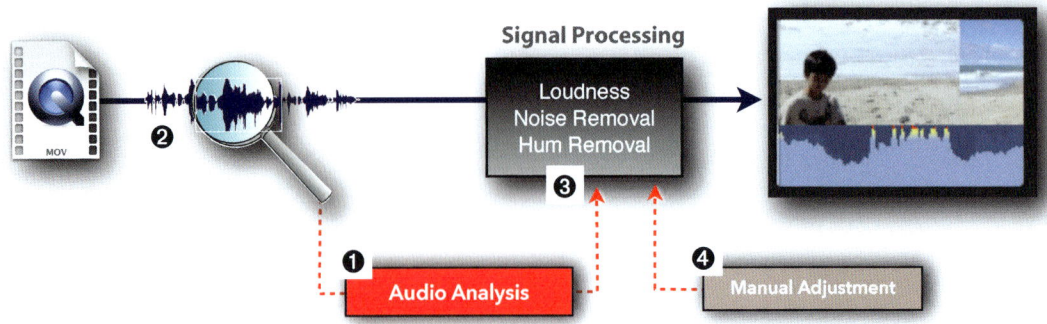

Here is the basic concept about the Audio Analysis Module:

▶ You can tell FCPx to analyze ❶ the audio signal of a Clip ❷ and look for three things:

- ☑ **Loudness**: Is the overall audio level in a good range or maybe there are too many peaks or the levels are too low?
- ☑ **Noise Removal**: Is there some constant background noise going on behind dialog?
- ☑ **Hum Removal**: Is there some noticeable 50Hz or 60Hz cycle hum present in the audio signal?

▶ The Analysis procedure can have three results:

- ☑ A signal has no problems and gets a checkmark. No action is taken.
- ⚠ A signal has problems in any of the three areas and gets a yellow badge.
- ☑ If a problem was detected, then FCPx is automatically trying to fix that problem by enabling that specific Module and adjusting its parameters ❸. It also gets the green checkmark.

▶ You can manually adjust the parameters of those three Modules ❹, disable the module if you don't like the fix at all, or want to delete the analysis data.

💀 Audio Component Clips only

Remember that the Audio Enhancements Module is only available on the individual Audio Components Clips (the first module ❺ on the Channel Strip in our mini-mixer model). That means that the Analysis procedure is performed on those specific Audio Component Clips.

The Enhancements Modules ❻ that are displayed in the Audio Inspector when a Summed Audio Clip is selected only lets you initiate ❼ the Analysis process or displays those Modules as a lookup from the actual Audio Component Clip (if the Channel Configuration has only a single Audio Component). Initiating the Analysis on a selected Summed Audio Clip will perform the Analysis on all its Audio Components.

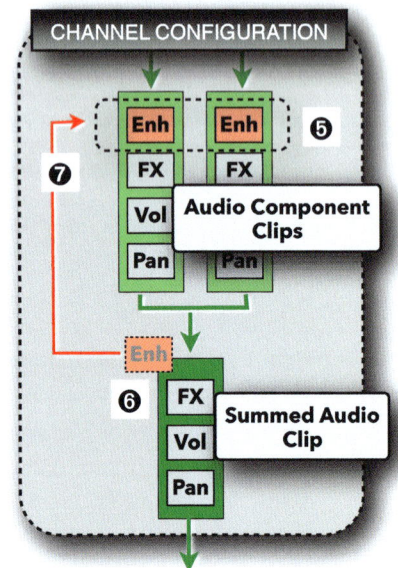

Next, I will introduce the Audio Analysis functionality by going through four dedicated steps and show examples what happens and what to look out for.

➡ #1 Operate Manually

You can use the Audio Analysis Module manually as a standard Effects Module without the analyzing procedure. The header displays the label "*Not Analyzed*" ❶.

Click on the "Show" button (mouse over the header) to reveal the three Modules and their parameters (**clicking** the "Show" button on their header).

Here are the available parameters. A module has to be enabled with the checkbox ☑ before you can adjust its parameter.

- ▸ **Loudness Amount** ❷: This controls the amount of compression that is applied to the signal (similar to the Threshold setting on a Compressor).
- ▸ **Loudness Uniformity**: This controls the dynamic range of the signal that is affected (similar to the Ratio setting on a Compressor). Has to be more than 0% for this module to have an effect.
- ▸ **Noise Removal Amount** ❸: This controls how much the background noise (air condition, wind, etc.) is reduced. Be careful, setting it too high might also affect the "good" signal by cutting in and out.
- ▸ **Hum Removal Frequency** ❹: You can select a radio button to remove either the 50Hz (European power cycle) or 60Hz (US power cycle).

➡ #2 Analyze

There are multiple ways to initiate the Analysis process. It seems that the "*Auto Enhance Auto*" feature works the same as "Analyze and fix audio problems".

- ▸ Analyze and Fix:

  This analysis is applied to the entire Clip, which means all the Audio Components inside those Clips

  - 📌 **During Import**: In the Media Import Dialog, enable the checkbox for the "*Analyze and fix audio problems*" ❺. Every file that you import now will be analyzed.
  - 📌 **During Drag & Drop**: The same checkbox is available in the **Preferences ➤ Import**, which applies to all files that you import via drag and drop.
  - 📌 **Event Clip**: Select any Event Clip(s) in the Browser and choose from the Main Menu **Modify ➤ Analyze and Fix** or **ctr+click** on the Event and choose that command from its Shortcut Menu. It slides out a sheet that contains the checkbox "*Analyze and fix audio problems*" ❻.

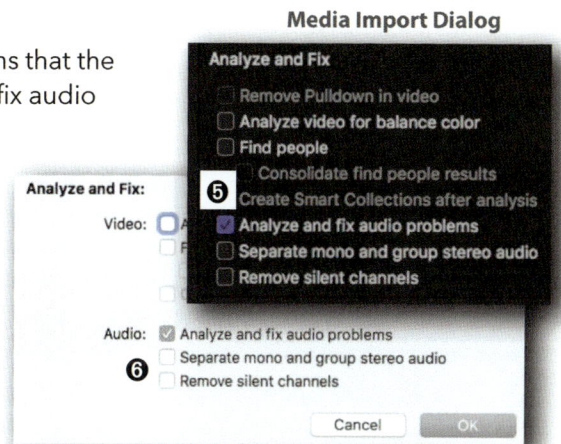

- ▸ Auto Enhance Audio:

  This command is applied to whatever Clip is selected in FCPx, for example, individual Audio Component Clips. Selecting a Summed Audio Clip in the Inspector or the Event Clip or Timeline Clip will analyze all its Audio Component Clips.

  - 📌 **Click** the Magic Wand 🪄 icon ❼ in the Audio Analysis Module
  - 📌 Select *Auto Enhance Audio...* ❽ from the Enhancements Menu button below the Viewer Pane
  - 📌 Use the Key Command **opt+cmd+A**

Pay close attention to the various icons and the current selection to understand what is currently displayed and how to interpret that. Here are a few examples.

Example 1

This is a screenshot with a Clip that contains a single Audio Component (stereo).

I selected the Summed Audio Clip ❶ 🖼, but because this Clip has only a single Audio Component Clip ❷, the Audio Inspector displays the complete Audio Enhancements Module ❸. As we have just learned, this is a lookup of the Audio Component Clip.

▸ The Audio Analysis header has changed the label from "*Not Analyzed*" to "*Fixed*" ❹ and indicates that with the green checkmark ✅.

▸ ⬛✅ The Loudness and Hum Removal Modules left disabled and have the green checkmark, which means that they are ok, no actions were required.

▸ ☑✅ The Noise Removal Module is enabled and also has the green checkmark, which means that FCPx detected a problem and has fixed it by setting the Amount slider to 50%.

▸ ✅ Now the Audio Component Clip also shows that green checkmark on the waveform ❷.

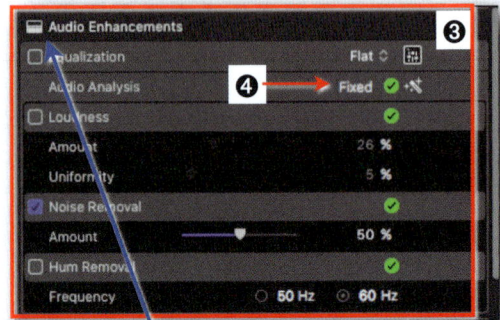

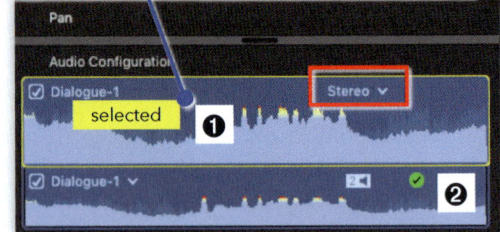

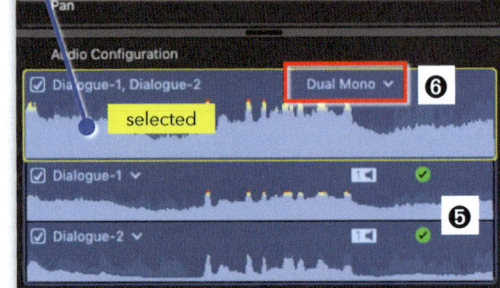

Example 2

This is a Clip that has two Audio Component Clips ❺ as you can see on the Channel Configuration button (Dual Mono ❻).

▸ I also selected the Summed Audio Clip, but this time, the Audio Enhancements Module only displays the header.

▸ It still displays the label Fixed ❼ and the green checkmark ✅

▸ Both Audio Component Clips ❺ also display the green checkmark on their waveform to indicate that they were either ok in the first place or have been fixed.

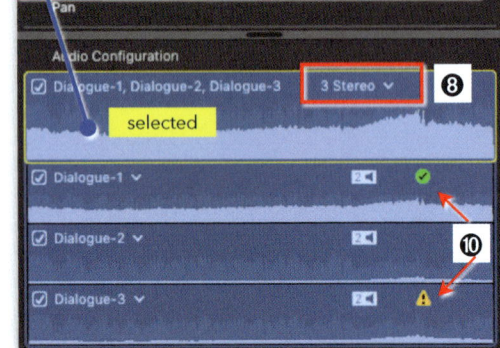

Example 3

This is a Clip that has three Audio Component Clips as you can see on the Channel Configuration button (3 Stereo ❽).

▸ I also selected the Summed Audio Clip and you can see that only the header of the Audio Enhancements Module is selected.

▸ The header displays the label "*Mixed*" ❾ with the special mixed icon 🔄, because of the different status of its Audio Component Clips ❿.

▸ All three Audio Component Clips have a different status indicated by their badges ❿. The first is ok, then second one is not analyzed yet, and the third one has detected problems that haven't been fixed yet.

Example 4

If the select Clip has detected problems that haven't been fixed yet, then it will display the yellow label "*Problems Detected*" with the yellow icon ⚠.

➡ #3 Modify Parameters

You can modify the results of the analysis that FCPx performed.

- ▶ **Adjust**: You can adjust the parameters ❶ of the Modules to see if you can improve the results. FCPx only uses math, but you can use your ears, which should be the ultimate judge.
- ▶ **Disable**: *Click* on the On/Off checkbox ❷ to disable ▢ a Module. You can still see the settings, but extremely dimmed ❸.
- ▶ **Reset**: When you mouse-over the header of a Module, the Reset Button ❹ ↩ appears. It has the same functionality as turning the On/Off Button off.
  - 🎚 *Click* the Reset Button ↩ on a module to turn that module off.
  - 🎚 *Click* the Reset Button ↩ on the Audio Analysis section ❺ to turn all three Modules off.

Once you have reset a Module, it shows either the green checkmark ✅ to indicate that the FCPx Analysis didn't require any action on that Module or it shows the yellow warning badge ⚠ to show that this Module was needed to fix a problem ❻.

You always can click on the magic wand ❼ 🪄 to re-instate all the corrections based on the FCPx Analysis.

Please note that any changes made in those Modules will be instantly reflected in the audio waveform of the Timeline Clip.

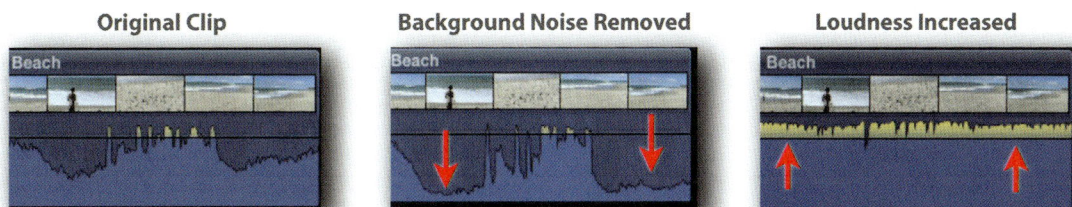

Original Clip   **Background Noise Removed**   **Loudness Increased**

➡ #4 Remove Analysis Data

There is one easy action that removes all the analysis data from a Clip (and all its Audio Component Clips):

From the Channel Configuration popup menu select the currently selected Channel Configuration again ❽.

Attention: Selecting a different Channel Configuration from the popup menu will reset all Modules in the Inspector for that Clip.

➡ Signal Flow

Let's have a look at our mini-mixer model to see where the Effects Modules are:

▶ As you can see on the Channel Strip, the FX Module is after the Audio Enhancements Module. That means, any level adjustments in the Audio Enhancements Modules will affect the signal processing in the Effects Module (i.e. Compressor Threshold).

▶ The Volume Fader is positioned after the Effects Module, which means it has no affect on the signal processing of the Effect Module(s).

▶ Inside a single Clip you can apply Effects to each individual Audio Component Clip and the Summed Audio Clip, to process the summed signal of all Audio Components in that Clip.

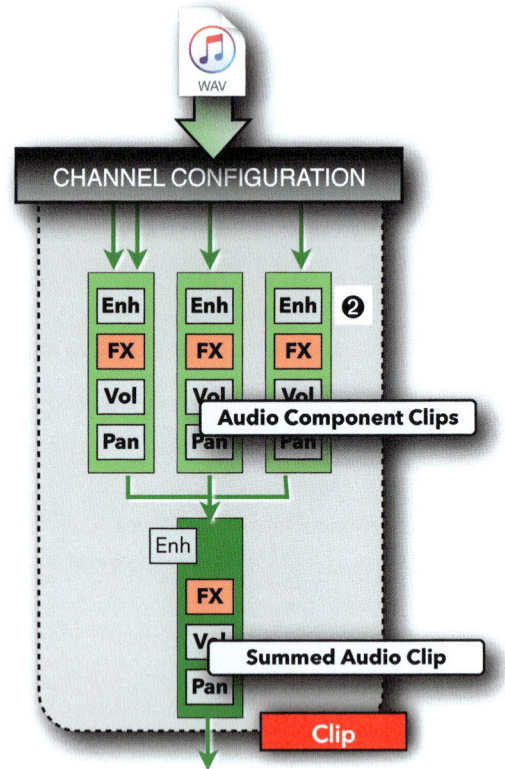

➡ Concept

Here are the basic rules and procedures about Effects:

▶ **Effects Browser**: You can only apply Effects that are available in the FCPx Effects Browser, a window pane, part of the Timeline Pane.

▶ **Apply Effect**: You add an Effect from the Effects Browser to one or multiple Timeline Clips on the Timeline.

  • As we know from our mini-mixer model, the Effect will be applied to either one of the Audio Component Clips or the Summed Audio Clip of that specific Clip.

▶ **Multiple Effects**: Use the same procedures to add more Effects to the Timeline Clips. You are adding more Effects to your Channel Strips to process the signal that passes through it.

▶ **Copy-Paste Effects Management**: FCPx has a sophisticated procedure to copy/paste Effects between Clips.

▶ **Edit Effects**: The editing of the Effects is done in the Audio Inspector.

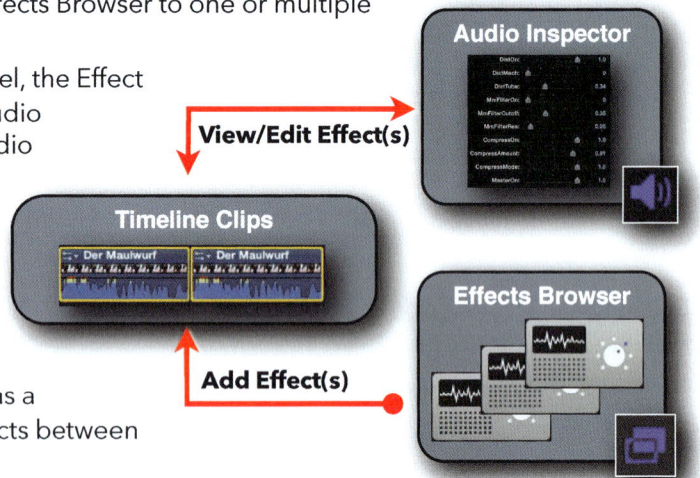

➡ Basic Steps

These are the simple steps of adding effects to a Clip:

☑ Open the Effects Browser
☑ Search for the Effects plugin
☑ Apply the Effect Plugin to the Clip in the Timeline
☑ Make adjustments (edit) for that effects plugin in the Audio Inspector

Effects Browser

Effects Browser ❶

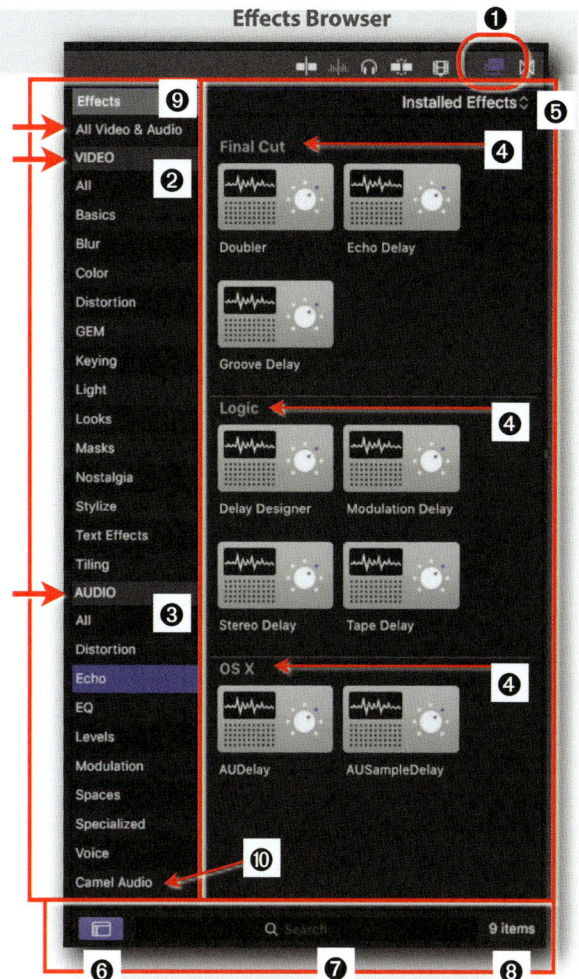

Toggle the Effects Browser with any of those commands:

🔘 **Click** the Effects Browser Button ❶ 🔳 in the Timeline Header

🔘 Main Menu **Window ➤ Show in Workspace ➤ Effects**

🔘 Key Command **cmd+5**

The Effects Browser has three sections:

🔘 **Sidebar**

▸ The Sidebar on the left lists various categories of effects. Each item is like a smart folder that restricts which effect is displayed in the Browser on the right.

▸ The Sidebar displays both Video ❷ and Audio ❸ Effects. This is the same location when looking for video effects.

🔘 **Browser**

▸ The Browser window displays the actual Effects Plugins based on the selection in the Sidebar.

▸ The Plugins are displayed alphabetically and organized in subgroups ❹ based on their origin or format (Final Cut, Logic, OS X, "Third Party").

▸ The popup menu in the upper corner lists "Installed Effects" ❺ and all currently open Libraries (to show Plugins that are stored with a Library).

🔘 **Status Bar**

▸ <u>Toggle Sidebar</u> ❻: The purple button 🔳 lets you toggle the Sidebar.

▸ <u>Search Field</u> ❼: The selection from the Sidebar already acts as a search restriction (unless you select *All Video & Audio* ❾). In addition to that, you can enter a name in the Search Field at the bottom of the Browser to filter the displayed Effect Plugins even more.

▸ <u>Found Items</u> ❽: The lower-right corner displays how many Effect Plugins are displayed based on the search criteria (Sidebar + Search Field).

These are the different groups ❹ of Plugins that are displayed in the Browser Window:

- **Final Cut**: These are little Effect Racks that contain one or more Effects from Logic and macOS. For example, the "Car Radio" Effect contains an EQ Plugin and a Distortion Plugin to achieve the car radio effect.

- **Logic** :These are the same excellent Effect Plugins that come with Logic Pro. (Please note that although Logic supports the AU plugin standard, those Logic Plugins are a Logic-specific format and not AU Plugins).

- **OS X**: These are the Effect Plugins in the standard AU format that come preinstalled with macOS.

- **"Third-party FX"**: Any additional AU Effect Plugin that you installed on your machine will be available in FCPx. The Plugins are listed by Manufacturer in the Browser and also in the Sidebar at the end of the categorized list ❿.

Apply and Edit Effects

CHANNEL CONFIGURATION

Audio Component Clips

Summed Audio Clip

Clip

➡️ *Apply Effects*

You can apply an Effect from the Effects Browser in two ways:

▶ *Drag* the Effect from the Effects Browser ❶ onto a Timeline Clip (one at a time).

▶ *Double-click* on the Effect in the Effects Browser to add it to one or multiple selected Timeline Clips at once.

🔮 Target Clip - Target Channel Strip

Now it is important to use our understanding about the difference between a Summed Audio Clip and an Audio Component Clip to determine exactly where to drag the Effect to and, therefore, determine where the signal processing takes place along the signal flow inside a Clip.

▶ **Summed Audio Clip**: *Dragging* the Effect onto a Standard (collapsed) Clip ❷ or on the Expanded Audio ❸ portion of that Clip, then the Effect will be placed in the Master Channel Strip ❹ in our mini-mixer model.

Summed Audio Clip

Audio Component Clip

▶ **Audio Component Clip**: When *dragging* the Effect onto a Clip in Expanded Audio Component view, then the Audio Component Clip ❺ you are dragging the Effect to determines on which of the corresponding Channel Strips ❻ you will place that Effect to.

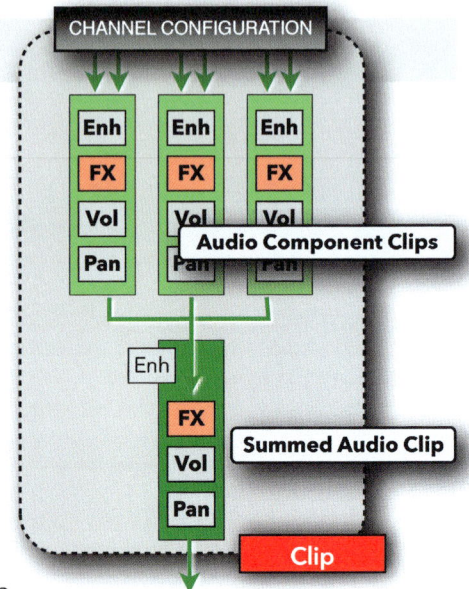

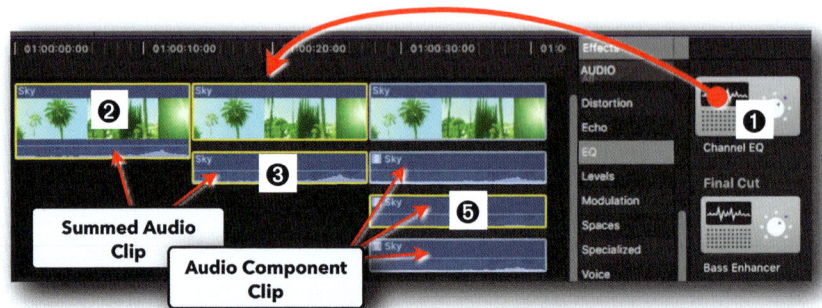

🔮 FX Badge [FX] and Mixdown Badge ⇥

▶ **Audio Component Clip**: Any Audio Component Clip that has at least one Effect applied to it will display an FX Badge [FX] ❼ on the waveform in the Audio Inspector.

▶ **Summed Audio Clip**: Any Summed Audio Clip that has at least one Effect applied to it will display an FX Badge [FX] ❽ on the waveform in the Audio Inspector, plus the Mixdown Badge ❾ in the upper-left corner (if the Clip has more than one Audio Component Clip). The Timeline Clip then will also display a Mixdown Badge ❿ ⇥.

Timeline Clip

Audio Inspector

🔮 Preview Effect

Select the Timeline Clip you want to hear with an Effect. Now, move the mouse cursor over an Effect in the Effects Browser and you will see the video play inside the Effects image with the Skimmer ⓫ enabled too. The audio signal plays back with that Effect applied to it in real time. While the Skimmer is visible, you can use the playback commands *spacebar*, *J*, *K*, *L*. How cool is that?

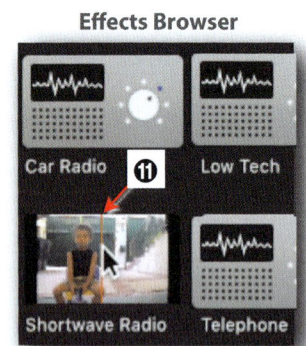

Effects Browser

➡ Interface

Once an effect is applied to a Timeline Clip, the effect itself with all its parameters can be displayed and edited in the Inspector (some parameters are also visible in the Animation Editor on the Timeline). Remember, the Inspector displays the Effects Module only for selected Timeline Clips. You cannot apply Effects directly to Event Clips (unless they are opened in a Timeline).

The Effects Module acts like a container with more modules listed inside, similar to an effects rack used in big recording studios.

Here is how you "unfold" the various layers of the Effects Module:

🔘 Effects Module

Click the Show/Hide Button ❶ (that appears when you mouse over the module) to toggle the expanded view, which displays the individual Plugins "inside" the Effects Module. Please note that this Module is also displayed when an Event Clip is selected, but it is disabled because you cannot add Effects to Event Clips.

▸ **No Plugins loaded**: When you expand the empty Effects Module, it displays the text "*No Effects Applied*" ❷, because no Plugin has been loaded yet to this Clip.

🔘 Plugin Module (Collapsed)

If you have an Effect applied to this Clip, then the Collapsed View of this Plugin Module has five elements:

▸ **On/Off Button ❸** ☑: Disable the checkbox to bypass the Plugin. The Effects Module itself also has an On/off Button to bypass all Plugins.

▸ **Name of the Plugin ❹**

▸ **Plugin Button ❺** 🔳 **Click** on the Plugin Button to open the Plugin Window as a separate floating window. The onscreen controls on that window are linked to its corresponding controls in the Inspector.

▸ **Show/Hide Button ❻**: **Click** the button to toggle the expanded view ❽ of the Plugin Module to display the Plugin parameters and controls.

▸ **Keyframe Menu ❼**: See the Automation chapter for details.

🔘 Plugin Module (Expanded)

The expanded view shows two more rows:

▸ **Preset ❾**: Final Cut Effects have various presets to choose from. Other Plugins also have a command to save your own Presets.

▸ **Parameters ❿**: The disclosure triangle lets you toggle the expanded view of all the controls for that parameters.

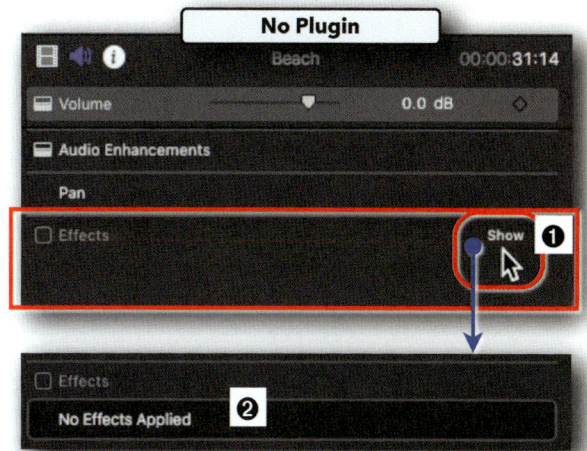

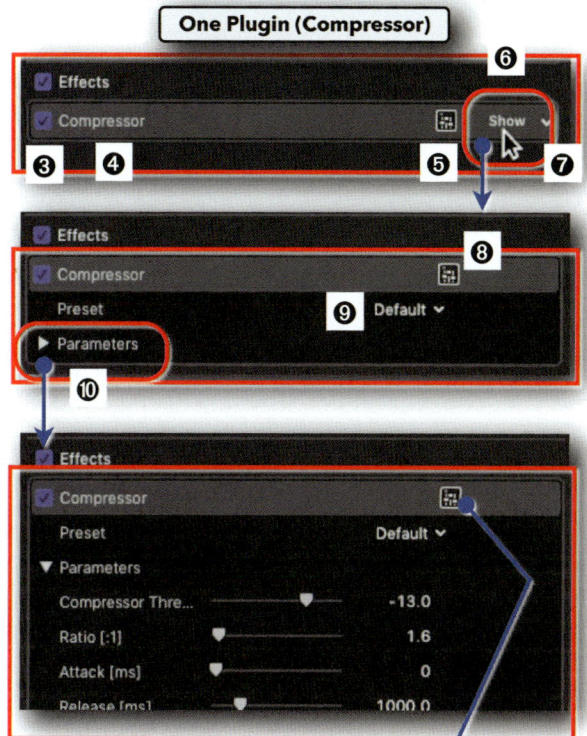

🍎 Final Cut Effects Module

Final Cut Effects are different from the other Plugins in the Effects Browser. They are macros, containing a group of multiple Plugins. The interface is, therefore, a little bit different

Final Cut Effects

▶ **Collapsed View**: The header has the On/Off Checkbox but no Plugin Button ❶ 🔲.

▶ **Expanded View**: The expanded view has a minimum of three rows:

- Preset ❷: The Preset Menu lists only Presets without any additional commands.
- Amount ❸: This slider controls the overall effect of all combined Plugins included in this Effect. It functions like a wet/dry control.
- Plugin Button ❹ 🔲: Each Plugin that is part of this Effect is listed with its own Plugin Button, so you can open it and adjust the settings individually in its own interface.

➡️ *Additional Edits*

There are a few additional tasks regarding the Effects Module

🍎 Edit multiple Plugins

You can select multiple Clips and edit their Plugins together as long as the Clip has the same Effects loaded. In that case, the Inspector Header displays "*Inspecting n Items*" ❺ instead of the name of the selected Clip.

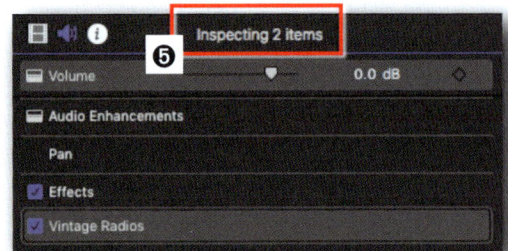

🍎 Reorder Plugins

Each newly added Effect is added as a new Plugin Module at the bottom. However, you can *drag* ❻ Plugin Modules up/down inside the Effects Module to rearrange their order, because the signal flow is from top to bottom and the sequence of how the signal flows from one Plugin into the next Plugin can make a big difference. For example, you might want to place any EQ before any Dynamics Plugins (Compressor or Limiter), or place any reverb after the Dynamics Plugins.

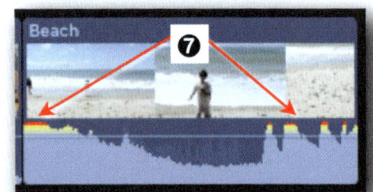

🍎 Audio Waveform

Any level change caused by a Plugin will be reflected on the Clip's waveform right away, so you can spot any potential clipping ❼.

🍎 Remove Plugins

To delete a Plugin, just *click* on it (or multiple) to select it (displays a yellow frame ❽) and press the *delete* key. You can undo that action.

There are other ways to remove Plugins as we will discover on the next page.

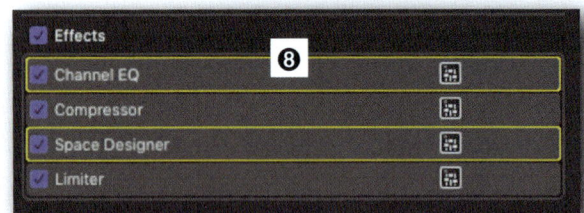

➡ Preset Management

▸ Changing a Parameter in a Plugin Module will add the label "(edited)" ❶ to the Preset name to indicate that what you hear is not the original Preset.

▸ You can save the Plugin settings as your own Preset by selecting "*Save Preset...*" ❷ from the Preset menu and enter a name in the entry box.

▸ The Custom Presets are displayed separately ❸ in the Preset menu above the Factory Presets.

▸ The custom Presets have the extension .aupreset and are stored in the location *~/Library/Audio/Presets/ EMAG/*. Any custom Plug-In Presets that are stored in Logic (at a different user location) are also listed in the Custom Preset section ❸.

▸ The Plugin Window also has a Preset selector ❹ that opens the same Preset Menu. The left-right arrows ❺ step through the Presets.

▸ To delete a custom Preset, select the command "*Reveal User Presets in Finder...*" ❷ and delete the Preset in the Finder.

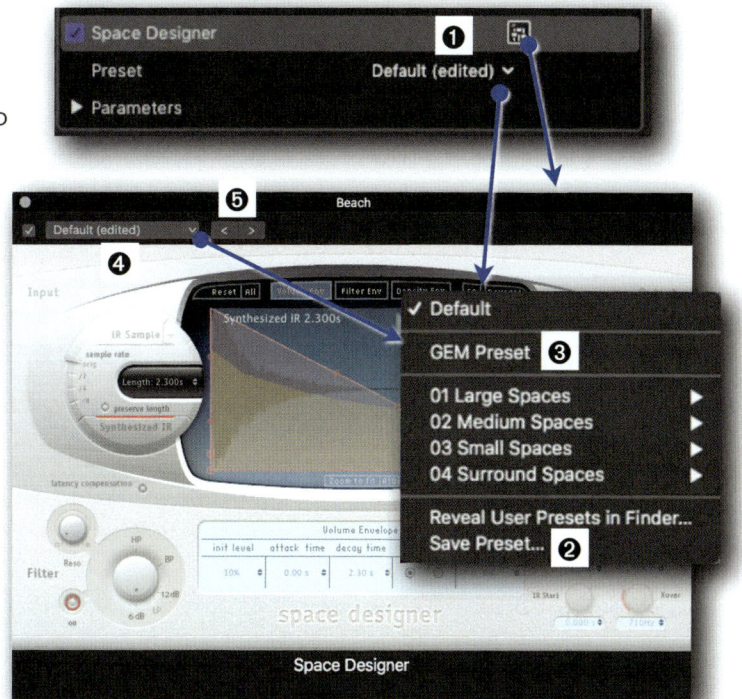

➡ Reset

Please note that the Effects Module has Reset buttons on multiple levels. That means, you can reset specific layers of the Effects Module. So, whenever you *click* on the Reset button, know exactly what level (what Parameters) are affected. Also, the Reset Button only appears when you mouse-over that section on the right (Parameters with active Keyframes are not affected by the Reset command!):

❻ **Effects Module**: This resets all the Plugins, everything inside that Effects Module.

❼ **Plugin Module**: *Click* on the selector to open a popup menu ❽ with the Reset Parameter command. This resets only that specific Plugin to its default setting.

❾ **Plugin Parameter**: This resets only that specific Parameter (and removes all its Keyframes) for that Plugin. Please note that the separate Plugin Window 🔲 has more parameters.

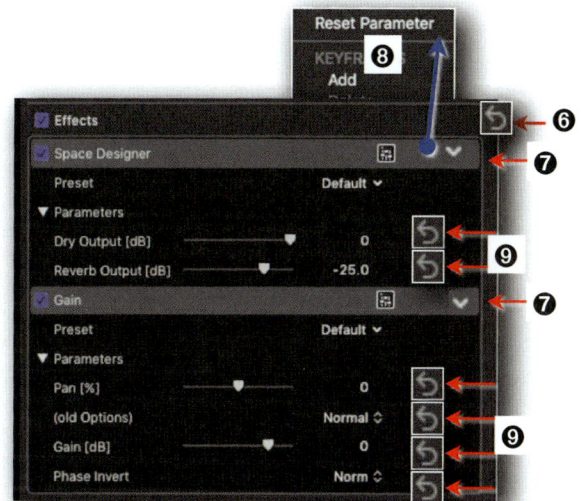

➡ Effects on Audio Subgroups

Audio Effects can be applied to single Clips very easily, even multiple Clips at once, but what if you want to apply an Effect (i.e. compressor) to a group of Clips that play at the same time (multiple Foley FX) or Clips that play one after another (a sequence of different music clips) and treat them as a so-called audio subgroup? FCPx doesn't provide a standard audio mixer with such a bussing feature.

To achieve that in FCPx, you use Compound Clips instead. This is not a trick or a workaround, it is the digital workflow with metadata that you have to adapt to. This might be even more flexible and powerful than the old (accustomed to and proven) workflows.

I will cover that in the Roles chapter.

Manage Effects

I already showed this diagram in the Editing chapter. Let's review these procedures that provides additional commands to add Effects to a Timeline Clip and explore them a little bit further:

Edit Menu

▶ **Copy**: When you select a Timeline Clip ❶ and use the standard copy command (*Edit* ➤ *Copy* or *cmd+C*), the entire Clip, including its Video and Audio Attributes are copied to the clipboard ❷. FCPx has two commands to use only the Audio and Video Attributes and "paste" them onto any existing Timeline Clips ❸.

▶ **Paste Effects** ❹: This command uses all Video and all Audio Attributes of the Clip that has been copied to the clipboard ❷ and adds them to the currently selected Timeline Clip(s) ❸. Default Attributes will be overwritten.

▶ **Paste Attributes...** ❺: This command opens a Dialog ❻ with a list of all the Video and Audio Attributes of the Clip on the clipboard ❷. You can pick which Attributes you want to add to the currently selected Clip(s) ❸ and which Default Attribute you want to overwrite.

▶ **Remove Effects** ❼:This command does two things. It removes all the Video and Audio Effects that have been added to the currently selected Timeline Clip ❸ (Added Attributes). In addition, all the Default Attributes that can't be removed are reset to their default setting.

▶ **Remove Attributes...** ❽: This command opens a Dialog ❾ with a list of all the Video and Audio Attributes of the currently selected Timeline Clip ❸. You can pick which Attribute you want to remove. Again, selected Added Attributes, (the added Video and Audio Effects) are removed and selected Default Attributes are reset to their default values.

▶ **Save Effects Preset**: The bottom of the Inspector has a button "Save Effects Preset" ❿ that saves all the current Attributes as a *Final Cut Pro Effects Preset* file that will be available in the Effects Browser, so you can apply it to any Timeline Clip.

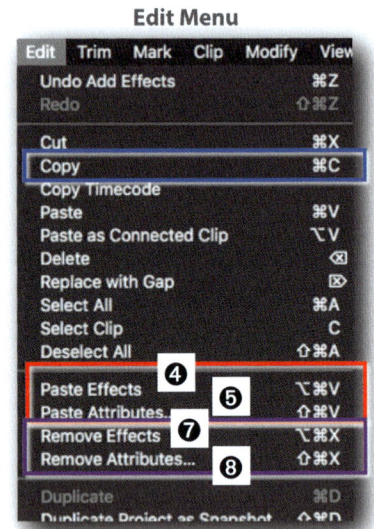

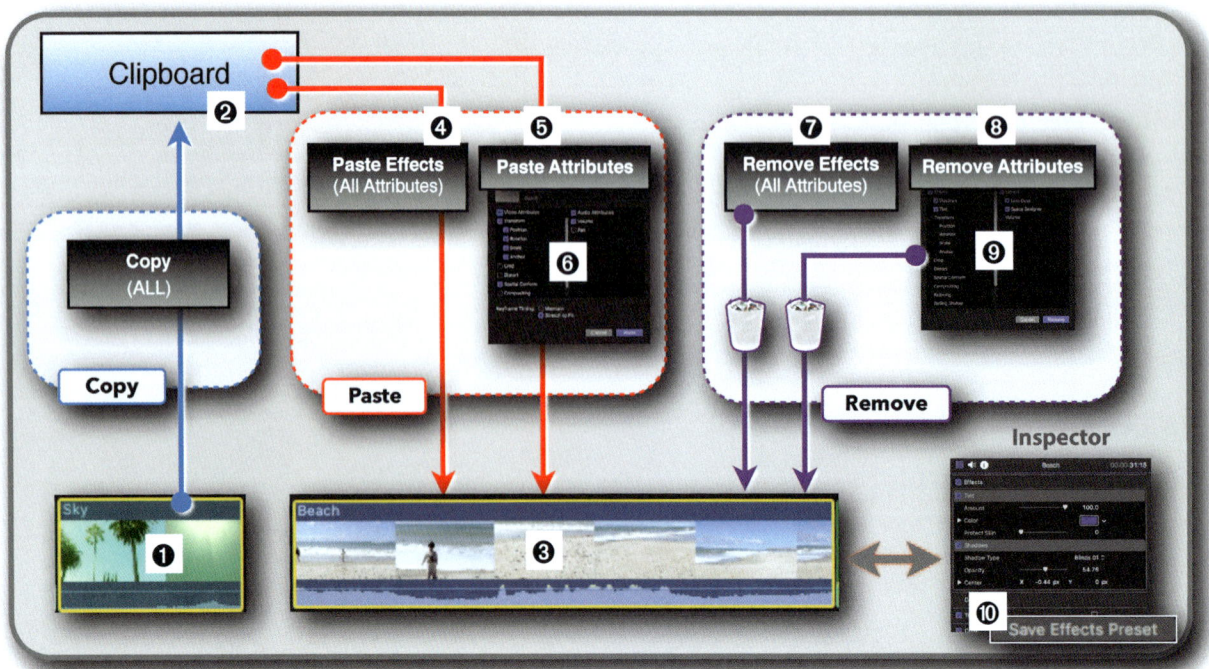

➡ Paste Attributes Dialog

Using the Paste Attributes command (**sh+cmd+V**) opens the Paste Attributes Dialog. It has three sections.

🌑 Copied From - Paste To

The top of the window displays the thumbnail and the name of the Source Clip ❶ (the one that was copied to the clipboard) and the Destination Clip ❷ (the one that is currently selected). If there is more than one Destination Clip selected on the Timeline, then it only indicates the number of Destination Clips without their names or thumbnails ❸.

🌑 Attributes Selection

All the available Attributes are listed in two columns (Video Attributes ❹ and Audio Attributes ❺). You can use the checkboxes to select/deselect individual Attributes or use the checkbox in the header to toggle all selections in that column.

The screenshot lists Effects ❻ as the first Attribute. This is the Effects Module that contains all the added Video and Audio Effect Plugins. Effects is only visible if the current Clip on the clipboard contains at least one Effect Plugin. Please note that Effect Plugins are added to any existing Effect Plugin on the Destination Clip without overwriting any existing Plugins. Selecting any Default Modules ❼ will overwrite the Parameters of those Default Modules.

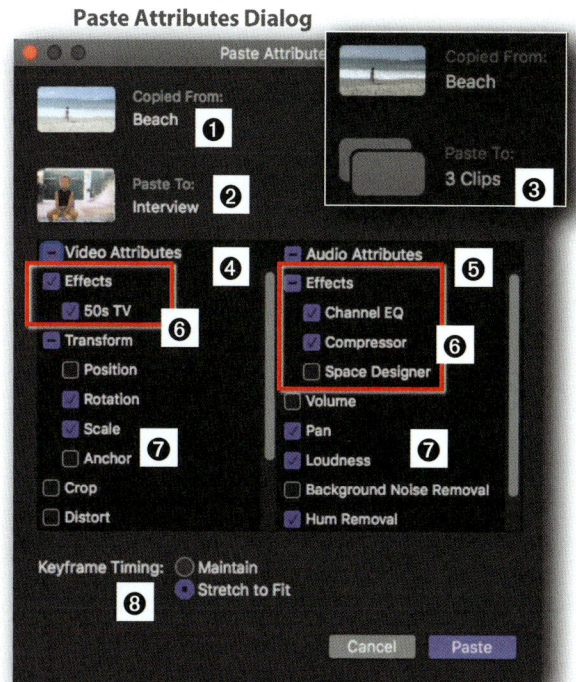

Paste Attributes Dialog

🌑 Keyframe Timing

There is an additional setting at the bottom of the window ❽. It determines the behavior if an Attribute contains Keyframes and how to apply the timing information if the Destination Clip has a different length as the Source Clip.

The following diagram shows the affect of both behaviors when copying a Source Clip that is 2 seconds long to a Destination Clip that is 3 seconds long or 1 second long.

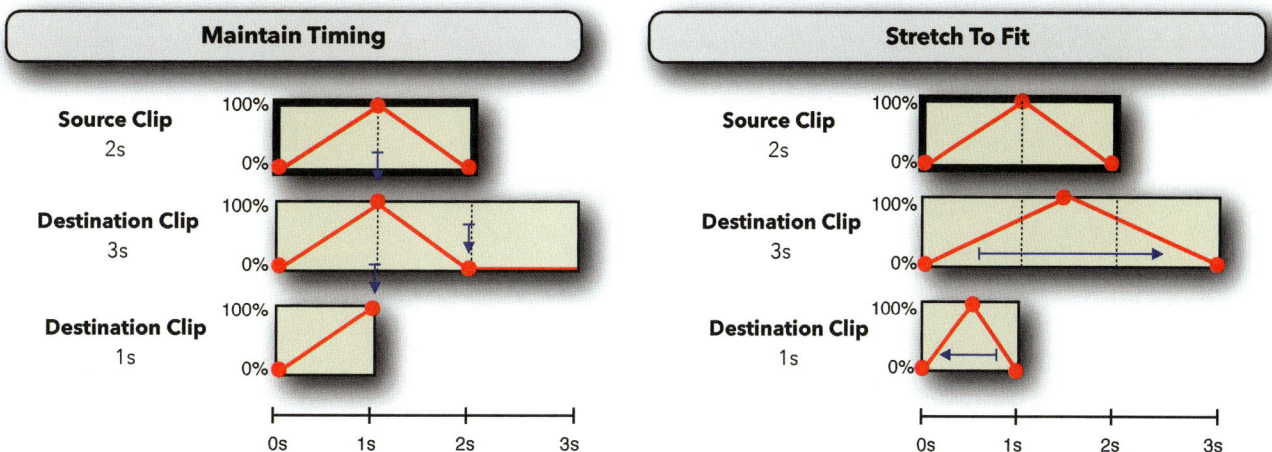

➡ Custom Effects Presets

This is a great feature to create and save your own custom Effects Presets to use in any Clip.

▶ **Save Effects Preset**: At the bottom of the Audio Inspector, click the "Save Effects Preset" button ❶.

▶ The Save Audio Effects Preset Dialog ❷ opens with the following elements.

- **Attributes** ❸: The center lists all the Modules that you have currently available in the Inspector ❹. Enable the checkboxes for those modules you want to save in that Preset.

- **Keyframes**: The Keyframe column indicates if there are any Keyframes ❺ used in that Clip.

- **Name** ❻: Enter a name for your custom Preset.

- **Category** ❼: Select any of the Audio Effects Categories you want to save the Preset to. The *New Category...* command opens a text field that lets you create a new Custom Category ❽. In this example, I have already created a new Category "GEM FX".

- **Save**: All the enabled settings are saved to this Preset.

- **Effects Browser**: The Custom Category is listed in the Sidebar ❾ of the Effects Browser with the custom Effects listed inside. Now you can apply that Effect to any Clip in any Project Timeline.

Audio Inspector

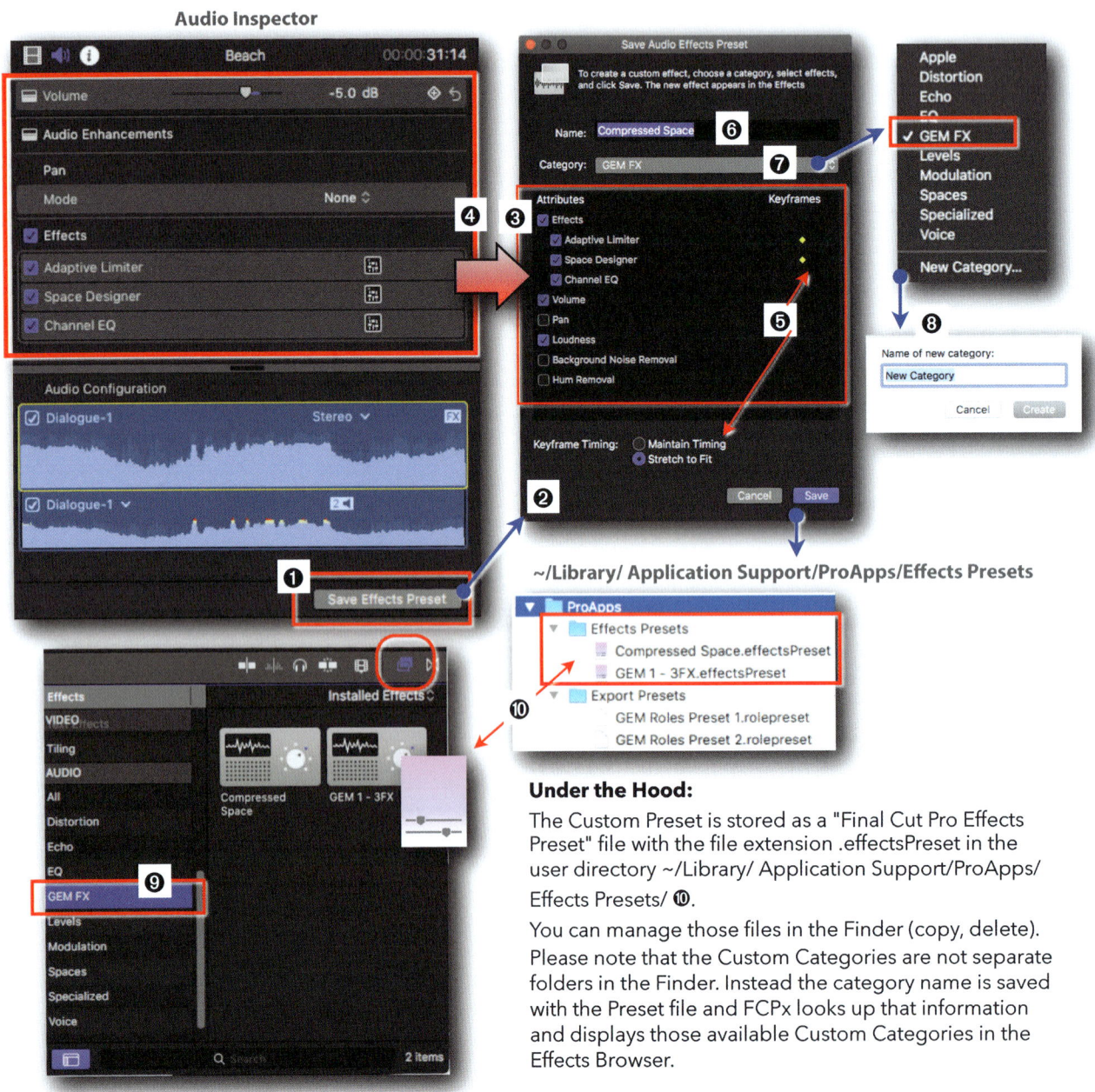

~/Library/ Application Support/ProApps/Effects Presets

Under the Hood:

The Custom Preset is stored as a "Final Cut Pro Effects Preset" file with the file extension .effectsPreset in the user directory ~/Library/ Application Support/ProApps/ Effects Presets/ ❿.

You can manage those files in the Finder (copy, delete). Please note that the Custom Categories are not separate folders in the Finder. Instead the category name is saved with the Preset file and FCPx looks up that information and displays those available Custom Categories in the Effects Browser.

Overview

Now on to the next module in the signal flow of a Clip, the Volume Module.

Here is a basic overview:

▸ Although the Volume Module ❶ is listed first in the Audio Inspector, it is actually placed in the signal chain after ❷ the Effects Module.

▸ The Summed Audio Clip ❷ and each Audio Components Clip ❸ "inside" a Clip have their own Volume control.

▸ Check the little icon on the left of the module that indicates if the currently selected Clip is a Summed Audio Clip ❹ 🗔 or one of the Audio Component Clips ❺ 🗔.

▸ The Volume Module only has a single slider ❻ and a numeric value display in dB next to it.

▸ The Volume can be adjusted between -∞dB (silence) and +12dB.

▸ Mousing-over ❼ the module will reveal the Reset Button ↺ and the Keyframe Button ◈. There is no Show/Hide button, because there are no more controls to reveal.

▸ Once you created Keyframes on a Clip, then those buttons ❽ will also be visible on the module ⟨ ⟩ ◈.

▸ The waveform on the Clip (Browser, Timeline, Inspector) is updated instantly to show any volume changes. This lets you check the level and possible clipping ❾ (red), which means that the audio level is to high and causes distortion.

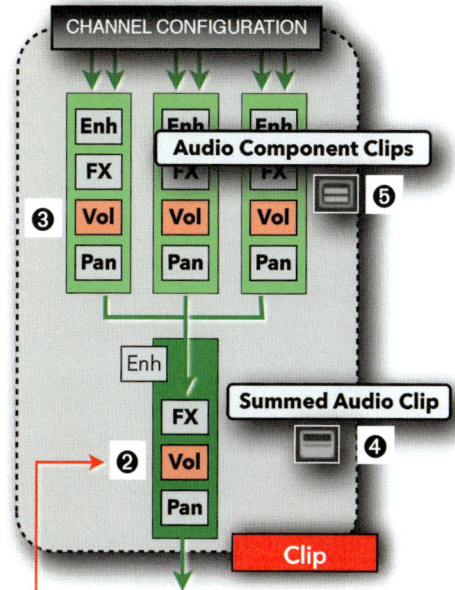

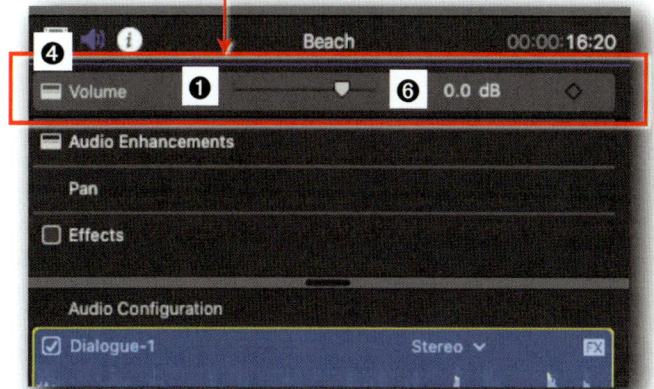

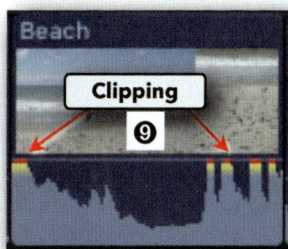

Adjust Volume

➡ *Volume Adjustments*

There are multiple ways to adjust the Volume for a selected Timeline Clip. Pick your favorite:

💀 Audio Inspector

The controls in the Inspector change the Volume of all the currently selected Event Clips or Timeline Clips.

> *Drag* the slider ❶ in the Inspector.
>
> *Click* the numeric value ❷, enter a dB value, and press *return*.
>
> *Drag* the numeric value up/down ❹. Two little up/down arrows appear while you move the mouse over. *Opt+drag* for a finer drag resolution.
>
> *Click* the Reset Button ❸ 🔄 to set the Volume back to 0dB.

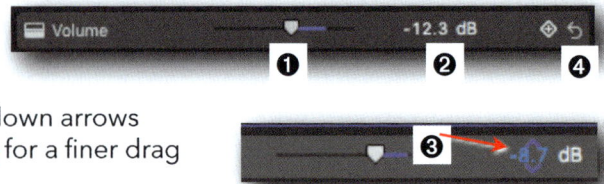

💀 Timeline

The Timeline Clips show a horizontal line ❺ on the waveform. Its vertical position reflects the current value of its Volume. More about that line in the Animation chapter.

> ▶ Mouse-over that line and the cursor changes to a double-arrow ❻ with a black help tag, displaying the dB value of that Volume line.
>
> ▶ *Drag* the Volume line up/down and the value changes accordingly.
>
> ▶ *Cmd+drag* to move with a finer resolution to set the value more precisely.

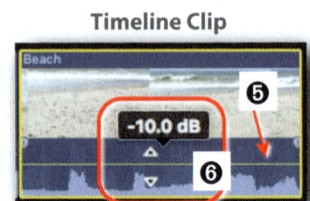

Timeline Clip

💀 Commands

There are many commands that let you quickly adjust the Volume of the currently selected Clips. They are available as Menu Commands ❼ (*Modify ➤ Adjust Volume ➤*) and as Key Commands (some of them are not assigned yet).

> ▶ **±1dB**: This command changes the Volume by 1dB increments.
>
> ▶ **Silence** (-∞dB): This is like dragging the Volume Slider all the way to the left, which is like muting or silencing the Clip.
>
> ▶ **Reset** (0dB): This is the same effect as clicking on the module's Reset Button 🔄 on the Volume Module ❹.
>
> ▶ **Absolute...**: This is a special command that is useful to set a group of selected Clips to a specific Volume value.
>
>> • When you use the command, the Timecode Reader changes to Numeric Input Mode (key focus)
>>
>> • The Timecode Reader now shows a symbol ❽ 📊 on the right and the number 0 on the left
>>
>> • Type a number value (plus and minus key if needed) and press return
>
> ▶ **Relative...** : This command, indicated by a different symbol ❾ 📊, is also useful for a group of selected Clips. The value you enter now will be applied as an offset to all Clips. For example, with a value of -10dB entered, a Clip with a value of 0dB will be set to -10dB and a Clip with the value of -5dB will be set to -15dB.

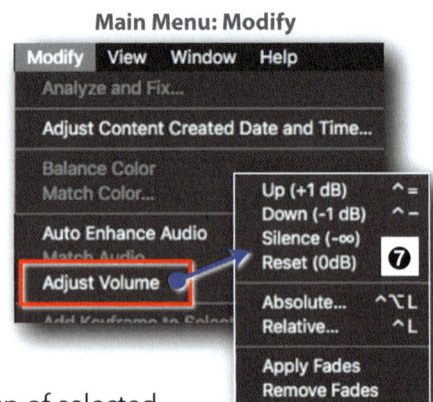

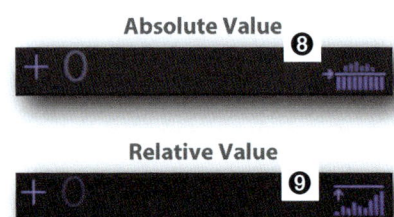

Main Menu: Modify

Absolute Value

Relative Value

🌐 Touch Bar

A quick way to adjust the Volume is by using the Touch Bar. The control is automatically displayed when you have one or multiple Timeline Clips ❶ or Event Clips ❷ selected:

📌 **Tab** the Speaker Button ❶ ❷ 🔊 and the view changes, displaying a long volume slider ❸ that you can adjust. The Fader disappears and shows "Relative Volume" when multiple Clips are selected. You can also **tap** the speaker buttons to incrementally change the volume. You can stay in this view, selecting different Clips that you might want to adjust to quickly make multiple Volume adjustments.

📌 **Tab** the Silence Button ❹ to set the volume to -∞dB. The slider jumps to the left-most position ❺.

📌 **Tab** the Close button to return to the previous view.

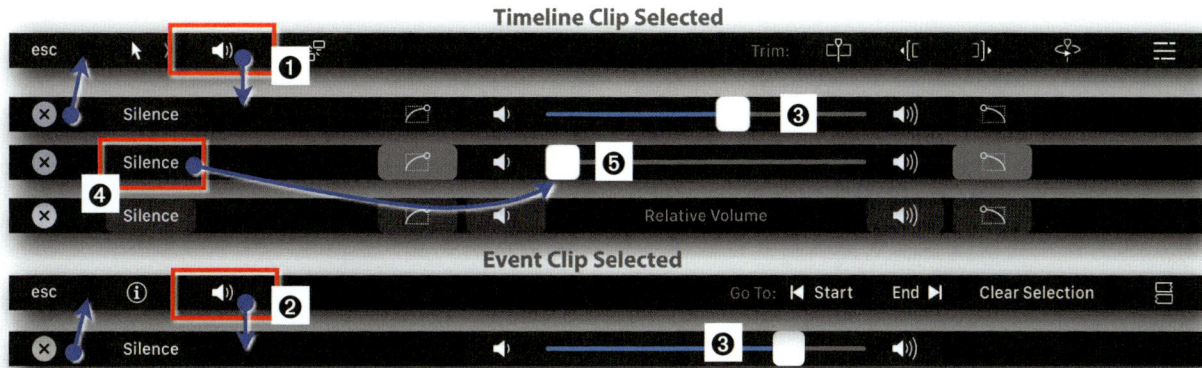

Timeline Clip Selected

Event Clip Selected

➡ Fades (Fade-in, Fade-out)

Technically, Audio Fades also belong to Volume adjustments. They are common procedure during editing. Here is how they are implemented in FCPx:

▶ Fades can only be applied to Timeline Clips and as a default, they don't have any Fades applied yet.

▶ **Fade Handles (off)**: When you mouse-over a Clip, a Fade Handle appears ❻ at the left and right border of the Clip on the line between the video and audio line. That means that there is no applied Fade on that Clip.

▶ **Fade Handles (on)**: If a Fade-in or Fade-out has been applied, then the Fade Handles are brighter ❼ and their position away from the left or right border indicates the length (the duration) of that fade.

▶ **Fade Curve**: A Fade Curve, similar to an Automation Curve, indicates the volume increase and decrease.

▶ If you move the mouse away from the Clip, then the Fade Handles disappears and only the Fade Curves ❽ indicate the existence of a Fade.

▶ Unlike any other Volume changes, the effect of any Fade (volume change) is not reflected on the waveform.

▶ **Fade Tool**: Moving the cursor over a Fade Handle changes the cursor from the Fade Tool ❾ to a double-arrow ◀▶.

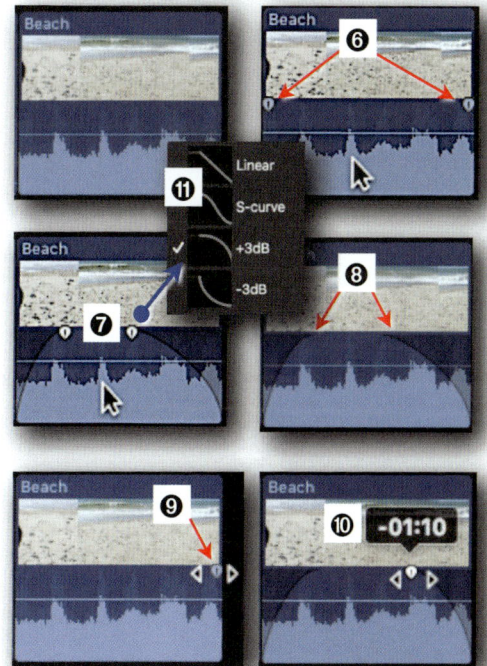

▶ **Fade Duration**: A black help tag ❿ appears while dragging a Fade Handle to show the duration of the fade.

▶ **Fade Curve**: *Ctr+click* on a Fade Handle to open a Shortcut Menu ⓫ with four different characteristics on how the volume increases and decreases (exponential, S-curve, etc.).

▶ The Fades are not displayed in the Inspector and can only be applied and edited directly on the Timeline Clip.

🌑 Commands

The Menu Command *Modify ➤ Adjust Volume ➤* ❶ contains two Fade related commands that are also available as Key Commands (not assigned yet).

▶ **Apply Default Fades**: Select one or multiple Clips and use this command to apply a Fade-In and a Fade-Out on those Clips with a default duration set in the *Preferences ➤ Editing ➤ Default Fade duration is* ❷. If a Clip has a Fade-in or Fade-out already set, then the command will be ignored.

▶ **Remove Fades**: Select one or multiple Clips and use this command to remove the Fade-in and Fade-out on those Clips (duration set to 0).

▶ **Toggle Audio Fade In/Out**: These two Key Commands (that are not assigned by default) can toggle any existing Fade-In or Fade-out separately. Be careful with its functionality, because it is not a bypass function. It toggles between *Apply* and *Remove*. That means, if no Fade has been applied yet, then it will apply the default fade, if the Clip already has a fade, then it will be removed, even if it is a manually drawn/adjusted Fade.

🌑 Cursor Tool

You can add Fades or adjust existing Fades manually with the following procedures:

▶ Position the mouse over a Fade Handle ❸ (that appears when you mouse-over a Clip) and *drag* it left or right.

▶ If the Fade Handle is at the edge of the Clip, then you have to position the mouse very precisely until it changes to the double arrow ◄─► (and not a Trim Tool).

▶ The length of the Fade is displayed in the black help tag ❹ in min:sec while *dragging* the Fade Handle. The Fade Curve follows accordingly.

🌑 Touch Bar

The Touch Bar also has some Fade controls:

🔊 *Tab* the Speaker Button ❺ [🔊] and the view changes, displaying a Fade-in Button ❻ [⟋] on the left and a Fade-out Button ❼ [⟍] on the right of the Volume Slider. You can stay in this view, selecting different Clips that you might want to adjust.

🔊 A dark ❽ Fade Button means that a Fade hasn't been applied yet to that Clip. *Tap* the Fade Buttons to apply a Fade with the default length set in the Preferences.

🔊 A light ❾ Fade Button means that a Fade has been applied (default or custom). *Tap* the Fade Buttons to remove that Fade.

Main Menu: Modify

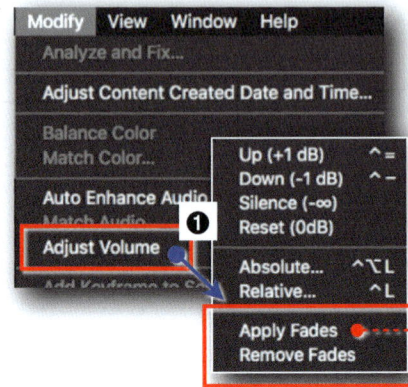

Preferences ➤ Editing

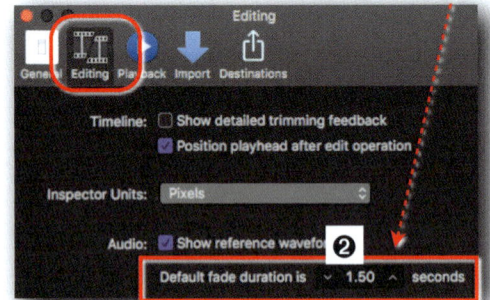

➡ Crossfades

A crossfade is another procedure that affects the volume of your Clip.

You can create a crossfade manually by fading out the audio of the outgoing Clip while fading in the audio of an overlapping incoming Clip. However, you can also let FCPx create the crossfade automatically, using Transition Effects. In this case, the controls for the fades are different.

Transition Inspector

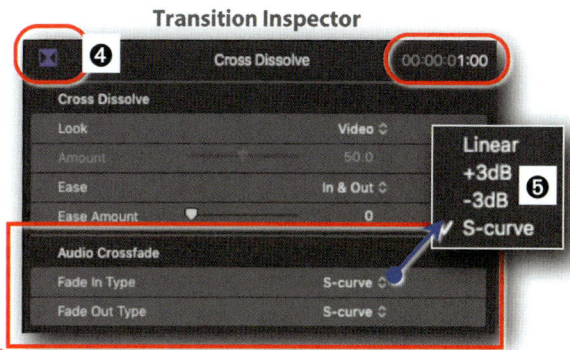

- ▸ You **drag** a Transition Effect ❶ from the Transition Browser ⋈ directly between two Timeline Clips that you want to crossfade.

- ▸ The Transition appears as a separate (gray) Clip ❷ on the Timeline.

Transition Browser

- ▸ You change the duration of the Crossfade by dragging the Edit Points of that Clip (the bottom left and right border ❸) or **tap** the Duration Button ⬚ on the Touch Bar to enter a number in the SMPTE Reader.

- ▸ Select the Transition Clip and open the Inspector ❹. It shows the video and audio properties of the crossfade. Here you can set the Fade Type from the popup menu ❺ separately for the Fade In and Fade Out.

➡ Mute

A Mute Button is a standard control found on virtually every channel strip of an audio mixer that, when enabled, silences that channel strip without the need of changing the Volume Fader.

Although FCPx doesn't have a mixer or channel strips (only a virtual representation), it still has a Mute Button. It is a checkbox placed on the Clip in the Audio Inspector. The functionality is a little bit different than a "Mute Button":

- ▸ Every Clip in the Audio Inspector has a checkbox ❻ in the upper-left corner that functions as a Mute Button.

- ▸ **Click** on that checkbox to toggle the audio signal of that Clip on or off.

- ▸ Pay attention to whether the checkbox belongs to the Summed Audio Clip ❼ (mutes all Components) or one of the individual Audio Component Clips ❽.

- ▸ Muting Audio Component Clips will remove that signal from the Summed Audio Clip, which shows a hyphen ▬ checkbox ❾.

- ▸ Muting the Summed Audio Clip (or all Audio Component Clips) will mute the entire Clip ❿. The Clips will be dimmed and the Timeline Clip will show a blank area ⓫ instead of the waveform.

Audio Inspector

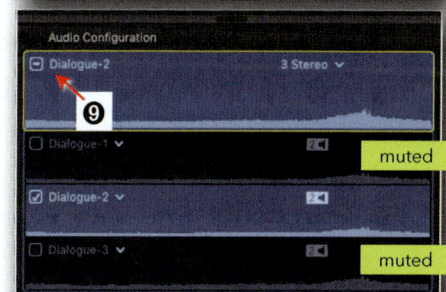

Timeline Clip

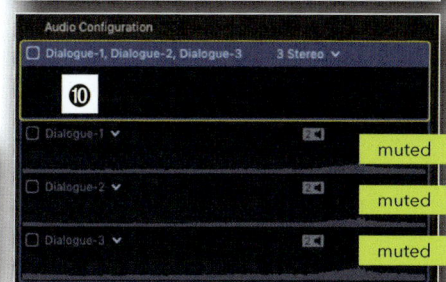

➡ *Solo*

The Solo Button is also a standard control found on virtually every channel strip of an audio mixer that, when enabled, lets you listen to those Channel Strips in isolation that have Solo enabled. All other Channel Strips are muted.

Because FCPx doesn't have a mixer or channel strips, the functionality is a little bit different.

▶ First, you select the Clip(s) you want to solo. Remember, this could be a Summed Audio Clip or individual Audio Component Clips.

- You can select a single Clip or multiple Clips, indicated by the yellow frame ❶ (has focus) or white frame ❷ (not key focus) around them.
- If no Clip is selected, then the red circle ❸ on the Playhead indicates the target Clip.
- If no Clip is selected and the Playhead is not positioned over any Clip, then the Solo Button is dimmed (almost not visible ❹) to indicate that you cannot use the Solo function.

▶ Enable the Solo Mode and it disables the audio of every Clip on the Timeline that is currently not selected. Use any of those commands:

Timeline Header

- 📌 ***Click*** the Solo Button ❺ 🎧 🎧 in the upper-right corner of the Timeline
- 📌 Key Command ***opt+S***
- 📌 Main Menu ***Clip ➤ Solo***

Timeline Header

All non-soloed Clips turn gray. You can still click edit and trim those Clips. This doesn't affect the current solo status of the Clips until you use the Solo command again to turn off Solo Mode.

▶ You can add (or remove!) Clips from the current group of soloed Clips with the special command:

- 📌 Menu Command ***Clip ➤ Add to Soloed Clips***
- 📌 Key Command (not assigned by default)

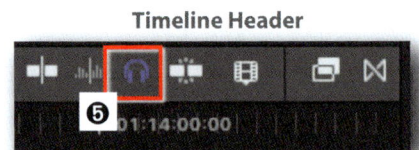

➡ *Reference Waveform*

The displayed waveform on a Clip can often be used to quickly identify specific locations in a Clip, i.e. a sudden audio burst of a gun shot or segments of dialog and silence. However, when you lower the audio level, the audio waveform is also lowered to reflect the actual signal level of the Clip. This could make it more difficult to identify those events.

Preferences ➤ Editing

To alleviate this problem, you can activate the Reference Waveform (***Preferences ➤ Editing ➤ Audio: Show reference waveform*** ❻) to display the waveform (with a maximum level) in the Clip in a lighter shade ❼ together with the actual waveform ❽. This lighter shade is very subtle, so you might have the brightness turned up on your computer to actually see it.

The Reference Waveform is displayed in the Event Clips, Timeline Clips, and the Clips in the Audio Inspector.

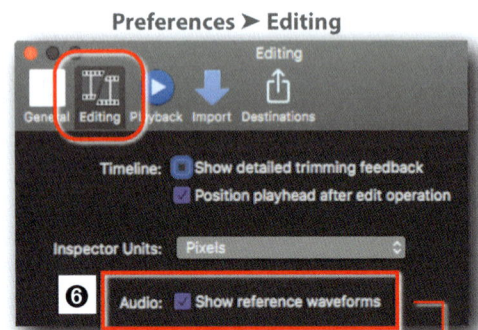

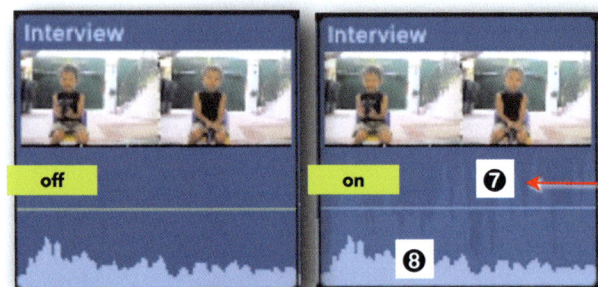

Concept

➡ Interface

Similar to the other modules, the Pan Module has nested elements that you have to make visible first.

▶ The Pan Module has only one row with the *Show* button and the *Reset* button on the right ❶ that appear when you mouse over it.

▶ When you click on the *Show* button another row appears ("Mode" ❷) with just one selector that opens a popup menu ❸ to choose one of the Pan Modes.

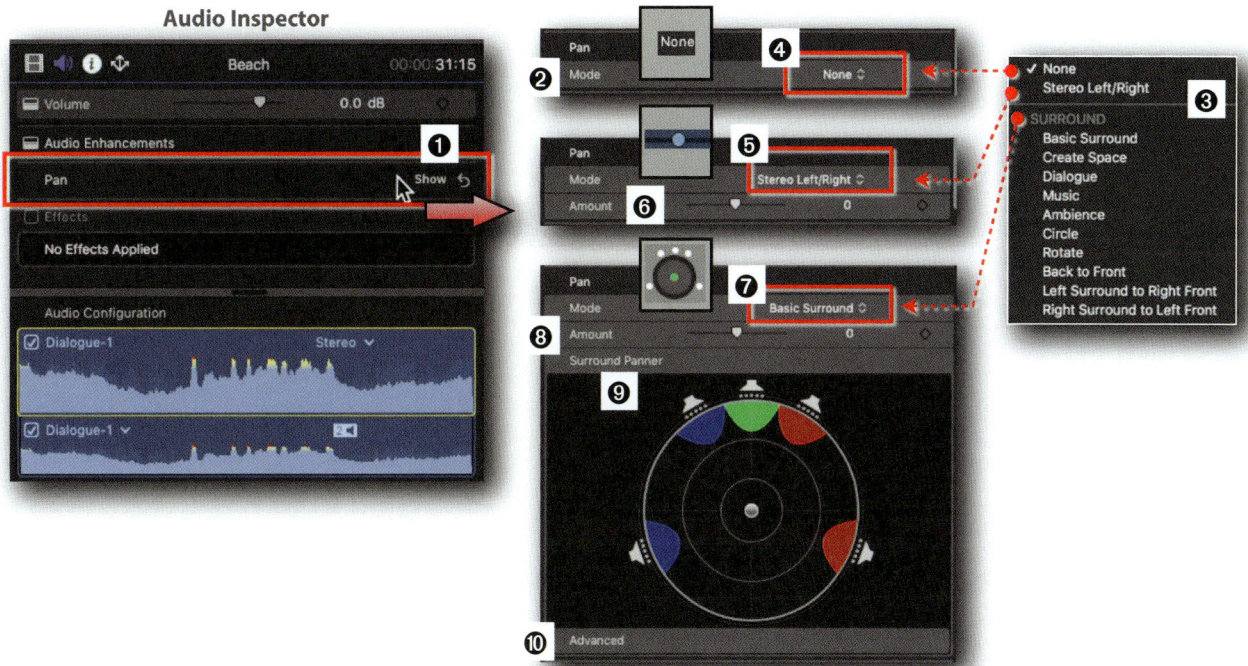

➡ Pan Modes

Although there are 12 items in the popup menu, they only represent three Pan Modes. I use the following three icons in my diagrams to demonstrate the various functionality on the next few pages.

None ❹: This is the default setting with no further controls. However, even without controls, FCPx still might do some channel matching. See below.

Stereo ❺: Selecting this setting opens another row with a single "*Amount*" slider ❻. Please note that this slider can function as a Pan Control or a Stereo Balancer (two completely different controls).

Surround ❼: The next 10 settings are Surround Presets that open the Surround Pan Mode, pre-configured for specific tasks as the preset names imply. It opens three more rows:

- Amount ❽: This functions as the master control.
- Surround Panned ❾: This is a graphical user interface to position a signal in the surround field.
- Advanced ❿: This reveals another "Show" button that opens a section with more detailed surround controls.

➡ *Easy Way*

The Pan Module can be extremely complex with all its possible configuration options. The key to stay on top of it and know where your signals end up is trying to understand the signal flow.

If you don't want to deal with that complexity that I will get into on the next few pages, you can leave the Pan Mode at its default setting "*None*". In that case, you only have to be aware of what FCPx is doing when you have a mismatch of channels. The means, the Channel Format (mono, stereo, or surround) is different between the source (input) the destination (output).

Here are three examples:

▶ The Channel Format of your Clip is different from the Channel Format of your Project.

▶ The Channel Format of your Project is different from the Channel Format you select in the Share Dialog when exporting separate tracks (see the Export chapter).

▶ The Channel Format "inside" a Clip is different, for example, if a Clip has multiple Audio Components that have different Channel Formats.

🔵 Mono Source

When a mono signal is matched to a stereo signal ❶, it gets distributed to both stereo channels but with a 3dB lower level. When matched to a surround signal ❷, the mono signal will be placed on the Center channel.

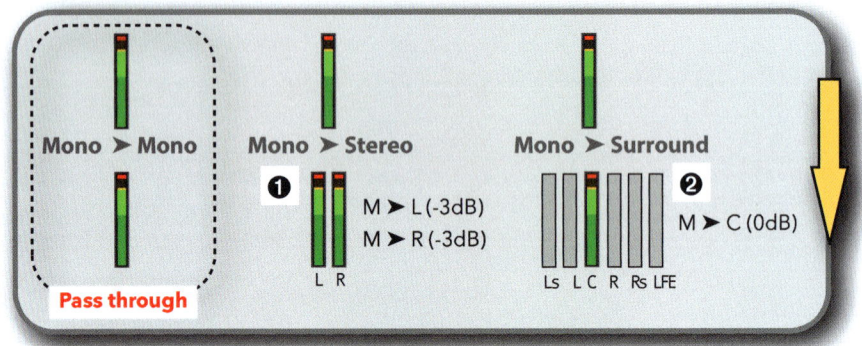

🔵 Stereo Source

When a stereo signal gets matched to a mono signal ❸, both signals are merged with a 6db reduced level. When matched to a surround signal ❹, the Left and Right channels are placed to their corresponding Left and Right channels in the surround format.

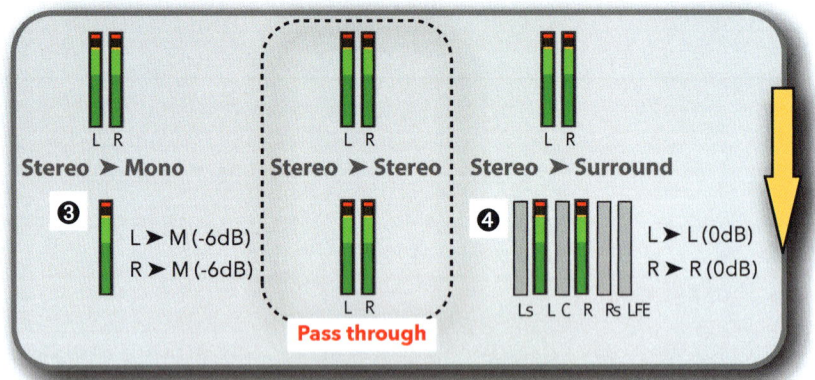

🔵 Surround Source

When matching a surround signal to a mono ❺ or stereo ❻ signal, all the surround channels are merged to mono or stereo. However, they are placed at different levels as I indicate on the diagram.

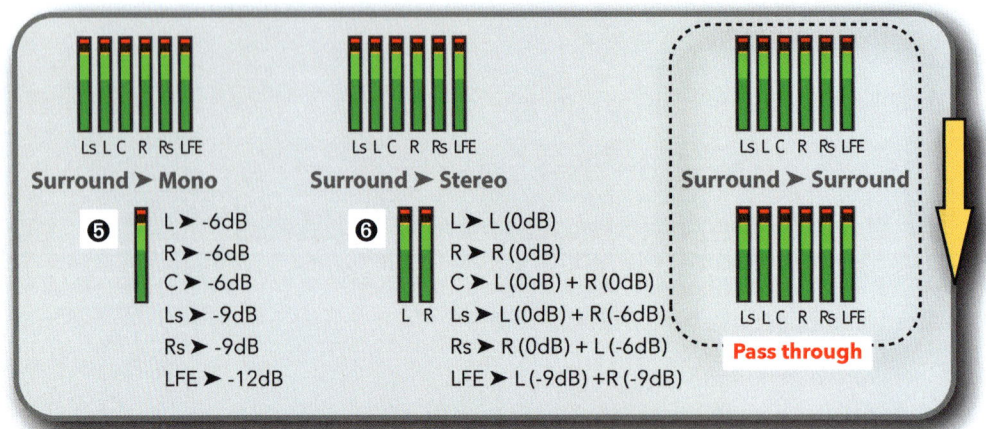

264   8 - Audio

➡ *Signal Flow Overview*

Now, let's dive into the signal flow to understand what is going on.

Here is the diagram that I used so far to demonstrate the reason why panning is so complex in FCPx.

☑ Each Clip that contains audio has two types of Clips, the Audio Component Clip ❶ and the Summed Audio Clip ❷.

☑ Each one represents a Channel Strip with a Pan Module ❸ for the individual Audio Component Clip and a Pan Module ❹ for the Summed Audio Clip.

☑ The output of the Pan Module ❺ on the Audio Component Clip's Channel Strip feeds to the Summed Audio Clip's Channel Strip ❻ and its own Pan Module.

☑ In addition, a Clip can have more than one Audio Component Clips (based on the Channel Configuration ❼), even with different Channel Formats (mono, stereo), all with their own Pan Module routed to the input of the Summed Audio Component.

☑ Now imagine that you can set an individual Pan Mode for the Audio Component Clips ❽ and select an individual Pan Mode ❾ for the Summed Audio Clip, pan all of them in various directions and you get the idea how complex the signal flow can get in just a single Clip.

☑ Now multiply that by each Clip ❿ you have in your Project, each one with their own complexity.

☑ At the end, you have a Project set to either Stereo or Surround, which imposes another stage where you have to figure out what happens to your signals regarding the Channel Format on the output of your Project.

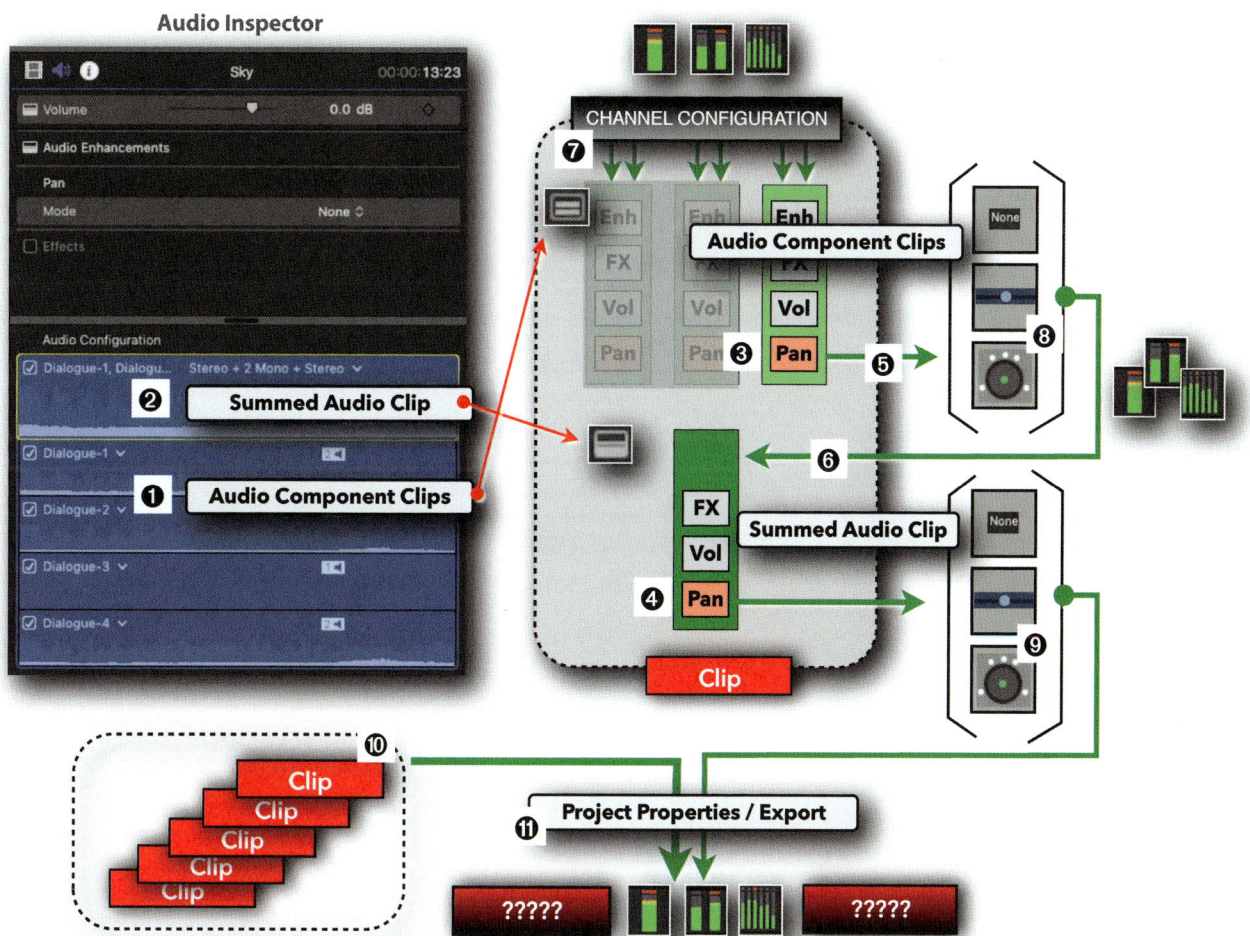

Signal Flow - Details

On the next few pages I will show the different scenarios and what to watch out for.

➡ *Basics*

Here is a look at a Clip with a single Audio Component with a focus on what happens at the Pan Module:

🔘 Audio Component Clip

▶ **Input ❶**: The Channel Format (the amount of channels) at the input of the Pan Module depends on how many Audio Channels are available in the Source Media File and how the Channel Configuration distributes those channels across one or multiple Audio Component Clips. An Audio Component Clip can have 1 channel, 2 channels, or 6 channels ❷. That's the input signal for its Pan Module.

▶ **Pan Mode ❸**: On the Pan Module, you can choose any of the three Pan Modes, *None*, *Stereo*, or *Surround*. That creates the first situation where you can have a possible mismatch of channels and then the question, how do their controls affect that mismatch.

▶ **Output ❹**: The output of the selected Pan Mode depends on the type of Clip:

- Event Clip: It is determined by the Pan Module's output ❹.

- Timeline Clip: It depends on what is set in the Project Properties ❺, *Stereo* or *Surround*.

🔘 Summed Audio Clip

▶ **Input ❻**: The Channel Format for the Pan Module input on the Summed Audio Clip depends:

- Event Clip: It is the highest channels number of any output of the Audio Component Clips ❹.

- Timeline Clip: It is either *Stereo* or *Surround*, depending on the current Project Properties ❺.

▶ **Pan Mode ❼**: Again, you can choose any of the three Pan Modes, *None*, *Stereo*, or *Surround*. And their controls determine the signal distribution.

▶ **Output ❽**: The output of the selected Pan Mode also depends on the type of Clip:

- Event Clip: It is determined by the Pan Module's output ❽.

- Timeline Clip: It depends on what is set in the Project Properties ❺, *Stereo* or *Surround*. ❾

🔘 Monitor/Export

The available Audio Interface for your monitoring and the selected setting for the File Export could also cause a Channel Mismatch.

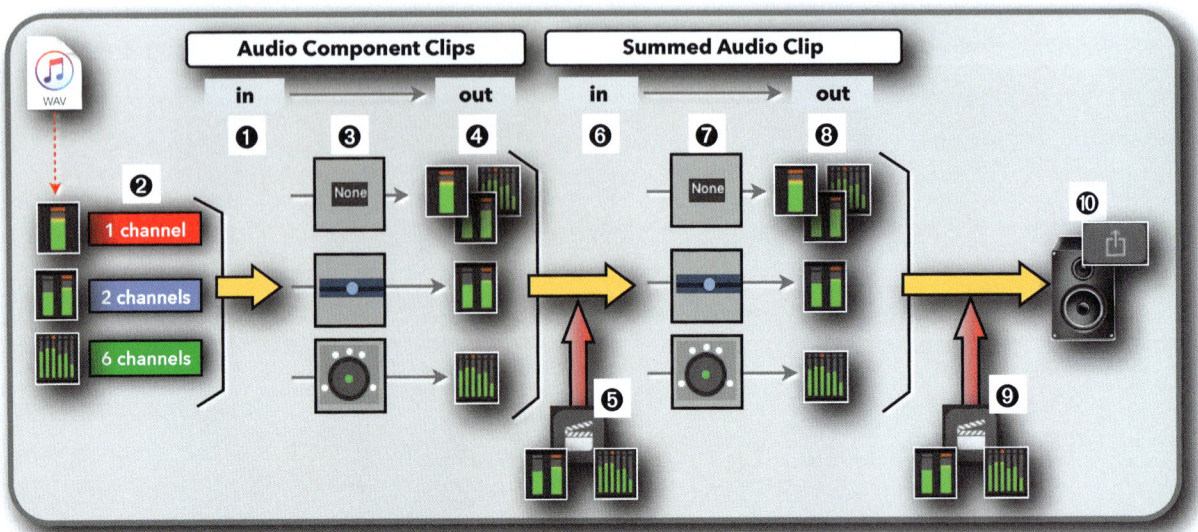

8 - Audio

➡ *Input - Output Scenarios*

Here are the 20 (!) different scenarios, how a specific input signal (1ch, 2ch, 6ch) gets routed to its output depending on the selected Pan Mode.

If you are not familiar with the difference between a Pan and a Stereo Balancer, I have written an article on my website LogicProGEM.com about that http://bit.ly/2lO4g89

The last category requires special attention, where the actual control (Pan Slider or Surround Panner) doesn't match the channels. For example, you have a 6-channel surround signal, but only a 2-channel pan control.

Pass-through (match)

If the Pan Mode is set to "None", then any channel on the input will pass through to the output

Pass-through (mismatch)

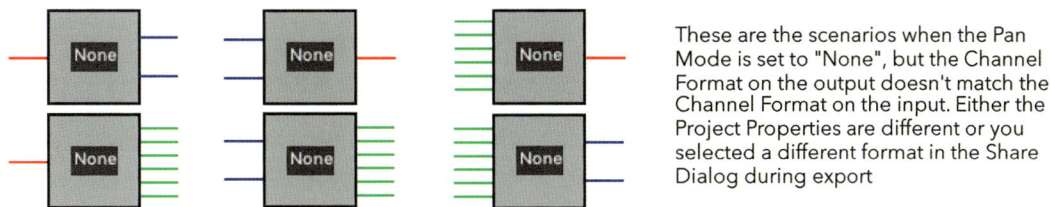

These are the scenarios when the Pan Mode is set to "None", but the Channel Format on the output doesn't match the Channel Format on the input. Either the Project Properties are different or you selected a different format in the Share Dialog during export

Position

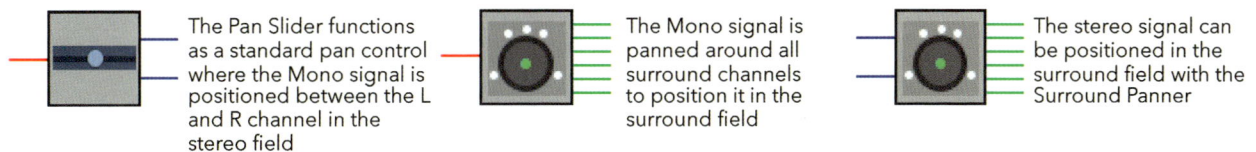

The Pan Slider functions as a standard pan control where the Mono signal is positioned between the L and R channel in the stereo field

The Mono signal is panned around all surround channels to position it in the surround field

The stereo signal can be positioned in the surround field with the Surround Panner

Balance

The Pan Slider functions as a Stereo Balancer, attenuating the Left or Right channel depending on the slider position

The Surround Panner controls the balance of the surround signal in the surround field

Special

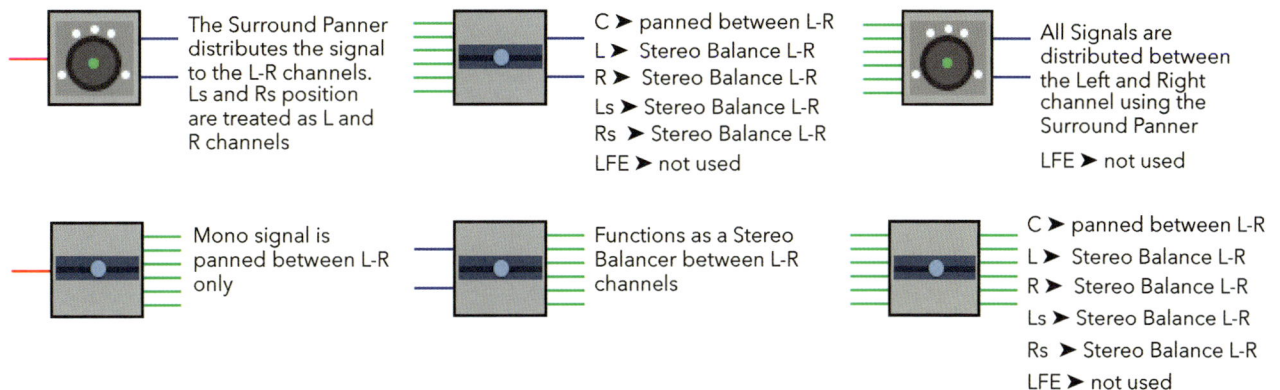

The Surround Panner distributes the signal to the L-R channels. Ls and Rs position are treated as L and R channels

C ➤ panned between L-R
L ➤ Stereo Balance L-R
R ➤ Stereo Balance L-R
Ls ➤ Stereo Balance L-R
Rs ➤ Stereo Balance L-R
LFE ➤ not used

All Signals are distributed between the Left and Right channel using the Surround Panner

LFE ➤ not used

Mono signal is panned between L-R only

Functions as a Stereo Balancer between L-R channels

C ➤ panned between L-R
L ➤ Stereo Balance L-R
R ➤ Stereo Balance L-R
Ls ➤ Stereo Balance L-R
Rs ➤ Stereo Balance L-R
LFE ➤ not used

➡ Event Clips

These are the possible combinations with an Event Clip.

- ▶ You can lookup the routing of each individual Pan Module on the previous page.

- ▶ Now you have to consider the different combinations when you put two Pan Modules (Audio Component Clip ❶ and Summed Audio Clip ❷) in series to figure out what happens inside a single Clip.

- ▶ There are three possible input scenarios (1ch ❸, 2ch ❹, 6ch ❺) depending on the Channel Configuration. I show that in the three main columns.

- ▶ Keep in mind that for Event Clips, the Project Properties settings (Stereo or Surround) has no affect.

- ▶ The output of the second Pan Module (Summed Audio Clip) has to match the Audio Interface (for listening to your Clip ❻) or the settings in the Share Dialog ⬆ (Mono, Stereo, Surround) when you export a single Event Clip.

➡ *Timeline Clip*

The routing for the Pan Module is slightly different with Timeline Clips:

▸ Because the Timeline Clips are located on a Project, they follow the Project Properties, Stereo or Surround.

▸ **Stereo ❶**: If the Project Property is set to Stereo, then the output of the Pan Module for the Audio Component Clip is stereo ❷ and, therefore, the input of the Pan Module for the Summed Audio Clip is also stereo, and also, its output ❸.

▸ **Surround ❹**: If the Project Properties are set to Surround, then those routings are set to Surround ❺.

▸ The input of the Pan Module is still determined by its Channel Format (1ch ❻, 2ch ❼, 6ch ❽).

▸ The selected Pan Mode determines how the Pan Module distributes those channels, and as you can see, there are quite a few scenarios.

▸ Again, the output of the second Pan Module (Summed Audio Clip) has to match the Audio Interface (for listening to your Clip) or the settings in the Share Dialog 📤 (Mono, Stereo, Surround) when you export a single Tracks.

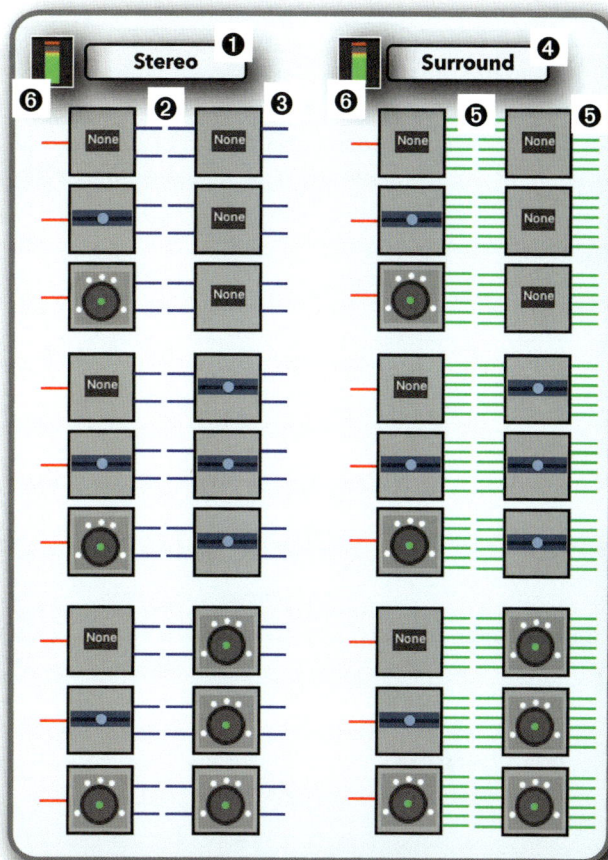

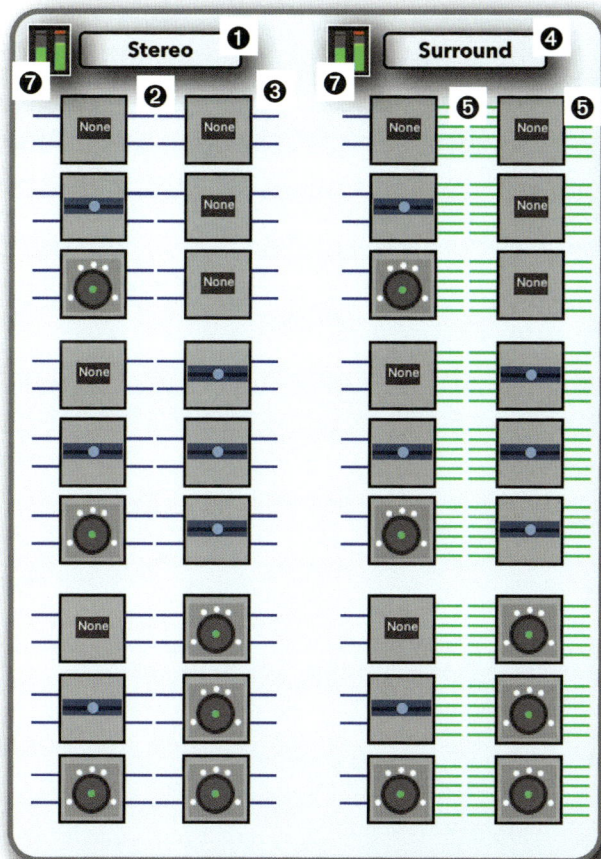

Although FCPx is foremost a video editing application, it provides a wide range of tools to deal with the audio aspect of a project on a very professional level without the need to "hand it over" to a separate audio application. But it doesn't stop there. FCPx also includes the tools to work in a surround sound project. The amount of controls that are available are quite extensive.

The topic of surround panning and mixing would be a separate manual all by itself so I'll cover only the important elements.

Two tips:

▸ Be aware of the concept, the architecture, and consequences (especially channel configuration).

▸ Just play around with the controls. The layout is quite visual and intuitive and when you look at your level meters at the same time, you'll see what is actually happening.

How to switch to Surround?

How to switch to surround? The answer is - you don't.

Instead, think of three elements that affect the audio routing:

☑ The **Clips**
☑ The **Project**
☑ The **Monitoring** (your speakers)

All three elements can be set independently and FCPx and macOS will automatically perform a down-mix or up-mix to map the input channels to the output channels.

- **Clips**: The audio content of every Clip can be set to any configuration (mono, stereo, surround) regardless if the Project itself is set to Stereo or Surround and regardless with what speaker setup you are listening to. The audio routing for each individual Clip is done in the Pan Module of the Audio Inspector as we discussed already.

- **Project** (export): As we know by now, you can change the Project Settings at any time and that includes the Project's Output Channel Configuration (Stereo or Surround). There is no need to go back and reconfigure the individual Clips. FCPx will automatically map the available input and output channels.

- **Monitoring**: Your hardware setup that you are listening to (mono, stereo, or surround speakers) is also independent from the Project Settings and the Clip's Audio Configuration. The output channels of your Project (stereo or surround) will be mapped to the selected Output Device in macOS (mono speaker, stereo speakers, or a surround sound setup).

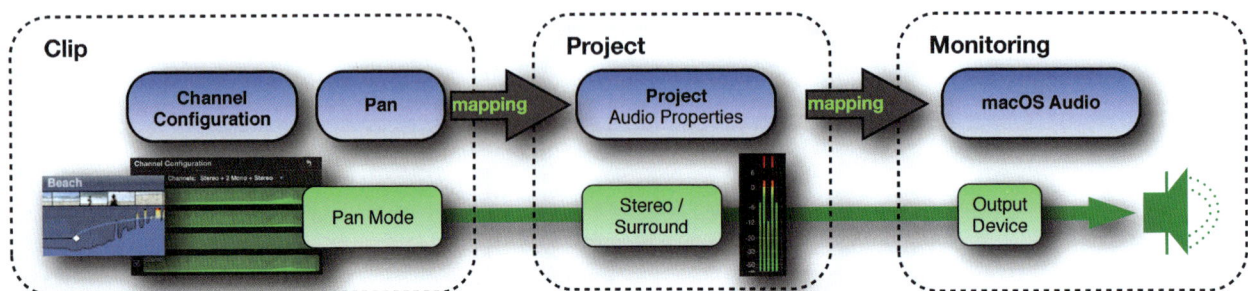

➡ Pan Mode

This is the important output routing configuration, available for each individual Clip in the Audio Inspector. The selection determines how the Clip's Audio Component Clips and its Summed Audio Clip, are routed to the Project's Output Channels:

- ▸ **None**: The Audio Components are routed directly to the available output.
- ▸ **Stereo Left/Right**: The Audio Components are routed to the left/right output channel and the slider "Pan Amount" determines the signal balance between the two channels.
- ▸ **"Surround"** (all others): Every other Preset provides the Surround Panner which reacts to the available controls in a specific way depending on the selected Preset (see below).

➡ Surround Panner

❶ **Mode**: The Pan Mode Preset is the important setting that determines the routing/panning of the audio channels. It displays the word "(edited)" once you change any of the parameters.

❷ **Amount**: The slider is actually a "macro" slider that is programmed differently for different Pan Mode Presets, i.e. moving the slider left and right rotates the "Sound Source" in the sound field or moves the control back and forth in the sound field.

❸ **Surround Panner**: Mouse-over this row to reveal the Show/Hide button to display the Surround Panner.

❹ **Sound Source**: Each of the five speaker represent a sound source in the surround setup. *Click* on it to toggle it on/off. The dots indicate how much sound is coming out of it.

❺ **Sound Source Controller**: Instead of changing the level of each sound source separately, this controller increases the level of the sound source (speaker) the more you are moving this "puck" (the gray circle) closer to a speaker.

❻ **Advanced**: Mouse-over this row to reveal the Show/Hide button to reveal the eight additional controls for the Surround Panner.

❼ **Keyframes**: The Pan Amount, the Sound Source controller, and all the Advanced controls can be keyframed. This is the place to "get creative in space".

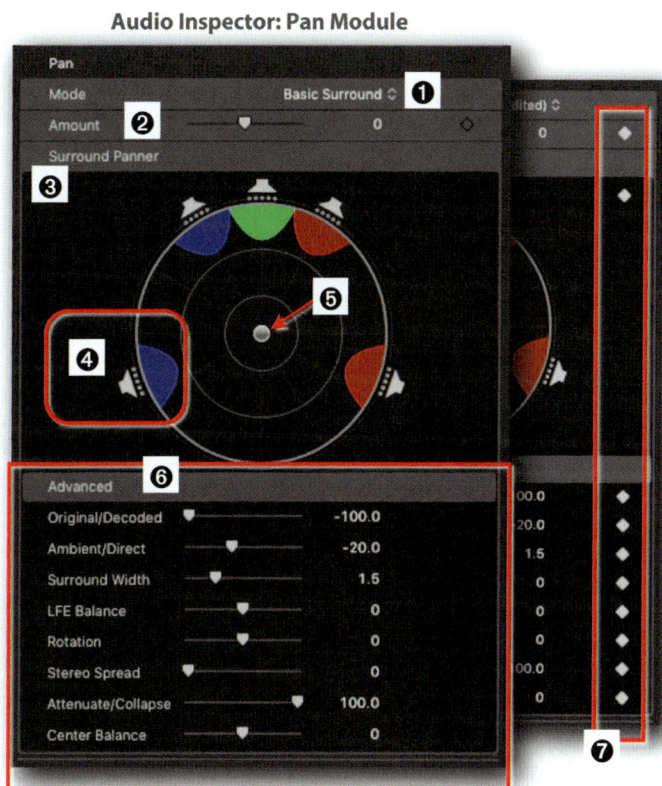

These are the elements on the surround panner:

- **Sound Field**

  The big circle area represents the sound field, the listening environment.

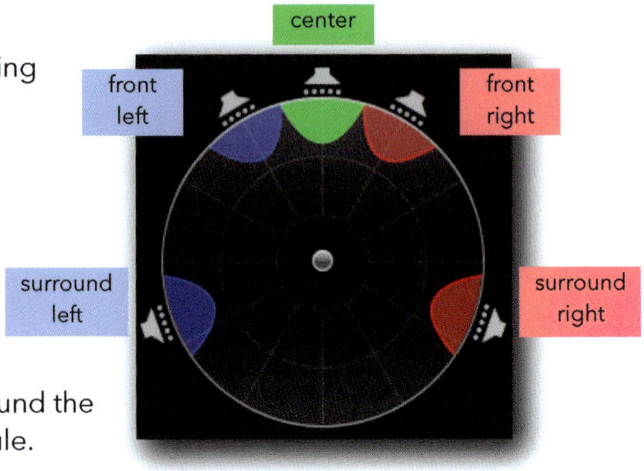

- **Input**

  The color areas represent the expected input sources. Be aware how FCPx assigns the Channel Configuration of your Clip to those 5 input sources.

- **Output**

  The speakers are placed in a typical surround setup around the sound field. They represent the Output of the Pan Module.

- **Sound Source Controller**

  That little gray circle (the puck) is the actual panner that determines how much of each individual input source gets distributed to each individual output source (the speaker). For example, moving that controller towards the left surround speaker sends more of the input signal to that output.

➡ *Pan Mode Presets*

Here is a description of the various Pan Mode Presets from the FCPx User Guide:

Create Space: Distributes the signal across the surround spectrum, with more signal to the center and front left and right channels. This setting is useful for making a general-purpose surround mix from any stereo source. The Pan Amount slider setting can be adjusted from 0 (no effect) to 100 (total surround field).

Dialogue: Pans more signal to the center channel of the surround spectrum so that the direct sound is in the center, while ambient sound is distributed to the other channels. This setting is best used for voiceover or other dialogue clips. The Pan Amount slider setting can be adjusted from 0 (no effect) to 100 (all sound to the center channel).

Music: Distributes a stereo mix signal evenly across the surround spectrum. This setting is best used for converting stereo music to a surround mix. The Pan Amount slider setting can be adjusted from 0 (no effect) to 100 (total surround field).

Ambience: Pans across the surround spectrum with more signal towards the surround channels and less signal to the front and center channels. This setting is useful for effects such as crowd noise or other outdoor environments. The Pan Amount slider setting can be adjusted from 0 (no effect) to 100 (total surround field).

Circle: Pans the sound in a circle around the surround spectrum like a bee buzzing around the listener's head. The Pan Amount slider adjusts the direction to the listener in degrees (-180 to 180).

Rotate: Pans around the surround spectrum as if the listener is turning in a circle. The Pan Amount slider adjusts the listener rotation in degrees (-180 to 180).

Back to Front: Pans from back to front across the surround spectrum. The Pan Amount slider setting can be adjusted from -100 (back) to 100 (front).

Left Surround to Right Front: Pans from left surround to right front across the surround spectrum. The Pan Amount slider setting can be adjusted from -100 (left surround) to 100 (right front).

Right Surround to Left Front: Pans from right surround to left front across the surround spectrum. The Pan Amount slider setting can be adjusted from -100 (right surround) to 100 (left front).

Surround Examples

Different Channel Configurations of the same Clip have completely different results in various Pan Modes:

Surround 5.1

Pan Mode:

Pan Amount:

Basic Surround

The incoming channels are labeled as surround and recognized as such. The Surround Panner treats them as surround channels and pans them correctly.

Stereo Left/Right

The Pan Module uses only the stereo L/R channels and ignores the other channels!

6 Mono

Basic Surround

The Surround Panner sees 6 incoming mono channels and assigns them to the center channel. They are folded into one signal and panned together.

Stereo Left/Right

The Pan Module uses all 6 mono channels and pans them as one summed signal.

➡ *Output Metering*

FCPx has three types of level meters: **Mono ❶** (1 channel), **Stereo ❷** (2 channels), and **Surround ❸** (6 channels). They switch automatically depending on whether the Project is set to stereo or surround or what Clip is selected. The meters are shown in two areas:

▸ **Viewer**: At the bottom of the Viewer **❹** (and Event Viewer). This meter (although very tiny) is always visible.

▸ **Timeline Pane ❶ ❷ ❸**: The Audio Meter Pane slides out on the far right of the Timeline Pane and can be resized proportionally with the rest of the panes. It can be toggled with:

- Key Command *sh+cmd+8*
- Main Menu *Window ➤ Show in Workspace ➤ Audio Meters*
- *Click* on the Small Audio Meters on the Viewer Pane **❹**

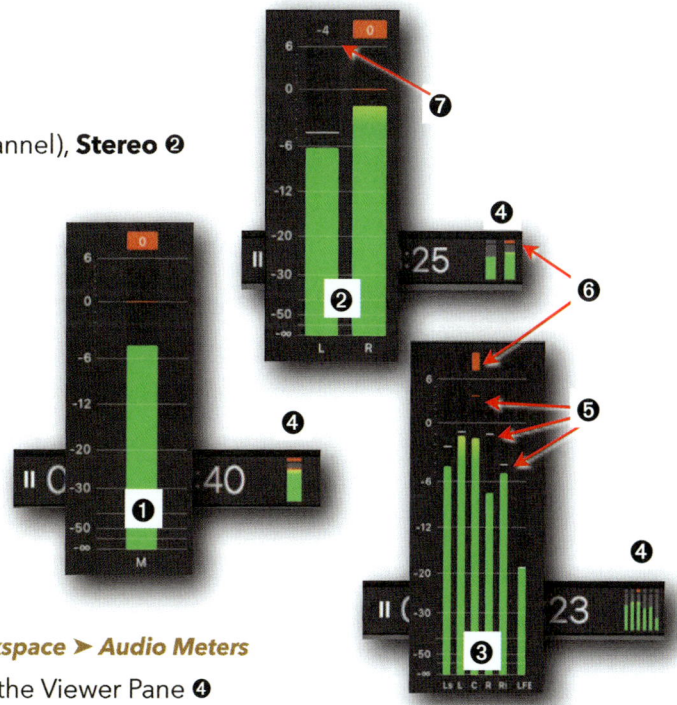

The meters have a "peak hold" line **❺** (2-4s) and a red "over" LED **❻** if the level went above 0dB. If the meter is big enough it displays the peak level in dB **❼**, which turns red if the level is above 0dB. This indicator can be reset by *clicking* on it or when you stop and restart again.

Roles is one of the key features in FCPx that plays a major "role" (so to speak) in every aspect of your video project. Although it relates to audio as well as video, it has the most impact when working on audio as we will see in this chapter.

Basics

As with many features that can get very complex, it is important to understand the basic concepts of Roles. In a nutshell, Roles are just text labels plus color that are attached to Clips as Metadata to describe their purpose (video clip, title clip, music clip, dialog clip, SFX clip, etc.). Based on that metadata, FCPx can treat Clips that are assigned to the same Roles as groups for all types of powerful metadata-based functionality.

> **Roles are Text+Color Labels attached to Clips as Metadata**

Here is a list of basic facts about Roles:

- **What are Roles**
  - ▶ A Role is just a text label plus a color
  - ▶ In addition to some default labels, you can create your own labels
  - ▶ Those labels, the Roles, are used to describe the purpose of Clips (video, title, dialog, music, etc.)
  - ▶ Roles can be freely assigned to Clips to label Clips based on similar purposes
  - ▶ You can assign only one Video Role and/or one Audio Role to a Clip

- **Metadata**
  - ▶ A Role, attached to a Clip, is part of its Metadata
  - ▶ Based on that Roles Metadata, FCPx can provide extremely powerful functionality for editing, routing, and exporting
  - ▶ That Metadata concept based on Roles, not only replaces a conventional audio mixer in FCPx, it provides functionality and flexibility that is not possible with a traditional mixer

- **Types of Roles**
  - ▶ Role Types: There are two types of Roles, Video Roles and Audio Roles
  - ▶ Main Roles: You can create your own custom Roles for each of these two types of Roles
  - ▶ Subroles: For each Main Role, you can create additional Subroles to further categorize a Clip's purpose in your video

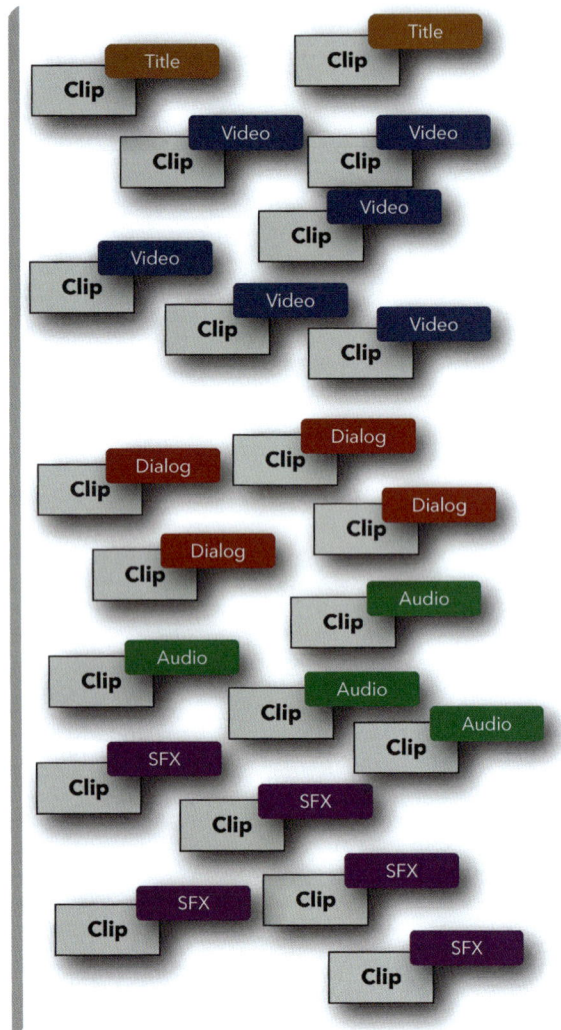

➡ Roles Everywhere

Roles are omnipresent in FCPx. In order to not get overwhelmed, you have to be clear about the main parts and functions first. Here is the basic structure:

- ▶ **Edit Roles**: The Role Editor ❶ is a special Dialog window that lets you manage all the Roles (add, edit, delete).

- ▶ **Assign Roles**: All the Roles that are available in the Role Editor are displayed in the two Assign Roles Menus. One is listing all the available Video Roles ❷ and one listing all the available Audio Roles ❸.

- ▶ **Access Menus**: If you select a Clip(s) ❹, FCPx provides commands ❺ in many places to access those Assign Roles Menus ❷ ❸ and choose one Role for each Clip. FCPx assigns a Role to each Clip by default.

- ▶ **Utilize Roles**: All these previous steps are just a necessary preparation to create the metadata that FCPx relies on to provide the functionality for editing, mixing, and exporting your video ❻.

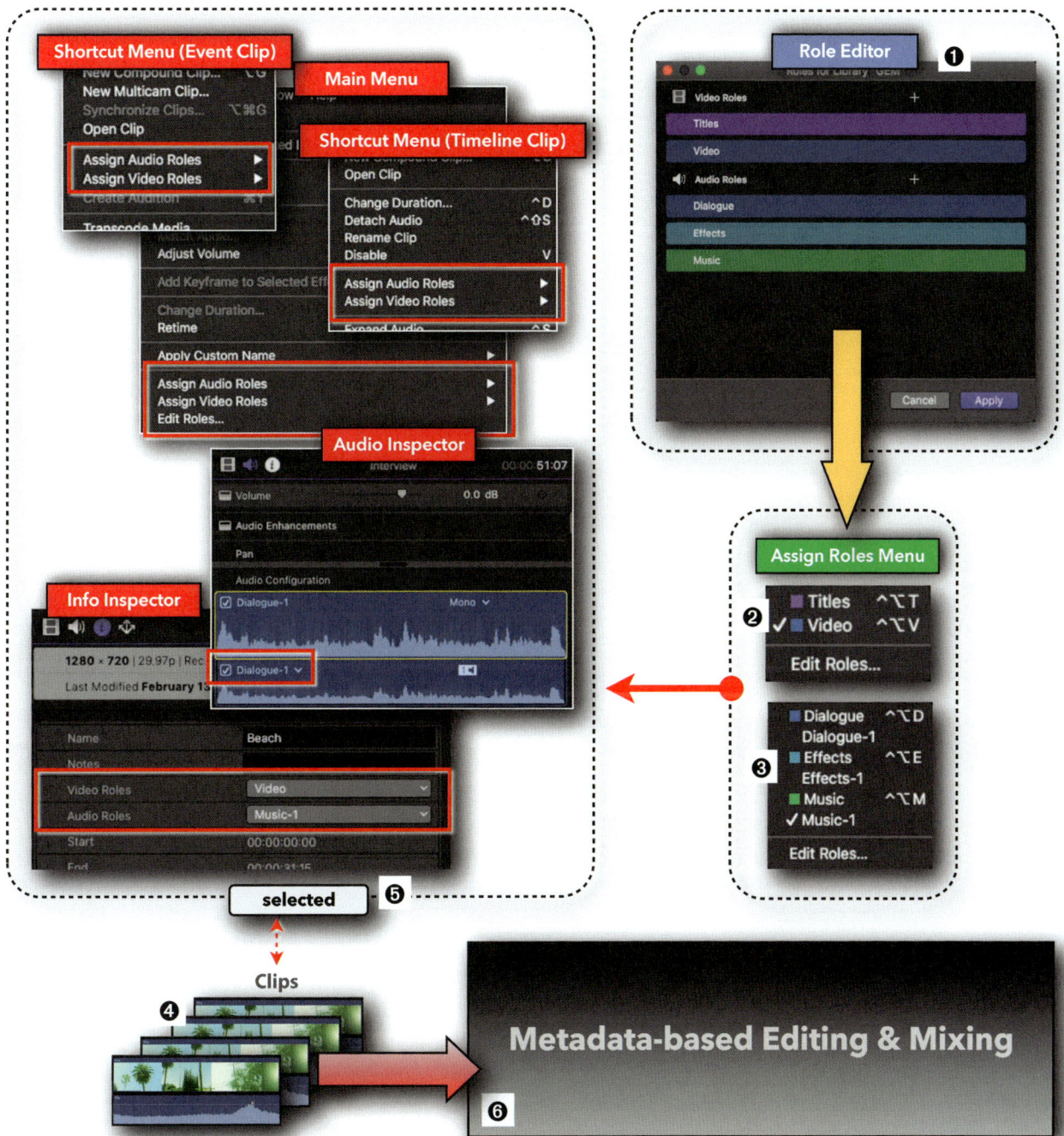

Role Editor

FCPx automatically has five default Roles created for any new Library that you start with. FCPx also automatically assigns one of those default Roles to every newly imported Clip. So technically, you don't have to do anything regarding Roles. However, you might want to customize those Roles and create new ones specifically tailored to your individual video project ... why? Remember, Roles are Metadata, and like with any other metadata, the functionality that is based on that metadata is only as good as the metadata itself.

There are three main tasks that involve Roles:

☑️ **Create the Roles**: In this step, you create the metadata, the text labels with their assigned color. Before you can assign any Roles, it has to exist. At any time you can add new Roles or change existing Roles (rename, merge, delete, change color, etc.).

☑️ **Assign the Roles**: This is the step where you assign (or reassign) one of the available Roles to a Clip. And again, if you want to label specific Clips with a unique Role, i.e. "Voiceover", you first have to create that Role in the Role Editor.

☑️ **Utilize the Roles Functionality**: Creating Roles and assigning them to Clips is only the prep work to use the powerful features in FCPx that are based on that metadata. For example, quickly organize your Timeline visually by Roles, create mix-downs, or export stems. Of course, during editing, you can fine-tune everything by creating new Roles or reassign Clips to different Roles.

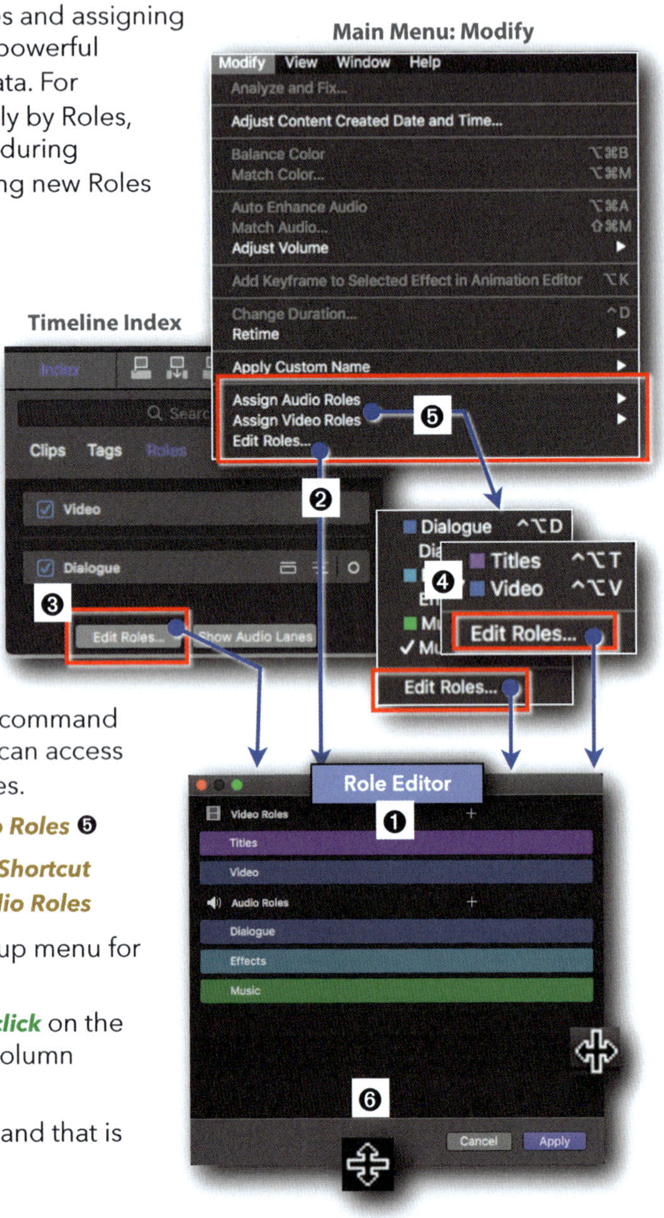

➡️ *Open the Role Editor Dialog*

The first step, creating and managing Roles is done in one place, the Role Editor Dialog ❶. There are multiple ways to open that window. Please note that this is a Dialog window, so you have to close it before you can continue with FCPx.

- Main Menu *Modify ➤ Edit Roles* ❷
- Open the Timeline Index in Roles View (*click* the Roles tab) and *click* the Edit Roles... ❸ button at the bottom of the window.
- The two Assign Roles Menus ❹ always list the command "*Edit Roles...*" at the bottom of the menu. You can access those Assign Roles Menus from different places.
  - Main Menu *Modify ➤ Assign Audio/Video Roles* ❺
  - *Ctr+click* on a Clip and choose from the *Shortcut Menu ➤ Assign Video Roles* or *Assign Audio Roles*
  - In the Info Inspector 🛈 *click* on the popup menu for Video Roles or Audio Roles
  - In the Clips View of the Timeline Index, *click* on the item in the Video Roles or Audio Roles column window
- "Edit Roles..." is also available as a Key Command that is not assigned by default.

Main Menu: Modify

Timeline Index

Role Editor

You can resize the Role Editor by dragging 🞥 its borders ❻.

➡ Managing Roles

This is the default view of the Role Editor Dialog when you open it in a new Library:

- ▸ **Role Types**: The window shows all the Roles grouped by the two Role Types, the Video Roles ❶ on top with the two default Roles "Titles" and "Video" and the Audio Roles ❷ below with the Roles "Dialogue", "Effects", and "Music".

- ▸ **Default Roles**: You can't delete or rename the five default Roles, only assign new colors to them, or add Subroles to them.

- ▸ **Add Roles**: *Click* on the Plus ❸ button in the Video Roles or Audio Roles section to create a new custom Role.

- ▸ **More Controls**: Moving the mouse cursor ❹ over a Role will reveal more controls: Show/Hide Subroles ❺, Add Subroles ❻, Assign Color ❼, Remove Roles ❽ (not available for default Roles).

Role Editor Dialog

☻ Color Assignment

Remember that a Role is metadata that includes two components, a text label (Role Name) and a color label. *Clicking* on the Color Button ❼ opens a little Color Palette with 12 colors that you can assign to a Role. The default Roles already have a default color assignment. These colors determine the colors of the Clip to quickly spot Clips, belonging to the same Role.

> *Attention*: If a Clip uses a Video and Audio Role that have different colors, then the Clip will appear in the color determined by its Audio Role. If you mute the Audio Clip, the Clip changes its color to the one assigned to the Video Role.

☻ Add New Role

When you click on the Plus button, a new bar is added at the bottom of the Video or Audio section with the Role name "Untitled" highlighted. Enter a name and press enter.

> *Attention*: Two things are different when you move the mouse over that Role, because this is a user-created Role: You can rename the Role and delete the Role.

☻ Rename Role

When you move the mouse cursor over a custom Role, various buttons appear and also the cursor changes to a Text Insertion Tool ❾ ⌶ The reason for that is that *clicking* on it will activate the name field so you can rename the custom Role.

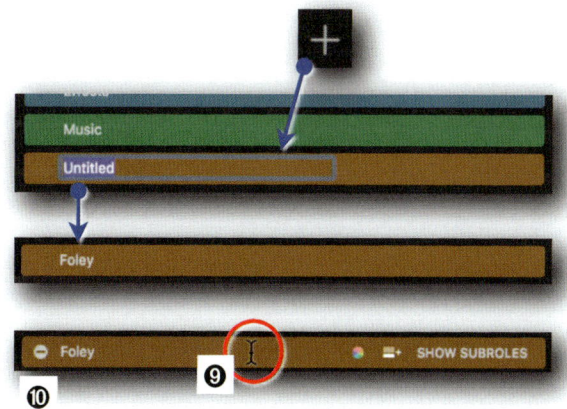

> *Attention*: All Clips that have that Role assigned to them will be updated with the new name of that Role.

☻ Remove Role

A user-created Role will show a Minus button ❿ ⊖ on the left that lets you delete that Role (and all its containing Subroles).

> *Attention*: When you *click* the Apply Button to close the Role Editor Dialog after you have deleted Roles, a sheet will pop up with a warning, letting you know that this action will remove that
Role assignment from any Clip that is using it in this Library. Those Clips will automatically be reassigned to one of the default Roles.

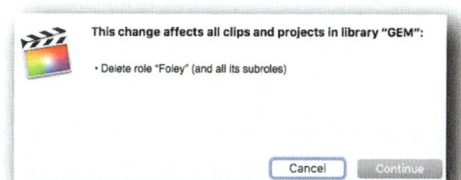

➡ *Managing Subroles*

⚙ Overview

Subroles is a great way to create more Roles, but have them grouped together under a parent Role (let's call it the "Main Role"). For example, if you want to label all the Clips with dialogue by the specific actor (Bob, Steven, Susan, etc. ❶) or a specific microphone (boom mic, lav mic, camera mic, etc.), you don't create additional Roles with the Plus button, instead you create nested Roles inside an existing Main Role (in this case the "Dialogue" Role). Those nested Roles are the so-called Subroles.

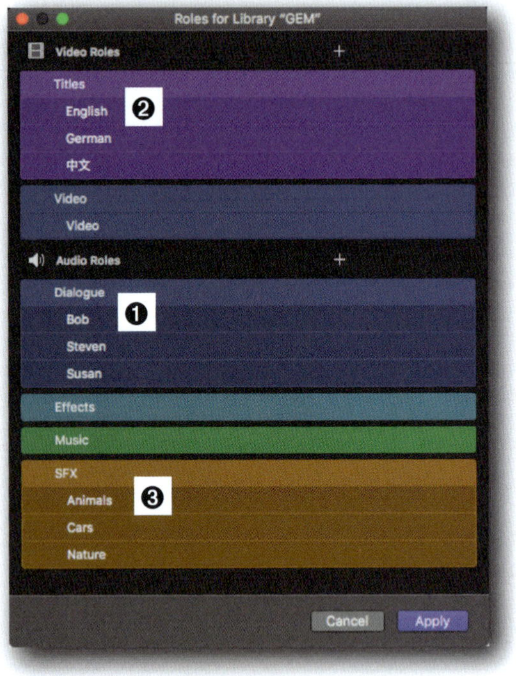

The screenshot on the right shows an example of what it could look like. You also might want to create different Subroles for the Titles cards you have in different languages ❷ or create individual Subroles for the different types of sound effects ❸, like all the car sounds, all the nature or animal sounds.

It is pretty much up to you how you want to structure and organize your Clips using Main Roles and Subroles, and as I mentioned, you can change your Roles (add more, rename them) during editing to optimize your workflow for the specific project you are working on.

Attention: Keep in mind that Roles created in the Role Editor are only stored with the current Active Library in FCPx. However, copying Clips that contain Roles that are not available in the Library you are copying to, will add those Roles to that Library.

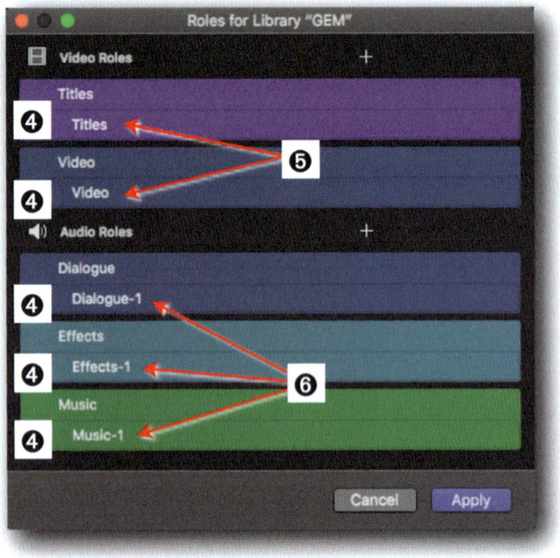

⚙ Default Subroles

Now, before creating our own custom Subroles, let's have a look at the default Subroles by moving the mouse over each individual Role and *clicking* the button "Show Subroles":

▸ **Default Subroles**: Each Main Role already has one Subrole created by default ❹.

▸ **Default Subrole Names**: If you look at the Subroles for the Video Roles type ❺ and the Subroles for the Audio Roles type ❻, you will see a different labeling method. This indicates the fundamental difference between the two Role types that I will explain on the next page.

▸ **Delete Default Subroles**: Unlike the default Main Roles (Title, Video, Dialogue, etc.) that you cannot delete, moving the mouse cursor over a default Subrole will reveal the minus button ⊖ on the left ❼, which indicates that you can delete a default Subrole (kind of).

• If the default Subrole is not used by any Clips, then you can delete it

• If the default Subrole is already used by a Clip, then you cannot delete it and get a warning dialog ❽ that it is used for "*Automatic Subrole Assignment*"

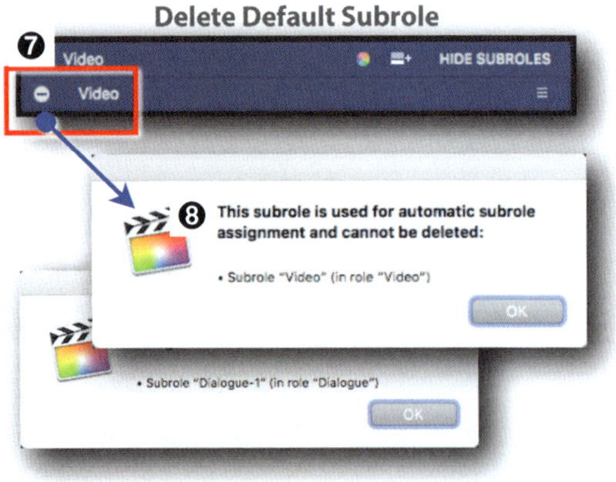

➡ *Automatic Subrole Assignment*

Let's pay attention to this term "*Automatic Subrole Assignment*". Is it just text in a dialog or maybe a hint to something bigger? I would argue that Clips are always assigned to Subroles and not their parent Main Roles. A Clip automatically "belongs" to a parent Main Role by being assigned to a Subrole

> **Clips are always assigned to <u>Subroles</u> (not the Main Roles)**

🟡 Observation 1

The first screenshot displays the Role Editor Dialog with the "Video" Role showing its default Subrole "Video" ❶ (same name!) and the "Dialogue" Role showing its Subrole "Dialogue-01" ❷.

Now, I import one media file in that Library and FCPx automatically assigns a Video Role and an Audio Role to that Clip. I select that Clip, go to the Main Menu *Modify* to look at the two Assign Roles Menus to check their assignments:

Default Subroles

- ▶ Audio Roll Assignment: FCPx assigned the Subrole "Dialogue-01" ❸ ☑ to the Video Clip. The Main Roles seem to be the one with the colored square and their Subroles listed underneath.

- ▶ Video Role Assignment: Here, the situation is not clear, because the Role (the Main Role) and its Subrole both have the same name "Video" ❶. However, the menu seems to list (for whatever reasons) only the Main Roles ❹ (the one with the colored square).

🟡 Observation 2

Now, on the second screenshot, I go back to the Role Editor and add two custom Subroles, the Subrole "Interior" ❺ to the Main Role "Video" and the Subrole "Boom Mic" ❻ to the Main Role "Dialogue".

I didn't change anything with the Roles assignment of the Clip, but if I select the Clip and look at the Assign Roles Menu again, something interesting has happened:

New Subroles

- ▶ Audio Roll Assignment: The Audio Clip is still assigned to the Subrole "Dialogue-1" ❼ (checked ☑) and I see the additional Subrole "Boom Mic". Everything is as expected.

- ▶ Video Role Assignment: Now look at this. Below the Main Role "Video", there are the two Subroles, the default "Video" and the newly added "Interior" ❽ (as you would expect). However, now the Subrole "Video" seems to be selected (checked ☑) and not the Main Role "Video" ❹ as before.

🟡 Conclusion

For some reason, if a Video Role only contains its default Subrole ❶, then the Assign Video Roles Menu only displays the Main Role ❹ with the checkmark ☑ next to it. This is the wrong impression, because the Clip is actually assigned to the default Subrole (which happens to have the same name as its parent Main Role).

➡️ **Color Code**

There are two little facts about the color for Subroles:

▸ Subroles cannot be assigned individual colors. They automatically inherit the color of their parent Main Role.

▸ There is a specific rule on how the Subroles are displayed in the Role Editor below their parent Main Roles:

    ☑️ The default Subroles ❶ are displayed first and then below the custom Subroles ❷, sorted alphabetically.

    ☑️ The custom Subroles have a slightly darker shade ❷.

    ☑️ Based on the color shading, you can see that the "Music" Role has multiple default Subroles ❸. More about that in a minute.

➡️ **Rename Subroles**

The simple process of renaming Subroles could get a little bit confusing when you are not aware of the underlying rules:

▸ **Custom Subrole Names**: You can rename a custom Subrole by *clicking* on the label and entering a new name. All the Clips with that Subrole assignment are updated accordingly. Remember that FCPx is based on databases? This is the beauty about that concept. One edit is just an update in a database record and all the relationships based on metadata is still intact.

▸ **Forbidden Names**: You cannot use the name that FCPx uses for its Automatic Subrole Assignment. You will be warned with the appropriate dialog ❹.

▸ **Default Subrole Name**: Renaming a default Subrole will convert it to a custom Subrole. FCPx might add the default Subrole again when it is assigning Subroles automatically during import or any changes in the Channel Configuration for an Audio Clip.

➡️ **Merge or Move Subroles**

This is another powerful procedure, courtesy of the underlying database structure with metadata.

▸ When you move the mouse cursor over a Subrole, a handle appears on the right ❺ ☰.

▸ If you drag that handle of a Subrole ❻ ("Synth Music") over another Subrole ❼ ("EDM"), then the source Subrole will be deleted and all Clips that were assigned to that source Subrole ("Synth Music") are now reassigned to the destination Subrole ("EDM"). Just an update in the database record.

▸ You can even merge Subroles across Main Roles.

▸ When you close the Role Editor, a warning dialog ❽ explains the action that FCPx will perform.

▸ You can also move a Subrole to a different parent Role by dragging it over that Main Role.

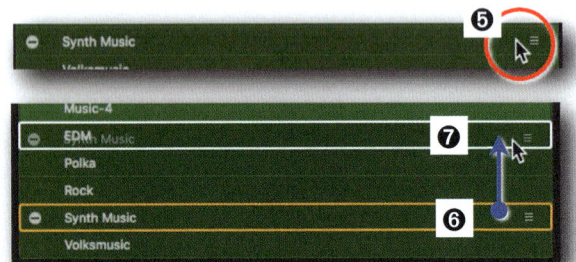

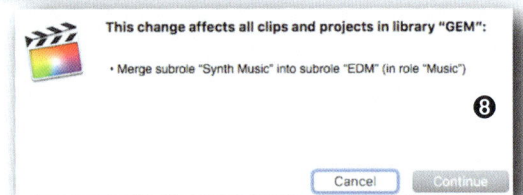

Assign Roles

Let me repeat the rules about metadata. The better you assign Roles to your Clips, the bigger the benefits are later on when using that metadata. So let's learn all the details about how to assign Roles to Clips.

➡ Basic Rules

Here is a summary of the rules regarding the assignment of Roles.

▶ A Role is a metadata that includes a text label (name of the Role) and a corresponding color label.

▶ Every Clip in FCPx has an assigned Role (now we know, it is actually one of the Subroles).

▶ A Standard Clip that has audio and video content will have two Roles. A Video Role assigned to the Video Clip and an Audio Role assigned to the Audio Clip.

▶ You can assign video-type Roles only to Video Clips (or Image Clips) and audio-type Roles can only be assigned to Audio Clips and Video Clips that contain audio.

▶ Every instance of an Event Clip or Timeline Clip contains its own Role. However, changing the Roles assignment of Clips inside Compound Clips and Multicam Clips will also affect their corresponding Clips.

▶ Audio Roles behave a little bit different, because the Subrole is not assigned to the actual Clip but to its Audio Component(s)!

➡ Video Clips vs. Audio Clips

Here is the important difference between the video-type Roles and audio-type Roles.

▶ **Video Portion**: The video content ❶ of a Standard Clip is always represented by a single video signal, the video (or the still image as a single frame). Therefore, a single video-type Role ❸ is assigned to the Clip.

▶ **Audio Portion**: The audio content ❷ of a Standard Clip is represented by Audio Channels. As we have already discussed in the Audio chapter, a Clip not only can have one Audio Channel or multiple Audio Channels, those Audio Channels are grouped differently, a procedure called Channel Configuration. And whatever Channel Configuration is selected for that Clip (in the Audio Inspector), you will have one or multiple so-called Audio Components ❹ (representing one or multiple Audio Channels).

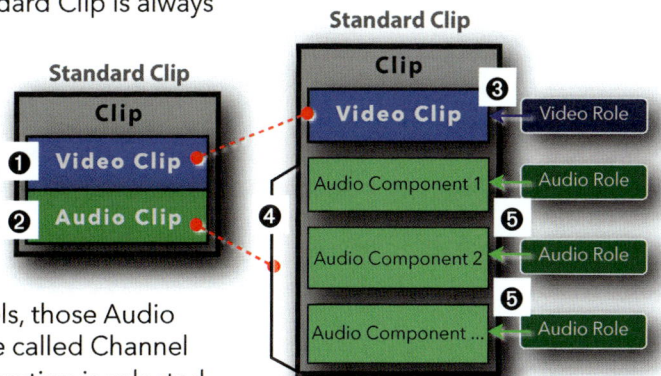

And here are the important facts:

☑ An Audio Role is not assigned to the Audio Clip!

☑ An Audio Role is also not assigned to the individual Audio Channel(s) of a Clip!

☑ Instead, <u>an Audio Role is assigned to the Audio Component</u>.

☑ If a Clip has more than one Audio Component, then each Audio Component has its own assignment to an Audio Role ❺ (and with Audio Role, I actually mean Audio Subrole).

☑ You can change (reassign) the assigned Subrole for each Audio Component of a Clip separately

☑ If you change the Channel Configuration (and most likely with it the amount of Audio Components), then that might also change (reset) the assignment of the Subroles.

> **Audio Roles are assigned to Audio Components**

➡ *Automatic Assignment*

Because each Clip in FCPx has to be assigned to a Role, FCPx takes care of that and automatically assigns Roles when Clips are created during the import of Source Media Files. The video portion of a Clip will have the "Video" Subrole assigned to it, but for the audio portion you have more control about the assignment.

🔵 Automatic Audio Roles Assignment

The settings on the right side of the Media Import Dialog (also available in the *Preferences ➤ Import*) determine how FCPx assigns the Audio Roles.

▶ **Automatically ❶** (Analyze): This option from the popup menu is the default. FCPx analyzes the file plus its metadata (i.e. ID3 tags in audio files) to determine the proper Role. It can choose only one of its three default Roles to make an assignment, but cannot use any of the custom Roles that you might have created in the Role Editor.

▶ **Default Roles ❷**: You can choose any of the three default Roles to have FCPx assign that Audio Role to all the source media files you import.

▶ **Custom Roles ❸**: If you added any custom Audio Roles in the Role Editor Dialog, then they will also be available in that popup menu for you to choose from.

▶ **iXML ❹**: If you import Source Media Files from a device that supports the iXML standard, then you can check this option and FCPx creates new Roles based on the iXML metadata included with those files and assigns those new Subroles to the corresponding Audio Components. Please note that the Main Role you selected in the popup menu ❷ ❸ will be used as the parent Audio Roles where those new Subroles are created under.

💀 Subroles vs. Audio Components

Here is an example of a media file with 6 audio channels. The three screenshots (Audio Inspector ➤ Audio Configuration) show three different scenarios if you choose any of these Channel Configurations. This demonstrates why default Audio Subroles are numbered.

- If you choose a Channel Configuration with one Audio Component ❺ (containing all 6 audio channels), then it needs only one Subrole (Music-1 ❻).

- If you choose a Channel Configuration with three Audio Components ❼ (each with 2 audio channels), then it needs 3 Subroles (Music 1, Music-2, Music-3 ❽).

- If you choose a Channel Configuration with six Audio Components ❾ (each with 1 audio channel), then it needs 6 Subroles (Music 1, ... Music-6 ❿).

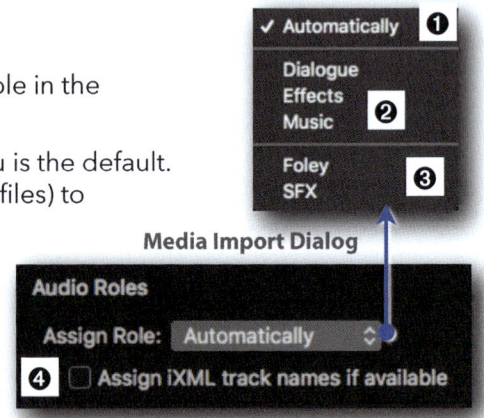

Media Import Dialog

Audio Inspector

➡️ *Manual Assignment*

Once FCPx creates a Clip and assigns it a default Role, you can change that assignment at any time by accessing the *Assign Video Roles* or *Assign Audio Roles* Menu. But be careful, there are a few "specific" behaviors that are not that obvious, but could potentially mess up your assignments (even without you noticing it).

First, here are all the places where you access those two popup menus:

▶ Change a specific Clip:

- *Ctr+click* on an Event Clip and choose from the *Shortcut Menu ➤ Assign Audio/Video Roles* ❶
- *Ctr+click* on a Timeline Clip and choose from the *Shortcut Menu ➤ Assign Audio/Video Roles* ❷
- In the Timeline Index, choose the *Clips* tab and select the Roles for any displayed Clip in the Video Roles or Audio Roles column ❸

▶ Change one or multiple selected Clips:

- Main Menu *Modify ➤ Assign Audio/Video Roles* ❹
- Key Command ❺ *ctr+opt+V* (for Video) or *ctr+opt+T* (Titles), *ctr+opt+D* (Dialogue), *ctr+opt+M* (Music), *ctr+opt+E* (Effects). This only works when a Clip is selected, but does not work when an Audio Component is selected
- In the Info Inspector 🛈 choose from the popup menu in the Video Roles and Audio Roles field ❻
- In the Audio Inspector 🔊, all the Audio Components are displayed at the bottom in the Audio Configuration section as Audio Component Clips (see Audio chapter for details about that). Each of those Audio Component Clips displays its current Subrole assignment ❼. *Click* on the selector 🔽 next to it to open the "*Assign Audio Roles Menu*" to select a different Audio Subrole

Menu Commands

Info Inspector

Timeline Index ➤ Clips

Assign Video Roles

Assign Audio Roles

Audio Inspector

➡ Possible Confusion

Remember two important facts we learned so far.

- ☑ Only Subroles are assigned to Clips
- ☑ For Clips with audio content, Subroles are assigned to the individual Audio Components Clip

🔘 Select Clip vs. Select Audio Component Clip

There is a little detail you have to be aware of regarding the *Assign Audio Roles Menu*. It is important as to what exactly is selected (Clip or Audio Component) when you choose any of the commands to open that menu.

- ▶ **Audio Component Selected**: If you select an Audio Component Clip ❶, then the menu has the Main Roles ❷ grayed out. Only the Subroles ❸ can be selected.

  - This makes sense, because only a Subrole can be assigned to an Audio Component Clip. The Main Roles are not needed for assignment.

- ▶ **Clip Selected**: If you select the actual Clip ❹, then the menu lets you select the Main Roles ❺ or their Subroles ❻. That still doesn't mean that you can assign a Main Role to a Clip. It just provides a convenience when assigning Audio Roles.

  - ☑ **Individual Subroles**: If you select a Main Role, for example, "Music", FCPx assigns individual Subroles to all the available Audio Component Clips in that Clip with those sequential numbers (Music-1, Music-2, etc. ❼).

  - ☑ **Same Subrole**: If you select a specific Subrole (i.e. "Music-2"), then FCPx assigns that one Subrole to all the available Audio Component Clips in that Clip ❽.

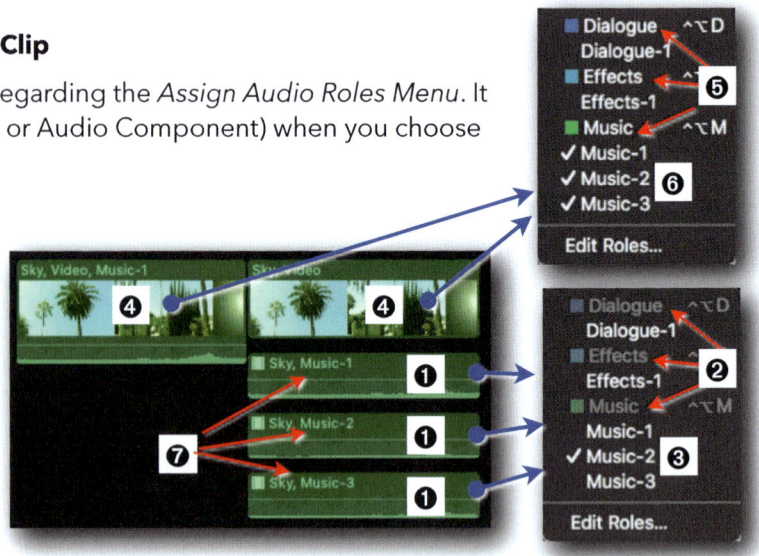

➡ Mixed Audio Roles

Usually, the Audio Components are assigned to individual Subroles that belong to the same parent Main Role. Therefore, they all have the same color in the Audio Inspector that shows the Summed Audio Clip and its Audio Component Clips.

However, if at least one of the Audio Component Clips of that Audio Clip belongs to a different parent Main Role ❾, then the Summed Audio Clip (or just the Clip if it is collapsed) is displayed in gray color ❿ to indicate that.

Attention: If you show Audio Components in the Timeline, then they will be sorted by their name of their subroles. In the two screenshots on the right you see the same Clip displayed in the Audio Inspector (original Audio Components order) and the Timeline (Audio Component Clips sorted by Subroles).

Remember, selecting a different Channel Configuration in the Audio Inspector will reset the Subrole Assignment back to a single Main Role with sequential Subroles.

The functionality of Lanes in the Timeline is based on Roles and Subroles. This is an area where you can see the power of metadata in action. As we will find out, there are not many controls, but a lot of little details that requires some attention or everything becomes confusing very fast.

Review

I want to review a few basics about the Timeline and Clip Appearance that we have already covered, but they are important for the understanding of what happens with Lanes.

🌐 Timeline Area

Here is a review on how the Timeline Area is divided into the various horizontal sections:

▶ **Primary Storyline ❶**: The Primary Storyline is that black strip in the middle of the Timeline that represents the Magnetic Storyline. Although you cannot stack multiple Clips on top of each other, you can "Expand" Timeline Clip, which displays it as a separate Clip stacked on top of each other.

▶ **Upper Area ❷**: The area above the Primary Storyline can only contain Connected Clips or Connected Storylines.

▶ **Lower Area ❸**: You can place any type of Clip here.

▶ **Lanes ❹**: The Lanes will appear in the Lower Timeline Area, following specific rules we will discover on the next few pages.

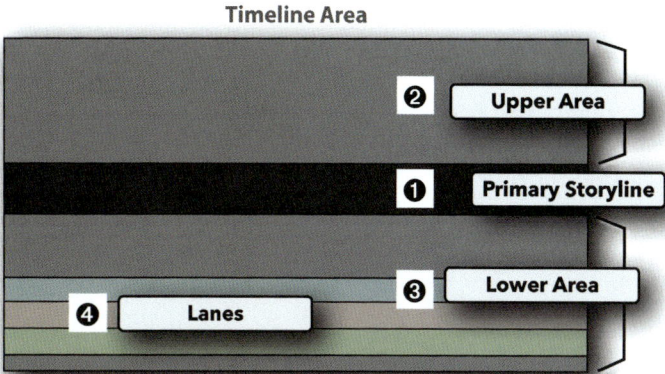

🌐 Timeline Clips

Now let's review a few things about the appearance of Clips on the Timeline, the so-called Timeline Clips.

The default appearance of a Clip has three sections. Please note that the Clip Appearance popover 🖼 lets you adjust those sections.

▶ **Header ❺**: The Header displays various Text (Clip Name, Roles) and Batches (🖼 🔊 💱 🗂).

▶ **Video ❻**: This section displays a thumbnail image if the Clip contains video or a still image. The section is blank ❼ if the Clip only contains audio.

▶ **Audio ❽**: This section displays a waveform if the Clip contains audio. If not, the section is blank ❾.

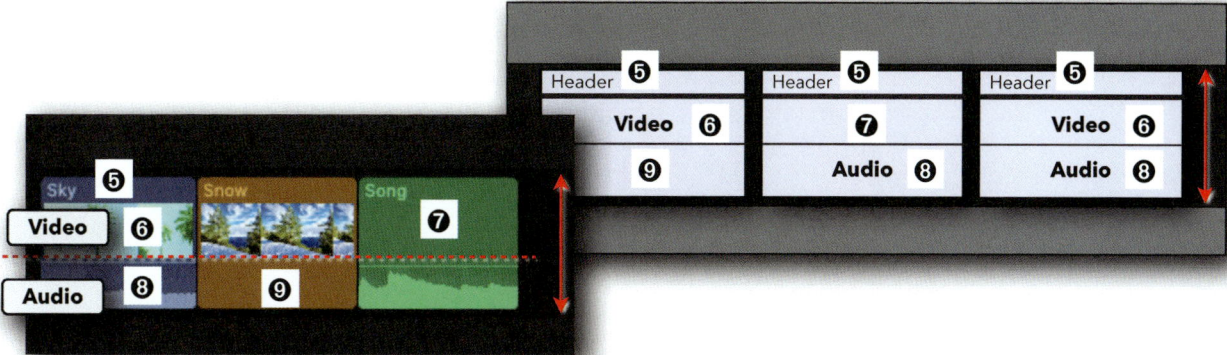

⚫ Clip Views

If you look closely at the following example, you can see that the elements of a Timeline Clip can be displayed in four different ways. We already discussed that earlier in this chapter, but I want to point it out again, because it is important for the understanding of what is displayed in Lanes.

▸ **Combined Video/Audio Clip ❶**: This is the default view with the three sections, Header, Video, Audio.

The other three appearances of the Clips are not as high, because they contain only two sections, the Header and either Audio or Video. A Clip changes to this view when using any of the two Expand commands "Expand Audio" ❷ or "Expand Audio Components" ❸ that you access by *ctr+clicking* on the Timeline Clip and selecting from its Shortcut Menu.

▸ **Separate Video Clip ❹**: This view shows the Header and Video

▸ **Separate Audio Clip ❺**: This view only shows the Header and Audio

▸ **Separate Audio Component Clip ❻**: This view shows the Header and the Audio Component(s). It has a badge in the header to distinguish it from the Separate Audio Clip ❺.

Please note that the Primary Storyline (the black strip ❼) expands vertically for all those Clips, because this is still considered one Clip, just viewed in its expanded form.

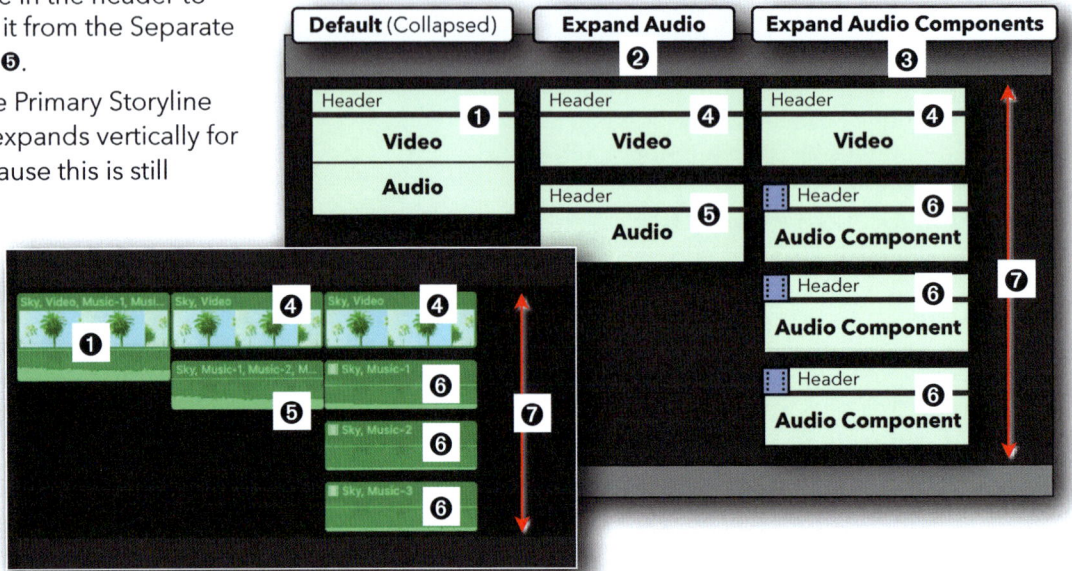

Here is the same example, but this time with a Timeline Clip that only contains audio. As we have seen before, the video section is blank ❽ in the default (collapsed) Video/Audio View. However, even in both expanded views, the Clip for the separate Video view ❾ is still created, it is just empty. Please note that the badge for the Audio Components is now a speaker symbol ◀.

If you select an expanded Clip, you will see a shaded area around them, indicating that they belong together. Even as Connected Clips, they "stay virtually attached to each other".

Clip Name

And here is another overview to show the relationship between Clips and Roles.

First, let's look at the Clip Appearance popover again (*click* on the Clip Appearance Button ❶ in the Timeline Header). The "*Show*" setting determines what text is displayed on the header of the Timeline Clip. A a default, only *Clip Names* ❷ is selected. As you can see, when you expand a Clip, all its expanded Clips display the same Name ❸, because they all "are" the same Clip.

Timeline

Clip Names and Clip Roles

Here is the same Timeline with the same Timeline Clips and their different Clip Views, but now I enabled the *Clip Roles* ❹ checkbox too. I also show the screenshots of the *Assign Audio Roles* popup menu, to show what is displayed in the menu (and why) when opening it from the various Clips Views.

▶ **Combined Video/Audio Clip ❺**: The Clip Header shows the Name ("*Sky*"), the Main Video Role ("*Video*"), and all Subroles that are assigned to all Audio Components of that Clip, even if they are not displayed in this combined view. The popup menu ❻ confirms that, all three Subroles for the three Audio Components are checked ✅.

▶ **Separate Video Clip ❼**: The Clip Header shows the Name ("*Sky*") and the Main Video Role ("*Video*").

▶ **Separate Audio Clip ❽**: The Clip Header shows the Name ("*Sky*") and all Subroles that are assigned to all its Audio Components, even if they are not displayed in this separate Audio Clip (that I call "Summed Audio Clip"). The popup menu shows the same three Subroles checked ✅.

▶ **Separate Audio Component Clip ❾**: All the separate Audio Component Clips show that name of the Clip ("*Sky*") and the individual Audio Subrole they are assigned to ("Music-1", "Music-2", "Music-3").

➡ Lanes Interface

It is extremely important to understand a few underlying concepts about Lanes, otherwise, Clips will just jump around when you click on things and you will have no clue why.

To avoid any potential confusion or roadblocks, I will introduce the Lanes feature step-by-step over the next few pages. Let's start with a quick overview of the interface.

▶ **Timeline Index**: All the controls for the Lanes are located in the Roles View ❶ of the Timeline Index (Main Menu *View ➤ Timeline Index ➤ Roles*).

▶ **Roles and Subroles**: The rows in the Timeline Index represent the Main Roles and Subroles. Please note that only those Roles are displayed that are assigned to any of the Clips that are placed on the current Timeline.

▶ **Video Roles ❷**: Although the Video Roles and Subroles are also listed in the Timeline Index, they don't have anything to do with the Lanes. Those rows only provide three controls:

- Select: *Click* on the row (or *sh+click* for multiple) to select Clips with that Role assignment.
- Mute ❸ ☑: Disable the corresponding Clips (has no effect on the export).

- Expand/Collapse ❹: If any Clip in the Timeline is assigned to a Video Subrole, then the button Expand/Collapse appears when mousing over the row.

▶ **Audio Roles**: You can drag the rows ❺ up/down to determine their order, which controls the vertical positioning of the Lanes ❻ in the Timeline.

▶ **Buttons ❼** ☑ ▭ ≡ ●: The various buttons on the rows for Audio Roles determine the appearance of the Lanes in the Timeline ❻.

▶ **Lanes**: The Lanes in the Timeline are displayed in the Lower Timeline Area ❽ and only affect the audio portion of a Clip.

▶ **Visual Guides ❾**: There are visual guides (shaded areas) in the Timeline that indicate which separated Clips "belong together".

Show/Hide Video Subroles — Timeline Pane — Shaded Area (Selected Clip)

Timeline Index

Mute Lanes — ❸

Show/Hide All Audio Role Lanes

Toggle Lane Focus
Show/Hide Subrole Lane
Show/Hide Audio Lanes

Understanding Lanes

As I mentioned already, Lanes can easily become confusing and it might be difficult to understand or to predict where individual Clips will be placed vertically on the Timeline. Because there are so many factors that you have to take into account, I'll try to explain that with seven examples.

#1 - Auto-Populate the Timeline Index

All the controls for the Lanes are located in the Roles View ❶ of the Timeline Index. So, the first thing you have to be aware of is, what does the Roles View display?

This what we know:

▶ Every Clip in FCPx has a Role and the Role's Color assigned to it.

▶ Remember, even if we say "Role", we know that a Clip is actually assigned to a specific Subrole that belongs to a parent Main Role.

▶ A Clip has either a Video Role or an Audio Role assigned to it, and if the Clip has audio and video content, then it will have two assignments.

▶ If the Clip has a Video Role and an Audio Role assigned to it, then the combined Video/Audio Clip shows the color of the Audio Role. The exception is when the audio portion is muted (Clip will show the Video Role color) or if it has more than one Audio Component and at least one is assigned to a Subrole belonging to a different parent MainRole (Clip will have a gray color).

This is what will happen:

▶ Whenever you place a Clip ❷ on the Timeline, the Roles View of the Timeline Index "looks up" ❸ its assigned Role and adds a corresponding row ❹ to the Roles View (if it wasn't there already).

▶ Every time you add a Clip to the Timeline that has a Role which no other Clip is assigned to, then that Role will be added to the Roles View.

▶ Changing the Role assignment of any existing Timeline Clip will update the Roles View accordingly (if necessary).

▶ This dynamic Roles View does also apply to the existing Subroles assignment of Clips. For example, if you have an Audio Clip that contains one Audio Component (i.e. Surround 5.1) and you change its Channel Configuration so its will have three Audio Components (3 x Stereo), then the available Subroles in the Roles View change accordingly too (you have to show the Subrole Lanes ▦ to see that).

Here is an example with a couple of Timeline Clips on the right ❷ and the Roles View in the Timeline Index on the left, showing individual rows ❹ for each Main Role that FCPx looks up from the Clip's Assignment. The matching color assignment will help as well as having the Role Names displayed on the Clip Header ❺.

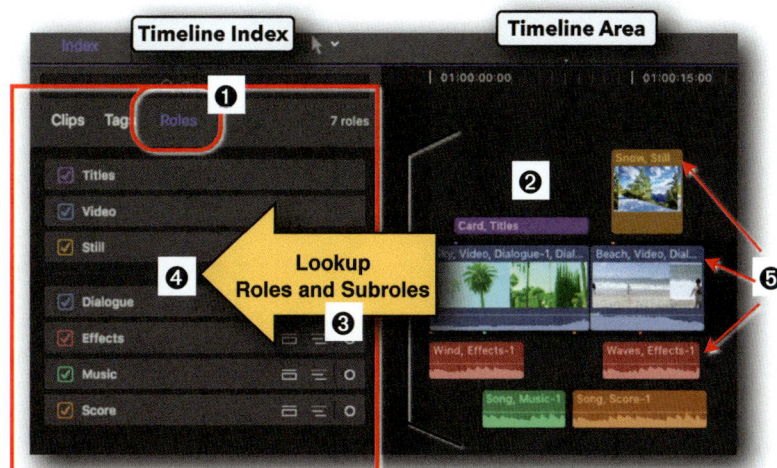

💀 #2 - Lanes are only for Audio Content

Remember the four views of a Standard Clip I showed earlier:

> ❶ *Combined Video/Audio Clip*
> ❷ *Separate Video Clip*
> ❸ *Separate Audio Clip*
> ❹ *Separate Audio Component Clip*

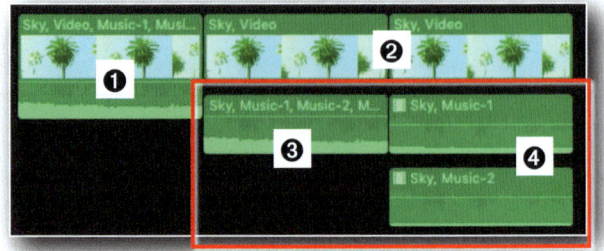

Only the last two, separate *Audio Clips* ("Summed Audio Clip") ❸ and *the* separate *Audio Component Clips* ❹ will be displayed on Lanes.

💀 #3 - Invisible Lanes

Here is a little-known fact that is important when trying to make sense out of how FCPx places Clips on the Timeline. FCPx already uses an invisible Lanes structure in the Lower Timeline Area, even if it doesn't show any Lanes. Here is an example:

▶ Example 1: The first screenshot shows a single Video Clip ❺ on the Primary Storyline with five Connected Audio Clips ❻ underneath in the Lower Timeline area. You can see the names of their assigned Roles in the Clip Header, which matches the names and colors of the Roles ❼ displayed in the Timeline Index to the left. All the four Audio Clips are placed on the Timeline next to each other, because they do not overlap and Lanes are not enabled yet.

▶ Example 2: The only thing I changed in the second Screenshot is the length or start time of the individual Audio Clips. In its usual fashion, FCPx avoids any "collision" by stacking the Clips vertically ❽. There are still no Lanes and the Timeline is still one gray area. However, this vertical stacking order is not random. Whenever a Clip has to be moved vertically out of the way, then the order of the Roles in the Timeline Index on the left ❾ functions as invisible lanes ❿ and determines the vertical arrangement in the Timeline area. If you **drag** the Roles ❾ up/down in the Timeline Index, the vertical arrangement in the Timeline area will follow accordingly.

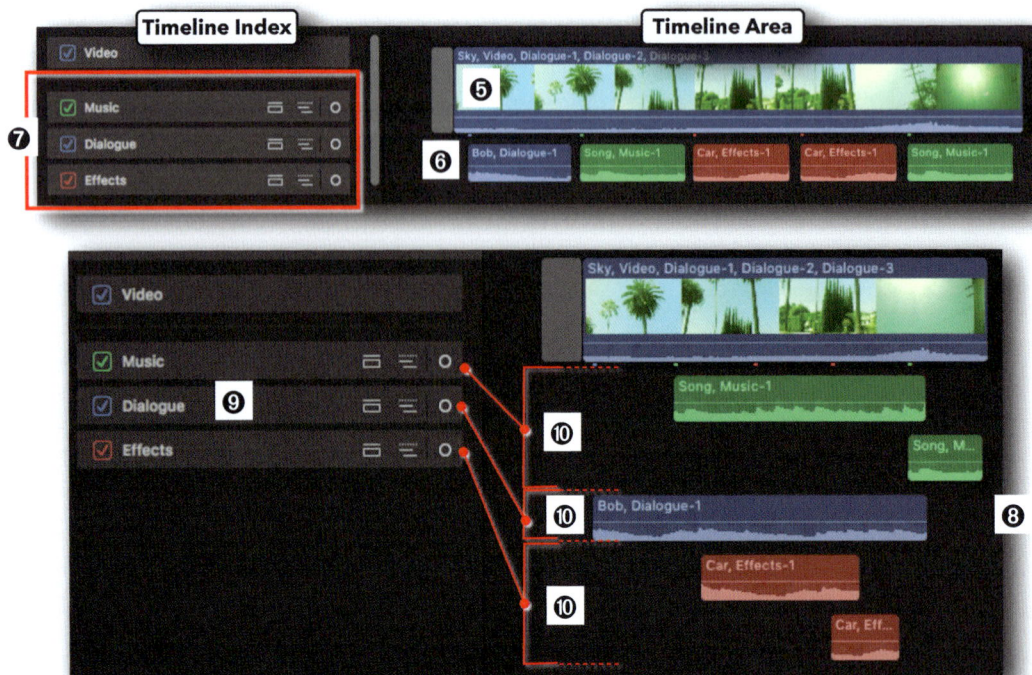

#4 - Basic Functionality

Now let's look at the basic functionality of the two buttons on the Audio Roles row:

Show/Hide Main Role Lanes

Show/Hide Subrole Lanes

Remember this diagram I used earlier to show the different views of a Standard Clip. Keep it in mind when we look a the functionality of Lanes:

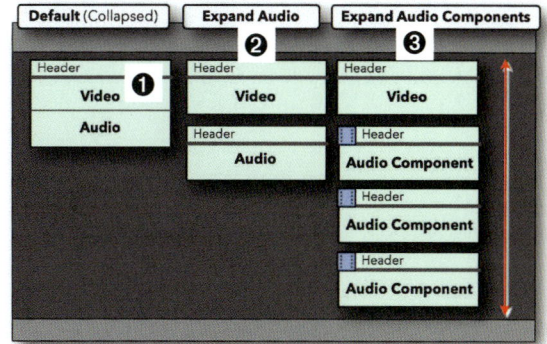

- A Combined Audio/Video Clip represents the video and audio content ❶.
- When Using the "**Expand Audio**" ❷ command, then that content is displayed as two separate Clips, the *Separate Video Clip* and *Separate Audio Clip* (which I call "Summed Audio Clip").
- When Using the "**Expand Audio Components**" ❸ command, then that content is displayed as the *Separate Video Clip* and one or many *Audio Component Clips*.

Now, here are the three variations for those two buttons:

▶ [icon] off [icon] off: **No Lanes ❹**
- ☑ The Combined Clip ❺ is displayed on the Primary Storyline
- ☑ This Clip has a Video Role and an Audio assigned to it, which are displayed in the Roles View ❿

▶ [icon] on [icon] off: **Show Main Role Lanes ❻**
- ☑ The Combined Clip expands into a "Separate Video Clip" and "Summed Audio Clip"
- ☑ The *Separate Video Clip* stays on the Primary Storyline
- ☑ A Lane ❼ is now visible that represents the parent Main Role ("Music") and is labeled with the Role Name
- ☑ The *Summed Audio Clip* is placed on that Lane "Music"

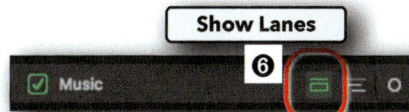

▶ [icon] on [icon] on: **Show Subrole Lanes ❽**
- ☑ The Clip expands into the Separate Video Clip and Audio Component Clips
- ☑ The *Separate Video Clip* stays on the Primary Storyline
- ☑ FCPx displays a Lane for each available Subrole ❾ ("Music-1", "Music-2", "Music-3")
- ☑ The *Audio Component Clips* [icon] are placed on their corresponding Subrole Lanes

You may have noticed that the two Lanes Buttons ▣ ▤ have a similar effect as the two Expand commands we just reviewed. While the Expand commands keep the separated Audio Clip(s) below the separate Video Clip (but still on the expanded Primary Storyline), the Lanes Buttons put the separated Audio Clip(s) on individual Lanes and only the separated Video Clip stays on the Primary Storyline.

> ▣ Show/Hide Main Role Lane = Expand/Collapse Audio
> **Summed Audio Clip ➤ Main Role Lanes**
> ───
> ▤ Show/Hide Subrole Lanes = Expand/Collapse Audio Components
> **Audio Component Clips ➤ Subrole Lanes**

🔵 #5 - Three Buttons

Lanes are very powerful, which can tremendously improve and speed up your editing workflow. However, the key is the understanding why FCPx arranges the Clips in a specific way and learn how to read the "information", based on how the Clips are organized

Here is the next example with a few more elements. This is what happens:

▸ FCPx looked up three Audio Roles ❶ from the existing Timeline Clips, which you can see in the Roles View on the left. "Dialogue" (blue), "Music" (green), and "Effects" (turquoise).

▸ **Turquoise**: Both buttons for the Effects Role (turquoise) are disabled ❷ ▣ ▤, which means those Clips ❸ on the Timeline (turquoise) are not expanded into Lanes. You can see them on the Primary Storyline with the full height, showing the video and audio content.

▸ **Blue**: The Dialog Role (blue) has only the first button enabled ❹ ▣. That means, all the blue Clips are expanded and show their Summed Audio Clip on the Lane labeled "Dialogue" ❻. Please note that the Lane expands vertically if Clips overlap on that Lane.

▸ **Green**: The Music Role (green) has both buttons enabled ❼ ▣ ▤, which expands the Role into the individual Subroles and displays them as separate rows ❽. For each separate Subroles row, FCPx creates a separate Subrole Lane ❾ in the Timeline with colored divider lines and the Subrole names shown on the left. Now, that Clip (green) is expanded and shows its individual Audio Component Clips. Please note that little filmstrip badge ▥ on the Clip Header that indicates that theses Clips represent Audio Components.

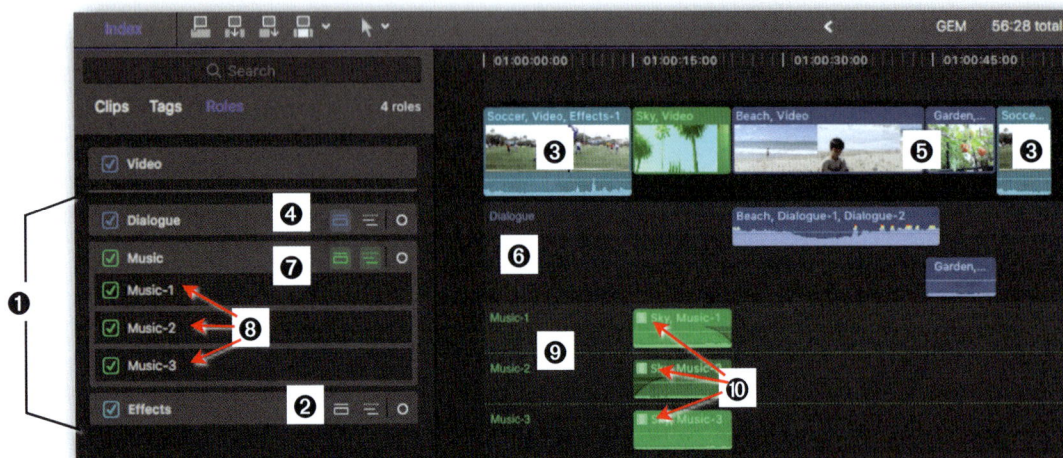

💡 #6 - Lanes and Connected Clips

Here is the next example that has Connected Audio Clips in the Timeline and a few other little twists that can easily be misinterpreted when you don't pay attention to the tiniest little details.

▶ **No Lane**: First, check the Roles View on the left. You can see by the two disabled buttons 🔲 🔳 that the Roles "Songs" ❶ (orange) and "Foley" ❷ (red) are not displayed as separate Lanes. Although the Timeline looks like it is divided by Lanes, these two Roles are just "surrounded" by Lanes. Their vertical position ❸ ❹, however, is still based on the order of the Roles in the Roles View ❺ (as we discussed earlier). Also, those non-Lanes have no Role labels ❻ on the left of the Timeline Area.

▶ **Connected Clips**: Once Connected Clips are displayed on Lanes, they look indistinguishable from Summed Audio Clips that belong to a separated Video Clip on the Primary Storyline (or a Connected Video Clip). The only indication is the Connection Point ❼ on its parent Clip on the Primary Storyline. In this example, in the lower right corner, the Clip "Beach"❽ is a Summed Audio Clip that "belongs" to the Beach Clip on the Primary Storyline, but the Clip below "Bob" ❾ is a Connected Audio Clip.

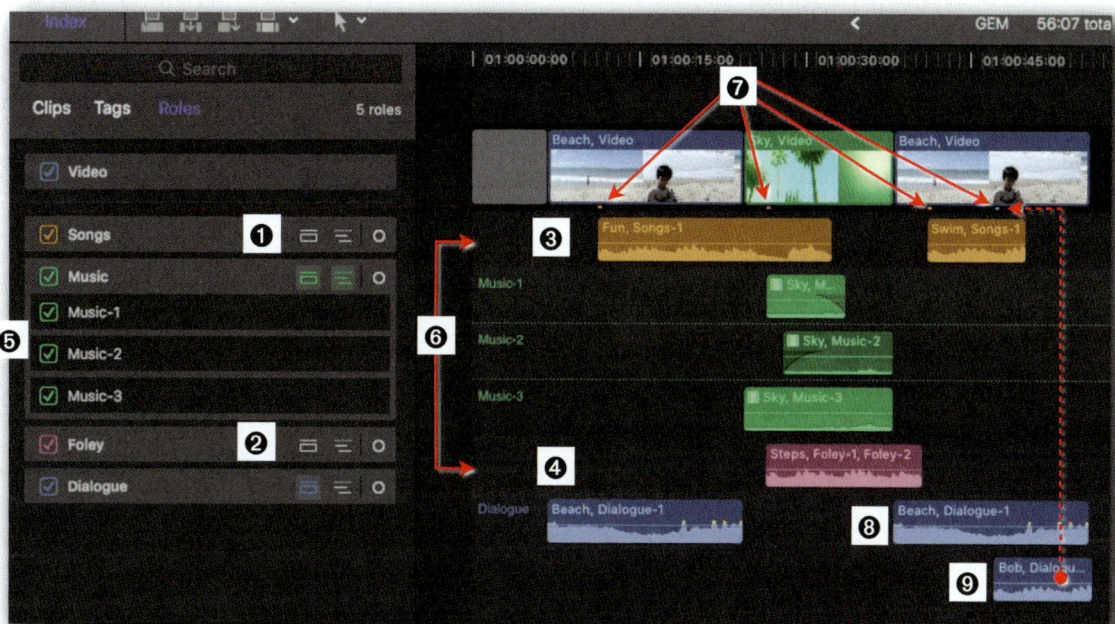

Here is an example with a lot of Connected Clips. On the left screenshot, you can only spot that by the tiny Connection Points along the Primary Storyline. On the right screenshot, I have all Clips selected (*cmd+A*), which brings up the Connection Lines that are better to follow. The Clips without the Connection Lines ❿ are the separated Summed Audio Clips that belong to a parent Video Clip on the Primary Storyline ⓫.

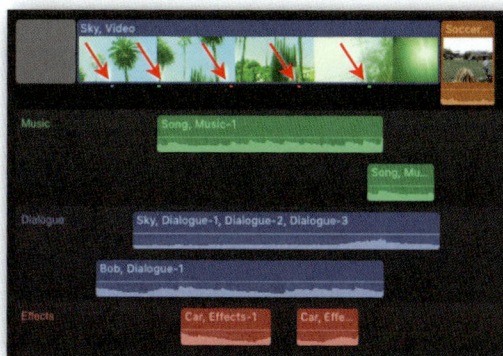

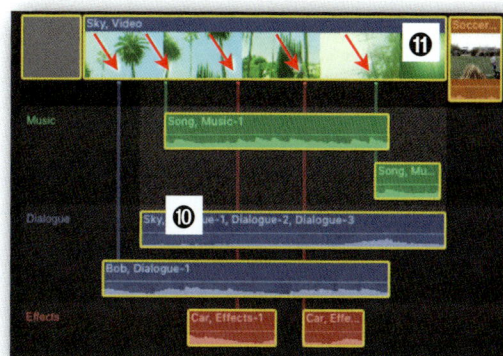

#7 - Mixed Clips

In this last example, I "mix" it up even more, with a "special" Clip. A quick review again about audio that we should be familiar with by now:

The audio content of a Standard Clip (Video Clip or Audio-only Clip) can be displayed in three forms:

- ☑️ A **"Combined" Clip** displays the audio content as a single waveform (combining all the included audio channels, hence the name "Summed Audio Clip") visible below the video thumbnail.
- ☑️ A **"Separated" Audio Clip** (use the *Expand Audio* command or enable the Show Lanes Button 🔲) also displays the audio content as a single waveform, the "Summed Audio Clip".
- ☑️ A **"Separated" Audio Component Clip** (use the *Expand Audio Components* command or enable the Show Subroles Lanes Button 🔲) shows an individual Clip for each Audio Component, which can be one or multiple Clips, depending on the selected Channel Configuration.

Usually, when a Clip has multiple Audio Components, all those Audio Components are assigned to separate Subroles that all belong to the same parent Main Role. For example, all the individual stereo stems of a mix in surround all belong to the parent Main Role "Music". Or the different tracks of a multitrack field recorder that are assigned to the various mics (boom mic, Lav1, Lav2, etc.) belong to the parent Main Role "Dialogue". In those cases, all the separate Audio Component Clips are assigned to the same parent Main Role.

However, if one Audio Component Clip is assigned to a different parent Main Role, then stuff is getting interesting:

- ▶ If you show no Lanes ❶ or Expand anything, then that Clip with that mixed Audio Components assignments is indicated by a gray-colored Clip ❷.
- ▶ If you show the Role Lanes ❸ 🔲, then that Clip will display all its separate Audio Component Clips, indicated by the badge 🎞️ on the corresponding Lanes ❹.
- ▶ If you show the Subrole Lanes ❺ 🔲 for that specific Role, then the Audio Components assigned to those Subroles will be placed on separate Subrole Lanes ❻, but the other Audio Components still appear on the other Lanes ❼ as Audio Components 🎞️.

Audio Inspector

If you look at that "mixed assignment" Clip in the Audio Inspector, you see in the Audio Configuration section that the **Summed Audio Clip** ❽ (the first waveform) is also displayed in gray and the individual waveforms below (representing the individual **Audio Component Clips** ❾) are displayed in the color, corresponding to their parent Main Role assignment. Please note that this is the original order of the Audio Components and is not affected by the Role order in the Timeline Index.

➡ *Controls*

Let's look at all the controls in the Roles View including all their variations with modifier keys that help you speed up your workflow.

Timeline Index

🟤 Sort

A few things to be aware of about this feature:

▸ You can **drag** the rows ❶ up and down in the Timeline Index to determine the vertical sorting order of how the Clips are displayed in the Timeline Area. Video Roles ❷ can't be dragged.

▸ You can also **drag** the rows for the Subroles ❸ to determine the order of how the different Audio Components are displayed.

▸ Please remember that Timeline Clips that are not located on Lanes also follow this vertical sorting order ("virtual lanes") based on their Role assignment.

🟤 Highlight

Clicking on a Role will highlight ❹ that row and highlights all Clips in the Timeline that are assigned to that Role. Please note, those Timeline Clips are not selected (no yellow frame), they are just shown in a brighter color.

The highlight functionality can be used independently from the Lanes feature, which means even if you don't display any Lanes in your Timeline Area, you can quickly highlight Clips that belong to the same Role(s) by clicking on those rows in the Timeline Index.

These are the available commands:

🔘 *Click* on a row (of a Role or Subrole) to highlight that row. *Clicking* on another row will deselect the previously selected row

🔘 *Sh+click* on a row will not deselect any other highlighted rows, so you can select a group of Roles

🔘 *Click* on the background of the Timeline Index to deselect any highlighted row

The Timeline Index shows the amount of Roles ❺ that are currently used (and displayed in this Roles View) at the top next to the Roles tab. If you highlight any Roles or Subroles, then it will display the total duration of the highlighted Clips.

🟤 On/Off

The On/Off checkbox disables all the Timeline Clips that belong to that Role or Subrole. For video, it means that those Clips will not be played (black) and makes any video "below" visible. For audio, it means that the audio is muted. If some of the Subroles are muted and some are not, then the Main Role displays a hyphen checkbox ▣. Clips that are turned off change their color to gray. This is different from disabling Clips (Key Command *V*), which keeps their color but dims it.

These are the available commands (they work independently for Video and Audio Roles):

🔘 *Click* to toggle the checkbox

🔘 *Cmd+click* to toggle all checkboxes in the Timeline Index

🔘 *Opt+click* an off button will function like a "solo-exclusive". Only the clicked Role will be set to on ☑ and all other Roles will be turned off ☐.

Please note that the on/off status is just for playback and has no effect during export.

☻ Show/Hide Audio Role Lanes ⬛⬛

I discussed that feature already in great detail. Here is just the effect when clicking with modifier keys:

- *Click* to toggle that specific button
- *Cmd+click* to toggle all buttons
- *Opt+click* enables that button and disables all other buttons (like exclusive functionality)

☻ Show/Hide Audio Subrole Lanes ⬛⬛

Here is the effect when clicking with modifier keys. Remember that enabling this button will also enable the Main Role Lanes Button.

- *Click* to toggle that specific button
- *Cmd+click* to toggle all buttons

☻ Show Audio Lanes Button

At the bottom of the Roles View is an additional button with the label "Show Audio Lanes". It is also available as a Key Command that is not assigned by default.

Please note that the button has three states and the label on the button changes accordingly:

- `Show Audio Lanes` ➤ `Hide Audio Lanes` *Click* to enable all Lane Buttons ⬛.
- `Hide Audio Lanes` ➤ `Show Audio Lanes` If all Lane Buttons ⬛ are enabled, then the label on this button changes to "Hide Audio Lanes". *Clicking* on it will disable all Lane Buttons. There is an exception. Any row that also has the Subroles Button ⬛ enabled will not be affected and stays enabled.
- `Collapse Subroles` ➤ `Hide Audio Lanes` If all rows have the Subrole Lane Button enabled ⬛, then this button changes its label to "Collapse Subroles". *Clicking* will disable all the Subrole Lanes Buttons ⬛, but leaves the Lanes Button enabled ⬛. The label now changes to "Hide Audio Lanes".

Here is an example of how this button could speed up your workflow.

The first screenshot ❶ shows a simple Timeline with a few Clips. Their embedded audio content is assigned to different Roles as you can see by their colors. Now with the simple click on the "Show Audio Lanes" button (or its Key Command), FCPx expands the Clips and places all their Summed Audio Clips on their corresponding Lanes based on the Clip's Role Assignment, as you can see on the second screenshot ❷. The third screenshot ❸ shows the similar result expanded Summed Audio Clips without Lanes when using the "Expand/Collapse Audio" command (on all selected Clips).

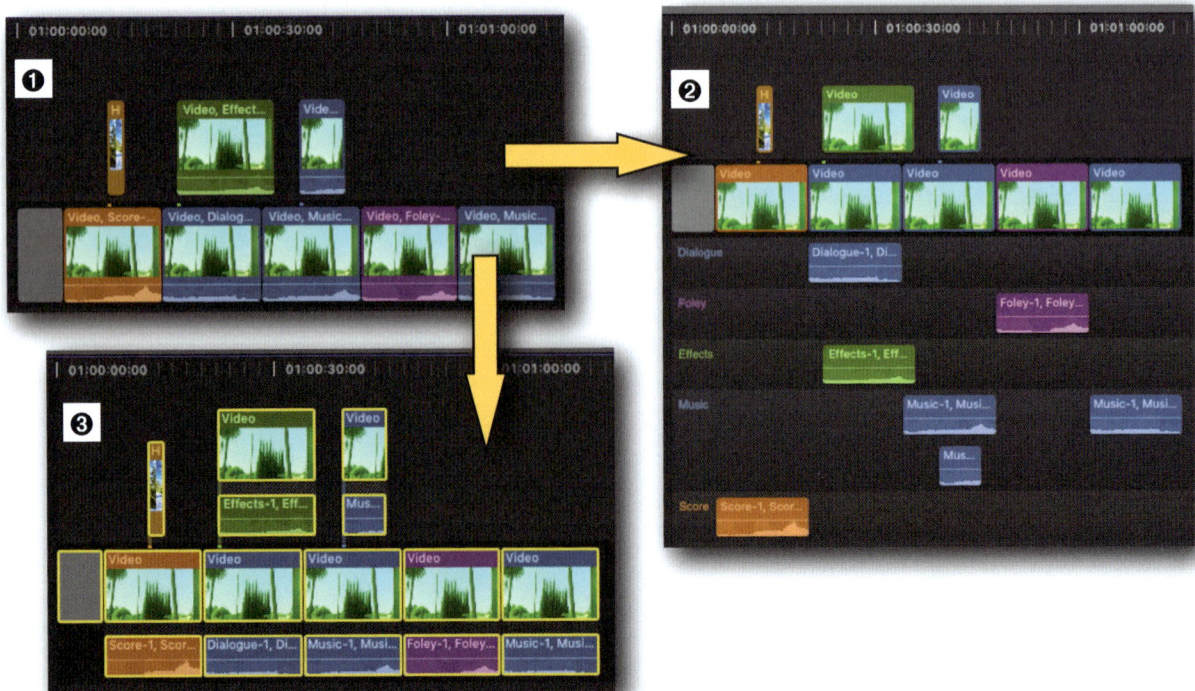

Focus Button

This is the one button we haven't talked about yet. It is very simple and very effective.

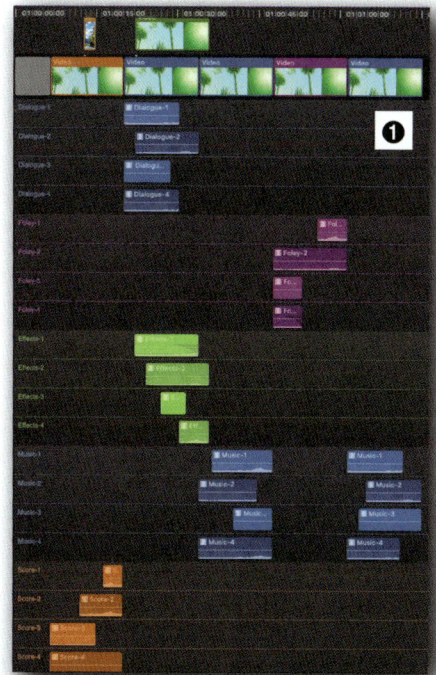

Here are two screenshots, one with the standard Timeline View ❶ (using Subrole Lanes) and the second screenshot ❷ where I enabled the Focus Button on the "Music" Role ❸.

- ▶ Whenever you have a lot of Clips in your Lower Timeline area (of course all assigned to Subroles), you can enable "Focus" for a specific Role (not Subroles) to better "focus" on the Clips belonging to that parent Main Role.
- ▶ All the non-focused Clips are minimized to small lines ❹ so the vertical space gets more manageable and only the focused Clips ❺ are displayed in their regular size.
- ▶ You still can edit the minimized Clips with the various Trim Tools ❻ and they even show the colored Edit Points.
- ▶ The Focus feature works on Lanes, but also if you don't use Lanes and just have a lot of Connected Clips going on in your Lower Timeline area.
- ▶ You can also enable Focus on more than one Role.

There are also click variations when using the usual modifier keys:

- 📌 **Click** to toggle the button. Any other Focus Button will be disabled
- 📌 **Sh+click** to enable or disable the button without affecting any other Focus Button
- 📌 **Ctr+opt+click** to disable all Focus Buttons

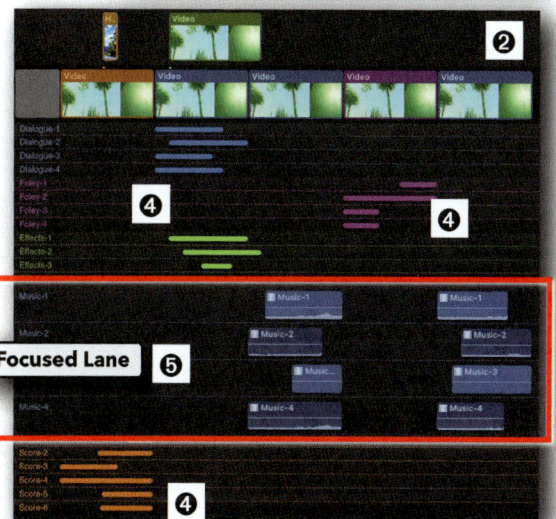

Lane Labels

A few things to note about the text label with the names for the Main Role Lanes or Subrole Lanes:

- ▶ The labels are always displayed on the left border ❼ of the visible Timeline Area.
- ▶ When scrolling horizontally in your timeline, those labels always stay fixed on that left border.
- ▶ If there are Clips at that location, then the label will be covered ❽.

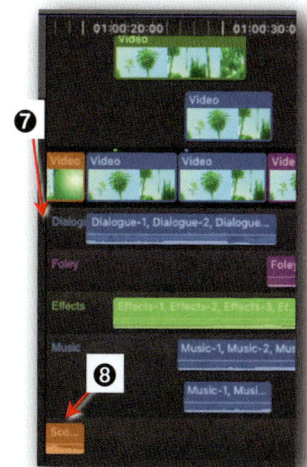

It's a Mixer

Many users are not happy that FCPx eliminated the conventional mixer layout and replaced it with the concept of Metadata. But what if I tell you that FCPx is still based on the same underlying concept of busses and routing like a standard mixer. The Metadata, especially Roles just add more flexibility to it.

Below is a signal flow diagram where I try to show how the Roles are nothing other than audio busses:

▶ As we have discussed already, when you create a new Library in FCPx, you can see in the Role Editor Dialog ❶ that it created three Main Roles (*Dialogue*, *Effects*, *Music*), each with a single Subrole (*Dialogue-1*, *Effects-1*, *Music*-1).

▶ Each of those Subroles represents a bus where you can route the audio signal to from any Clip. I call those "*Subrole Busses*" ❷.

▶ Each of the Main Roles is also represented by a bus. I call those "*Main Role Busses*" ❸.

▶ All those Main Role Busses are automatically routed to a Master Bus ❹, representing your main output that you hear ❺ when you play back your Project.

▶ Think of the Role Assignment on each Clip as an output routing ➕ to one of the *Subrole*

Busses. Changing the Role Assignment on a Clip means that you change the output routing of a Clip to a different Subrole Bus.

▶ Keep in mind that the Role Assignment is done on the Audio Component in a Clip, which means, each individual Audio Component can be routed to a different Subrole Bus ❻.

▶ Routing a Clip to a Subrole Bus will automatically route it to its parent Main Role Bus too.

▶ FCPx allows you to export the signal of ❼ any Subrole Bus or Main Role Bus with a quick selection in the Export Dialog (*cmd+E*).

▶ Please note that each bus in this diagram can represent a signal with one, two, or six audio channels depending on the Channel Format.

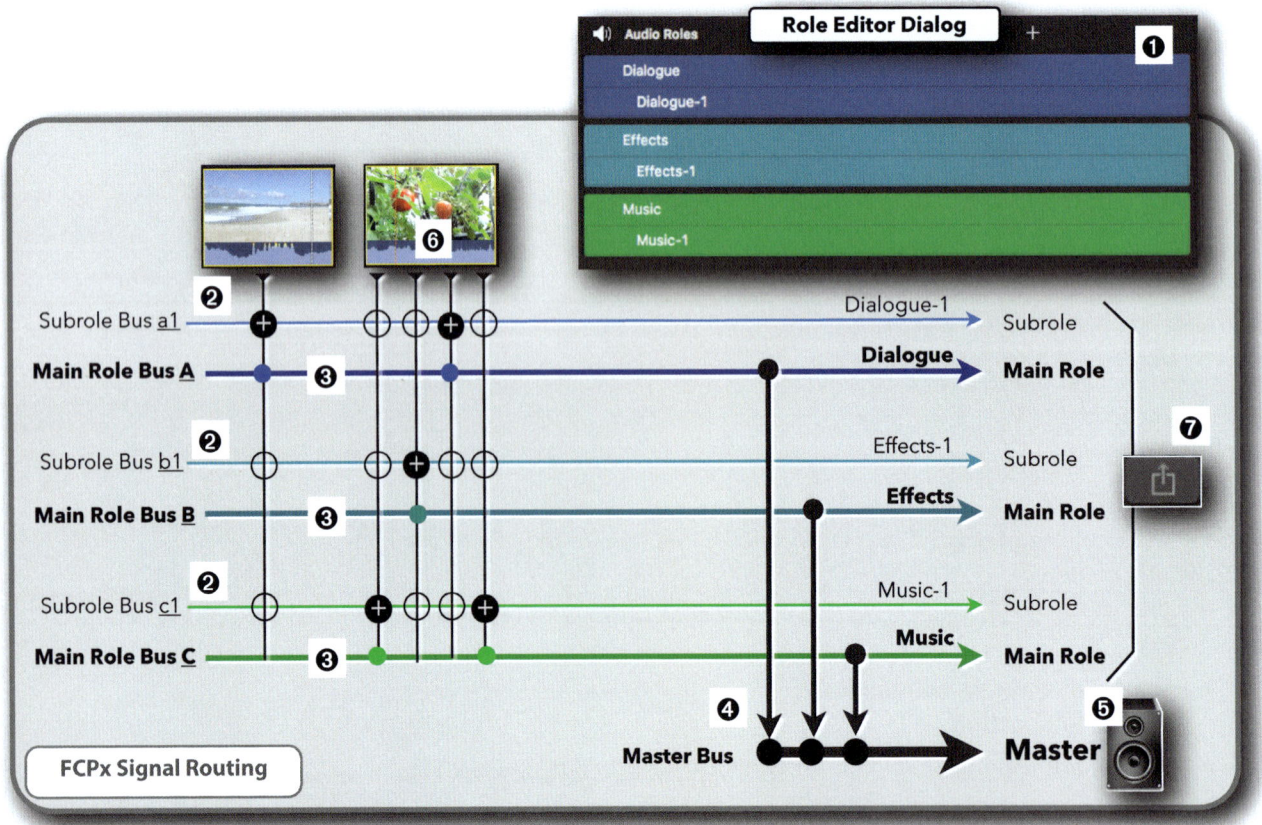

FCPx Signal Routing

➡ **Audio Components**

Here is an example that focuses on Audio Component Clips:

▶ The diagram shows three Clips, each one with a screenshot of the Audio Inspector, which displays the Audio Component Clips ❶ of the currently selected Clip.

▶ Remember, the waveform on top represents the Summed Audio Clip ❷, displaying the names of all the Roles that are assigned to its individual Audio Components.

▶ **Clip 1**: The first Clip ❸ has three Audio Component Clips that are assigned to three individual Subroles of the the same Main Role *Dialogue*. You see the routing to the appropriate three Busses ❹.

▶ **Clip 2**: The second Clip ❺ also has three Audio Component Clips. They are assigned to three individual Subroles of the same Main Role *Music*. You see the routing to the corresponding three Busses ❻.

▶ **Clip 3**: The third Clip ❼ is a little bit different. First of all, it has four Audio Component Clips, three of them are assigned to Subroles of the Main Role *Effects* ❽ and one is assigned to the Subrole *Music-2* ❾, which belongs to the Main Role Music.

💡 **Gray Colored Clip**

Look at Clip 3 again ❼. We already discussed the fact that, whenever the Audio Component Clips of a Clip don't belong to the same Main Role, then the Summed Audio Clip ❷ (the Timeline Clip or the Event Clip) turns gray. Now you can see the implication regarding the routing of those Audio Components. They are sent to different Main Role Busses ❽ ❾. This is something to pay attention to when exporting Roles or using Compound Clips for sub-mixing (creating stems).

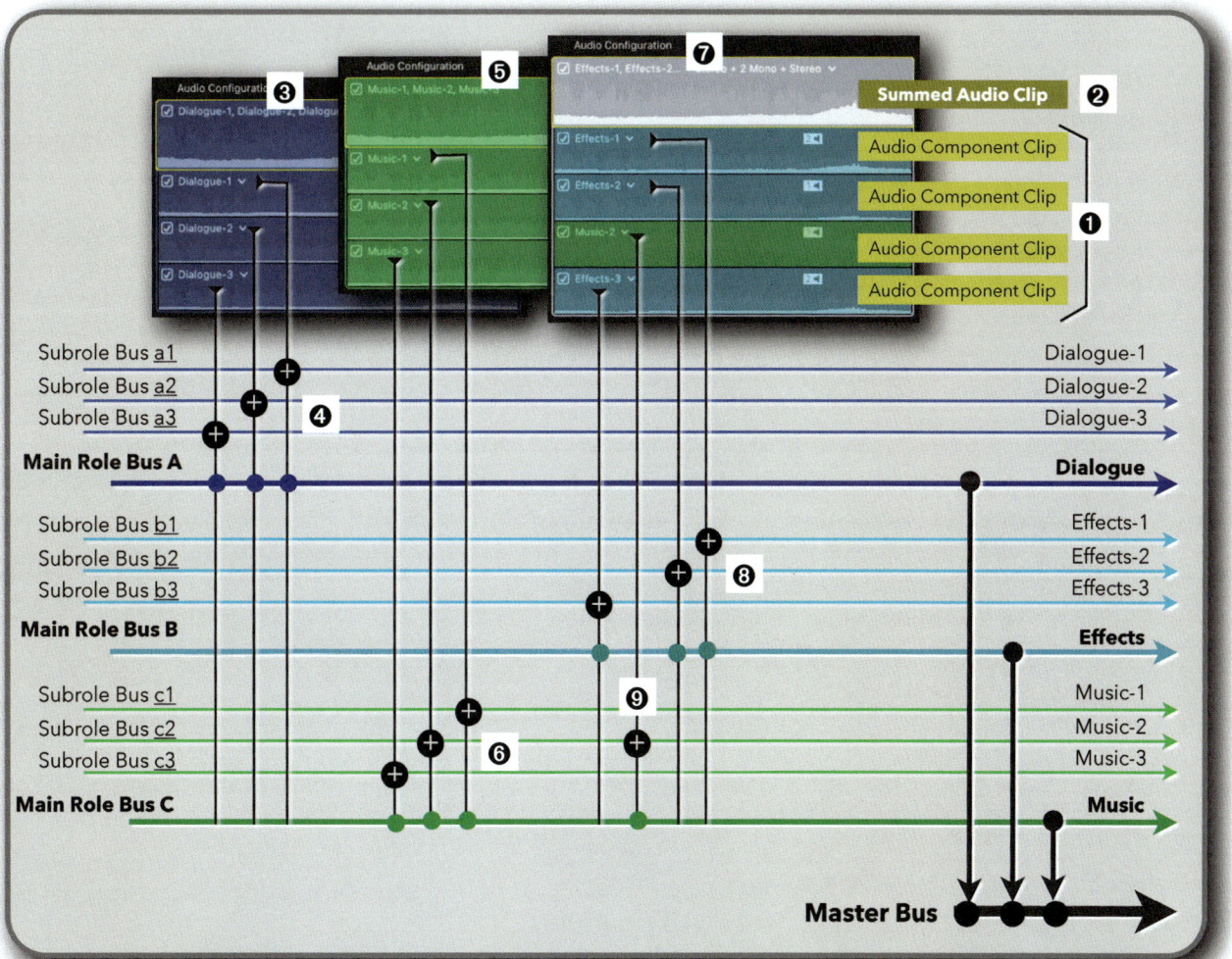

➡ *Channel Strips*

Now that we have the bus routing model of a mixer, let me add the Channel Strip model that I used in the Audio chapter to demonstrate the audio functionality inside a Clip. But first, we have to make two important modifications to that mixer model.

🔵 Simple Model

Here is a recap of the current model:

▸ Each Audio Component Clip inside a Standard Clip is represented by a Channel Strip ❶.

▸ Each Channel Strip has four Modules that you can access in the Audio Inspector ❷, *Audio Enhancements*, *Effects*, *Volume*, and the *Pan Module*.

▸ The output of each of those Channel Strips, the Audio Components Clips, feeds into a Master Channel Strip ❸, representing the Summed Audio Clip. This Channel Strip has three independent Modules (*Effects*, *Volume*, *Pan*) that let you adjust the summed signal of all Audio Component Clips.

▸ The output of the Summed Audio Clip is sent to the output of your Project together with the output of all other Clips in your Project.

🔵 Advanced Model

I make the following two adjustments for a more advanced model:

▸ **Output Routing**: As we have seen on the signal flow diagram, each Audio Component Clip can be routed individually to a Subrole Bus by selecting a Subrole ❹, representing that bus. Therefore, I add a fifth module on those Channel Strips, the Output Routing ❺, which is actually the Role Assignment Menu ❻ that you can access for each Audio Component Clip. For example, right on the Audio Component Clips 🔽 in the Audio Inspector ❹.

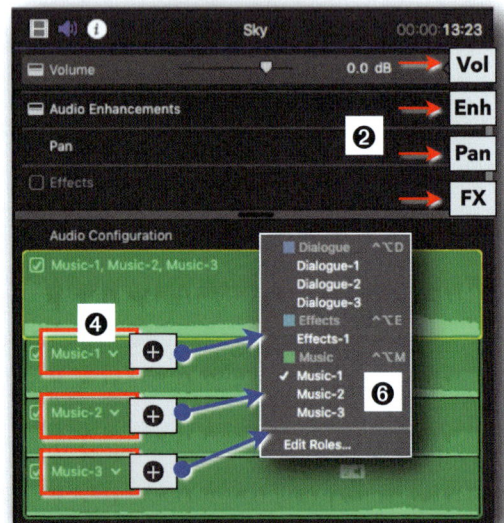

▸ **Summing Audio Clip**: In the simple model, I pretended that the Summing Audio Clip is a Channel Strip that sums ❸ all the outputs of the Clip's Audio Components. However, as we have seen on the signal flow diagram, each Audio Component can be routed individually to separate busses. In this advanced model, think of the Summed Audio Clip ❼ as a multi-channel signal processor. That means, the signal processing that you adjust on the Summed Audio Clip is applied to all signals coming from the Audio Components Clip ❺, going to the busses ❽. *Please note*, if you apply an Audio Effect ❾ 🟩 to the Summed Audio Clip, a Mixdown Badge ❿ 🔁 is added to the Summed Audio Clip if the Clip has more than one Audio Component. More about that later.

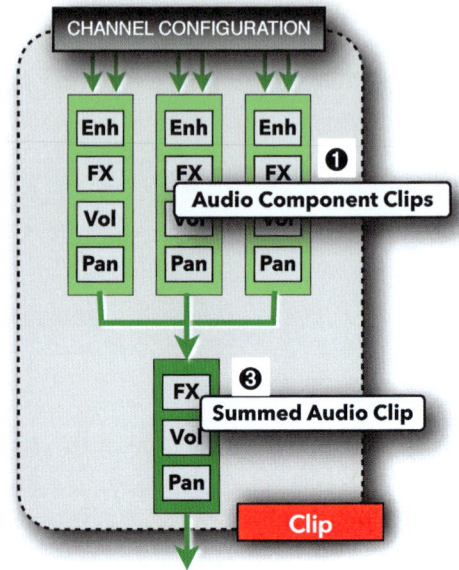

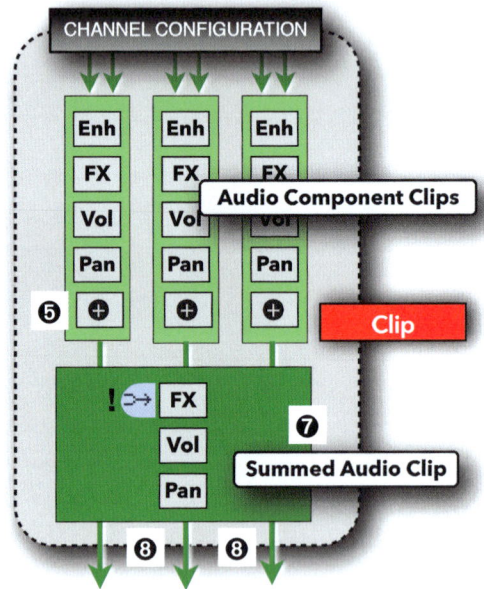

CHANNEL CONFIGURATION

Audio Component Clips ❶

Summed Audio Clip ❸

Clip

CHANNEL CONFIGURATION

Audio Component Clips

Clip ❺

Summed Audio Clip ❼

❽ ❽

Audio Inspector

➡ Complete Signal Flow Diagram

And here is the complete picture of the signal flow diagram with the example of a single Clip.

▸ The Source Media File ❶ contains the audio material in the form of a specific amount of Audio Channels.

▸ The Channel Configuration ❷ arranges the Audio Channels into groups called Audio Components (the Audio Component Clips).

▸ Each Audio Component Clip provides various modules ❸ to process the audio signal.

▸ The Role Assignment Menu ❹ lets you route the output of each Audio Component Clip to a specific Subrole Bus ❺ (Subrole) and FCPx automatically routes it to its parent Main Role Bus ❻ too, which is routed to the Master Bus ❼, and that's what you hear on your speakers ❽.

▸ The Summed Audio Clip also provides modules ❾ for further signal processing that affects all the signals coming from its Audio Component Clips ❿ on the way to the busses ❺ ❻.

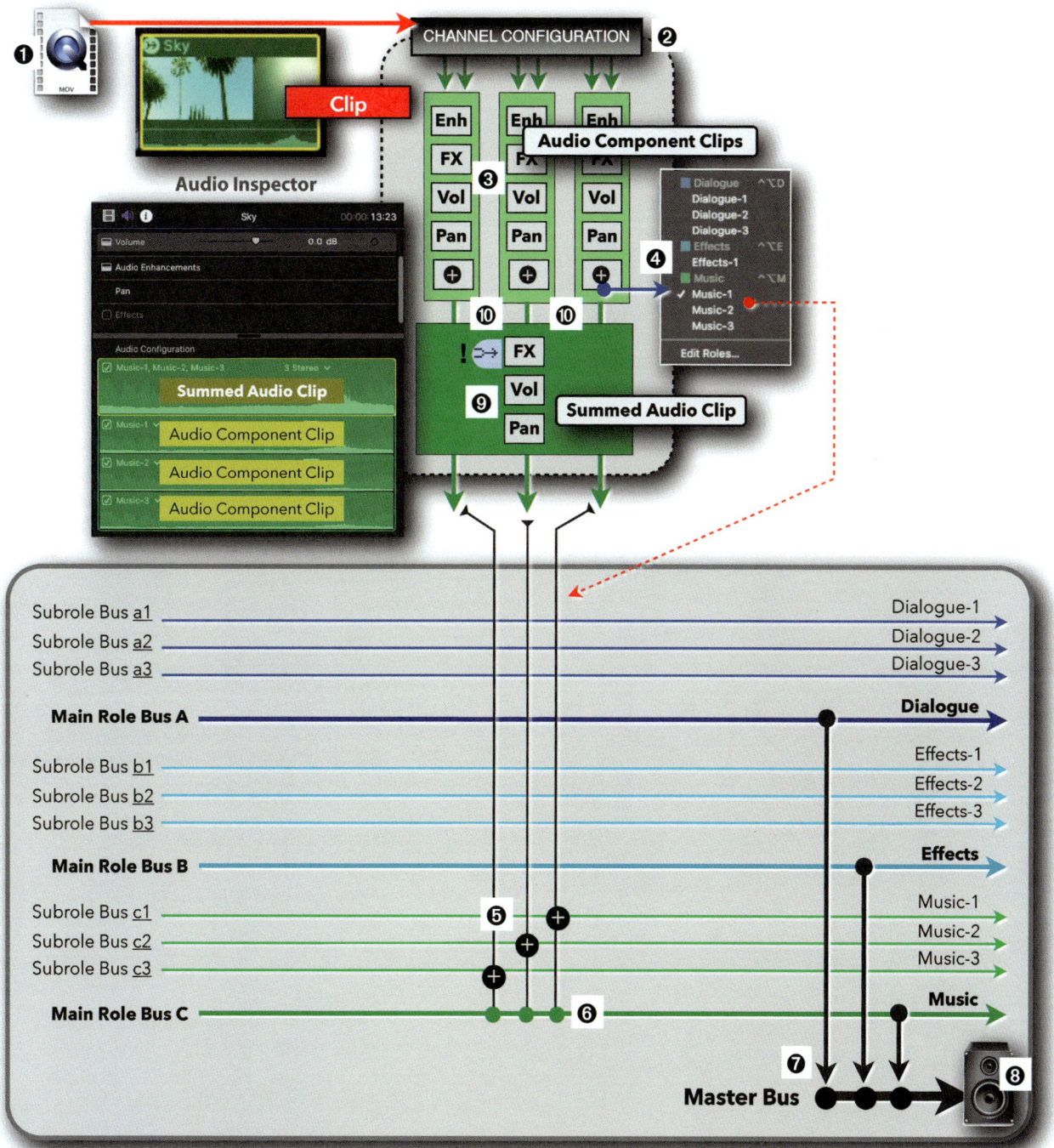

Compound Clips

I will cover the Compound Clips together with the other types of Clips (Multicam Clip, Synchronized Clip, Audition Clip, etc.) later in the Clips chapter. However, I want to discuss this special type of Clip here in the Roles chapter, because it provides some very powerful features regarding Roles.

➡ Roles - Compound Clips - Signal Routing

There are only a few settings when using Roles with Compound Clips, but their "consequences" are quite dramatic. For example, changing a selection in a popup menu reroutes the signal flow under the hood without any obvious indication of what just happened. For the proper understanding, I will explain those "consequences" step-by-step on the next few pages with an example.

⚫ #1 - Standard Clips

Here is a simple example of a Timeline Project with seven Clips ❶:

▸ Each Clip is assigned to one of five Subroles (*Sam*, *Bob*, *Rock*, *Pop*, *Folk*) ❷.

▸ These are the five Subroles belonging to the two parent Main Roles *Dialogue* (blue) and *Music* (green).

▸ The signal flow diagram shows the standard routing. Every Clip is routed (by the Role Assignment) to a specific Subrole Bus ❷, which is automatically routed to its parent Main Role Bus ❸. All the Main Role Busses are automatically routed to the Master Bus ❹, and

that is what you hear when playing back your project ❺.

▸ The Export feature in FCPx ❻ lets you export individual Roles. That means, you can export the signals on a specific Subrole Bus, which means, export only the Clips that are assigned to that Subrole, for example, *Bob*, *Sam*, or *Rock*, etc. Or you can export all the signals on a Main Role Bus to export the audio of all the Clips belonging to the parent Main Role *Dialog* (*Bob* and *Sam*) or *Music* (*Rock*, *Pop*, *Folk*).

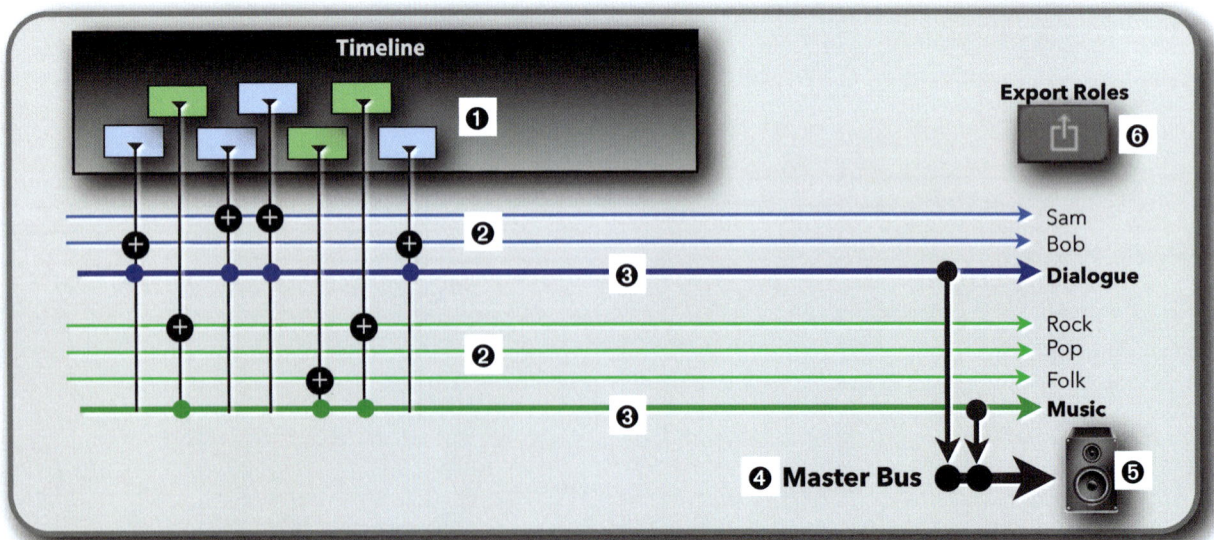

No Level Controls on Busses

There is one problem in this setup. Once a Clip is routed to a bus, there is no level control anymore along the bus routing (Subrole Bus ❷, Main Role Bus ❸, Master Bus ❹). If you want to adjust, for example, the level of all Clips assigned to *Bob*, or adjust all the Clips belonging to the parent Main Role *Music*, you have to do that in each individual Clip ... unless you use Compound Clips.

🌑 #2 - Compound Clips (Role Components)

In this example, I selected all seven Clips and made a Compound Clip (*opt+G*). This replaces all seven Clips on the Timeline with a single Clip, the Compound Clip. In this diagram, we concentrate on the changes regarding the audio signal routing:

▶ **Role Assignments**: The Role Assignment of the individual Clips ❶ enclosed in the Compound Clip did not change.

▶ **CC Busses**: The Compound Clip creates its own busses for each Subrole that is used by its enclosed Clips. I call them "CC Busses" ❷.

▶ **CC Main Busses**: Those CC Busses are routed to (what I call) "*CC Main Busses*" ❸ that, again, only exists inside the Compound Clip.

▶ **Compound Clip**: Those *CC Main Busses* function as the audio input of that Compound Clip ❹. The same way I used a Channel Strip model to demonstrate what is going on inside a Standard Clip, I can also use that model for a Compound Clip to better demonstrate its functionality.

▶ **Role Component Clip**: In the Standard Clip, you had one or multiple Channel Strips that

represented the Audio Components. In the Compound Clip, each *CC Main Bus* ❸ is represented by a single Channel Strip called a "Role Component" ❺. In this example, we have the Role Components, *Dialogue* and *Music*.

▶ **Summed Roles Clip**: Like with the Standard Clip where all Audio Components are controlled by the Summed <u>Audio</u> Clip, in the Compound Clip, all the Role Components are processed by the Summed <u>Roles</u> Clip ❻.

▶ **Additional Subrole Busses**: Each *CC Main Bus* that is going through its individual Role Component ❺, is routed to a newly created Subrole Bus ❼ named after the Main Role (*Dialogue* and *Music*), which is automatically routed onto its regular Main Role Bus ❽ of the Project.

As you can see, now you have a separate audio control (Channel Strip ❺) for each Main Role (Role Component) and even a control (Channel Strip) for the sum of both Main Roles ❻ (Summed Role Clip).

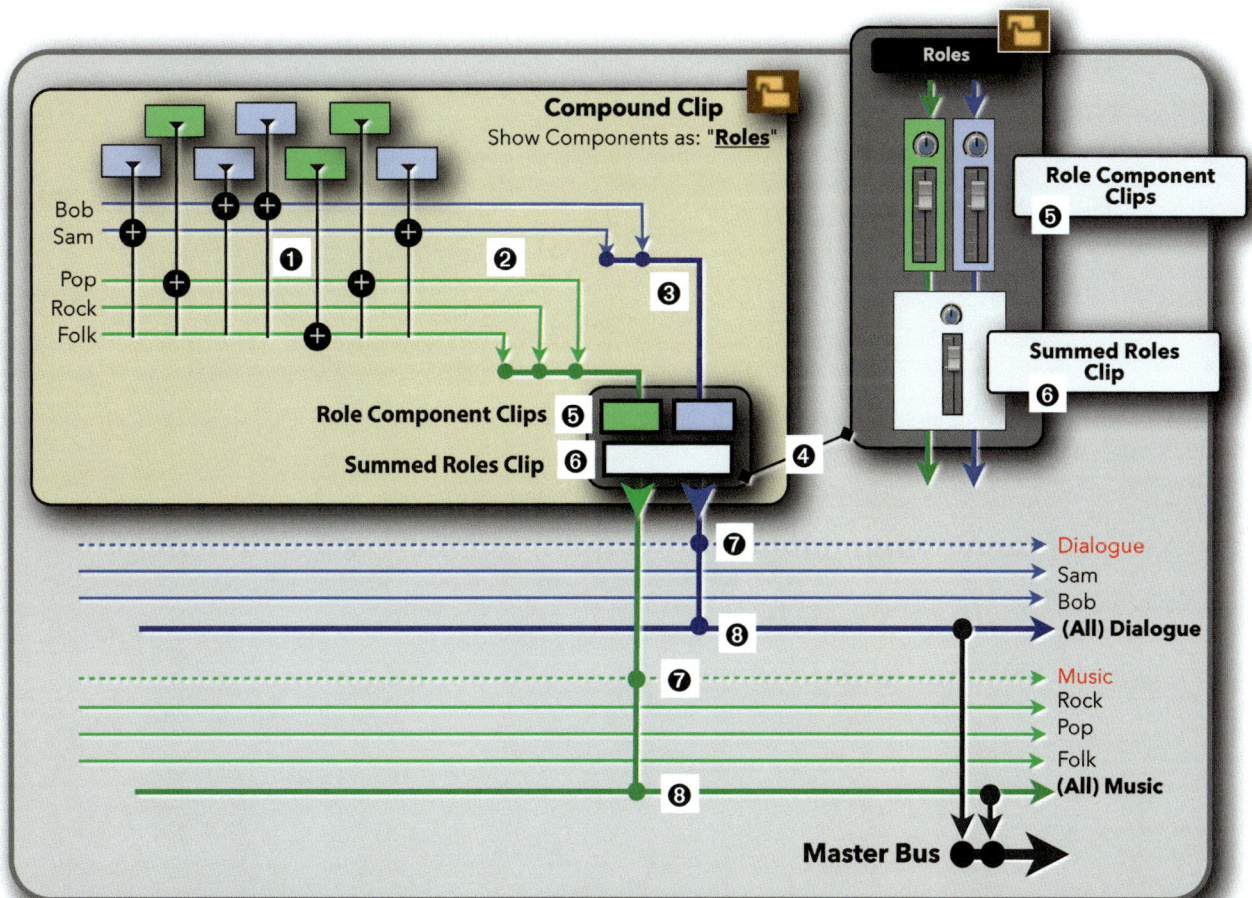

💀 #3 - Compound Clips (Subrole Components)

Here is another twist:

"Show Components as"

The diagram I just showed is only one of two ways a Compound Clip can route the audio of its embedded Clips. When you select the Compound Clip and display it in the Audio Inspector, you can see that little popup menu ❶ in the upper-right corner of the Summed Role Clip (the top waveform) that looks like the Channel Configuration Menu. Here, it determines what type of Components to use, *Roles* or *Subroles* ❷.

The diagram on the previous page showed the configuration where each individual <u>Main Role</u> (used inside the Compound Clip) is represented by a Component Clip. In this case, when selecting "Subroles" ❷, each individual <u>Subrole</u> (used in the Compound Clip) is represented by a Component Clip.

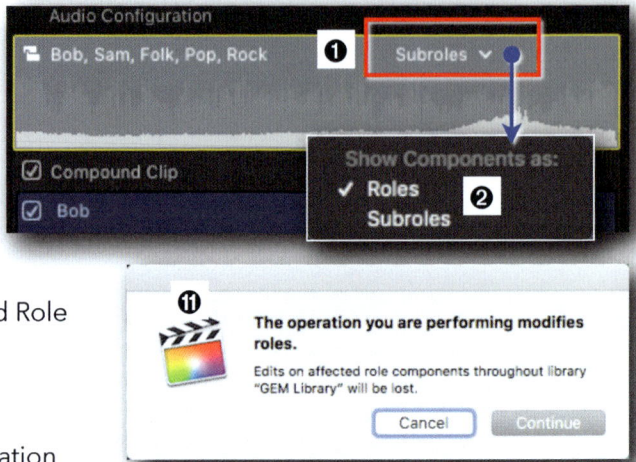

- ▸ **Role Assignments**: The Role Assignment of the individual Clips ❸ enclosed in the Compound did not change.

- ▸ **CC Busses**: Again, the Compound Clip creates its own internal busses for each Subrole that is used by its enclosed Clips, the "CC Busses" ❹.

- ▸ **Subrole Component Clip**: Now each of the *CC Busses* is routed to Subrole Component Clips ❺ inside the Compound Clip. Of course, each one represents a Channel Strip ❻ with full audio processing controls over those audio signals.

- ▸ **Summed Roles Clip**: All those Subrole Components are processed by the Summed Roles Clip ❼ with its own signal processing modules.

- ▸ **Bus Routing**: The output of each Subrole Component Clip ❺ is routed directly to its corresponding Subrole Bus ❾ (Bob, Sam, Rock, etc.) and also to its parent Main Role Bus ❿, which are routed to the Master Bus.

Switching the option between Roles and Subroles prompts a Warning Dialog ⓫ that any edits on the Role Components will be lost.

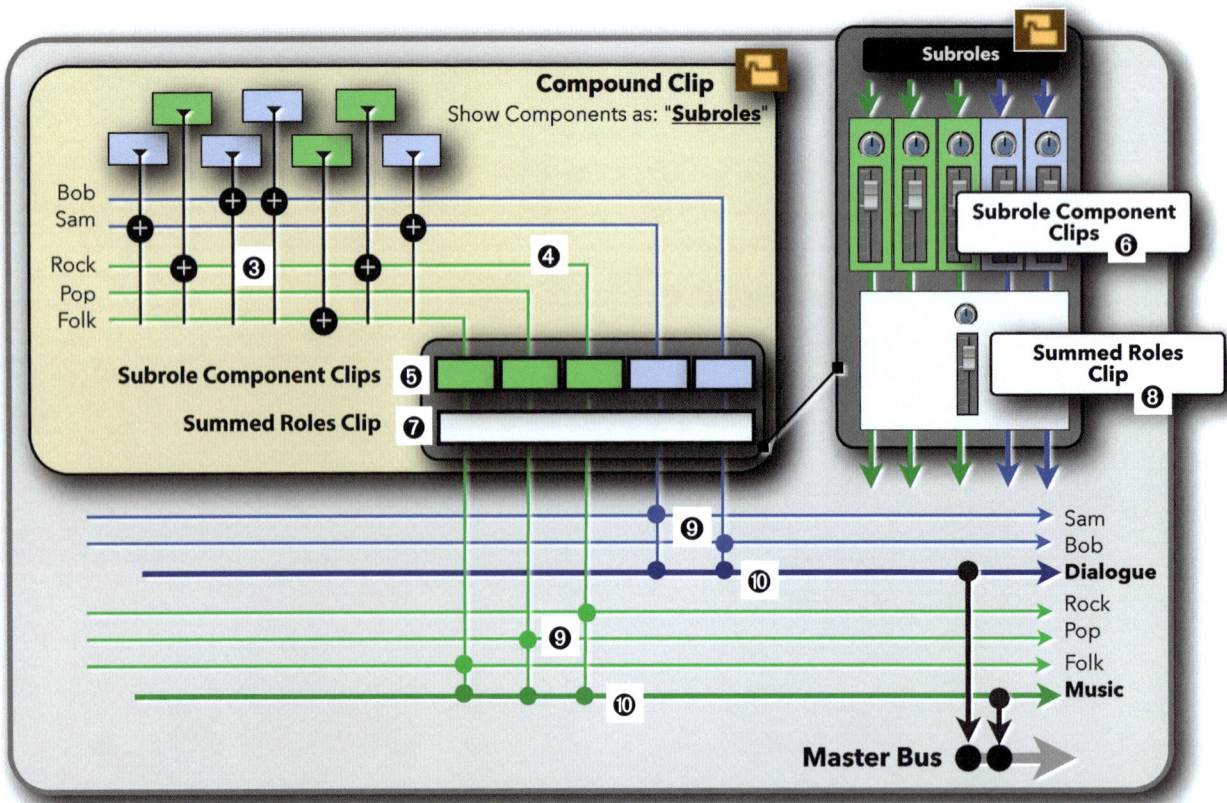

➡ *Audio Inspector*

Here is another look at the Audio Configuration section in the Audio Inspector.

▶ **Show Components as**: The little popup menu in the upper-right corner of the Clip in the Audio Inspector can have two functions:

- Standard Clip ❶: The popup menu shows all the available Channel Configurations that determine the amount of Audio Components in that Clip.

- Compound Clip: The popup menu lets you switch between Roles Components ❷ and Subroles Components ❸ as we just discussed.

▶ **Gray Summed Clip**: The Summed Clip turns gray if the Components in that Clip belong to different parent Main Roles.

▶ **Summed Roles Clip**: The Summed Roles Clip doesn't have an on/off checkbox like the Summed Audio Clip. Instead, the section has an additional row underneath with the label

"*Compound Clip*" ❹ that has a checkbox to mute that Compound Clip. The Compound Clip icon ❻ 🔲 on the header also tells you that this it as a Compound Clip.

▶ **Roles Assignment**: Please note that for Compound Clips there is no popup menu ❼ selection for the Role Assignment next to the Component names. As we have seen on the previous signal flow diagram, these are fixed routings. However, you can "open" a Compound Clip and change the Role Assignment of its enclosed Clips ❽.

▶ **Channel Strips**: Always keep in mind that each Clip, the Component Clips ❾ and the Summed Clip ❿, represent Channel Strips. Click on the Clip and the Audio Inspector displays all the available signal processing controls above for that specific Clip.

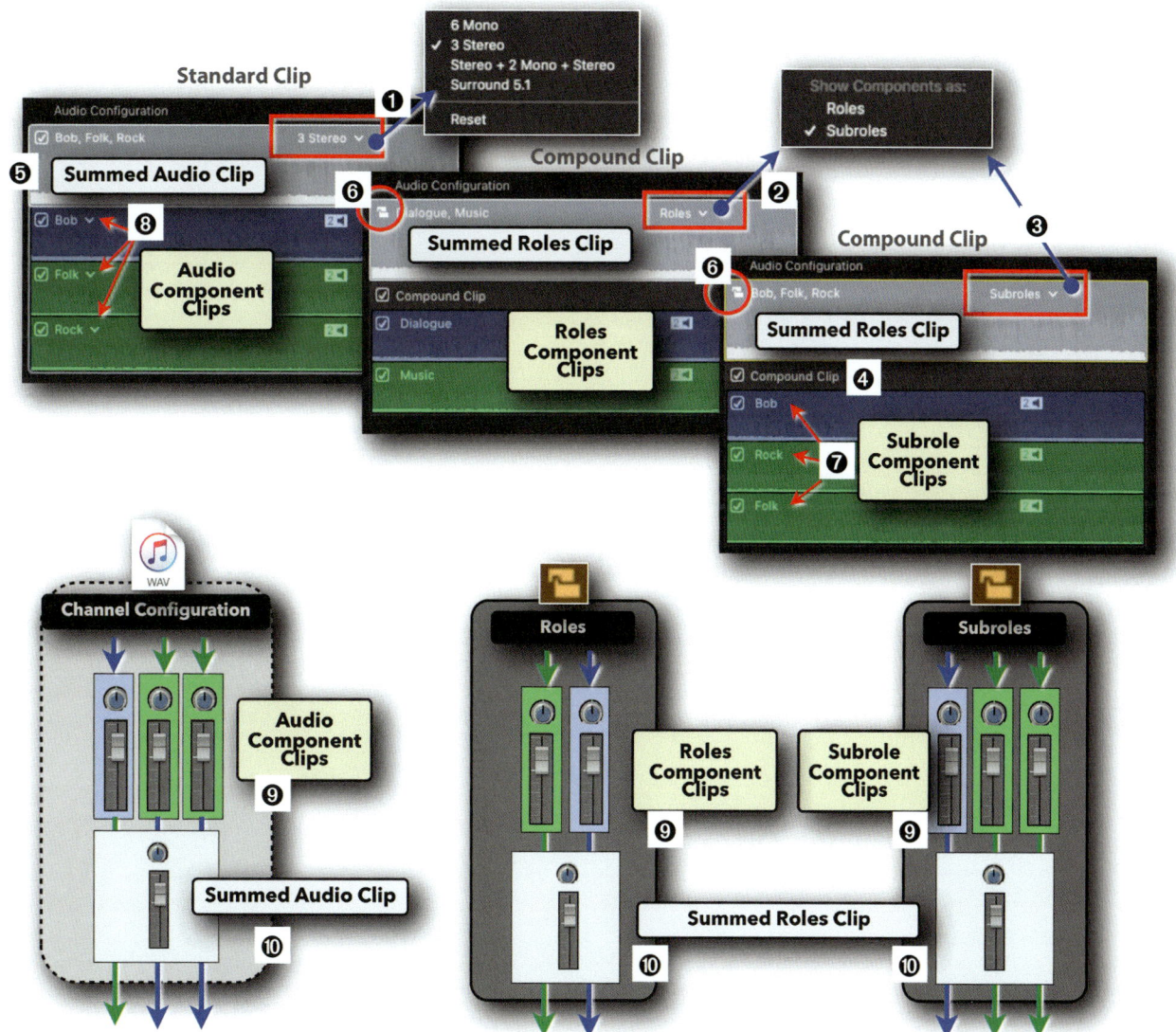

➡ Indicators

There are so many possible variations with different types of Clips, different Role assignments, and configurations that it becomes very important to quickly identify the little interface "hints" to see what is going on in your Project.

Here are just a few examples to point out the various badges, different color indications, and important elements.

👤 Example 1 - FX Badge

This example is a Compound Clip, indicated by the Compound Clip icon ❶ 🖻. It has three Subroles Component Clips with two of them having Effects loaded, which is indicated by the FX Badge ❷ [FX] on those Clips ❷.

👤 Example 2 - Mixdown Badge

This is the same Clip, but instead of having Effects loaded on the Component Clips, now I have loaded an Effect on the Summed Roles Clip, indicated by the FX Badge ❸ [FX] The Mixdown Badge ❹ ⇢ (more on that on the next pages) appears in three places, the Effects Module, the Summed Component Clip, and the Clip on the Timeline ⇢.

Another little change is that instead of the individual Subroles (*Folk*, *Pop*, *Rock*), the Main Role *Music* is displayed on the header of the Summed Clip.

This procedure also applies to Standard Clips.

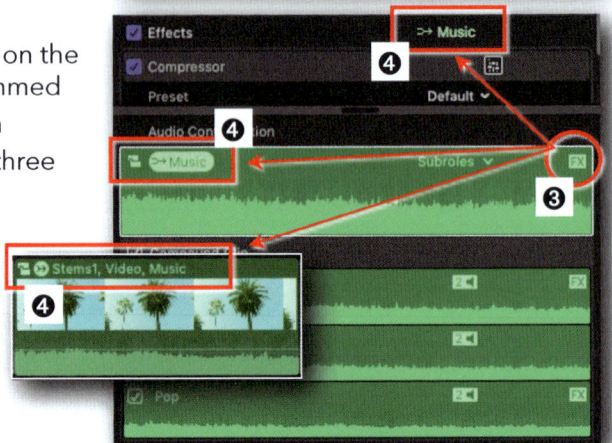

👤 Example 3 - Gray Clips

In this example, no Effects have been applied yet, but the Components now belong to different parent Main Roles. This is indicated by the gray color of the Summed Roles Clip ❺ and the the gray color of the Timeline Clip ❻ (and Event Clip).

This gray color indication also happens with Standard Clips that have Audio Components belonging to different parent Main Roles.

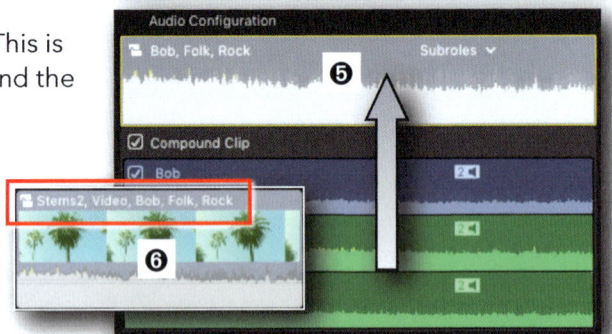

👤 Example 4 - "Mixed Audio"

Now with this "gray" Clip, when I add an Effect on the Summed Role Clip ❼ [FX] I will see the Mixdown Badge ❽ ⇢ as expected. However, something else changed. The name of the Main Role is not *Music*, because the Components belong to *Music* and *Dialogue*. Instead of listing both names, FCPx creates a new Main Role named "*Mixed Audio*" (maybe the term "Mixed Roles" would be more obvious).

There is one more little detail. If you open the Roles Assignment Menu from the Timeline Clip, you will see a new Main Role in the popup menu "Mixed Audio" ❾. This is technically the (made up) Role assigned for that Compound Clip. In case you wonder, this "new" Role is not displayed in the Role Editor.

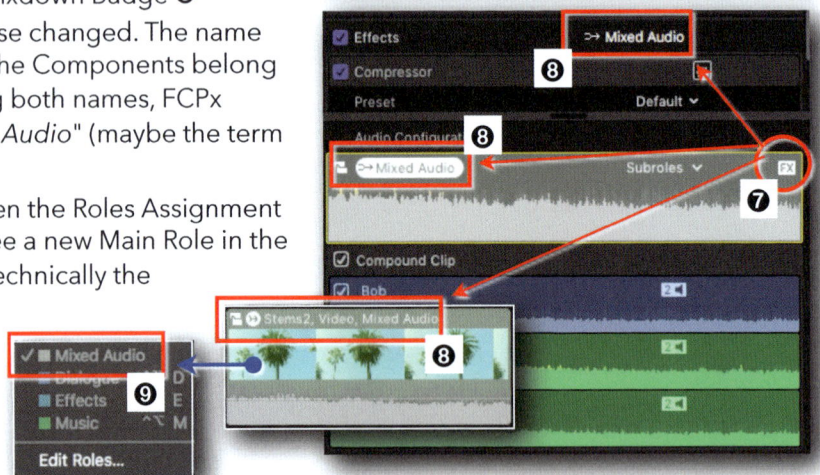

➡ Compound Clips and Lanes

Compound Clips behave a little bit different with Lanes. Here is an example with four Clips to demonstrate that:

🔘 ⬜ off ⬜ off: **No Lanes ❹**

- ▸ **❶ Clip 1**: This is a Standard Clip with three Audio Components assigned to Dialogue Roles (blue).
- ▸ **❷ Clip 2**: This is a Standard Clip with three Audio Components assigned to Music Roles (green).
- ▸ **❸ Clip 3**: This is a Compound Clip 🗀 containing two Clips, one of the Clips has three Audio Components assigned to Dialogue Roles (green) and the other Clip has three Audio Components assigned to Music Roles (blue). That's why the Clip on the Primary Storyline is gray. The Compound Clip is set to "Roles Components" in the Audio Inspector.
- ▸ **❹ Clip 4**: This is the same Compound Clip 🗀 but this one is set to "Subroles Components".

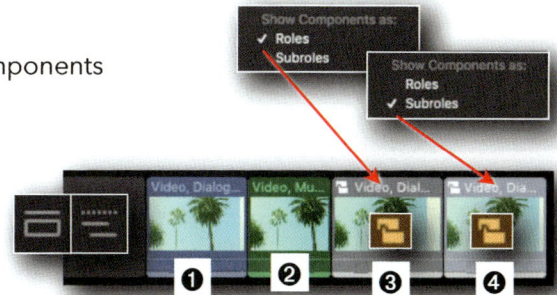

🔘 ⬜ on ⬜ off: **Show Main Role Lanes**

- ▸ **Standard Clip**: FCPx creates a separate Lane for each Main Role ❺ (Dialogue, Music), names them after those Main Roles, and places all <u>Summed Audio Clips</u> on their corresponding Lane based on their Role assignment.
- ▸ **Compound Clip (Roles Components)**: The Roles Components 🎞❻ are displayed on the Main Role Lanes.
- ▸ **Compound Clip (Subrole Components)**: All the Subrole Components 🎞❼ are placed (stacked!) on the Main Role Lanes.

🔘 ⬜ on ⬜ on: **Show Subrole Lanes**

- ▸ **Standard Clip**: FCPx creates a separate Lane for each Subrole ❽, names them after those Subroles, and places all <u>Audio Component Clips</u> 🎞 on their corresponding Lane based on their Role assignment.
- ▸ **Compound Clip (Role Components)**: The Roles Components 🎞❾ are still displayed on the Main Role Lanes ❿.

  Attention: Please note that here is an exception. Usually, FCPx only shows the Subrole Lanes and not the Main Role ❿ Lanes when the Subrole Lanes ❽ button is enabled.
- ▸ **Compound Clip (Subrole Components)**: Subrole Components 🎞⓫ are displayed on their individual Subrole Lanes.

Final Signal Flow Model

One last thing. So far, I introduced two models in the form of slightly different diagrams to describe the "signal routing" inside a Clip in FCPx. I also presented a bus routing scheme to describe what happens with the overall signal in your Project. If FCPx had a standard mixer interface with the common buttons and controls found on a real mixer, then the whole signal flow would be much easier to follow and to understand. Instead, the entire signal flow is based on Metadata. Yes, this makes it much more flexible and powerful, but at the same time, more difficult and complex (as you might have noticed by now).

The reason I use different models and not just one, is the difficulty to demonstrate the functionality with a simple diagram. First of all, different models help to demonstrate the functionality of a specific aspect, while "leaving aside" other aspects of the big picture, but also, while I try to unfold the signal flow in FCPx, I found it necessary to introduce the elements step-by-step. Now, that we gathered all the bits and pieces together, I want to introduce a final third model that combines all.

🔵 Model 1 - Clip Signal Flow

This was the first mode I used to introduce the signal flow "inside" a single Clip. We learned that each Clip contains one or multiple Audio Components ❶ with various Modules to process the audio signals (similar to Channel Strips) that are routed to a Summed Audio Clip ❷ (like a submix Channel Strip) with its own Modules to process the summed signal.

🔵 Model 2 - Component Clip Routing

The first model didn't show the details about the output routing. In this Roles chapter, we learned that you can assign each Component to a specific Subrole that functions as an output bus. This model illustrates that with the additional routing module ❸ on the Channel Strip. However, now we have to think of the Summed Audio Clip as one big Channel Strip ❹. Each audio signal (coming from the Components ❸) will have the same setting (that you adjust in the Audio Inspector for the Summed Audio Clip ❹) applied, when going through that Summed Audio Clip before reaching its bus ❺.

🔵 Model 3 - Summing Clip Routing

This is the final model that explains the signal routing we discussed earlier:

▸ The Summed Audio Clip is still considered a single unit ❻ with its controls available in the Audio Inspector.

▸ Think of the "inside" of that single unit (Summed Audio Clip) as parallel signal paths running through. Each one is coming from an individual Component output feeding into the Summed Audio Clip. The diagram shows individual Channel Strips ❼ for each path.

▸ The controls on those Channel Strips, no matter how many signal paths, are <u>linked together</u>. That means, the Audio Inspector shows only one control (i.e. Volume), but that value is applied to each individual signal path ❼.

▸ The individual outputs of those signal paths ❽ on the Summed Audio Clip are routed to their assigned Subrole Busses.

▸ The output of all Components are summed together and create an additional signal path (linked Channel Strip ❾) with its output routed to the Main Role Bus ❿ representing the Component's parent Main Role.

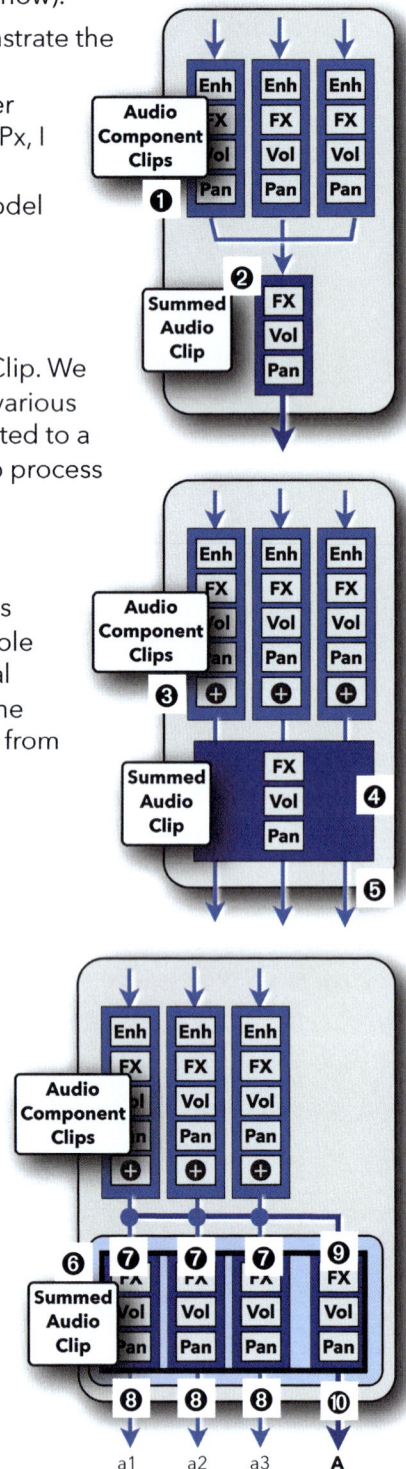

➡ *Mixdown Badge*

Now let's use the model 3 and demonstrate some of the advanced functionality to understand what is actually going on under the hood.

🌑 #1 - Single Audio Component

This is the most basic configuration of a Standard Clip. The signal that is going to the Subrole Bus (a1) ❶ is the same as the one going to the Main Role Bus (A) ❷.

🌑 #2 - Multiple Audio Components

Each of the three individual Components is routed to a Subrole Bus (a1, a2, a3) ❸ and the sum of all Components is routed to the Main Role Bus (A) ❹.

🌑 #3 - Multiple Audio Components + Summed FX

This is the same setup, but now I have added an Effect to the Summed Audio Clip. As we have learned already, this will add the Mixdown Badge ➻ ❺ to the Clip. Based on the model I use, there is technically no difference regarding the routing, with or without FX. However, the difference regarding the processing could be quite substantial. For example, if you added a Compressor or Limiter and export the Main Role and the individual Subroles, then mixing all the individual Subroles together later is not the same as the (summed) Main Role!

🌑 #4 - Mixed Audio Components

In this example, the Audio Components are routed to Subroles (a1, a3, b1) that belong to different parent Main Roles (**A**, **B**). As we have already learned, the Clip turns gray to indicate that. The signal flow inside the Summed Audio Clip has changed. You have a signal chain that sums all the Components belonging to the Main Role **A** ❻ and all that belong to Main Role **B** ❼.

🌑 #5 - Mixed Audio Components + Summed FX

As you can see in this example, adding an FX to the Summed Audio Clip doesn't change the signal flow. Please note that this scenario is indicated by three things:

☑ Clip is gray ❽

☑ Mixdown Badge ➻ ❾ is displayed on the Clip

☑ The Clip is assigned to a new Main Role "Mixed Audio" ❿ that is displayed in the Roles Assignment popup menu

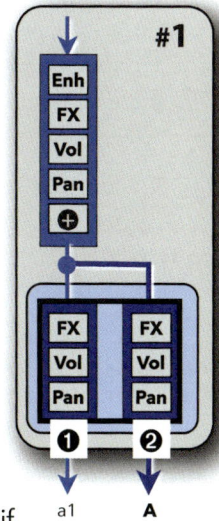

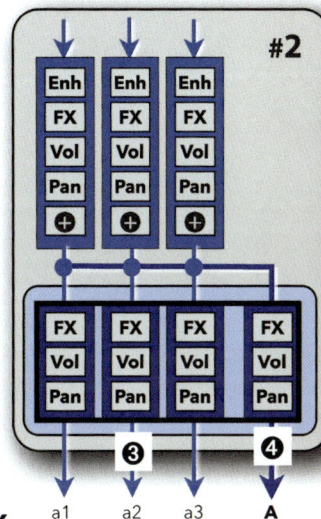

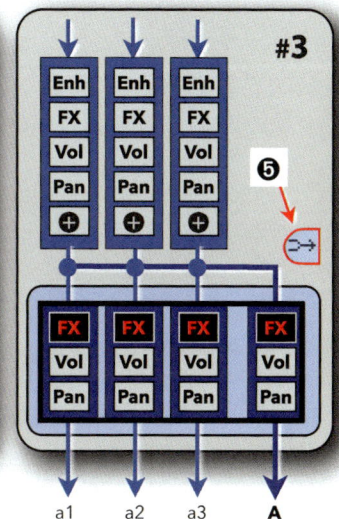

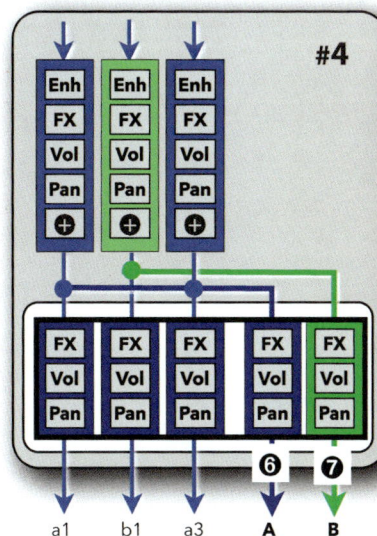

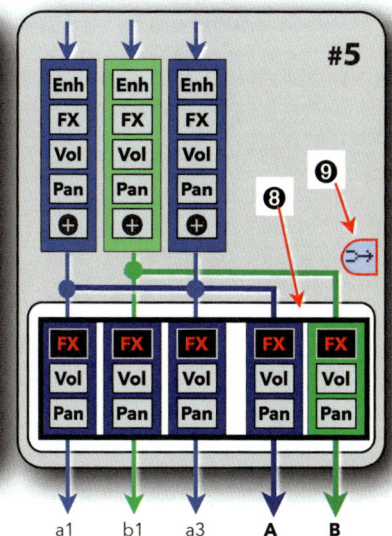

Roles Assignment Menu

➡ *The Complete Picture*

Here is the final diagram that shows everything connected together. Now you can follow the individual signals to see what elements they "go through".

▸ I have three Clips. One with a single Audio Component ❶, one with three Audio Components ❷, and one with three Audio Components belonging to different parent Main Roles ❸.

▸ The output of the Audio Components that represent an individual signal path inside the Summed Audio Clip will be routed onto the Subrole Bus ❹ according to their individual Role Assignment ❺.

▸ Remember, on the earlier diagrams I showed that each Clip was also automatically routed to the parent Main Role Bus ❻. Now you can see where that signal is coming from. It is the output of the signal path ❼ that sums the output of all the Audio Components in that Clip together.

▸ The third Clip is assigned to Subroles belonging to different parent Main Roles and, therefore, you have two signal paths ❽ representing those summed signals. These are the two signals that are automatically routed to each Main Role Bus ❻.

▸ When you open the Share Dialog (***cmd+E***) 🔲 and select a destination for exporting individual Roles (see the Export chapter for details), you have a popup menu with different options ❾. These are exactly those busses you see in the diagram ❿, the available Subrole Busses and the available Main Role Busses (marked with the label. "All").

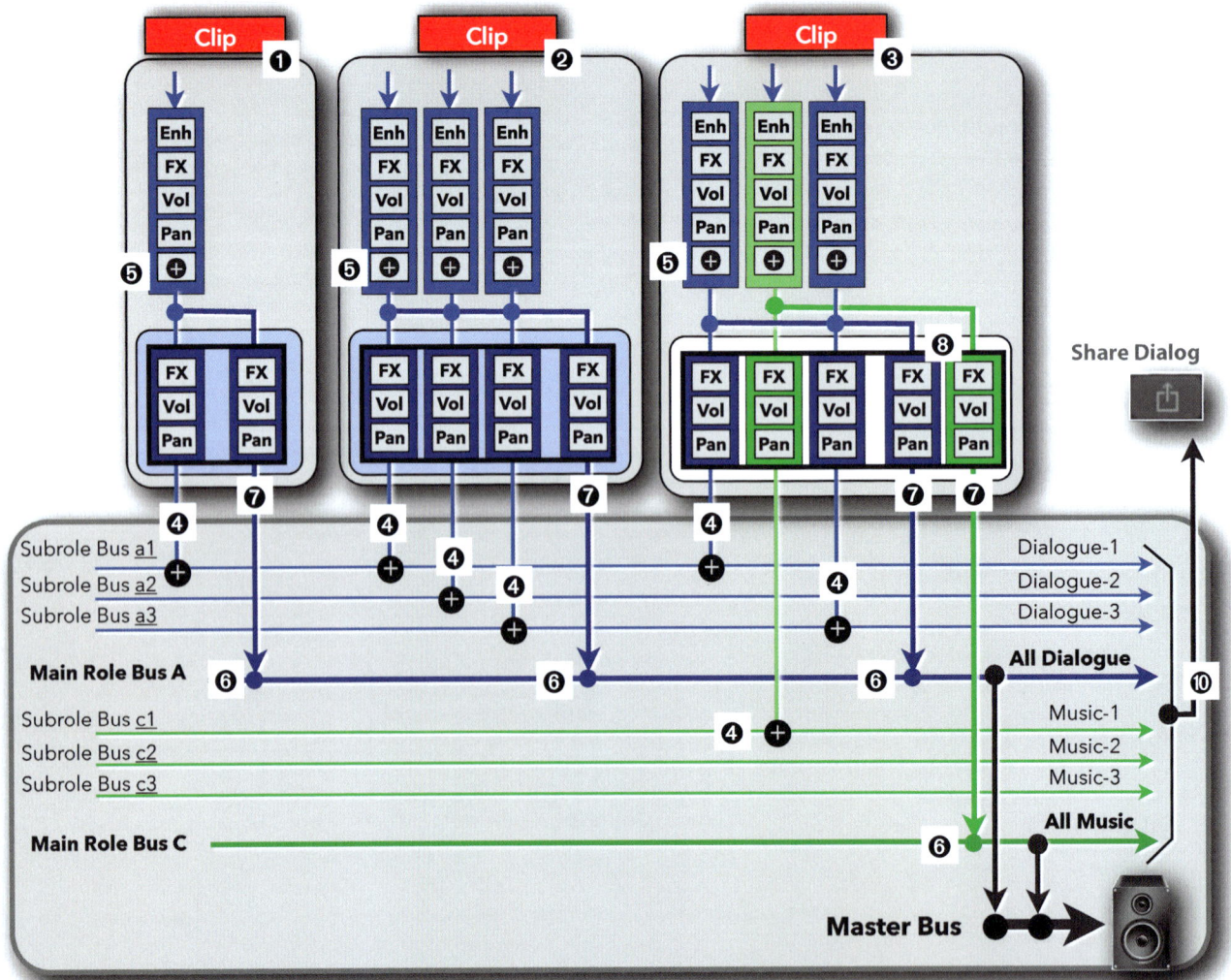

Share Dialog

Export Roles

The main elements we use in FCPx to create our video are Clips. However, FCPx uses a lot of different types of Clips for different purposes and, in this chapter, we will look at what they are, how they differ, and what they can be used for.

Standard Clips

Although the term "Clip" can be used for any of those types of Clips, most likely it refers to the most common and most used type of Clip, the so-called **Standard Clip**.

Here is a quick review about the Standard Clip:

☑ A Standard Clip is referenced to a single Source Media File on your drive and is created when importing that file.

☑ The Source Media File can be an image file ❶, a video file ❷, or an audio file ❸.

☑ Depending on the media file, the Clip can have either video content ❹, audio content ❺, or both ❻ ❼.

☑ Regardless of the content, the Standard Clip is displayed as a single Clip showing the content (video frame ❹ ❻ and/or audio waveform ❺ ❼) on its thumbnail image.

☑ A Standard Clip can appear in the Browser Pane as an Event Clip ❽ and in the Timeline Pane as a Timeline Clip ❾.

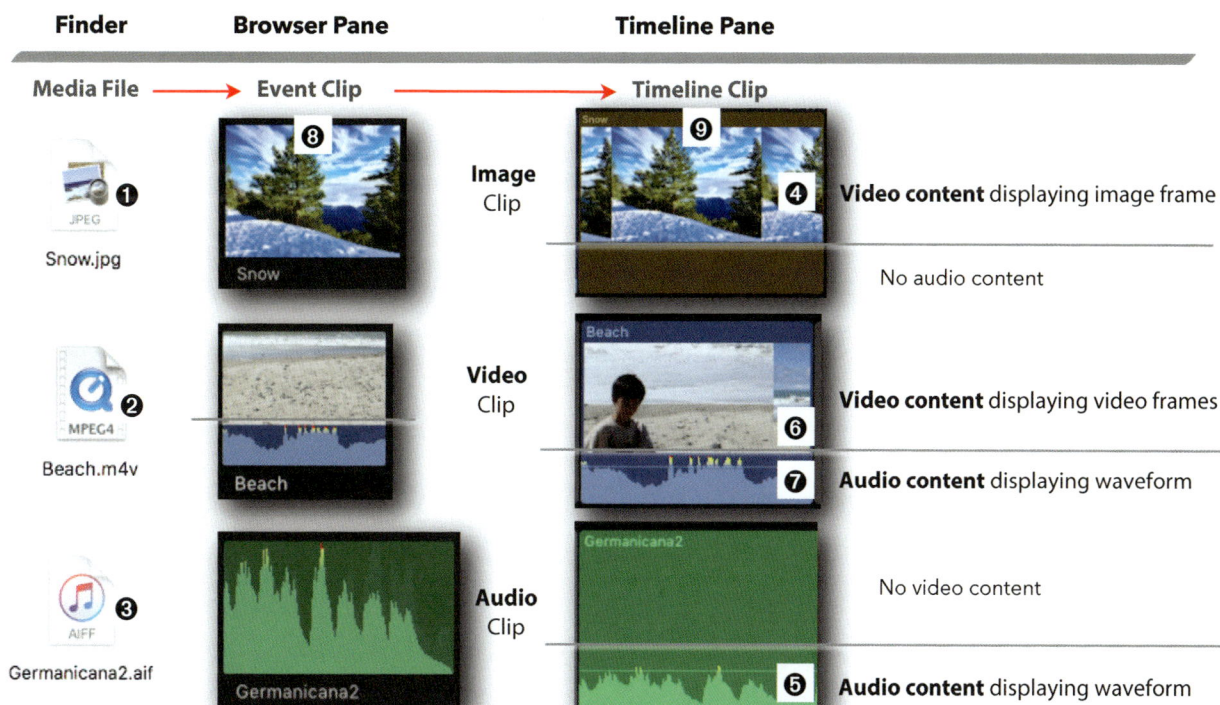

Open Clip

A Standard Clip appears as one unit, one object. That provides all the advantages of editing a single Clip without editing its video and audio components separately. However, FCPx still provides the tools to edit the components that are "inside" a Standard Clip, individually.

▶ **Expand Clip**: We discussed all the details in the Audio chapter how to expand ❶ a Standard Clip to edit all its audio content separately.

▶ **Open Clip**: This is another option I briefly mentioned at the beginning of the book, the ability to "open" a Clip and display its content on a Timeline.

Expand Audio

➡ *Open Clip*

You can open a Standard Clip either from the Browser ❷ or from the Timeline ❸. In both ways, you **ctr+click** on the Clip and choose from the **Shortcut Menu ➤ Open Clip** ❹. It opens up in the Timeline with the video content displayed on the Primary Storyline ❺ and the audio content attached as Connected Clips ❻.

🥎 Event Clip

The Timeline Header displays the path of this nested Clip, the Event the Clip is stored and the name of the Clip: "*EventName | ClipName*" ❼.

The popup menu for the Timeline History also displays the path and even shows the icon for a Compound Clip 🖿 ❽. More about that in the Compound section later in this chapter.

🥎 Timeline Clip

If the Clip was trimmed, then the unused portion (media handles) is dimmed ❾.

The Timeline Header and the Timeline History Menu display the path, this time, as the Project the Clip is placed on and the name of the Clip: "*ProjectName | ClipName*" ❿.

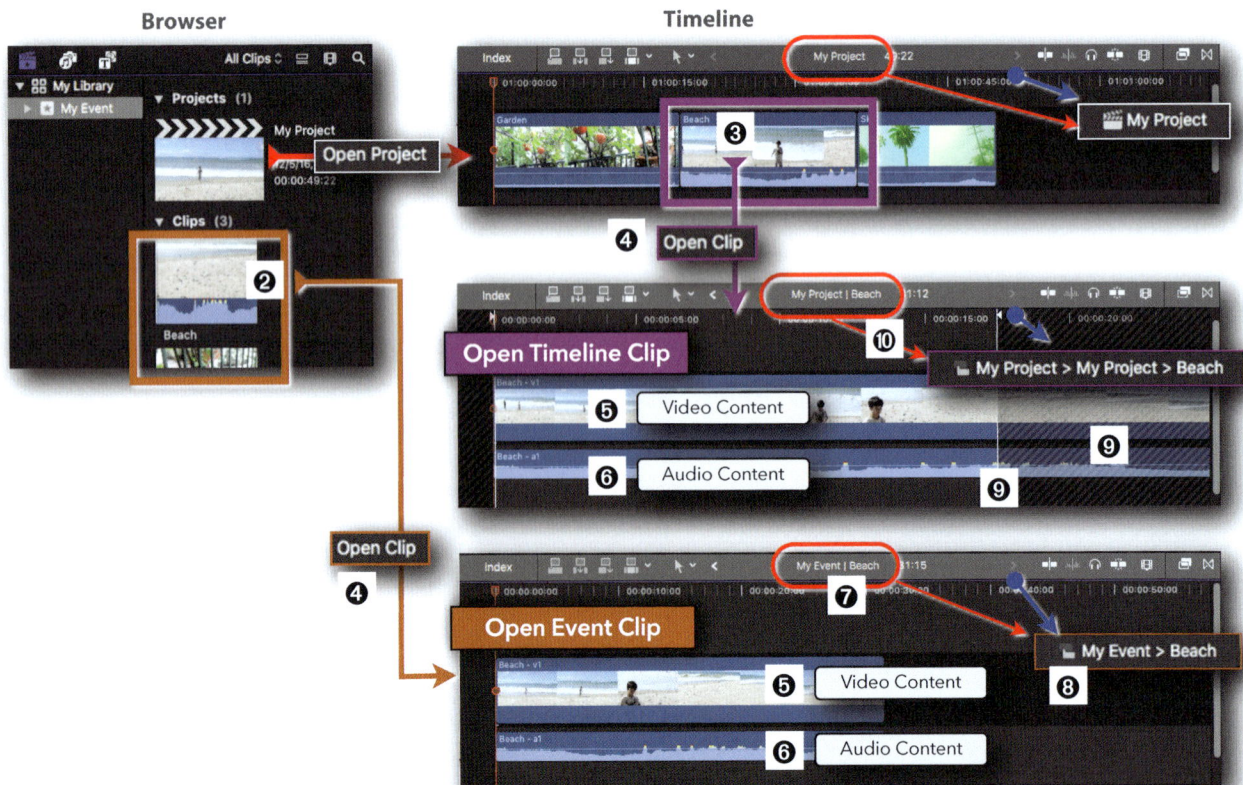

Transitions

⚉ Basics about Transitions

▸ Two adjacent Clips create a hard cut, which means, the last frame of the outgoing Clip ❶ is followed by the first frame of the incoming Clip ❷.

▸ When applying a transition effect to that cut, the frames from the outgoing Clip gradually change/blend into the frames of the incoming Clip.

▸ The transition will be automatically applied to the video and/or audio content of a Clip.

▸ The properties of such a transition determine how long the transition will be and what type of visual effect is used.

▸ A transition can be used in three areas:

  ● **Crossfade**: A crossfade is the typical transition between two adjacent Clips ❸.

  ● **Fade-in**: A Fade-in is the transition from "nothing" (silence, black, white) into the Clip. That is usually the beginning the Primary Storyline or Connected Storyline ❹.

  ● **Fade-out**: A Fade-out is the transition from the Clip into "nothing" (silence, black, white). That is usually the end of the Primary Storyline or Connected Storyline ❺.

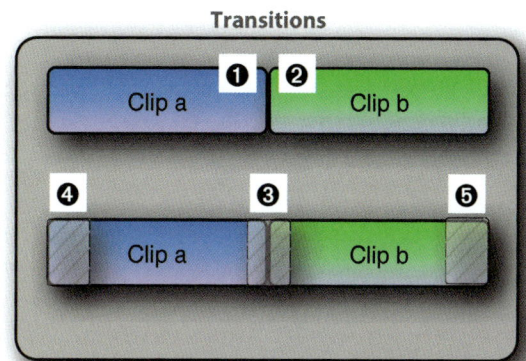
Transitions

⚉ Transitions in FCPx

▸ A Transition in FCPx is an individual Clip, a so-called Transition Clip that is placed upon existing Clips where you want to apply the transition.

▸ The Transitions Browser ❻, a window pane that is part of the Transition Pane, contains all the various Transition Clips to choose from.

▸ Transitions can only be placed on Clips of a Storyline ❼ (Primary Storyline or Connected Storyline).

▸ Placing a Transition on a Connected Clip will automatically wrap that Clip first into a Connected Storyline (more about those later in this chapter).

▸ Transitions are applied to the video and audio content of a Clip unless the audio content is separated by "Expand Audio" or "Detach Audio".

▸ Because Transitions are considered Clips, they can be treated like Clips. You can Trim the Edit Points, change the duration, delete them, *opt+drag* to copy, etc.

▸ The properties of a selected Transition Clip are displayed in the Transition Inspector ◳ ❿ where you can edit its properties.

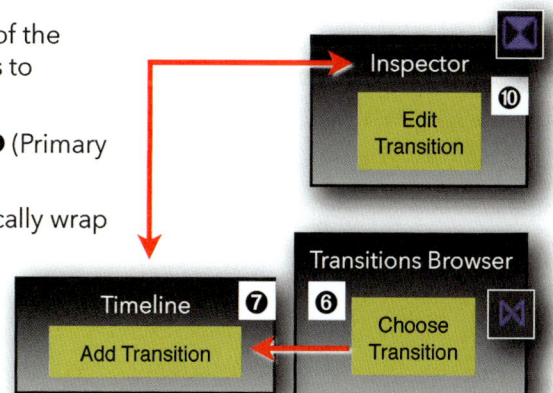

➡ *Transitions Browser*

To apply a Transition to a Clip you have to open the Transitions Browser that contains a wide variety of pre-installed Transitions to choose from.

The Transitions Browser is a window pane that opens on the right side as part of the Timeline Pane. Please note both, the Transitions Browser and the Effects Browser, share his window pane. It can display only one Browser at a time. Toggle the Transitions Browser with any of the following commands:

Transitions Browser

- *Click* on the Transitions Browser Button ⧓ ❶ in the upper-right corner of the Timeline Header
- Main Menu *Window* ➤ *Show in Workspace* ➤ *Transitions*
- Key Command *sh+cmd+5*

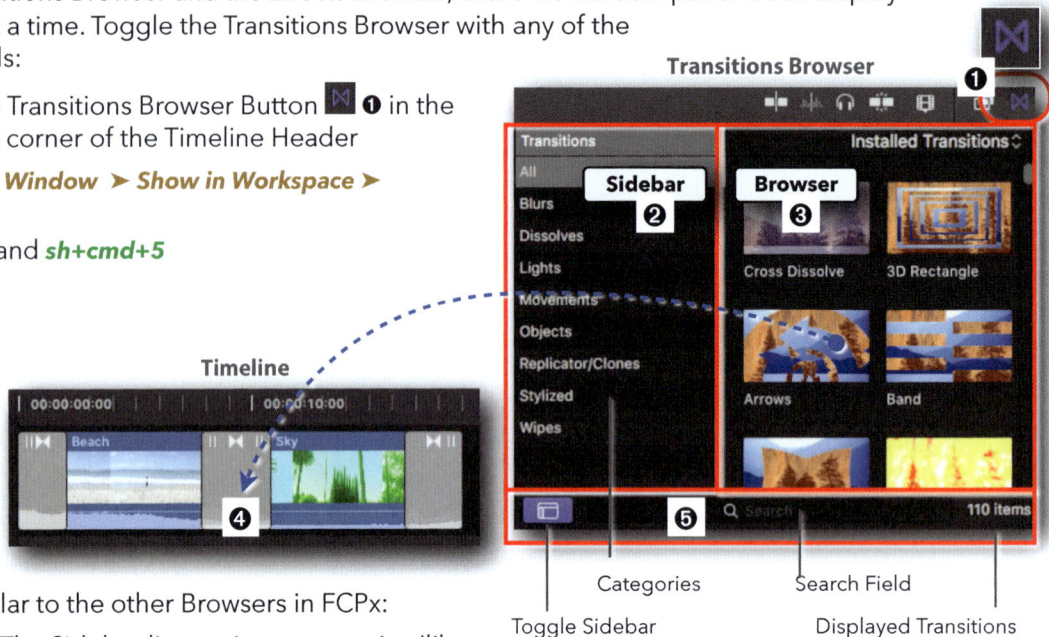

Timeline

🌑 Interface

The interface is similar to the other Browsers in FCPx:

- **Sidebar ❷**: The Sidebar lists various categories (like folders) to show only the Transition in that Browser that belong to that category.

- **Browser ❸**: The Browser displays all the Transitions based on the selection made in the Sidebar. The Clip image provides a visual indication of the effect. You can *drag* that image, representing the Transition Clip, directly on a Timeline Clip ❹.

- **Status Bar ❺**: The Status Bar contains three elements. The button on the left lets you toggle the Sidebar, the Search Field lets you narrow the displayed Transitions in the Browser by entering a name, and the number on the right displays the amount of the currently displayed Transitions.

🌑 Preview

You can preview a Transition by skimming over the image, moving the mouse cursor (it turns into the orange Skimmer ❻) from left to right. This will simulate the Transition in the Viewer to give you an idea of what the transition will look like before you apply it.

🌑 There are three types of Transitions:

- **FCPx Transitions**: These are simple transitions based on basic parameters.

- **Motion Transitions - pre-installed**: These are effects that are created with Apple's motion-graphics application Motion 5. FCPx comes installed with many Motion effects and if a Transition is one of those, then the Shortcut Menu (*ctr+click* on the Transition) will display the command "*Open a copy in Motion*" (if you have Motion installed on your computer). You cannot overwrite one of the installed effects, that's why FCPx creates a copy of that effect first and then opens that copy in Motion. (To learn how to use this app, check out my book "Motion 5 - How it Works".)

- **Motion Transitions - custom created**: If any effect in the Browser is based on one of the Motion effects that you've created, then the Shortcut Menu will display "*Open in Motion*". It lets you adjust and overwrite the effect in Motion. You have to then re-apply the effect to the Timeline in FCPx.

Add/Replace a Transition

There are different procedures to apply a Transition Clip:

▶ *Drag* a Transition to the Clip: You can drag a Transition Clip from the Transitions Browser directly onto the Timeline Clip. A ghost Clip will indicate the drop-position before you release the mouse.

▶ *Double-click* a Transition: When double-clicking on a Transition Clip in the Browser, it will be applied to both ends of all selected Timeline Clips.

▶ Apply Default Transition: You can choose any Transition to make it the "Default Transition". From now on, you can just use a command to apply that default Transition (without a trip to the Transitions Browser). Define the Default Transition by *ctr+-clicking* on the Transition in the Browser and select "Make Default". Please note that the name of the selected Transition will actually be displayed in the menu command. Now you can use any of the two commands to apply that Transition to the selected Clip(s):

> Main Menu *Edit ➤ Add "Name of the Transition"*
> Key Command *cmd+T*

▶ Copy-Paste: You can *opt+drag* an existing Transition Clip in the Timeline to copy it to a different Clip or use the copy - paste commands to paste it to the selected Clip(s).

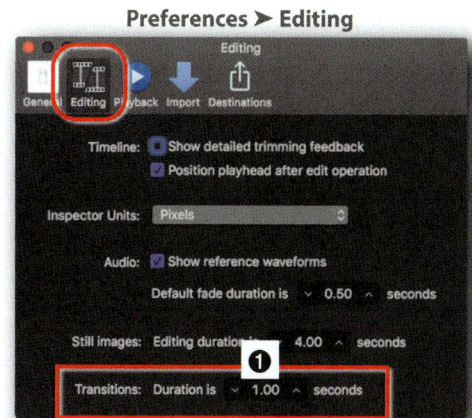

Transition Duration

You set the default duration of a Transition in the *Preferences ➤ Editing* ❶.

Trim Transitions

There are quite a few cursor tools for trimming a Transition Clip using various Click Zones, the areas you are moving the cursor over:

▶ The Transition Clip appears as a gray Clip ❷ without any image, but any waveform is still visible at the bottom.

▶ **Ripple Edit**: The upper-left ❸ and upper-right ❹ corner of the Transition Clip indicates a handle that you *drag* to ripple-edit the Clip underneath without changing the Transition Clip. The cursor changes to the Ripple Left and Ripple Right Tool.

▶ **Roll Edit**: In the center on top of the Transition Clip is another handle that lets you perform a Roll Edit ❺ of the underlying Clips without changing the Transition Clip itself. The cursor changes to the Roll Edit Tool.

▶ **Duration Edit**: Moving the cursor over the left or right border ❻ of the Transition Clip will change it to the Resize Tool that lets you change the duration of the Transition Clip. Or press *ctr+D* and enter a duration in the Timecode Reader (Main Menu *Modify ➤ Change Duration...*).

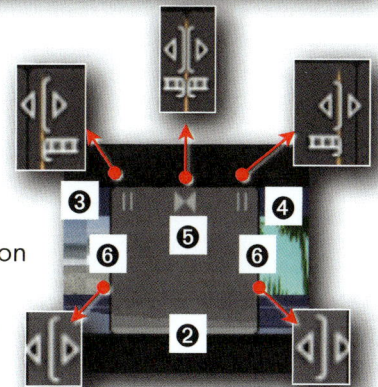

Precision Editor

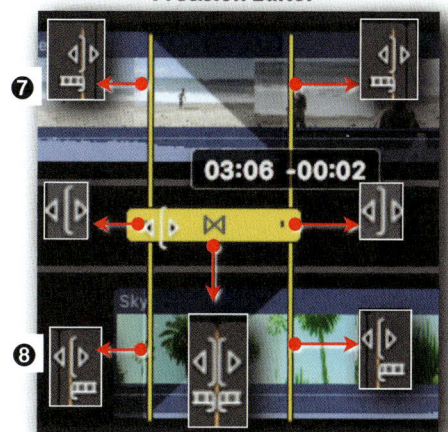

Double-clicking on a Transition Clip will open the Precision Editor that lets you perform the Ripple Edits, the Roll Edit, and the Duration Edit with a full view of the outgoing ❼ and incoming ❽ Clip on their separate lanes. Watch the mouse cursor when you move over the specific handles to see what edit you are performing.

Make Default

Preferences ➤ Editing

Precision Editor

➡️ *Edit Transition Properties*

You can view and edit the properties of a single or multiple selected Transition in the Inspector ▣ to fine tune the Transition effect.

▸ **Name and Duration ❶**: The Inspector Header displays the name of the selected Transition and its current duration.

▸ **Video Properties ❷**: The upper section of the Transition Inspector shows the video properties. The available parameters, of course, depend on the individual Transition.

▸ **Audio Properties ❸**: The bottom section shows the Fade-in and Fade-out type. Select any of the four curves ❹ from the popup menu.

▸ **Onscreen Controls**: Some Transitions also provide onscreen controls in the Viewer to adjust their settings visually.

Transition Name · Transition length · Transition Inspector

🟡 Media Handles

There is one important factor that has to be considered when applying Transitions between two Clips. A Transition requires that there is enough "media handle" available on the Clip border to create the transition, depending on the length of the transition.

If there isn't enough Media Handle available, then an Alert window ❺ will pop up that gives you two options.

▸ **Cancel ❻**: The Transition uses only the available media for the transition effect regardless of the required transition length.

▸ **Create Transition ❼**: The Clips will be moved (rippled) to provide enough handle to apply the current Transition. This will shift the remaining Clips on the Timeline to the left at the transition point.

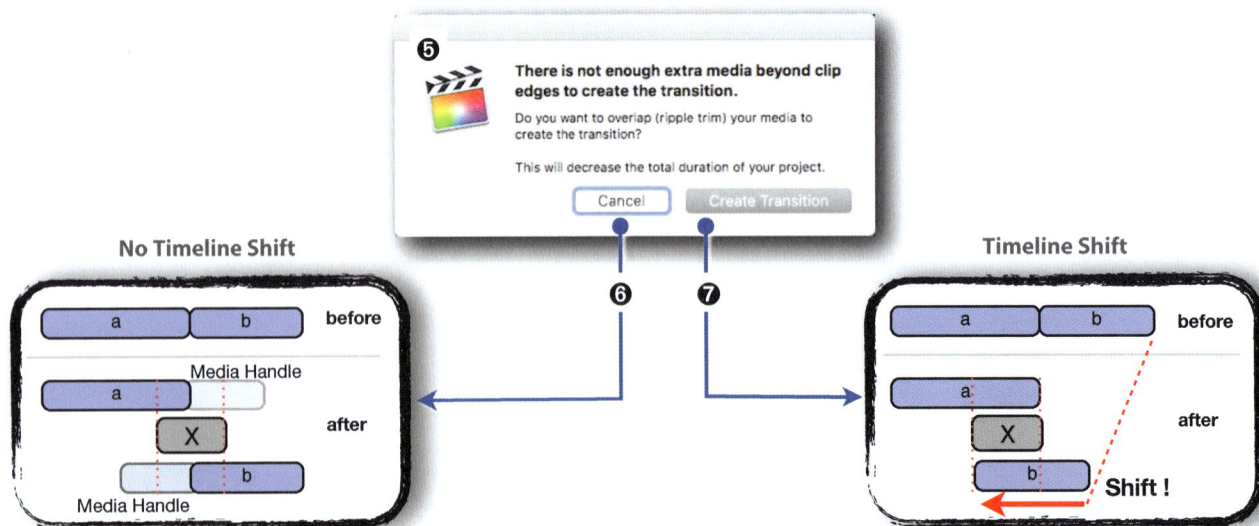

🟡 Flow Transition

FCPx has a new Transition "Flow" that can smooth out jump cuts between two Clips using its magical "optical flow frame blending".

Titles

Titles are a special type of Clip that you use in the Timeline for anything related to customized text in your video, e.g. front titles, end credits, lower third, etc. Here are some basic facts about them:

▶ Title Clips don't refer to any Media Files.

▶ Title Clips are generated by FCPx and are based on effects created in Apple's Motion app (the ones that come with FCPx).

▶ FCPx comes with a wide variety of Titles preinstalled and they are available from the Titles and Generator Browser ❶.

▶ Most of the Title Clips are semitransparent, showing the text and their objects on top of any other video clip without blocking the rest of the frame. Some Titles have full frame graphics with no transparency.

▶ You edit Title Clips like any other Clip and customizes their properties (their appearance) in the Inspector 🅃 and in the Viewer via onscreen controls.

➡ Titles Browser

Let's start with the Titles Browser. FCPx considers Titles as content and, therefore, the Titles Browser, which lists all the available Titles, is located in the Browser Pane, the same area where you access your other content (Event Clips, Music, Photos, etc.).

You can toggle the Titles Browser with the following commands:

📌 *Click* on the Titles and Generator Browser button 🅃 ❷ in the upper-left corner. This button also toggles the Sidebar

📌 Key Command *opt+cmd+1*

📌 Main Menu *Window* ➤ *Go To* ➤ *Titles and Generators*

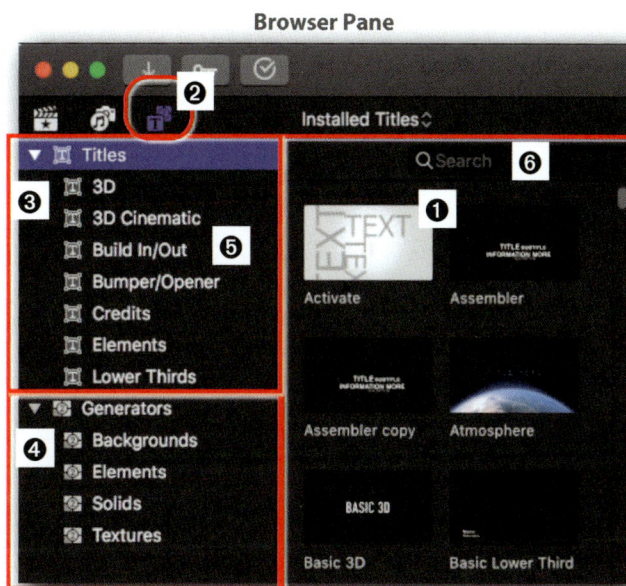

Browser Pane

🌐 Interface

The interface is similar to the other Browsers in FCPx:

▶ **Sidebar**: The Sidebar lists two items with disclosure triangles. "Titles" ❸ contain all the categories for "Titles" and "Generators" ❹, which list all the categories for the available Generators. Selecting any of the seven categories in the Sidebar shows only the Titles in that category in the Browser on the right ❶.

▶ **Browser**: The Browser displays all the Titles based on the selection made in the Sidebar as interactive images. Scroll further down and you will see Titles grouped by themes. The Clip image provides a visual indication of the effect and you can *drag* that image, representing the Title Clip, directly onto the Timeline. The search field ❻ on top lets you filter out the Titles in the Browser based on your text entry.

▶ **Skimming**: Moving the mouse cursor left-right (Skimming) over a Title image will simulate the Title effect in the Viewer to give you an idea of what the Title will look like ❼.

▶ **Shortcut Menu**: *Ctrl+click* on a Transition to open its Shortcut Menu with a command for editing the Title effect in Motion. The command depends on if it is a pre-installed effect (*Open a copy in Motion*) or your own created Title effect (*Open in Motion*).

➡ *Use Titles*

Before adding a Title Clip to your Project Timeline, be aware of how it "reacts" to other Clips.

- ☑ **Primary Storyline**: When placing a Title Clip on the Primary Storyline, then its transparent background will be black.
- ☑ **Connected Clip**: When placing a Title Clip as a Connected Clip or Connected Storyline, then the underlying video clip will act as the background.
- ☑ **Stacked Title Clips**: Everything except the text and its used objects in the Title Clip are transparent, so you can stack multiple Title Clips on the Timeline.

🌐 Add Titles

Here are the different procedures on how to add a Title Clip to the Timeline (the default length is 10s):

- ▶ **Double-click**: You can simply add a Title Clip to the Timeline by *double-clicking* on a Title in the Browser.
  - This adds the Title as a Connected Clip at the current Playhead position.
  - If a Title is selected in the Timeline, then the Title from the Browser will replace that one.
- ▶ **Drag & Drop**: *Drag* a Title from the Browser onto the Timeline:
  - <u>Outside</u> a Storyline: Will become a Connected Clip.
  - <u>Between</u> two Clips on a Storyline: Will insert the Title and moves other Clips to the right.
  - <u>On top</u> of an existing Clip: Will replace the existing Clip according to the selection from the popup window. You can even create Auditions with Titles. This way you can create different Titles that you can decide on later or create Titles in different languages to select for different exports later.
- ▶ **Add Buttons/Commands**: Use the buttons ❶ on the Timeline header or their corresponding Key Commands (*Q*, *W*, *E*, *D*) to add a selected Title to the Timeline.
- ▶ **Default Title**: Use one of the commands to add the Basic Title or Basic Lower Third as a Connected Clip at the current Playhead position. You can assign any Title as the Basic Title or Basic Lower Third by *ctr+clicking* on the Title and selecting from the Shortcut Menu.
  - 📌 Main Menu *Edit ➤ Connected Title ➤ Basic Title* (*ctr+T*)
  - 📌 Main Menu *Edit ➤ Connected Title ➤ Basic Lower Third* (*sh+ctr+T*)
- ▶ **Move/Copy**: You can use the standard procedures of *dragging* (movie) and *opt+dragging* (copy) Title Clips on the Timeline or use the copy-paste commands directly in the Timeline.

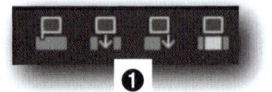

🌐 Appearance

This is what the Title Clips look like in the Timeline and the Timeline Index.

- ▶ A Title Clip will have the Video Role "Title" assigned to it by default and appears in that color, purple.
- ▶ The Title Clip only shows a solid color ❷ and is displayed as a narrow Clip ❸ when used as a Connected Clip.
- ▶ The Timeline Index lists the Title Clips like any other Clips with their own icon 🅣 ❹. You can search for the phrase "Title", add notes ❺ to them, and even filter out all the Title Clips by selecting the Titles button ❻ at the bottom of the Timeline Index.

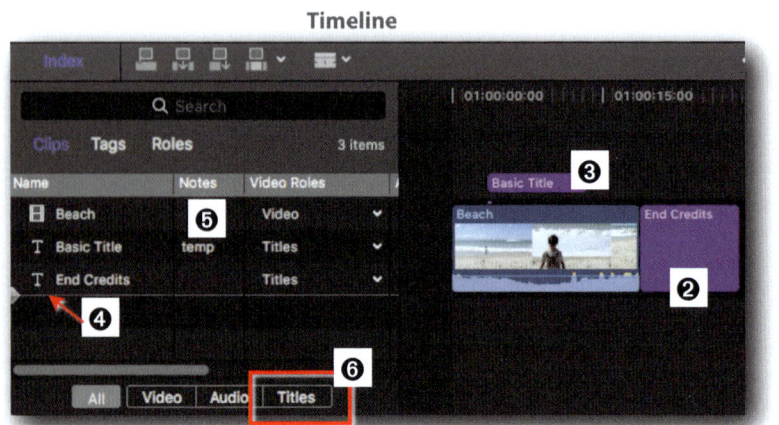

➡️ *Edit Title Clips*

Because Title Clips are Clips, they can be edited with similar procedures as Standard Clips.

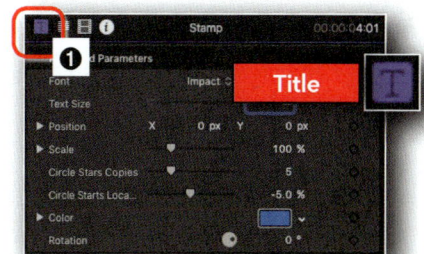

🌑 Delete Titles

A simple edit is to delete the Title Clip. As with any other Timeline Clip, select the Title Clip(s) and press the **delete** key.

🌑 Trim

If the Title contains just a static text, then trimming will change the length of that image. If a Title, like many of them, contains motion, then shorten or lengthen the Clip means speeding up or slowing down the built-in motion.

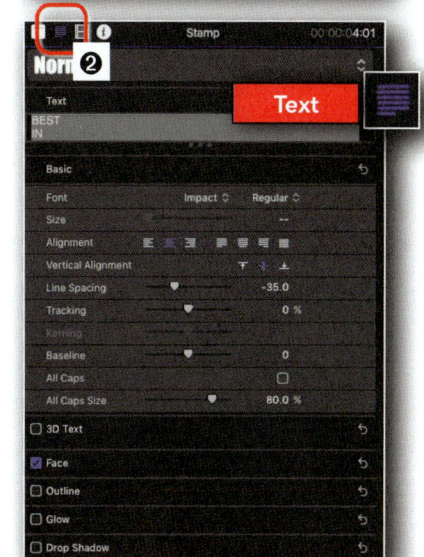

🌑 Transition

You can apply Transitions on Title Clips as long as they are on a Primary Storyline or Connected Storyline.

🌑 Edit Effect (Inspector)

You modify the Title effect (*what is displayed and how*) in the Inspector. In addition, the text entry and placement of objects are also available in the Viewer directly with the convenience of onscreen controls. If available, Keyframes can be used to further automate the already built-in motion.

When selecting any Title Clip in the Timeline, the Inspector shows the attributes of that Clip grouped in four windows to edit every aspect of the title appearance:

▸ **Title Inspector ❶**: This window contains the main parameters that make up the Title. Therefore, its content varies from Title to Title. These are the parameters that are "published" from the Motion effect, which means, Motion allows to alter specific attributes of that Title effect.

▸ **Text Inspector ❷**: This window contains all the controls related to the text in that Title Clip from the actual text entry to all the various text attributes, the text formatting. Please note that pasting text in this field will only paste the text but not any format that the text might have. However, pasting text directly in the Viewer via the onscreen controls will also paste any text formatting (and overwrites any existing text format).

▸ **Video Inspector ❸**: This window contains the usual modules. Here you can modify the look of the Title and even add video Effects to it.

▸ **Info Inspector ❹**: This window is the same as any other Clip. Keep in mind that you can add Metadata like Notes, or change the name of the Titles Clip.

Title Editing with the Touch Bar

The Viewer provides onscreen controls for most of the Titles too, so you can edit them directly on the video frame. In addition, if you select the onscreen control, the Touch Bar provides many controls to quickly edit the text-related attributes of the Title.

▶ **Title Clip View ❶**: This is the main view with five buttons that appears when you select the onscreen control in the Viewer. *Tapping* on any of the buttons changes to the following views:

▶ **Text Formatting Button ❷** [A ⟩]: This button switches to a view with various format controls.

▶ **Font Size Button ❸** [ᴀA ⟩] This button switches to a view that lets you adjust the font size with a slider. *Tapping* on the letter A on the left or right will change the size incrementally.

▶ **Kerning Button ❹** [A\V ⟩]: This button is only visible if you have clicked between characters in the text on the Viewer. It lets you adjust the text kerning (distance between characters).

▶ **3D Button ❺** [3D]: This button toggles the Text between 2D and 3D. Enabling 3D will display the onscreen control for the three axes.

▶ **Color Button** [⊙]: This button switches to the color view that itself can have four different views depending on which button you tap. Here is how it works:

● **Result ❺**: The first color button on the left displays the resulting color based on what you set with the other four buttons on the right.

● **Hue ❻ - Saturation ❼ - Brightness ❽**: You have three buttons to set the hue, saturation, and brightness individually. One of the buttons is always extended into a wide slider that lets you set that parameter. *Tapping* on any of the other two buttons will extend that control to the big slider so you can set that control. The previous slider is minimized to a button, showing its setting. You see the position of the slider with a little white bar ❾ on the button.

● **Color Presets ❿**: This button works as a toggle. When you *tap* on it, it switches to a view with 11 color buttons. *Tap* on one of the buttons to select that color (the view closes) or *tap* on the Preset button again to return to the main color view.

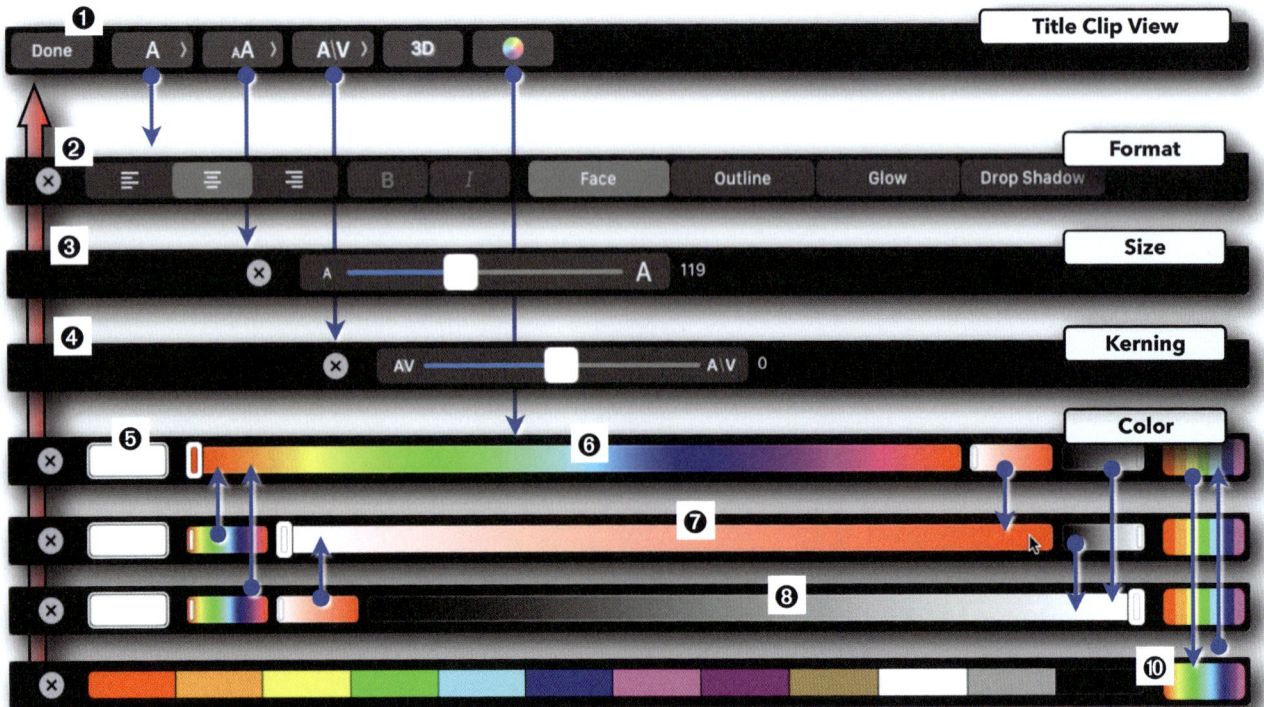

➡ Basic Titles

As we have seen in the Transition section, FCPx provides a command that lets you apply a user definable default Transition. For Titles, there are two commands that let you apply two often-used Titles without opening the Title Browser, "*Basic Title*" and "*Basic Lower Third*".

Basic Title	Basic Lower Third

🔘 Define Default Title and Lower Third

You can define any Title in the Titles Browser to be the Default Title or the Default Lower Third. **Ctr+click** on a Title in the Browser and choose from the **Shortcut Menu ➤ Make Default Title** or **Make Default Lower Third**.

Title Shortcut Menu

> Make Default Title
> Make Default Lower Third
> Open a copy in Motion

🔘 Basic Title

Add a Basic Title with any of the two commands:

- 📌 Main Menu *Edit ➤ Connect Title ➤ Basic Title*
- 📌 Key command *ctr+T*

There are three scenarios:

- If no Title Clip is selected: This will add a Basic Title as a Connected Clip in the Timeline at the Playhead position.
- If one Title Clip is selected: This will replace the currently selected Title Clip with the new Basic Title Clip.
- If more than one Title Clip is selected: A new Title Clip will be created at the Playhead position.

Move the round onscreen control to position the text on the frame.

Click to edit the text onscreen or edit it in the Inspector with more options.

🔘 Basic Lower Third

Add Basic Lower Third with any of the two commands:

- 📌 Main Menu *Edit ➤ Connect Title ➤ Basic Lower Third*
- 📌 Key command *sh+ctr+T*

There are three scenarios:

- If no Clip is selected: This will add a Basic Lower Third as a Connected Clip in the Timeline at the Playhead position.
- If one Title Clip is selected: This will replace the currently selected Title with the new Basic Lower Third Title.
- If more than one Title Clip is selected: A new Basic Lower Third will be created at the Playhead position.

Move the round onscreen control to position the text on the frame.

There are two Text entry fields (Title, Descriptions). Click to edit the text onscreen or edit it in the Inspector with more options.

Generators

Generators are a special type of Clip that you use in the Timeline for background, placeholders, or some special purposes like a Timecode Reader. Here are some basic facts about them:

▶ Generator Clips don't refer to any Media Files.

▶ Generator Clips are generated by FCPx and are based on effects created in Apple's Motion app (the ones that come with FCPx).

▶ FCPx comes with a wide variety of Generators preinstalled and they are available from the Titles and Generator Browser.

▶ Generator Clips that contain objects are semitransparent, displaying the objects on top of any other video clip without blocking the rest of the frame. Background Generators, on the other hand, have no transparency. Usually you would place other semitransparent Clips (i.e. Title Clips) on top of Generators.

▶ You edit Generator Clips like any other Clip and customize their properties (their appearance) in the Inspector and in the Viewer via onscreen controls.

➡ *Generator Clips vs. Title Clips*

Generator Clips work pretty much the same as Title Clips. Here are a few things to be aware of:

▶ **Source**: The Generator Clips are also listed in the Titles and Generators Browser.

▶ **Preview**: You can also skim over the Generator to see a preview of that effect in the Viewer.

▶ **Adding**: Adding Generators to the Timeline works the same as adding Title Clips.

▶ **Editing**: Editing Generator Clips follows the same procedures as Title Clips or any other Clips.

▶ **Roles**: Generator Clips are assigned the Role "Video" ❶ by default.

▶ **Appearance**: Generator Clips display their video content on the Clip thumbnail ❷.

▶ **Inspector**: The Inspector has three tabs, Generator Inspector 🔘 ❸, Video Inspector 🔲 ❹, Info Inspector 🛈 ❺.

▶ **Viewer**: Many Generators also provide onscreen controls in the Viewer.

▶ **Timeline Index**: Generator Clips also have their own icon 🔘 ❻ in the Timeline Index.

Default Generator

The "*Gap Clip*" ❼ (*opt+W*) and the "*Placeholder Clip*" ❽ (*opt+cmd+W*) are also Generator Clips. The Placeholder Clip, however, is special, because it functions as the Default Generator. You can define any other Generator as the Placeholder Clip by *ctr+clicking* on the Generator in the Browser and selecting "*Make Default Generator*". Now you can select it by using its Key Command *opt+cmd+W* or select from the Main Menu *Edit ➤ Insert Generator ➤ "NameOfDefaultGenerator"* without opening the Titles and Generators Browser.

Compound Clips

Remember, we discussed the concept of a "Package File" that macOS uses in the Finder in the FCPx Concepts chapter. This is a file that looks like a file on the "outside", but it is actually a folder, a container, that includes other files inside. The concept of a Compound Clip is similar. A Compound Clip looks like a Clip on the outside, but it is actually a container (with a Timeline) that includes other Clips (placed on that Timeline) inside. Therefore, it functions more like a mini Project.

> **A Compound Clip is a Project disguised as a Clip**

A few basic things about Compound Clips before we look at the details:

▶ You can create Compound Clips using Timeline Clips ❶ in the Timeline or using Event Clips ❷ in the Browser.

▶ The *Create New Compound Clip* command is available from the Main Menu *File ➤ New ➤ Compound Clip...* ❸, from the Shortcut Menu ❹ when *ctr+clicking* on the Event Clip or Timeline Clip, or as Key Command *opt+G*.

▶ The Settings Sheet that opens next is different when creating the Compound Clip in the Timeline ❺ (just the name and the Event assignment) or in the Browser ❻, which provides the similar settings when creating a Project.

▶ Once you've created a Compound Clip, it will have a "Modify" ❼ button in the Info Inspector that opens ❽ that same Settings Sheet, similar to a Project when you need to change its Properties.

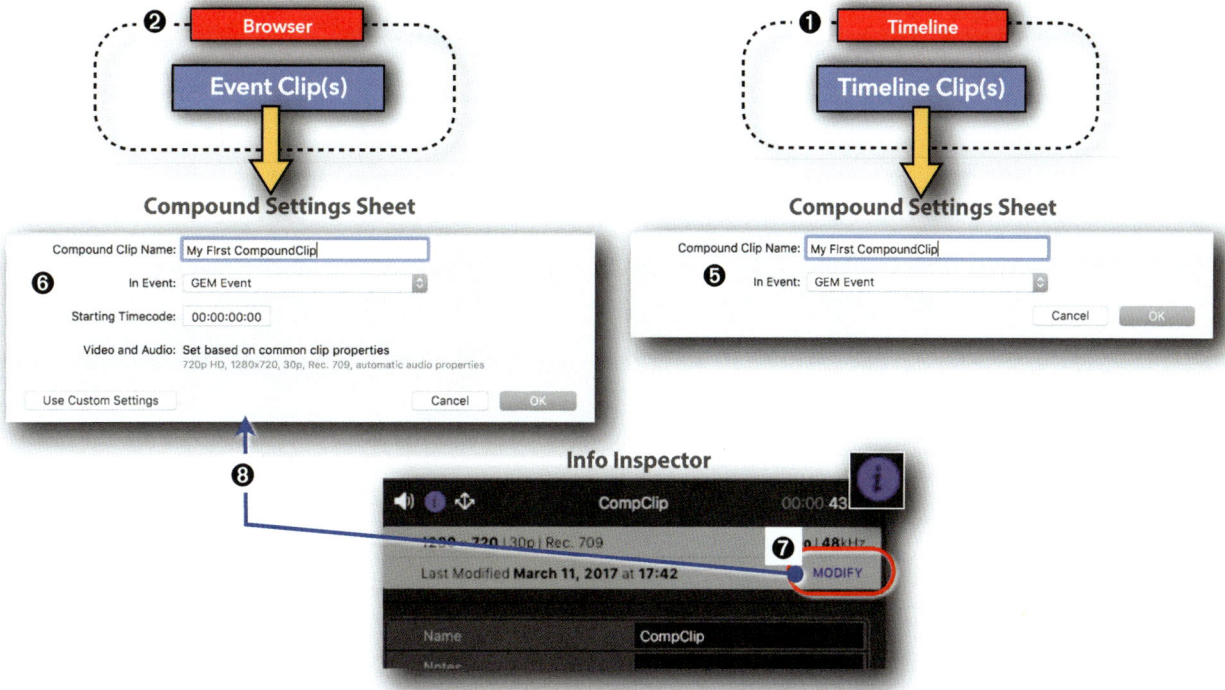

Main Menu: File

Clip: Shortcut Menu

Browser ❷
Event Clip(s)

Timeline ❶
Timeline Clip(s)

Compound Settings Sheet

Compound Clip Name: My First CompoundClip
❻ In Event: GEM Event
Starting Timecode: 00:00:00:00
Video and Audio: Set based on common clip properties
720p HD, 1280x720, 30p, Rec. 709, automatic audio properties
Use Custom Settings   Cancel   OK

Compound Settings Sheet

Compound Clip Name: My First CompoundClip
❺ In Event: GEM Event
Cancel   OK

❽

Info Inspector

CompClip   00:00:43
720 30p Rec. 709   48kHz
Last Modified **March 11, 2017** at **17:42**   ❼ MODIFY

Name   CompClip

➡ *Compound Clip: Project Timeline*

The Timeline is where the Compound Clip is being used the most and where it's the easiest to understand. For example, you are in your Project and the Clip structure is already very complex. There might be a few Clips on the Primary Storyline and a few Connected Clips that make up a logical unit or section in your video. The Compound Clip command can "group" those Clips together so when you want to move or copy that section, you only have to deal with one Clip, making sure that nothing about those Clips gets messed up. You treat that whole group of Clips as one Clip, a Compound Clip.

▸ Here is an example of a section of Clips ❶ that you want to group together as a Compound Clip. Be careful with a few rules regarding the placement of the Clips you want to group together: Grouping only Connected Clips ❷ together is safe. You can freely select any Connected Clips and the grouping will not affect other clips. Other non-selected Connected Clips will be rearranged vertically (just visually) to maintain a nice visual placement of the Clips. However, if you have Clips on the Primary Storyline in your group selection, make sure that they are connected and they don't have Connected Clips that "hang over" unselected Clips on the Primary Storyline. This would shift the unselected Clips in the Primary Storyline!

▸ Select the command "*New Compound Clip*" and give it a name ❸.

▸ All the previously selected Clips are now packed into that single Compound Clip ❹ ❺. The length of the Compound Clip ranges from the left border of the leftmost selected Clip to the right border of the rightmost selected Clip.

▸ The Clip has the "Compound Clip" icon ⬛❻ in front of its Clip name "Compound Clip". You can rename the Clip in the Inspector.

▸ To view the content of the Compound Clip (the inside ❼), use the command *Open Clip*. You can also **double-click** on the Clip to open it in the Timeline.

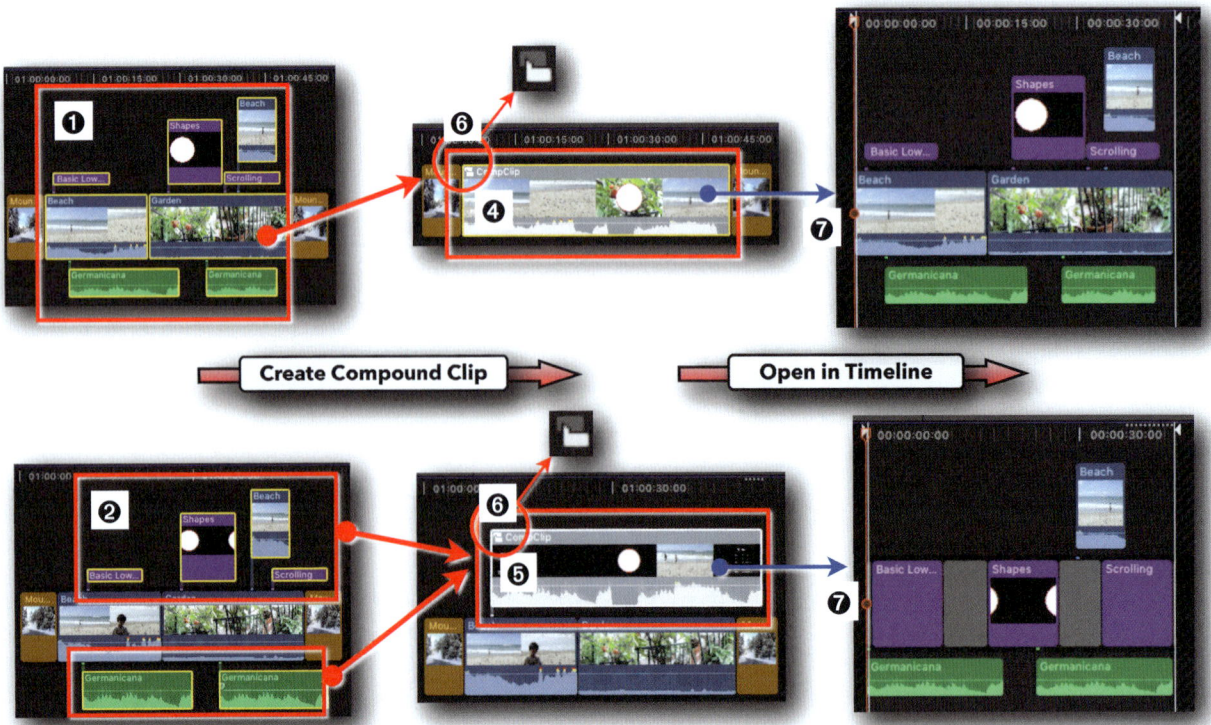

Configuration Sheet

Compound Clip Name: GEM Clip

In Event: GEM Events   ❸

Cancel   OK

Create Compound Clip   Open in Timeline

➡ *Compound Clip: Event Clip*

Creating Compound Clips in the Timeline makes sense from a practical point of view. Even the technical aspect of "looking inside" a Compound Clip by opening it in the Timeline now makes sense once we understand the bigger picture of FCPx. But why do we need Compound Clips in the Event? Isn't the Browser just for prep work before you start your actual Project? That includes collecting media files (import) and organizing them (adding metadata). That prep work can now be taken a little bit further with Compound Clips. In the Browser, you can already create little mini-Projects by combining Event Clips as Compound Clips to do some "pre-editing".

Here is the procedure for creating a Compound Clip in an Event:

⚙ Selection

You can differentiate three different kinds of selections:

▸ **No Clip is selected**

This creates an empty Compound Clip, kind of an empty container that you prepare to fill up later.

- ☑ From the Libraries Sidebar ⬛, select the Event ⬕ in which you want to place the newly created Compound Clip.
- ☑ Use any of the commands:
  - 📌 Key Command *opt+G*
  - 📌 Main Menu *File ➤ New ➤ Compound Clip...*

▸ **One Clip is selected**

If you only put one Clip into a Compound Clip, isn't that redundant? Yes, unless you want to add to that Compound Clip later or apply effects to that one enclosed Clip (which is not possible with Standard Event Clips). Remember, in the Metadata chapter, I mentioned the trick to trim an individual Event Clip and save it as a Compound Clip, so it functions as a "real" Subclip (without the need of Keywords and Metadata).

- ☑ In the Browser, select the Event Clip.
- ☑ Use any of the commands:
  - 📌 Key Command *opt+G*
  - 📌 Main Menu *File ➤ New ➤ Compound Clip...*
  - 📌 *Ctr+click* on the Event Clip and choose from the *Shortcut Menu ➤ New Compound Clip...*

▸ **Multiple Clips are selected**

Because there is no timeline when you just select random Clips from the Browser, they will be placed sequentially in alphabetical order on the Primary Storyline inside the Compound Clip.

- ☑ From the Libraries Browser, select all the Clips that you want to include in the Compound Clip.
- ☑ Use any of the commands:
  - 📌 Key Command *opt+G*
  - 📌 Main Menu *File ➤ New ➤ Compound Clip...*
  - 📌 *Ctr+click* on the Event Clip and choose from the *Shortcut Menu ➤ New Compound Clip...*

⚙ Settings

Once you use the command, the Compound Clip Settings Sheet ❶ will slide out. And isn't that interesting? This window has the same settings as the window for creating a new Project. That pretty much proves the point that a Compound Clip is simply a mini-Project. Just enter a name ❷ for the Compound Clip and set its Properties.

When you select the Compound Clip later and open the Info Inspector, you will also see the same Modify button when you select a Project in addition to the displayed Video and Audio Properties ❹. *Clicking* on *Modify* opens that Settings Sheet again if you need to make changes to its Properties later.

Compound Settings Sheet

Info Inspector

Editing Compound Clips

Please note that a Compound Clip in the Browser (Event Clip) and a Compound Clip in the Project Timeline (Timeline Clip) are different regarding what you can do on its inside when using the "*Open Clip*" command..

➡ Compound Clips in the Browser

When "opening a Compound Clip", you can freely edit its content.

> **Edit Clips**: All those tools that are usually not available for Event Clips, like adding Video and Audio Effects and adding Keyframe Automation are available to the Event Clip once it is contained inside a Compound Clip in the Libraries Browser.

> **Remove Clips**: Of course, you can also delete Clips from the Compound Clip's Timeline. After you packed an Event Clip inside a Compound Clip, you can even delete the original Clip from the Browser without affecting the Compound Clip. All those nested Clips are copies (a new record in the Event database) that inherited all the properties and don't rely on their parent Event Clips anymore.

> **Add Clips**: You can add more Clips to a Compound Clip's Timeline. The source for Clips to be added to the Timeline is always the Browser (besides duplicating existing Clips). This enables you to add a Clip from Event B to a Compound Clip on Event A because once you open a Compound Clip in the Timeline, you can select a different Event in the Browser.

➡ Compound Clip in the Project Timeline

Here are two examples that show the restrictions regarding shortening or lengthening the content inside a Compound Clip. Please note the white border lines left ❶ and right ❷.

> This is the original Compound Clip ❸ in the Project Timeline and I use the "*Open Clip*" command to switch the Timeline Pane to show the content ❹ (the inside) of the Compound Clip.

> When you open a Compound Clip in the Timeline and shorten ❺ its content, then the length of the Compound Clip stays the same. However, the audio will stop playing and the video will be transparent ❻ (black) from the right border of the shortened nested Clip.

> When you open a Compound Clip in the Timeline and lengthen a Clip or add ❼ a Clip that exceeds the right border of the Compound Clip ❽, then the extra length will be ignored (it is marked as a dark gray cross-hatched area) and the length of the Compound Clip stays the same ❾. In this example you see the added audio over that portion on the waveform ❿ of the Compound Clip. The only way to change the length of that Compound Clip is the regular way, trimming the "outside" with the trim tool. After all, the Compound Clip acts like a regular Clip regarding the editing techniques.

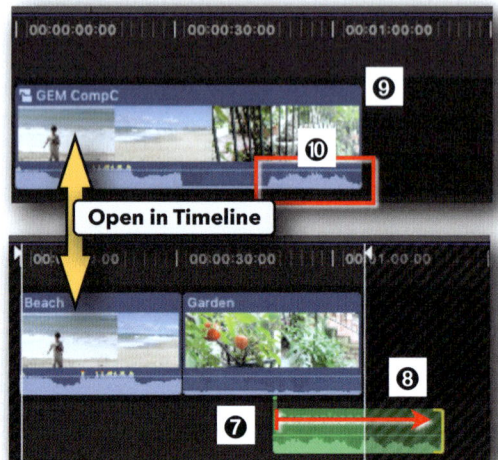

➡ *Event Clip - Timeline Clip: Linked* Relationship

Remember, once you drag an Event Clip to the Timeline, it becomes its own Timeline Clip. The Timeline Clip carries its reference to its parent Event Clip, but, other than that, is completely independent. Adding any effects to it will not affect its parent Event Clip. The Clips were only referenced but not linked.

However, Compound Clips stay linked once you move them from the Browser to the Project Timeline. Any adjustment (except trimming) on the Browser will update the Compound Clip on the Project Timeline and vice versa.

💡 Unlink Compound Clip

The only way to "unlink" a Compound Clip on the Project Timeline from its parent Compound Clip on the Libraries Browser is by using the Command in the Main Menu *Clip ➤ Reference New Parent Clip*. This will just create a copy of the selected Compound Clip on the Timeline and places it in the Bowser with the same name and the suffix "copy".

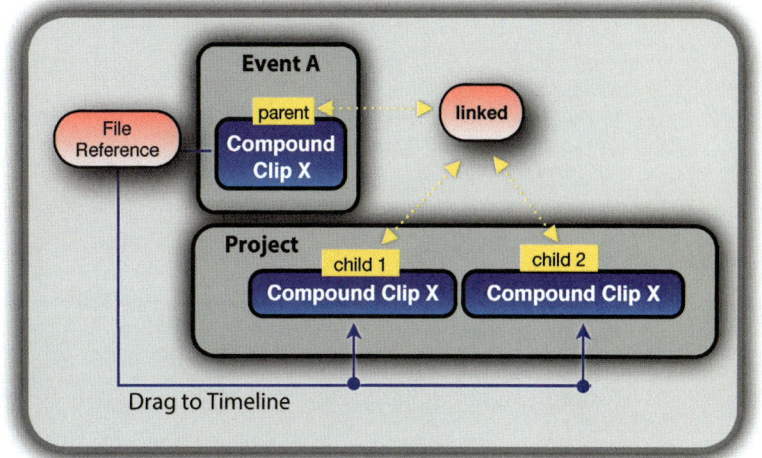

➡ *Break Apart a Compound Clip*

There is also a command to reverse a Compound Clip and disassemble it into its individual Clips with the command "*Break Apart Clip Items*" (not available for Compound Clips in the Browser):

- Key Command *sh+cmd+G*
- Main Menu *Clip ➤ Break Apart Clip Items*
- *Ctr+click* on the Compound Clip in the Timeline and choose from the *Shortcut Menu ➤ Break Apart Clip Items*

➡ *More Tricks*

Compound Clips are extremely versatile and powerful. Here is more functionality:

- ▶ You can put Compound Clips into Compound Clips, nest them.
- ▶ Compound Clips can also be used in Auditions.
- ▶ "Compound" is a Metadata value for "Clip Type" that lets you create Smart Collections for them.
- ▶ You can use the Timeline Index to display the content of a Compound Clip as with any other Project Timeline.

- ▶ The Inspector will also display the Properties of Compound Clips. The File Location lists "(Multiple Files)" because it has references to all the Media Files of the containing Clips.
- ▶ We have already seen the the powerful feature in the Roles chapter how to create Stems and submixes using Roles and Compound Clips.

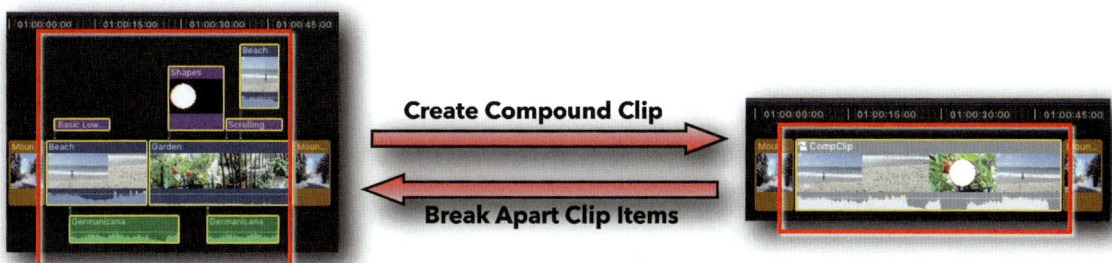

Standard Clip vs. Compound Clip

One of the main features in FCPx is: No need to split the video and audio content into two clips when importing a video file (Source Media File). FCPx automatically creates a single Event Clip, which is one "nested" Clip that packs together the video content as a Video Clip and the audio content as an Audio Clip in a single package. If you think about it, this Standard Clip behaves almost like a Compound Clip.

This is the Browser, displaying the Event Clip "Beach". You can see on the thumbnail that the video clip contains audio information. Use the *Open Clip* command to "look inside".

Now, the Timeline displays the content of the Event Clip "Beach". It contains one video clip and one connected audio Clip. Please note that the individual Clips have "-v1" and "-a1" in their name to indicate what track it is.

This is the same "Beach" clip dragged onto a Project Timeline. We can see that it contains video and audio content and we are able to "look inside" with the *Open Clip* command.

Here is the result when opening the Timeline Clip in the Timeline. We see one video clip and one audio clip as a Connected Clip. Please note the length restriction with the two white border lines on the left and right.

Once you open a Standard Clip (Event Clip or Timeline Clip) in the Timeline, you can treat it like a Compound Clip and edit the content, trim it, add or remove Clips or add effects. At that state, even FCPx seems to be confused what type of Clip that is.

▸ The Standard Clip itself lists its Standard Clip icon 🎞 ❶ and not the Compound Clip icon 🗂.

▸ If you look at the Timeline History Menu (*click* on the History Buttons ◁ ▷ in the Timeline Header), then FCPx lists the Clip ("Beach") with a Compound Clip icon 🗂 ❷.

▸ Once you start editing the content of a Standard Clip, you will see the "Modify" button ❸ listed in the Info Inspector. This button is listed for Projects, Compound Clips, and Synchronized Clips. In this case, the Settings Sheet opens up with the "Synchronized Clip" settings ❹.

That means, the *Beach* Clip is a Standard Clip, displayed with a Compound Icon and the settings of a Synchronized Clip. Makes sense, right?

Synchronized Clips

A Synchronized Clip is a special type of Clip, like a variation of a Compound Clip. It can only be created in the Browser.

FCPx can synchronize multiple Clips (video and audio clips) that were recorded during the same take but came from different sources (camera, external recorder). It automatically analyzes and syncs those clips together into a Compound Clip. The analysis process is based on various factors like timecode, creation date, audio content, or added markers. If the analysis doesn't find any sync point, then the files will be lined up at their start time.

Create a Synchronized Clip

- ☑️ Select the Event Clips that you want to synchronize.
- ☑️ Use any of the following commands.
  - 🎚️ Key Command *opt+cmd+G*
  - 🎚️ Main Menu *Clip ➤ Synchronize Clips...*
  - 🎚️ *Ctr+click* on one of the selected Clips and choose from the *Shortcut Menu ➤ Synchronize Clips...*
- ☑️ A new Synchronized Clip will be created in the Libraries Browser with the name *"NameOfFirstClip - Synchronized Clip"*

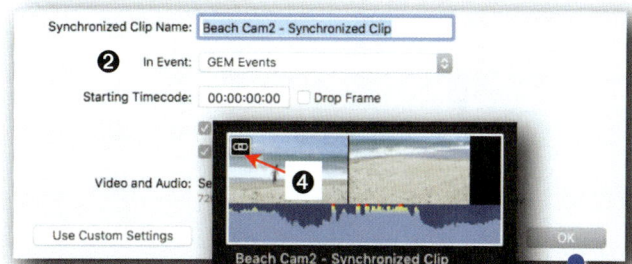

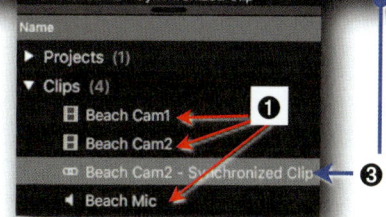

➡ Synchronized Clip

Synchronized Clips are similar to Compound Clips, where you select multiple Clips and "stuff" them inside a new Clip that functions as a container with its own timeline.

However, while a Compound Clip puts all the Clips next to each other on its timeline the Primary Storyline, a Synchronized Clip will stack the Clips inside on top of each other, based on their sync.

Here is an example to demonstrate that:

- ▸ I have two Video Clips (Beach Cam1 and Beach Cam2) and one Audio Clip (Mic) in the Browser. I select the three Clips ❶ and use the Synchronize Clips command, which will prompt the Dialog Sheet ❷ similar when creating a Compound Clip.

- ▸ The newly created Synchronized Clip ❸ will be listed in the Browser with the special synchronized icon, which is also displayed in the video thumbnail ❹.

- ▸ Opening the new Synchronized Clip in the Timeline will show how FCPx synced the Clips together. One Primary Storyline ❺ with two Connected Clips ❻.

- ▸ If you look at the Audio Inspector for that Clip, you will see the Audio Components listed accordingly under Storyline ❼ and Connected ❽. You can easily mute specific audio or apply effects to them.

- ▸ You can search for "*Synchronized*" in the Timeline Index.

Audio Inspector

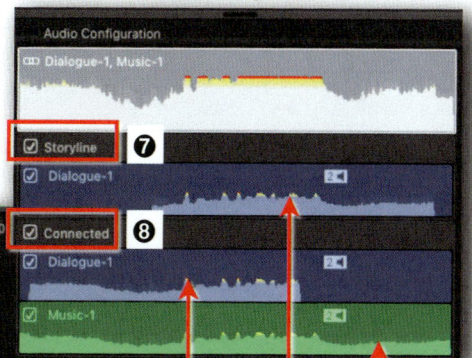

Timeline

Layered Graphic Clips

FCPx allows you to import layered Photoshop images that keep their individual layers. However, Layer Masks and Layer Effects are not imported. You have to merge them in Photoshop before importing them into FCPx. The layers retain the alpha channel.

Here are the simple rules and procedures:

▶ You import the .psd file that contains the layers into FCPx like any other media file, same rules and procedures.

▶ FCPx detects if the file contains layers and creates a special type of Clip, a "Layered Graphic Clip" indicated by its own "stacked" icon 🗇 **❶**.

▶ Technically, a Layered Graphic Clip is similar to a Compound Clip, a Clip that contains other Clips. When you open the Clip in the Timeline, you will see that the individual Layers are Connected Clips **❷** to the Background Layer on the Primary Storyline **❸**. The Timeline Index shows the individual layers as image Clips **❹**.

▶ All the rules and editing techniques apply as with any other Compound Clip or Project Timeline: Shift, trim, remove individual layers or apply any video effects to individual layers in the Video Inspector.

▶ You can even add additional Clips to the Layered Graphic Clip. This, however, will ultimately convert it to a Compound Clip. Its stacked icon will change to a Compound Clip icon 🗁.

▶ Layered Graphic Clips can, of course, be added to other Compound Clips, Auditions and even MultiCam Clips.

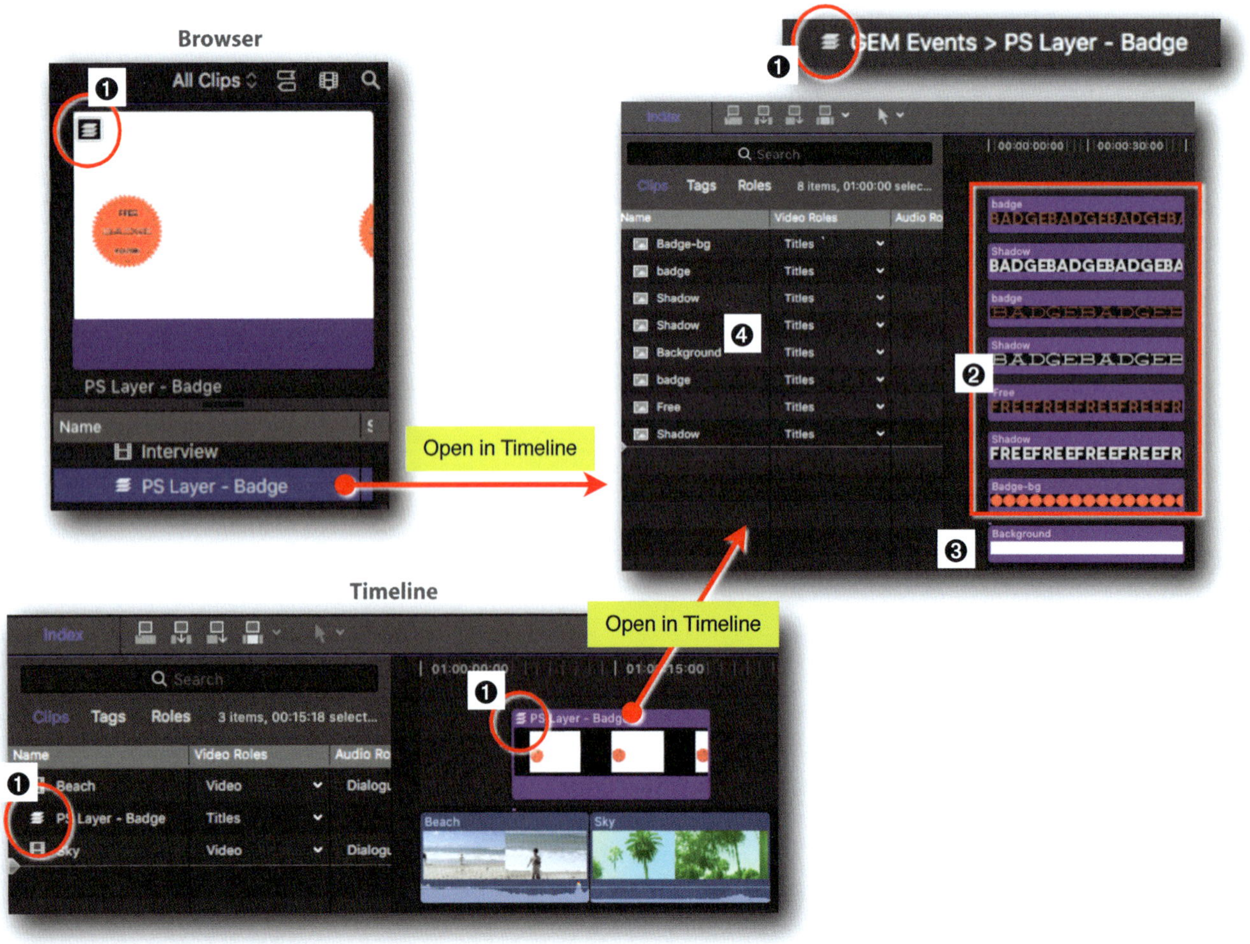

Browser

Open in Timeline

GEM Events > PS Layer - Badge

Open in Timeline

Timeline

Audition Clips

Audition is an extremely useful and very powerful feature. With this tool, you take existing Clips and group them together into an "Audition". Don't confuse that with a Compound Clip, which becomes a separate Clip containing other Clips nested inside on a Timeline. An Audition Clip, on the other hand, is not a Clip, it has no properties, it doesn't show up in the Inspector either. It's just an indicator that you can replace the current Clip with any of the alternate Clips that exist in this group. In other words, when you look at an "Audition" Clip, it appears as an individual Clip marked with an "Audition" icon ◢ ❶. This lets you know that you have alternate Clips attached in that Audition group, which you can use in place of the current Clip.

▶ An Audition is not a Clip, just an organizational tool.

▶ You can group multiple Clips ❷ into an Audition Clip.

▶ Auditions can be created in the Libraries Browser and on the Timeline.

▶ The Audition icon ◢ ❸ indicates that you are looking at one specific Clip that can be swapped out with any other Clip in that Audition group.

▶ A Clip marked with the Audition icon can be edited as usual (trim, add Markers, Keywords, adding FX, editing, etc.).

▶ You can add any Clip into an Audition: Standard Clip, Compound Clip, Titles, etc.

▶ Audition Clips can help you to:

　　☑ Group different takes ❹ from the same scene to quickly determine which one fits best.

　　☑ Have duplicates of the same Clip with different effects.

　　☑ Switch between Title cards ❺ in different languages.

　　☑ Switch between different Audio Clips ❻ (songs) for background music.

▶ An Audition Clip can be placed on the Primary Storyline, as a Connected Clip to the Primary Storyline or on a Connected Storyline. You can even put (one or multiple) Audition Clips into a Compound Clip, that itself can be placed again into an Audition - Did I mention that Audition is a powerful feature?

▶ Please note that if you use Audition Clips on the Timeline and switch between different Clips from that Audition, the rest of the sequence might shift on the right if the Audition Clips have different lengths. (Magnetic Timeline!)

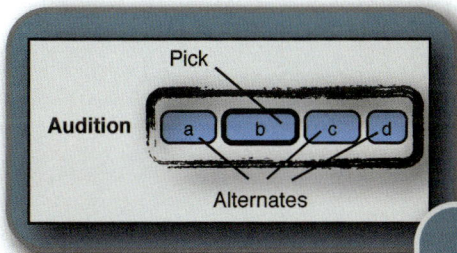

An Audition is a group of Clips. The visible Clip is called the "**Pick**" and the other Clips are the "**Alternates**".

When used on the Timeline, a Clip (Pick) belonging to an Audition can be swapped with any of the Alternates in that Audition.

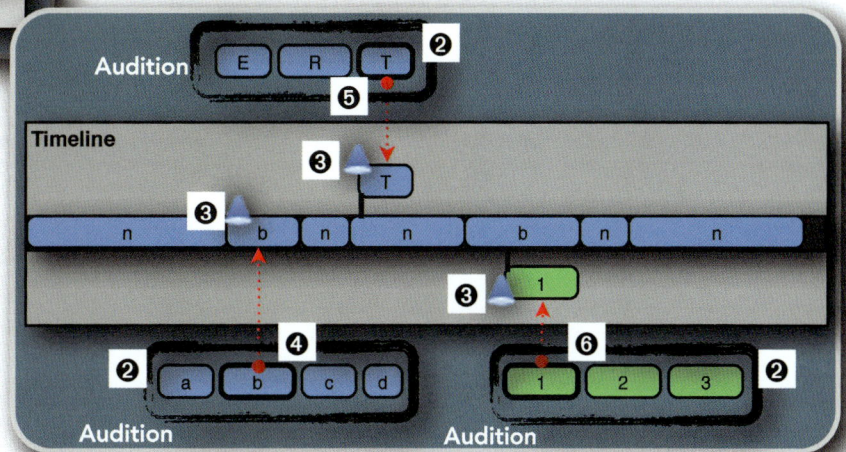

A Clip belonging to an Audition is marked with the additional Audition icon.

Please note: The Audition doesn't represent a timeline itself, just a group of Clips. However, Clips in that group can have a timeline, i.e. Compound Clips.

Workflow

To work with Auditions is very easy, just keep a few rules in mind:

- 🟡 **Create** an Audition
  - In the Browser, create an Audition as part of the preparation to move it later to the Project Timeline.
  - On the Timeline, create an Audition at any time during the editing process.
- 🟡 **Change** the Content of an Audition Clip

  At any time, you can add more Clips to the Audition or remove Clips from the Audition. You can add new Clips to an Audition only from the Libraries Browser, not the Timeline.

- 🟡 **Edit** as usual

  Any edit applied to the current Clip in an Audition (Pick) stays with that Clip. You can switch to a different Clip in the Audition and edit that one, etc.

- 🟡 **Finalize**

  You can leave the Audition in your Project as long as you want (keep your options open). Or, you can "Finalize" an Audition if you don't need the Alternates anymore. This discards all the Alternates and leaves the Pick as a regular Clip. You cannot export Alternates from the Audition. The workaround would be to duplicate the Audition and finalize it with the different Pick.

➡️ *Audition Window*

You can manage an Audition directly in the Browser or on the Timeline with Menus and Key Commands. However, the Audition Window (a floating window) provides a nice visual interface to manage the group of Clips inside the Audition.

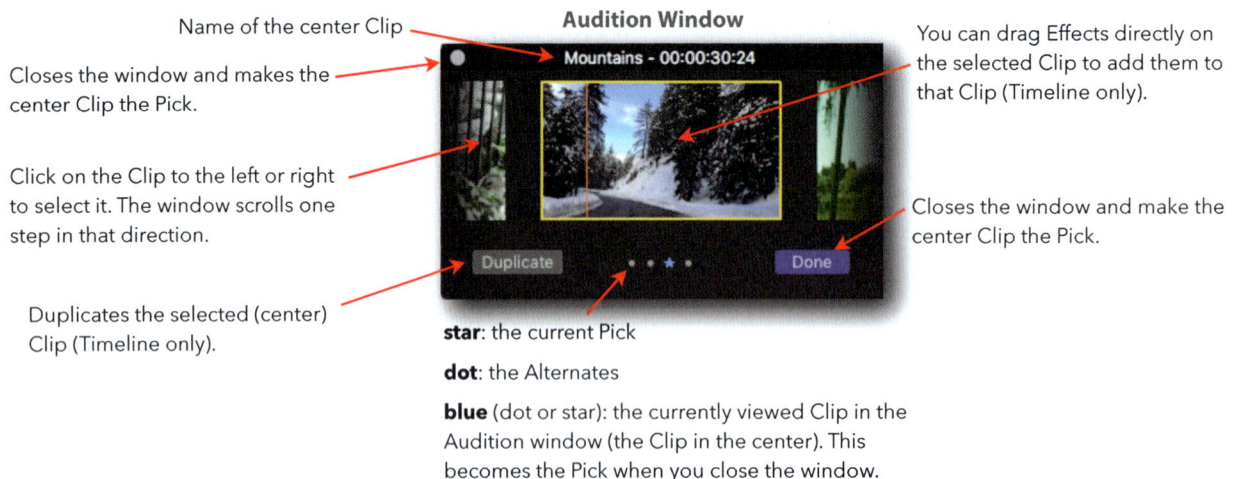

Name of the center Clip

Closes the window and makes the center Clip the Pick.

Click on the Clip to the left or right to select it. The window scrolls one step in that direction.

Duplicates the selected (center) Clip (Timeline only).

Audition Window

Mountains - 00:00:30:24

Duplicate   • • ★ •   Done

You can drag Effects directly on the selected Clip to add them to that Clip (Timeline only).

Closes the window and make the center Clip the Pick.

star: the current Pick

dot: the Alternates

blue (dot or star): the currently viewed Clip in the Audition window (the Clip in the center). This becomes the Pick when you close the window.

Open the window by *clicking* on the Audition icon ◤ of a Clip. You can have only one Audition Window open at a time. Close any Audition window first before opening another one.

The window displays a maximum of three Clips. You can step through the available Clips on the left or right, one at a time, by *clicking* on them or using the Key Commands *ctr+ArrowRight* or *ctr+ArrowLeft*.

The Audition Window is just a display tool that can be used for Auditions in the Browser or Auditions in the Timeline. The same way Event Clips and Timeline Clips are slightly different due to their purpose and the way you use them, Auditions in the Browser and in the Timeline are also slightly different. That means that some functions in the Audition Window might not be available for Browser Auditions or Timeline Auditions.

You can manage Auditions in three areas:

- ... in the **Browser** for Auditions made of Event Clips
- ... on the **Timeline** for Auditions made of Timeline Clips
- ... in the **Audition Window** to manage Auditions in the Event or Project Timeline

➡ *Audition in the Libraries Browser*

The following are the procedures available when you use Audition in the Browser.

🟡 **Create an Audition**

Select at least two Clips you want to group together into an Audition and choose any of these commands:

- Key Command *cmd+Y*
- Main Menu *Clip ➤ Audition ➤ Create*
- *Ctr+click* on the Clip and choose from the *Shortcut Menu ➤ Create Audition*

🟡 **Add to an Audition**

You cannot add a new Clip to an existing Audition in the Libraries Browser. If you have an Audition with Clip a+b+c, you can select that Audition and any new one (Clip d) and use the Create Audition command again. This creates the new Audition with Clip a+b+c+d. Just delete the other Audition (a+b+c). Please note that you don't delete any Event Clips when you delete an Audition in the Libraries Browser (different story in the Timeline, see below).

> **Be Careful:**
> Using any of the two commands "Replace and add to Audition" or "Add to Audition" (from theMain Menu *Clip ➤ Audition ➤*) will add the currently selected Clip in the Libraries Browser to the Clip in the Timeline that has the Playhead parked at. This is regardless of what window has key focus at that moment.

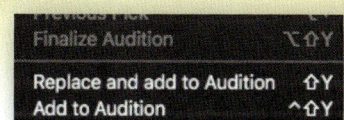

🟡 **Select a different Pick**

Select the Audition Clip and use any of these commands:

- Key Command *ctr+ArrowRight* or *ctr+ArrowLeft*
- Main Menu *Clip ➤ Audition ➤ Next /Previous Pick*
- *Ctr+click* on the Clip and choose from the *Shortcut Menu ➤ Next /Previous Pick*

🟡 **Open Audition Window**

Select the Audition Clip and use any of these commands:

- Key Command *Y*
- Main Menu *Clip ➤ Audition ➤ Open*
- *Ctr+click* on the Clip and choose from the *Shortcut Menu ➤ Open Audition*
- *Click* on the Audition icon in the filmstrip, not the one in the list.

➡️ Audition in the Timeline

🟡 Create Audition

Creating an Audition in the Timeline is a little bit different. Let's look at two scenarios. The first one is for creating an Audition in the Timeline and the second one is when adding Event Clips to existing Timeline Clips.

> ▶ **Timeline to Timeline**
>
> You cannot create an Audition from two or more Clips on the Timeline the way you can in the Browser. The only way to create a new Audition in the Timeline is to select a single Timeline Clip and FCPx then creates a new Audition, containing the selected Clip and a duplicate of that Clip. There are two commands with a different outcome:
>
> - Duplicate as Audition ❶: The duplicate Clip is an exact copy with all the Effects that the original Clip might have.
>   - 📌 Key Command **cmd+Y**
>   - 📌 Main Menu *Clip ➤ Audition ➤ Duplicate as Audition*
>
> - Duplicate from Original ❷: The duplicate Clip has all Effects removed that the original Clip might have.
>   - 📌 Key Command **sh+cmd+Y**
>   - 📌 Main Menu *Clip ➤ Audition ➤ Duplicate from Original*

> ▶ **Browser to Timeline**
>
> Here is how to add an Event Clip (or an existing Audition) from the Browser onto a Timeline Clip. This is the same action as replacing a Timeline Clip with a different Event Clip. When you do that, the Event Clip will not be added to the Timeline right away. Instead, the Timeline Clip will turn gray and the cursor gets a green "add" icon 🟢 to indicate that the Clip you are "holding" with your mouse gets added to that grayed Clip. If you release the mouse, a popup menu ❸ gives you a list of choices:

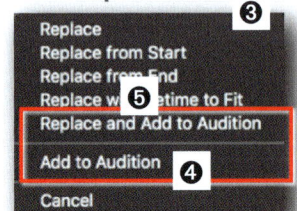

> - ☑️ **Add to Audition ❹**: If the current Clip is already part of an Audition, then the new Clip will just be added as an Alternate. If the current Clip is a regular Clip, then an Audition will be created with the existing Clip becoming the Pick and the new Clip the Alternative.
>
> - ☑️ **Replace and add to Audition ❺**: This is the same procedure with the difference that the newly added Clip becomes the Pick.

The same two commands are also available from the Main Menu *Clip ➤ Audition ➤* ❻. When you use these commands, then the source Clip (the one that will be added) is the one currently selected in the Browser and the destination Clip is the one that is selected (white frame) in the Timeline or shows the red dot 🔴 on the Playhead.

🟡 Add Timeline Clip to an Audition

You cannot add a Timeline Clip to an existing Audition in the Timeline. Only Event Clips (or entire Auditions) from the Browser can be added to an Audition Clip in the Timeline.

🟡 Edit the Pick (Clip)

Edit the Audition Clip as if it was an individual Clip.

🟡 Preview

This command will open the Audition Window and starts playing the Audition with a two second preroll from the previous Clip on the Timeline.

- 📌 Key Command **ctr+cmd+Y**
- 📌 Main Menu *Clip ➤ Audition ➤ Preview* ❼
- 📌 **Ctr+click** on the Audition and choose from the *Shortcut Menu ➤ Audition ➤ Preview*

🌑 Select a different Pick

Same as in the Libraries Browser. Select the Audition Clip and use the command:

- 📌 Key Command *ctr+ArrowRight* or *ctr+ArrowLeft*
- 📌 Main Menu *Clip ➤ Audition ➤ Next/Previous Pick* ❶
- 📌 *Ctr+click* on the Audition and choose from the *Shortcut Menu ➤ Audition ➤ Next/Previous Pick*

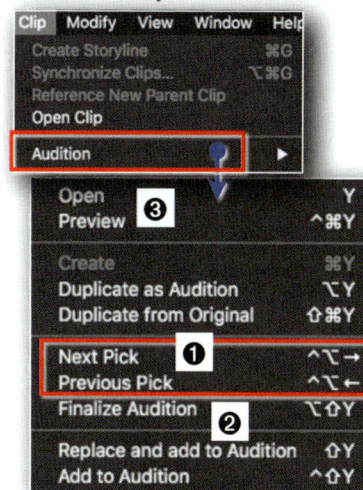

🌑 Finalize Audition

You can leave the Audition in your Project as long as you want (keep your options open) or you can "Finalize" an Audition if you don't need the Alternates anymore. This command discards all the Alternates and leaves the Pick as a regular Clip. Select the Audition Clip and the following commands:

- 📌 Key Command *sh+opt+Y*
- 📌 Main Menu *Clip ➤ Audition ➤ Finalize Audition* ❷
- 📌 *Ctr+click* on the Audition and choose from the *Shortcut Menu ➤ Audition ➤ Finalize Audition*

🌑 Open Audition Window

Select the Audition Clip and use any of the commands:

- 📌 Main Menu *Clip ➤ Audition ➤ Open* ❸ or use *Clip ➤ Audition ➤ Preview* to open the Audition window and start playing right away.
- 📌 Shortcut Menu *Audition ➤ Open Audition* or use *Clip ➤ Audition ➤ Preview* to start playing right away.
- 📌 Key Command *Y* or use *ctr+cmd+Y* to open the Audition window and start playing right away.
- 📌 *Click* on the Audition icon 🖼 ❹ on the Timeline Clip (not on Event Clips).

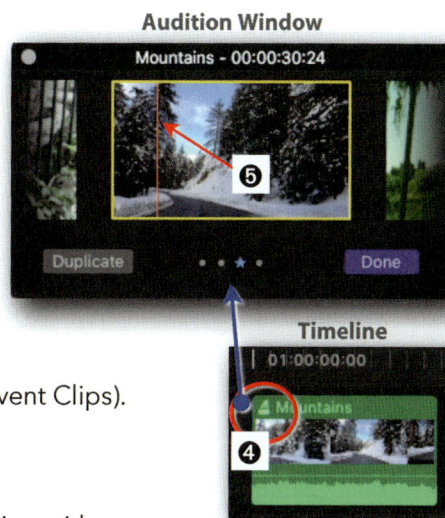

Audition Window

🌑 Audition in the Audition Window

Although you can perform most of the commands related to the Audition without opening the Audition Window, it provides a better visual feedback. Please note that the following commands are only valid when the Audition Window has key focus (indicated by a highlighted close button in the upper-left corner).

- ▸ **View**: The Clip is visible and plays in the center thumbnail and also in the Viewer.
- ▸ **Skimming**: Skimming is automatically active for the center Clip when moving the curser over the thumbnail. In addition, when the red Skimmer ❺ is visible, you can use the standard playback commands. Press *spacebar* (play/stop) or *J, K, L*.
- ▸ **Preview**: The Preview command (*Clip ➤ Audition ➤ Preview* ❸ or *ctr+cmd+Y*) plays back the Clip with a two second preroll. The Audition Window displays "Auditioning" ❻ in the header while playing.
- ▸ **Edit**: You can apply Effects by *dragging* them from the Effects Browser directly onto the center Clip.
- ▸ **Duplicate**: The Duplicate button ❼ functions as "Duplicate as Audition" (with effects).
- ▸ **Change**: *Click* on the left or right thumbnail to scroll to the next Clip or use the Key Command *ArrowLeft* and *ArrowRight*.
- ▸ **Remove**: Just select the thumbnail (center) and press the *delete* key.

Concept

Maybe you won't shoot a multi-camera interview or a TV-show and maybe you are not working on a multi-camera setup for a feature film, but since nowadays every smart phone owner technically carries an HD camera around, the possibilities are endless.

▶ Maybe you and your buddies went to a concert that you all recorded on your iPhones from different angles.

▶ Maybe at the dance recital some other parents also taped your little girl's performance from different angles.

▶ Maybe your two nieces taped aunt Mary's cake making, pointing one iPod at the cake and one at her face explaining the process.

▶ Maybe at the wedding shoot, uncle Bob (due to his alcohol intake) unintentionally created some additional shaky "handheld" footage that you can combine as a different angle with your official Clips.

You get the idea. MultiCam editing is for everyone and FCPx provides the easy to use tools to edit MultiCam shots.

The basic technique behind MultiCam is that you have a scene or event shot with more than one camera at a time from different angles. But as I mentioned, you can use MultiCam for different non-traditional situations. Now let's first look at the concept before learning how to use it.

What you are doing with a MultiCam Clip is this: You have multiple Clips that you want to sync together, to treat them as one "über"- Clip, but still have the tools to control the individual Clips. Sounds pretty much like a "Compound Clip" or a "Synchronized Clip". Although it is a different type of clip called "MultiCam Clip", its behavior is very similar to a Compound Clip. This has the advantage that once you are familiar with the basic concept of the various Clips in FCPx (including Compound Clips), learning to use MultiCam Clip is pretty easy.

Make sure that you're always aware of the different types of Clips and what you can do with them.

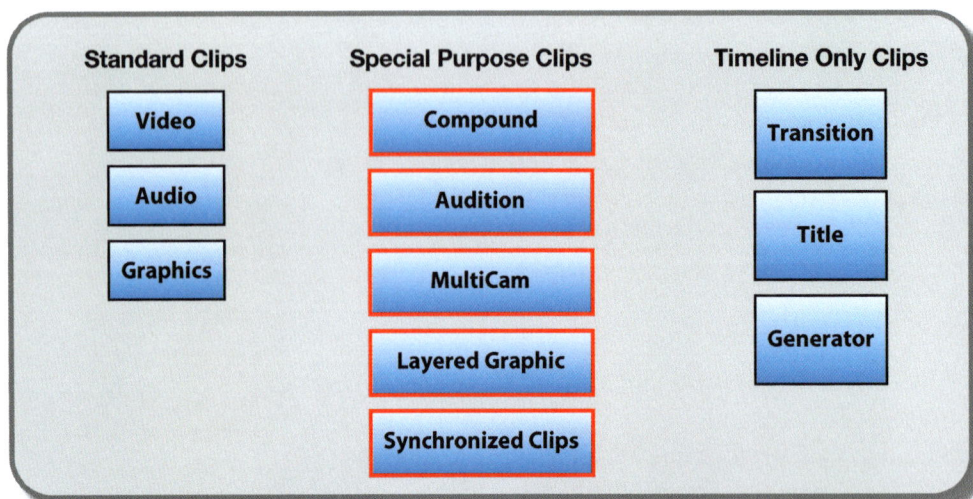

Standard Clips	Special Purpose Clips	Timeline Only Clips
Video	Compound	Transition
Audio	Audition	Title
Graphics	MultiCam	Generator
	Layered Graphic	
	Synchronized Clips	

First, a few diagrams to understand the concept of how MultiCam is implemented in FCPx.

❶ MultiCam Clip: Starting at the Libraries Browser, you select multiple Clips and create a new MultiCam Clip, which incorporates all those individual Clips into one single (easy to handle) Clip. For the moment, think of it as a Synchronized Clip with added functionality.

❷ Angle Editor: A new interface element called the "Angle Editor" lets you edit the structure of the MultiCam Clip and its content. This looks and behaves like a Timeline, where the individual Clips are displayed on separate tracks, called "Angles". However, you won't find a Primary Storyline or anything "magnetic" in here.

❸ Angle Viewer: Another new interface element, called the "Angle Viewer", lets you view all those individual Clips in a special Viewer. It is made of individual mini Viewers, one for each Angle in the Angle Editor. It is like a multi display video board.

As a second function, the Angle Viewer lets you switch and cut between different Angles of the MultiCam Clip for picture editing.

❹ Timeline: And finally, as with any other Clip in the Browser, you can drag the MultiCam Clip to the Timeline of a Project for your picture edit where it can be treated like any other Clip in addition to the unique editing features the MultiCam Clip provides. You can cut between the available Angles to choose the "Active Angle" for any given moment in your video. Think of an Audition Clip where, instead of choosing one "pick", you could switch between different picks during the duration of the Clip. Once placed on a Timeline, you can still access the Angle Viewer (for viewing, switching, and cutting between Angles during editing) and the Angle Editor (to tweak the content and structure of the MultiCam Clip). The parent-child relationship (yellow) is explained on the next page.

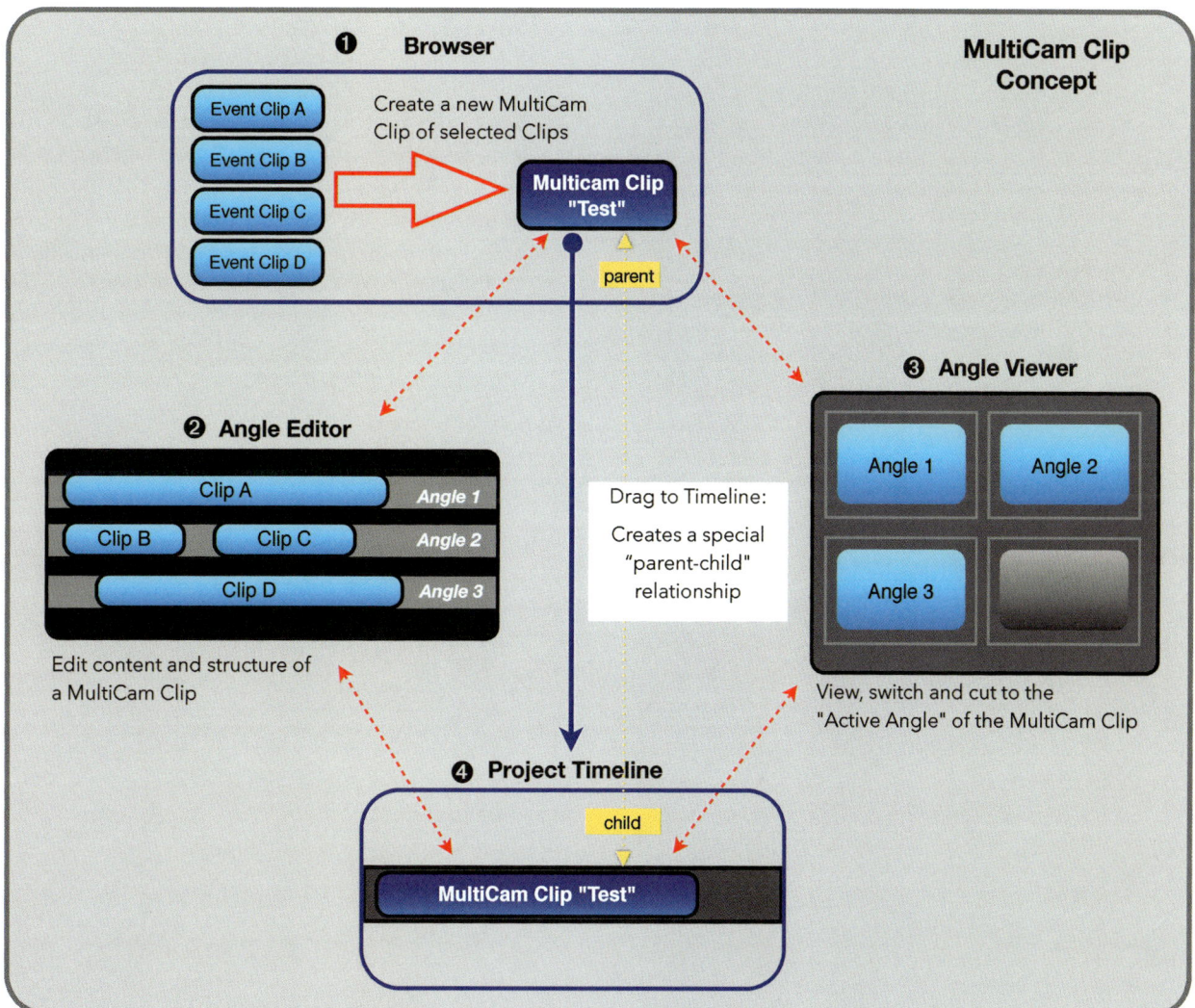

➡ *Editing*

Be careful with the term editing in regards to the "Angle Editor" and "Angle Viewer".

🔵 **Angle Editor**: Here you "edit" the content and structure of the MultiCam Clip. This has nothing to do with the picture edit where you arrange and "edit" various Clips on the Timeline. The Angle Editor is mainly a tool to prepare the MultiCam Clip before it gets used on the Timeline. You can open up the Angle Editor from a MultiCam Clip on the Timeline for tweaking, but be aware of the possible consequences (see parent-child relationship).

🔵 **Angle Viewer**: Although mainly a display tool for MultiCam Clips, the Angle Viewer also provides "editing" tools. This kind of editing is for the actual picture editing where you can choose the right audio and video content from "inside" the MultiCam Clips to switch or cut to specific Angles, called the "Active Angle".

➡ *"Parent - Child" Relationship*

This is a very important detail to understand before using MultiCam Clips because it can seriously mess up your Projects if you are not aware of that concept. The simple step of dragging a Clip from the Libraries Browser to the Timeline needs to be understood in that context.

▶ **Standard Clips**: When you drag an Event Clip to the Timeline ❶, a new Timeline Clip is created that inherits all the properties of that Event Clip. After that, both Clips (Event Clip and Timeline Clip) are independent. Any edits on the Event Clip ❷ doesn't affect the Timeline Clip ❸ and vice versa. Their only connection is their common File Reference ❹ ("where did I originate from?").

▶ **MultiCam Clips**: MultiCam Clips seem to behave the same way. You can drag a MultiCam Clip from the Browser to one or many different Projects. From now on, they are all independent Clips. Changes of the MultiCam Clip in the Browser ❺ don't affect copied MultiCam Clips

in the Project Timeline ❻ and vice versa. However, this is only true for the "outside" of the MultiCam Clip (the wrapper), but NOT for the "inside", its content, the Clips that are contained inside the MultiCam Clip (visible in the Angle Editor). That content ❼ is not independent between the Event Clip and Timeline Clip versions. There is a parent-child relationship. Any MultiCam Clip copy (child) ❽ on a Timeline is still connected to its original MultiCam Clip (parent) ❾ in the Browser. Opening the Angle Editor ❿ from any of those related MultiCam Clips and making changes will affect all other MultiCam Clips in that "relationship", because they access that same content.

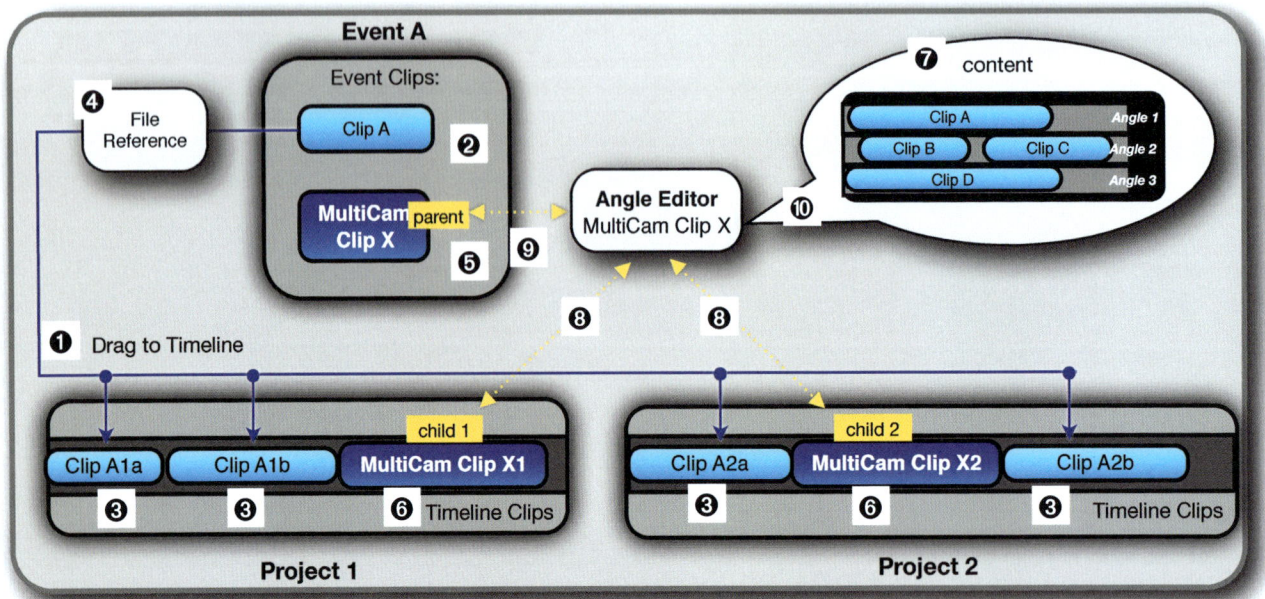

Create a MultiCam Clip

Let's start with the first step of creating a MultiCam Clip. Please note that MultiCam Clips can only be created in the Browser. The procedure is similar to creating a Compound Clip. Select all the Clips in the Browser that you want to combine in the MultiCam Clip and choose one of the following commands to copy them into a MultiCam Clip (it is a real copy, so you could delete the original Clips after you created the MultiCam Clip without affecting the MultiCam Clip):

- Main Menu *File ➤ New ➤ New Multicam Clip ...*
- *Ctr+click* on any of the selected Clips and choose from the *Shortcut Menu ➤ New Multicam Clip...*
- Key Command "New Multicam Clip" is not assigned by default

A Sheet ❶ will slide out that is similar to the one we know from the Compound Clip ❷. I put the two screenshots next to each other. As you can see, the MultiCam Clip configuration has all the parameters ❸ from the Compound Clip plus a few more that are specific to the MultiCam Clip ❹ .

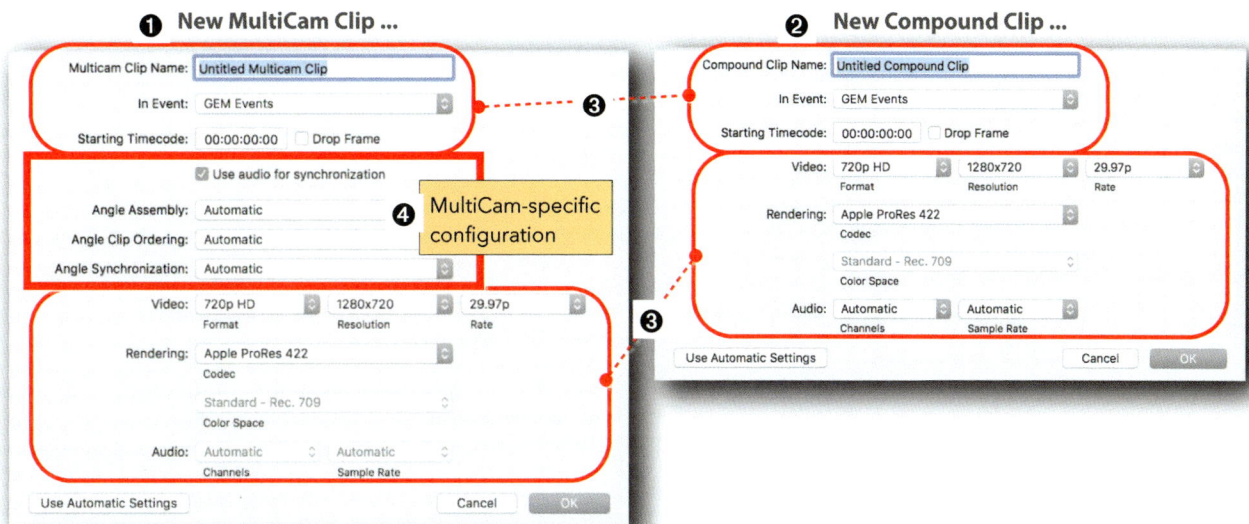

The important thing is to realize that you define new Video and Audio properties for the MultiCam Clip (as we did with Compound Clips and as we did with a new Project.) Please be aware of their similarities:

- **Project**: A Project is represented by a Timeline that contains many Clips.
- **Compound Clip**: A Compound Clip can be opened in a Timeline that contains many Clips.
- **MultiCam Clip**: A MultiCam Clip can be opened in a special Timeline (called Angle Editor) that contains many Clips.

➡ What's in it?

The following items are allowed to be inside a MultiCam Clip:

- ☑ A mix of multiple Clips of any kind (video, audio, graphics)
- ☑ A mix of multiple Clips of different Frame Size, Frame Rate, and Codec
- ☑ You can't put a MultiCam Clip inside another MultiCam Clip

Next, we will look at those MultiCam Clip specific settings in the Configuration window.

➡ MultiCam Specific Configuration

These are the settings that determine how the individual Clips are synchronized and laid out in the Angle Editor:

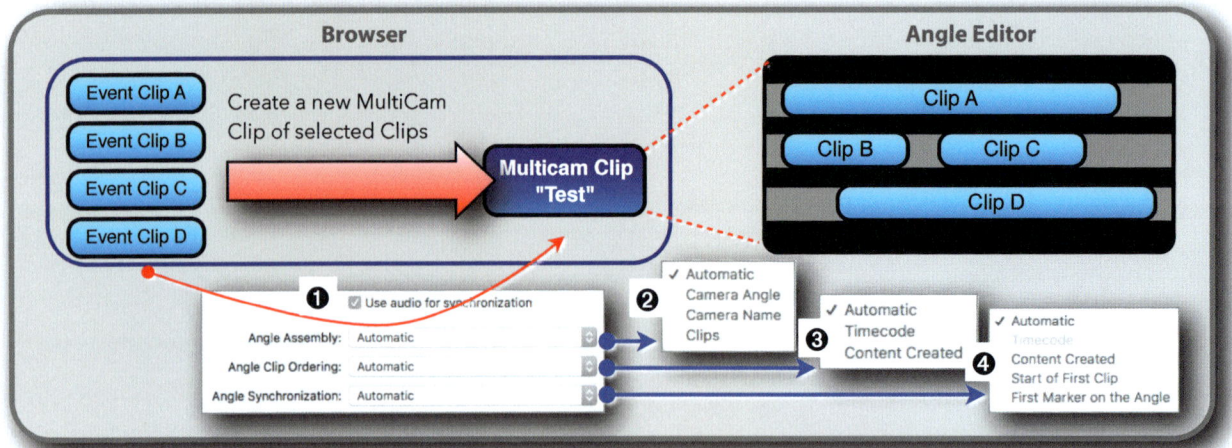

🔵 Use audio for synchronization ❶

This analyzes the audio waveform and uses that information to synchronize the Clips. It's also a useful way to sync audio only Clips with video Clips. Although quite accurate, it can be very time consuming.

🔵 Angle Assembly ❷

How are the "Angles" (the lanes, or tracks) created (can be changed later):

- ▶ Automatic: FCPx automatically creates Angles based on the most valid data (metadata) it can find.
- ▶ Camera Angle: Creates different Angles for different "Camera Angle" metatdata in the Clips, if available.
- ▶ Camera Name: Creates different Angles for different "Camera Name" metatdata in the Clips, if available.
- ▶ Clips: Creates different Angles for each Clip.

🔵 Angle Clip Ordering ❸

How are the Angles ordered in the Angle Editor (can be re-arranged later):

- ▶ Automatic: Creates the order automatically based on the available data.
- ▶ Timecode: Ordered by Timecode start of each individual Clip. Preferred method if the Clips have Timecode.

- ▶ Content Created: Ordered by the Date and Timestamp metadata recorded by the camera.

🔵 Angle Synchronization ❹

The important aspect of how the Clips are synchronized to each other (can be adjusted later):

- ▶ Automatic: Uses the best of all available choices below (analyzing audio waveforms).
- ▶ Timecode: This is the fastest and most accurate method (if the timecode between the cameras was set properly). FCPx even detects Timecode breaks of Clips that belong to the same Angle or Camera and places them on the same Angle lane with gaps in between.
- ▶ Content Created: Uses the Date and Timestamp metadata that was created by the camera (not as accurate).
- ▶ Start of First Clip: Syncs each Clip to its first start frame.
- ▶ First Marker on the Angle: This is useful when you created a marker for a clapper slate at the beginning of a take. You can set the markers roughly and have the audio synchronization checked. This way, FCPx uses the waveform synchronization only around the markers to fine tune the sync without performing a complete waveform analysis.

When you click OK, FCPx analyzes the data and creates a MultiCam Clip. It copies the Event Clips into the MultiCam Clip and places them onto the Angles, based on the configuration.

The newly created MultiCam Clip has its own MultiCam icon ▦, a four-square. It is displayed in various places:

- ▶ **❶ Browser List View**: You can search for the phrase "MultiCam"
- ▶ **❷ Browser Thumbnail**
- ▶ **❸ Timeline Clip**
- ▶ **❹ Timeline Index**: You can search for the phrase "MultiCam"
- ▶ **❺ Timeline History Menu**
- ▶ **❻ Angle Viewer**

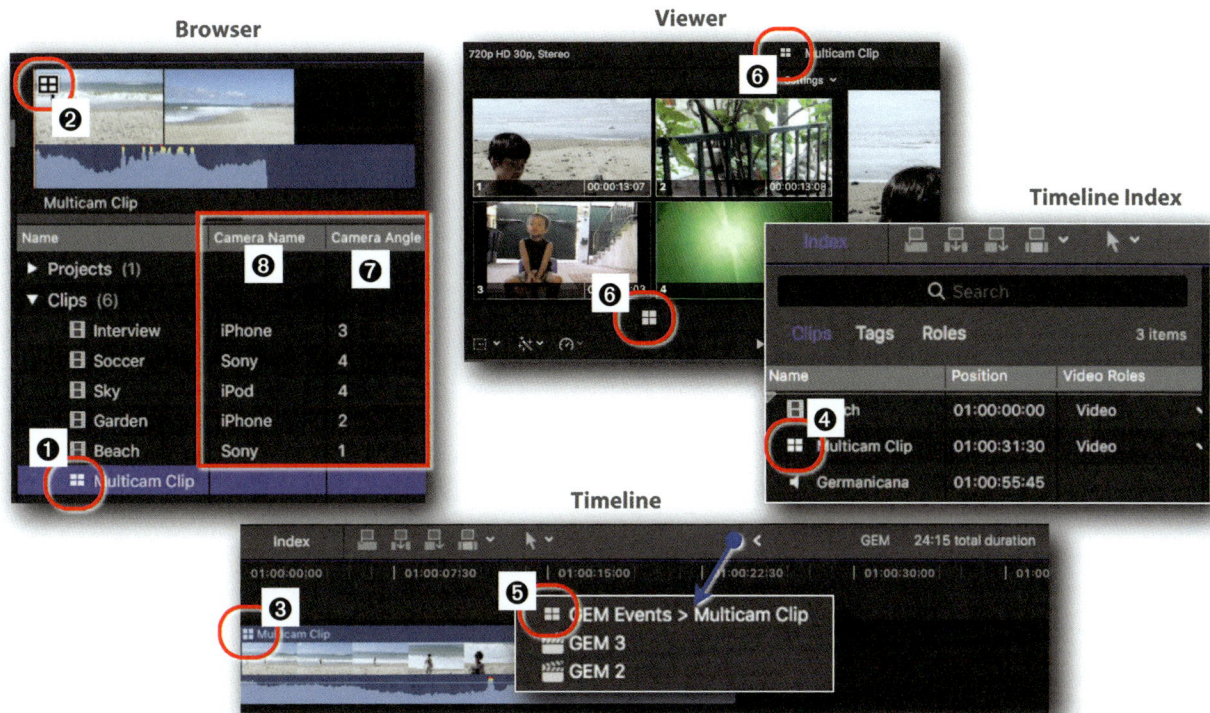

Browser

Viewer

Timeline Index

Timeline

➡ *Preparation for MultiCam Clips*

Here are a few things you can prepare before you create the MultiCam Clip.

☑ Make sure that the timecodes are synchronized between the different cameras when you are using this feature.

☑ Record audio on all cameras when possible, even if you don't use that source. You can still use it for audio synchronization.

☑ Make sure the Date and Time are set correctly on the cameras. You can later fix an incorrect Date and Timestamp with the command *Modify ➤ Change Content Created Date and Time*. This can also be used for still images. If a graphics Clip has the same date and time as the other Angles, then the length of the graphics clip will be adjusted to the full length of the Angle.

☑ There are three specific Metadata that FCPx can use to arrange different Clips in the MultiCam Clip:

- ▶ **Camera Angle ❼**: You can edit that metadata for each Clip in the Browser's List View or in the Inspector.

- ▶ **Camera Name ❽**: You can edit that metadata for each Clip in the Browser's List View or in the Inspector.

- ▶ **Camera ID**: This is a metadata that is created by some Cameras. It can't be edited, but FCPx can use that information during the creation of a MultiCam Clip.

Edit a MultiCam Clip - Angle Editor

The Angle Editor is the tool for editing the content of a MultiCam Clip. Remember, those changes affect the "parent" MultiCam Clip in the Browser and all its "child" copies in all Projects!

🌑 Open Angle Editor

Use any of the following commands to open a MultiCam Clip in the Angle Editor:

📌 ***Ctr+click*** on the MultiCam Clip in the Browser or Timeline and choose from the ***Shortcut Menu ➤ Open in Angle Editor***.

📌 ***Double-click*** on the MultiCam Clip in the Browser or Timeline.

📌 Key Command for "Open Clip" (unassigned by default).

➡️ *Interface Elements*

The Angle Editor is just the Timeline Pane, displaying the MultiCam Clip with special interface elements:

Angle Editor

Timeline Header: The header displays the name of the MultiCam Clip.

Video Monitor Icon: Click on it to select the Angle as the current video output. The icon 🖥️ turns purple 🖥️ and the entire Angle turns gray. This is the same as selecting "***Set Monitoring Angle***" from the Angle Menu.

Audio Monitor Icon: ***Clicking*** on it turns the audio for this Angle on 🔊 or off 🔇

This is the same as selecting "***Monitor Audio***" from the popup menu.

Angle Name: The name for each Angle is created automatically (numbered), but can be renamed.

Angle Menu: Various commands, specific for the Angle Editor.

🌑 Other Elements

▶ The Timeline History buttons (arrows on the Timeline Header `<` `>`) or Key Command ***cmd+[*** and ***cmd+]*** work in the same way as with any other Timeline.

▶ Skimming is always on.

▶ The "Clip Skimming" feature (***View ➤ Clip Skimming*** or Key Command ***opt+cmd+S***) also works. If selected, it skims only the one Clip (video and audio) that you mouse over, ignoring the current Video and Audio Monitor selection.

🌑 Output of the Angle Editor

The settings for Video and Audio monitoring in the Angle Editor has no affect on the actual MultiCam Clip. It is only for monitoring while working in the Angle Editor, i.e. monitoring the audio output of two Angles to check if they are in sync.

When Playing or Skimming (not Clip Skimming), this will be the output of the Angle Editor:

▶ **Video**: The one Angle that has the video icon selected 🖥️ which makes it the "Monitoring Angle".

▶ **Audio**: The sum of all the Angles with the speaker icon activated 🔊, "Monitor Audio".

- ▶ **Set the Video Monitor**: Only one Angle can send video
  - 🎱 *Click* on the Video Monitor icon 🖥
  - 🎱 From the Angle Menu 🔽 choose "*Set Monitoring Angle*"
  - 🎱 Key Command *sh+V* while skimming over the Angle

- ▶ **Set the Audio Monitor**: You can activate more than one Angle
  - 🎱 *Click* on the Audio Monitor icon 🔊
  - 🎱 From the Angle Menu choose "*Monitor Audio*"
  - 🎱 Key Command *sh+A* while skimming over the Angle

Here is a diagram that shows what is displayed in which Viewer:

- ▶ Play mode and Skimming behave the same.
- ▶ Clip Skimming always plays the skimmed Angle with one exception: When Clip Skimming over a Monitored Angle, then it behaves like regular Skimming.

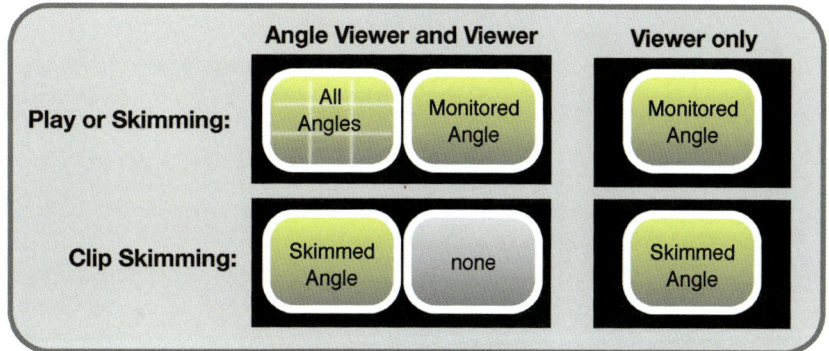

	Angle Viewer and Viewer		Viewer only
Play or Skimming:	All Angles	Monitored Angle	Monitored Angle
Clip Skimming:	Skimmed Angle	none	Skimmed Angle

➡ *Edit Tasks*

- ▶ **Position Tool**: The cursor changes to the Position Tool ▶ when switching to the Angle Editor.

- ▶ **Rename Angle**: The name for the Angle is set automatically during the creation of the MultiCam Clip (uses Angle Name, or Camera Name or Clip Name of the Event Clips). *Click* on the name and type a custom name.

- ▶ **Reorder Angles**: *Drag* the Handles on the right edge of the Angle up or down.

- ▶ **Add Angle**: *Click* on the selector 🔽 and choose "*Add Angle*" to add a new empty Angle below. You can now drag Clips onto it.

- ▶ **Delete Angle**: *Click* on the selector 🔽 and choose "*Delete Angle*". Please note that this affects the parent and child MultiCam Clip. If any Clip of the deleted Angle was used, a black placeholder Clip will be inserted in those Projects to avoid any time shift on the Timeline.

- ▶ **Move Clips**: You can freely move existing Clips on an Angle or between Angles. Remember, no "Magnetic Timeline" here. These are Tracks!

- ▶ **Add, Remove, Edit Clips**: You can drag new Clips from the Libraries Browser or Media Browser (Titles and Generators), trim those Clips, add Effects to individual Clips and even add Transitions between adjacent Clips. *Ctr+click* on the Clip to use Video and Audio Animation.

- ▶ **Disable Clips**: You can disable selected Clips. Main Menu *Clip ➤ Disable*, Shortcut Menu or Key Command *V*.

- ▶ **Synchronize Clips**: You can change the sync between Angles by moving their Clips manually. You can also sync them automatically:

  - On the reference Angle you want to sync to, choose from the popup menu "*Sync to Monitoring Angle...*", a two-up display opens in the Viewer. Set the Playhead on the Monitoring Angle to the frame that you want to sync to (i.e. a clapper). Now skim over the Angle that you want to sync. The left Viewer displays that video. Skim to this sync point (i.e. the clapper on this shot) and click the mouse. Now the Clip on this Angle will move the line up with the frame of the first Clip. - Click Done.

  - Select "*Sync Angle to Monitoring Angle*" on an Angle that has the out of sync Clip(s). This will compare those waveforms to the waveform of the Monitoring Angle and syncs those Clip(s).

UNAVAILABLE: because the Angle Editor is not exactly like a Timeline, the following features are not available: Solo Clips, Ripple Edit, Precision Editor, Connected Clips, Detach Audio, Break Apart Clip Items, and Change Duration.

Use a MultiCam Clip - Angle Viewer

The Angle Viewer has two functions: It is a special multi-display Viewer and an interactive interface for editing Angles in your Project Timeline.

➡ *Concept*

Each Angle in a MultiCam Clip is displayed in its own frame in the Angle Viewer.

▸ **64 Angles**: A MultiCam Clip can contain up to 64 individual Angles. That means, you can create a maximum of 64 lanes or tracks in your Angle Editor.

▸ **16 Displays**: The Angle Viewer can display up to 16 Angles at one time. This means that FCPx could play up to 16 video streams at the same time. Check if your hardware can handle such a data throughput.

▸ **Banks**: All the available Angles are organized in Banks. You can set the size of a Bank to 2, 4, 9, or 16. If the number of Angles in a MultiCam Clip is higher than the number of your chosen Bank size, then FCPx creates multiple Banks, i.e. for a MultiCam Clip with 7 Angles and a Bank size of 4, the created Banks would be Bank1: Angle 1-4 and Bank2: Angle 5-7.

▸ The Angle Viewer can only display one Bank at a time. However, all the available Banks are displayed as little icons at the bottom of the Angle Viewer and you can switch between the Banks by *clicking* on their icons to switch the Angle Viewer and display that specific Bank (see next page).

▸ Square or stacked layout: The Angles are arranged in a square layout (2x2, 3x3, 4x4). When you *drag* the divider line between the Angle Viewer and the Viewer to the left, the layout changes so all the Angles are displayed in a stacked way.

▸ The order of the displayed Angles in the Angle Viewer follows the order of the Angle lanes in the Angle Editor.

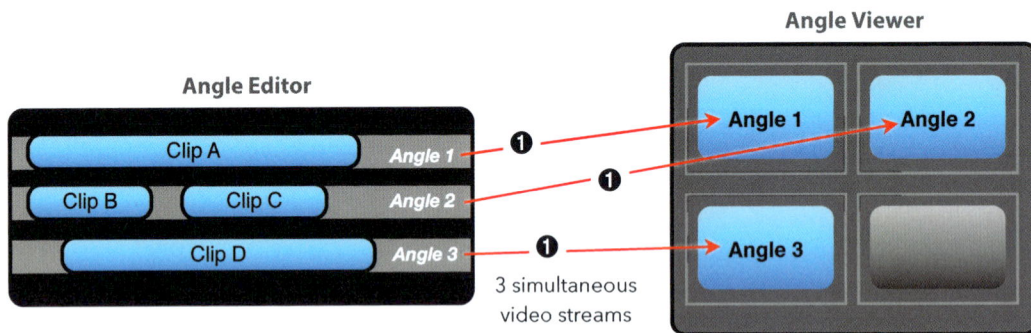

When you play or skim through a MultiCam Clip, all the Angles (individual Clips) in the Angle Viewer are played simultaneously. However, you have to be aware that each Angle represents a separate data stream ❶ and you have to check if the computer/graphics card/hard drive(s) can handle all those streams. Here are a few numbers ❷: If you transcode your footage in FCPx to Optimized Video, one stream (1 angle) requires about 20MB/s.

Transcoding your media files to Optimized Media (during import or later) will definitely improve the efficiency of your data stream. A checkbox in the Preference window "Create optimized media for multicam clips" ❸ is doing that transcoding step automatically. Also, set the Quality in the Vlewer's View Menu to "*Better Performance*" ❹ or use Proxy Media ❺.

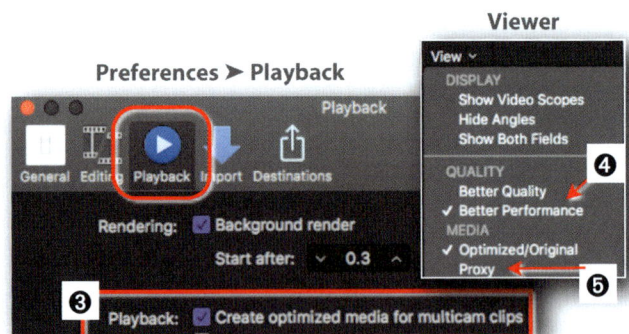

Toggle the Show/Hide Angle Viewer with any of the three commands:

- Key Command *sh+cmd+7*
- Main Menu *View ➤ Show in Viewer/Event Viewer ➤ Angles*
- From the upper-right corner of the Viewer, click the selector [icon] and choose *View Menu ➤ Show/Hide Angles* ❶. The Event Viewer can display its own Angle Viewer which can play, of course, only a selected MultiCam Clip in the Libraries Browser.

The Angle Viewer slides out from the left of the Viewer Pane, becoming part of it by squeezing the standard Viewer frame to the right. Here are the various interface elements:

▶ **Header ❷**: The Viewer header indicates what is "feeding" the Viewer, displaying either the name and the icon of an Event Clip [icon] or a Project [icon].

▶ **Settings Menu ❸** [icon]: Select how many Angles to display at a time, or "how many Angles are in one Bank" (2, 4, 9, 16), i.e. if you have 4 Angles in your Clip and choose to display 2, then you end up with two Banks of 2 Angles. You can also drag the divider line between the Angle Viewer and Viewer left to create a Stacked Angle View.

- Overlays - Timecode: Select if you want to display the Clip's timecode in each Angle.

- Overlays - Display Name: Select if you want to display the name of the Clip, the Angle (Angle or Camera ID), or None.

4 Angles in a 4x1 Bank: [icon]
4 Angles in a 2x2 Bank: [icon]
4 Angles in 9x1 Bank: [icon]
Stacked Angle View: [icon]

▶ **Bank ❹**: The Bank icon(s) lets you switch between banks if there are more than one. They also indicate which Angle is the Active Angle. This is the Angle from which the current video and/or audio content is selected and played.

▶ **Switch Mode Buttons ❺**: The selected icon is highlighted to indicate which of the three modes is active for displaying and editing (see next page for editing details): Video + Audio [icon], Video only [icon], Audio only [icon].

▶ **Viewer Frames ❻**: The individual Viewer frames indicate by their color coded border and the icon in the upper-right corner which one is playing audio and/or video at the current Playhead position (yellow - blue - green). This is called the Active Angle. The Bank icon ❹ also displays the colored content information besides letting you switch between banks (if there are more than one). This is a really elegant interface. If you have Bank2 selected, but Bank1 has the Active Angle, then you would still see that Active Angle information indicated by the colored segments of the tiny Bank icon.

▶ **Viewer ❼**: The selected Angle in the Angle Viewer is the active video output that is shown in the Viewer on the right.

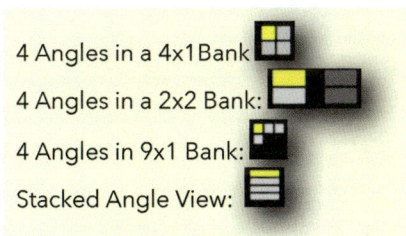

As I pointed out at the beginning of the chapter, you have to be aware of the different instances of a MultiCam Clip.

▶ **MultiCam Clip in the Browser**: This is where the MultiCam Clip was created. It is the parent-clip.

▶ **MultiCam Clip on the Timeline**: Once you drag a MultiCam Clip onto a Project Timeline, it becomes a child-clip.

Editing the "inside" (dependent)

Regarding the content of the MultiCam Clip (the inside structure), all versions are dependent on the same content of the MultiCam Clip. Parent-Child relationship. Either the parent-clip or child-clip will display and edit the same content in the Angle Editor.

Editing the "outside" (independent)

Regarding the treatment of the Clip (what to do with it), the different instances are independent. For example, when you set the Active Angle of a MultiCam Clip in the Libraries Browser to the second Angle and then drag that Clip to the Timeline, it becomes a child-clip. Now, changing the Active Angle in this child-version on the Timeline will not change the Active Angle of the parent-clip in the Browser. And also, changing the Active Angle of the parent-clip in the Browser will not affect the child-clip afterwards. In that regards, they are independent.

Also any trimming and processing (video and audio) of the MultiCam Clip is independent for each copy of the MultiCam Clip on the Timeline. Only the processing of the individual Angles in the Angles Editor applies to all copies of the MultiCam Clip.

➡ *Active Angle*

This is the main task of the editing that you are doing in a MultiCam Clip. You decide which of the available Angles will be displayed. That Angle becomes the "Active Angle". There is a big difference if the MultiCam Clip is in the Libraries Browser or on the Timeline.

● **Browser**: You can choose only one Active Angle for that MultiCam Clip, although Video and Audio can come from separate Angles. The bottom line is that you can only make one choice at a time which is valid for the entire Clip. This is more like a default Angle. That information gets carried over when you drag the MultiCam Clip to the Timeline.

● **Timeline**: Once the MultiCam Clip is placed on the Timeline (as an independent child-clip), you can switch between Angles at any time during the duration of the Clip as part of your picture edit.

The procedure is similar to a director of a life TV show who watches the monitors of the different camera feeds: "Camera 1, now cut to Camera 3, back to Camera 1 in 5 seconds", etc.

▶ The Angle Viewer represents that wall of Monitors .

▶ A click with the mouse on an Angle in the Angle Viewer (or a key command) at a specific time is your instruction when and where to cut to.

▶ You can click in pause mode while the Playhead is parked at a Timeline position or you can perform the cutting on-the-fly in play mode while the Playhead is moving.

➡️ *Switch Mode Buttons*

Before you click on any Angle, you have to make sure what "Switch Mode" the cursor is in. This is determined by the three Switch Mode buttons in the upper-left corner of the Angle Viewer. Click on one of three icons to change the mode:

Video and Audio: *Click* on the first icon or select it with the Key Command *sh+opt+1*

In this mode, the cursor switches the whole Angle, Video and Audio.

Video Only: *Click* on the second icon or select it with the Key Command *sh+opt+2*

In this mode, the cursor switches only the Video content, leaving the audio at the previous Active Angle.

Audio Only: *Click* on the third icon or select it with the Key Command *sh+opt+3*

In this mode, the cursor switches only the Audio content, leaving the video at the current Active Angle.

Three kinds of Active Angles

Having the option to switch audio and video separately creates three types of Active Angles. You can see in the Angle Viewer by the colored border and the colored icon in the upper-right corner of the frame what content (video, audio) is coming from what Angle at any time.

Active Angle: video + audio   Active Angle: video only   Active Angle: audio only

➡️ *Switch or Cut*

Switch

If a MultiCam Clip is selected in the Browser, then the mouse cursor displays the standard Pointer Tool 👆 when moving over the Angle Viewer. You just switch the default Active Angle for the MultiCam Clip. Alternatively, use the number keys to switch Angles (numbered from top to bottom): *1*, *2*, *3*, ...

Switch Tool

Cut

If a MultiCam Clip is selected in the Timeline, then the cursor changes to a Blade Tool ◆ when moving over the Angle Viewer. *Clicking* now on an Angle will not switch but will actually create a (special) cut on the MultiCam Clip at that Timecode position. Alternatively, use the number keys to cut to different Angles: *1*, *2*, *3*, ...

If you just want to switch to a different Angle while editing a MultiCam Clip in the Timeline, hold the *opt* key, which changes the cursor to a Pointer Tool (Switch action). This also works with the number keys *opt+1*, *opt+2*, *opt+3*, ...

You can perform the switch and cut action in two ways:

- ▶ **Step-by-Step**: Position the Playhead where you want to switch or cut and use the command.
- ▶ **On-The-Fly**: Let the Playhead run (play mode) and perform the commands live while you're watching.

Use a MultiCam Clip - Timeline

We just covered all the functionality for the MultiCam Clip in the Angle Viewer. Now, let's look at what we can do with a MultiCam Clip once it is placed on the Timeline. This is where the Clip is used the most.

➡ Interface Elements

Here are the various elements.

▶ The Clip displays the MultiCam icon ⊞ to identify it as such ❶.

▶ The name of the Clip ❷ depends on the setting in the Clip Appearance window ❸:
  - Clip Names
  - Angles: If video and audio content come from a different Angle, then both Angle names will be displayed
  - Clip Roles

▶ Shortcut Menu: *Ctr+click* on the Clip will open its Shortcut Menu ❹. Besides the command "*Open in Angle Editor*", you can set the *Active Video Angle* and *Active Audio Angle* from the submenu.

▶ Other editing commands are also available from the Shortcut Menu like the Video and Audio Animation ❺.

▶ In addition to that, you can set the Active Audio Angle and Active Video Angle ❻ in the Info Inspector ⓘ when you have a Metadata View selected that displays those two properties.

Angle Clip

Next, we will learn the details about cutting a MultiCam Clip. Please be aware that cutting to a different Angle on a MultiCam Clip DOES NOT cut or split the MultiCam Clip into two separate Clips like on other Clips. The MultiCam Clip technically remains a single Clip and still can be edited and trimmed like a Standard Clip. The "cuts" on a MultiCam Clip creates segments, each segment representing a specific Angle of the MultiCam Clips. They are like special "Angle Clips".

➡️ Through Edit (Angle Clip)

When you cut to a different Angle on the MultiCam Clip, a dotted "Through Edit" line divides the Clip and indicates that audio or video "continues" on either side of that edit point.

Here is an example of how the MultiCam Clip edits could look in your Timeline (just for demonstration purposes).

- ▶ This is the full MultiCam Clip (blue) without any edits ❶. One Angle is selected. Like any other Clip, you could place it wherever you want: On the Primary Storyline, Connected Clip, Compound Clip, Audition, etc.

- ▶ Making an Angle cut ❷, produces the dotted Through Edit line ❸. Now this is important. It is still the same Clip. Note the rounded corner of the other regular Edit Points.

- ▶ This is how the MultiCam Clip could look after adding more Angle cuts ❹. It is still one continuous Clip! The Through Edits create these special "Angle Clips", segments of a MultiCam Clip.

- ▶ In the Timeline Index, instead of the single MultiCam Clip, each individual Angle Clip ❺ is listed (with the same name) with the *Active Angle* column ❻ indicating its used Video Angle and Audio Angle(s). You can even add Notes ❼ to the individual Angle Clips.

Timeline

Timeline Index

➡️ Trim Edits:

When you move your mouse over a Through Edit, the cursor changes to a Roll Tool ❽. Dragging the line will change to a yellow Edit Point ❾ and you can perform a Roll Edit between "Angle Clips".

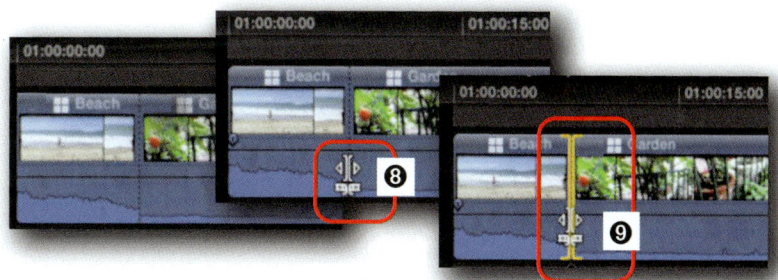

🏆 Other Editing Techniques

You can use most of the other editing techniques for trimming Clips as well:

- ▶ Use the Trim Tool 🔲 for Ripple Edits, Slip and Slide, etc.

- ▶ Precision Editor, Expand/Collapse Audio/Video, Transitions (at the edges of the MultiCam Clip) are all available.

- ▶ You can connect other Clips to the MultiCam Clip or apply effects to it.

- ▶ Delete Edit Points to have the previous Angle continue to the next Through Edit.

- ▶ Moving other Clips onto the Through Edit point will insert that Clip and changes the edit point from a Through Edit to a regular Edit Point.

Multi-channel Audio

I covered the topic of Multi-channel Audio in FCPx and its elegant implementation in the Audio chapter. This is already an extremely powerful feature, but when combined with MultiCam Clips, it's getting even better.

Here is an example to demonstrate the functionality.

- ▶ This is a single MultiCam Clip with three Through Edits , showing the individual Angles ❶. The two "cuts" switch from Angle 1 (Beach) to Angle 2 (Garden) to Angle 3 (Sky).
- ▶ The Playhead is parked at Angle 1 and that's why the Angle Viewer ❷ has the yellow frame and icon, indicating that video and audio is coming from this Angle.

Now let's look at the Audio Inspector ❸ and see what is going on there if you select any segment ❹ (Angle Clip) of the MultiCam Clip in the Timeline:

- ▶ All Angles are displayed with their Audio Components (if they were enabled in the Angle Editor).
- ▶ The Audio Components are grouped by Angles with the Angle showing their own header ❺ with their names and a checkbox to enable/disable their Audio Component.
- ▶ Each Audio Component is displayed with the typical elements like checkbox, Role assignment, channel indicator, FX (if applied).
- ▶ The Audio Components for the currently selected Angle are enabled by default ❻.
- ▶ The Summed Audio Clip ❼ (the top waveform) displays the sum of all enabled Audio Components and the Roles of all included Audio Components.
- ▶ The command Expand Audio Components ❽ is also available for each individual Angle on the MultiCam Timeline Clip (*ctr+click*) and, of course, those Audio Components ❾ correspond to what is displayed in the Inspector ❸.

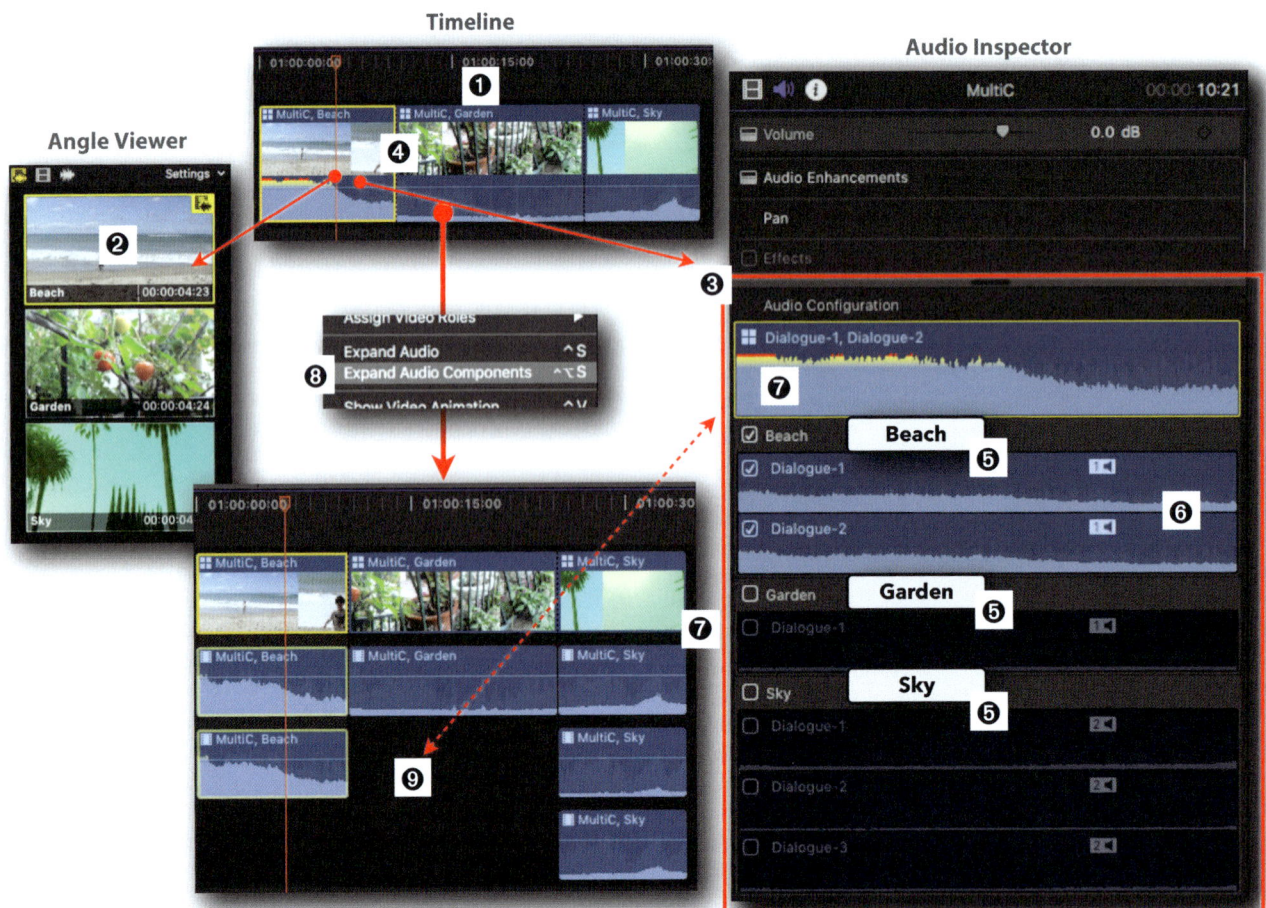

10 - Clips

➡ *Advanced Audio Editing*

Although FCPx provides an extremely flexible and easy to use implementation for audio editing, it can get quite complex if you take advantage of all the features. So make sure to understand the underlying concept and terminology and review the Audio chapter for a detailed explanation of Audio Channels, Audio Components, and Channel Configurations.

Here are a few examples:

- ▸ If you have multiple Angles selected as your audio source, then you will see all those Angles in the Angle Viewer showing the green audio icon 🟩 and the green frame in addition to the Angle with the yellow fame and icon 🟨 ❶.

- ▸ You can freely trim the beginning and end of an individual Audio Component, and even overlap ❷ those Audio Components.

- ▸ *Drag* a Range with the Range Tool 🔲 ❸ and disable only that portion of the audio (*V*). Repeat the procedure to "cut out" multiple sections.

- ▸ Adjust the audio level by *dragging* the volume line and/or the Fade Handles ❹ or select a Range first and adjust the level for that section.

- ▸ Use Audio Animation ❺ with Keyframes on individual Audio Components.

- ▸ Only those Audio Components are displayed on the Timeline that are selected in the Inspector. However, you can still disable an entire Component with the Disable command on the Timeline (*V*).

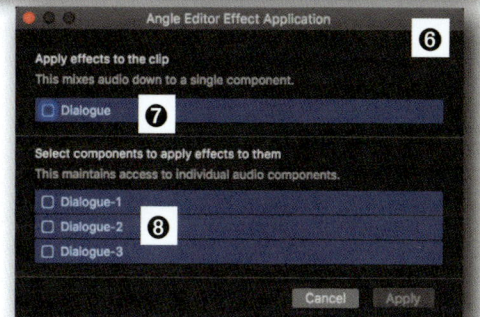

🔘 Audio Effects

I showed the difference in the Audio chapter when applying Audio Effects to the individual Audio Component or to the Summed Audio Clip. With MultiCam Clips, that concept gets one level more complex, because you can apply Effects on the Angle Editor <u>and</u> in the Timeline separately!

- ▸ **Angle Editor**: When you *drag* an Audio Effect over a Clip in the Angle Editor, then the "Angle Editor Effect Application" dialog ❻ opens (if the Clip has more than one active Audio Component). It gives you the option to apply the effect to the Summed Clip ❼ (top) and/or to individual Audio Components ❽. The FX Badge 🅵🆇 will be placed on the corresponding Clip. However, that Effect Badge is not visible in the Audio Component in the Timeline. It is kind of a premix that you do in the Angle Editor!

- ▸ **Timeline**: You can apply Audio Effects to the Summed Audio Clip or its Audio Components 🅵🆇 ❾. The same rules apply as we discussed in the Audio chapter regarding the Mixdown Badge 🔗 ❿.

🔘 Roles

Of course, you can take advantage of all those complex audio editing situations by using Roles and Lanes as I explained in the Roles & Lanes chapter.

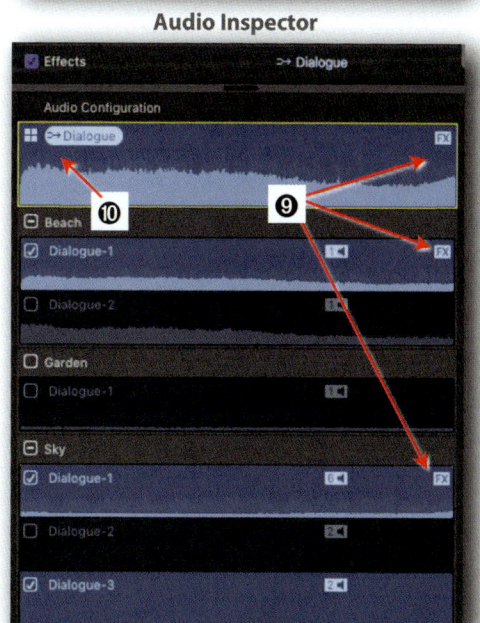

Audio Inspector

Connected Storyline

Before I explain this feature, let's make sure we are clear on how the track-less Timeline in FCPx works. It comes down to two questions:

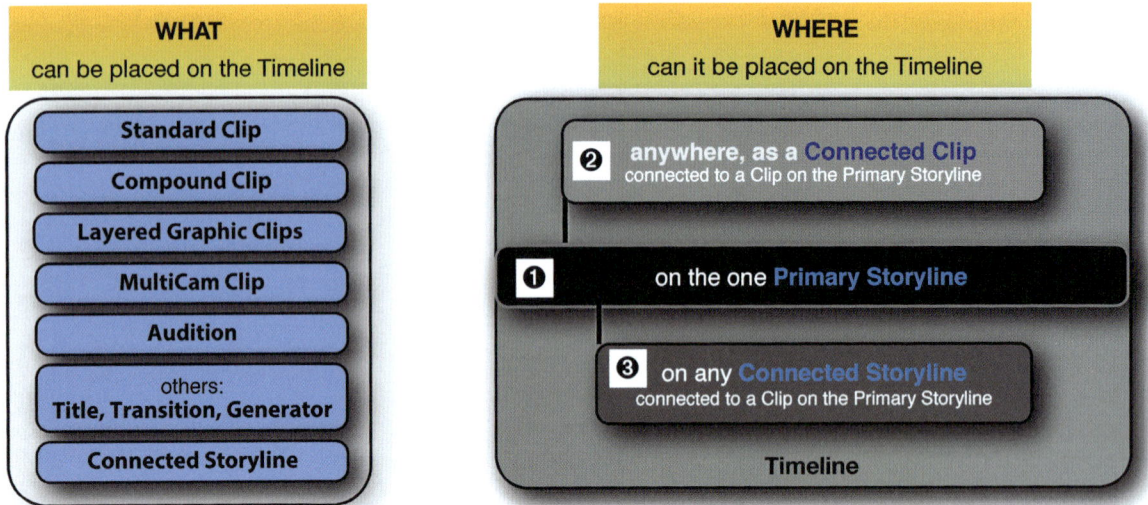

❶ Any item can be placed on the Primary Storyline except a Connected Storyline.

❷ Any item can be placed outside the Primary Storyline but must be connected to a Clip on the Primary Storyline.

❸ Any item can be placed on a Connected Storyline that is itself connected to a Clip on the Primary Storyline.

The function of a Connected Storyline should not be confused with a Compound Clip. Here are the main differences:

▶ A Connected Storyline is like a container, that can "group" multiple Clips together. The Clips don't have to be connected (gaps in between) but can not overlap. Space between Clips will be filled with Gap Clips in the Connected Storyline.

▶ You cannot select Clips that are located on the Primary Storyline to create a Connected Storyline.

▶ The Connected Storyline is not a "nested" Clip. Instead of putting Clips "inside" something, they stay on the same Timeline level, just "tied together" with a "see through" frame. Therefore, the Connected Storyline doesn't have any properties on its own and no command to "Open in Timeline" (Clips on the Connected Storyline of course can have that command).

▶ All the editing features from the Primary Storyline also apply to the Connected Storyline. Please note that Effects are not added to the Connected Storyline, they are added to the individual Clips placed on the Connected Storyline. Remember, it is just a frame, not a Clip by itself like the Compound Clip.

▶ You can add any Clip onto it, but only on that one single lane. No stacked Connected Clips like the Primary Storyline.

▶ Dragging a Connected Storyline (a) onto a Connected Storyline (b) will just add the containing Clips from (a) in that sequence onto (b).

▶ Transitions work for all ins and outs. Please note that dragging a transition to any Connected Clip will wrap it automatically into a Connected Storyline first (because Connected Clips cannot have transitions).

So basically, a Connected Storyline is just a sequence of Clips. As a whole, these Clips can be treated like one Connected Clip and individually they can be edited as if they would be on their own Primary Storyline.

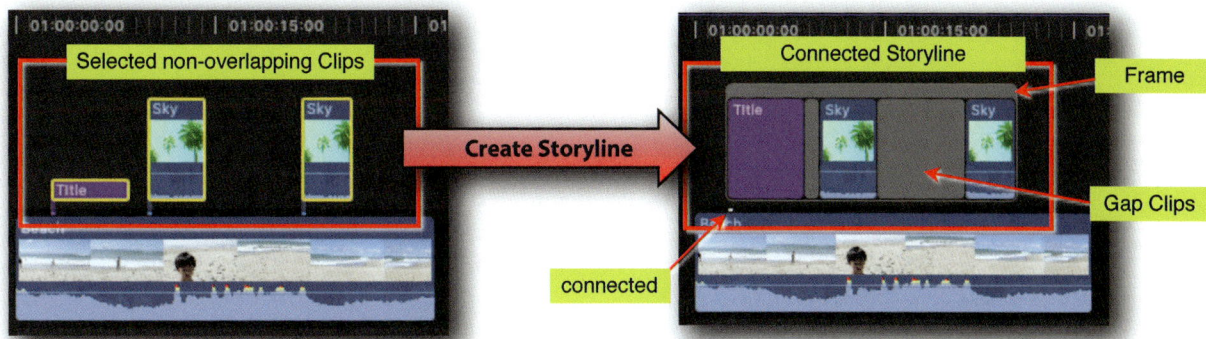

➡ Create a Connected Storyline

Select any non-overlapping Connected Clips (even existing Connected Storylines) and use any of the following commands:

- Key Command *cmd+G*
- Main Menu *Clip ➤ Create Storyline*
- *Ctr+click* on the Connected Clip and select from the *Shortcut Menu ➤ Create Storyline*

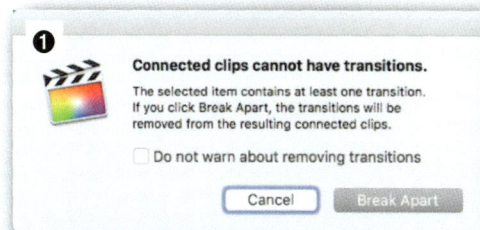

➡ Editing Connected Storylines

Most of the edit commands follow standard FCPx rules with a few specialties to be aware of.

- **Trimming**: Trimming the left or right border of a Connected Storyline actually trims the Clip at that location.

- **Add/Remove Clips**: The same procedures apply as with the Primary Storyline (exception: no Connected Clips allowed). Just drag Clips in or out of the Connected Storyline(s).

- **Merge Connected Storylines**. Moving one Storyline over another will just move the Clips over into one frame. If you move the Storylines only partially over the other one, then they stay individual Storylines, just visually rearranged.

- **Detach Audio**: Of course, this command also works on Clips inside the Connected Storyline. It extracts the audio portion of the selected Clip, putting it as an audio-only Connected Clip to the Primary Storyline and leaves the now "video only" Clip inside the Connected Storyline.

- **Break Apart Clip Items**: This command completely resolves the Connected Storyline into its individual Clips as Connected Clips to the Primary Storyline. If the Connected Storyline

has transitions, then an Alert Window ❶ warns you that Connected Clips can't have transitions and they will be lost. Make sure to select the frame of the Connected Storyline and not the Clips inside when initiating this command from the Main Menu *Clip ➤ Break Apart Clip Items* or by using the Key Command *sh+cmd+G*.

- **Lift from Storyline**: This command moves a single selected Clip on the Primary Storyline into a Connected Clip. Multiple Clips will turn into a Connected Storyline (leaving Gap Clips on the Primary Storyline). Use the Key Command *opt+cmd+ArrowUp* or command from the Main Menu *Edit ➤ Lift from Storyline*.

- **Overwrite to Primary Storyline**: This command works the same as with a single Clip (except audio only Clip). You can *drag* a Connected Storyline onto the Primary Storyline with the Select Tool (insert) or the Position Tool (overwrite). The frame will disappear and all the Clips will end up on the Primary Storyline. You can also use the Key Command *opt+cmd+ArrowDown* or the command from the Main Menu *Edit ➤ Overwrite to Primary Storyline*.

11 - Animation (Automation)

Basics

Just to be clear, in this chapter we are not talking about animation as in video animation, like cartoons or Pixar movies. The topic here is "Automation", the automatic change of specific Parameter Values in a Clip when playing back that Clip. Instead of using this common term "Automation", FCPx uses the term "Animation".

Math Background

First, let's look at some math background to see what we are dealing here with.

It is all about applying a parameter value to a Clip, i.e., setting the volume level, setting the amount of blur, scale, etc. Let's look at two scenarios:

▶ ❶ Applying one fixed value (y) for a parameter (a constant value). That value doesn't change for the duration of the Clip and is, therefore, time independent. No time information (x) is necessary.

▶ ❷ Applying different values (y) for that parameter over time (variable values) for the duration of a Clip. Now, for each parameter value we need the timing information (x), "what parameter value at what time?"

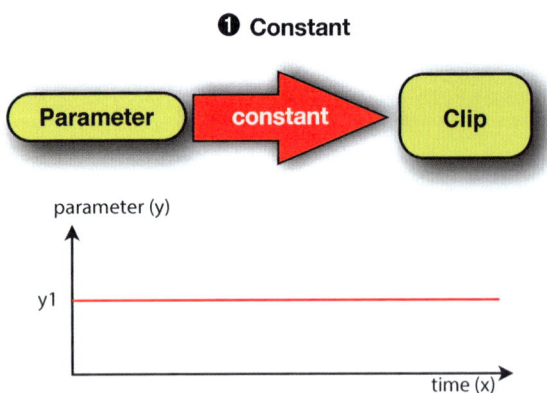

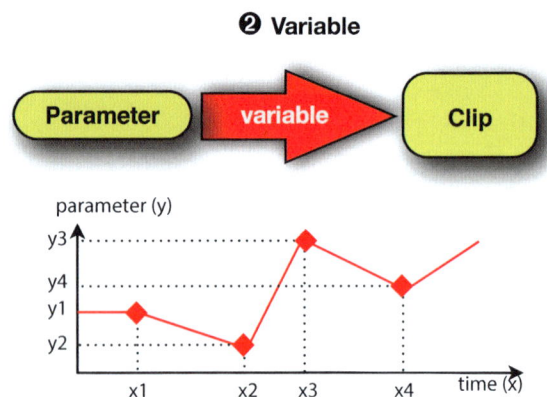

❶ **Constant**

❷ **Variable**

What we see here is a mathematical function (x-axis and y-axis), where the x-axis represents the timeline of the Clip and the y-axis represents the value of the parameter over time. The red line (the function) is a result of x/y coordinates connected together.

❶ In this example, the x/y coordinate is special, because for any x value (time) the Parameter value (y) is the same, creating a straight line, parallel to the x-axis.

❷ In this example, the parameter value changes over time. The graph shows 4 discrete x/y coordinates (x1/y1, x2/y2, x3/y3, x4/y4). Connecting those coordinates results in the function.

Your math teacher calls those red dots ...	In video applications, the dots are known as ...	In audio applications, the dots are known as ...
x/y Coordinates	**Keyframes**	**Nodes or Control Points**

➡ *Keyframes - Interpolation*

So a Keyframe is simply an x/y coordinate that carries two values:

- 🔘 **Time Stamp**: The time stamp (x value) or time address on that Clip
- 🔘 **Parameter Value**: The specific parameter value (y) of the Clip at that time address (x)

However, there is one more technicality we have to be aware of: **Interpolation**

- ▶ **Graph ❸**: This graph has four keyframes (a, b, c, d). Imagine the Clip is playing (moving along the x axis from left to right) and the keyframes represent the volume level of the dialog. The volume is set to 0dB (**a**) until it reaches keyframe **b**, which has a value of -6dB, so the level drops. When the Clip reaches keyframe **c**, which has the value +5dB, the level jumps to +5dB until it reaches keyframe **d** with the instruction to lower the volume level to -5dB.

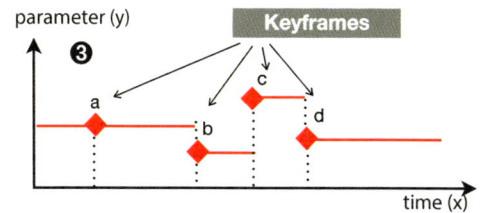

  This would be an example of a switch. The value of the first keyframe stays constant until the Clip reaches the second keyframe where it switches to the new value, etc. This, however, is not what the function looks like when we "connect" the keyframes. Instead of a sudden value change at each new keyframe, the value is actually changing gradually to reach the next keyframe.

- ▶ **Graph ❹**: If you look at this graph, it means that there are not only 4 keyframes, but an infinite amount of keyframes each representing discrete values (x/y coordinate). The system automatically creates those "invisible" keyframes, a procedure also known as "Interpolation".

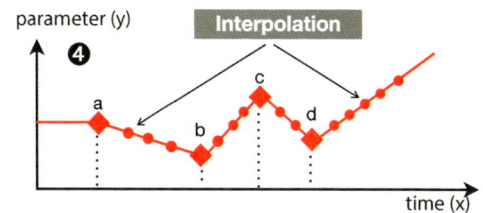

Here is a quote from the FCPx User Guide about keyframes: "*The word keyframe comes from the traditional workflow in the animation industry, where only important (key) frames of an animated sequence were drawn to sketch a character's motion over time. Once the keyframes were determined, an in-between artist drew all the frames between the keyframes.*"

That "in-between artistry" is called interpolation. Maybe this is why Apple uses the terms "Audio Animation" and "Video Animation" in FCPx to describe the changing of parameter values over time instead of using the term "Automation".

Conclusion

A Keyframe is always a value pair of time address (x) and parameter value (y) that belongs to a parameter of a Clip on the timeline. The series of keyframes for one particular parameter creates a graph ("Automation Line") with the interpolation taking place between the Keyframes.

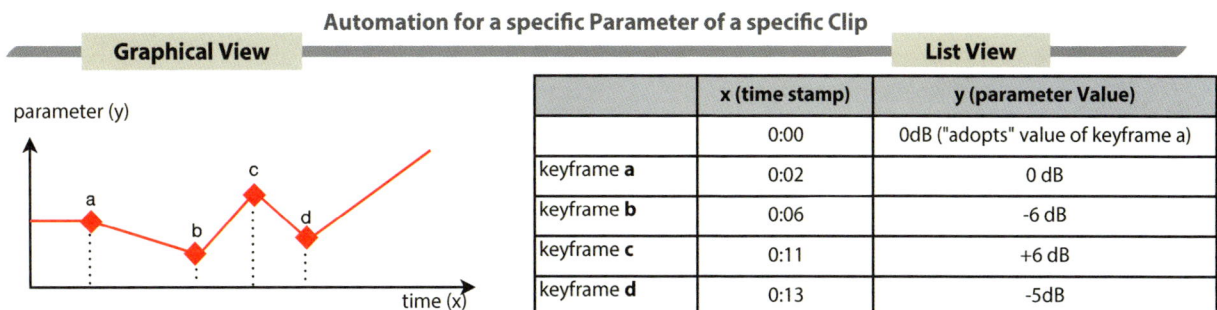

Automation for a specific Parameter of a specific Clip

Graphical View

List View

	x (time stamp)	y (parameter Value)
	0:00	0dB ("adopts" value of keyframe a)
keyframe **a**	0:02	0 dB
keyframe **b**	0:06	-6 dB
keyframe **c**	0:11	+6 dB
keyframe **d**	0:13	-5dB

Create Keyframes

When thinking about Keyframes, think about the Clip, because Keyframes belong to a specific Clip, stored with the Clip. Each Clip has a list of Parameters (properties) that can carry multiple keyframes (value pair of SMPTE Address and Parameter Value):

▶ The top level is a Clip, the selected Clip ❶. What you are doing in the next step affects only that Clip.

▶ The next level is a selected Parameter ❷ for that Clip. What you are doing in the next step affects only the selected Parameter of the selected Clip.

▶ A Parameter has at least one value (the fixed default value). A fixed value doesn't change during the Clip and is, therefore, not assigned to a time value. If you are changing only one existing value, then that is the constant value for the selected Parameter of the selected Clip. No Keyframes required.

▶ To have the Parameter change to a different value at a specific time address (x) ❸, move the Playhead to that position on the selected Clip, create a Keyframe ❹, and change its Parameter value (y) ❺. This Keyframe now stores that value pair (x/y). Of course you can change its x or y value at any time or delete the Keyframe all together.

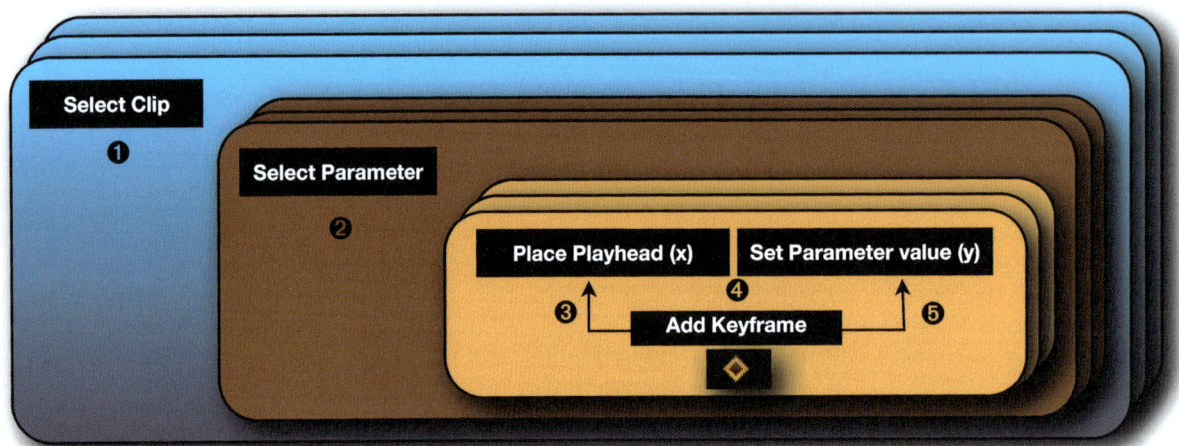

🟡 **Create New Keyframe**: These are the steps of creating a new Keyframe(s):

❶ Select the Clip
❷ Select the Parameter
❸ Place the Playhead
❹ Add the Keyframe
❺ (optional) Adjust the Parameter Value (y)
❸ Place the Playhead to the next position
❹ Add another Keyframe or adjust the Parameter Value ❺ (which automatically adds a new Keyframe)

🟡 **Edit Existing Keyframe**: These are the steps for editing any existing Keyframes:

❶ Select the Clip
❷ Select the Parameter
❹ Select the Keyframe
❸ Move its position or ❺ change its Value

• **_Attention_**: Changing the Parameter in the Inspector while in Play Mode moves the whole Automation Line up or down.

FCPx has three areas where you can create/edit Keyframes. These are just different user interfaces (graphic view, list view) accessing the same data (in the database of your Library). Those user interface elements are:

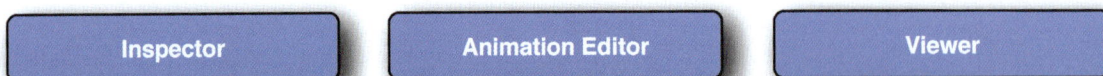

Inspector	Animation Editor	Viewer

Inspector

The Inspector doesn't provide an automation graph like we've seen before. Instead, you are adding/editing Keyframes, one Keyframe at a time.

▶ The position of the Keyframe's location (x -axis) is determined by the current Playhead position.

▶ Changing the position (time location) of an existing Keyframe is not possible in the Inspector.

▶ Changing the Parameter of an existing Keyframe is done right there with the controls in the Inspector.

Dynamic Keyframe Area

Let's quickly review the Inspector's interface. Keep in mind that the Audio Inspector and Video Inspector are context sensitive (depending on specific conditions of the elected Clip) and also depend on if you move the mouse cursor over a specific area or not. The Keyframe Area ❶ is located on the right side of the Inspector next to the parameter values. If there are no Keyframes set yet and the mouse is not moved over that area, then it is blank ❺. You don't notice that it is even there. You have to move the mouse over that area and then various buttons will pop up ❷, indicating the status of its Keyframes or buttons appear and disappear depending on what Keyframes have been programmed.

🌑 Adding first Keyframes

These are the steps for adding the very first Keyframes in the Inspector:

☑ Select the Clip in the Timeline that you want to add a Keyframe.

☑ Place the Playhead on the Timeline over that Clip where you want to create the Keyframe.

☑ Select the Module ❸. Effects Module (and some other modules) have their Parameters hidden by default. Make them visible by *clicking* any *Show* Button ❹ or the Parameter disclosure triangle.

☑ Move the mouse over the blank ❺ Keyframe Area and a diamond with a plus sign appears ◈ ❻. *Click* on that "Add Keyframe Button".

☑ <u>Congratulations</u>, you just added a new Keyframe to that parameter (indicated by the now solid diamond button ◆ ❼) with the current value at the current Playhead position. That data is now stored with the Clip.

☑ You can still change the Parameter value of that Keyframe by adjusting that Parameter Value ❽ if you haven't moved the Playhead yet and that Keyframe Button is still visible.

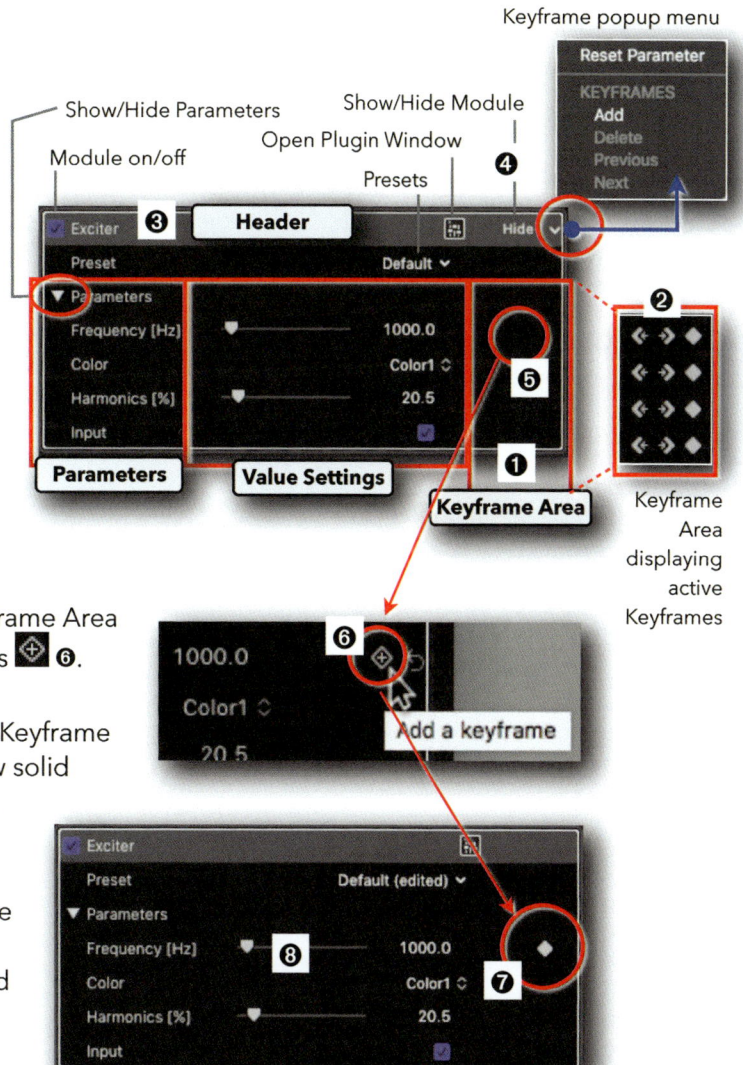

Keyframe popup menu

Show/Hide Parameters
Show/Hide Module
Open Plugin Window
Module on/off
Presets

Parameters
Value Settings
Keyframe Area
Keyframe Area displaying active Keyframes

Add a keyframe

Keyframe Buttons

Here is a closer look at the Keyframe Area with all those different Keyframe Buttons.

First of all, think of the Keyframe Area in the Inspector as a grid of three (invisible) columns that displays the various Keyframe Buttons. Here are the appearances, the meaning and the functionality of those buttons:

Inspector: Effects Module

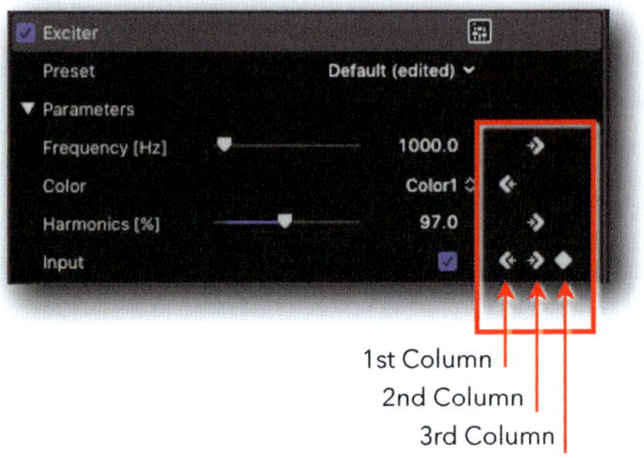

1st Column
2nd Column
3rd Column

1st Column

This button indicates that the Clip has an existing Keyframe for this Parameter to the <u>left</u> of the current Playhead position.

When you move the cursor over that button, it lights up. *Clicking* on it will move the Playhead to the left, to the position of that Keyframe.

If that area is blank, then the Clip has no Keyframes for this Parameter to the left of the current Playhead position.

2nd Column

This button indicates that the Clip has an existing Keyframe for this Parameter to the <u>right</u> of the current Playhead position.

When you move the cursor over that button, it lights up. *Clicking* on it will move the Playhead to the right, to the position of that Keyframe.

If that area is blank, then the Clip has no Keyframe for this Parameter to the right of the current Playhead position.

3rd Column

If that area is blank, then the Clip has no Keyframe for this Parameter at the current Playhead position.

Moving the cursor over that blank area will change it to the "*Add Keyframe Button*" (diamond with the plus sign). *Clicking* on it will add a Keyframe at the current Playhead position with the current Parameter value.

This button (solid diamond) indicates that the Clip has a Keyframe for that Parameter at the current Playhead position. The currently displayed Parameter value is the value for this Keyframe.

Moving the cursor over that solid diamond button will change it to the "*Remove Keyframe Button*" (diamond with a minus sign). *Clicking* on it will remove that Keyframe.

Depending on what Keyframes are programmed for what Parameters at what Timeline position of a Clip determines what button is displayed in which column. If you play back your Project, you can see those buttons appear and disappear based on those conditions.

Interface

The so-called "*Animation Editor*" is the user interface in FCPx that lets you add/edit Keyframes - graphically. Remember, there are three different ways to enter parameter values:

▶ **Inspector**: The Inspector provides a simple data entry interface, which is sufficient when adjusting a "constant" value for a parameter.

▶ **Animation Editor**: The Animation Editor provides a graphical interface. This is much more useful when entering or changing parameter values throughout the duration of a Clip, the Keyframes.

▶ **Viewer**: This is a third option that lets you change Parameter values with onscreen controls directly on the video frame. More about that later in this chapter.

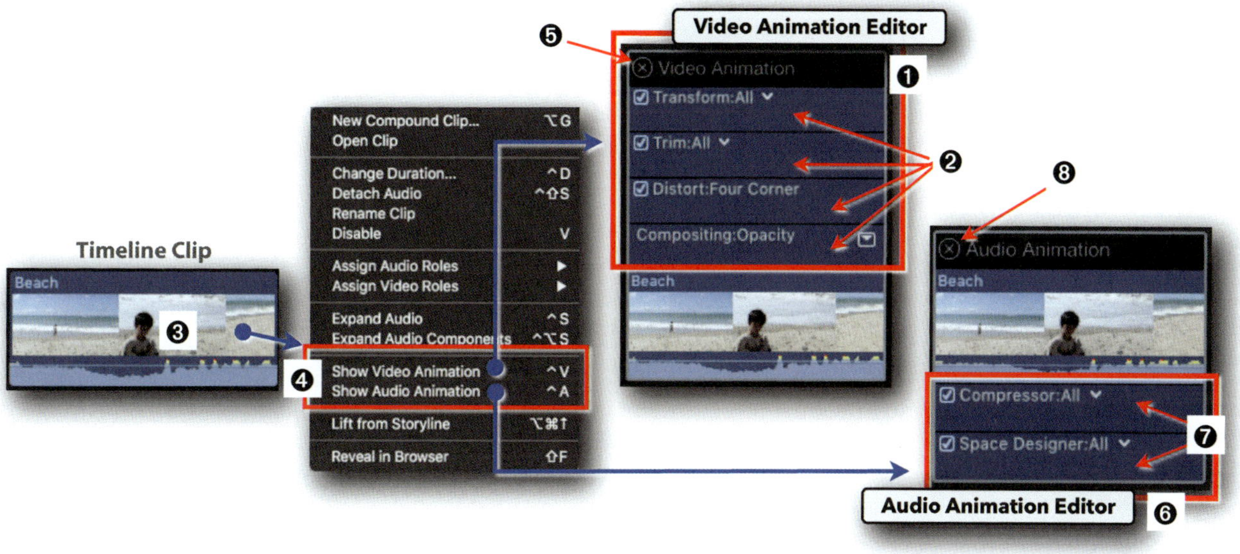

Video Animation Editor

The Video Animation Editor ❶ is an extended area above the Timeline Clip. All the Modules from the Video Inspector (for the selected Clip) are displayed as individual Animation Lanes ❷. You can toggle that area with the following commands:

- *Ctr+click* on the Clip ❸ and select from the *Shortcut Menu ➤ Show/Hide Video Animation* ❹
- Main Menu *Clip ➤ Show/Hide Video Animation*
- Key Command *ctr+V*
- *Click* the X button ❺ ⊗ on top of the Clip to hide the Animation Editor

Audio Animation Editor

The Audio Animation Editor ❻ is an extended area below the Timeline Clip. All the Effects Modules from the Audio Inspector (for the selected Clip) are displayed as individual Automation Lanes ❼. You can toggle that area with the following commands:

- *Ctr+click* on the Clip ❸ and select from the *Shortcut Menu ➤ Show/Hide Audio* ❹ *Animation*
- Main Menu *Clip ➤ Show/Hide Audio Animation*
- Key Command *ctr+A*
- *Click* the X button ❽ ⊗ on top of the Clip to hide the Animation Editor

A Clip can only display the Video Animation Editor (above) or Audio Animation Editor (below), not both at the same time.

➡ **Animation Lanes**

Here is a closer look at those Animation Lanes:

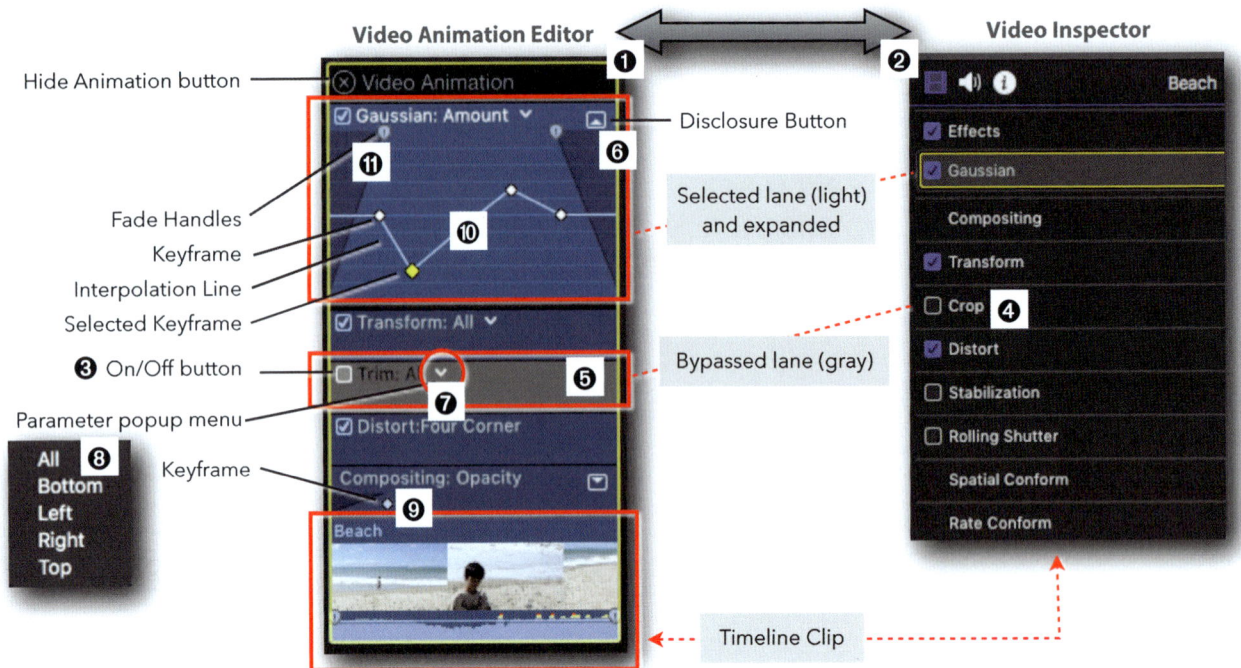

Video Animation Editor   ❶   ❷   **Video Inspector**

Hide Animation button ⟶

Disclosure Button ⟶

Selected lane (light) and expanded

Fade Handles
Keyframe
Interpolation Line
Selected Keyframe

❸ On/Off button ⟶

Bypassed lane (gray)

Parameter popup menu ⟶

All ❽
Bottom
Left
Right
Top

Keyframe ⟶

Timeline Clip

🏆 Lane Selection

A few things to know about the lanes:

▶ The order of the Animation Lanes in the Animation Editor ❶ corresponds to the order of the Modules in the Inspector ❷ (with a few exceptions).

▶ Selecting a lane in the Animation Editor will select that Module in the Inspector and vice versa. It will appear with a little bit lighter color.

▶ Toggling the on/off ❸ button on the lane will toggle the corresponding module in the Inspector ❹. The lane of a bypassed module (off) turns gray ❺.

▶ The Modules that don't have Keyframe functionality are not listed in the Animation Editor (Spatial Conform, Rolling Shutter, Audio Enhancements, etc.).

▶ You can expand only one lane by clicking on the Disclosure Button 🔽 ❻ (or *double-clicking* the header). It will collapse another expanded lane. Please note that the button will only appear when the Parameter Menu ❽ has an item, other than "All", selected.

🏆 Parameter Menu

A Module can only be displayed by a single Animation Lane. If the Module has more than one Parameter (i.e., Position, Rotation, Scale, Anchor), then a selector 🔽 ❼ on the lane opens a popup menu ❽ to choose which Parameter to display on that lane. The option "All" displays the Keyframes of all Parameters.

🏆 Expand/Collapse Lane 🔽 🔼

Some lanes have a Disclosure Button ❻ in the upper-right corner that expands the lane vertically to provide more functionality. You can also *double-click* on the lane header to toggle.

▶ **Collapsed**: You can add and delete Keyframes ❾. *Dragging* the Keyframes is limited to the horizontal directions (move to different time position). The parameter value (vertical direction) has to be edited in the Inspector.

▶ **Expanded**: Besides adding and deleting Keyframes ❿, the *dragging* works in horizontal (time value) and vertical (parameter value) directions, however, limited to one direction at a time. The lane now also displays Fade Handles ⓫ for some Parameters.

Managing Keyframes

Finally, the connection between the math function ❶ with its x/y coordinates and what it looks like in FCPx in the Animation Editor ❶ with Keyframes.

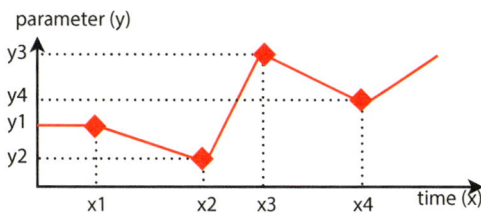

❶ **Mathematical Function**

❷ **Animation Editor**

➡ Adding Keyframes

There are a lot of operations, actions, and visual indications when working in the Automation Editor. Take your time to learn those little details to better understand the procedures.

🌑 Single Line (no Keyframe)

With no Keyframe added yet, the Automation Lane shows one horizontal line that represents the value of that parameter.

▶ Moving the mouse over the line (Clip is not selected) will change the cursor to an up/down arrow ⬍ ❸.

▶ If the Clip is selected (yellow frame), then, in addition to the double arrow cursor, a black help tag ❹ displays the value of that line (parameter value).

▶ *Dragging* the line up/down (at that moment the Clip gets selected), changes that value, with the help tag displaying the corresponding value. This is the same as adjusting that value in the Inspector.

🌑 Adding a Keyframe - Animation Editor

You have several options on how to add a new Keyframe in the Animation Editor:

▶ **Cursor**: *Opt+click* on the Automation Line to add a Keyframe at that position. Pay attention to a few details of what happened:

• Holding down the *option* key when moving the cursor over the Automation Line will change the cursor to the pointer with a tiny Plus Keyframe icon ⬚ ❺.

• The black help tag is displayed if the Clip is selected.

• *Clicking* on the Automation Line will add that Keyframe ⬚ ❻ on the Automation Line and the cursor appearance changes to the pointer with the solid Keyframe icon ⬚ ❼, because you are now pointing at an existing Keyframe.

• *Clicking* on that Keyframe will select it and it changes from white ⬚ to yellow ⬚ ❽.

▶ **Command**: The Keyframe will be added on the Automation Line at the current Playhead position when using the following commands.

🔲 Key Command *opt+K*

🔲 Main Menu *Modify* ➤ *Add Keyframe*

⚫ Adding a Keyframe - Inspector

I already showed you how to create a Keyframe in the Inspector, however, there is a condition you have to be aware of:

▶ **No Keyframes exist**: If the Clip has no Keyframes for a specific Parameter yet, then moving the cursor over the Parameter of a Module will show the *Add Keyframe Button* ◆ ❶ on that row. However, changing the Parameter value (moving a slider, enter value field, or selecting a menu item) will not create a Keyframe. It will move the existing Automation Line in the Automation Editor just up or down.

▶ **Keyframes exist**: If the currently selected Clip has at least one Keyframe for a Parameter, then changing the value of that Parameter with any of the controls ❷ in the Inspector will automatically add a new Keyframe ❸ at the current Playhead position with that value without the need to click the *Add Keyframe Button* ◆.

▶ **Either way**: The following actions will add a new Keyframe(s) no matter if one already exists or not:

📌 ***Click*** on the *Add Keyframe Button* ◆ ❶ that appears when you move the mouse over the Parameter row of a Module (if that button doesn't appear, then it means that you cannot automate that Parameter).

📌 The Audio Effects and Video Effects have a selector ⌄ in the upper right corner of the Module row ❹. It opens a popup menu with the command "Add" ❺. Please note that this command creates a Keyframe for <u>every</u> Parameter in that Module at the current Playhead position.

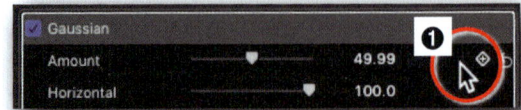

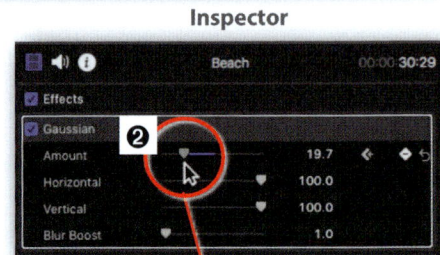

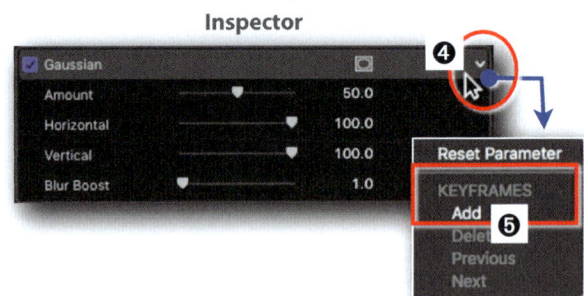

Inspector

Inspector

➡ Navigation with Keyframes

You can move the Playhead to a specific Keyframe. Those navigation commands relate to the Keyframes of the selected Animation Lane. The commands won't work if the Playhead is outside the selected Clip or the Parameter is set to "All":

▶ <u>To move the Playhead to the Keyframe on the left of the current Playhead position:</u>

📌 Key Command ***opt+;***

📌 Main Menu *Mark* ➤ *Previous* ➤ *Keyframe*

📌 In the Inspector, move over the header of an Effects Module and ***click*** on the selector ⌄ ❻ for the Keyframe popup menu and select ***Previous*** ❼

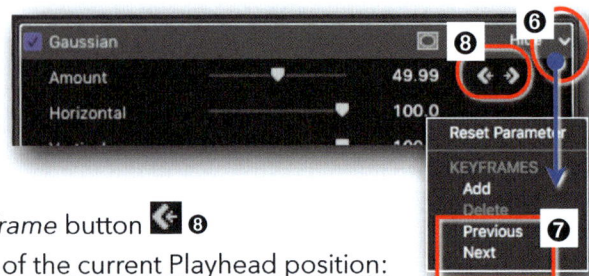

📌 In the Inspector, ***click*** the *Move to Previous Keyframe* button ← ❽

▶ <u>To move the Playhead to the Keyframe on the right of the current Playhead position:</u>

📌 Key Command ***opt+'***

📌 Main Menu *Mark* ➤ *Next* ➤ *Keyframe*

📌 In the Inspector, move over the header of an Effects Module and ***click*** on the selector ⌄ ❻ for the Keyframe popup menu and select ***Next*** ❼

📌 In the Inspector, ***click*** the *Move to Next Keyframe* button → ❽ of the Parameter

➡ Selecting Keyframes

There are different ways to select Keyframes:

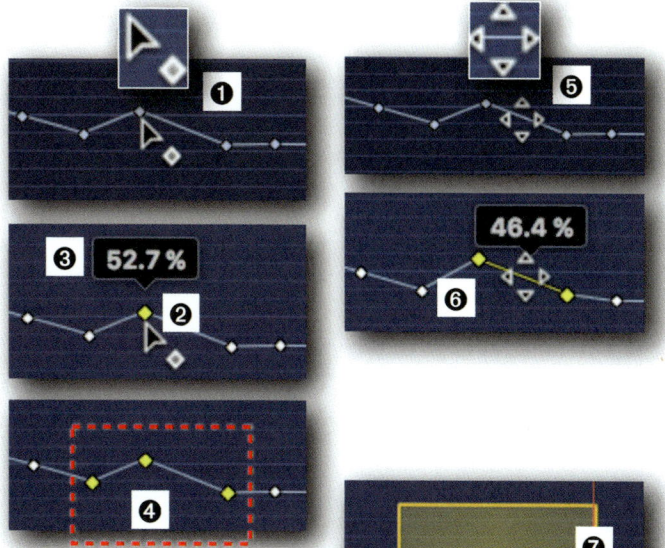

▶ **Keyframes**

- 📌 Move the cursor over a Keyframe and it changes to the pointer with the solid Keyframe icon 📍 ❶.

- 📌 *Click* on a Keyframe to select it and it turns yellow ◈ ❷. The black help tag ❸ displays the Parameter value of that Keyframe.

- 📌 *Sh+click* a second Keyframe to select all the Keyframes ❹ between the already selected Keyframe(s) and the one you sh+clicked on.

▶ **Automation Line**

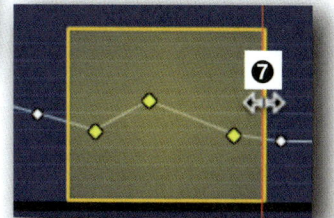

- 📌 Move the cursor over an Automation Line (between two Keyframes) and it changes the pointer to the four-arrow cursor tool ⬌ ❺.

- 📌 *Click* on the Automation Line to select it and it turns yellow ❻. The black help tag shows the Parameter value at the position you clicked on, which, of course, is different depending on where along the line you clicked.

▶ **Range**: *Drag* horizontally on the Animation Lane to create a yellow range ❼. All Keyframes inside that range are selected. You can drag the borders of the range to extend it left or right, and also, *drag* inside the range to move it left/right as it is. This range is used for special Keyframe editing.

▶ **Deselect**: *Click* on the Automation Lane background to deselect any selected Keyframe or selected Automation Line.

➡ Editing Keyframes

Now let's look at all the various commands on how to edit existing Keyframes:

⚙ Copy/Paste Keyframes

The standard copy (cut) paste procedure can also be used to move or copy existing Keyframes.

- ▶ Select one or multiple Keyframes and use any of the following commands to copy them to the clipboard:
  - 📌 Key Command **sh+opt+C**
  - 📌 Main Menu *Edit* ➤ *Keyframes* ➤ *Copy* ❽

- ▶ Select the Animation Lane of a Parameter on the Clip where you want to paste the Keyframe(s) and position the Playhead over that Clip at the target position. Use any of the following commands to copy them to the clipboard
  - 📌 Key Command **sh+opt+V**
  - 📌 Main Menu *Edit* ➤ *Keyframes* ➤ *Paste* ❽

🌑 Move Keyframes

First, a few things to pay attention to when moving Keyframes:

▶ You can drag the Keyframe(s) or the Automation Line.

▶ Moving the cursor over a Keyframe adds the solid Keyframe icon to the pointer 🔻❶, moving over an Automation Line will change to the four-arrow cursor 🔹❷.

▶ The movement is limited to one direction at a time. Which direction depends on if you start dragging horizontally or vertically.

▶ The Cursor Tool changes accordingly to show either the up/down 🔻 arrow or the left/right arrows ◀▶.

▶ The black help tag displays the value of the Keyframe while moving it. When moving vertically, it displays its Parameter value, when moving horizontally, it displays its SMPTE position.

▶ You can't move a Keyframe horizontally beyond the position of any adjacent Keyframe or the borders of the Clip.

Keyframe up/down

- **Drag** the Keyframe up/down 🔻 ❸
- If multiple Keyframes are selected ❹, then dragging one will move all selected Keyframes. Dragging a group all the way to the top or bottom will set all Keyframes to max or min value, losing their relative value to each other
- Select the Keyframe(s) and use the Key Command **opt+ArrowUp** or **opt+ArrowDown**
- **Opt+cmd+drag** a Keyframe up/down will move the entire Automation Curve
- If the Playhead is positioned at that Keyframe, then you can adjust its Parameter value in the Inspector to move that Keyframe up-down

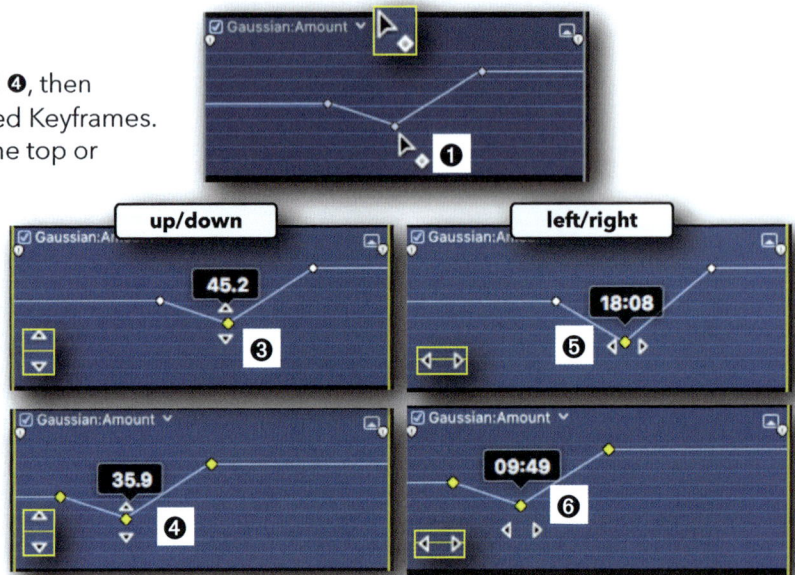

Keyframe left/right

- **Drag** the Keyframe left/right ◀▶ ❺
- If multiple Keyframes are selected, then dragging one will move all selected Keyframes ❻

Automation Line up/down

- **Drag** an Automation Line up/down 🔻 ❼ to move the Keyframes on the left and right of that line
- **Cmd+drag** a line will move the line vertically with a finer resolution for more precise adjustments
- **Opt+cmd+drag** an Automation Line up/down will move the entire Automation Curve

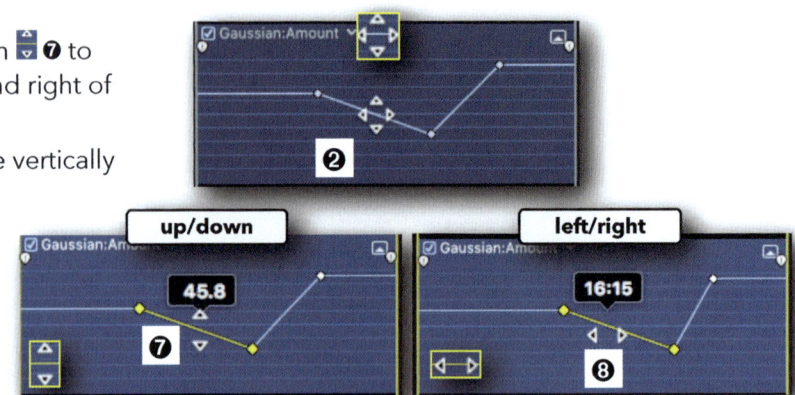

Automation Line left/right

- **Drag** an Automation Line left/right ◀▶ ❽ to move the Keyframes on the left and right of that line

Range Editing

I already showed that you can drag a range ❶ on the Animation Lane to select multiple Keyframes. This has a special functionality for editing.

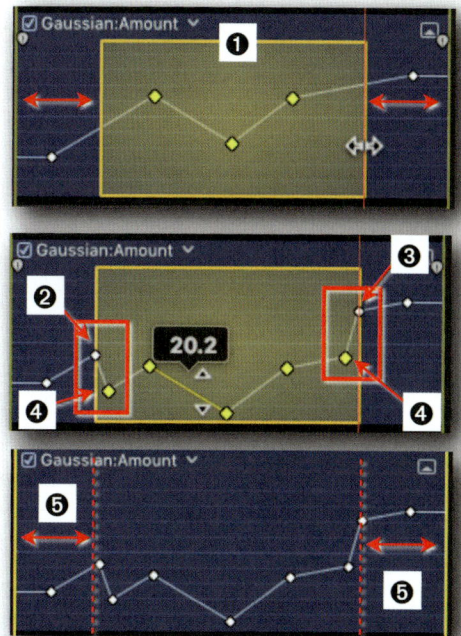

▶ *Dragging* the Animation Line (not the Keyframe) inside the Range up or down will create 4 new Keyframes.

▶ Two of those Keyframes are created exactly on the selection border, one on the left ❷ and one of the right ❸. They stay fixed during the movement and function as anchors or hinges.

▶ The other two Keyframes are created about 15 frames away from those anchor Keyframes, inside ❹ the range selection. These two Keyframes act as the first and last Keyframe in that group that are moved up and down with the other Keyframes inside the range selection.

▶ These four Keyframes guarantee that you can drag the Automation Curve inside the range selection ❶ without affecting the position of the Automation Curve outside ❺ the range selection.

▶ You can only move vertically.

Delete Keyframes

There are several ways on how to delete Keyframes:

⚲ Key Command *sh+opt+delete* will delete any selected Keyframe(s)

⚲ Key Command *sh+opt+X* will delete any selected Keyframe(s) and moves them to the clipboard

⚲ Menu Command *Edit ➤ Keyframes ➤ Delete Keyframe*

⚲ *Ctr+click* on a Keyframe and a single-item Shortcut Menu ❻ opens with the command "*Delete Keyframe*" or "*Delete Keyframes*" if you have multiple Keyframes selected. *Click* on it

⚲ In the Inspector, move over the header of an Effects Module and *click* on the selector 🔽 ❼ for the Keyframe popup menu and select *Delete* ❽

⚲ *Click* the Delete Keyframe Button ⊟ in the Keyframe Area of the Inspector

Reset Keyframes ↺

There is a special "relationship" between the Reset command and Keyframes. Please note that the Effects Module has Reset buttons on multiple levels. That means, you can reset specific layers of the Effects Module. So, whenever you click on the Reset button, know exactly what Parameters are affected. The Reset Button only appears when you mouse-over that section on the right:

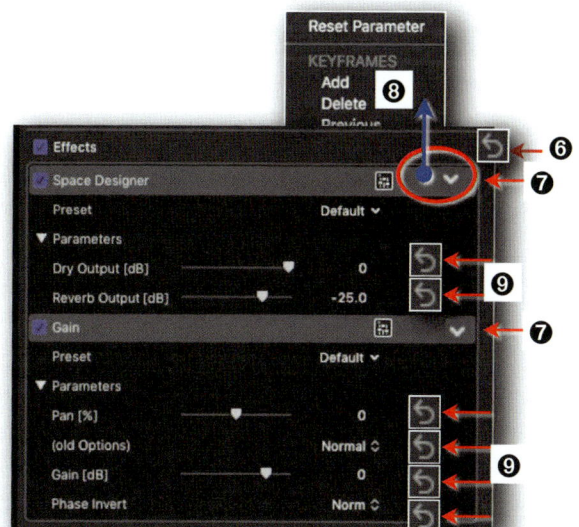

• ❻ **Effects Module**: This resets all the Plugins, everything inside that Effects Module - <u>except Parameters with Keyframes</u>

• ❼ **Plugin Module**: *Click* on the selector 🔽 ❼ to open a popup menu ❽ with the *Reset Parameter* command. This resets only that specific Plugin to its default setting - <u>except any Parameters that have Keyframes</u>.

• ❾ **Plugin Parameter**: This command resets only that specific Parameter for that Plugin and it is the only reset command that also resets all the Keyframes for that Parameter, which means, they will be deleted.

➡ Automation Line Shape

The Automation Line (or Automation Curve), the interpolation between Keyframes is straight ❶ by default. However, there are two methods to bend that straight line.

▶ **Ctr+click** on an Animation Line to open a Shortcut Menu with four curve options ❷. This menu is only available for Video effects, not for Audio effects. It determines the shape of the line between two Keyframes. You can further adjust how much the line will bend by cmd+dragging the line horizontally.

▶ **Cmd+drag** the line horizontally between two Keyframes. A little curve icon appears with the cursor ☝ to indicate the curve functionality. Now, when you move the mouse left or right, the linear line will be shaped towards an S-form. There are two different scenarios:

☑ When no shape was selected from the Shortcut Menu (default = linear), then the curve tool bends the straight line toward a S-shaped line. This is the same shape as the "Ease" curve ❸ from the Shortcut Menu.

☑ When a shape has been selected from the Shortcut Menu, then using the shape tool can bend that shape more or less, depending on the horizontal direction of the mouse movement. The selected shape from the menu has a 50% "bend" and the shape tool allows you to adjust that shape between 100% (= max) to 0% (= linear).

On the side are screenshots of the four different shapes when adjusted to 100%. Please note that the term "Ease in" ❹ relates to the Keyframe on the right of a line and the "Ease out" ❺ refers to the Keyframe on the left. The "Ease" ❸ shape is basically a combination of both.

➡ Fade Handles

Fade Handles are those two little dots at the upper left and right border on some of the extended Animation Lanes.

▶ **Volume Lane**: This is where the Fade Handles are the most useful. You can drag the handle to create a quick audio fade-in ❻ or fade-out ❼ without creating Keyframes and shaped lines. You have two controls:

   🔘 **Drag** the Handle to set the length of the fade, the Fade Area. The black help tag displays the SMPTE time for reference.

   🔘 **Ctr+click** on the handle to open a Shortcut Menu ❽ to choose from four different shapes.

▶ **Other Video or Audio Effect Lanes**: Not all Effects have Fade Handles. If available, they function as a layer on top of the Animation Line with their Keyframes to ease in and out the programmed effect. These handles are always linear ❾ without any curve options.

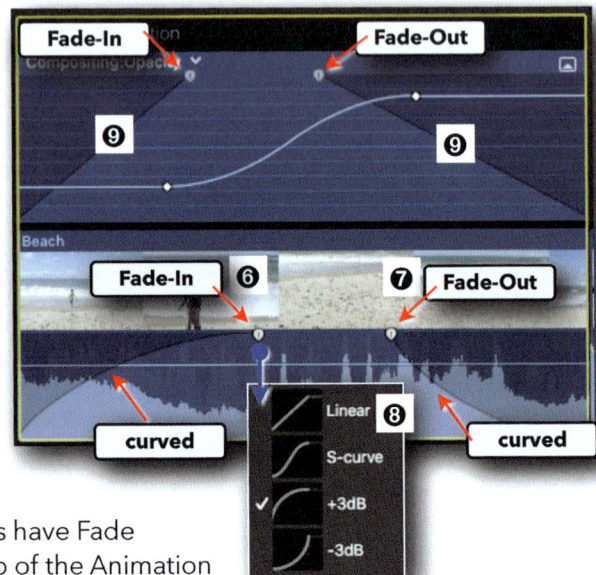

Animation Editor Summary

Let's have a final look at the Animation Editor:

The individual Animation Lanes are displayed in "Collapsed View" as a default and if they have a Disclosure Button ❶, then they can be opened to an Expanded View. Not all Parameters have that Disclosure Button ❷ and it is also not displayed if the Parameter popup menu is set to "All".

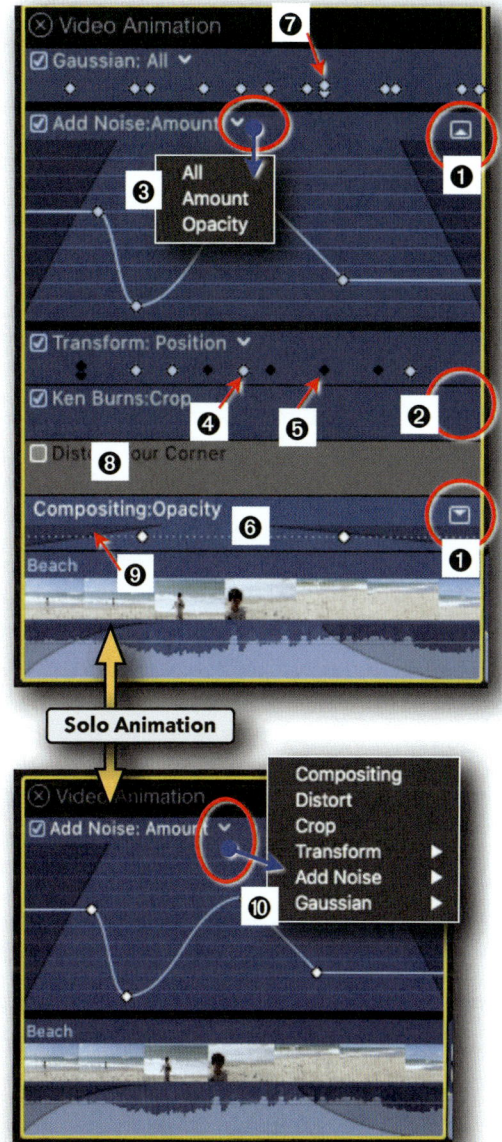

🔵 Expanded View

▶ New Keyframes can be added and existing ones can be moved vertically and horizontally. The Automation Lines can be moved too.

▶ You can expand only one Animation Lane (effect). The command will collapse any currently expanded lane.

🔵 Collapsed View

▶ New Keyframes can be added but existing ones can only be moved horizontally. Any change to the Parameter value has to be done in the expanded view or the Inspector.

▶ If the Effect has more than one Parameter, then the Module will have a selector ☑ next to its name that opens a popup menu to choose one of the other Parameters ❸. Only one Parameter at a time can be displayed as an expanded lane.

▶ Keyframes for the active Parameter are bright ❹ and can be edited. Keyframes from other Parameters (not visible) are displayed as dark dots ❺ and cannot be edited. You have to switch to that Parameter first to make them active.

▶ A selected lane displays a dotted line ❻ that represents only the time axis with no representation of the Parameter Value (y-axis).

▶ If "All" Parameters are selected for the lane, then all Keyframes from all Parameters are visible in bright and two Keyframes from different Parameters at the same position are displayed as double diamonds ❼. It is possible to move the Keyframes but hard to know which Parameter they belong to.

▶ Bypassed Effects (checkbox unselected) are displayed by a grey Animation Lane ❽.

▶ Fade areas are visible in expanded and collapsed view ❾.

➡ Solo Animation

If you have a lot of Video or Audio Effects in your Clip, then the Animation Editor could stack up pretty high using a lot of real estate in your timeline window. For that situation, FCPx provides a simple command that lets you limit the Animation Editor (individually for each Clip) to display only one Animation Lane at a time. This feature is called "Solo Animation". Now, the selector next to the name opens a popup menu ❿ listing all the Animation Lanes and their Parameter to switch to.

Toggle Solo Animation with any of the following commands:

🎚 Menu Command *Clip* ➤ *Solo Animation*

🎚 Key Command *sh+ctr+V*

Viewer - Onscreen Controls

Onscreen Controls are the third way, in addition to the Inspector and Animation Editor, to create and edit Keyframes.

▶ ❶ The Inspector provides a simple numerical entry of Keyframes.

▶ ❷ The Animation Editor uses a graphical interface in the form of an x/y function for Keyframe management.

▶ ❸ Onscreen Controls, on the other hand, let you "draw" the Keyframes and other data, superimposed over the video in the Viewer. As with the controls in the Animation Editor, most of the Onscreen Controls are also available in the Inspector. Some parameters, however, can only be adjusted with Onscreen Controls.

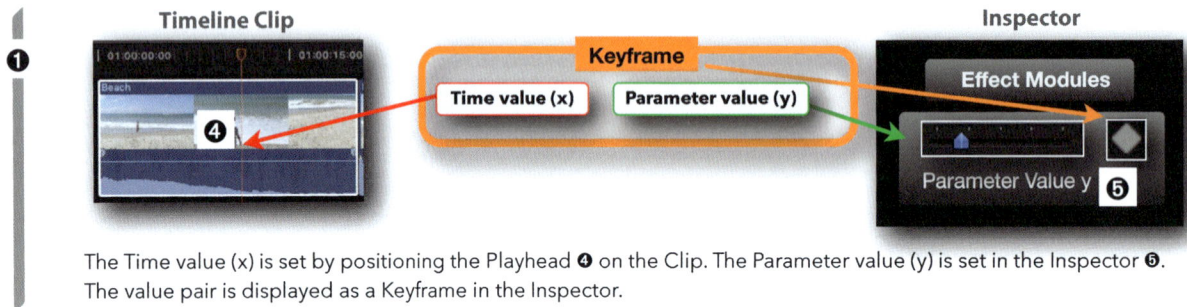

The Time value (x) is set by positioning the Playhead ❹ on the Clip. The Parameter value (y) is set in the Inspector ❺. The value pair is displayed as a Keyframe in the Inspector.

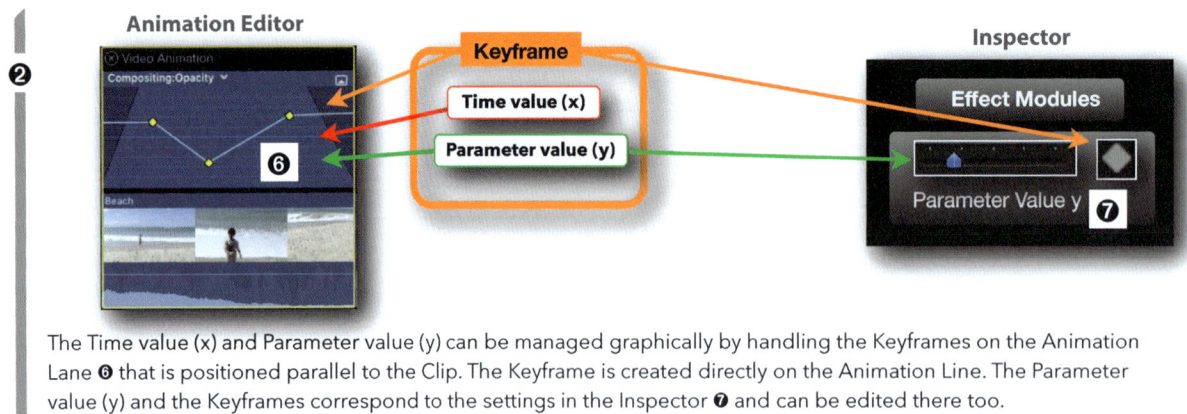

The Time value (x) and Parameter value (y) can be managed graphically by handling the Keyframes on the Animation Lane ❻ that is positioned parallel to the Clip. The Keyframe is created directly on the Animation Line. The Parameter value (y) and the Keyframes correspond to the settings in the Inspector ❼ and can be edited there too.

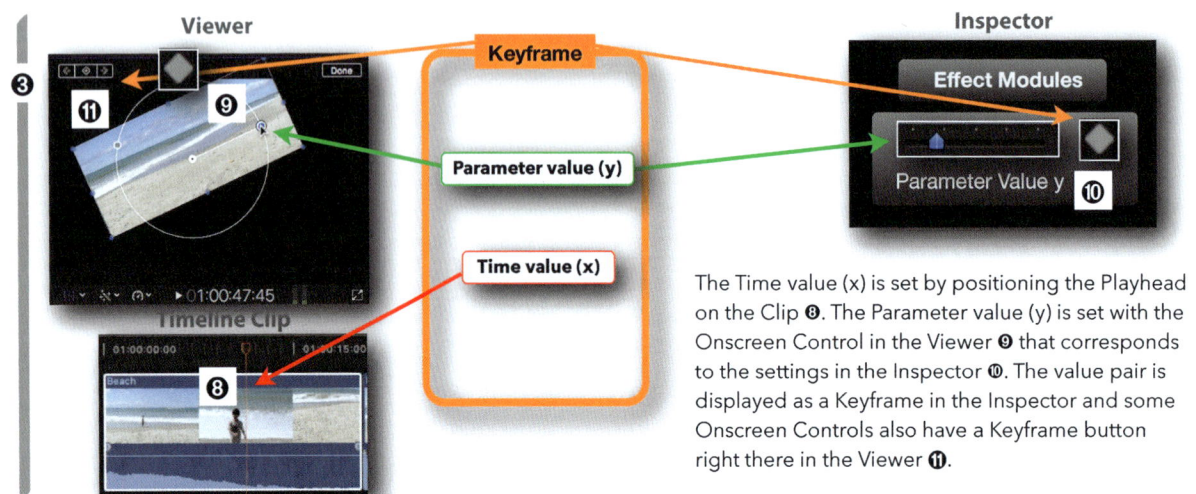

The Time value (x) is set by positioning the Playhead on the Clip ❽. The Parameter value (y) is set with the Onscreen Control in the Viewer ❾ that corresponds to the settings in the Inspector ❿. The value pair is displayed as a Keyframe in the Inspector and some Onscreen Controls also have a Keyframe button right there in the Viewer ⑪.

Mechanism

Onscreen Controls are most useful when adjusting Parameters that represent position information on the screen, the video frame. This could be an object (text, image) or an effect (transition, transform, etc.).

If you want to place an object in the upper left corner of the picture, you have to enter the x and y coordinate of that position in the Parameter value field in the Inspector. But what are the exact values for x and y? It would be much easier if you could just place the object in the Viewer over the image where you want it to be. This is basically what Onscreen Controls are for, an intuitive, graphical interface (kind of *WhatYouSeeIsWhatYouGet*).

The Onscreen Control, in the shape of a circle, arrow, or line that indicates its purpose, corresponding with the Parameter values in the Inspector. Moving the Onscreen Controls will change the Parameter values in the Inspector and vice versa.

▶ **Fixed Value**: You can use the Onscreen Control to adjust the value(s). Those values stay for the duration of the Clip or Transition, for example, a fixed position on the screen.

▶ **Variable Value**: You can make the adjustment with the Onscreen Control and assign them to a time position, storing that information as a Keyframe. Move the Playhead to the next time position, create another Keyframe, or adjust the Onscreen Control at that address, which creates the Keyframe(s) automatically. This is basically the same Keyframe process as we have seen before. Some Keyframes store multiple Parameter values, in other situations, you have to create multiple Keyframes in more complex situations. And again, the interpolation creates all those invisible "in-between values" between two Keyframes, providing a smooth "animation" with just a few clicks. Here are three examples:

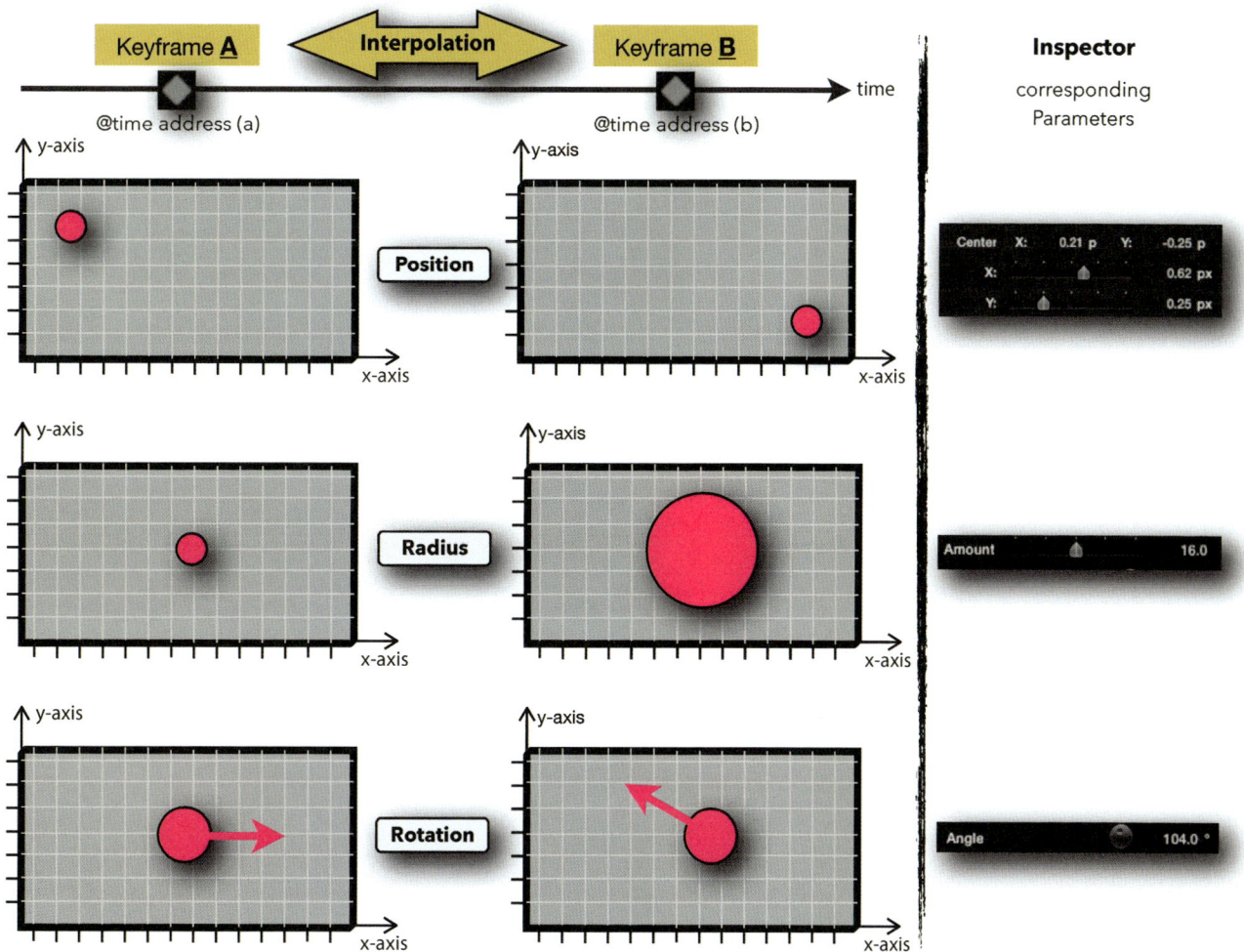

Modules with Onscreen Controls

Let's look at some Modules that have Onscreen Controls. I've grouped them together in three sections:

❶ Default Video Modules for a Clip

These are the Modules in the Inspector that every Timeline Clip (video) has by default:

- ▶ Transform
- ▶ Crop
- ▶ Distort

❷ Additional Video Effects for a Clip

These are the user-added Modules that are grouped together in the "Effects" section at the top of the Inspector. Every Video Effect applied to a Clip will show up here for further tweaking.

❸ Transition Modules

This Inspector view doesn't display the properties of a regular Clip. It displays the properties of a Transition Clip, placed between two Clips on the Timeline. When you select a Transition, this is the view of the Inspector that displays its Properties for further adjustments. Please note the "Transition" tab ❹ one the Inspector header.

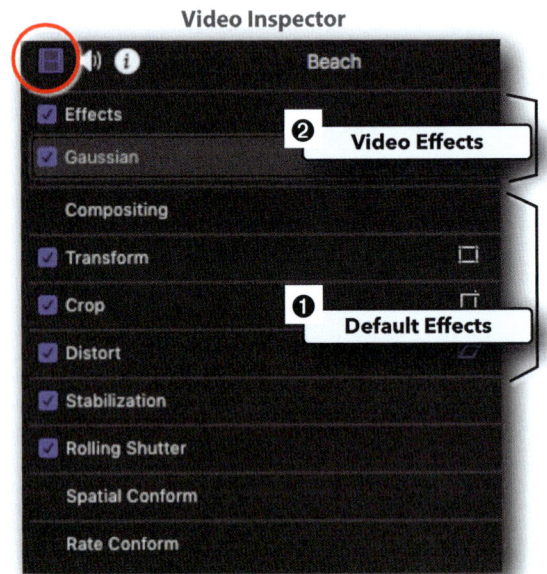

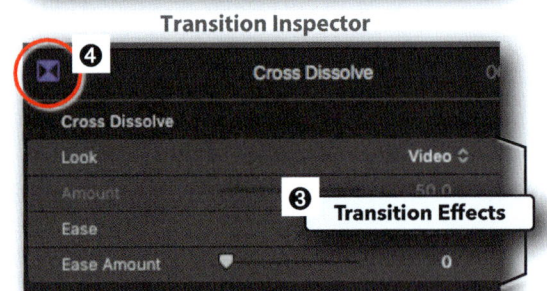

➡ *Onscreen Controls - Button*

The Viewer has a little button ❺ in the lower left corner with two functions:

- ▶ The icon lets you toggle to have the Onscreen Controls visible in the Viewer or not. If the icon is gray, then the onscreen controls for that effect are not visible. If the icon is purple, then those Onscreen Controls are visible in the Viewer. The status of that icon corresponds to the icon button ❻ of that Module in the Inspector.

- ▶ Next to the icon is a selector ▼ that opens a popup menu ❼. Here you can switch between the three effects, which of the controls you want to display.

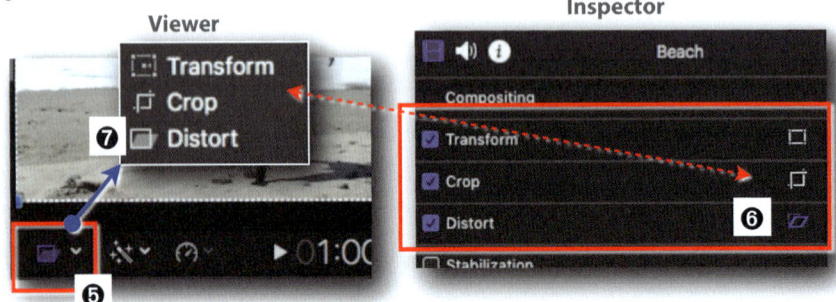

Those three video effects can only be applied to Timeline Clips and that's why that button is only available in the Viewer and not in the Event Viewer.

Transform

The Transform Parameters (Position, Rotation, Scale, and Anchor) can be set visually via the onscreen controls ❶ without dealing with the actual pixel and percentage values in the Inspector ❷.

The Viewer provides its own Keyframe Buttons ❸ in the upper-left corner to setup animated effects even quicker.

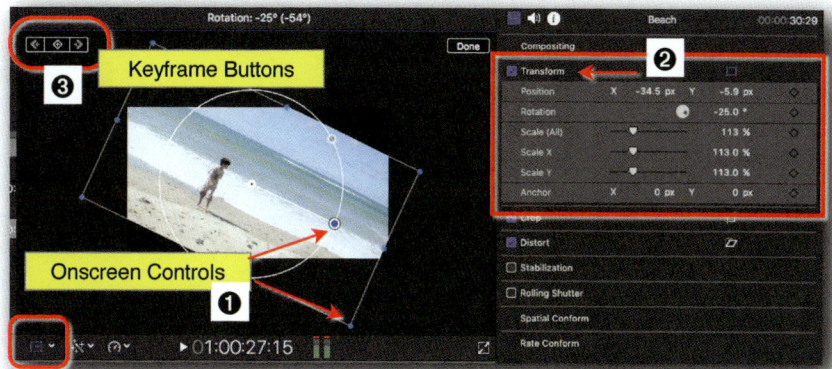

Crop

The Crop Module actually has three types of Modules ❹ built in: Trim, Crop, Ken Burns.

Trim and Crop also provide onscreen Keyframe controls and Ken Burns makes programming of the typical Ken Burns effect very easy with its intuitive Onscreen Controls ❺.

Distort

The Distort Module provides mainly the Handles ❻ as Onscreen Controls to distort the shape of the frame.

This Module also has its own onscreen Keyframe Buttons ❼ in the Viewer.

Color

I cover the Color Modules in the next chapter. Here is an example of Onscreen Controls ❽ to create a color mask.

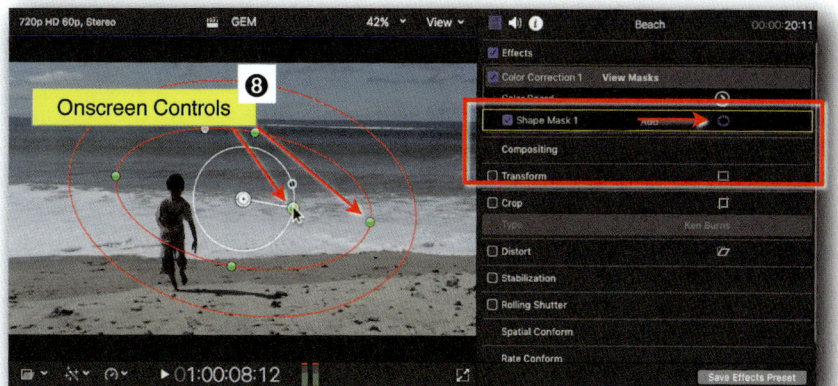

Video Effects

In this chapter, I will cover the tools that are available to alter the video in any shape and form (of course in a non-destructive way). This includes everything other than the actual sequencing of the Clips (the way you "organize" them on the Timeline). Video Effects alter the "look" of the Clips. The one exception are the Retime Effects which don't alter the look but rather the sequence and the playback speed of the frames. Maybe that's why it is not listed in the Inspector, but I included it in the Video Effects chapter anyway. Color has its separate section because of its complexity.

The way the Modules are organized in the Video Inspector appears to be by the order of most often used. However, I want to group them in a different way, by priority.

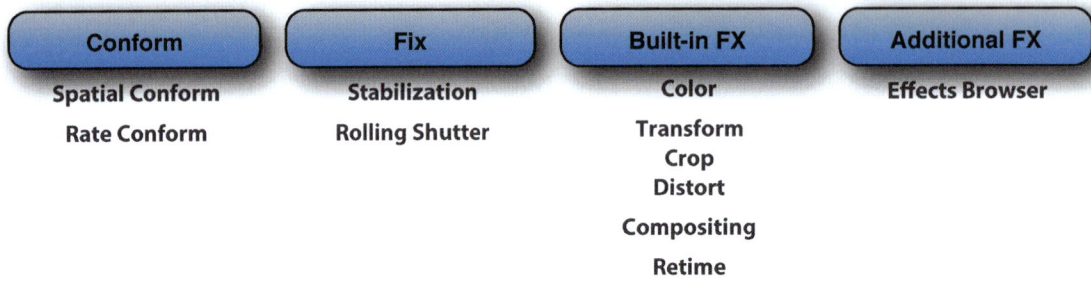

Conform	Fix	Built-in FX	Additional FX
Spatial Conform	Stabilization	Color	Effects Browser
Rate Conform	Rolling Shutter	Transform	
		Crop	
		Distort	
		Compositing	
		Retime	

Conform

This is the first step where you have to make sure that the video plays "correctly" in your Project regarding the size and the speed.

Fix

The next step lets you fix some issues regarding shaky video and other artifacts.

Built-in FX

This is the area where you get creative and mess around with the video, using a set of built-in Modules that are always available in the Inspector.

Additional FX

Finally, you can add additional Effect Modules from the Effects Browser. You can even add your own custom made Effects (from Motion) to treat your video even further.

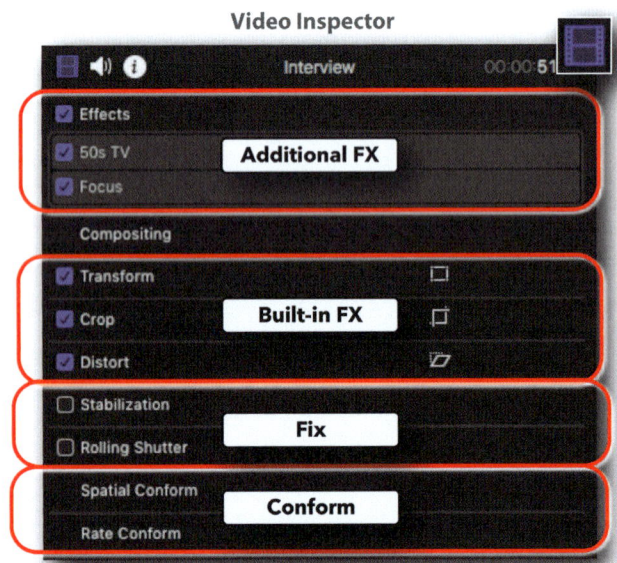

Conform

FCPx allows you to have mixed-format media in your Project's Timeline (video and audio). You just drag whatever format the Clips have onto the Project's Timeline and FCPx adjusts them based on your settings how to do the "conform". However, it is a good idea to choose the Project's format based on how you want to export your final video at the end.

There are two Conform Modules available, Spatial Conform and Rate Conform. They represent the two main parameters of a video format:

▶ **Spatial Conform - Frame Size**: How big is the image, also known as the pixel resolution in "Width x Hight", i.e. 1280x720

▶ **Rate Conform - Frame Rate**: How fast are the frames played back, measured in frames per second, i.e. 24fps

➡ *Spatial Conform*

Original Clip	None	Fill	Fit

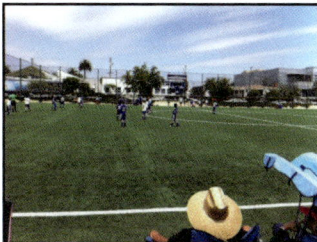

This is an example of a Clip that has a higher resolution than the Project's resolution (red frame). The three examples to the right demonstrate the effect of the three available Conform Types.

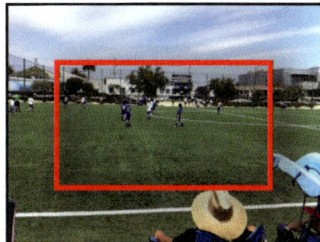

The Clip will not be resized. However, if the Clip's frame size is bigger than the Project's frame size, then it appears cropped because the Project "uses" only a portion of it. If the Clip's frame size is smaller, then black bars will fill the "empty" space.

The Clip's frame is resized to fill the Project's frame size. The Clip might get cropped on either side to fill the frame.

The Clip's frame is resized to fit the Project's frame size at least horizontally or vertically. The Clip will not be cropped. The "empty" space of the Project's frame will be black or transparent if there is an overlaying Clip in the Timeline.

➡ *Rate Conform*

FCPx performs a frame-sampling method to match the Clip's frame rate to the Project's frame rate in the event that they are different. The Rate Conform Module provides a popup menu to choose the best-fitting option. The line above the Frame Sampling, displaying the frame rate numbers, is only visible if a conversion is performed. Please note that both Conform Modules have no Bypass button.

From the official FCPx User Guide

Floor: Final Cut Pro truncates down to the nearest integer during its calculation to match the clip's frame rate to the project's frame rate.

Nearest Neighbor: Final Cut Pro rounds to the nearest integer during its calculation to match the clip's frame rate to the project's frame rate. The Nearest Neighbor option reduces artifacts at the expense of visual stuttering. Rendering is required.

Frame Blending: Creates in-between frames by blending individual pixels of neighboring frames. Slow-motion clips created with Frame Blending appear to play back more smoothly than those created with the Floor or Nearest Neighbor setting. This setting provides better reduction of visual stuttering, but you may see some visual artifacts. Rendering is required.

Optical Flow: A type of frame blending that uses an optical flow algorithm to create new in-between frames. Final Cut Pro analyzes the clip to determine the directional movement of pixels, and then draws portions of the new frames based on the optical flow analysis. Choosing the Optical Flow option results in better reduction of visual stuttering, and Final Cut Pro spends a significant amount of time to fix visual artifacts.

Fix

These two Modules need the analysis data that was created with the "Analyze and Fix" command. If you have shaky video footage or the Rolling Shutter artifacts in your video, you can activate these two Modules and play with the available parameters to see if you can fix those issues.

➡ Stabilization

There are three independent sliders ❶ to set the Stabilization parameters. The higher the value, the more you compensate any camera motion. A value of 0 turns that parameter off and a maximum value of 5 is the maximum value for the strongest transformation.

If you choose the InertiaCam Method ❷, then the module only provides the Smoothing slider.

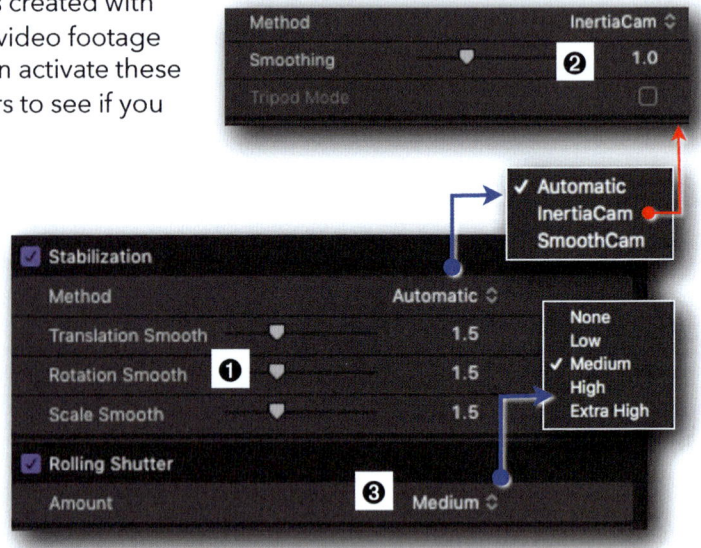

Here is the explanation from the official FCPx User Guide about the functionality of those Stabilization parameters:

From the official FCPx User Guide

Automatic: Allows Final Cut Pro to choose the most appropriate stabilization method.

InertiaCam: Applies stabilization optimized for video footage that has camera moves such as pans and zooms. Use the Smoothing slider to adjust the amount of the InertiaCam effect. Note: When you choose InertiaCam, Final Cut Pro analyzes your video footage and, depending on the results of the analysis, provides a Tripod Mode checkbox that creates the effect of a static camera that is mounted on a tripod.

SmoothCam: Applies the default stabilization method described above, allowing you to adjust the translation, rotation, and scale parameters:

- Adjust left, right, up, and down movement of a shot (x and y axes): Drag the Translation Smooth slider.

- Adjust rotation around the center point of the image: Drag the Rotation Smooth slider.

- Adjust forward or backward camera or lens movement (z axis): Drag the Scale Smooth slider.

➡ Rolling Shutter

The Rolling Shutter Module ❸ has only a single parameter with a popup menu where you can choose from five settings from "none" to "Extra High".

➡ *Basic Stuff First*

🌐 Onscreen Controls

Most of the parameters of the three Modules are much easier to manipulate with onscreen controls ❶ than with the entry of numeric values. For example, why would you figure out the x/y coordinates on the video frame when you can click on a control/handle in the video and *drag* it to the new position in the frame?

For that reason, the Viewer provides a button ❷ that lets you turn on any of those three on-screen controls without even opening the Inspector (The Viewer has its own Shortcut Menu ❸ that displays the Controls). The same buttons are also available on the Modules in the Inspector ❹. You can select (turns purple), to display only one of the Effects in the Viewer at a time ⬚⬚⬚. Keyframe controls ❺ are also available on-screen.

🌐 Frames

Before we discuss the individual parameters for Video Effects, let me point out that we have to be aware of THREE different frames. A little detail that can easily be overlooked.

▶ **Viewer Frame ❻**: This is just the window pane of the GUI. You resize it by resizing the FCPx window or the divider lines between the window panes. Its size has no effect on the video itself, it is just a display parameter.

▶ **Project Frame ❼** (Canvas): This is the frame that is determined by the Project Settings, the Video Properties (Format, Resolution). It represents the available Canvas, the area where you can place your Clips. This will become the size (resolution) of the QuickTime movie when you export your Project.

▶ **Clip Frame ❽**: This is the size and shape of the Clip that is placed on the Project Frame.

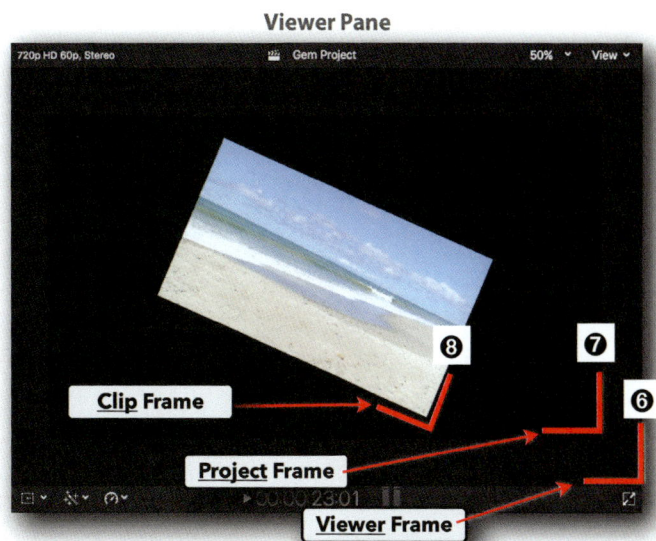

As we have already seen in the Spatial Conform Module, if the Clip Frame resolution is higher than the Project Frame resolution, then part of the Clip will be cropped. If the Clip resolution is lower, then the portion of the Project Frame that is not covered by the Clip will be black or transparent. So the important step is, how is the Clip Frame placed on the Project Frame?

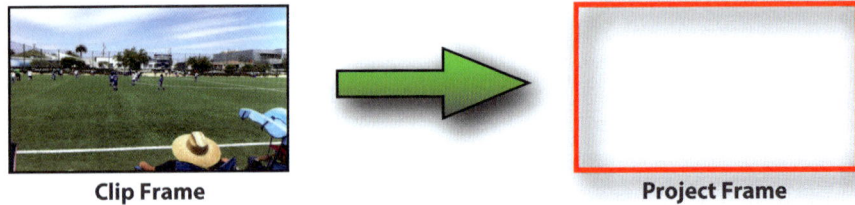

Clip Frame   **Project Frame**

The Transform, Crop, and Distort Modules let you mess with the dimensions and position of the Clip Frame in relation to the Project Frame. So whenever there is a value for x/y coordinates, we have to be aware if those coordinates are related to the Clip Frame or the Project Frame.

This is just the frame of the Project, determined by its resolution, i.e. 1280x1080
No Clip is displayed inside.

Now a Clip is displayed inside the Project frame. The size of the Clip is filling the frame of the Project.
Clip and Project Resolution are the same in this example.

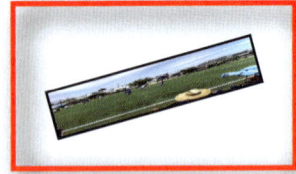

The frame of the Clip is smaller than the frame of the Project and also the Clip has a different aspect ratio (distorted) and orientation (rotation).

🟤 Project Frame Zoom

In the upper right corner of the Viewer Pane is a popup menu that controls the zoom level ❶ of the Project Frame. You can also use the Key Commands *cmd+plus* and *cmd+minus* (make sure the Viewer has Key Focus). Set the value to "Fit" to have the Project Frame automatically adjust its zoom level to match the Viewer Frame whenever you resize the Viewer window.

A little white frame ❷ will be displayed in the Viewer if the Project Frame is zoomed in so much that the Viewer Frame can't display the whole Project Frame. The white frame now represents the Project Frame and the red frame inside represents the Viewer Frame, indicating which portion of the Project Frame is visible ❸. You can even *drag* that red frame inside the white frame to move it to the section of the Project Frame you want the Viewer to display.

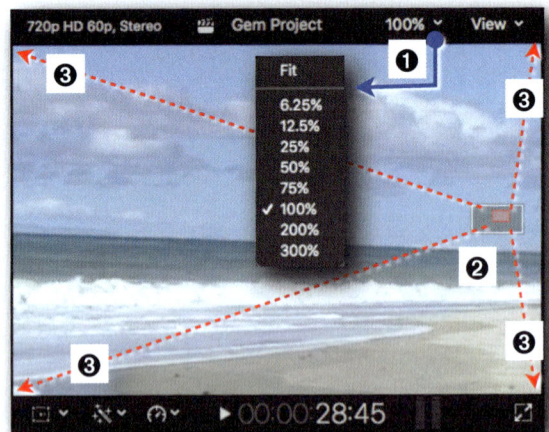

🟤 Controls

Changing the values with the onscreen controls ❹ in the Viewer will change the values (and the visual controls) in the Inspector ❺ and vice versa. Most controls in the Inspector can be changed with a slider, by entering a numeric value, or by *dragging* a value up and down. You can automate the values with Keyframes from the Inspector and also from the Viewer. Use the multi-level Reset 🔄 commands to reset individual controls or the entire Module. The bypass buttons ☑◻ let you quickly do an A/B comparison to view the Clip with or without the Effect.

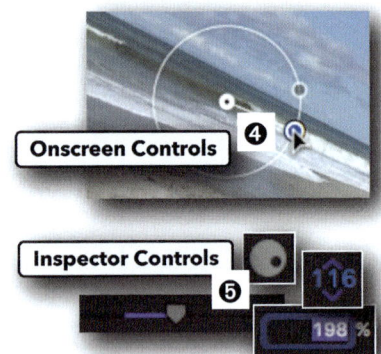

➡ *Transform* ⊡

The Transform Module lets you change the following aspects of the Timeline Clip, the **Size** of the image (the Clip Frame), the **Position** of the image (Clip) relative to the Project Frame, and the **Rotation**.

Transform					
Position	X	0 px	Y	0 px	◇
Rotation		●	-22.0 °		◇
Scale (All)	——— ▽		246 %		◇
Scale X	——— ▽		178.19 %		◇
Scale Y	——— ▽		246.0 %		◇
Anchor	X	0 px	Y	0 px	◇

🔘 Scale (X, Y)

The following controls resize the image (Clip Frame).

- *Drag* any of the blue handles in the four corners of the image to change the image size while maintaining the aspect ratio. (This is the same as moving the Scale Slider in the Inspector).
- *Opt+drag* has the same function, but the handle in the opposite corner is fixed while dragging.
- *Sh+drag* lets you resize the image freely without any aspect ratio restrictions.
- *Drag* either one of the two blue handles in the middle of the <u>left side</u> or <u>right side</u> to change only the horizontal image size. This changes the aspect ratio. It is the same as moving the X Slider in the Inspector.
- *Opt+drag* has the same function but the handle on the opposite side is fixed while dragging.
- *Sh+drag* will also move the vertical size to maintain the aspect ratio.
- *Drag* either one of the two blue handles on the <u>top side</u> or <u>bottom side</u> of the image to change the vertical image size. This changes the aspect ratio. It is the same as moving the Y Slider in the Inspector.
- *Opt+drag* has the same function, but the handle on the opposite side is fixed while dragging.
- *Sh+drag* will also move the horizontal side to maintain the aspect ratio.

X, Y: the same value   **X, Y**: NOT the same value

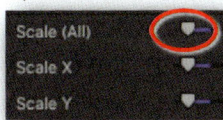

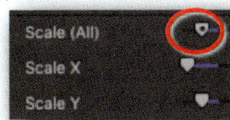

Scale (All)	⬭
Scale X	▽
Scale Y	⬭

Scale (All)	▽
Scale X	⬭
Scale Y	⬭

🔘 Anchor (X, Y)

The Anchor (the big round puck in the middle) is the "reference point" of the image. Its default

position is in the center of the image (Anchor: x=0, y=0). Any other value positions that anchor off-center. Moving the image on the Project Frame will move the Anchor with the image. The Anchor also functions as the rotation point or axis when you rotate the image.

The Anchor position (Anchor: X, Y) is not available as an on-screen control.

🔘 Position (X,Y)

While the Anchor coordinates define the position of the anchor on the Clip Frame, the Position coordinates define the position of the Anchor on the Project Frame (moving the Clip with it). Its default position is in the center of the Project Frame (x=0, y=0).

Think about it, the actual placement of the image is a result of both coordinates, Anchor (Clip/image related) and Position (Project related). Just play around with it to fully understand the relationship.

To change the Position in the Viewer, either *drag* the Anchor or *click+drag* anywhere in the image.

🔘 Rotation

This control lets you rotate the whole image on its axis. The Anchor point functions as the axis. The onscreen control provides the rotation handle next to the Anchor point. When you click on it, the control turns blue and a concentric circle appears. The further you drag the rotation handle away from the center, the bigger the circle will be and the finer the rotation control will be. A second dot on the circle indicates the previous rotation position.

If you hold down the shift key while dragging (*sh+drag*), then the rotation handle turns yellow and will latch to a fixed rotation value (0°. 45°, 90°, 135°, etc.).

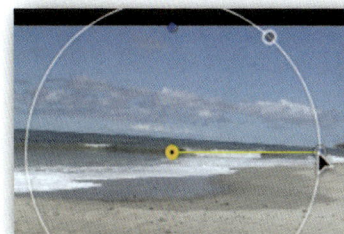

➡ Crop

The Crop Module provides three options:
Trim - **Crop** - **Ken Burns**

They can be selected from the Module's popup menu or from the top of the Viewer.

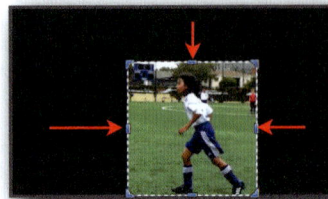

The "unused" black area will be transparent for any Clip that is placed underneath it.

Viewer

Video Inspector

Trim

You can trim the four sides of the image independently with the 4 controls in the Inspector (Left, Right, Top, Bottom).

The same four controls can be changed with the onscreen controls in the Viewer, which provide a few extra features:

- *Drag* a side handle to move only that side.

- *Opt+drag* a side handle to move that side and its opposite side together.

- *Sh+drag* to move all the sides except the opposite side while retaining the aspect ratio of the image.

- *Drag* a corner handle to trim the image without restriction of the aspect ratio.

- *Opt+drag* a corner handle to move opposite sides together.

- *Sh+drag* a corner handle to leave the opposite corner handle fixed while moving all sides together and, therefore, retaining the aspect ratio of the image.

- *Click+drag* the window to move the selection over a different position of the Clip.

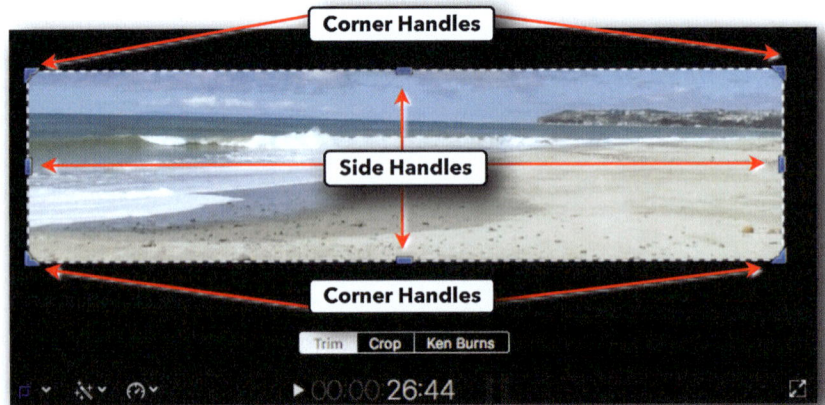

Pay attention to the yellow "guide lines" that indicate when you crop half or you are in the center, etc.

💀 Crop ❶

This is basically a "Trim+Scale" effect.

After you made the trim and hit "Done" ❷ or play, the selection will be scaled to fit the Project Frame. Additional cropping might occur if the aspect ratio of the trim doesn't fit the aspect ratio of the Project.

You can trim the four sides of the image independently with the 4 controls in the Inspector (Left, Right, Top, Bottom).

The onscreen controls in the Viewer, however, only provide the corner handles ❸:

- **_Drag_** a corner handle to change the image size while retaining its aspect ratio. The opposite corner is fixed.

- **_Opt+drag_** a corner handle to change the image size while retaining its aspect ratio. But this time, the center of the selection is fixed.

- **_Click+drag_** the window to move the selection over a different position of the Clip.

Pay attention to the yellow "guide lines" that indicate when you crop half or you are in the center, etc.

💀 Ken Burns ❹

The Ken Burns effect is nothing other than two different crop (and scaled) settings of an image that move towards each other. It is a very common effect to create a movement with still images, but can also be used on Video Clips.

This time, there are no controls ❺ in the Video Inspector but a very intuitive and easy to use interface, using the onscreen controls in the Viewer.

The Viewer has four controls:

- ❻ The green rectangle is the crop setting used as the first frame of the Clip. The same resize and reposition rules apply.

- ❼ The red rectangle is the crop setting that will be the last frame of the Clip. The big arrow indicates the direction of the movement. You can see the actual frame in the Viewer for the start and end frame when you **_click_** the red or green frame by clicking on it.

- ❽ **_Click_** the Swap Button ⟲ to reverse the movement.

- ❾ **_Click_** the Play Button ▶ to preview the Effect, which starts with the green cropped selection and moving towards the red cropped selection over the duration of the Clip. In case of a still image, you can speed up or slow down the movement by changing the length of the Clip.

- ❿ **_Click_** the Done Button Done to complete the setting.

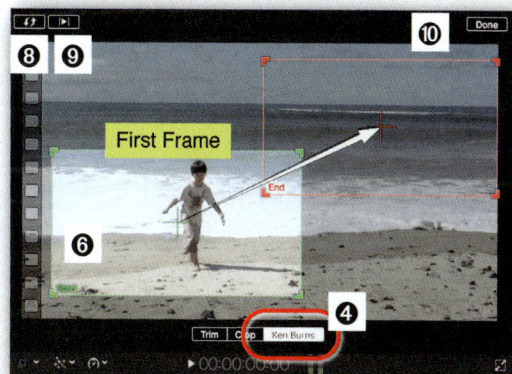

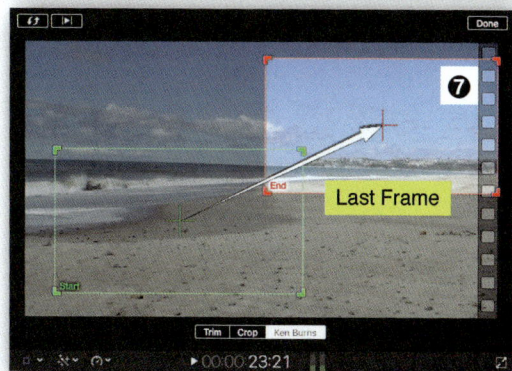

🌀 Distort

The Distort Module is similar to the Transform Module. You trim the image and the "unused" black area ❶ of the Viewer becomes transparent. The difference, however, is that the left-right and top-bottom sides of the image don't have to stay parallel while trimming. The image can be squeezed and stretched freely in all directions.

▶ **Inspector Controls ❷**: Instead of defining the position of the sides of a Clip, this time you define the position of the four corners with their X/Y coordinates.

▶ **Onscreen Controls ❸**: The model below shows what's happening. You can move either one of the four corner ❹ or side handles ❺ (red). The black handles and sides stay fixed while the orange handles and sides get dragged with it like if they were tied on a rubber band.

Of course, you can *click+drag* the whole selection over the image.

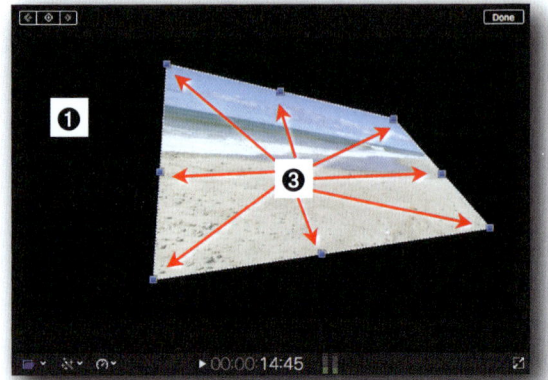

➡ Color

I cover the Color Modules later in this chapter.

Dragging a corner   Dragging a side

● dragged handle
● moves with it
● stays fixed

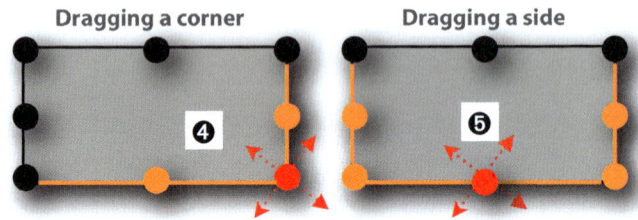

➡ *Compositing*

The Compositing Module ❻ is used to quickly combine (overlay) one or more Clips without the need of the more time consuming Keyer Effect from the Effects Browser. The term "compositing" means overlaying or combining video frames. The available settings determine the "how it is done" and what the resulting video will look like.

The most important step before applying any settings is the placement of the videos. When you stack Clips (containing video content) in FCPx (videos or still images), then the top video always has priority, meaning it blocks the video underneath. It doesn't matter if the Clip is placed on the Primary Storyline or as a Connected Clip.

Remember science class? "An object can be transparent, translucent, or opaque." The object here is the top level video and the question is how much of the video signal of the Clip underneath does the top Clip let through. You can have areas in the top video (alpha channel, keys) that are fully transparent, meaning they let the video below through. Or you can set conditions that the whole video or part of it is partially transparent, meaning some of the underlying video gets through, ending up with a mix or blend of both video signals. The level of transparency is set with the Opacity value. I will get into much more details about this topic in my book "Motion 5 - How it Works".

▶ **Opacity ❼**: 100% Opacity means fully blocked (opaque object), 50% means both video signals are mixed equally, and 0% means fully see-through with the effect that all the signal from the bottom video goes through and nothing from the top video is visible.

▶ **Blend Mode ❽**: This popup menu provides a long list of settings that apply the Opacity level to portions of the video signal (i.e. specific colors). A great place to experiment.

▶ **Keyframe**: The Opacity level can be automated with Keyframes to change the effect over time.

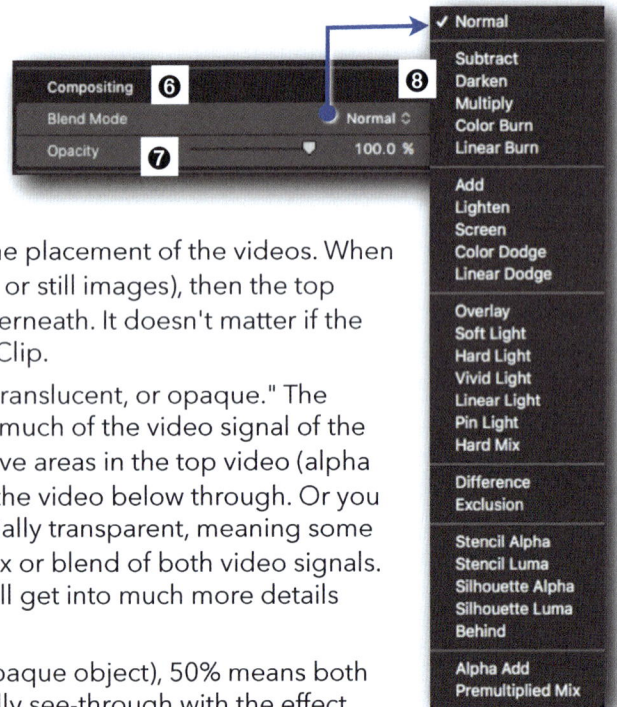

Additional Video Effects

All the additional Video Effects that you can apply to Clips are available in the Effects Browser ❶. *Click* on the Effects Browser Button ❷ or open it directly with the Key Command *cmd+5* or Main Menu *Window ➤ Show in Workspace ➤ Effects*.

The Effects are organized in categories ❸ that you can select from the Sidebar. Search for a specific effect by typing its name into the search field ❹ at the bottom of the Browser. I cover the details of the interface in the Audio chapter.

Timeline Pane: Effects Browser

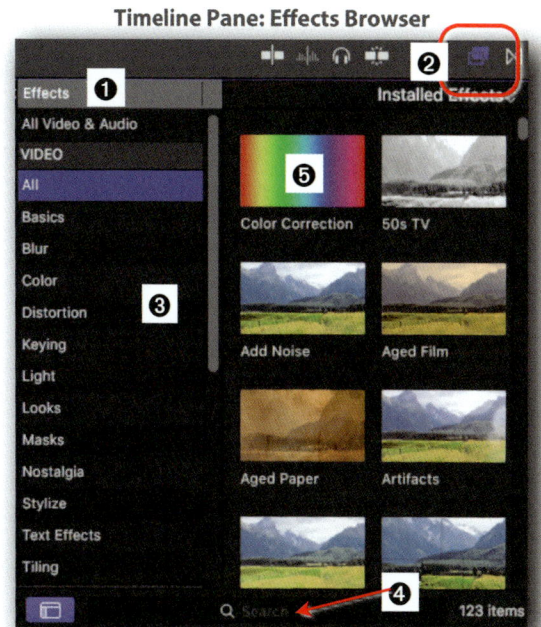

▶ **Preview Effects**: Select a Timeline Clip and then skim over the effects image ❺ in the Browser. This will let you preview the effect in the Viewer to see what it looks like for that Clip. The width of the Effect image represents the length of the selected Timeline Clip. The SMPTE Reader in the Viewer displays the relative time from the beginning of the Clip.

> *Tip*: Hold down the *option* key and drag left-right to adjust the primary control of that specific effect.

▶ **Add Effect**: These are the procedures on how to apply Effects to a Clip:

- *Drag* the Effect image from the Browser over the Clip in the Timeline.
- *Double+click* on the Effect image to add it to the selected Clip(s) in the Timeline.
- You can copy-paste all the Effects (*opt+cmd+V*) or a selection of specific Attributes (*sh+cmd+V*) from one Clip to another (or multiple Clips). This is the same procedure I explained in the Audio Effects chapter.

▶ **Edit Effects**

- Inspector ❻: That's where most of the parameters are available, including the Keyframe settings ❼.
- Video Animation: This is mainly for Keyframe editing (discussed in the Animation chapter). Use the Fade Handles to smooth the in and out of a specific effect.
- Viewer Onscreen Controls: Some parameters might be available as onscreen controls in the Viewer.
- Motion: Most of the Effects originate from Motion and can be further adjusted in the Motion app. *Ctr+click* on the Effect image and use the command to open the Effect in Motion (if installed on your machine).

▶ **Sequence of Effects**: If you add multiple Effects to a Clip, then the order of those effects can affect the final look of the video. To change the order:

Video Inspector

- *Drag* the Effect Modules in the Inspector.
- *Drag* the lanes in the Video Animation Editor of the Timeline Clip.

▶ **Reset - Bypass - Delete**

- Reset: The Inspector has a hierarchy of different Reset levels. Reset a parameter, reset a Module, reset the whole Effects rack. Make sure to choose the right Reset Button ❽ for the action you want.
- Bypass: Each module can be bypassed with the checkbox ❾ in the Inspector or the Video Animation lane.
- Delete: Just select the module in the Inspector or the Video Animation lane and press *delete*.

Retime

Basics

The Retime Effect is a video effect that is not listed (available) in the Inspector. Retiming means, applying one of the following effects to a whole Timeline Clip or a section of a Timeline Clip:

- **Fast-motion or slow-motion**: Change the playback speed, resulting in a new constant speed
- **Speed-ramping**: Change the playback speed, resulting in variable speed

- **Reverse, Rewind**: Play backwards
- **Instant Replay**: Repeat playback
- **Freeze Frame**: Playback the same frame over time

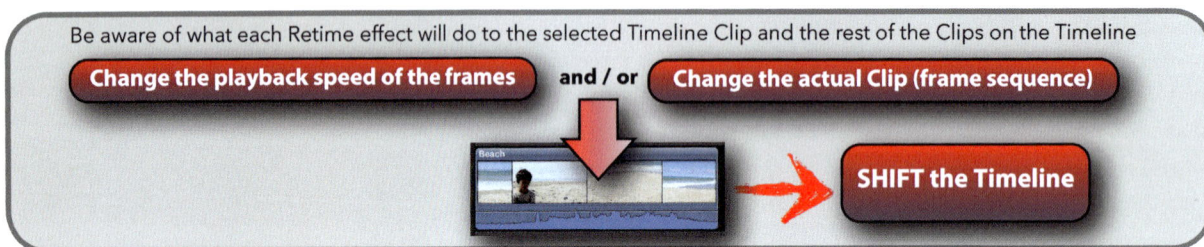

Be aware of what each Retime effect will do to the selected Timeline Clip and the rest of the Clips on the Timeline

Change the playback speed of the frames and / or **Change the actual Clip (frame sequence)**

SHIFT the Timeline

Here is the basic workflow:

☑ From the Timeline Clip, select a Clip Range, the whole Clip or multiple Clips ❶.

☑ Select from the Main Menu *Modify ➤ Retime ➤* ❷ or *click* the Retime Button ❸ 🕐 on the Viewer to open the Retime Menu ❹ listing all the Retime Effects.

☑ Enable the Retime Editor ❺, a visual Timeline Clip extension, displaying various on-Clip Controls.

☑ You can toggle the Retime Editor independently for any selected Clip from the same Retime Menu or with the Key Command *cmd+R* ❻.

☑ The Retime Editor with the colored Speed Segments lets you further adjust the speed via the additional popup menus ❼, the Custom Speed Popover ❽, and set the speed by dragging the Retime Handle ❾.

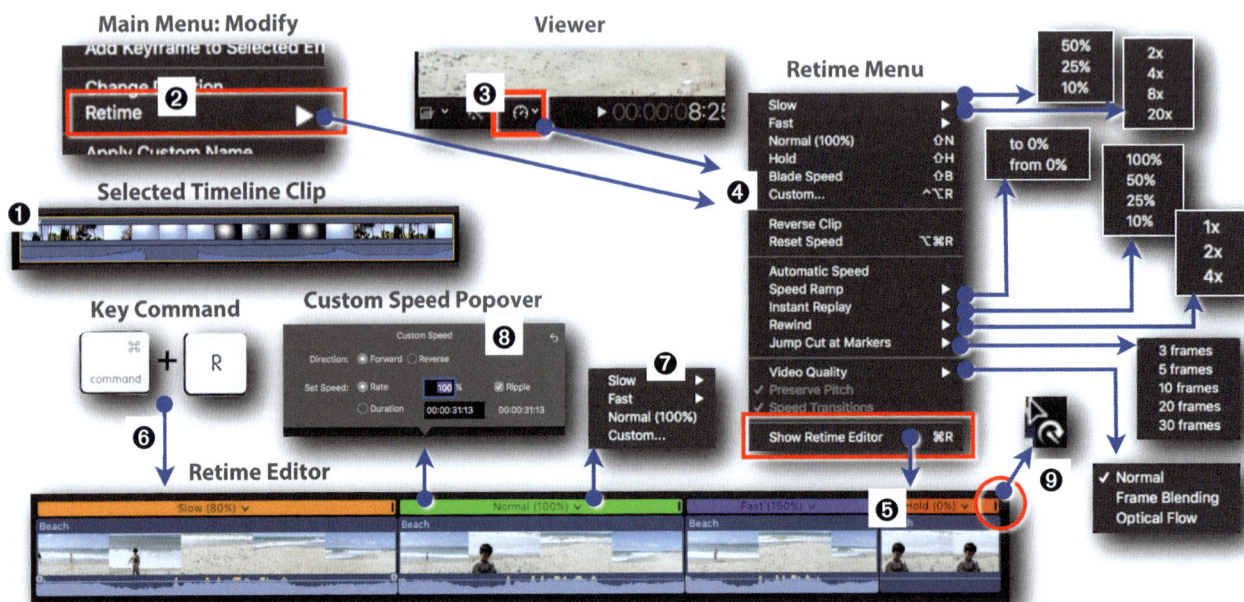

12 - Video Effects

Retime Editor

The Retime Editor is just an expanded view of the selected Timeline Clip, a colored bar on top of Clips, to display the Retime related on-Clip controls. The command, Show Retime Editor, toggles this bar on and off. Selecting any Retime command from the menu will automatically show the Retime Editor for the selected Clip. Unfortunately, there is no indication in the Timeline if a Clip has an applied Retime Effect once the Retime Editor is closed. A workaround: select all Clips and toggle Retime Editor on *cmd+A*, *cmd+R*.

Show/Hide Retime Editor

These are the commands to toggle the Retime Editor on the selected Timeline Clip(s):

- Key Command *cmd+R*
- Main Menu *Modify ➤ Retime ➤ Show/Hide Retime Editor*
- *Click* on the Retime Button 🕸 and select from the *Retime Menu ➤ Show/Hide Retime Editor*
- Enabling any Retime Effect on a Clip will automatically show the Retime Editor

Interface

These are the main interface elements for the Retime Editor:

- **Retime Bar ❶**: The Retime Editor is basically just the added Retime Bar on top of the Clip that contains the various controls.

- **Color**: The various color indicates the playback speed of the Clip:
  - Green: Original speed (100%)
  - Orange: Slower speed (< 100%)
  - Blue: Faster speed (> 100%)
  - Red: Freeze Frame (0%)

- **Retime Handle ❷**: On the far right of the Retime Bar is the Retime Handle (a tiny vertical bar). *Drag* that handle to manually lengthen (time expand) or shorten (time compress) the Clip.

- **Custom Speed Popover ❸**: *Double-click* on the Retime Bar to open the Custom Speed Popover that provides a few controls to quickly adjust the speed.

- Direction: You can play back the Clip forward or backwards
- Set Speed - Rate: Enter a percentage value for the playback speed
- Ripple: If enabled, then the Clips on the right move accordingly. If disabled, then no Clips are shifted on the Timeline. Either a Gap Clip is added (fast playback) or the Clip gets shortened (slow playback)
- Set Speed - Duration: Enter a specific duration for the length of the Clip
- Reset: The Reset Button ↩ sets all the controls to their default value

- **Retime Menu ❹**: *Click* on the selector ⌄ to open a mini Retime Menu with the four basic controls, including the Custom command that opens the Custom Speed Popover.

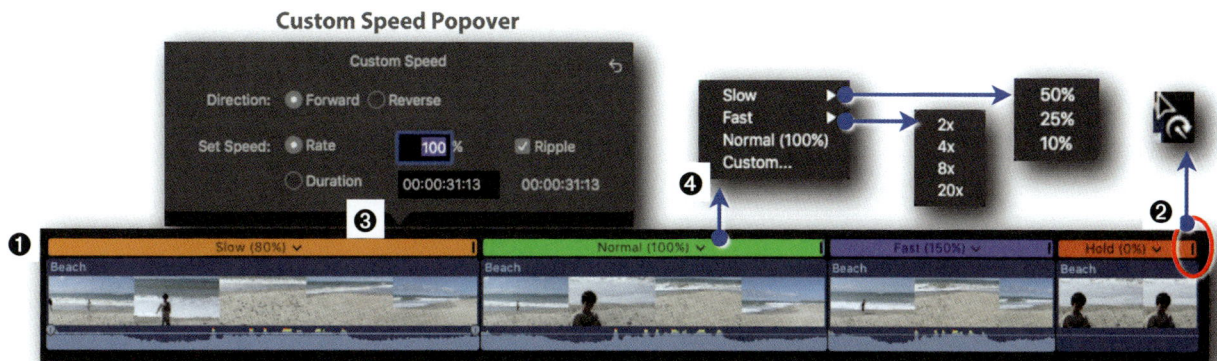

Custom Speed Popover

⚫ Entire Clip or Clip Range

You can apply a Retime Effect to an entire Clip or to a Clip Range:

▶ **Entire Clip**: Select one or multiple Clips and choose a Retime command, which will be applied to all selected Clips.

▶ **Clip Range**: *Drag* a range ❶ with the Range Tool (*R*) and then select a Retime Command to apply that playback speed to only that range ❷. This creates the so-called Speed Segments ❸.

⚫ Speed Segments ❸

A Speed Segment is the section on a Clip that lets you set the playback individually. This enables you to set different playback speeds along a single Clip without cutting it up in smaller Clips. The individual Speed Segments on a Clip can be identified by their separate Retime Bars.

⚫ Speed Transition

A Speed Transition ❹ is the gray area on the Retime Bar between two Speed Segments, which many Retime effects add automatically. These transitions create a smoother change in playback speed between adjacent Speed Segments. A Speed Transition between a forward and backward playing Speed Segment is not possible.

You have some control over the Speed Transition:

▶ **Speed Transition on/off**: The Retime Menu has a command "*Speed Transitions*" ❺ that turns them on or off for the currently selected Clip(s).

▶ **Trim ❻**: You can trim the length of the transition by *dragging* the left and right edge of that gray area.

▶ **Speed Transition Popover**: *Double-click* on the Retime Handle ❼ to open a popover ❽ that lets you remove that Speed Transition. Please note that you can only disable a Transition if a Speed Transition has been enabled for that Clip in the Retime Menu ❺. The second control on this popover lets you edit the Source Frame ❾.

⚫ Source Frame 🎞

The Source Frame, the little filmstrip icon determines which frame of the Clip is the last frame of a specific Speed Segment and, therefore, sets the position where one Speed Segments ends and the adjacent one starts.

▶ *Drag* the Source Frame left or right to move it

▶ You see the Speed Segment to the left and to the right of the Source Frame update accordingly while dragging

▶ The Viewer displays that frame while dragging

▶ *Double-click* the Source Frame to hide it

Speed Segments

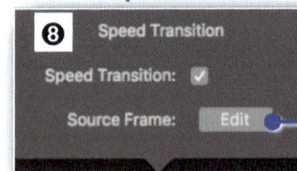
Retime Menu

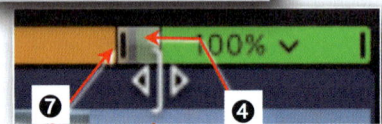
Popover

Retime Handle ❻ Trim Tool Speed Transition ❹

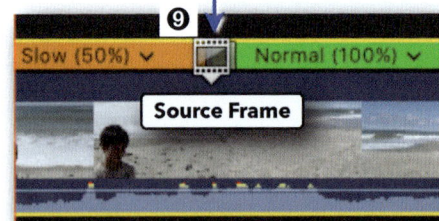
Source Frame

Retime Effects

Now let's go over the various Retime Effects. There are multiple procedures and menus on how to apply a Retime Effect, so we will start with an overview about those available procedures.

☑ Step #1 - **Select Target**: Like with any other effect, you have to first select the target that you want to apply the Retime Effect to. Please note that the Retime Editor doesn't have to be visible yet. It will be automatically shown on the Clip once you apply a Retime Effect.

- Select a single Clip ❶
- Select multiple Clips
- Select a Clip Range (with the Range Tool). You can make a selection across Speed Segments and/or multiple Clips
- Select a Speed Segment. *Click* on an individual Retime Bar (not the text) to only select that Speed Segment

☑ Step #2 - **Select the Effect**: Once you selected the target clip(s) or range, you choose the Retime Effect from the Retime Menu ❷ that you can access from two places:

- Main Menu *Modify* ➤ *Retime* ➤ ❸
- *Click* on the Retime Button ❹ at the bottom of the Viewer
- The Retime Effects are also available as Key Commands. Search for "Retime" in the Command Editor Dialog (*opt+cmd+K*)

☑ **Retime Editor**: If the Retime Editor ❺ is visible on a Clip, then you can apply some Retime Effects directly on the Clip with the following commands:

- *Click* on the selector ❻ of the Retime Bar to open a mini Retime Menu with the basic Slow/Fast/Normal commands
- *Double-click* on the Retime Bar to open the Custom Speed Popover ❼ that provides some of the Retime Effects
- *Drag* the Retime Handle ❽ to graphically adjust the speed of that Speed Segment

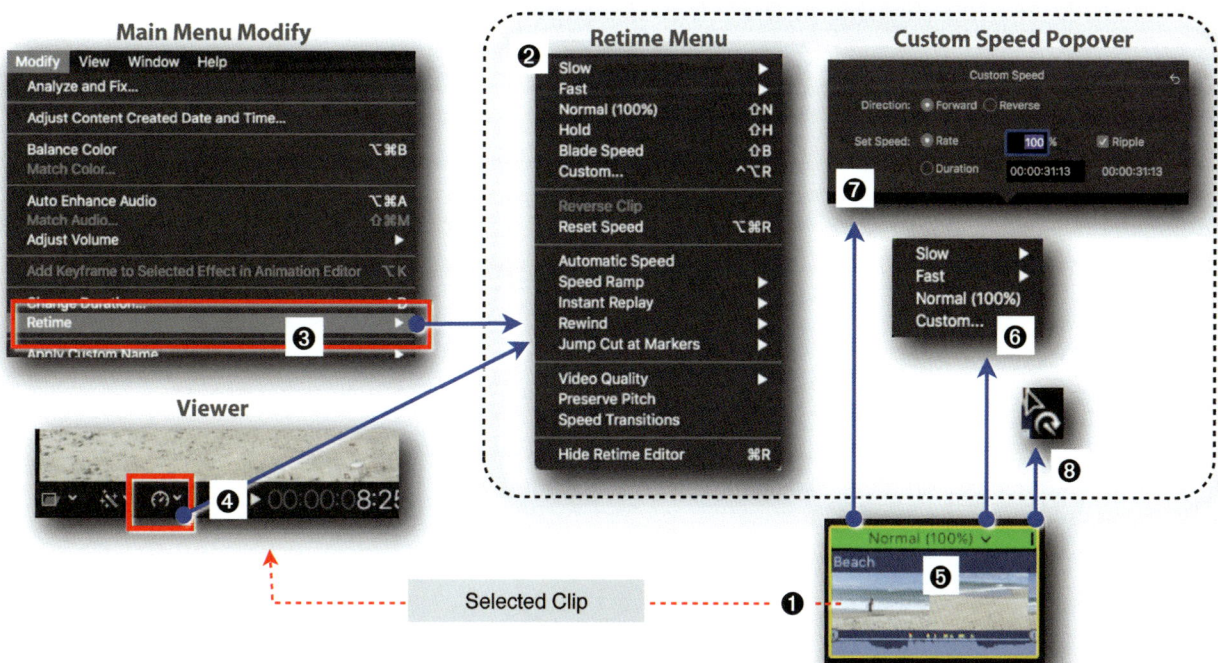

➡ Fixed Playback Speed

The first section ❶ in the Retime Menu contains all the commands that let you apply a fixed speed to a Speed Segment.

Retime Menu

💀 Slow

The submenu ❷ provides three options to set the speed to 50%, 25%, or 10% of the normal speed. The Speed Segment gets longer and the percentage value is indicated in the Retime Bar, which turns orange ❸.

💀 Fast

The submenu ❹ provides four options to set the speed to twice, 4 times, 8 times, or 20 times the normal speed. The Speed Segment gets shorter and the percentage value is indicated in the Retime Bar, which turns blue ❺.

💀 Normal (100%)

This command sets the selected Clip/Range back to its original speed, indicated by the color green ❻ and the number "100%".

💀 Hold

The hold command creates a so-called Hold Segment ❼ (red color) at the current Playhead or Skimmer, which is like a 2 second freeze frame. Please note that this type of freeze frame is still part of the Clip as a Speed Segment. The other Freeze Frame command in FCPx creates a separate Clip.

Custom Speed Popover

Freeze Frame Command

Preferences

- ▶ Select a frame on an Event Clip and the command from the Main Menu *Edit ➤ Connect Freeze Frame* (*opt+F*) will insert that frame as a Connected Clip (Still Image) at the current Playhead position with the length set in the *Preferences ➤ Editing ➤ Still Images* ❽.

- ▶ When the Timeline has Key Focus, then selecting from the Main Menu *Edit ➤ Freeze Frame* (*opt+F*) will insert a Still Image at the current Playhead position with the frame at that position and the length set in the *Preferences ➤ Editing ➤ Still Images*.

💀 Blade Speed

The Blade Speed command (*sh+B*) simply cuts a Clip into two Speed Segments at the current Playhead or Skimmer Position.

💀 Custom

The Custom command opens the same Custom Speed Popover ❾ that you also can access by *double-clicking* on the Retime Bar. However, the difference here is that you can have multiple Clips and/or Speed Segments selected to apply the changes you make in the popover to all those selected Clips.

Enter a specific percentage value (Rate) or a specific length (Duration). If the *Ripple* checkbox ❿ is enabled, then any adjacent Clips on the right move according to the Magnetic Timeline concept. If disabled, then a Gap Clip will be added (when a Clip ends too early due to the faster speed) or the Clip will be shortened (when the Clip lasts too long due to the slower speed).

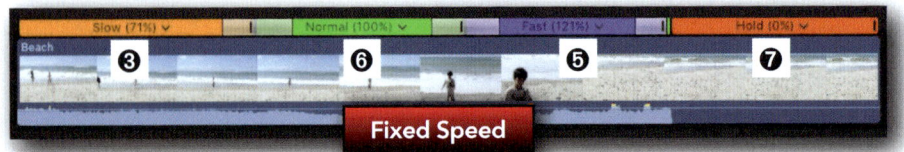

➡ Reverse Clip

The Reverse command plays the Clip backwards (frames are in reverse order). The Speed Segment has a line of left arrows to indicate the reverse order ❶.

The Reverse effect can only be applied to a whole Clip. However, you can apply Retime Effects to a section of the reversed Clip in a second step and create separate Speed Segments.

➡ Speed Ramp

There are two variations ❷ for the Speed Ramp Effect:

- 🔘 To speed up a Clip, select from the Retime Menu **_Speed Ramp ➤ from 0%_**.
- 🔘 To slow down a Clip, select from the Retime Menu **_Speed Ramp ➤ to 0%_**.

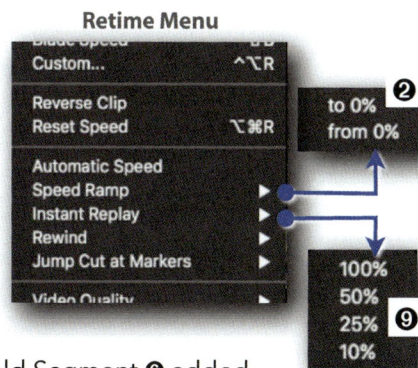

The command will divide the Clip or the Range into four Speed Segments ❸ with increasing or decreasing percentage values (b1, b2, b3, b4) plus the two unaltered Speed Segments ❹ at the beginning (a) and end (c). If you selected a Range ❺, then you will have a short (red) Hold Segment ❻ added for the 0% Segment at the beginning (from 0%) or at the end (to 0%) of the Ramp.

To create a finer resolution, apply the command again to each segment to divide them again and adjust the percentage values accordingly.

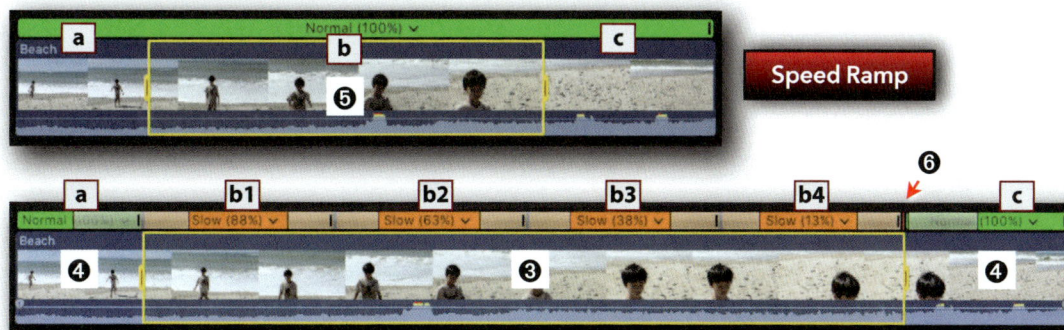

➡ Instant Replay

Here is an example when Instant Replay is applied to a Clip Range ❼. Please note that this effect changes the sequence of the existing frames:

- ☑ The section up to the end of the Clip Range stays untouched (a+b).
- ☑ At end of the Clip Range, FCPx repeats the section of the Clip Range (b) with the speed change (b-slow) ❽ selected in the submenu ❾ of 100%, 50%, 25%, or 10%.
- ☑ That new section (b-slow) will have a Title Clip ❿ added as a Connected Clip.
- ☑ The remaining section of the Clip after the Clip Range plays after the replay section (c).
- ☑ A Speed Transition is added at the end of the replay section.
- ☑ Of course you can adjust the Speed Segments and Speed Transition manually.

➡ Rewind

Here is an example when the Rewind Effect is applied to a Clip Range. Please note that this effect changes the sequence of the existing frames:

Retime Menu

- ☑ The section up to the end of the Clip Range stays untouched (a+b).
- ☑ At the end of the Clip Range ❶, FCPx repeats the Clip Range based on the speed factor set in the popup menu (1x, 2x, 4x) ❷ and reverses that Speed Segment ❸.
- ☑ After that, the section of the Clip Range repeats again (b) ❹, followed by the remaining section after the Clip Range of that Clip (c) ❺.
- ☑ Again, you can adjust the Speed Sections manually.

➡ Jump Cut at Markers

This Retime Effect is useful to cut out a few frames here and there to shorten a Clip. However, instead of actually splitting the Clip and ending up with multiple Clips to trim, you can do this elegantly with Speed Segments and, therefore, leave the actual Clip intact. Here is the procedure:

- ☑ Add Markers ❻ on the Clip where you want to create a Jump Cut.
- ☑ Have the Clip selected and choose from the "Jump Cut at Markers" command submenu how many frames ❼ you want to cut out at each Marker position.
- ☑ FCPx inserts a very short Speed Segment ❽ at each Marker with a very high speed factor that looks like you've cut the equal amount of "frames" you've selected in the popup menu. As you can see in my example, where I zoomed in on the speed segment, it has a speed factor of 3,000 ❾.

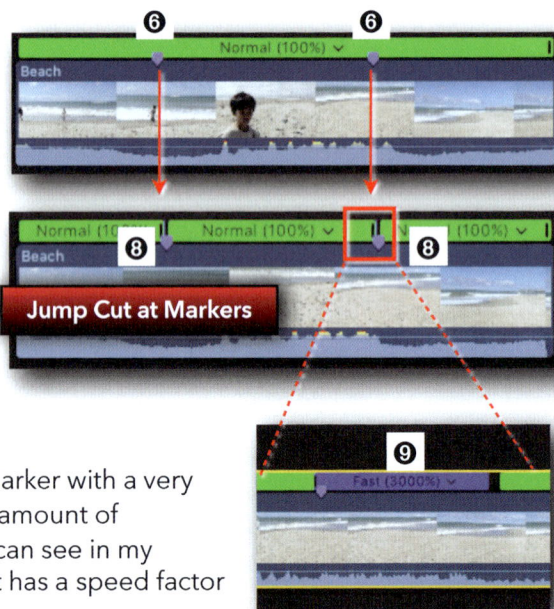

➡ Automatic Speed ❿

This is a special Retime command that plays back the Clip with the native frame rate of the original Source Media File. For example, if a Camera had a speed effect applied to the clip with 240 fps, but your Project is set to 25fps.

➡ Reset Retime Effects

There are several ways to undo Retime Effects:

🟡 Undo

This is the easiest command. Just use the Undo command (**cmd+Z**) to undo any Retime Edit you just applied.

🟡 Normal (100%)

You can select a whole Clip, multiple Clips, or a selected Range (even across multiple segments and Clips) and use the Retime Command *Normal (100%)* ❶. It sets all the segments to 100% speed.

🟡 Reset Button

The Custom Speed Popover has a Reset Button ❷ 🔄 that removes all the Retime Effects from the Speed Segment(s) or the entire Clip(s), depending from where you opened the popover.

🟡 Reset Speed

The *Reset Speed* ❸ command can only be used on a whole Clip or multiple selected Clips. It removes all the Retime Effects from that Timeline Clip(s). Please note that any Title Clip created by the Instant Replay command will not be removed.

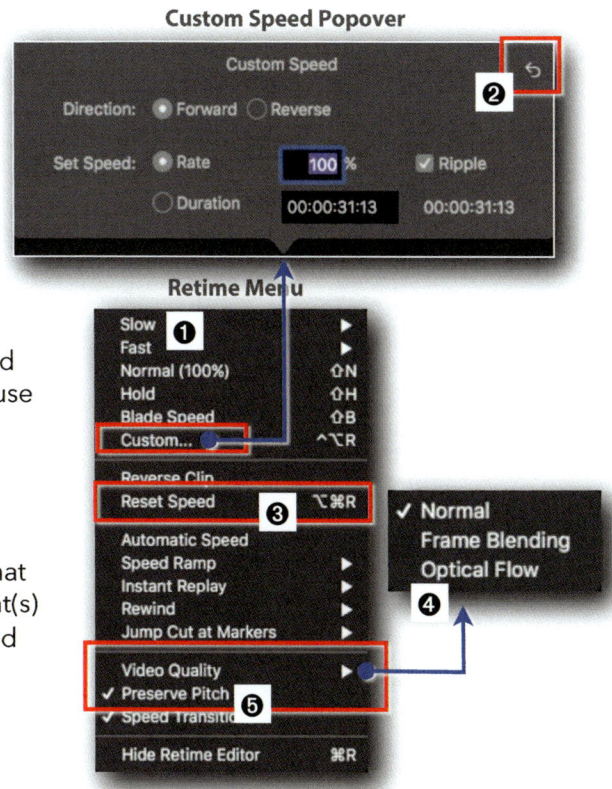

Custom Speed Popover

Custom Speed

Direction: ● Forward ○ Reverse

Set Speed: ● Rate `100` % ☑ Ripple

○ Duration 00:00:31:13   00:00:31:13

❷

Retime Menu

Slow ❶ ▶
Fast ▶
Normal (100%) ⇧N
Hold ⇧H
Blade Speed ⇧B
Custom... ^⌥R
Reverse Clip
Reset Speed ❸ ⌥⌘R
Automatic Speed
Speed Ramp ▶
Instant Replay ▶
Rewind ▶
Jump Cut at Markers ▶
Video Quality ▶
✓ Preserve Pitch ❺
✓ Speed Transition
Hide Retime Editor ⌘R

✓ Normal
Frame Blending
Optical Flow
❹

➡ Video Quality

Of course, speed manipulation has an affect on the video quality of the Clip. Although FCPx can compensate for any artifacts, the more extreme the speed changes are, the higher the chance you might notice artifacts.

The Video Quality item in the Retime Menu provides three options in its submenu ❹ to choose the one that is more suitable for any given video material.

Video Quality Presets (FCPx Documentation)

Normal: *The default setting. Frames are duplicated, and no frame blending is applied to the slow-motion clip. No rendering is required.*

Frame Blending: *Adds in-between frames by blending individual pixels of neighboring frames. Slow-motion clips created with Frame Blending appear to play back more smoothly than those created with the Normal (duplication) setting. Rendering is required.*

Optical Flow: *Adds in-between frames using an optical flow algorithm, which analyzes the clip to determine the directional movement of pixels and then draws portions of the new frames based on the optical flow analysis. Only the portion of the clip used in the project (the media between the clip start and end points) is analyzed. Rendering is required.*

➡ Preserve Pitch

The "Preserve Pitch" option ❺ in the Retime Menu is enabled by default. This maintains the original pitch of the audio signal regardless of any speed changes to the Clip. For example, avoid the typical Mickey Mouse effect when speeding up the playback, or the big monster effect when slowing down the speed.

Last final note on Retime Effects

Retime Effects can be applied to any Clip (Storyline, Connected Clip, Compound Clip, Audition), but always pay attention to a possible shift of the subsequent Clips in the Storyline.

Basics

Color correction is the step in your video production where you adjust the color of your Clips or segments of a Clip for many different reasons. This could be for correcting any errors in color balance or exposure, to make different Clips in your edit that were shot on different days or on different cameras look more similar, or even manipulate the color of the video in a more creative way, like special effects.

FCPx provides three built-in tools that let you perform color correction for slightly different purposes:

Quick Fix	**Match**	**Create**
Correct errors in the video i.e. exposure and color balance	Match the look of a reference frame to other clips for consistency in the video	Change the look of the video to achieve different tones all the way to extreme effects

The way those three tools are implemented in FCPx could be a little bit confusing. First of all, they are listed in the Video Inspector under the Effects Module ❶ where usually the effects are listed that you manually add from the Effects Browser 🔲 These three tools, however, only show up in the Inspector when you first use their corresponding commands in the Enhancement Menu ❷ that opens when *clicking* on the Magic Wand Button ❸ 🪄 at the bottom of the Viewer Pan (in addition to the Main Menu and Key Commands).

Also, you have to pay attention to which Clips those modules can be applied to.

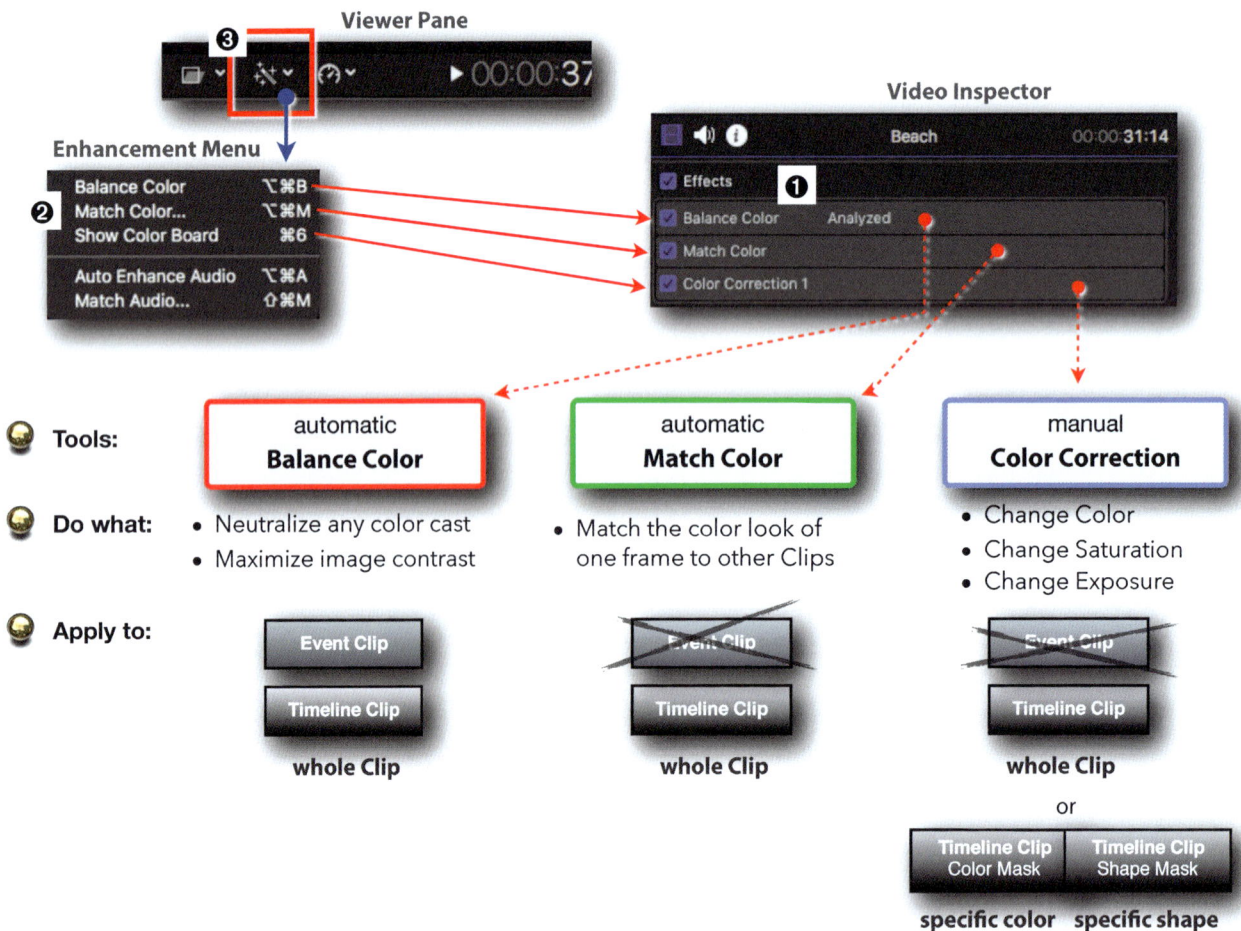

　　　　　12 - Video Effects

Color Balance (Automatic Color Correction)

This is the first of the three tools that lets you apply a quick color correction to selected Clips that FCPx performs automatically based on its own analysis. This is similar to the "Enhancement" button in Apple's Photos app, where you don't have to deal with (or know about) the individual parameters and just tell the app *"make the picture look better"*.

The feature is basically just an on/off switch to tell FCPx "<u>with</u> color correction or <u>without</u> color correction". However, you have to pay attention to a few little details.

Analyze for Balance Color - OPTIONAL

This is a little checkbox we discussed in the Import chapter. It tells FCPx to analyze the video file during import and check its color. Here is the important mechanism and functionality about this checkbox that needs to be understood when using the Color Balance feature.

▸ When you import a video file ❶, you will see the checkbox "Analyze video for balance color" ❷ in the Media Import Dialog.

▸ If enabled, FCPx analyzes the video file for color balance issues and stores that data as a separate file ❸ with the name of the Clip and the file extension .cbal in its corresponding Event folder inside the subfolders "*Analysis Files/Color Adjustment Files*".

▸ The command "Analyze and Fix..." ❹ which is available from the Main Menu *Modify* and from the Shortcut Menu when *ctr+clicking* on an Event Clip ❺ (not a Timeline Clip ❻), opens a Sheet with the same checkbox ❼ "Analyze for balance color". This lets you perform the

analysis to create that *cbal* file ❸ any time after the import. The .cbal file will be deleted if you delete the Clip in the Browser.

▸ Please note that the analysis itself only creates the file, but doesn't perform any color correction on your Clip ❺ ❻.

▸ The Color Balance Module shows the label "*Analyzed*" ❽ if it finds the cbal file for that Clip, if not, it shows "*Not Analyzed*".

▸ If you enable Balance Color ❾ for the Event Clip ❺ or Timeline Clip ❻, FCPx looks for the .cbal file to use it for applying color correction. If the file is not there, then the color correction is performed without the data in that file.

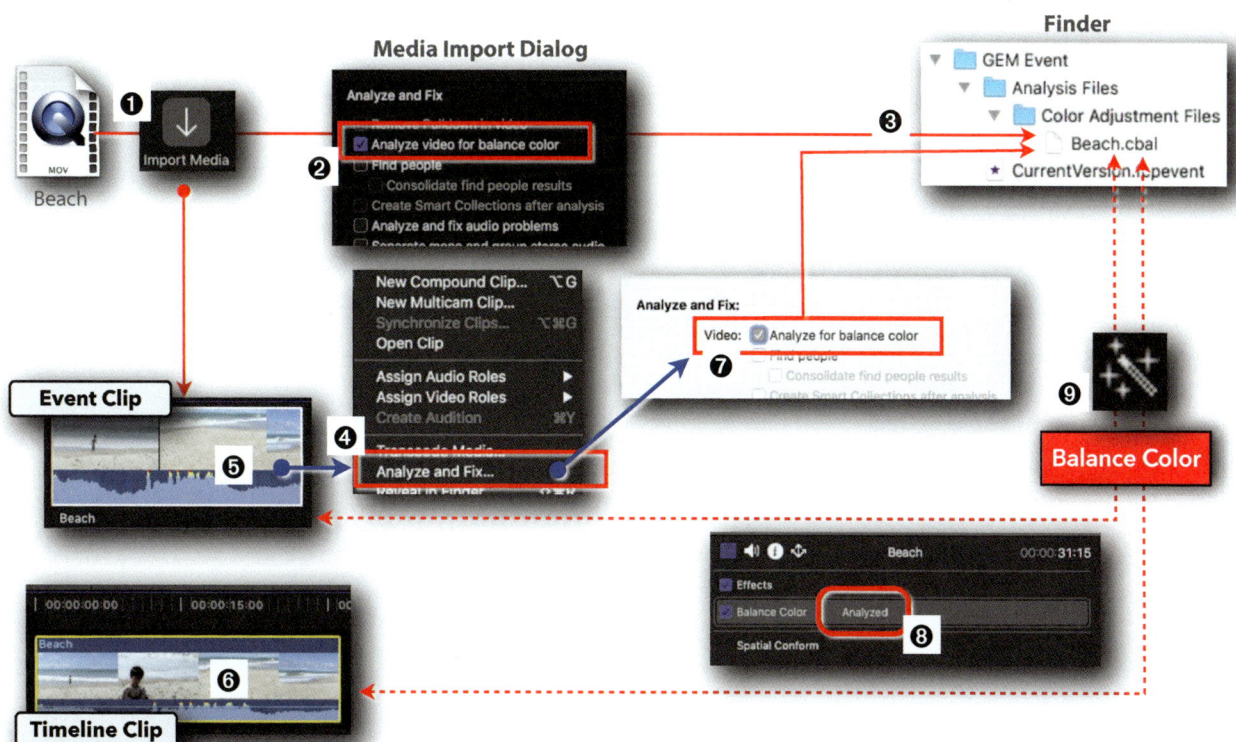

➡️ *Automatic Color Balance Procedure*

Now that we know the role of the (optional) *cbal* file, let's look at the procedure on how to use the Automatic Color Correction.

🟡 Step 1 - Default

As a default, neither the Event Clip, nor the Timeline Clip show the Balance Color Module in the Video Inspector. For the Event Clip, there is only the Spatial Conform Module visible ❶, no Balance Color Module is available.

🟡 Step 2 - Command

To use the Balance Color feature, you have to select the Clip (Event Clip or Timeline Clip) and enable it the first time with any of the following commands.

- 📌 Main Menu *Modify* ➤ *Balance Color*
- 📌 Key Command *opt+cmd+B*
- 📌 At the bottom of the Viewer, *click* on the Magic Wand Button 🪄 and select *Balance Color...* from the Enhancement Menu ❷

🟡 Step 3 - Added Module

Once you have enabled Balance Color on a Clip, the Video Inspector will add the Effects Module ❸ with the Balance Color Module "inside" (pay attention to the Show/Hide procedure to show/hide nested modules and their parameters).

🟡 Step 4 - Analyzed?

Once the Balance Color Module is added to the Effects Module, you will see the label "Not Analyzed" ❹ if FCPx couldn't find the *cbal* file for that Clip, or it shows the label "Analyzed" ❺ if it finds the *cbal* file.

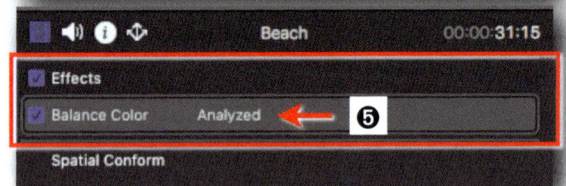

🟡 Step 5 - Color Corrected

Once you used the Balance Color Command (Step 2), FCPx applies a color correction to the Clip with or without the *cbal* data. The results just might be better with FCPx having analyzed the file before.

🟡 Step 6 - Toggle

Once you applied the automatic color correction to the Clip, you can use the checkbox ❻ ✅ ⬛ on the Balance Color Module to toggle the correction (before - after), and maybe leave it off, if the result isn't useful. Please note that the Balance Color Module is part of the Effects Module, so disabling the Effects Module will also disable the Balance Color Module, indicated by a gray checkbox ✅ ❼.

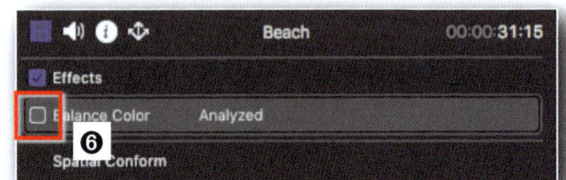

🟡 Step 7 - Others

The Balance Color setting is independent for each instance of a Clip (Event Clip, Timeline Clip). However, if you analyze an Event Clip after you dragged it to the Timeline, then that newly created *cbal* file will be used for any Balance Color procedure on Timeline Clips that are referenced to that Event Clip.

➡ *Functionality*

The FCPx User Guide gives a few explanations about the functionality of the automatic color balance:

> **From the FCPx User Guide**
>
> FCPx takes a video frame of the Clip as a **reference frame** and ...
>
> ... samples the darkest and lightest areas of the image's luma channel and adjusts the shadows and highlights in the image to neutralize any color casts.
>
> ... adjusts the image to maximize image contrast, so that the shot occupies the widest available luma range.

🔘 Analyzed

The analysis process extracts color balance information for the entire Clip.

Moving the entire Event Clip to the Timeline:
When adding an entire Event Clip or a section of the Clip (Subclip) to the Timeline, the Color-balancing feature chooses a reference frame from the selection that is closest to being correctly balanced and applies that setting to the Timeline Clip.

Moving only a Subclip to the Timeline: Timeline Clips that derived from different sections of the same (analyzed) Event Clip are each optimized for that individual section.

Two frames from the same Clip, Color Balance on

🔘 Not Analyzed

The reference frame is determined by the Playhead position. If the Playhead is parked outside the selected Clip, then the Clip's middle frame is used.

Look at the sample below that shows the effect of different Color Balance results depending on what frame the Playhead is parked at:

Two frames from the same Clip, Color Balance <u>off</u>

Color Balance <u>on</u>: Playhead parked at the <u>L</u> frame

Color Balance <u>on</u>: while Playhead parked at the <u>R</u> frame

Color Match

The concept of matching color is fairly simple: You have a video or even a graphics file with a look that you really like (i.e. the tone, the color, etc.) and apply that look to other Clip(s) without having to find out what combination of Color, Saturation, and Exposure made up that special look and then having to manually recreate that look. It's more like "whatever she had, I want to have too".

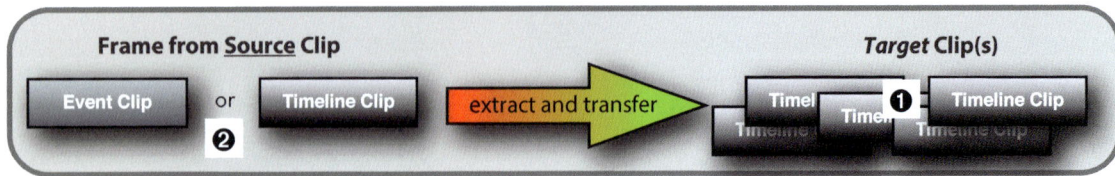

FCPx provides a nicely implemented graphical interface that is super easy to use. Please note that you can apply Match Color only to Timeline Clips ❶ as the target, but you can use either a Timeline Clip or an Event Clip as the source ❷.

☑ First, select the Clip (the Target) on the Timeline that you want to adjust its color and place the Playhead to a frame that you will use as a preview.

☑ Activate Match Color with any of the following commands:

- Main Menu *Modify* ➤ *Match Color...*
- Key Command *opt+cmd+M*
- At the bottom of the Viewer, *click* on the Magic Wand Button ✨ and select *Match Color...* ❸ from the Enhancement Menu ❶

☑ Two things will happen:
- The Video Inspector will add the Match Color Module ❹ inside the Effects Module.
- The Viewer changes to the "Match Color" split view (Source left ❺, Target right ❻) with the following Instruction at the bottom: **Skim to a frame you want to match, and click to preview ❼**.

☑ Skim over any Clip (the Source) in the Browser or on the Timeline to find the frame that you like as the reference. The cursor now has a little camera icon ❽ to indicate Match Color Mode.

☑ *Click* on a Clip (the Source) to preview that frame on the left Viewer ❺, which will automatically apply that color scheme to the viewer on the right ❻ (the Target), where you parked the Playhead at. The gray "Apply Match" button turns purple ❾.

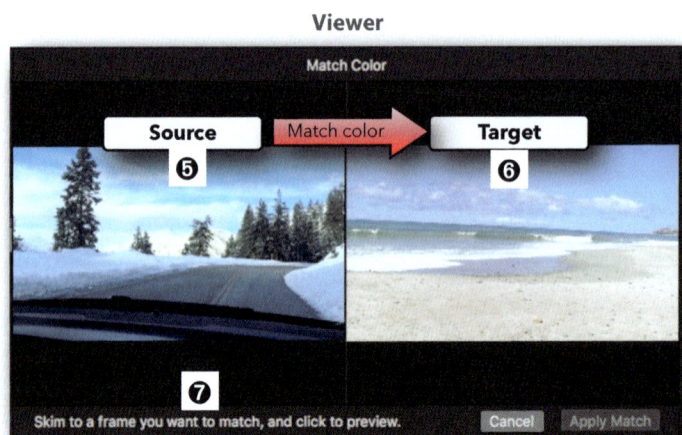

☑ You can continue to "skim around" to find the perfect source frame and *click* again to preview that color applied to the target Clip.

☑ Finally, if you found the perfect match, *click* the purple "Apply Match" ❾ button and the color correction is applied to the target Clip. The Viewer returns to its normal view.

☑ The Match Color Module in the Video Inspector has the "*Choose...*" ❿ button, that initiates the match Color process again by *clicking* on it.

☑ You can use the checkbox ☑ ◻ on the module ❹ to toggle the effect on/off or select the module and delete it entirely.

Color Correction

Color Correction, or often referred to as Color Grading, is the manual process of altering or enhancing the color of your video (unlike Color Balance and Color Match). It requires knowledge and skills to do it right. There are different reasons why you want to do color correction:

▶ You have problems with the look in the original video that wasn't captured right. Too bright, too dark, not enough contrast, not enough color, too much of some color, etc.

▶ You want to give the video a specific look, i.e. warm, harsh, over-saturated, old style, b/w, etc.

▶ You want to create special effects by changing the look of the video to an extreme.

▶ You want to do any of the above treatments but apply it only to a specific color or a specific area in your video frames.

➡ Basic Layout

The following diagram shows the basic concept of Color Correction in FCPx.

▶ The first thing you would notice is that there is not one Color Correction (Module), but as many as you want.

▶ The Color Correction Modules are in series, the output of the first Module feeds the input of the next one.

▶ Each Correction Module can be bypassed individually or all together with the main Effects Module checkbox selection.

▶ The signal flow in each Color Correction Module goes through three Sections:

☑ **Color Adjustment**: This is the main section, the Color Board. Adjustments can be saved and recalled as Presets.

☑ **Color Mask**: If activated, the section restricts the Color Adjustment to a selected Color in the video.

☑ **Shape Mask**: If activated, the results of the first two Sections can be further restricted to an adjustable area on the frame. You can create multiple Shape Masks to define multiple areas on the frame. Each Shape Mask can be animated via Keyframes (i.e. to follow a moving object through the Clip). Note: Each Shape Mask will have the same Color Adjustment. You have to create separate Color Correction Modules with individual Color Adjustments and Shape Masks to follow objects with different color treatments.

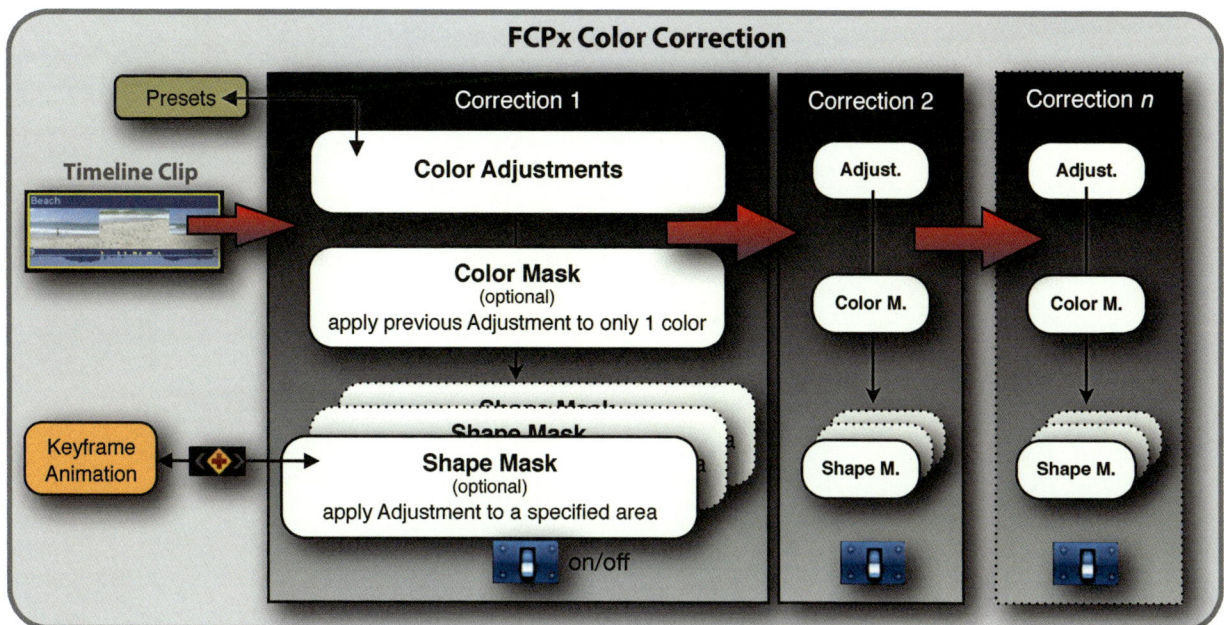

➡ Color Correction Interface

There are a few "technicalities" about the interface of the color correction that you have to be aware of before starting your color correction. First, color correction in FCPx is performed in the Video Inspector in two areas

> ### Color Correction = Color Correction Module ❶ + Color Board ❷

🔮 Color Board ❷

This is a special view of the Inspector (displayed in the Inspector Pane) that provides all the controls for the actual color corrections. You can access the Color Board with any of the following commands:

- 📌 Main Menu *Window* ➤ *Go To* ➤ *Color Board*
- 📌 Key Command *cmd+6*
- 📌 At the bottom of the Viewer, *click* on the Magic Wand Button 🪄 and select *Show Color Board* ❸ from the Enhancement Menu
- 📌 *Click* on the right arrow 🔘 ❹ in the Color Correction Module ❶ of the Video Inspector

🔮 Color Correction:

"Color Correction" is a Video Effect that is available in the Effects Browser ❺ 🎨, listed in the Color ❻ category of the Browser's Sidebar. That Color Correction Module has to be loaded in the Effect Module of the Video Inspector to perform any color correction on that Clip. As with any other Effects, you can load it (apply it) multiple times to a Clip.

- ▸ Open the Effects Browser and *drag* ❼ the Color Correction Effects onto the Timeline Clip or *double-click* it to apply it to all selected Timeline Clips.
- ▸ If a Clip doesn't have a Color Correction Module loaded yet, then opening the Color Board ❷ and making a change ❽ will automatically load the first Color Correction Module ❶ to the Clip.

You can configure the color correction by selecting a Clip and accessing ❾ its Color Correction Module in the Video Inspector for the special Color Mask and Shape Mask features. All the controls for the color correction itself are available in the Color Board, that you open with any of the commands listed above. The Color Board has a small left-arrow ❿ ◀ in the upper-left corner to switch the Inspector view back to the Video Inspector ❶.

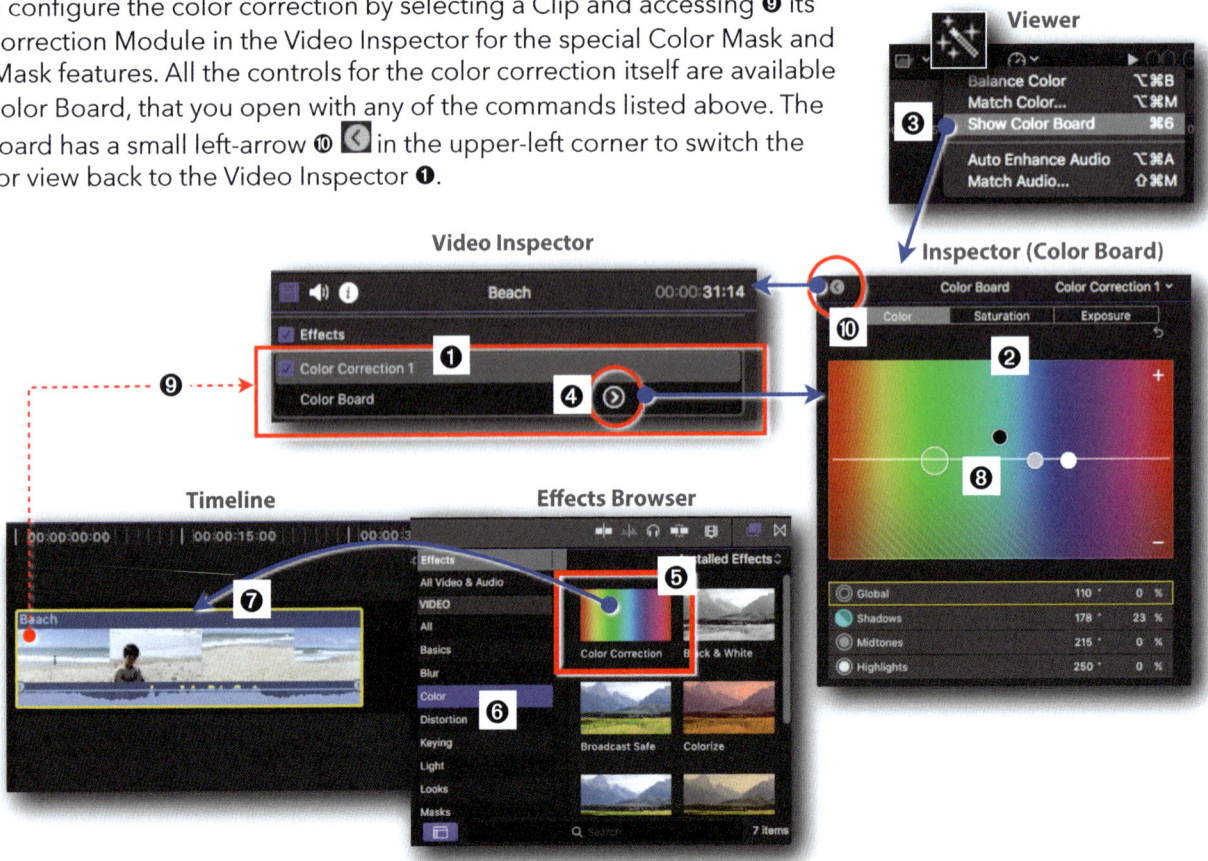

➡ Color Adjustment (Color Board)

As a default, the Color Adjustment applies to the entire (selected) Timeline Clip (if neither Color Mask nor Shape Mask is active). Although you could apply the Color Balance and Color Match to multiple selected Clips at once, the Color Correction Module can only be applied to one selected Timeline Clip at a time. If you have multiple Timeline Clips selected, then the Color Correction Module won't be displayed in the Video Inspector ❶.

Inspector: Color Board

The actual color adjustments are done in the Color Adjustment window, called the "Color Board" ❷. This is an alternate view in the Inspector Pane.

I listed the command on the previous page how to switch to the Color Board:

The Color Board has three tabs to make separate adjustments for:

▶ **Color ❸** - Key Command *ctr+cmd+C*

▶ **Saturation ❹** (chroma) - Key Command *ctr+cmd+S*

▶ **Exposure ❺** (luma) - Key Command *ctr+cmd+E*

Ctr+tab to step cycle the three tabs (or *sh+ctr+tab* to step backwards)

Here is the Color Board with the GUI elements that are the same for all three tabs:

This popup menu lets you switch to different Color Correction Modules (if available) without going back to the Inspector first, and also add a new Color Correction Module.

Resets only the current tab of the Color Board that is visible.

Click on the tab to switch the view between:

Exposure

Saturation

Color

Drag the 4 individual onscreen controls for:
Global - Shadows - Midtones - Highlights

Numeric values for the 4 separate controls:
Global - Shadows - Midtones - Highlights

Slide the values up/down with the mouse or *click* on it and enter the numeric value directly.

Preset menu to save and recall Color Correction Presets.

➡ Controls

Each of the three tabs in the Color Board provides four onscreen controls to manipulate four areas of the selected Clip individually:

▶ **Global**: This affects the whole clip.

▶ **Shadows**: This affects only the dark areas of the Clip (dark circle control).

▶ **Midtones**: This affects only the midtone areas of the Clip (gray circle control).

▶ **Highlights**: This affects only the bright areas of the Clip (bright circle control).

To set a control:

- **Drag** the control up and down (in all tabs) or left and right (only in the Color tab).

- The numeric values of the four controls that are displayed at the bottom are changing accordingly while you are moving the control. The currently selected control is highlighted in that list.

- Use the **ArrowUp** and **ArrowDown** key for the selected control (in all tabs) or the **ArrowLeft** and **ArrowRight** key (only in the Color tab).

- The value list for the Color tab indicates the color setting in their circles and even has a little minus sign to point to a negative % value, e.g.

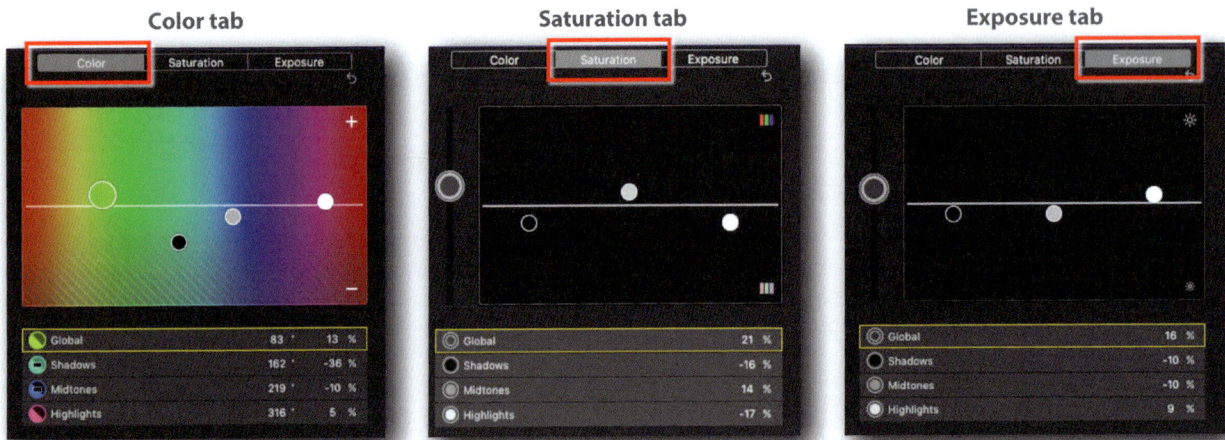

Color tab   **Saturation tab**   **Exposure tab**

🔘 Inside Mask / Outside Mask

If the Color Correction Module has an active Color Mask or Shape Mask, then the Color Board will display two extra buttons at the bottom of the window: **Inside** and **Outside**. That means that in each of the three tabs you can define separate Color Adjustments for the inside of that Mask and for the outside of that Mask.

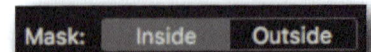

➡ Presets

The Preset button in the lower right corner opens the Preset popup menu:

▶ A Preset includes the settings of all three tabs in the Color Board. If a Mask is present, then it applies to the Inside or Outside depending on what button is selected at that moment.

▶ The current settings can be saved as a user Preset with the "Save Preset…" command.

▶ User Presets are listed alphabetically at the end of the list after the factory presets.

▶ The Custom Presets (XML files with the extension .*cboard*) are stored in your user directory */Library/Application Support/ProApps/Color Preset/*

➡ Color Mask

By default, the Color Board settings are applied to the entire clip (whole video frame). However, you can restrict the settings to a specific color. For example, you might have a blue sky that you want to enhance in your clip or a colored shirt that you want to tone down without affecting any of the other colors. The procedure is straight forward.

🔵 Activate the Color Mask

Click on the mini-viewer icon 🔲 ❶ that appears when you mouse over the Color Correction Module. Select "*Add Color Mask*" ❷ 🖊 from the popup menu, which will add a Color Mask Module ❸ below. You can select the Color Mask Module and press **delete** if you want to remove the Color Mask.

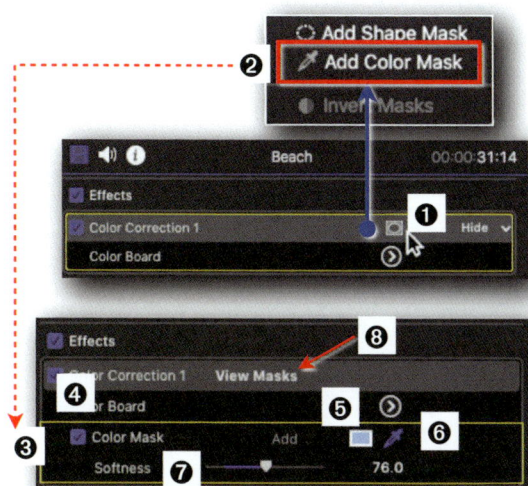

The Color Mask module has the following sections:

- ❹ Checkbox ☑🔲 to bypass the Mask
- ❺ Color Well to display the masked color
- ❻ Eyedropper 🖊 to toggle the mouse cursor between arrow and eyedropper
- ❼ Edge Softness slider and numeric value
- ❽ The Color Correction Module displays a button labeled "*View Masks*" that lets you view the Color Mask Alpha Channel

🔵 Define the Color Mask

☑ Select the Timeline Clip and position the Playhead at the frame containing the color you want to mask.

☑ Activate the eyedropper 🖊

☑ **Click** on the area in the Viewer to define the color you want to mask (the color well ❺ in the module will change to that color).

☑ Or you can **drag** the eyedropper. Now you can see two concentric circles that increase

the more you drag them open. The outer circle determines the range of variations in the selected color. The procedure is similar to defining the area for the alpha channel of an image. The more you drag the circle open ❾, the more colors are included. Also, a bigger area of the image might be affected by the mask. Once you release the mouse you will see the effect (have some color settings made in the Color Board prior to setting the mask).

☑ You can repeat the click color or drag color range until you can see the result you want.

🔵 Refine the Color Mask

☑ <u>Remove color shades</u>: **Opt+drag** with the eyedropper over a color in the image that you want to remove from the Color Mask. The eyedropper icon displays a little minus sign while holding down the option key.

☑ <u>Add color shades</u>: **Sh+drag** with the eyedropper over a color in the image that you want to add to the Color Mask. The eyedropper icon displays a little plus sign while holding down the shift key.

☑ <u>Adjust the color mask edges</u>: Move the edge softness slider.

☑ **Opt+drag** the Edge Softness slider to see the isolated effect. White is the mask area, black is outside the mask, and the levels of gray are the transparent mask areas.

🔵 Inside Mask / Outside Mask

Remember that in the Color Board you can define a color setting for the Mask area (Inside) and everything else but the Mask area (Outside).

➡ Shape Mask

You can restrict the settings of the Color Board to a specific shape on the frame. For example, you might want to enhance the skin color of a specific face (Inside Mask) or you may want to change the color of everything but the face (Outside Mask). A Color Mask wouldn't do it because the face has different color shades that could also be present somewhere else in the frame.

This is the procedure:

🟡 Activate the Shape Mask

Click on the mini-viewer icon 🔲 ❶ that appears when you mouse over the Color Correction Module. Select "*Add Shape Mask*"❷ from the popup menu, which will add a Shape Mask Module ❸ right below.

The Color Shape Module shows only one row with the following controls: Bypass checkbox ☑ 🔲 ❹, a selector ❺ for the popup menu with the Mask Blend Modes ❻ (*Add*, *Subtract*, *Intersect*) ❺, a button ❼ 🔳 to toggle the onscreen controls ❽ on the Viewer that lets you create the shape, and the Keyframe buttons ❾ 🔲🔲🔲.

You can create multiple Shape Masks, i.e. to define two or three shapes. Keep in mind that all Shape Masks inside one Color Correction Module have the same Color Board setting. For different color settings in different shapes, you have to create additional Color Correction Modules.

The Color Mask Module has the ability to store the Shape Mask data in Keyframes. This way you can animate the shape, i.e. change the shape over time to follow a moving face or object. The Shape Mask keyframes will show up as an Animation lane called "Color" in the Animation Editor (see Animation Chapter for details).

🟡 Onscreen Controls

The onscreen controls provide multiple handles ❽ to form the Shape Mask. This is a perfect example on how to use a complex keyframe set efficiently. This time, the Keyframe is not a value pair of time value (x) and parameter value (y), but a set of parameters (y1a, y1b, y1c, y1d, y1e) assigned to a specific time value (x1). Instead of figuring out all these coordinates, you just form the shape and store it as a Keyframe. Then move the Playhead to the next position, adjust the shape and store it as another Keyframe, etc.

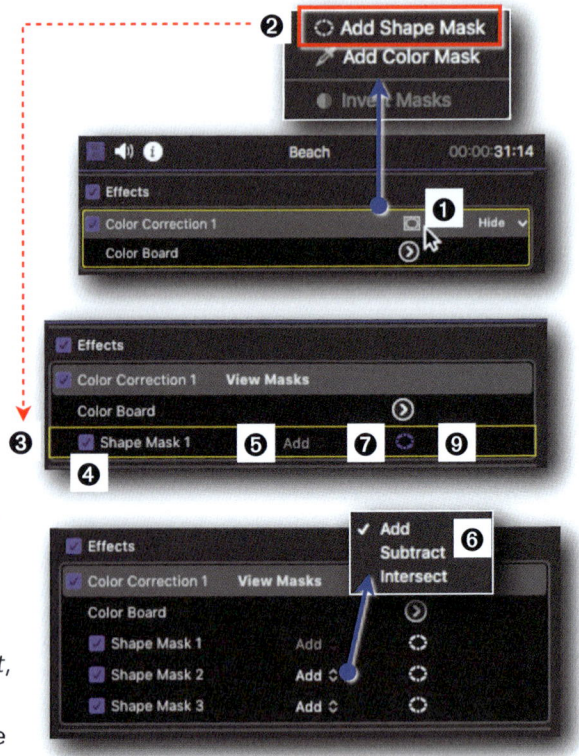

Onscreen Controls

Roundness

You can morph the form from a circle to a rectangle

Position

Moves the whole shape

Edge Softness

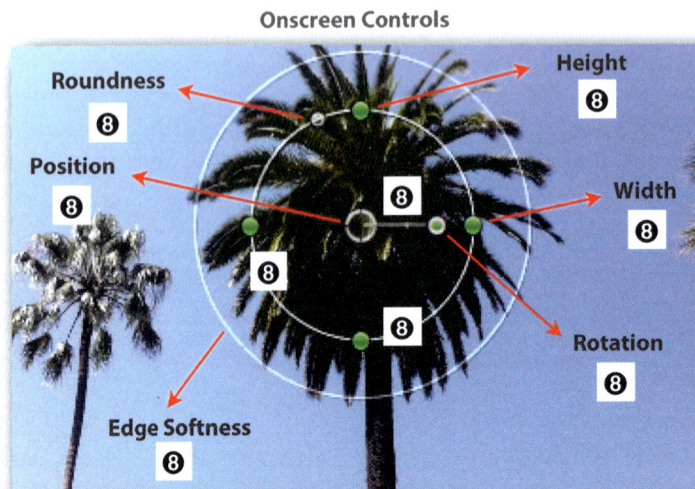

Height

Moves the top and bottom handle at the same time

Width

Moves the left and right handle at the same time

Rotation

Rotates the shape

Dragging the outer circle affects the edge of the shape (inner circle). Drag to the center creates a harder transition to the color correction. Drag away from the center creates a softer transition.

➡ Combined Color Techniques

▶ **Combine a Color Mask and Shape Mask**: This is very useful if you have an object that you color masked to treat a specific color (a red Shirt). But if the scene has a red car in the background that you don't want to be affected then you can overlay the red Color Mask with a Shape Mask for the shirt and animate its movements.

▶ **Multiple Color Correction**: You can overlay multiple corrections. For example, different color-masked objects that are shape-masked. You can easily play around with different layers by bypassing specific modules.

▶ **Transition Correction**: It is easy to transition in and out of Color Corrections by cutting up the Timeline Clips and adding Transitions between the Clips.

➡ Mask Blend Modes

If you need to use multiple Masks, you have to determine the order (you can drag the individual modules up/down to rearrange the order) and the Mask Blend Mode, using the popup menu ❶ selector on the Module:

▶ **Add**: The effect will be applied to the inside of the mask shape selection

▶ **Subtract**: This will remove the effect from the area inside the mask shape, including overlapping areas with other masks

▶ **Intersect**: The effect will be applied to any area inside the mask shape that overlaps with other masks that are set to "Add"

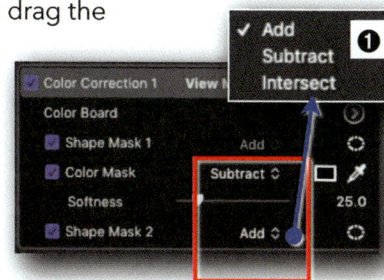

➡ Reset and Delete

The Color Module has multiple "levels" of resets that show up when you mouse over those modules. This could be either a Reset Button 🔄 or the "Reset Parameter" command in the popup menu that opens up when clicking on the selector ⌄.

▶ **❷ Effects Module**: This is the Master Reset that resets all Effect Modules "inside" that Effects Module.

▶ **❸ Color Correction Module**: Each Color Correction Module can be reset separately with the *Reset Parameter* command.

▶ **❹ Shape/Color Mask Module**: Each Color Mask Module and Shape Mask Module has its separate *Reset Parameter* command.

▶ **❺ Parameter**: The row for the Softness parameter has its own Reset Parameter 🔄.

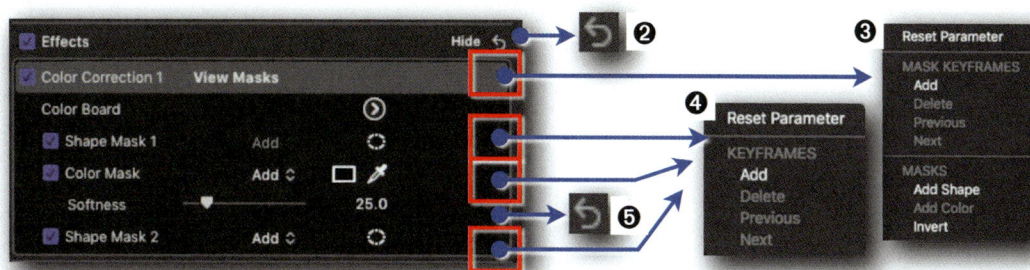

You can delete each individual Shape Mask Module and Color Mask Module or an entire Color Correction Module by clicking on its header. Once it shows the yellow frame, press the **delete** key. You can Undo this step (**cmd+Z**).

Video Scopes

Video Scopes are tools that provide realtime measurements for the video signal of your Clip (luma and chroma level). This is important when dealing with broadcast video requirements or when looking at your signal in a more mathematical way to spot potential problems. Of course, this requires practice and experience. The details are going beyond the scope (no pun intended) of this manual.

FCPx has three different Scopes that can be viewed one at a time or all together in different arrangements.

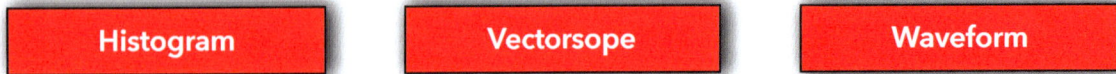

Histogram	**Vectorsope**	**Waveform**

Toggle the Scope window with any of the following commands (it remembers the Scope that was last selected)

- **Click** the View Selector in the upper-right corner of the Viewer and choose **Show/ Hide Video Scopes**
- Key Command **cmd+7**
- Main Menu **View ➤ Show in (Event) Viewer ➤ Video Scopes**

You can also use the following commands to access a specific Scope directly in the Viewer (not the Event Viewer).

- Histogram Scope: **Ctr+cmd+H**
- Vectorscope Scope: **Ctr+cmd+V**
- Waveform Scope: **Ctr+cmd+W**

Viewer Pane

➡ Scope Configuration

In addition to the actual scope ❶, you have to pay attention to three areas in the Scope View:

- ▶ **Color Space ❷**: The upper-left corner displays the current Color Space the Scopes are calibrated to (Rec. 601, Rec. 709, Rec. 2020). This is the color space of the signal that you view in the Viewer, an Event Clip or a Project.
- ▶ **View Menu ❸**: This menu lets you choose what and how you view the various Scopes.
- ▶ **Settings Menu ❹**: In the upper-right corner is the tiny Scopes Button 📊 **Click** on it or **ctr+click** on the scope to open its scope-specific Settings Menu. Select a specific view setting which and how to display the Scopes. The three commands below switch to any of the three Scopes ❺ and the remaining settings ❻ are specific for the currently viewed Scope.

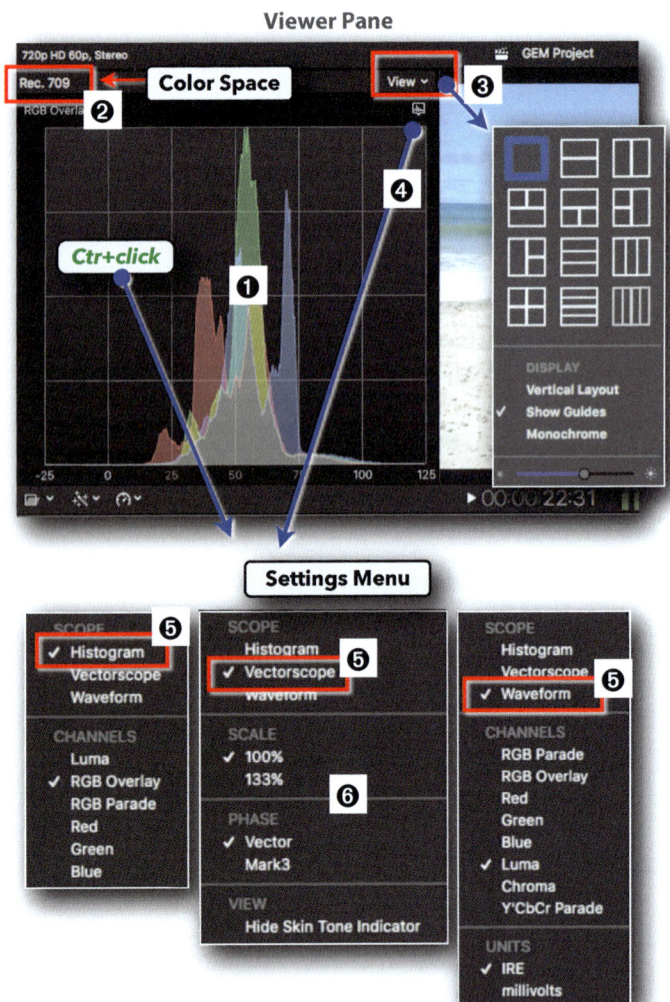

➡ *What do I see?*

As I mentioned before, the use of Scopes requires some math knowledge and a background in video technology. Here are just a few explanations from the FCPx User Guide to get started:

🌑 Histogram

Displays the lightness and darkness of the image on a chart from left (dark) to right (light), with the vertical axis representing the density of pixels.

The Histogram provides a statistical analysis of the image by calculating the total number of pixels of each color or luma level and creating a graph that shows the number of pixels at each percentage of luma or color. Each increment of the scale from left to right represents a percentage of luma or color, and the height of each segment of the Histogram graph shows the number of pixels that correspond to that percentage.

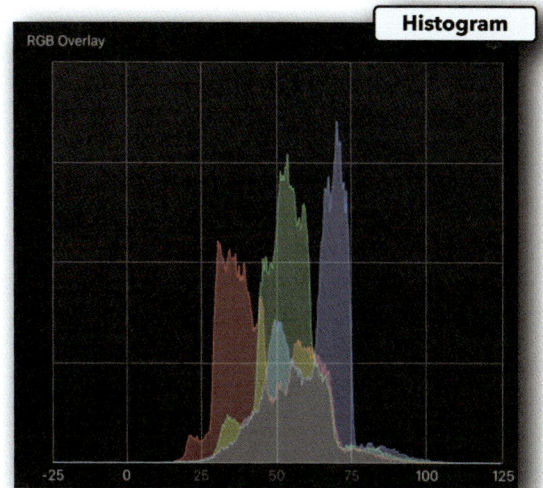

🌑 Vectorscope

This type of scope is the most abstract of the three.

The Vectorscope shows the distribution of color in the frame on a circular scale. The color in your video is represented by a series of connected points that fall somewhere within this scale. The angle around the scale represents the hue displayed, with targets indicating the primary colors of red, green, and blue and the secondary colors of yellow, cyan, and magenta. The distance from the center of the scale to the outer ring represents the saturation of the color being displayed. The center of the scale represents zero saturation, and the outer ring represents maximum saturation.

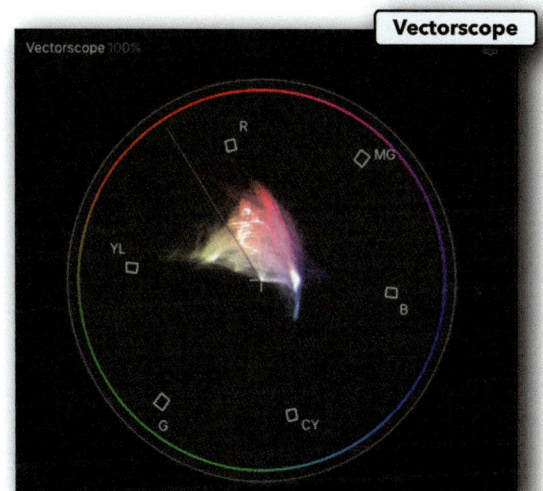

🌑 Waveform

The x-axis represents the width of the video frame and the y-axis the exposure (luma), saturation (chroma), or other parameters from the popup menu.

The Waveform Monitor shows the relative levels of luma and chroma in the clip currently being examined. These values are displayed from left to right, mirroring the relative distribution of luma and chroma levels from left to right in the image. Spikes and dips in the displayed waveforms correspond to light and dark areas in your picture. The waveforms are also tinted to match the color of items in the video.

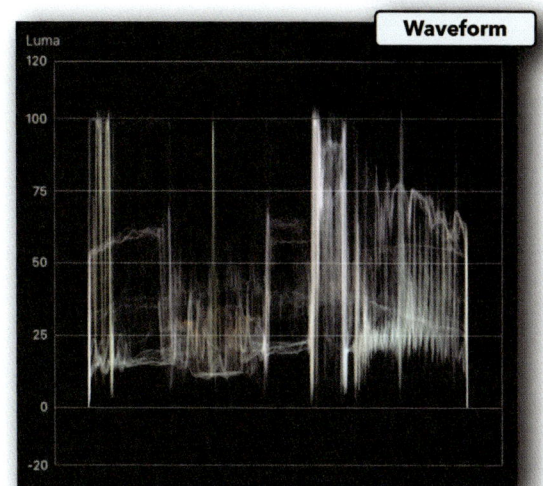

Basics

Once you are done editing your project, you have to do the final step and "export" it. This is the process of saving the project to a differently formatted file for a specific purpose.

- Play the file with a specific app other than FCPx. For example, QuickTime Player, iTunes, on the web, etc.
- Play the file on a specific device. For example, iPad, Apple TV, etc.
- Use the file on a specific application to further work on it. For example, Compressor, Pro Tools, etc.

➡ *Export vs. Share*

The Export process is common in most content-creation applications where you work on a project in a proprietary format (video, song, graphics, etc.) and at the end, export it to a file format that can be opened (read, played) by other applications. Although this step is similar in most applications, the terminology varies. These are the most often used commands.

- ▶ **Save as...**
- ▶ **Export...**
- ▶ **Share...**
- ▶ **Bounce...**

It seems that Apple has tried to establish the term "Share" in all of their apps, and even has a system wide Share Button 📤 now found on their desktop applications (macOS) and also on their iDevices (iOS).

➡ *Three Export Procedures*

FCPx provides three different export procedures. They are all listed under the File Menu.

Main Menu

❶ Export XML... ❶

This procedure is actually called an "Export". It creates an XML file of your Project or Event that can be used by other applications for specific tasks.

Share ❷

This is the main export procedure that creates a media file of your Project (or Event Clip) in a wide variety of different formats. The command has a dynamic submenu ❸ that lists all the (pre-configured) Destinations.

Send to Compressor ❹

This is an "internal handshake" command. The current Project will be "handed over" internally on your computer to Apple's Compressor app (if installed) and opens there automatically, ready to be used in that app. Compressor 4 provides more detailed settings and formatting options to create specific media files.

To learn more about this cool "Swiss army knife" app, check out my book "Compressor 4 - How it Works"

Share Concept

The concept of exporting a Project or even an Event Clip in FCPx using the Share command is very elegant and simple but yet extremely powerful. It uses so-called "Destinations".

Destinations = Export Presets

- FCPx provides 13 Destination Types ❶ plus a special Destination Type, the "Bundle" ❷.

- These Destination Types are available in the FCPx Preferences window under the Destinations tab ❸ by selecting the "Add Destination" ❹ item in the Sidebar on the left or by *clicking* on the Plus button ⓿ ➕ ➖

- Each of the 13 Destination Types, representing a specific kind of export preset, provides a set of parameters for that procedure. The default values for those parameters can be modified later.

- The Sidebar ❺ on the left represents the list of the actual Destinations (Presets that contain the export instructions) that are used to export your Project (or Event Clip). A default selection of seven Destinations is already listed there.

- To add new Destinations to the Sidebar, *drag* any Destination Type from the right side onto the Sidebar ❻ or by *double-clicking* on a Destination Type. You can move the items in the Sidebar around to arrange them in the preferred order and also rename them. Please note that you can *drag* a specific Destination

Type multiple times to the Sidebar. They then become individual Destinations of the same type that you can configure differently.

- The content of the Sidebar is displayed (mirrored) in two locations in FCPx, representing the actual Share commands. The Share Menu ❼ in the File Menu and the popover that opens when *clicking* on the Share Button ❽ 🔼 in the upper-right corner of the FCPx Workspace window. Later, you initiate an export by selecting any of those Destinations in those menus.

- The "Add Destination" ❾ command in both locations ❼ ❽ opens the Destinations Preferences window ❸ with the "Add Destination" item ❹ selected in the Sidebar.

- Delete any Destination from the Sidebar ❺ by selecting it and *click* the Minus button ⓿ ➕ ➖ in the lower-left corner or simply hit the *delete* key.

- Configure any Destination in the Sidebar ❺ by selecting it. Its parameters are now displayed in the right pane.

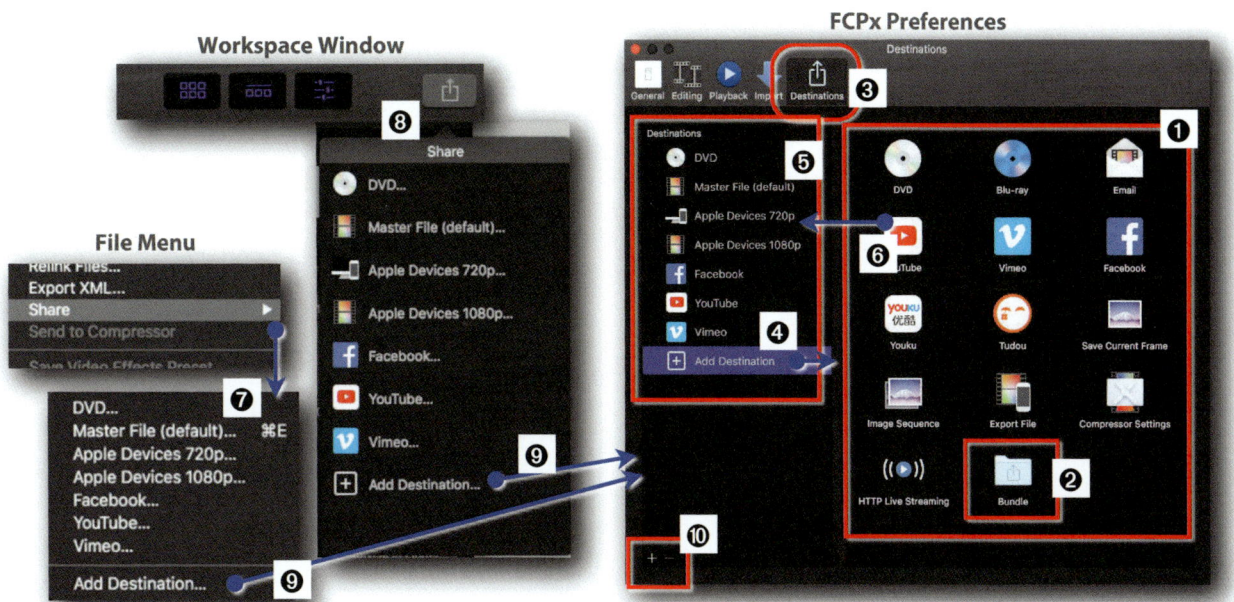

Workspace Window

File Menu

FCPx Preferences

Destinations and Bundles

➡ Configure a Destination

Configuring the Destinations is very simple:

☑ ❶ Go to the *Preferences* ➤ *Destinations*.

☑ ❷ In the Sidebar, *click* on the Destination that you want to configure.

☑ ❸ The right pane now displays all the available parameters and their current values for that Destination where you can make the necessary adjustments. No Save command is required.

☑ Later, when you actually use a specific Destination from the Share Menu for exporting a Project, you again have the opportunity to adjust the parameter values before actually starting the export.

Preferences ➤ Destinations

➡ Configure a Bundle

A Bundle is a special Destination, like a macro. It is displayed as a folder that can include multiple Destinations. The concept is pretty simple. When you export a Project to a Bundle, that Project will be exported to all the Destinations in that Bundle at once. For example, you can publish a Project to multiple social media sites (even different accounts on the same social media site) or export a Project with different resolutions (low, medium, high).

The setup could not be simpler:

❹ Open the *Preferences* ➤ *Destinations* window.

❺ *Click* the "Add Destination" in the Sidebar.

❻ *Drag* the Bundle Type ❻ on the right to the Sidebar on the left ❼. The Bundle in the Sidebar is actually a folder with a disclosure triangle.

❽ *Drag* any Destination Type on the right onto that Bundle folder.

❼ You can even *drag* existing Destinations ❾ from the Sidebar onto that Bundle folder.

The standard commands are available as expected: Re-order by *dragging* Destination up and down, *opt+dragging* for duplicating. Select and delete or *click* and rename. Everything is straight forward and very logical. Of course, you can configure each Destination in a Bundle by selecting it and configuring it the same way.

Preferences ➤ Destination

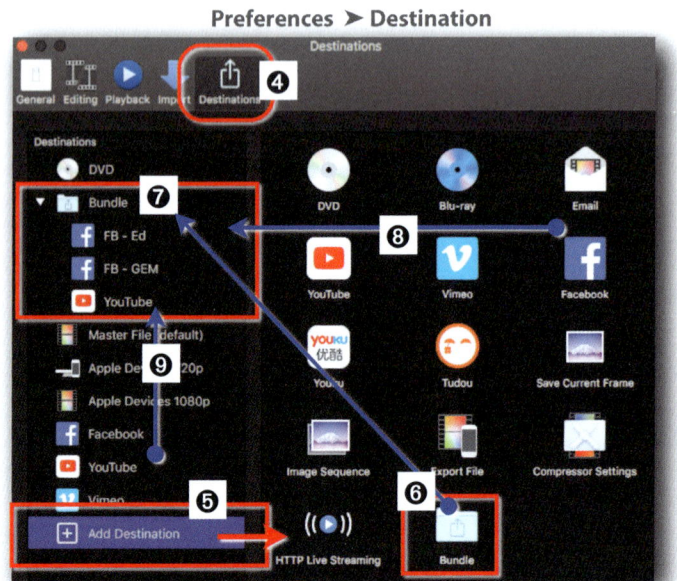

Configuration Window

Now let's look at each Destination Type's parameters that are displayed in the right pane.

➡ **Export File** ▫Export File

This might be the most used export Destination. It exports the Project as a new Media File. The configuration pane has seven parameters with popup menus to choose their values from. The displayed values vary, depending on the setting of the first parameter, the Format. The value items on the Format popup menu are divided into three groups:

▸ **Format ❶**: This popup menu has three sections, "Mastering", "Publishing", and "Broadcast". Please note that if you choose Publishing, the Destination Icon changes from filmstrip ❷ ▫ to iPhone ❸ ▫.

  ▫ Mastering ❹: Any of the three options can be used when exporting the Project as a master file, the final product of your video edit.

  ▫ Publishing ❺: Any of those three options will also create a media file. They are optimized for playing on specific devices: Apple Devices (.m4v), Computer (.mp4), Web Hosting (.mov).

  ▫ MXF ❻: This is a Broadcast delivery standard.

▸ **❼ Video codec, Resolution**, and **Audio file**: The available options and popup menus vary, depending on what option you chose for the Format parameter. "Faster Encode" makes use of Intel's "Quick Sync" feature (5x faster on modern Macs)

▸ **❽ Include chapter markers**: The enabled checkbox embeds any Chapter markers that you created in your Project in the exported video file (can be viewed in the QuickTime Player).

▸ **❾ When done**: This popup menu provides different options that determine what happens when the export procedure is done. Besides doing nothing, you can choose an app like QuickTime Player or Compressor to automatically open with the new file. The menu also lists all the playlists of your iTunes Library ❿, so you can choose to add the new file directly to one of those playlists.

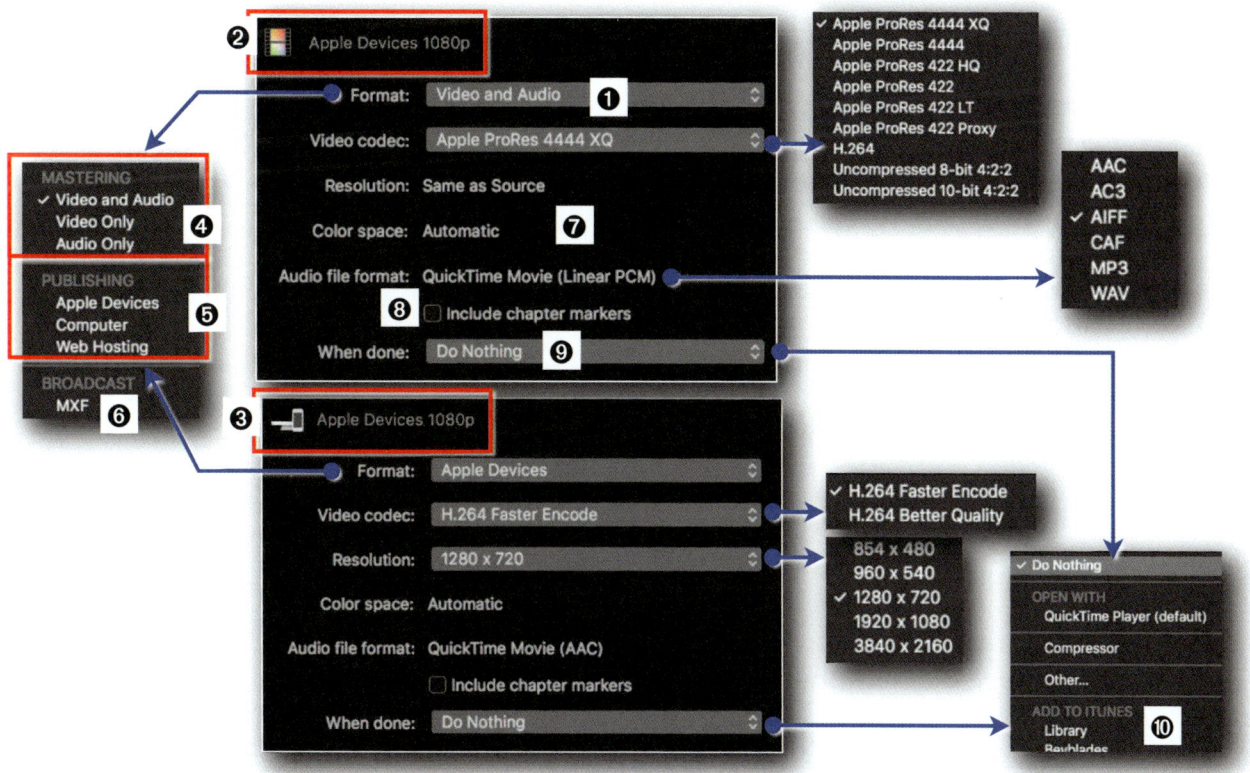

→ You Tube YouTube **Facebook** Facebook **Vimeo** Vimeo **Youku** Youku **Tudou** Tudou

These five Destination Types enable you to export your project and publish it directly to one of the social media sites. No extra step is needed to do the publishing after the export. The Destination settings can also include your login information. The settings page for the five social media sites are similar.

▸ When you drag the Destination Type to the Sidebar for the first time, a login window will open. Here you can enter the name and password for the account you plan to upload the video to. With the checkbox "Remember this password in my keychain" you can store the login info so you don't have to enter it every time you export to that Destination. FCPx has to be open during the upload.

▸ **Sign In ❶**: This button opens the same login window, in case you want to change it later.

▸ **Resolution ❷**: The available items on this popup menu are similar for all four Destinations.

▸ **Compression ❸**: Choose between "*Better quality*" and "*Faster encode*". It is the same menu for all five.

▸ **Site Specific**: The last parameter values are specific for the individual social media sites. For example, set the Privacy settings ❹ (who can see your video) or the Category ❺ that YouTube provides.

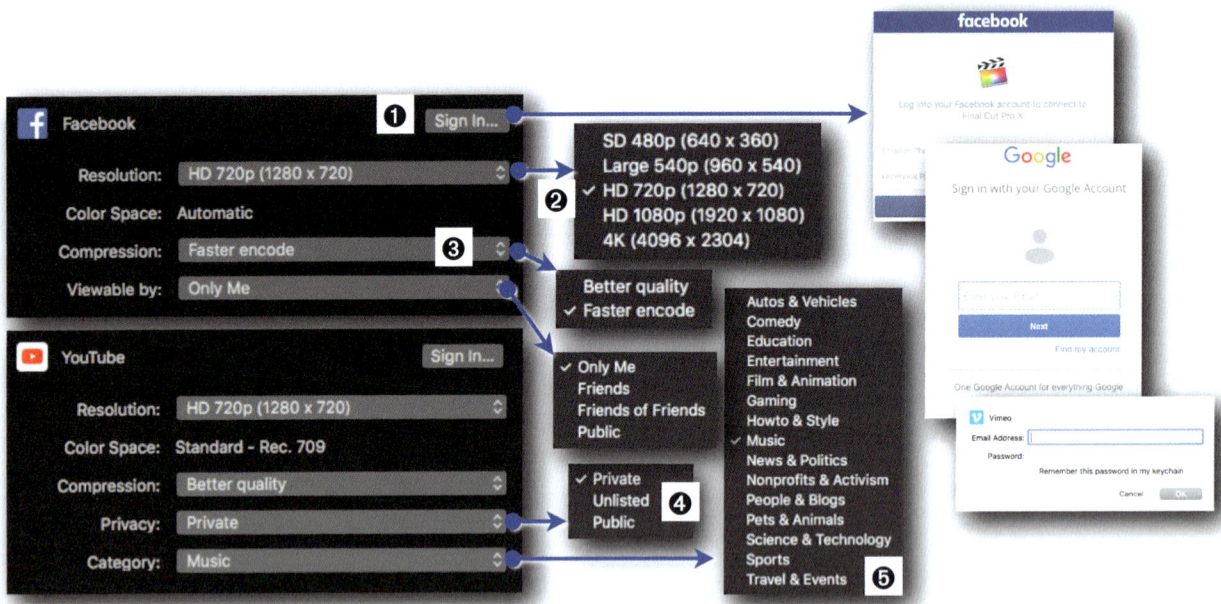

→ Email Email

The Email Destination is very convenient when you quickly want to attach your exported video file to an email. The configuration page provides only two parameters:

▸ **Resolution ❻**: Select from the popup menu.

▸ **Compression ❼**: Better quality or Faster encoding.

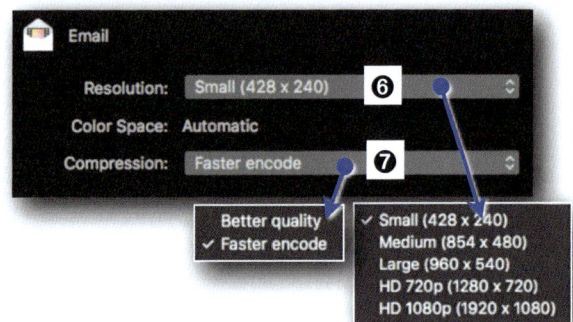

Once the encoding is done, a new email will open in the Mail app with the exported media file attached and the Project name in the Subject line.

➡ **DVD / Blu-ray**

These two Destinations let you create a video DVD or video Blu-ray from your Project. It even provides basic authoring tools ❶ right in the Configuration pane with some animated templates. Please note that you can use the Chapter Markers ❷ that you created in the FCPx timeline of your Project as subtitles.

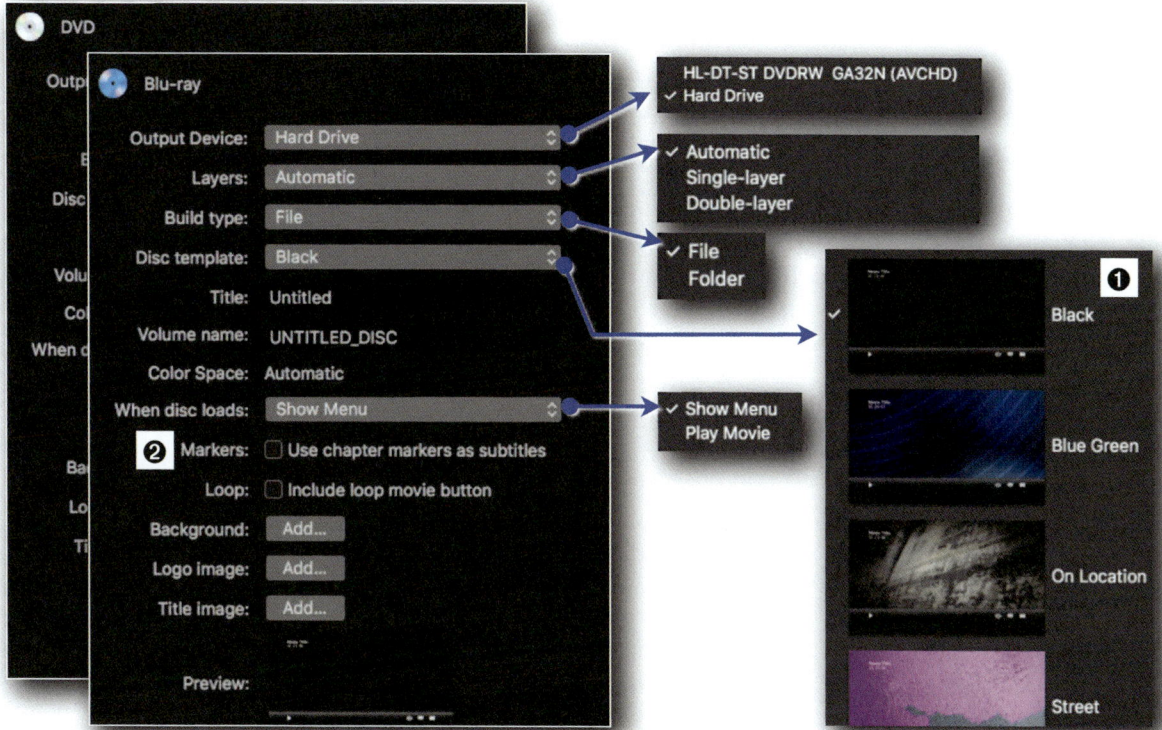

➡ **Save Current Frame**

This is the easiest Destination. It lets you export the current frame at the parked Playhead position. Choose a specific graphics file format from the popup menu ❸.

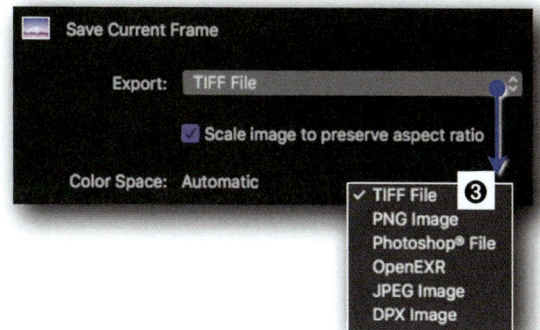

➡ *Image Sequence* Image Sequence

This Destination is used to create a series of images (individual frames) from your video project to be used in an animated video scene. The popup menu lets you choose the image format **❶**.

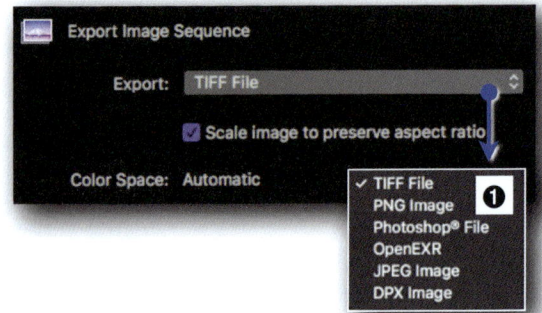

Export Image Sequence

Export: TIFF File

☑ Scale image to preserve aspect ratio

Color Space: Automatic

✓ TIFF File
PNG Image   **❶**
Photoshop® File
OpenEXR
JPEG Image
DPX Image

➡ *HTTP Live Streaming* HTTP Live Streaming

This Destination is used to create the media and html files required to make your video available on a website via HTTP Live Streaming.

The export can create up to three files, optimized for streaming over Cellular, **❷** WiFi **❸**, or Broadband **❹**.

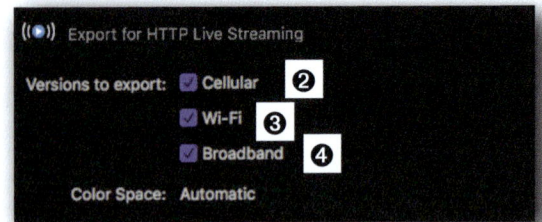

((●)) Export for HTTP Live Streaming

Versions to export: ☑ Cellular **❷**

☑ Wi-Fi **❸**

☑ Broadband **❹**

Color Space: Automatic

➡ *Compressor Settings* Compressor Settings

I mentioned earlier that the File menu provides a separate Export command "Send to Compressor". This allows you to open the current project in Compressor and perform the actual export in the Compressor app which provides more detailed configuration options.

The "Compressor Settings" Destination, on the other hand, utilizes the power of Compressor without opening the app. Compressor has its own pre-configured export presets, called "Settings". FCPx lets you use those settings by assigning one of those specific Settings to a Compressor Settings Destination. And that is the only available parameter in the configuration page. It opens the Settings window **❺** where you can choose which Compressor Setting you want to assign to that Destination.

Apple Devices 4K   Change.

Create output with dimensions up to 4K.

❺

Q Search

Built-in
15 Groups

Add to iTunes Library
1 Setting

Apple Devices
4 Settings

Apple Devices 4K
Create output with dimensions up to 4K.

Apple Devices HD (Best Quality)
Create output with dimensions up to 1080p for best quality playback.

Apple Devices HD (Most Compatible)

Cancel

Of course if you don't have Compressor installed on your computer, you will get a friendly reminder to go to the App Store and purchase Compressor for just $49.99.

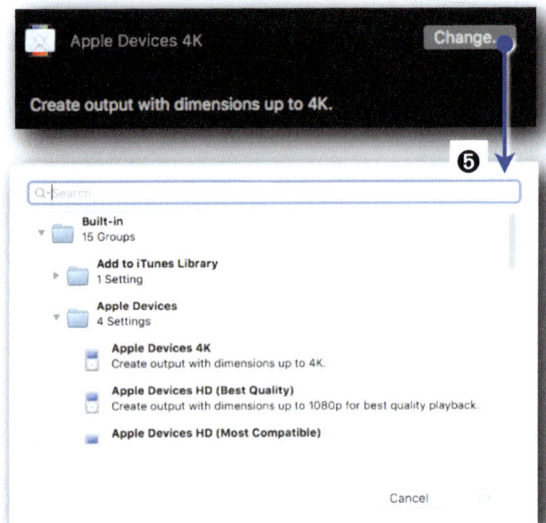

Preferences ➤ Destinations

➡ *Bundle*

The configuration page for a Bundle is different, because, as we have already seen, a Bundle is technically not a Destination but a collection of individual Destinations. Therefore, the configuration page displays all the parameters of all the included Destination's configuration pages grouped by Destination. This lets you make adjustments in one long list ❶.

You can also select a Destination ❷ inside a Bundle to display only that configuration page.

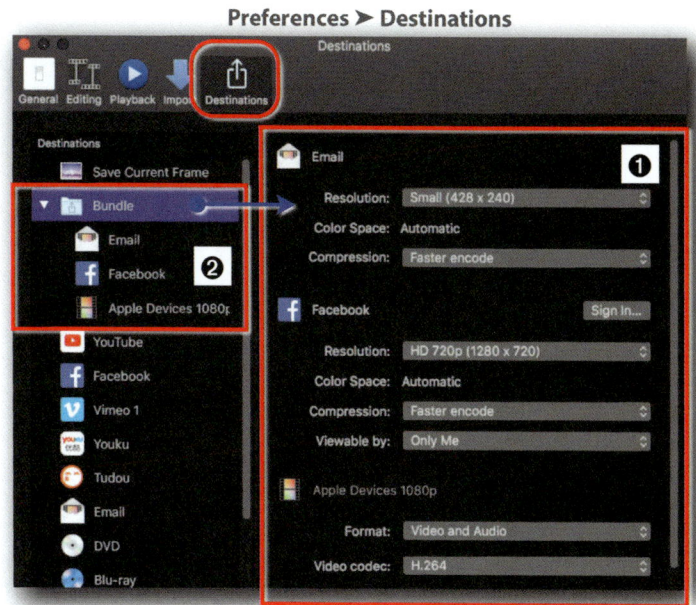

Attention

Please keep in mind that all the settings you configure for the various Destinations can be modified during the actual export (in the Share Dialog ❸) when you use any of the Destinations. This makes sense, because you don't have to go back to the Preferences window for that. However, as we will see in the next section, any changes made for a Destination during the export will be saved to that Destination ❹.

So be aware, the Destination you configure in the Preferences window ❹ can be overwritten in the Share Dialog ❸.

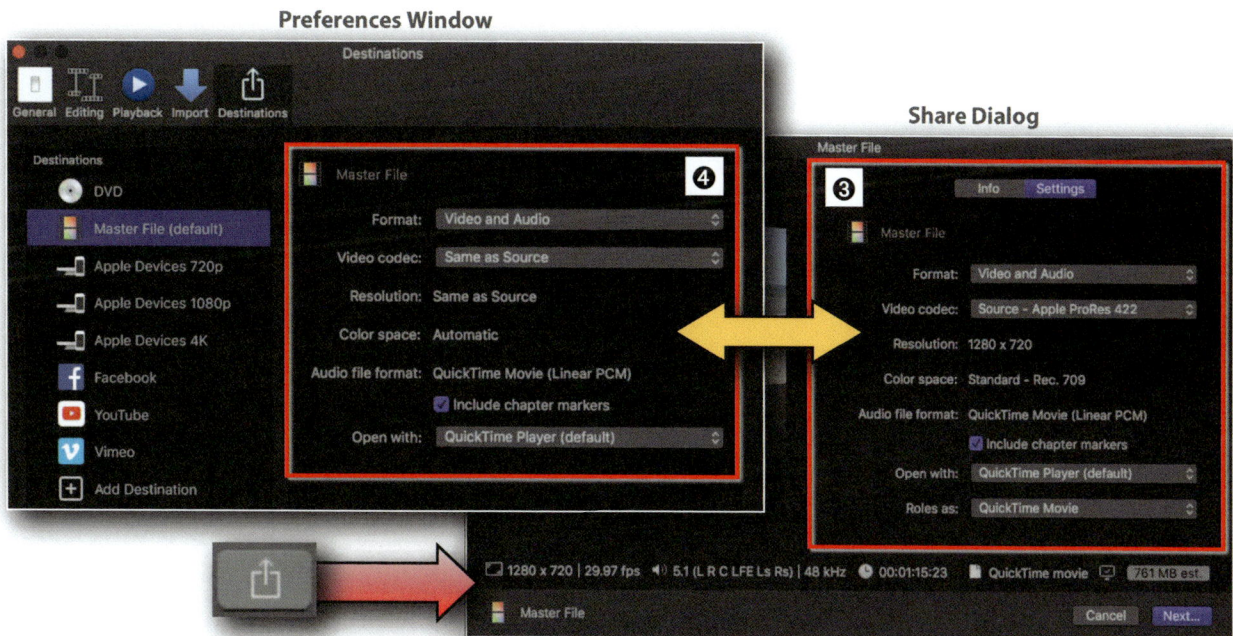

Preferences Window

Share Dialog

Shortcut Menu

Ctr+click on any Destination in the Sidebar to open the Shortcut Menu with some additional commands:

▸ **Revert to Original Settings**: This command changes the parameter values of the currently selected Destination(s) to the values of the original Destination Type.

▸ **Make Default**: Select any Destination and use this command to make it the "default" Destination. The Destination will have the additional ("default") ❶ next to its name and in the *File ➤ Share ➤* submenu. The Destination indicates that it can be selected with the Key Command **cmd+E** ❷ without the need to access the Share Menu.

▸ **Duplicate** (*cmd+D*): Duplicates the selected Destination(s).

▸ **Delete** (*cmd+delete*): Deletes the selected Destination(s).

▸ **New Bundle From Selection**: Select any Destinations (standard *cmd+click*) to move them into a new Bundle.

▸ **Restore Default Destinations**: This removes all your custom Destinations in the Sidebar and restores the initial list of Destinations that were there after a new FCPx install. You will be warned ❸ about those "consequences".

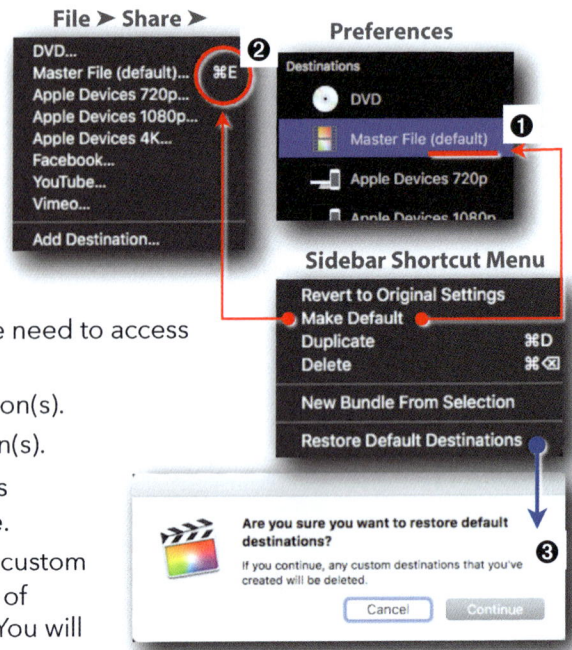

➡ *Destinations: Import - Export*

Destinations can easily be exchanged with other FCPx users or between different computers. It is so simple, it doesn't even require a separate command.

▸ **Export**: Just *drag* a Destination from the Sidebar ❹ of the Destinations Preferences to a Finder window ❺ or the Desktop. A FCPx Destination file ❻ will be created that includes all the settings. The file, with the *.fcpxdest* file extension can be moved to any location to be imported to any FCPx application.

▸ **Import**: Just drag a FCPx Destination file ❻ from the Finder into the Sidebar ❼ of the Preferences window, which will create a new Destination based on the file's configuration. The mouse cursor will show the green add sign and a ghost image of the file.

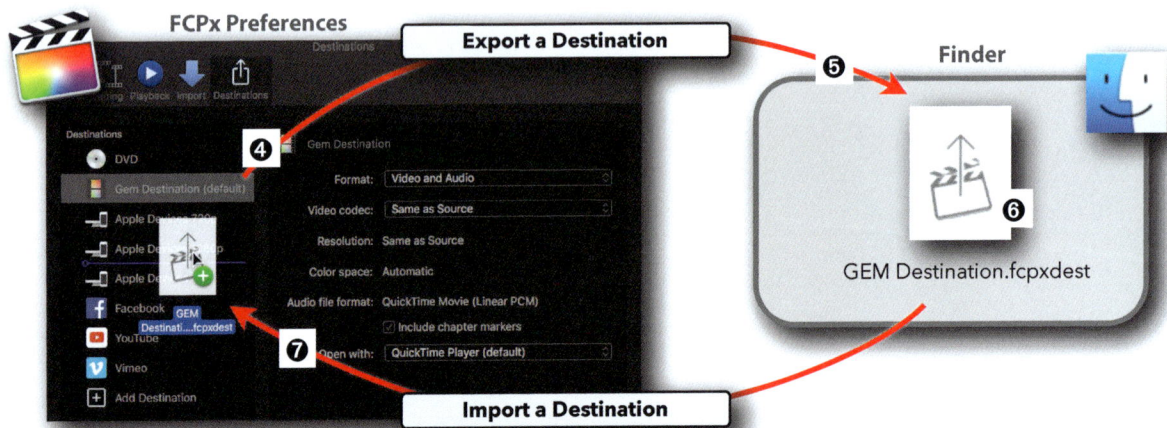

13 - Export (Share)

Share a Project

Now let's look at the actual export procedure when using any of those Destinations.

➡ **Export Steps**

- ☑ Choose **what** to export.
- ☑ Choose **how** to export by selecting a Destination from the Share Menu or use the Key Command *cmd+E*.
- ☑ Adjust the "how to export" in the Share Dialog.
- ☑ Start the export process.

What to Export

First, here are the source options, what to export:

Browser Pane

Entire Project

You can export the entire Project in two ways:
- Select the Project in the Browser Pane ❶.
- Have the Project open in the Timeline Pane ❷ and the Timeline Pane selected (has key focus).

Timeline Pane

Section of the Project

You can select only a section ❸ of your current Project in the Timeline Pane if you want to export only that portion of it. *Drag* the Range on the Primary Storyline with the Range Tool 🔲 or by defining an in-point and out-point with the Key Commands *I* and *O*. The duration of the Range is displayed in a yellow font ❹ in the Timeline Header.

Event Clip

You can also export a single Event Clip ❺ in the Browser Pane by selecting it and using the Share command. This is very useful, especially with Compound Clips that you created in the Browser Pane.

Section of an Event Clip

You can also set a ClipRange ❻ on the Event Clip to export only that section of the Event Clip.

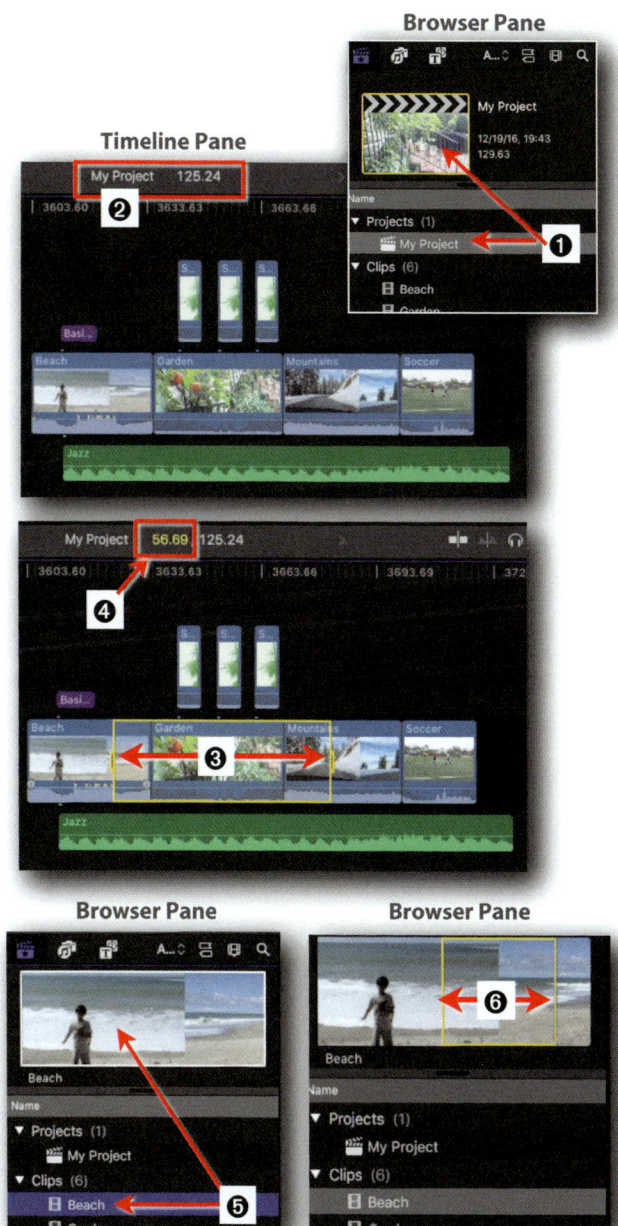

Browser Pane

Browser Pane

Share Dialog

Once you've selected the source (what you want to export) and have selected the Destination from the Share Menu, the next window will pop up, the Share Dialog. This is where you make the final adjustments before starting the export process.

➡️ *Setup*

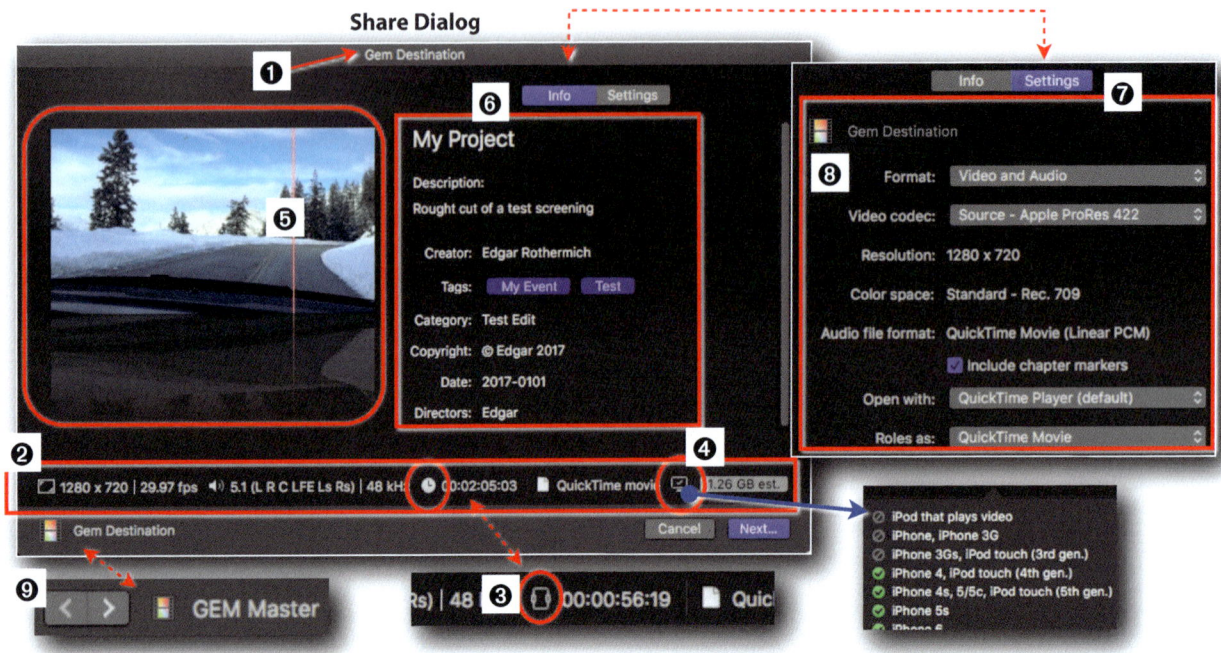

Share Dialog

▶ **Window Title**: The window title displays the name of the Destination ❶ you chose for the export.

▶ **File Information**: The strip at the bottom ❷ displays what format the exported file will have. The frame size and frame rate, audio channels and sample rate, duration, output file type, and the estimated file size. If you export a Range of your Project or Clip, then the icon next to the displayed duration is a range icon ❸ 🔲 instead of a clock icon 🕐.

▶ **Compatibility**: Some Destinations will display the Compatibility Icon ❹ 🖥. When you mouse over it, a popover will appear, listing all the devices that can play the exported file.

▶ **Video**: Move the mouse over the Viewer ❺ to skim the video that you are about to export. Video Skimming is always on, but Audio Skimming has to be enabled in the View Menu (Key Command *sh+S*).

▶ **Info Tab**: Under the Info Tab ❻, you can view and modify the Share Attributes, which are preconfigured in the Share Inspector ⬇ (I discussed this feature in the Organize Clips chapter). These are metadata that will be embedded in the exported file.

▶ **Settings Tab**: This Tab ❼ shows all the parameters from the Configuration window of that Destination, which is displayed in the upper-left corner ❽. Please note that any changes made here will also change the Destination configuration in the Preferences window.

▶ **Bundle**: If the current Destination is a Bundle (with multiple Destinations), then the bottom of the Share Dialog displays two arrows that let you step through the individual Destinations ❾.

▶ **Share or Next button ❺**: The button that starts the final export process is labeled Next or Share depending on the current Destination. An additional window may prompt you to select a file location in the Finder.

Export Roles

Roles have a huge workflow advantage when it comes to exporting your project in FCPx. Some of the following examples would be either extremely time consuming or not possible at all when using in other editing software, including FCP7.

▶ Create Stems very easily with one export process by creating separate audio files of your audio tracks during the export based on their assigned Roles. For example, music, dialogue, sound effects.

▶ Create alternate audio files for different languages.

▶ Create video exports using only specific title cards based on Roles assignment (language,

territory, etc.).

▶ Create separate audio and video files of your export or a combined quicktime file.

▶ Create automatic down-mix and up-mixes in mono, stereo, and surround.

▶ Manage export configurations for Roles as customizable Presets.

➡ **Share Dialog**

All the export settings regarding the Roles are configured in the Share Dialog when you're about to export your Project or Event Clip. Here are the basic procedures and rules.

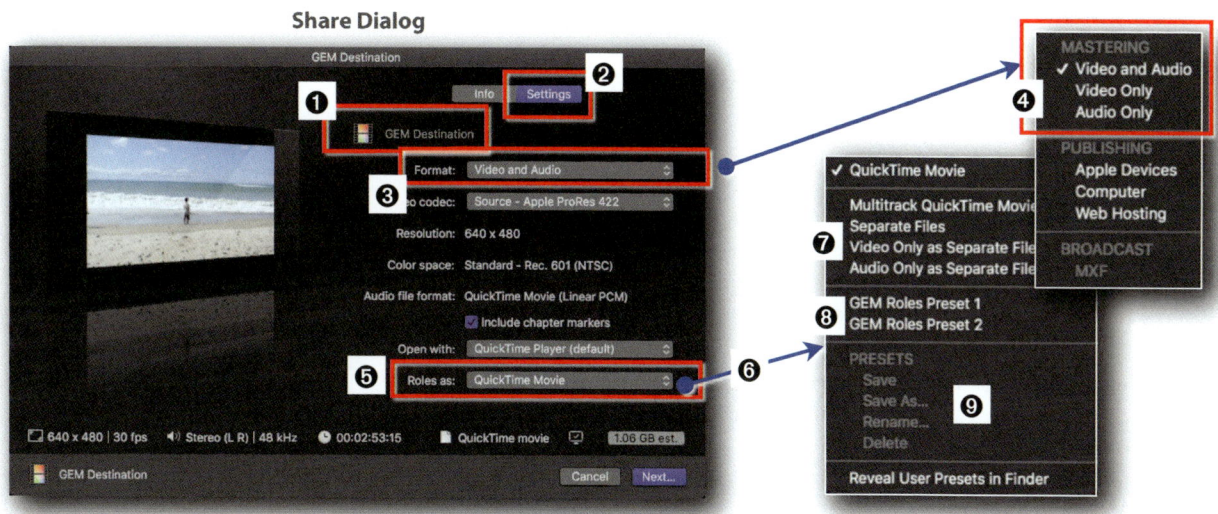

Share Dialog

☑ Select the Project you want to export and choose a Destination from the Share Menu by *clicking* on the Share Button 🗗 in the upper-right corner of the Workspace or from the Main Menu *File ▶ Share ▶*.

☑ Roles can only be used with the Destination Type ❶ **Export File** 🔳

☑ Once you chose a Destination and the Share window opens up, select the Settings tab ❷.

☑ The Format ❸ popup menu lists six options. Only the first three options under "*Mastering*" ❹ and "*MXF*" can be used for Roles.

☑ Selecting any of the first three options creates a pre-selection that lets you export "Video and Audio", "Video Only", or "Audio Only".

☑ If any of these three Formats is selected, an additional item "*Roles as*" ❺ will be displayed at the bottom of the Share Window.

☑ This opens the Roles Export Preset window ❻ that lets you select a pre-configured default ❼ or a user ❽ Preset. The window also provides the commands for managing Presets ❾.

☑ Once you select a specific Preset, the Share Window will disclose additional controls with the option to further customize the Roles export settings.

➡ Roles Export Preset Window

Here is an overview of the Roles Preset popup menus:

"Roles as" popup menu

- ▶ **No Roles**: ❶ *QuickTime Movie* is the default section. Everything is exported regardless of their Role assignment.
- ▶ **Default Presets**: ❷ These four items are the default Presets which are often used Roles export configurations.
- ▶ **Custom Presets**: ❸ This section lists all your custom Presets that you configured. Of course, this section is only visible if you have created any of your own Presets.
- ▶ **Preset Management**: ❹ The section with the header PRESETS lists all the commands that let you manage your user Presets. Presets are stored with the file extension *.rolepreset* in your user directory *~/Library/Application Support/ProApps/Export Presets*. When you create your own Presets for the Roles Export, you have to start with one of the four default Presets (or a custom Preset that was based on one of those four). Be aware if you choose either the "Multitrack QuickTime" Preset or a "Separate Files" Preset to create your own custom Preset. You cannot change that export type later.

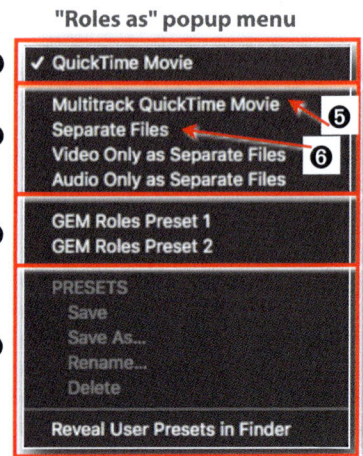

➡ Roles Export Settings

Before getting into the configuration settings, you have to be familiar with the basic concept of Roles export. Think of it as three different options:

🟡 QuickTime Movie - single Track ❺

This is the default export procedure that ignores any existing Roles and just exports a standard QuickTime Movie file containing a single video track and a single audio track ❼. Please note, the term "track" refers to the separate "container" inside the QuickTime file. One audio track can still have multiple audio channels (stereo, surround).

The bottom of the Share Window that lists all the format settings, displays "QuickTime movie" ❽.

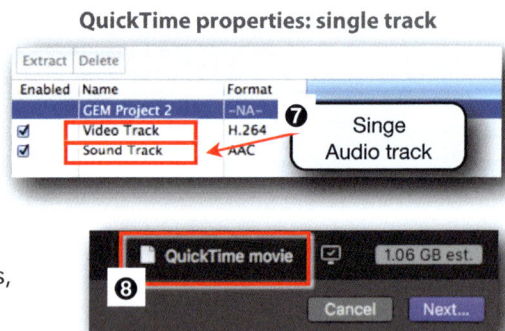

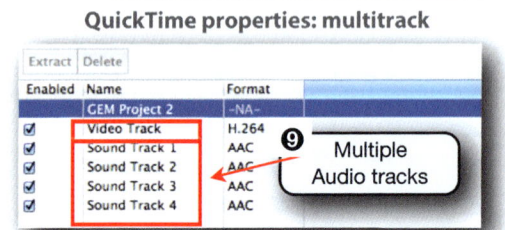

QuickTime properties: single track

🟡 Multitrack QuickTime Movie - multiple Tracks ❻

This export option also creates a single Quicktime Movie file. This time, however, the Roles that are assigned to video clips and audio clips can be used to create individual Tracks for specific Roles (or a group of Roles). This can create a QuickTime movie file with one video track (defined by the video Roles) and multiple audio tracks ❾ (defined by the Roles).

QuickTime properties: multitrack

The bottom of the Share Window that lists all the format settings, displays "QuickTime movie" ❽.

🟡 Separate Files - multiple Files

This export option creates multiple media files (video and/or audio), one file for each Role (or group of Roles) defined in the export configuration. The bottom of the Share Dialog that lists all the format settings, now displays "n files" ❿.

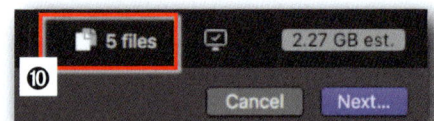

➡ *Roles Configuration*

Whenever you select a default or user preset from the "Roles as" popup menu, the area below extends, displaying various popup menus and controls to configure the export behavior based on Roles.

▶ **Rows**: You will see a maximum of five rows with popup menus depending on your selection (use the vertical scroll bar on the right if there are more rows). Each row represents a separate track (when using a QuickTime file option) or separate files (when using the Separate Files option) that will be exported.

▶ **Video Roles and Audio Roles**: The rows on top of that section represent the files/tracks exported for Video Roles ❶ followed by the files/tracks exported for Audio Roles ❷.

▶ **Select Roles**: When you click on a selector 🔽, the popup menu opens

- The menu shows a list of all the Main Roles ("All ...") and Subroles that are in use with your current Project.
- Video Roles ❸ and Audio Roles show their separate menu items ❹ (or Event List) that you are about to export.
- Selecting an item from that menu adds a checkmark to the item and the names of all the checked menu items (Roles and/or Subroles) will be listed on the menu button ❺ of that row divided by commas.
- You can open the popup menu again and select more Roles or Subroles.
- *Click* on a checked item in the menu to deselect it.

- All those selected Roles and Subroles for a specific row are exported to that particular file (or track) that this row represents.
- Remember, the popup menu doesn't list all the available Roles that you defined in FCPx, only the Roles that are used in your Project that you are about to export.

▶ **Audio Formats**: If a row represents an Audio Role, then a second popup menu will be displayed next to it ❻. This lets you configure if the Audio Clips belonging to those Roles will be exported in mono, stereo, or surround. Depending on the Project (or Event Clip), this will automatically perform a down-mix or up-mix, which is extremely powerful to quickly export files in various audio formats.

▶ **Add File (row)**: The two buttons at the bottom "*Add Video File*", "*Add Audio File*" ❼ add a new row to the list with an unassigned popup menu.

▶ **Remove File**: Moving the mouse over a row will display a minus button ❽ that lets you delete that row.

▶ **Edit**: If you made any changes to the current Preset, the word "(edited)" ❾ will be added to the Preset name in the *Roles as* popup menu to indicate that you better save (or save as) the current Preset setting.

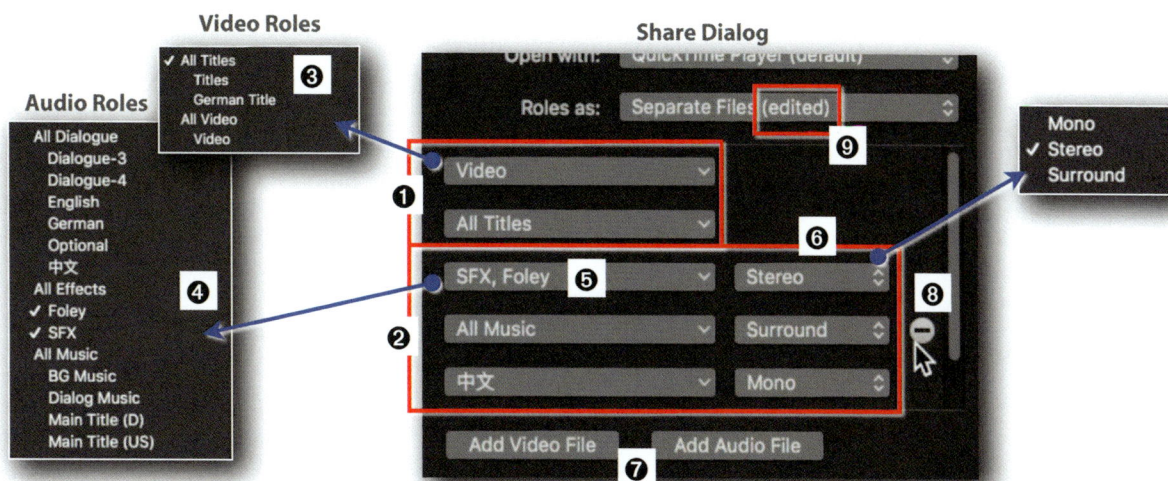

Monitor

You can think of the whole export procedure as three steps: before - during - after.

Before the Export	**During** the Export	**After** the Export
You select **What** to export and by choosing the Destination you decide **HOW** to export it.	Once the export starts, it is running in the background and you can continue to work on your Project. Changing the Project during the export won't affect the output file.	FCPx keeps a history of the exports and where the exported files are located.

During the Export

All export tasks are processed in the background and are GPU accelerated. Once you start the process, you can continue your work in FCPx and don't have to wait for the export to finish.

During the Export process, you can monitor its progress in two locations:

Workspace Window

Background Tasks Window

Progress Indicator

The Background Tasks Button ❶ is located in the upper-left corner of the FCPx Workspace window. This button changes to a dynamic pie chart to indicate any ongoing background tasks, including Sharing Tasks. It displays a checkmark if the process is completed. You can *click* on the button to open the Background Tasks Window ❷.

Background Tasks Window

You can toggle the Background Tasks Window with the following commands:

- *Click* on that Background Task Button ✓
- Key Command *cmd+9*
- Main Menu *Window* ➤ *Background Tasks*

The Background Task Window displays all the individual processes with a progress bar if a process is still going on. If you have multiple ❸ Sharing processes going on at the same time, then each one is listed with their own progress bar ❹ and percentage number ❺ in addition to the total Share process on top. Click the Cancel Button ❼ on the right of each process to cancel it.

macOS Notification

Notification

If you have Notifications enabled for FCPx in the System Preferences, then you will see a FCPx Notification ❽ in the upper-right corner of your screen when a process is done.

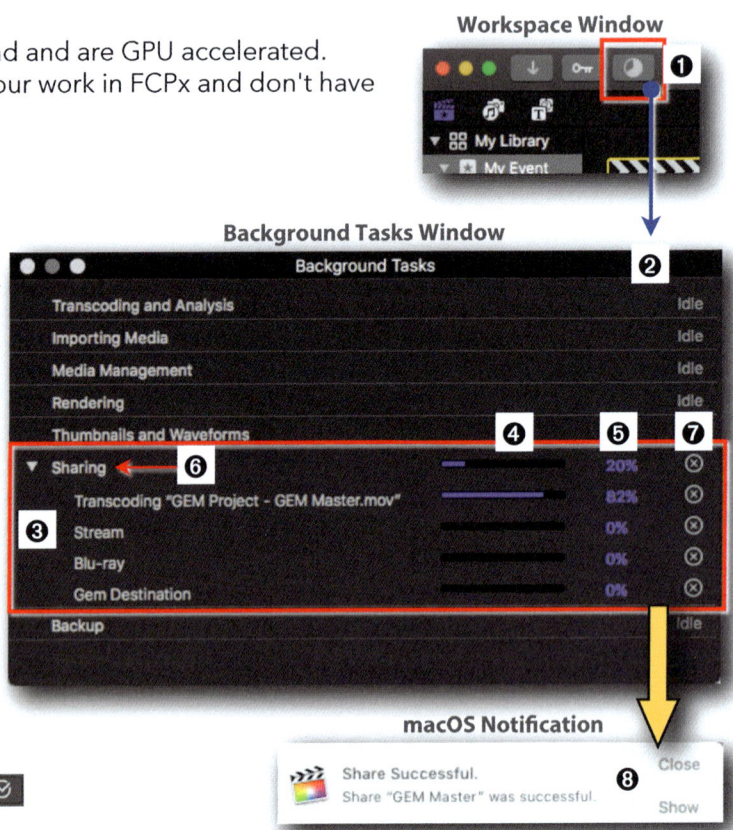

After the Export

Even after an Export is done, FCPx keeps track of those tasks.

➡ *Share Inspector*

Click on the Share Button ❶ in the Inspector Pane to show the Share Inspector.

> ▸ **Share Attributes**: The main area in the Share Inspector displays all the Share Attributes ❷ based on the selection from the popup menu ❸ . These are exactly the Attributes that are displayed under the Info Tab of the Share Dialog ❹ that we just saw.

> ▸ **Share History**: The area below ❺ shows the Share History for the currently selected Project or Event Clip. It keeps tracks of all the exports you have initiated. Each export is listed as a separate list item with the date of the export and a selector that shows the command "Reveal in Finder".

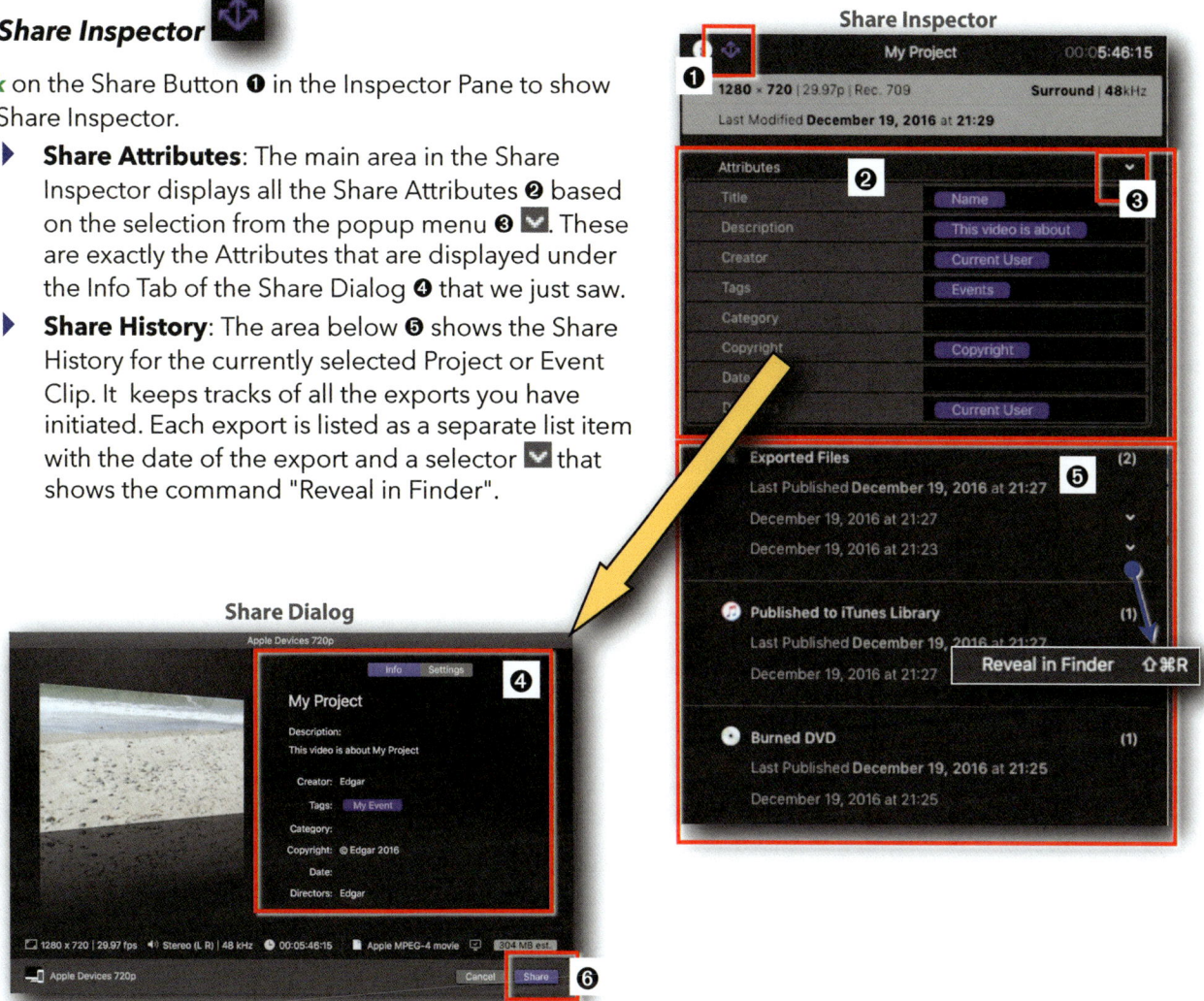

Share Inspector

Share Dialog

➡ *Share Location*

If the Share Inspector has a "Share" button ❻, then that file will be saved inside the Library File, the package file following these rules:

- Each Event Folder inside the Library File has a folder named "Shared Items" ❼.
- For each Project or Event Clip that you share, FCPx creates a folder with a 22digit name inside the Shared Items folder.
- Inside each folder is an XML file named "SharedStatus.plist" that stores all the information regarding the Share procedures for this Project or Event Clip.
- The newly created files based on the Share instructions are also shared in that same folder.

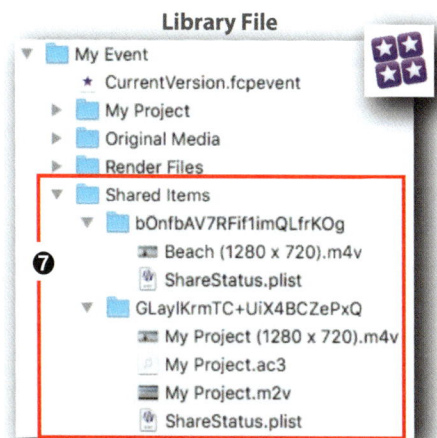

Library File

Relink Media

Missing Files

What happens when something goes wrong and a Clip won't play? Instead, you get a red "Missing File" warning and the Clip is listed in the Browser with a warning sign in its icon ⚠️. Uh oh!

🔘 FCPx Concept

Before we start to panic, let's recap the underlying mechanism in FCPx to understand what that means:

▶ Whenever you import a Source Media File (video, audio, still image) into a specific Event in your FCPx Library, FCPx creates a Clip, that is linked to that Source Media File.

▶ Every Clip in FCPx is actually a record entry in one of the databases that make up your FCPx Library.

▶ All the attributes, metadata, and parameters that describe that Clip are just fields, entries in the database record.

▶ One of those entries of a Clip is the pathname to its linked Source Media File, so if you play back that Clip, FCPx knows where the actual Source Media File is stored to play it back.

🔘 Source Media File is missing

When a Source Media File can't be found:

▶ A missing Source Media File doesn't change anything to the database record that represents that Clip. All its attributes, its applied effects, everything is still there stored in the database.

▶ FCPx temporarily replaces the Clip (that has the missing file) with a "Placeholder", which is actually a Generator Clip.

▶ Nothing changes (shifts) on your Timeline. You can even continue to edit with that red placeholder Clip, even add Effects to it.

▶ The red placeholder Clip represents the database record for that "troubled" Clip, until FCPx finds the missing file. Then everything is back to normal, as if nothing had happened.

Here is an example where all the warning signs pop up when a Clip can't find its referenced Source Media File.

➡ **Other Missing "Things"**

Besides a Clip that has lost its linked Source Media File, there are other items that can go missing, which is indicated by various icons in FCPx. Here are a few:

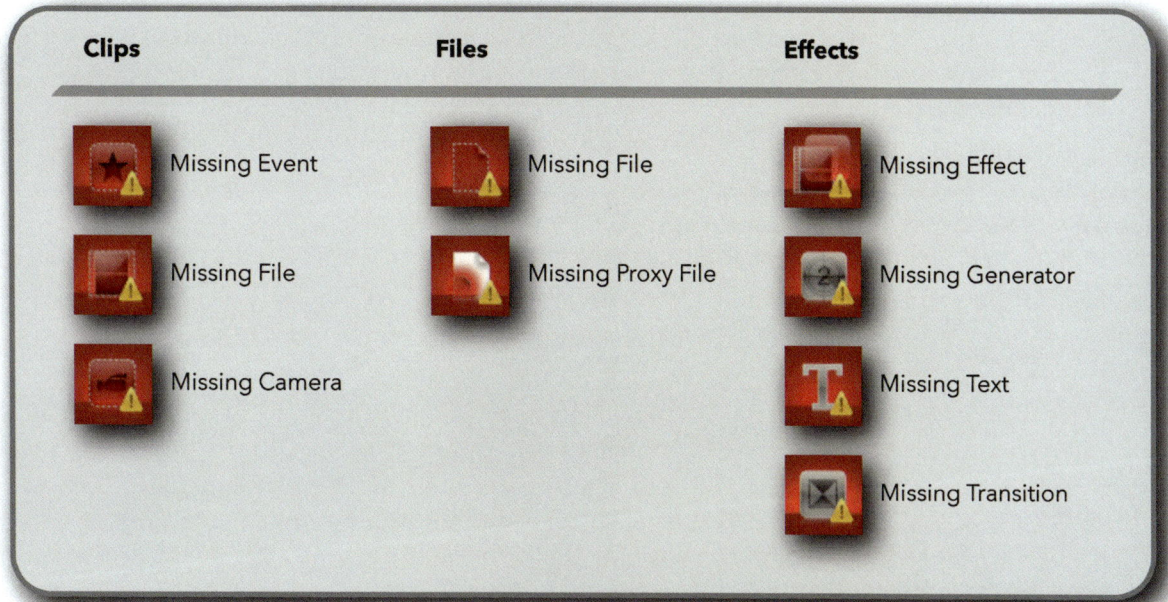

Clips	Files	Effects
Missing Event	Missing File	Missing Effect
Missing File	Missing Proxy File	Missing Generator
Missing Camera		Missing Text
		Missing Transition

➡ **How to Reconnect Source Media Files?**

There are many reasons why a Clip can't find its linked Source Media File and how to relink that connection.

▶ If a drive was not properly mounted where the Source Media File is stored on, then just mounting the drive will automatically reconnect the Media. The expected file location (as it is stored in the Event database) is displayed in the Inspector in the Clip's Info tab so you can see which drive is missing.

▶ If the Media File was deleted, renamed, or moved, then you have to manually relink the file with the "Relink Files..." procedure that we discuss next.

➡ **Relink Why?**

Don't think of the Relink feature only as a troubleshooting tool. You can use it when ...

▶ ... you "have to"
link to a (missing) Source Media File.

▶ ... you "want to"
link to a (different) Source Media File.

Here are some of the reasons why you have to, or want to relink files:

☑ **Deleted** file: The media file got deleted, it is not there anymore

☑ **Updated** file: The file got updated by a different application (i.e. Photoshop tweak, external color correction, etc.)

☑ **Renamed** file: File name doesn't match anymore

☑ **Moved** file: Now the path is different, because a file got moved or any of the parent folders got renamed

☑ **Swap** a file: You want to intentionally replace the current file with a different (better, updated, alternate) file

Relink Files Dialog

Here is a simple step-by-step example on how to relink files:

☑ Select the Event Clip or Timeline Clip that you want to relink.

- You can relink one Clip at a time or a whole batch of Clips (i.e when an entire folder got relocated).
- You can relink missing files (the ones with the yellow warning triangle) or any "valid" Clip, that you want to link to a different Source Media File.

☑ In my example, I have four missing Event Clips that I have selected in the Browser ❶ (Game1, Game2, Game3 - goal, Game4).

☑ Now I select the command from the Main Menu *File ➤ Relink Files...* ❷, which opens the Relink Files Dialog ❸. The command is also available as a Key Command, but it is not assigned.

☑ The four previously selected Event Clips are now listed in the section labeled "*Original Files*" ❹. What exactly is displayed depends on the selection of the Relink radio button ❺:

- **All**: The list shows all the files that you have selected when opening the Relink Files Dialog.
- **Missing**: From all the Clips that you have selected, only the ones that has a missing file are listed.

☑ **Files not Clips**: Please pay attention to the title is says "Original <u>Files</u>" and not Clips. The names here are the names of the linked Source Media Files of the previously selected Clips. This information comes from the Event Clip database where the Metadata "filename" stores the name of the Source Media File during the original import and referencing of that file. In this example, I renamed the Clip "Game3" to "Game3 - goal" ❻, but in the Relink Files Dialog it is listed as its original file name "Game3".

☑ **Pathname**: Moving your mouse over any file name will open a tooltip window ❼, displaying the name of the assigned Event and the pathname of its Source Media File. Remember, this is the pre-defined location where FCPx expects the file to be! The reason you get a missing file message is that FCPx cannot find the file in that location.

☑ The bottom of the list shows the same location info ❽ when you select one file. When you select more than one file, then you get an "Example" message with the pathname of one of the files in the list ❾.

☑ The next step is to locate the file(s) by clicking on the *Locate* button ❿:

- **Locate Selected...**: If you select any (or all) files in the list, then the button shows *Locate Selected*.
- **Locate All...**: If you don't select any files, then the button shows *Locate All* and you start searching for those files on the list.

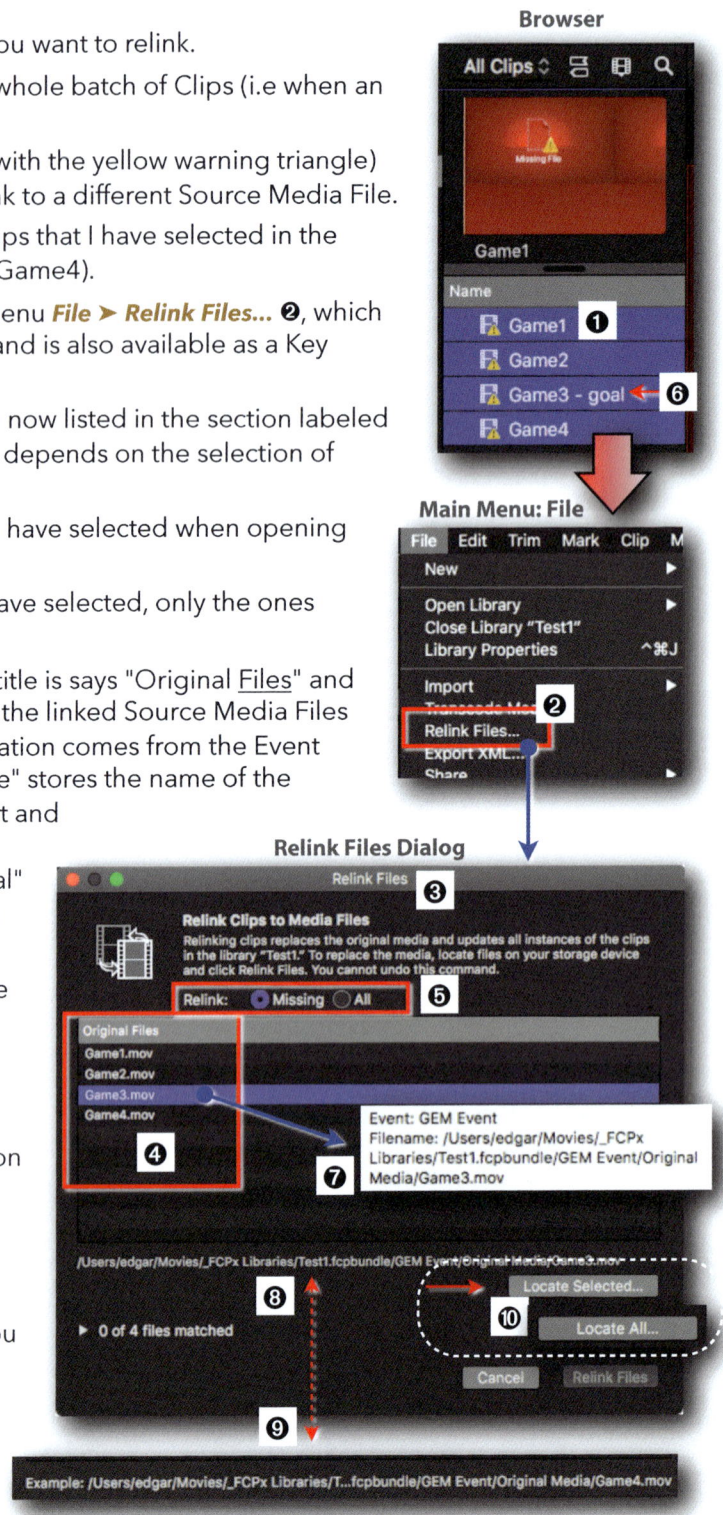

Browser

Main Menu: File

Relink Files Dialog

Once you clicked the "Locate ..." ❶ button, a Sheet ❷ will slide out under the Relink Files Dialog. Navigate to the folder where (you think) the new to-be-linked Source Media Files are located (FCPx looks for matching files that are closest to the original directory). To continue with my example, I navigated to a folder that contained the four media files. However, instead of the "Game1" file, there is a file named "Game-Test". This should simulate a name change of a file.

➡ *Relink Files Dialog: Multiple files selected*

This is the scenario, when you have more than one file selected in the "Original Files" list ❸ of the Relink Files Dialog and click the Locate Button. The Sheet displays a section with two lines, a pathname and an instruction that can be toggled with the Options button ❹.

▸ **Pathname**: The line can only display one pathname, therefore, the line starts with the word "Example" followed by the pathname of one of the previous files.

▸ **Instruction**: The line shows how many files have a match (in this example, "3 of 4 files found"), and tells you to *click* the "Choose" button to verify those matches.

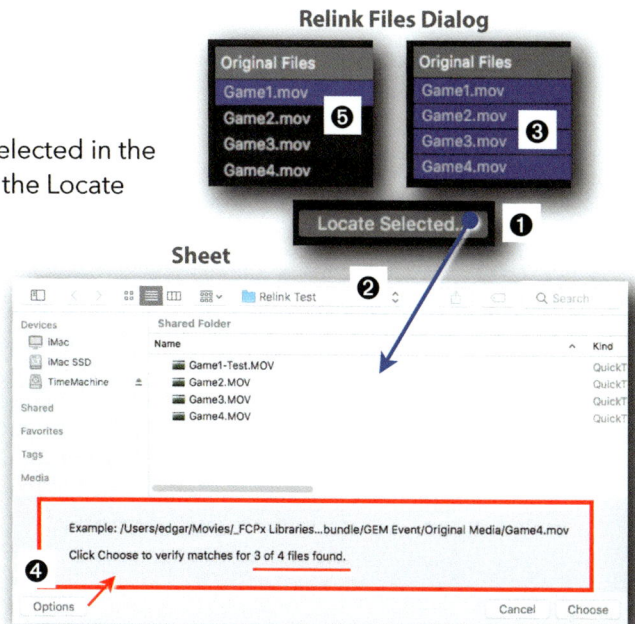

➡ *Relink Files Dialog: Single file selected*

This is the scenario, when you have only a single file selected in the "Original Files" list ❺ of the Relink Files Dialog and click the *Locate* Button. Now there are different outcomes depending on the following conditions. Pay attention to the information displayed in the two lines on the Sheet:

🌑 **Match ❻**

FCPx identifies a matching file at the Finder location:

▸ **Pathname**: This is the pathname of the file it found as a match.

▸ **Instruction**: The first name in this line is the "Name of the file selected in the Relink File Dialog" and the second name is the "Name of the file found by the Locate command". Clicking the "Choose" button will verify the match.

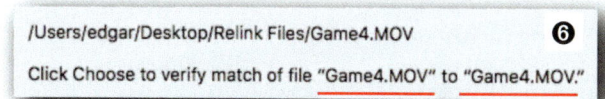

🌑 **No Match ❼**

FCPx cannot find any file on your drive that matches the one you are looking for:

▸ **Pathname**: This is the pathname of the file that is missing.

▸ **Instruction**: The instruction just tells you to select a different folder (or drive) for FCPx to look for.

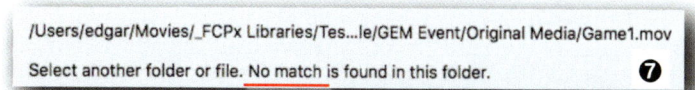

🌑 **No Match - different file ❽**

FCPx cannot find any file on your drive that matches the one you are looking for, so you click on a different file in that Sheet to match it to.

▸ **Pathname**: This is the pathname of the file that is missing.

▸ **Instruction**: The first name in this line is the "Name of the file selected in the Relink File Dialog" and the second name is the "Name of the file you clicked in the Sheet". *Clicking* the "Choose" button will verify the match, which tells FCPx, despite that fact that this might not be the original file, to match it anyways. See restrictions below.

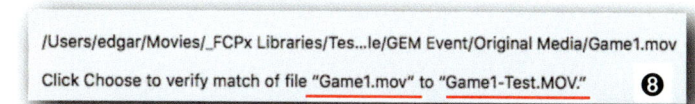

Relink Files Dialog

Original Files
Game1.mov
Game2.mov ❺
Game3.mov
Game4.mov

Original Files
Game1.mov
Game2.mov ❸
Game3.mov
Game4.mov

Locate Selected... ❶

Sheet ❷

/Users/edgar/Desktop/Relink Files/Game4.MOV ❻
Click Choose to verify match of file "Game4.MOV" to "Game4.MOV."

/Users/edgar/Movies/_FCPx Libraries/Tes...le/GEM Event/Original Media/Game1.mov
Select another folder or file. No match is found in this folder. ❼

/Users/edgar/Movies/_FCPx Libraries/Tes...le/GEM Event/Original Media/Game1.mov
Click Choose to verify match of file "Game1.mov" to "Game1-Test.MOV." ❽

➡ *Relink*

Now comes the final step, the actual "relinking". In the previous step on the Sheet that slid out underneath the Relink Files Dialog, you just selected the "Matched Files". After you *click* the "Choose" button on the Sheet, the following will happen:

▶ The Sheet will close and the Relink Files Dialog now displays in the line below the Locate button how many matches have been found ❶ on the Sheet you just closed. For example, "3 of 4 files matched".

▶ This text line has a disclosure triangle ❷ that opens another list underneath.

▶ The list has two columns:

  • **Original Files ❸**: This column shows the name of the original files (that have been moved from the list on top ❺).

  • **Matched Files ❹**: This column shows the name of the files that have been matched to the missing files on the left.

Relink Dialog

▶ You can select any of the files and press the *delete* key to remove them from the list and put them in the upper list ❺ again so you can locate a different file for it.

▶ If you have any unmatched files left in the upper list, then you can repeat the Locate procedure to find those matches.

▶ If you are ready, click the "Relink Files" ❻ button to do the "relinking".

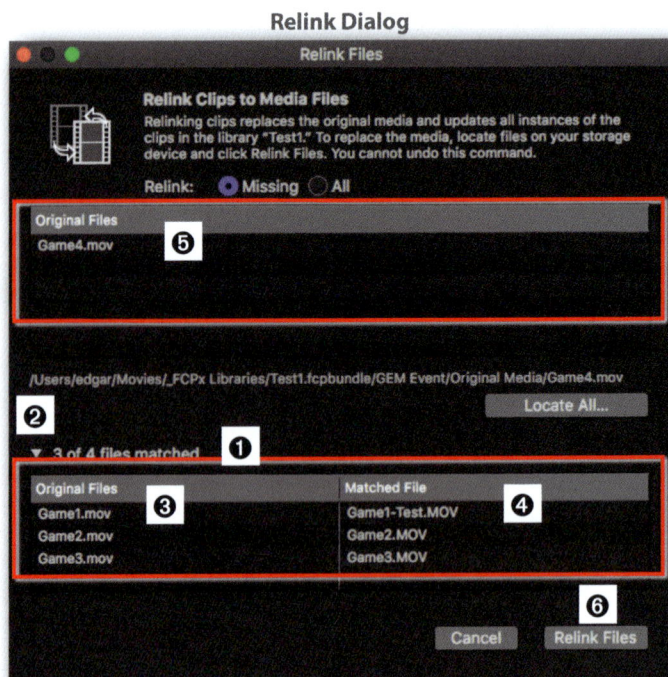

As I mentioned before, a Relink is like a new file import with the exception that it links to an existing Event Clip or Timeline Clip (an existing database record). You just update the entry for the linked file.

🌐 Referenced Files

Please note that relinked files are only referenced files (alias). You have to use the consolidate command **File ➤ Consolidate Event Media...** to place an actual copy of those files into the Event folder of your Library.

🌐 What files can be relinked

Any files with the same media type (audio, video), same frame rate, similar audio channel configurations and a duration at least as long as the Clip it is linking to can be linked. Resolution and Codec can be different. You will be prompted with an Alert window "Incompatible file" ❼ in case there is a mismatch.

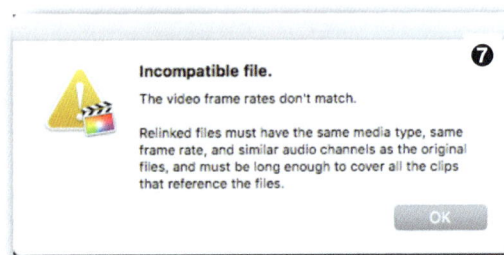

🌐 Transcoded Media

There is one important setting you have to keep in mind when dealing with missing files (and trying to relink them). Each Media File can also exist as two additional transcoded versions (Optimized and Proxy). You can switch at any time from the View Menu in the Viewer. A Missing Proxy warning ❽ just means that you selected to use Proxy files and haven't transcoded the Source Media Files yet. Also, when relinking files, make sure to update the transcoded files too!

Key Commands

Most applications have built-in Key Commands (also known as "keyboard shortcuts") and many apps even let you re-assign them to customize what key combinations (so -called Key Equivalents) trigger what command. FCPx has arguably one of the most sophisticated editors, the "Command Editor", that provides the interfaces for assign key equivalents to commands.

➡ Overview

Here is the basic functionality:

Main Menu

- ▶ **Command Set**: The list of all the assigned Key Commands in FCPx is called a Command Set.

- ▶ **Default**: FCPx has one Default Command Set that is listed in the Main Menu *Final Cut Pro ➤ Commands ➤ Default* under the section "Command Sets" ❶. It is selected by default.

- ▶ **Custom Command Sets**: You can modify that Default Command Set to create your own Command Sets and save them under a specific name, which is added to the Menu under the section *Final Cut Pro ➤ Commands ➤ Custom Command Sets* ❷.

- ▶ **Switch Command Set**: You can quickly switch between Command Sets by selecting them from the Menu. The currently active Command Set has a checkbox ✅ next to it.

- ▶ **Command Editor**: The Main Menu *Final Cut Pro ➤ Commands ➤ Customize ...* ❸ (*opt+cmd+K*) opens the Command Editor, a Dialog window that lets you view, edit, and manage the Command Sets. It recognizes your keyboard (full keyboard ❹ or laptop keyboard ❺) and displays exactly that keys layout.

- ▶ The *Import...* and *Export...* commands ❻ in the menu let you import and export Command Sets. They are stored as XML files with the file extension *.commandsets*. A Save Dialog lets you save the file to any location on your drive. This makes it easy to exchange Command Sets between users or different workstations.

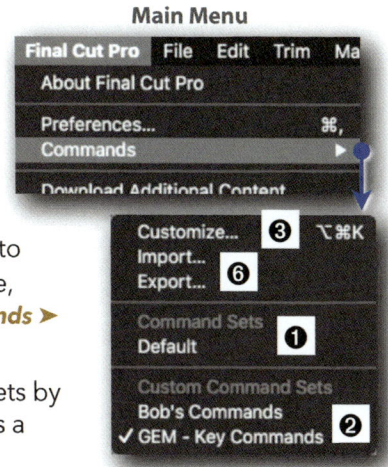

Command Editor (laptop keyboard)
Command Editor (full keyboard)

Command Editor

The Command Editor window is divided into 4 areas:

▶ **Header ❶**: The Header contains popup menu and various controls

▶ **Virtual Keyboard ❷**: This is the interactive keyboard layout that lets you view and assign key equivalent to specific commands.

▶ **Command List ❸**: This section lists all the Key Commands grouped by color-coded categories

▶ **Key Detail ❹**: This section switches its view depending on if you selected a Command in the Command List or a key on the Virtual Keyword.

▶ **Resize**: You can resize the the Virtual Keyboard by dragging its window border or corners ❺.

🌀 Command List Pane

The Command List lists all the available Key Commands. It has a Sidebar on the left and a Browser to the right.

▶ **Command Groups (Sidebar) ❻**: This area lets you restrict what is displayed in the browser on the right. You have three grouping options:

- All FCPx Commands ❼: Select this option to display all FCPx Key Commands

- Main Menu Commands ❽, only the ones assigned to commands in the various Main Menus, or display Key Commands grouped by functionality (Editing, Effects, etc.).

- Workflow Groups ❾: These are eleven groups based on specific tasks you are performing in FCPx. They have a color code that is also used to the assigned keys on the virtual keyboard to better identify the type of task.

▶ **Command Browser ❿**: This is the browser area that displays a list of all the Key Commands based on the selection in the Sidebar on the left. It has three columns (Command, Modifiers, Key). You can *click* their header to set a specific sort order. You can restrict the list even further by applying a search phrase in the search field ⓫ in the upper right corner of the Command Editor.

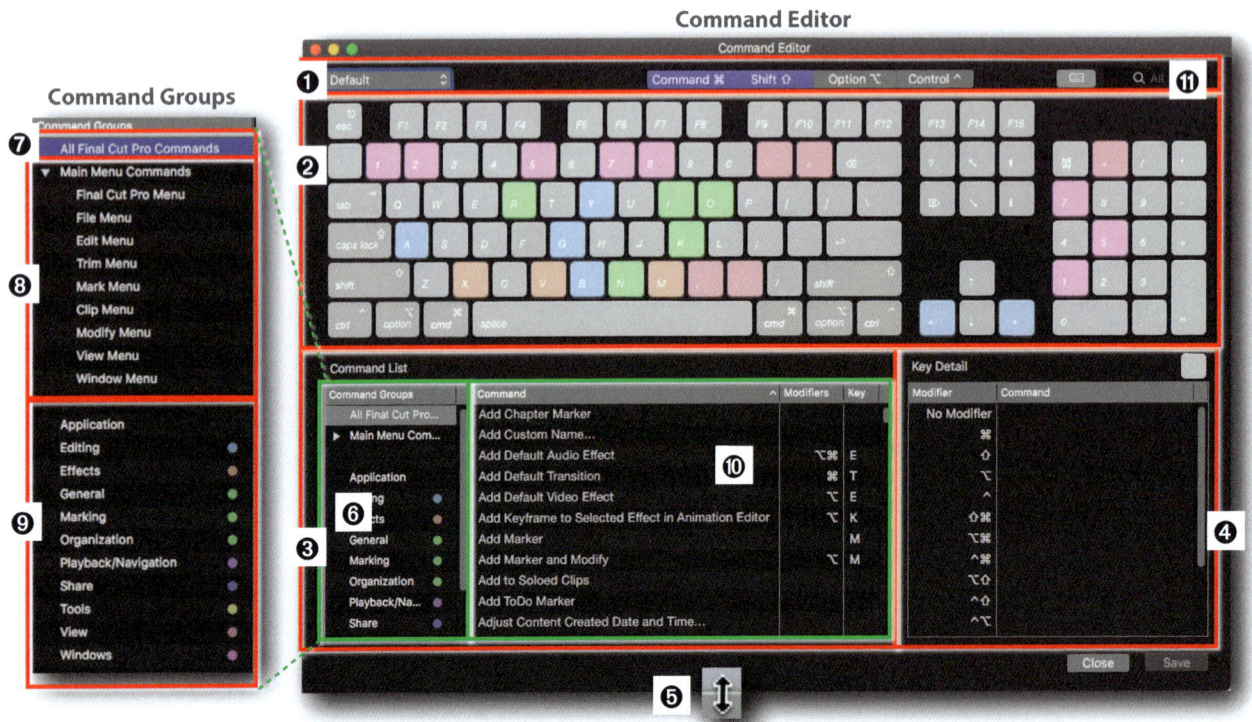

Command Editor

14 - Last But Not Least

🌐 Detail Pane

This area in the lower right can automatically switches between two different views depending on if you selected a Command in the Command List or a key on the Virtual Keyword.

> ▸ **❻ Command Detail**: If you select any Command in the Command Browser **❶**, then this area will display a short description **❷**, explaining the function of that Key Command.

> ▸ **❼ Key Detail**: If you *click* any key on the Virtual Keyboard, then this area displays all the possible Modifier Key combinations ("Key Equivalents") for that key and the commands that are currently assigned to those Key Equivalents **❸**. This way, you can see immediately which key equivalents are not assigned yet.

>> • The color-code of the Command indicates the Command Group.
>> • A White font indicates a default assignment and a black indicates a custom assignment.
>> • The upper-right corner shows the Key **❹** that is selected.

Key Detail Pane (Key Detail)

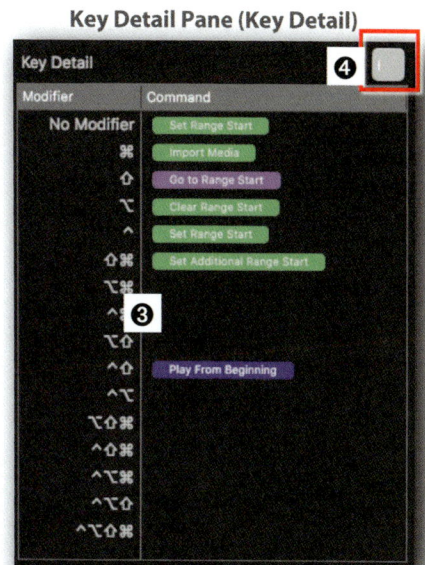

Key Detail Pane (Command Detail)

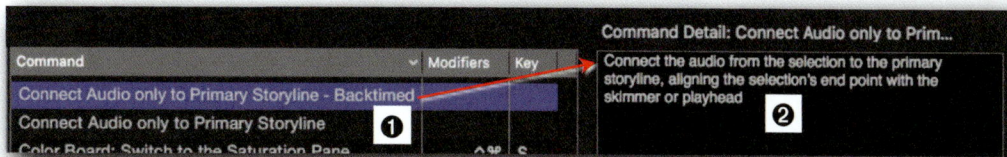

🌐 Virtual Keyboard

The color of a key **❺** indicates if it is assigned to a Command. You can enabled the four buttons **❻** in the header to simulate the status of having specific modifier keys pressed with a key.

> ▸ **Gray**: The key is assigned
> ▸ **Color**: The key is assigned and the color indicates its Command Group.

Commands

▶ **Add Key Command**: To assign a key equivalent to a command, simply select the Command from the Command Browser and press the key combination on your real keyboard. You will get an alert window if that key assignment is already used ❶ or if it is reserved ❷.

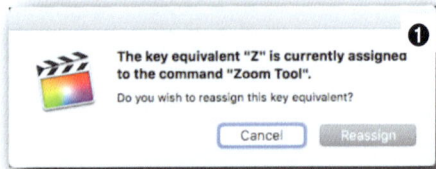

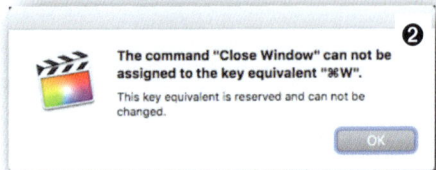

▶ **Re-assign**: *Drag* a Key on the Virtual Keyboard over a different Key or drag the Token (the colored label representing the actual Command) from the Key Detail List to a new key on the Virtual Keyboard. The mouse cursor will have the green plus sign and the ghost image of the token ❸.

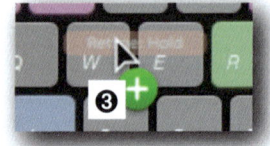

▶ **Delete Assignment**: *Drag* the key from the Virtual Keyboard outside the window. The mouse cursor will show the Token for that command and an x sing ❹ to indicate that the assignment will be deleted when you release the mouse.(in a puff of smoke) or select the Command in the Command Browser and press *delete*.

Other Controls

And here are is more functionality.

▶ **Popup Menu**: The popup menu ❺ in the left upper corner is similar to the Main Menu *Final Cut Pro ➤ Commands ➤* with the additional commands to Delete and Duplicate a Command Set. Please note that you can only name a Command Set when you duplicate it.

▶ **Search Field**: The magnifying glass icon in the upper-right corner pops up a menu where you can select the field you are searching (Key Equivalent is the actual Keystroke, i.e. *sh+cmd+S*).

▶ **Keyword Highlight**: *Click* the Keyboard Highlight ❼ button [⌨] to only show the keys on the virtual keyboard that are related to the currently selected Command Group ❽ in the Command List Sidebar.

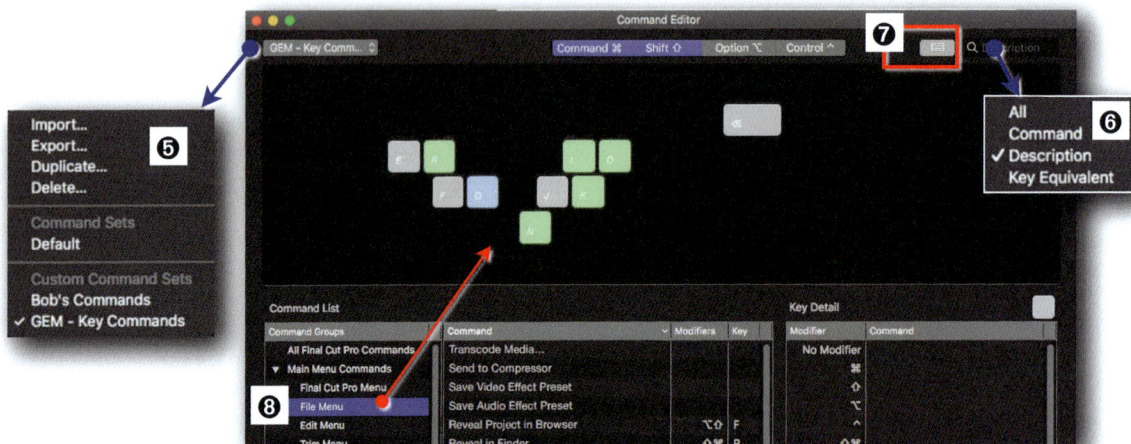

Touch Bar

Wait, wait ... before you skip over this chapter because you don't have a MacBook Pro with a Touch Bar and, therefore, think you can't use this feature, think again.

Yes you Can

As of the beginning of 2017, Apple's new Touch Bar technology is only available on the late 2016 MacBook Pro models. No information has come forward if and when Apple will also release a standalone Touch Bar enabled keyboard to use with your desktop Mac. But in the meantime, there are a few "options" on how you can still use Logic's Touch Bar features.

➡ Touché

This is the easiest and quickest solution to get Touch Bar functionality onto your desktop computer. Touché is a little (free) app that puts a floating window, the size of the Touch Bar, on your screen and works virtually the same, just clicking instead of tapping.

This is not just a gimmick to play with some of the Touch Bar functionalies. It is actually useful, even if you don't have the real Touch Bar (yet).

Here is the download link for Touché and a few other solutions to check out:
- https://red-sweater.com/touche/
- https://www.duetdisplay.com
- https://github.com/bikkelbroeders/TouchBarDemoApp/releases

System Configuration

Before using the Touch Bar, you can configure a few options in the System Preferences.

🌑 Control Elements

The Touch Bar has a maximum of three control areas:

▶ **Esc Button** `esc` **or Close Button** ⊗ **❶**: Always on the left is either the Close button to return to the previous view or the esc button, that represents the old physical esc key.

▶ **App Controls ❷**: These are the controls of the currently selected (focused) app.

▶ **Control Strip ❸**: These are the macOS system controls original assignable to the F-keys.

🌑 Main Layout

You can choose from three main layouts for the Touch Bar from the *System Preferences ➤ Keyboard ➤ Touch Bar shows* popup menu **❹**. The *System Preferences ➤ Keyboard ➤ Press FN key to* popup **❺** determines the layout that is temporarily displayed when holding down the fn key. The options in this popup menu change depending on what is selected for the Main Layout.

▶ **App Controls with Control Strip ❻**: fn key switches to Expanded Control Strip or F keys. *Tap* the left arrow **❼** in the Control Strip to expand to the Expanded Control Strip

▶ **Expanded Control Strip ❽**: fn key switches to Show App Controls or F keys

▶ **App Controls ❾**: fn key switches to Show Control Strip or F keys

🌑 Basic Functionality

▶ **Switch Button**: *Tap* on a button that represents a command or a switch to toggle that switch.

▶ **Slider Button**: *Tapping* on a button that represents a slider will switch the view to display a slider and a Close button ⊗ to switch back to. *Tap-hold* to display the slider so you can drag left-right and adjust the value.

▶ **Gestures**: Various touch screen gestures might be implemented depending on the app.

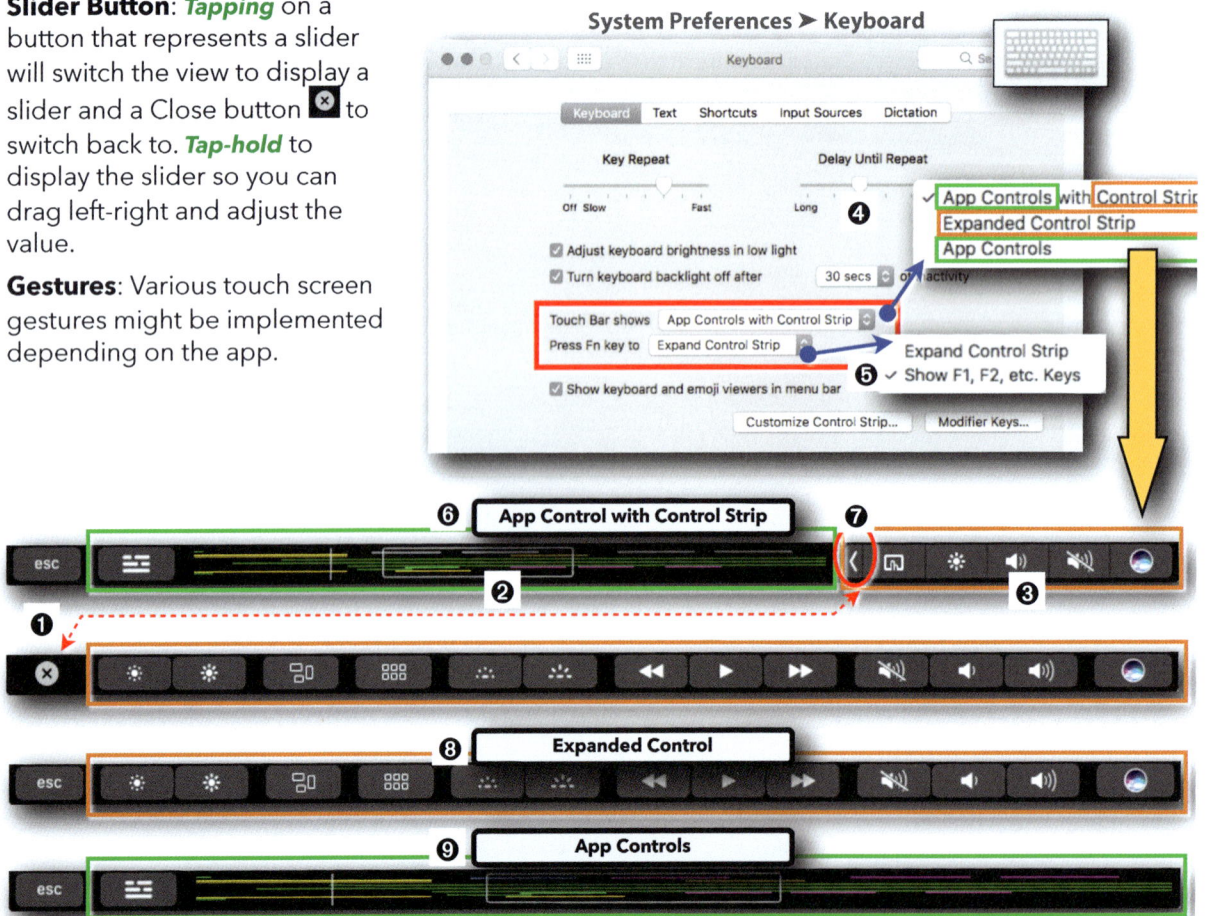

System Preferences ➤ Keyboard

❻ App Control with Control Strip ❼

❷

❸

❶

❽ Expanded Control

❾ App Controls

➡ *Customize Control Strip*

The *Customize Control Strip...* button ❶ at the bottom of the **System Preferences ➤ Keyboard** opens a window ❷ that lets you drag those elements down to the Touch Bar to configure the Control Strip View of the Touch Bar.

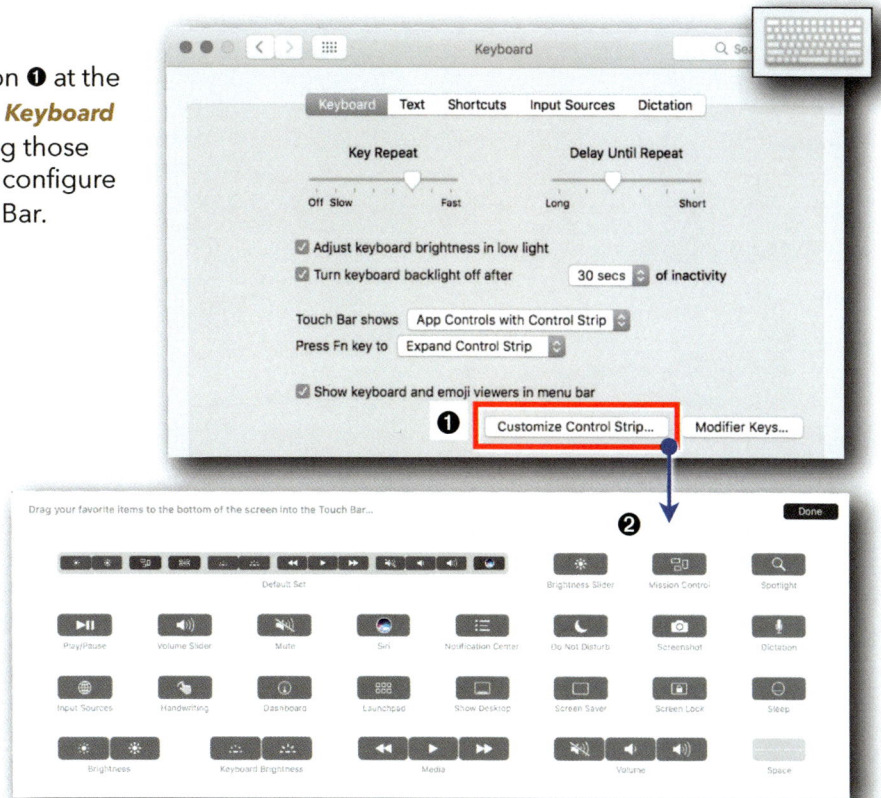

➡ *Touch Bar Zoom*

There is one rather hidden Touch Bar feature that might be useful. Enable the checkbox ❸ in **System Preferences ➤ Accessibility ➤ Zoom ➤ Enable Touch Bar zoom** and whenever you *tap-hold* (a little bit) a control on the Touch Bar, the entire Touch Bar will be displayed at the bottom of the computer screen.

This feature provides a few additional adjustments:

▶ **Standard Procedure**: Whenever you touch or drag with your finger on the Touch Bar the Touch Bar appears on the computer screen.

▶ **Adjust Zoom**: Hold the *command* key on the keyboard and use the two-finger pinch gesture on the Touch Bar to change the size of the on-screen Touch Bar.

▶ **Drag and Tap**: While *sliding* with one finger on the Touch Bar, *tap* with a second finger to generate a *tap* at the position of the first finger.

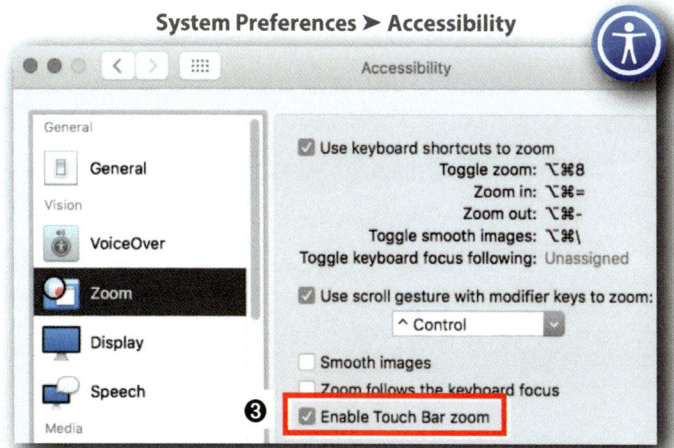

Final Cut Pro - Touch Bar Implementation

The great thing about the Touch Bar is that all its functionalities are optional. It doesn't add anything new to FCPx, it just provides an alternative to perform specific tasks using the Touch Bar. First, this requires some getting used to, but you will find that it can actually speed up your workflow in FCPx and enhances the way you work and interact with the FCPx interface.

➡ Main Views vs. Sub Views

Main Views `esc`

The main concept is that the Touch Bar View (what is displayed on the Touch Bar) automatically changes, depending on what window in FCPx has currently key focus or what object (i.e. Clip) is selected. These are the *Main Views*, which usually have the esc Button `esc` on the far left.

Sub Views ⊗

Many of the Main Views have buttons that switch to different views with additional controls. Let's call them "*Sub Views*", which usually have the Close Button ⊗ on the left that switches back to its corresponding Main View. Switching the key focus in FCPx can automatically close a Sub View and switch back to the corresponding Main View.

➡ Unsupported

There are only a few areas in FCPx that support the Touch Bar. If there are no controls available for the currently selected window or object in FCPx, then the Touch Bar is blank, only showing the escape button.

➡ Text Entry and Dialog Buttons

The Touch Bar automatically displays the buttons on most of the Dialog windows and when key focus is on a text field to enter a name for an object (Clip, Project, etc.), then you can enable the word suggestions.

Text Entry

Save Dialog: New Library / Export XML

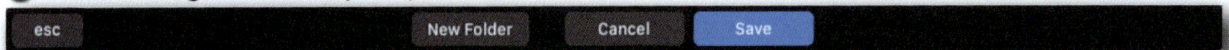

Import Dialog: Import XML

Open Library from Backup

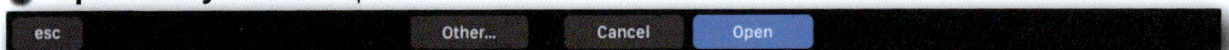

➡ *Browser*

When you are in the FCPx Browser, the Touch Bar could display three different Main Views, depending on if you selected the Library Sidebar, a Project, or an Event Clip.

🔵 **Browser - Library Sidebar selected**

esc		↓ Import	★ New Event	🎬 New Project	

If the Library Sidebar is selected, then the Main View on the Touch Bar displays three buttons that correspond to three of the commonly used commands in the Library Sidebar of the Browser:

▸ **Import**: *Tap* to open the Media Import Dialog (***cmd+I***)

▸ **New Event**: *Tap* to create a new Event in the currently active Library (***opt+N***)

▸ **New Project**: *Tap* to create a new Project in the currently active Library (***cmd+N***)

🔵 **Browser - Project Selected**

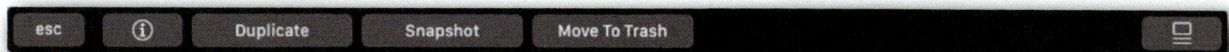

esc	ⓘ	Duplicate	Snapshot	Move To Trash	🖥

If a Project is selected in the Browser, then the Main View on the Touch Bar displays five buttons:

▸ ⓘ **Info Inspector**: *Tap* to open the Info Inspector for the selected Project (***cmd-4***)

▸ **Duplicate**: *Tap* to trigger the command "*Duplicate Project*" (***cmd+D***)

▸ **Snapshot**: *Tap* to trigger the command "*Duplicate Project as Snapshot*"(***sh+cmd+D***)

▸ **Move To Trash**: *Tap* to move the selected Project(s) to the Trash (***cmd+delete***)

▸ 🗄 🖥 **Toggle Filmstrip/List**: *Tap* to toggle the Browser between Filmstrip View and List View (***opt+cmd+2***)

🔵 **Browser - Clip Selected**

esc	ⓘ	🔊		Go To:	◄ Start	End ►	Clear Selection	🖥

If an Event Clip is selected in the Browser, then the Main View on the Touch Bar displays six buttons:

▸ ⓘ **Info Inspector**: *Tap* to open the Info Inspector for the selected Project (***cmd-4***)

▸ 🔊 **Volume**: *Tap* to switch to the Sub View ➤ Volume

▸ ◄ Start **Go to Start**: *Tap* to move the Playhead to the start of the selected Event Clip (***home***)

▸ End ► **Go To End**: *Tap* to move the Playhead to the end of the selected Event Clip (***end***)

▸ Clear Selection **Clear Selection**: *Tap* to remove any current selection(s) on the Event Clip (***opt+X***)

▸ 🗄 🖥 **Toggle Filmstrip/List**: *Tap* to toggle the Browser between Filmstrip View and List View (***opt+cmd+2***)

🔊 **Volume**

✕	Silence		🔉 ━━━━━●━━━ 🔊	

✕	Silence		🔉 Relative Volume 🔊	

▸ Silence **Silence**: *Tap* to set the Volume to -∞dB. This is a single command and not a toggle!

▸ **Volume Slider**: *Slide* the white knob to adjust the volume. The slider is replaced by a label "Relative Volume" if multiple Clips are selected

▸ 🔉 🔊 **Volume Buttons**: *Tap* on the left and right button to increase/decrease the volume incrementally

➡ *Timeline*

The Timeline has one Main View with three of its buttons switching to Sub Views:

🌑 Timeline Pane

If the Timeline Pane is selected, then the Main View on the Touch Bar displays eight buttons:

- ▸ **Tool Selector**: *Tap* to switch to the Sub View ➤ Tool Selector
- ▸ **Volume**: *Tap* to switch to the Sub View ➤ Volume
- ▸ **Unlink Connected Clips**: *Tap-hold* to temporarily unlink Connected Clips when moving Clips on the Primary Storyline (` key) 🌑
- ▸ **Trim to Playhead**: *Tap* to trim the start or end of the selected Clip to the Playhead position, whatever is closer to the Playhead position (*opt+*)
- ▸ **Trim Start to Playhead**: *Tap* to trim the start of the selected Clip to the Playhead position (*opt+[*)
- ▸ **Trim End to Playhead**: *Tap* to trim the end of the selected Clip to the Playhead position (*opt+}*)
- ▸ **Play Around**: *Tap* to play back the Clip at the Playhead position (*sh+?*)
- ▸ **Timeline Overview**: *Tab* to switch to the Sub View ➤ Timeline Overview

- • **Tool Selector**

Tap any of the seven buttons to switch the mouse cursor to that Edit Tool. The View automatically returns to the Main View - Timeline.

- • **Volume**

- ▸ **Silence**: *Tap* to set the Volume to -∞dB. This is a single command and not a toggle!
- ▸ **Fade Handles**: *Tap* to enable/disable the default Fade-In and Fade-Out.
- ▸ **Volume Buttons**: *Tap* on the left and right button to increase/decrease the volume incrementally.
- ▸ **Volume Slider**: *Slide* the white knob to adjust the Volume. The slider is replaced by a label "Relative Volume" if multiple Clips are selected.
  - • The Volume controls add some speedy functionality when working with Volume Automation:
    If at least one Keyframe is placed on the Volume Curve, then (only in pause) *tapping* on the Fader will create a Keyframe at that Playhead position, or you can *slide* the knob to create a Keyframe and adjust it vertically right away. Use the command Next/Previous Keyframe (or *drag* the Skimmer) to quickly step through the existing Keyframes and adjust them with the Touch Bar Slider.

-  **Timeline Overview**

The Touch Bar presents a user interface with the following functionality

- ▶ **Touch Bar**: The area from the left to the right shows the entire Timeline in FCPx displaying the various color-coded Clips for a quick overview of your Project.
- ▶ **Zoom Range**: The frame with the two handles indicates the Zoom Range, the section that is currently visible in FCPx in the Timeline Pane (the section you are zoomed in). *Slide* the center of the frame to move the Zoom Range left/right.
- ▶ **Zoom Handles**: *Slide* the left and right handle of the Zoom Range to zoom-in or zoom-out on the Timeline. They also update to any zoom changes you make in the Timeline Pane.
- ▶ **Playhead**: The white vertical bar indicates the Playhead position.

🌑 Transition Clip

If a single Transition Clip is selected on the Timeline, then the Main View on the Touch Bar displays a special button in addition to the Edit Tool Button and the Timeline Overview Button:

- ▶   **Transition Duration**: *Tap* this button and the SMPTE Reader changes to the Numeric Input Mode, so you can directly type a duration for the selected Transition Clip on your keyboard.

➡️ *Viewer - Onscreen Title Clips*

If you select any onscreen control on the Viewer for a Title Clip, then the Main View on the Touch Bar displays up to five buttons to adjust the various parameters for the Title Clip. This is an example where the Touch Bar definitely adds functionality and speed to your FCPx workflow. See the Color chapter for more details.

- **Text Formatting**

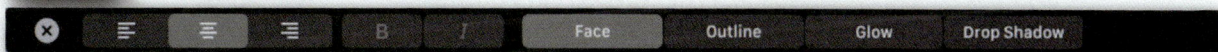

- **Font Size**

- **Kerning**

- **Color**

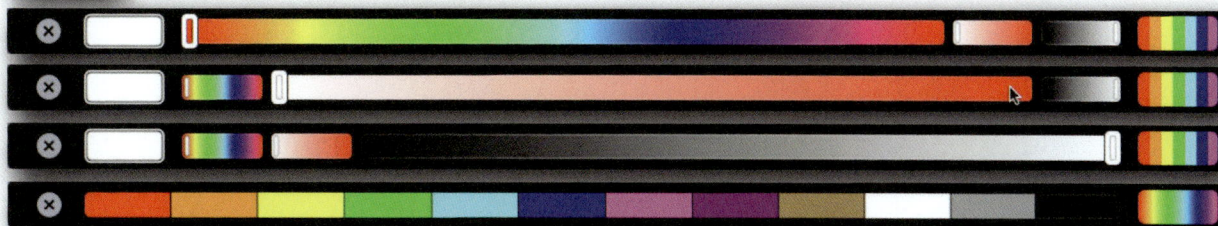

Preferences

Most of the Preferences settings I covered already throughout the book in the chapter that relates to those settings. Here is a list of all the individual settings.

Opening the Preferences window is standard with all Apple apps. The Key Command is *cmd+,* and the menu command is listed in the apps menu *Final Cut Pro X ➤ Preferences*

➡ General Preferences

The General Preferences window has only three settings:

🟡 **Time Display**

This setting determines what format is used to display time values in FCPx.

> ▸ **HH:MM:SS:FF ❶**: This is the standard SMPTE format

> ▸ **HH:MM:SS:FF + Subframes ❷**: This is the standard SMPTE format including the subframes

> ▸ **Frames ❸**: Old-school time when film was on reels, measured in actual frames

> ▸ **Seconds ❹**: This shows the seconds with milliseconds after the decimal point

The setting affects the following areas:

- ☑ SMPTE Reader
- ☑ Browser List View
- ☑ Info Inspector
- ☑ Timeline Ruler
- ☑ Timeline Header
- ☑ Timeline Index Position Column
- ☑ Help Tag (when the *View ➤ Browser ➤ Skimmer Info* is enabled)

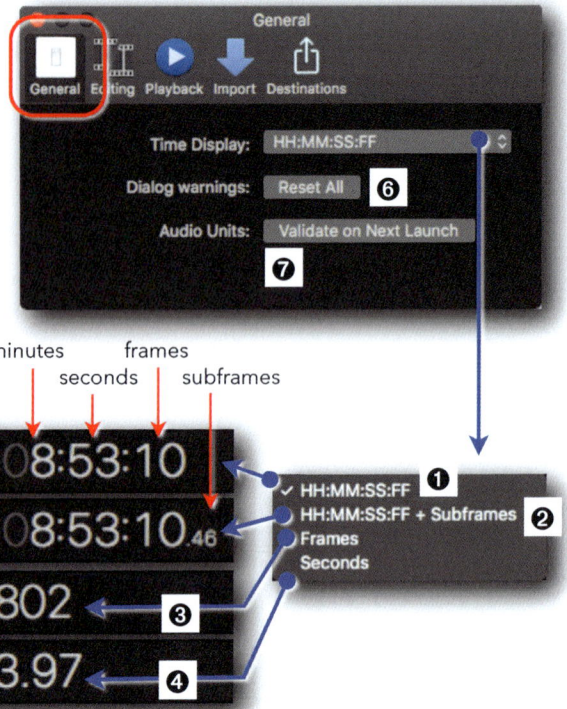

🟡 **Dialog Warnings**

Some Warning Dialogs in FCPx have a checkbox "Do not show again" ❺, so you won't see that dialog the next time FCPx wants to warn you about that specific issue. *Clicking* on this button "Reset All" ❻, resets all those settings and shows those Dialogs again.

🟡 **Audio Units**

When you launch FCPx the first time, or after you install a third-party AU Plugin, FCPx will perform a test on the installed AU Plugins and informs you of any Plugins that fail the test.

If you click on this button "Validate on Next Launch" ❼, FCPx will repeat that test on all installed third-party AU Plugins the next time you launch FCPx ❽.

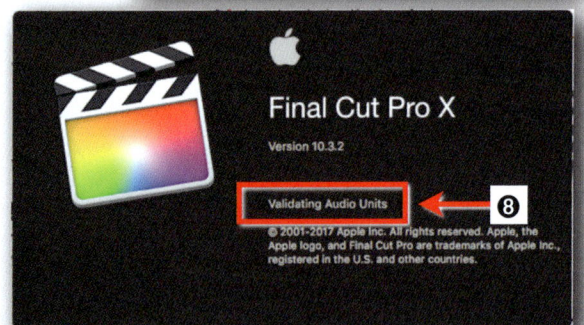

➡️ *Editing Preferences*

The Editing Preferences window includes the following settings:

🔵 **Timeline ❶**

Please note that other settings in this window also affect the editing on the Timeline, not just these two:

▸ **Show detailed trimming feedback** ☑️ ⬛: When enabled, the Viewer will show a so-called "Two-up Display" when you perform any trim edit. The left display shows the last frame of the left Clip and the right display shows the first frame of the right Clip at the Edit Point. You can temporarily turn off the Two-up Display by holding down the *option* key while trimming. Using the *option* key when the feature is disabled, toggles the Viewer from displaying the "last frame left Clip" to the "first frame right Clip".

▸ **Position playhead after edit operation** ☑️ ⬛: If you want to keep the Playhead position regardless of the edit you are performing, then leave this setting unchecked. In enabled, and you add a new Clip to the Timeline, the Playhead will move to the end of the new Clip.

🔵 **Inspector Units ❷**

Video Effects like Transform, Crop, or Distort have parameters that let you control the position of the Clip. This popup menu lets you choose if you want to display those position values as Pixels ❸ or Percentage ❹.

🔵 **Audio ❺**

Two settings regarding the audio editing:

▸ **Show reference waveforms** ☑️ ⬛: The displayed waveform on a Clip (Event Clip or Timeline Clip) can often be used to quickly identify specific locations in a Clip, i.e. a sudden audio burst of a gun shot or segments of dialog and silence. However, when you lower the audio level ❻, the audio waveform is also lowered to reflect the actual signal level of the Clip. This could make it more difficult to identify those events. When this reference checkbox is enabled, the waveform is displayed with a maximum level in a lighter shade ❼ (which is very subtle) together with the actual waveform ❽.

▸ **Default fade duration is [seconds]**: When you select one or multiple Timeline Clips and use the command *Modify ➤ Adjust Volume ➤ Apply Fades*, a Fade-In and a Fade-Out will be added on those Clips with a default duration of the value you entered in this field. This value also applies when using the Fade Handle Buttons on the Touch Bar to add Default Fades.

🔵 **Still Images ❾**

▸ **Editing duration is [second]**: The value you enter here is used as the default duration for any new Clip of a Still Image you add to the Timeline or any Freeze Frame you create on the Timeline (Main Menu *Edit ➤ Add Freeze Frame*).

🔵 **Transitions ❿**

▸ **Duration is [seconds]**: The value you enter here is used as the default duration for any new Transition Clip you add in the Timeline.

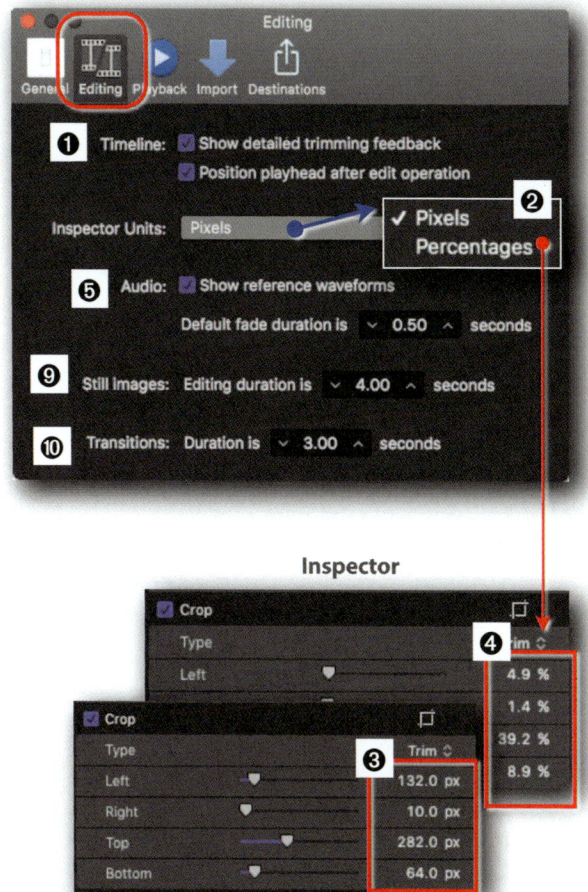

➡️ *Playback Preferences*

🌑 **Rendering ❶**

▸ **Background render** ☑️⬛: The checkbox toggles between manual rendering and automatic rendering. Please note that I use the term "automatic rendering" instead of "background rendering". Technically, the rendering doesn't happen in the background while you are working in FCPx in the foreground. You actually have to stop any editing before FCPx starts the processing of the render file. That means, you just tell FCPx to "automatically" start rendering when FCPx is in "idle mode".

▸ **Start after**: Here you set the idle time (up to 999sec) that determines how long FCPx is waiting after your last interaction with FCPx before it starts the render process. This makes sure that no CPU power is used for rendering while working in FCPx. Of course the render process can stop and pick up at any time. If you quit FCPx while still rendering, then a little window ❷ pops up, reminding you that it cancels the tasks, but rendering will automatically pick up again when you launch FCPx the next time.

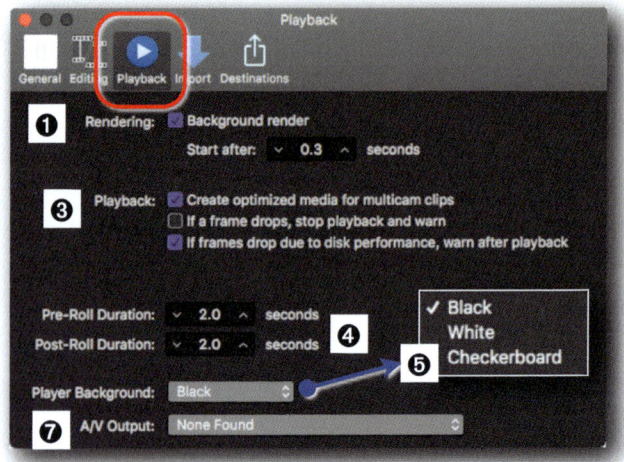

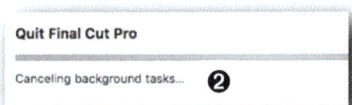

🌑 **Playback ❸**

▸ **Create optimized media for multicam Clips** ☑️⬛: If enabled, FCPx transcodes (during import or later) your media files to Optimized Media (Apple ProRes 422) to improve the efficiency of your data stream when using MultiCam Clips.

▸ **If a frame drops, stop playback and warn** ☑️⬛: Shows a Warning Dialog

▸ **If frames drop due to disk performance, warn after playback** ☑️⬛: Shows a Warning Dialog case

🌑 **Pre-Roll / Post-Roll Duration ❹**

The Play Around command (*sh+?* or *tap* the dedicated button ⌨️ on the Touch Bar) starts playing from the Playhead or Skimmer position. It starts earlier by the amount set here in the Pre-Roll Duration field and continuous to play beyond the Playhead or Skimmer position by the amount set in the Post-Roll Duration field. Enable Loop Playback (*cmd+L*) for repeating that section until you press stop.

🌑 **Player Background ❺**

You can choose from three different backgrounds that are displayed when the frame size of the Clip doesn't fill out the size of the Project Frame ❻ or for transparent Clips.

🌑 **A/V Output ❼**

Any external audio/video device or monitor connected via third-party video interface hardware will be displayed in this popup menu to select as an optional output.

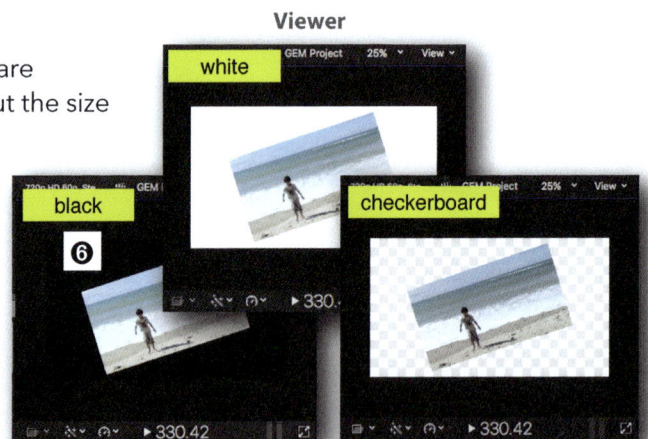

14 - Last But Not Least

➡ Import Preferences

There are some important little details about the Import Preferences window ❶ you have to pay attention to:

- ▸ The settings here are the same that you find in the Media Import Dialog (*cmd+I*).
- ▸ Whatever changes you make in this Preferences window (☑ ◼) will be the default when you open the Media Import Dialog.
- ▸ However, whatever changes you make to the checkboxes (☑ ◼) in the Media Import Dialog, will then be the default in this Preferences window, the next time you open it. That means any new settings in Media Import will update this Import Preferences window.

- ▸ The settings in this Preferences window will apply to any media file import when you *drag* files directly into FCPx without using the Media Import Dialog.

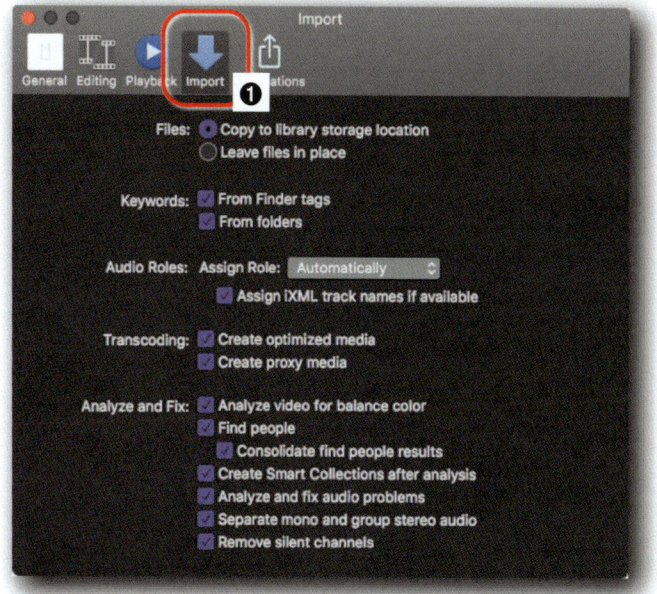

➡ Destination Preferences

The Destinations Preferences window ❷ functions more like a configuration window than a typical preferences window. Here, you can set up the various Destinations ❸ that are then displayed in the Share Menu ❹ (*File ➤ Share ➤*) that you use to export your Projects or Event Clips.

Please note that the menu command *File ➤ Share ➤ Add Destination...* ❺ directly opens this Destinations Preferences window. ❻

See the Export chapter for more details

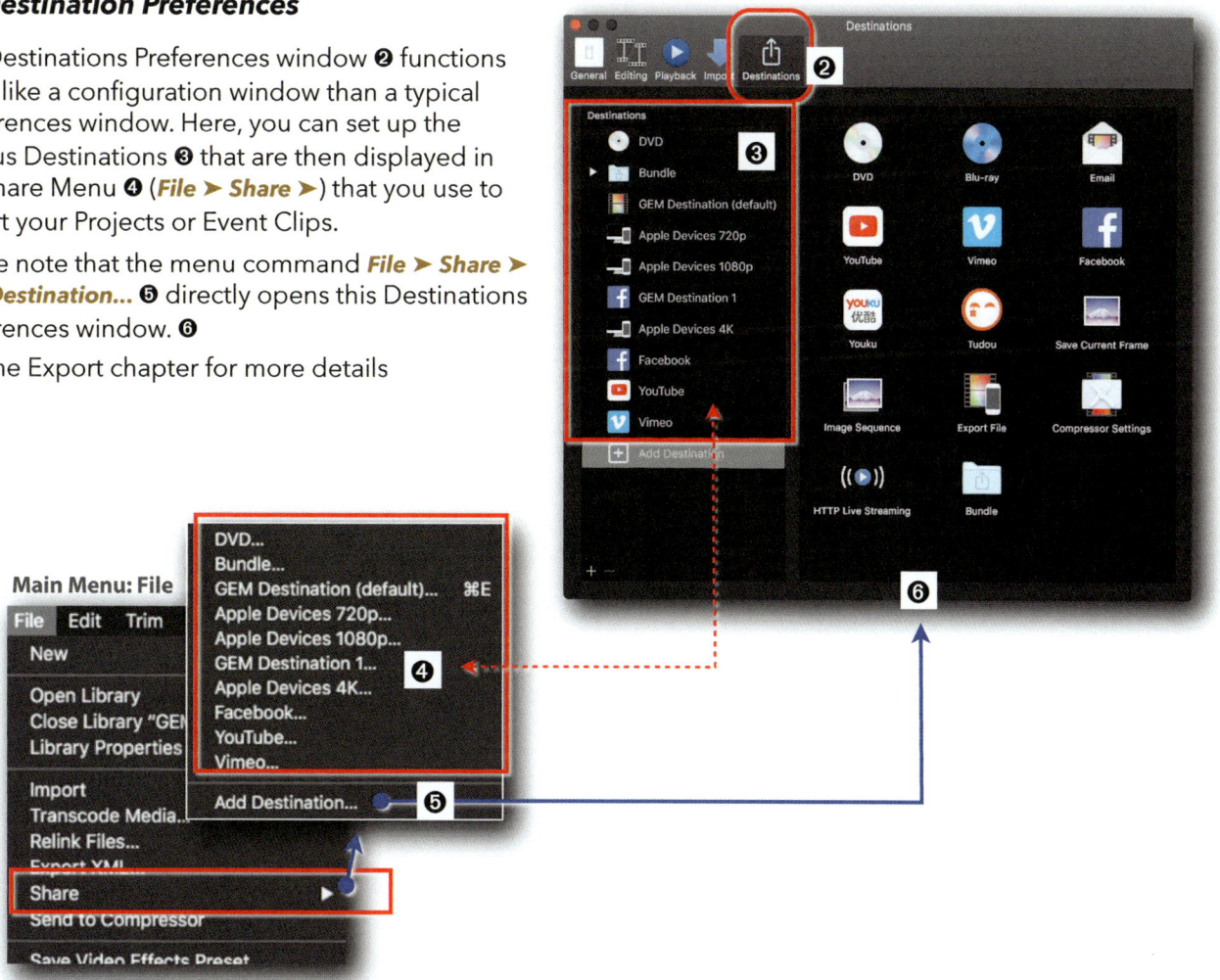

Conclusion

This concludes my manual "*Final Cut Pro 10.3 - How it Works*".

If you find my visual approach of explaining features and concepts helpful, please recommend my books to others or maybe write a review on Amazon or the iBooks Store. This will help me to continue this series.
To check out other books in my "Graphically Enhanced Manuals" series, go to my website at:
www.DingDingMusic.com/Manuals

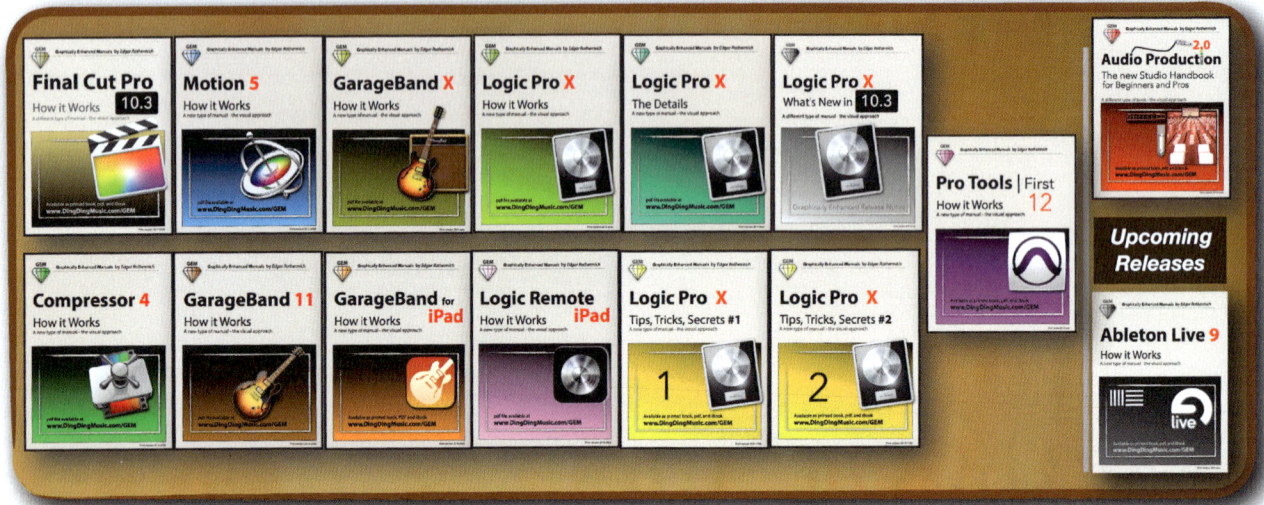

To contact me directly, email me at: GEM@DingDingMusic.com

More information about my day job as a composer and links to my social network sites are on my website:
www.DingDingMusic.com

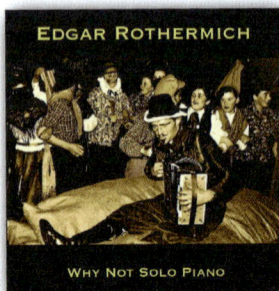

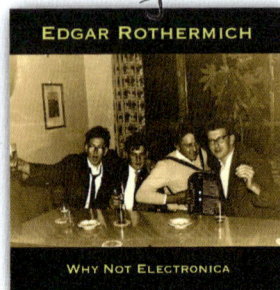

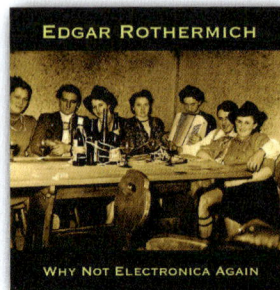

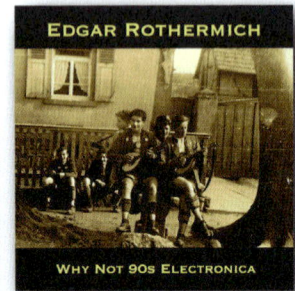

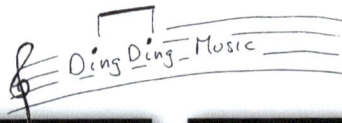

Listen to my music on SoundCloud

Thanks for your interest and your support,

Edgar Rothermich